Red Hamlet

The Life and Ideas of Alexander Bogdanov

James D. White

Haymarket Books
Chicago, IL

First published in 2018 by Brill Academic Publishers, The Netherlands
© 2018 Koninklijke Brill NV, Leiden, The Netherlands

Published in paperback in 2019 by
Haymarket Books
P.O. Box 180165
Chicago, IL 60618
773-583-7884
www.haymarketbooks.org

ISBN: 978-1-64259-048-7

Distributed to the trade in the US through Consortium Book Sales and
Distribution (www.cbsd.com) and internationally through Ingram
Publisher Services International (www.ingramcontent.com).

This book was published with the generous support of Lannan
Foundation and Wallace Action Fund.

Special discounts are available for bulk purchases by organizations and
institutions. Please call 773-583-7884 or email info@haymarketbooks.org
for more information.

Cover design by Jamie Kerry and Ragina Johnson.

Printed in the United States.

10 9 8 7 6 5 4 3 2 1

Library of Congress Cataloging-in-Publication data is available.

Red Hamlet

Historical Materialism Book Series

The Historical Materialism Book Series is a major publishing initiative of the radical left. The capitalist crisis of the twenty-first century has been met by a resurgence of interest in critical Marxist theory. At the same time, the publishing institutions committed to Marxism have contracted markedly since the high point of the 1970s. The Historical Materialism Book Series is dedicated to addressing this situation by making available important works of Marxist theory. The aim of the series is to publish important theoretical contributions as the basis for vigorous intellectual debate and exchange on the left.

The peer-reviewed series publishes original monographs, translated texts, and reprints of classics across the bounds of academic disciplinary agendas and across the divisions of the left. The series is particularly concerned to encourage the internationalization of Marxist debate and aims to translate significant studies from beyond the English-speaking world.

For a full list of titles in the Historical Materialism Book Series
available in paperback from Haymarket Books, visit:
https://www.haymarketbooks.org/series_collections/1-historical-materialism

For Nijole

Contents

Preface

Alexander Bogdanov was a Russian philosopher, scientist, political activist, novelist, pioneer of system theory and a physician who founded the first institute of blood transfusion in Soviet Russia. Nikolai Bukharin said of him that he was 'without doubt one of the greatest and most original thinkers of our time'. By rights Bogdanov should occupy a prominent place in the modern history of Russia and the history of European Marxism, but because he fell foul of Lenin, the role he played in the Russian revolutionary movement and his contribution to the various spheres of knowledge in which he was involved, have been deliberately obscured.

The present study of Bogdanov sets out to reconstruct his system of thought, examining the way his ideas originated and evolved, and showing the contexts in which they developed. Although this is first and foremost an intellectual biography of Bogdanov, it does not treat Bogdanov's ideas in isolation from his life and political involvements. Bogdanov's political activism is the complement of his thought. It was the factor that determined that his characteristic ideas should arise and the factor that determined their character. Bogdanov himself viewed his own personality as a synthesis of the philosopher and the revolutionary, of the thinker and the activist. On several occasions in his writings he returns to the theme of Shakespeare's *Hamlet*, which he regarded as a work of genius. Bogdanov saw the character of Hamlet, not in terms of the conventional interpretation, as a person who hesitated to take decisive action, but as a peculiar combination of a warrior and an aesthete. For Bogdanov Hamlet was a person whose upbringing had been the art of warfare, one appropriate to the descendant of Vikings, but whose inclinations were towards culture and the arts. Clearly Bogdanov saw himself in this same light, as the incarnation in a single person of the spirit of revolution and that of philosophy. Bogdanov's German biographer Dietrich Grille noticed this partiality for Shakespeare's play and referred to Bogdanov as 'the Red Hamlet'. Because it suggests the synthesis of ideas and political action that was central to Bogdanov's character, I have used Grille's phrase as the title of this book.

The approach I have taken in this book is historical, that is, I have traced chronologically the evolution of Bogdanov's ideas from his first publication in 1897 to his final lecture in 1927. This method is appropriate, as it is able to reveal the connection between episodes in Bogdanov's life to what he wrote at the given time. It is also apt because in the development of Bogdanov's ideas there are a number of recurrent themes which appear throughout his writings and form the central core of his thinking. Some of the chapters consist mainly of expositions of Bogdanov's ideas, as for example the chapters on 'empirio-monism' and 'tectology'. Other chapters, like those on the 1905 revolution and Bogdanov's expulsion from the Bolshevik Centre, have a fair amount of historical narrative. The two types of chapter tend to alternate, so that the exposition of Bogdanov's thought is punctuated by passages about his life and activities.

The method adopted here can also be described as 'multi-disciplinary'. Although Bogdanov was involved in several fields of knowledge – philosophy, natural science, medicine, economics, political theory etc. – it would be wrong to treat these various fields separately. Just as Bogdanov's ideas show continuity over time, they also show continuity between disciplines. Central themes in Bogdanov's thinking repeat themselves in the different disciplines which he pursued. The most obvious example of this is his use of tectology, his universal science of organisation, in economics, political science and medicine. To appreciate the range and depth of Bogdanov's thinking requires that all its ramifications be examined. I have not written either to defend or decry Bogdanov's ideas, but to expound them as accurately and as objectively as possible.

The main source used in the present work is the extensive corpus of Bogdanov's writings. In doing this I have been helped enormously by the bibliography of Bogdanov's works by John Biggart, Georgii Gloveli and Avraham Yassour, which is an essential companion for anyone doing research on Bogdanov. I have also been greatly helped by my extensive correspondence with John Biggart, who has been unstinting in his advice and provision of Bogdanov materials.

Until 1918 Russia used a different calendar from Western Europe. The dates of the Russian (Julian) calendar were twelve days behind the Western (Gregorian) in the nineteenth century and thirteen days in the twentieth. Rather than give both versions of every date, I have used the Russian calendar in those cases where the events take place in Russia, and the Western calendar where the events take place in Western Europe.

I have used a modified version of the Library of Congress system of transliteration from Russian in the Bibliography, since this will facilitate the identification of the sources used. In the body of the text, however, where there exist generally accepted forms of proper names, I have used these rather than the forms that a strict adherence to the Library of Congress system would have dictated (Berdyaev instead of Berdiaev, Lunacharsky instead of Lunacharskii, Trotsky instead of Trotskii etc.). In the text, for the sake of readability, I have omitted the soft sign in transliterated Russian terms (Proletkult instead of Proletkul't).

My gratitude goes to Georgii Gloveli, Francis King, John Lowrie and Ian Thatcher for the help they have given me and the materials they have put at my

disposal. I owe special thanks to Douglas Huestis, with whom I have corresponded on the subject of Bogdanov's illness and death. As well as translating Bogdanov's *The Struggle for Viability*, Professor Huestis had researched Bogdanov's
biography and had collected a number of documents relating to Bogdanov's
life, which he kindly made available to me. I have also profited greatly from my
discussions on Bogdanov's ideas with David Rowley.

This book would have been impossible but for the resources of the Soviet
Studies section of Glasgow University Library, which has been continually
enriched by the acquisitions made by the librarians in charge. I am also deeply
grateful to the staff of Inter-Library Loans department for scouring the libraries
of the world to obtain for me the items that were not in GUL.

JDW
2017

CHAPTER 1

Tula

1 Early Life

Reminiscing on his early life, Alexander Bogdanov considered himself to have an ordinary middle-class background. His grandfather had been a sexton in Vologda, and his father, Alexander Alexandrovich Malinovsky, had also studied to be a priest. But before taking holy orders he was sent on a course of teacher's training in Vilna (now Vilnius) and became a primary school teacher in Sokolko, a small town with a population of three and a half thousand people in the adjacent province of Grodno. Before its incorporation into the Russian Empire, Sokolko had been a Polish town, and under Russian rule had a mostly Catholic and Jewish population.[1] Alexander Malinovsky had married a girl from the local minor gentry, Maria Komarowska, by whom he had six children (three boys followed by three girls) who survived into adulthood. The second of the surviving children was Bogdanov (Alexander Alexandrovich Malinovsky) who was born on 10 August 1873.[2] Five days later he was baptised in the Sokolko Orthodox parish church of St Alexander Nevsky. In 1878 the Malinovsky family left Sokolko for Mologa in the Yaroslavl province, where Bogdanov began his education.[3]

In Bogdanov's family background one is struck with the parallels with that of his rival Lenin. Lenin was born just three years earlier. He was the third of six surviving children, and his father too was a schoolteacher, later a school inspector. But the contrast between the two situations is even greater than the similarities. Whereas Lenin had grown up in a supportive family environment with parents who took great pains with the upbringing of their children, giving them attention and encouragement, Bogdanov's parents were strict and authoritarian, but undermined their authority by quarrelling incessantly. This deprived their children of the stable domestic environment which they needed. It was not, Bogdanov recalls, that his parents were bad people; it was just that they were incapable of sorting out their differences in a rational way. He adds that, in accord with Freudian principles, he always took the side of his mother against the authoritarian figure of his father. He believed too that as the second

---

1 Chlebowski and Walewski 1890, pp. 26–7.
2 Neizvestnyi Bogdanov 1995, 1, p. 25.
3 Letter from V.S. Klebaner to Douglas Huestis 31 May 1995.

eldest of the children he was to some extent shielded from the worst of his father's outbursts of anger, the brunt of this being borne by his elder brother Nikolai, who took it upon himself to protect his younger siblings.[4]

Both Bogdanov and Nikolai were highly intelligent and precocious children and learned to read very early. They were fortunate in having access to the library of the local school where their father taught. Both boys became voracious readers and spent much of their time devouring books and journals in the school library. Bogdanov recalls that he read Tolstoy's *Anna Karenina* when he was only seven, much to the annoyance of his father who considered him too young to be reading 'romances'. The young Bogdanov, in his turn, was disturbed less by his father's prohibitions on his reading than by the lack of consistency and predictability with which these prohibitions were exercised. The erratic conduct of his father left Bogdanov feeling he had been treated unreasonably and unjustly.[5]

The precocity of the two eldest boys led to a curious kind of reversal of roles with their parents. Bogdanov recalls remonstrating with his father in an attempt to make him understand the futility of arguing with his mother over trifles and allowing quarrels to gain in vehemence. In a manner which Bogdanov thought immature, his father refused to accept responsibility for the situation, putting the blame firmly on his wife. In retrospect when Bogdanov analysed the failings of his father, he was inclined to attribute them to weakness of character. He was a man who was frustrated in his ambitions. He had tried to make good the deficiencies in his education by reading a great deal after qualifying as a primary school teacher, but had been unable to advance in his career beyond becoming a school inspector. He had submitted articles to a newspaper, but they had been rejected. In Bogdanov's opinion, his father was a failure because he did not have the determination and application to succeed.[6]

Bogdanov was more charitably inclined towards his mother. He believed that she had married too early, giving birth for the first time when she was only eighteen. There had then followed a succession of ten children, four of whom died in infancy. This, in Bogdanov's opinion, had placed an intolerable strain on her nervous system and made it difficult for her to cope with the fraught domestic situation. Infant mortality was a common phenomenon in those days, and occurred in Lenin's family as well as in Bogdanov's. Bogdanov was six years old when his younger brother Vladimir died and was deeply distressed by the loss, which plunged the entire family into grief and despair. The trauma was

---

4   Neizvestnyi Bogdanov 1995, 1, p. 25.
5   Neizvestnyi Bogdanov 1995, 1, p. 26.
6   Neizvestnyi Bogdanov 1995, 1, p. 25.

repeated four years later with the death of the infant Dmitry. The only con-
solation available to the stricken family was its religious faith. To the young
Bogdanov, however, God seemed to move not only in mysterious, but in unfeel-
ing ways, to take the life of his infant brothers. One feels that if Bogdanov's had
been a stronger family unit, it would have been better placed to withstand the
kind of crises which such bereavement brought about.[7]

Looking back on his childhood, Bogdanov thought that it had influenced his
later attitudes in a number of ways. The strict but arbitrary behaviour of his
father had made him an implacable opponent of authoritarianism. The irre-
sponsibility and fecklessness of both parents had made it necessary for all of
the children to work things out for themselves and to become independent and
self-sufficient, though Bogdanov believed that in this there also lay the danger
of becoming too individualistic, a fate which he thought had befallen his elder
brother Nikolai. The tragedies Bogdanov had experienced so early in life went,
he says, to form his early childish ideal of a life without pain and death, an ideal
he was not entirely to relinquish in adult life.[8]

At the local school Bogdanov was an outstanding pupil. He had such a gift for
mathematics that his father once deputised him to teach a class in arithmetic,
his father only being in attendance.[9] Because of his academic ability, Bogdanov
was able to gain a state scholarship to proceed to secondary education, which
at that time was fee-paying and would have been an impossible expense for his
modestly paid father. At school Bogdanov was able to receive no financial help
from his family, and from the third year onwards he had to take up tutoring
other pupils to earn some money.[10]

Between 1886 and 1892 Bogdanov attended the secondary school or *gimnaziya* in Tula. He studied there as a scholarship pupil and a boarder.[11] The
curriculum in *gimnaziya* was distinguished by its inclusion of the classical languages Latin and Greek. It also included religion, Russian, mathematics, history,
the natural sciences and foreign languages. Bogdanov recalls that attending the
gimnaziya was like living in barracks or a prison and that the malevolent and
obtuse way the school was run taught him by experience to fear and detest
those in power and to reject authorities.[12] This may well have been the case,

---

7   Neizvestnyi Bogdanov 1995, 1, pp. 25, 29–32.
8   Neizvestnyi Bogdanov 1995, 1, pp. 25–6, 32.
9   Bogdanova-Malinovskaia, N.B. 1928, Ob A.A. Bogdanove-Malinovskom (Dlia Instituta
      Mozga).
10   Prot'ko and Gritsanov 2009, p. 17.
11   Nevskii 1931, p. 372.
12   Neizvestnyi Bogdanov 1995, 1, p. 18.

but being away at school must have been a welcome escape from his chaotic life at home. It is symptomatic that when the school holidays came round and the pupils returned home, Bogdanov did not do so, but stayed on at school throughout the summer vacation.

I.I. Sobolev was another boy who remained at school over the holidays, and this allowed him to get to know Bogdanov quite well. Sobolev's reminiscences provide a vivid portrait of Bogdanov in his schooldays and confirm that he was something of a prodigy. According to Sobolev, Bogdanov had a phenomenal memory and a marvellous ability to carry out complex arithmetical and algebraic calculations in his head. He was an outstanding chess player and could even play without looking at the board. He was unbeatable unless he conceded some pieces to his opponent in advance; only then would he sometimes lose. He did extremely well at his studies, and in the senior classes began to specialise in the natural sciences. Nevertheless, Bogdanov still maintained a wide range of interests, and, according to Sobolev, read many books on Russian literature as well as a large number of books in French and German.[13]

It was at the *gimnaziya* in Tula that Bogdanov made a lasting friend in Vladimir Alexandrovich Rudnev (who later took the pseudonym Bazarov), a doctor's son and a native of Tula.[14] Despite the rigours of the *gimnaziya* regime, Bogdanov graduated from it with a gold medal.[15] In 1892 Bogdanov and Rudnev both entered Moscow University to study in the Natural Sciences Department of the Faculty of Mathematics and Physics. They both also joined the student society at the university.

2   Radicalisation

In Russian universities student societies took the form of *zemliachestva*, that is, groups of students from the same town or geographical area, so that quite often they would be composed of circles of friends who had attended the same school. The *zemliachestva* were products of the innate collectivism of Russian society and were encountered not only among students, but also among workers who had left their native villages to work in the towns. *Zemliachestva* provided an element of familiarity in a strange environment and gave their members support and assistance in the difficulties that might arise. They were a

---

13   Sobolev 1992, pp. 218–19.
14   Nevskii 1931, p. 191.
15   Neizvestnyi Bogdanov 1995, 1, p. 18.

convenient form of organisation for young people from the provinces in adjusting themselves to the unfamiliar surroundings of a large Russian university.

The material support which *zemliachestva* could provide became more important after 1884 when the new University Statute, which removed the universities' autonomy, also increased the fees, with a view to making the entrance of students from poorer families more difficult. The measure did not have the desired effect; poorer students continued to enter the universities, and the financial burdens imposed on them led the students to place even greater reliance on the help provided by the *zemliachestva*. The collection and distribution of money therefore became an increasingly important function of the *zemliachestva* and much attention was devoted to the organisation of their funds. In addition to the fund set up by each *zemliachestvo*, money was also contributed to a central fund for purposes involving the student body as a whole. This central fund was administered by a committee comprising of representatives from each of the constituent *zemliachestva*.[16]

By the early 1890s the functions of the *zemliachestva* began to extend, as the need was felt by the students for aspects of education not provided by normal university courses, such as moral precepts and social responsibility. To cater for this kind of self-education the *zemliachestva* formed libraries and arranged inter-*zemliachestva* meetings. To signalise this, the central fund was re-named the Union Council (*Soiuznyi sovet*) and the body which administered it, the Union of *Zemliachestva* (*Soiuz zemliachestv*).[17]

The part played by *zemliachestva* in radicalising the student body in the late 1880s and early 1890s was a very important one. They were capable of turning students who were largely indifferent to politics into avowed opponents of the existing regime within a short space of time, owing to the peculiar environment in which they operated. For while the *zemliachestva* could afford the student moral support and material help, the same university regulations which had made membership of the *zemliachestva* almost essential had at the same time made such membership a punishable offence, by outlawing any independent student organisations. Officially *zemliachestva* did not exist and could not be so much as spoken about, so that their meetings had to take place in the utmost secrecy, thus instilling in the students the habits and techniques of conspiracy. For some students, joining a *zemliachestvo* was the first step towards joining a revolutionary organisation. A contemporary writer described the process as follows:

---

16   Byvshii student 1896, p. 491.
17   Ibid.

It is not difficult to imagine how such a state of affairs must have acted upon each fresh, sincere nature, even that completely untouched by social influences. It emerged that the most innocent institution, set up only for mutual aid and intellectual development, was an enemy of the social order. But what kind of social order could it be that prohibited such useful organisations? This question was naturally posed by many, many people. On this basis was developed and nurtured the spirit of protest, which, according to the level of a person's intellectual development, extended to wider and wider formulations, to more extensive oppositionist activity. One could adduce many examples in support of what has been said. There are not a few people whose names have become well known: Alexandrovich, Ulyanov, Łukasiewicz, Novorussky etc., etc., who began their activities in *zemliachestva*.[18]

The writer is referring to the group of students, including Lenin's elder brother Alexander, who attempted unsuccessfully to assassinate the tsar Alexander III in 1887.[19] Lenin, in fact, joined the revolutionary movement by the same route; he was forced to leave Kazan University in December 1887 for participation in the Samara-Simbirsk *zemliachestvo*, which helped organise a demonstration against the provisions of the University Statute of 1884.[20]

On entering Moscow University Bogdanov joined the Tula *zemliachestvo* and became its representative in the Union of *Zemliachestva*. Although there had been student disturbances at Moscow University in 1890, Bogdanov's first two years of study passed in relative tranquillity. However, the authorities were becoming increasingly suspicious of student activities at this time because the first Social-Democratic circles appeared at Moscow University during the winter of 1891–2, involving students from the Kazan and the Ekaterinoslav *zemliachestva*. Whereas the Kazan *zemliachestvo* confined itself to organising student study groups, members of the Ekaterinoslav *zemliachestvo* began to conduct propaganda amongst the Moscow workers.[21] A number of workers' circles were quickly formed, mostly from workers at engineering works and railway workshops, and by September 1893 a rudimentary form of organisational structure had emerged so that the workers' circles were presided over by a group of six people, only some of whom belonged to the Ekaterinoslav *zemliachestvo*. It consisted of the two doctors A.N. Vinokurov and S.I. Mitskevich, plus M.N. Man-

---

18   Staryi student 1895, p. 310.
19   See White 1998.
20   Khait 1958, pp. 189–91.
21   Sanburov 1978, pp. 96–7.

delshtam (Liadov), E.I. Sponti and the railway worker S.I. Prokofiev. To maintain regular contact with the workers' circles, of which there were about a dozen, it was decided to form a Central Workers' Circle consisting of one representative from each circle established in the various factories and workshops. Members of the workers' circles, in their turn, carried on propaganda work among the remaining workers in the places of work, so that the total number of workers involved was quite considerable.[22]

The success of the Moscow Social-Democrat organisation, which began to refer to itself as the 'Workers' Union', soon attracted the attention of the police, who decided in December 1894 to use the occasion of demonstrations at Moscow University to carry out the arrest of both student radicals and the organisers of workers' circles. As an activist in the Union Council of *zemliachesva*, Bogdanov was one of those caught up in the mass arrests. Although Vinokurov and Mitskevich from the Workers' Union were captured in the raid, Liadov and Sponti managed to evade arrest, as did most of the worker members of the organisation.[23]

The student demonstrations in which Bogdanov had been involved had been precipitated by events surrounding the death of tsar Alexander III on 20 October 1894. There were hopes throughout Russia that the accession of Nicholas II would inaugurate an era of liberal reforms. In the brief interlude of uncertainty, N.S. Berdyaev, the chief of the Moscow Okhrana, looked on the students as a potential threat to public order and political stability. His apprehensions were increased when the students, being no less prone to 'senseless dreams' than their elders, drew up a petition to present to the new tsar. The petition requested: 1. the return of university autonomy; 2. academic freedom; 3. unimpeded access to university education for all who had completed secondary education without regard to nationality, creed or gender; 4. reduction in tuition fees and 5. freedom for student organisations. The petition, with its allusions to the repressive policy of the tsarist government in several spheres of Russian life, was regarded by Berdyaev as highly inflammatory.[24]

The Okhrana tried in every way to stop the students presenting their petition. An interdict was placed on all student meetings and members of the Union Council were placed under close scrutiny. Finally, on 27 October Berdyaev appeared at a Union Council meeting held in the apartment of one of the students and took the names of all 21 students who were present. To this list Berdyaev added the names of other students, who for some reason or other

---

22   Mitskevich 1906, p. 12; Sanburov 1978, pp. 100–1.
23   Mitskevich 1937, p. 194.
24   Byvshii student 1896, p. 493.

had fallen foul of the Okhrana, arriving at a total of about fifty. The list included Bogdanov and his friends from the Tula *zemliachestvo*, Rudnev, S.N. Stavrovsky and P.G. Smidovich. It also included Vinokurov, Mitskevich and the medical student who was Plekhanov's nephew and later to head the Soviet Commissariat of Health, N.A. Semashko. Having discovered the 'ringleaders' of the student movement, the Okhrana decided to exile them to the provinces at the earliest opportunity.[25]

If Berdyaev was concerned to prevent student disturbances, his list of suspected trouble-makers was extremely defective. In 1894 the attention of most students was taken up with self-education and discussions about Russia's future economic development. They had no interest in encouraging student rebellions which would inevitably end in the dissolution of their organisations. The Union Council was completely opposed to any open confrontation with the authorities. So too were the students who belonged to Social-Democratic groups, as this would jeopardise their contacts with the workers. Not only Bogdanov and his friends, but also Mitskevich and Vinokurov were in favour of maintaining order and tranquillity at the University. There was, however, a group of student radicals who were determined to use any excuse to bring about confrontation and encourage disturbances among the students.

Such an opportunity was soon to present itself. The Moscow University authorities required the eminent historian Vasily Kliuchevsky, the chairman of the Russian History and Antiquity Society, to make a speech in commemoration of Alexander III. Kliuchevsky, who was well known and respected for his liberal views, found himself in an awkward situation. He could either win the applause of liberal opinion but risk his career with a speech critical of the deceased emperor, or he could make a diplomatic speech, and risk being accused of hypocrisy. Kliuchevsky chose the latter course, and on 28 October at a meeting of the Russian Historical and Antiquity Society delivered an oration full of praise for Alexander III, marvelling at the way 'the will of the tsar expressed the thoughts of the people and the will of the people became the thought of the tsar'. Kliuchevsky had assumed that as his speech had been made within the confines of a Historical and Antiquity Society meeting, it would go no further. However, it was printed in pamphlet form as well as being published in the *Proceedings* of the Society. In this way it became widely known among the students at the university. They were astonished and dismayed that Kliuchevsky could speak as he had done about thirteen years of reaction.

A young Moscow schoolteacher called Ivan Ivanovich Skvortsov, later generally known as Skvortsov-Stepanov, who was associated with the Vyatka *zem-*

liachestvo, devised a method of demonstrating the disapproval of the student body for Kliuchevsky's hypocrisy. The students bought up some two hundred copies of the pamphlet version of Kliuchevsky's speech and to each copy attached a duplicated sheet on which was printed Fonvizin's fable of the fox who praised the dead lion for its 'love of cattle'. On the title page of the pamphlet was inscribed 'Second edition, enlarged and emended'. The students then distributed the new edition of Kliuchevsky's speech through the post. It was decided to arrange a protest demonstration at Kliuchevsky's regular lecture on 30 November.[26]

Despite the entreaties of the Union Council to the contrary, the demonstration went ahead. On the appointed day students from various faculties crowded into Kliuchevsky's lecture, and when the historian mounted the dais, he was greeted with a cacophony of whistles from his opponents and applause from his supporters. The tumult continued for several minutes, the applause eventually triumphing over the whistles, when most of the crowd departed and Kliuchevsky was left to deliver his lecture to his history students. The incident was reported to the Rector, though without any mention of the counter-demonstration by Kliuchevsky's supporters, and the University authorities began enquiries to discover who the instigators of the disturbance had been. Skvortsov-Stepanov was not discovered, but several students noticed at the lecture were held responsible and were disciplined accordingly. Three of them were expelled from the University.[27]

The investigation made by the University authorities into who had instigated the demonstration had been so cursory and the punishment to those deemed guilty so arbitrary that the Union Council had difficulty in restraining the students from violence. The Union Council accordingly requested that the case of the disciplined students be re-examined. This was done on 2 December, but the original verdict was allowed to stand. The Union Council thereupon repeated the request for the case to be re-opened with the warning that the dissatisfaction might erupt into violence. The university authorities, however, refused to accede to the request.

The students, who had assembled in the chemistry laboratory, were incensed at this uncompromising stance, and were kept in check only by the presence of detachments of troops placed round the University. Persuaded by the Union Council, they agreed nevertheless to ask the professors to intercede with the University authorities to re-open the case and see to it that justice was done.

---

26   Byvshii student 1896, p. 494; Nechkina 1974, p. 350.

27   Nechkina 1974, p. 351.

On receiving word that some of the professors, including Kliuchevsky, had consented to do this, the students dispersed.

That night, however (2–3 December), all the students whose names appeared on Berdyaev's list were arrested and taken to the Butyrki Prison. No specific charges were brought against them, but from the night of 4 December batches of students were sent to the provinces, sentenced to a period of banishment of three years. Bogdanov and his friends were sent back to Tula. None of them at that time was a committed revolutionary; on the contrary, they had been expelled from the University despite being advocates of moderation and conciliation.

The demonstration against Kliuchevsky was an important episode in Bogdanov's biography for launching his career as a revolutionary. But it is also a significant landmark in the formation of the group of people who would become his associates in that revolutionary career. They included his friend from Tula Rudnev (Bazarov), the man who had so abruptly precipitated him into the oppositionist camp Ivan Skvortsov-Stepanov, and the members of the Moscow workers' circle Mitskevich and Liadov. One can also include here an indirect victim of the episode, Kliuchevsky's postgraduate student M.N. Pokrovsky. In 1894 Pokrovsky broke off relations with his former teacher and after a short sojourn in the liberal camp, joined Bogdanov, Skvortsov-Stepanov and the rest as a Social Democrat.

3   Back in Tula

Tula, the town in which Bogdanov had been educated and now his place of banishment, was unlike most provincial towns in Russia in that it had been an industrial centre from the seventeenth century. Peter the Great had founded the Imperial Armaments Factory in Tula and it was the manufacture of firearms as well as samovars that formed Tula's traditional industries. At the beginning of the 1890s the government decided to re-equip the army with a new rifle. The Imperial Armaments Factory was consequently re-tooled and the work force expanded, so that by 1897 the Factory employed over ten thousand workers, the neighbouring Cartridge Factory employing around three thousand.[28]

The gunsmiths of Tula were not, however, a modern industrial labour force. Most carried on their trade as a handicraft industry almost exactly as they had done during the years of serfdom. Even in the 1890s a considerable propor-

---

28   Bynkina 1963, p. 8; Istoriia tul'skogo oruzheinogo zavoda 1973, p. 91.

tion of the gunsmiths produced gun components in villages around Tula and resisted attempts to induce them to work under the same roof in a factory.[29] The armament workers had lost few of their peasant attributes by virtue of their occupation. The same was true of those engaged in tho making of oamo vars. These too were manufactured as a cottage industry or in small industrial concerns. The traditional work force in Tula was in consequence conservative, quiescent and largely impervious to political propaganda.[30]

From the 1880s new industries began to develop in Tula, creating a different type of work force, some of whose members were recruited from other industrial centres in Russia. In 1883 the Ammunition Factory was opened, which by 1898 employed 3,600 workers. In the second half of the nineteenth century, moreover, there was a rapid expansion in the mining industry around Tula, and in 1896 a cast-iron foundry was built outside the town at Kosaya Gora, financed by Belgian capital. Bogdanov's arrival in Tula, therefore, coincided with something of an industrial upsurge and the leavening of the traditional work force with newcomers with less conservative attitudes.[31]

The labour movement in Tula owed its existence not only to incoming workers but also to members of the intelligentsia who, like Bogdanov, had been exiled there for political offences. In the 1880s the workers' circles which had been established were inspired by People's Will, but Social-Democratic circles began to appear at the beginning of the 1890s, set up by workers exiled from St Petersburg for political activities in the capital. It was these workers who ensured that, prior to Bogdanov's arrival in Tula in 1894, a Social-Democratic movement already existed there. It was within this movement that Bogdanov's attitudes to workers' organisations were formed, attitudes which he retained for the rest of his life and which permeated his thinking. These pioneers of Social-Democracy in Tula are of considerable importance to the study of Bogdanov's intellectual development.

During the years 1891–2 there arrived in Tula a group of workers banished from St Petersburg, including G.A. Mefodiev, V.V. Buianov and N.I. Rudelev, all of whom became involved in the local workers' circles and greatly influenced the development of Social-Democracy in Tula. These workers had previously belonged to one of the first Social-Democratic organisations in St Petersburg, which is associated with the name of M.I. Brusnev.

In 1889 Mikhail Brusnev, a student at the St Petersburg Technological Institute, and V.S. Golubev, a student at St Petersburg University, were invited to take

---

29   Istoriia tul'skogo oruzheinogo zavoda 1973, p. 49.
30   Bynkina 1963, p. 8.
31   Bynkina 1963, p. 11.

part in the running of a number of workers' circles which had previously been organised by some Polish students. These were study circles which provided instruction in such subjects as history and political economy; they were also concerned with raising the workers' political awareness, and discussed working conditions, workers' organisations and how these might campaign to improve living conditions. Between 1889 and 1890 the number of such circles in Brusnev's organisation increased to over 20 in various workplaces throughout the city.

At the end of 1890 the network of workers' circles was given an organisational structure. Each circle had its own organiser from among the workers and its own fund to which the workers contributed. This money was used to buy books or support the workers during strikes. Each month the workers' circle fund paid a donation to a central fund which was administered by a Central Workers' Circle, a committee of delegates from the local workers' circles and one representative from the group of intelligentsia, which included Brusnev and L.B. Krasin, who was to become a close associate of Bogdanov. The worker members of the Central Workers' Circle included G.A. Mefodiev and V.V. Buianov, who were exiled to Tula at the start of the 1890s.

A characteristic feature of the Brusnev organisation was the amount of initiative taken by the workers themselves and the point of principle made of this by the members of the intelligentsia involved in the workers' circles. It was understood by both workers and intelligentsia in the organisation that the 'liberation of the working class was the affair of the working class itself' and that the intelligentsia had no special part to play.[32] Their role was to educate the workers and teach them the skills necessary to organise themselves, but when this was done the workers would have no further need of the intelligentsia. Golubev stated: 'As regards our role as intelligentsia, we understood it to be an auxiliary one and one concerned with leading the movement temporarily'.[33] According to Brusnev the aim of the organisation was:

> to liberate the workers' movement from the leadership of the intelligentsia, an unreliable and inconsistent leadership, frequently at odds with the ideology of the working class. The idea that the liberation of the working class was the affair of the working class itself was introduced by us into all the workers' circles and was completely assimilated by our workers, even by those who were not in positions of leadership.[34]

---

32   Brusnev 1923, p. 10.
33   Nevskii 1925, p. 302.
34   Brusnev 1928, p. 69.

This was the approach to workers' organisations which Buianov and Mefodiev brought to Tula. It was to be one which was later to be encountered by Bogdanov when he came into contact with the Tula workers' movement.

The organisation that Buianov and Mefodiev established in Tula was a replica of the one they had known in St Petersburg. Workers' study circles set up in various enterprises sent representatives to a central body. There were about fifty workers in the various workers' circles. One of them, Nikolai Polosatov, later recalled the kind of instruction that he obtained from former members of the Brusnev group. His memoirs show clearly that the St Petersburg organisation had not been purely Social-Democratic, but had retained some remnants at least of People's Will ideology. According to Polosatov:

> We began going regularly to Buianov's place, where he gave us short lectures on the history of the workers' movement in Russia, on Khalturin ... on 1881, on what the Narodniki stood for, and why the tsar was assassinated ...[35]

While Buianov represented the People's Will current within the Brusnev organisation, Mefodiev's lectures were much more in keeping with Social-Democratic thinking. As Polosatov recalled:

> Mefodiev told us about Marxism; he said that there would come a time when the workers would take everything into their own hands and they would take charge of everything. I asked him about the peasantry and he said that they would not go along with the workers for a long time, but that eventually they would side with the workers and form a close alliance with them. They would then exchange their produce for the goods we made. As I remember, I asked what would happen to the tsar, because he would then no longer be necessary. Mefodiev said that the tsar would be got rid of, or there would be no tsars in general by that time, and that we would have a republic like the Americans had with a president at its head.[36]

Until his arrest in April 1892 and the collapse of his organisation Brusnev maintained close contact with the workers' circles in Tula, which, he recalled, 'were organised on the model of those in St Petersburg'. He added, however, that they

---

35   Polosatov 1923, p. 25.
36   Polosatov 1923, pp. 25–6.

had a serious weakness in that there was 'a shortage of intelligentsia to take charge of them'.[37] Though the workers' circles in Tula continued to exist after the arrest of Buianov and Mefodiev, which followed that of Brusnev, the need for help from members of the intelligentsia was still acutely felt. The situation was alleviated in December 1894 when Ivan Saveliev, a worker from the Armaments Factory, came across Bogdanov. As Bogdanov recalled in 1918:

> In the mid 1890s of the past century in Tula a young worker by the name of Ivan Ivanovich Saveliev set about organising workers' circles at the Armaments and Ammunition factories ... In this provincial town he had searched for a long time and without success for *intelligenty* who could do propaganda work until he found me ...[38]

It is important for an understanding of Bogdanov's thought to realise that he was not only the inheritor of the Brusnev organisation in Tula but of the Brusnev conception of workers' organisations as well. The idea put forward by Brusnev and Golubev, that the intelligentsia played an auxiliary part in the workers' movement, and that the object of educating the workers was to make them completely independent of the intelligentsia, was also an idea which guided Bogdanov. It formed the basis for his conception of Party Schools at Capri and Bologna and for his ideas on proletarian culture in Soviet times. It was given theoretical expression in his philosophical works. Indeed, for Bogdanov, the inadequacies of the intelligentsia, their individualism and their consequent metaphysical view of the world, contrasted with the collectivist and monist outlook of the workers. The theme runs through Bogdanov's works from the earliest to the latest. It was a conception that was based on Bogdanov's actual experience of the workers' movement, from the mainstream of Social-Democracy in Russia.

According to Bogdanov in an autobiographical article published in 1923, he was introduced to Ivan Saveliev by O.N. Tilicheeva, a teacher at the *feldsher* school, soon after his arrival in Tula. By the beginning of 1895 a workers' study group had been assembled in which Bogdanov taught political economy. The group, however, was not successful and in the summer a second group was formed with sixteen members, and this remained in existence until it was dissolved by a series of arrests in 1899.[39]

---

37   Brusnev 1928, p. 75.
38   Bogdanov 1918a, p. 10.
39   Bogdanov 1923, p. 16.

In May of 1895 Skvortsov-Stepanov was arrested, not for his part in organising the Kliuchevsky demonstration, but because of his contact with a terrorist
group which was planning to assassinate Nicholas II. The group was betrayed
and its members arrested. Skvortsov-Stepanov was imprisoned for six months
and banished for three years to Tula. As Skvortsov-Stepanov had been studying
economics in his spare time and had taught himself German to read Marx in the
original, he willingly joined Bogdanov in teaching the workers in the group.[40]
By 1896 the number of study circles had multiplied and to the teaching staff
there had been added Rudnev and a Cossack student Mariia Pavlovna Poliakova
who, like the rest, had been sentenced to banishment in Tula.[41]

At the home of his friend Bazarov, Bogdanov made the acquaintance of Natalia Bogdanovna Korsak, a medical orderly and midwife who was working in
the medical practice of Bazarov's father. Born on 24 January 1865, and eight
years older than Bogdanov, she was soon to become his fiancée. Natalia was the
daughter of a minor noble of the Orel province, and had received a 'domestic
education'. In 1882 she had been licensed to teach, but had not found teaching to her taste. Her ambition had been to become a doctor, but she had been
twice refused admission to the university to study medicine, once because of
her youth, and on the second occasion because of the restriction on women
entering university. She was, however, able to qualify as a medical orderly (*feldsher*) and a midwife, and it was as a midwife and nurse that she was employed
in Rudnev's medical practice. In Natalia Korsak Bogdanov had a knowledgeable
companion who could assist him in his political and literary activities. Natalia's
memoirs also suggest that, at least in the early days, she was able to help Bogdanov out financially.[42]

The study groups in which Bogdanov taught met in secret, usually out of
doors. In the summer meetings would take place in the woods and fields around
Tula; in colder weather they would assemble nearer to the town, in the Pet-
rovsky Cemetery. One worker later described his first encounter with Bogdanov's study circle, and in so doing gives an early pen portrait of Bogdanov
himself.

> We went on towards Gosteevka and soon on a knoll we saw some low
> bushes growing around a small hollow. This was known as the Baskov
> Thicket. As we approached it we caught sight of a figure at the side of the
> hollow. This turned out to be one of our friends, N.A. Polosatov. He told us

---

40   Krivtsov 1929, p. 8; Pokrovskii 1929, p. 4.
41   Bogdanov 1923, pp. 16–17.
42   Belova 1974, pp. 11–12; Malinovskaia 1928.

that an *intelligent* had arrived, and soon we came upon a small group of our workmates sitting in a little glade among the bushes. Seated in their midst was a young man in a dark red Russian shirt gathered around the waist. He had a kindly face with expressive, intelligent eyes. He gave us a friendly greeting and we joined the others on the grass.[43]

Teaching in the workers' study circles had the effect of transforming Bogdanov and his friends from followers of People's Will to Social Democrats. As Bogdanov explained:

We, the members of the intelligentsia, adopted a well-defined Marxist, Social-Democrat outlook only at the beginning of 1896. Before that Bazarov and I held People's Will views. Skvortsov-Stepanov and Poliakova arrived with that same viewpoint. What quickly decided us was the very nature of our work and the spirit of the workers' circles.[44]

According to Bazarov, this did not mean that Bogdanov subscribed to the views of the classic writers of the Narodnik school, Lavrov and Mikhailovsky; in the way he viewed historical development he was much closer to Marx than to these writers, since he saw the proletariat rather than the radical intelligentsia as the main force behind the Russian revolution. Nevertheless, in his outlook there were still some survivals of Narodnik ideology. Prominent among these were the recognition of the peasant commune as a possible basis for socialist development and the acceptance of political terror as an addition to the mass revolutionary movement of the working class. In 1895 Bogdanov still defended these two Narodnik supplements to Marxism, but in the following year he renounced them as he adopted an increasingly consistent Marxist point of view.[45] According to Bogdanov, a decisive factor in his own conversion to Marxism and that of Bazarov and Skvortsov-Stepanov was reading Lenin's article 'The Economic Content of Narodism and the Criticism of it in Mr Peter Struve's Book' (1895).[46] As Bogdanov did not indulge in honorific mentions of Lenin, the statement can be taken at face value.

---

43   Sokolov 1923, p. 19.
44   Bogdanov 1923, p. 17.
45   Bazarov 2004, p. 106.
46   Bogdanov 1923, p. 17.

4   The Short Course of Economic Science

It was Bogdanov's lectures in the workers' study groups which provided the stimulus for his first published works. Bogdanov makes it clear that the workers had a considerable input into how these works originated. He recalled:

> I commenced teaching in the first study circle with the legal books that I had at my disposal, Karyshev's *Economic Discourses*, Ivaniukov's *Course of Political Economy* etc. The unsuitability of these works was soon apparent, and, on Saveliev's advice, I began to put together special lectures from which there emerged *A Short Course of Economic Science*. The breadth and variety of the questions asked by the workers compelled me to re-examine my world outlook as a whole, and it was this which gave rise to my first work of philosophy *The Basic Elements of the Historical View of Nature*. This work, however, was not used directly in the courses.[47]

In an earlier memoir Bogdanov recalled in rather greater detail how his first works had been conceived, emphasising the interconnection of economic with philosophical questions. Referring to the Tula workers he stated that:

> Their questions and comments on what we were reading soon convinced me that the books I had selected did not satisfy their needs, and in particular were ill-suited for their way of thinking. Explanatory reading soon became a boring prologue to lively discussions which often went far beyond the topics we had been reading about. In these discussions certain tendencies kept appearing, all of their own accord, and a definite direction began to emerge, which prompted the searching mind of the young lecturer to seek to connect as links in a complex chain of development phenomena relating to technology and economics with their concomitant forms of spiritual culture. Thus there arose the need to make up my own course of lectures in which the material was arranged in just such a connection. The result was *A Short Course of Economic Science*, which was later published after some extensive cutting operations by the censor.[48]

According to Bazarov, the system for teaching in the workers' study circles was based on the practice of the 'University Extension' movement: there would be

---

47   Bogdanov 1923, p. 16.
48   Bogdanov 1918a, p. 10.

lectures followed by seminars in which the students could consolidate what they had learned by asking questions and participating in discussions.[49] Bogdanov emphasised that the workers he taught were not passive recipients of knowledge, but were a perceptive and demanding audience.[50]

Bazarov's memoirs are instructive in explaining how the approach adopted by the *Short Course* was arrived at. Bogdanov's objective was to 'democratise' Marx's doctrine. By democratisation, as opposed to its popularisation, he meant presenting his subject in such a way that it would be widely accessible without any simplifications or distortions, and this not only in its conclusions, but also in its methods. To present *Das Kapital* in this manner was a considerable challenge, the biggest obstacle being the first chapter of the first volume which dealt with the concept of value using Hegelian dialectics,[51] an approach clearly resistant to any attempt at 'democratisation'. Bogdanov, however, thought that for the purpose of conveying Marx's ideas it was unnecessary to expound them in Hegelian terms. As Bazarov pointed out, the approach adopted in the *Short Course* was not only significant for its effectiveness in making Marx's ideas accessible, but also for being a novel scholarly interpretation of Marx's doctrine.

Because it was intended to be accompanied by lectures, Bogdanov's textbook served as an outline of the course, with numerous headings and subheadings, each topic being treated in a summary fashion. The clarity of the exposition comes from Bogdanov's profound knowledge of his subject. In explaining what Marx meant by 'exchange value', for example, Bogdanov had realised that the different forms of exchange described by Marx, which culminated in the exchange of goods for money, represented historical stages in the evolution of the capitalist system.[52] This allowed him to expound Marx's ideas in *Das Kapital* historically, and to show the workings of the economic systems that had preceded capitalism. Bogdanov's book traces the history of economic development, chiefly in Western Europe, through primitive communism, slavery, feudalism and finally, capitalism in its free competition and monopolist stages.

A prominent feature of Bogdanov's book is that the author does not confine himself to economics in the narrow sense. In dealing with the successive eco-

---

49   Bazarov 2004, p. 107.

50   Bogdanov 1918, p. 10.

51   The version of *Capital* that Bogdanov and his friends had at their disposal was the Russian translation by Nikolai Danielson. This translation was of the first German edition of 1867, and had reproduced faithfully all the Hegelian terminology of the original (later progressively eliminated by Marx in the second German and the French editions).

52   Bogdanov 1897, pp. 39–45.

nomic systems he includes descriptions of the contemporary political orders, and also of important intellectual developments of the time. In doing this, Bogdanov displays an extensive knowledge of the slave system of the ancient world and the political orders that went with it. He shows an obvious sympathy for Athenian democracy, and admiration for Greek philosophy, but deplores the fact that even a great thinker like Plato could not envisage a world without slaves.[53]

The *Short Course* concluded by giving an outline history of economic thought from its beginnings until the present time. It did not, however, include any mention of Marx or his commentators, such as Karl Kautsky or Nikolai Sieber. Obviously, here there had been considerations of censorship.

In retrospect, what is most significant about this first edition of Bogdanov's most popular book is that it contains none of his own philosophical ideas. Topics that Bogdanov would later treat philosophically, such as the division of labour, the distinction between organising and executory functions, the function of machines, are mentioned, but on a purely economic plane. In this respect the first edition of the *Short Course* is unique.

When the *Short Course* had undergone all the corrections that Bogdanov thought necessary to make it accessible to his intended audience, he prepared it for publication. In this connection it was necessary for Bogdanov to choose a suitable pseudonym for himself as author. He resolved this by using his fiancée Natalia's patronymic – 'Bogdanov', which he continued to employ throughout his literary career.

Before the book could be published, however, it had to be submitted to the censor for approval, and Skvortsov-Stepanov, who had the reputation among the group for being something of an authority on getting things past the censor, was entrusted with editing the manuscript with this in view. However, Skvortsov-Stepanov's efforts were largely unsuccessful, because the book was published only after it had been seriously distorted by substantial cuts in the text. According to Bazarov, for example, the chapter on 'surplus value' was excised entirely (though many references to surplus value remain in the text); Natalia mentions the removal of a long footnote on kulaks. It remained for Skvortsov-Stepanov to collate and send to the publisher the sections of the book that had been spared by the censor.[54]

Despite the severity of the censor's cuts, the overall character and design of the *Short Course* ensured that it made the impact that Bogdanov hoped for.

---

53   Bogdanov 1897, p. 54.
54   Bazarov 2004, p. 108; Memoirs of Nataliia Bogdanovna Korsak (Malinovskaia).

This is shown by the review of the book by Lenin that was published in 1898 in the journal *Mir Bozhii*. Lenin introduced his review by saying that his object-ive was to draw attention to the outstanding merits of this book, as well as to indicate some places where improvement was possible. In his judgement, of all the guides to the subject of political economy that were available, this was the best. Lenin praised the clarity of the book's exposition, and admired the way in which the author had arranged his material chronologically, characterising the periods of economic development in their proper sequence: primitive clan communism, feudalism, guilds and, finally, capitalism. This, Lenin declared, was exactly how one ought to expound political economy.[55]

Lenin went on to say that the outstanding merit of the *Short Course* was that the 'author adhered consistently to historical materialism'. In dealing with a given period of economic development he would relate this to the political institutions of the time, to the structure of the family and to the main cur-rents of social thought. The author would explain how the particular economic system gave rise to a certain division of society into classes and showed how the interests of these classes were reflected in, for example, certain schools of economic thought. In Lenin's judgement, the *Short Course* would be of great benefit both to teachers and students of political economy.[56]

Having discussed at some length the merits of Bogdanov's book, Lenin craved the indulgence of the 'venerable author' to be allowed to mention some minor points that might be introduced by way of improvement. Some of these concerned terminology used or topics that might be mentioned, and included the suggestion that more examples might be taken from the Russian situation.

5   The Basic Elements of the Historical View of Nature

As Bogdanov recalled, it was while teaching in the workers' study circles in Tula that he worked on his first philosophical book, *The Basic Elements of the Histor-ical View of Nature*, published in 1899. This was a significant work, because there appear in it for the first time ideas that would later become characteristic of Bogdanov's philosophical system. Whereas in the *Short Course* Bogdanov had rejected the approach of Hegelian dialectics in expounding Marx's economics, in *Basic Elements* he showed that Hegelian dialectics were also unnecessary in dealing with broader philosophical questions. Bogdanov was looking for a

---

55   Lenin 1958–65, 4, p. 36.
56   Lenin 1958–65, 4, pp. 37–8.

method that would be universally applicable, that would be 'monist' – and dialectics did not conform to this criterion. As he explained: 'The word "dialectics" suggests facts of development which are characteristic ... only of living nature ... plus the fact that it indicates precisely "development in contradictions", which is even less a universal fact'.[57] The approach adopted in *Basic Elements* was to argue that nothing was static, and that everything was in a constant state of flux, interacting with its environment. What passed for stability or immobility was in fact the result of a moving equilibrium of countervailing forces. This phenomenon of the 'moving equilibrium' could be observed in all spheres of existence. This was, Bogdanov explained, why he had called this approach to reality 'historical' rather than 'dialectical'.

The area in Marxist philosophy where Hegelian dialectics had been most prominently deployed was in explaining the rapid change from quantity to quality, as Georgii Plekhanov had done in the 1880s. Bogdanov showed that this could be done more simply and convincingly in terms of moving equilibrium. Such rapid changes, he argued, were examples of 'crises', such as 'When water boils, a string breaks, a patient man lashes out after one too many insults'. The essence of a crisis was the triumph of one of the contending forces over another.[58]

In *Basic Elements* Bogdanov attempts to tie together the phenomena of the inorganic world, living things and human society to form a unified or 'monist' system. To do this he makes use of the two important principles which have revolutionised science in recent times. One of these is Darwin's theory of natural selection, and the other is the law of the conservation of energy as formulated by Robert Mayer, Rudolf Clausius, James Joule, Hermann Helmholtz and Wilhelm Ostwald.[59]

In discussing social questions in *Basic Elements*, Bogdanov elaborated on a topic he had only touched upon in the *Short Course*. This was the emergence within primitive society of two groups of people, a minority who gave orders and a majority who carried out orders. The people who organised were also the ones who decided on how the resources of the community were to be distributed, and in the process took care to favour themselves. These divisions were strengthened in feudal society, in which it was the feudal lord who was the organiser and who distributed the social product, and it was the vassals who carried out the orders. This division into organisers and executors would become a constant feature of Bogdanov's later writings.

---

57   Bogdanov 1899a, p. 18.
58   Bogdanov 1899a, pp. 53–9.
59   Bogdanov 1899a, pp. 33, 39.

A second element in Bogdanov's treatment of social questions in *Basic Elements* that would constantly reappear in his later works was the subject of morality. Bogdanov explained the emergence of morality historically. In primitive societies infringements of established customs were dealt with by expelling the perpetrators from the community or by putting them to death. In all cases the penalty was crude and immediate. As society became more sophisticated the existing order was maintained in a more indirect way, by prohibitions of behaviour that would violate customary law. The modern concepts of morality were nothing more than the internalised forms of these prohibitions.[60]

Although not outwardly polemical, Bogdanov's rejection of Hegelian dialectics and his explanation of changes of state by means of 'crises' contradicted the interpretation of Marxist philosophy propounded by Plekhanov, who was at that time regarded as the leading authority on the subject. Plekhanov had coined the term 'dialectical materialism' to characterise the method adopted by Marx and Engels, which he believed to have Hegelian roots, and he had laid special emphasis on what he considered to be the revolutionary content of Hegel's philosophy: the doctrine that changes in quantity led to changes in quality.

In fact, Plekhanov was aghast when he read *The Basic Elements of the Historical View of Nature* in the autumn of 1901, declaring Bogdanov's philosophy to be a 'decisive rejection of materialism', a view he communicated to Lenin. Plekhanov thought that Bogdanov's book should be condemned in print, but, unwilling to undertake the task himself, he delegated it to his follower L. Akselrod (Ortodoks).[61] Ortodoks, however, was preoccupied with family matters at the time and was unable to write the desired review. It was only three years later that she finally managed to fulfil Plekhanov and Lenin's request and publish an article in *Iskra* denouncing Bogdanov's ideas.

6 The Second Edition of the Short Course

In 1899, the same year as *The Basic Elements* was published, there appeared a second edition of Bogdanov's *Short Course of Economic Science*. In the foreword to the book Bogdanov explained that since the appearance of the first edition he had been engaged in writing *The Basic Elements of the Historical View of Nature*, a work that expounded the essence of the monist outlook. Writing the *Basic Elements*, he said, had led him to the conclusion that there was a neces-

---

60   Bogdanov 1899a, pp. 194–7.
61   Iovchuk and Kurbatova 1973, pp. 128–31.

sity and a possibility to expound economic science in a more consistent and more monist way. He also said that he wanted to take into account Bazarov's book *Productive Labour and Value-Creating Labour*.[62]

In his book Bazarov argued that in *Das Kapital* Marx had given too little weight to the activity of the merchant in the creation of value. While he agreed with Marx that the labour of transporting goods was value-creating labour, he argued that, in certain socio-economic conditions, the labour which facilitated the circulation of commodities, which transferred goods from the producer to the consumer, was also socially-necessary labour, and therefore labour which created value. Bazarov's argument on the importance of merchants in economic development was taken up by Bogdanov in the second edition of the *Short Course*. There he has an extensive section devoted to 'merchant capitalism', which he regards as defining a whole era in economic history. Bogdanov considers that the roles of the merchant and the usurer are closely related, and in the case of the Russian situation it is the kulak who performs the part of the usurer, and by charging exorbitant interest on his loans deprives the peasant of his land.[63]

The second edition of the *Short Course* was a more philosophical work than the first. It devoted increased attention to the distinction that emerged in the course of historical development between people who organised and those who carried out orders.[64] There was also an indication of how this distinction would be overcome; in discussing machine production, Bogdanov drew attention to the fact that machines increasingly took on the executory function that had formerly been characteristic of workers, whereas the workers who supervised the machines acted more and more in the capacity of organisers.[65]

In the second edition of his book Bogdanov was more systematic in the treatment of the successive economic orders. Each one is discussed under four main heads: the productive relations of the given order, its forms of distribution, its social psychology and the factors for change within it, factors which would bring about its evolution into the succeeding form of economic organisation. Different factors come into play at different stages of economic development. With his more schematic treatment of the subject his disquisition on the slave system of the ancient world and its associated intellectual developments that had graced the first edition were sacrificed.

---

62   Bogdanov 1899, p. 1; Bazarov 1899.
63   Bogdanov 1899, p. 134.
64   Bogdanov 1899, p. 24.
65   Bogdanov 1899, p. 236.

Whereas the stages that Marx famously listed in his *Contribution to the Cri-tique of Political Economy* were the Asiatic, ancient, feudal and modern bour-geois, Bogdanov's scheme was more varied; he distinguished two main eras of economic development: the era of natural economy and the era of exchange economy. To the first era belonged: primitive clan communism, the patriarchal clan system and the feudal order. The second era embraced the periods of merchant capitalism and industrial capitalism. The book devotes as much space to pre-capitalist as it does to capitalist forms of economic organisa-tion.[66]

In characterising the relation of mankind to nature in primitive clan group-ings Bogdanov makes the general point that man is a social animal, that con-temporary science does not know of any people either in the past or in the present who did not or do not live in society. In the struggle with nature it is impossible to dispense with the help of others. The basic relations of produc-tion in the clan group were simple cooperation. Primitive distribution had an organised communist character. There was no trace of individual private prop-erty; what was produced together was distributed together and immediately consumed. There was no accumulation.[67]

As regards the social psychology of clan society Bogdanov held that it knew neither masters nor slaves. But neither did it know freedom; it was in thrall to nature. There was equality of distribution, but there was very little to dis-tribute. There was brotherhood, but such relations did not extend beyond the confines of the narrow clan group. Someone who did not belong to the given clan could not count on any help from the little society. On the contrary; he was likely to be seen as an enemy and hunted down like an animal. The close natural bond between the members of the clan, with the virtual absence of psychical differences between them, led to the fact that personality was impossible to dis-tinguish from the group. A person did not have an individual will; there existed only the will of the clan.[68]

With the transition to patriarchal clan organisation of society came the beginnings of a settled existence based on agriculture and herding. This gave the possibility of sustaining a much larger social group. Within this group the characteristic of productive relations was the distinction between what Bog-danov termed 'organising labour' and 'executory labour', that is between the functions of giving orders and carrying them out. In this era there emerges the relationship of domination and subordination, which Bogdanov considers to

---

66   Bogdanov 1899, pp. 24–5.
67   Bogdanov 1899, pp. 31–3.
68   Bogdanov 1899, p. 34.

be a special form of the division of labour. Within the confines of the clan the family begins to define itself, grouped around patriarchs, who have the function of organisers of labour.[69]

The patriarchal clan epoch saw the beginnings of distribution based on exchange, as commodities began to be traded for each other. The organiser of production, moreover, came to view himself as the owner of the commodities which went for exchange, and in this way private property gradually emerged.[70]

The emergence of the organising and executory functions also had an impact on the social psychology of the patriarchal clan society. It fostered a view of the world termed by Bogdanov 'natural fetishism'. Causality was explained by assuming that there must be an organising will behind whatever existed in the natural world. Natural phenomena were credited with having souls or spirits. People saw these everywhere: in stones, in plants, in flames, in the wind, in water, and so on.[71]

Increase in population and the extension of exchange relations led to the transformation of the patriarchal clan system into feudalism. The process was by no means universal, and Bogdanov indicated that in some areas, such as in Switzerland, Southern Germany, the Pyrenees and the territories of the South Slavs, agricultural communism survived into the feudal period.[72] In describing the serf labour characteristic of the feudal economy, Bogdanov was able to draw upon examples from the fairly recent Russian past, mentioning labour service (*barshchina*) and payments in kind (*obrok*). These were concepts that would have been familiar to Bogdanov's audience, since the Tula armaments industry had formerly run on serf labour.[73]

Bogdanov attached great importance to the social psychology of the feudal period. It was an era in which science was the handmaiden of religion. The church's doctrines represented absolute truth. And since the absolute truth was given, there was no point in trying to discover new truths; one should try only to reveal further the truth that had been handed down. Any critical thought was classed as heresy, and all intellectual activity was subordinated to a higher authority.[74] In later works Bogdanov would often return to discussing these authoritarian attitudes as an illustration of something that was the exact opposite of what he believed the attitude to truth should be.

---

69   Bogdanov 1899, p. 39.
70   Bogdanov 1899, p. 49.
71   Bogdanov 1899, pp. 51–2.
72   Bogdanov 1899, p. 78.
73   Bogdanov 1899, p. 81.
74   Bogdanov 1899, p. 93.

What drove the forces for development within feudal society was the intens-
ification of the division of labour and with it the increased possibility for the
exchange of products. This extension of exchange encouraged the emergence
of a class of people whose main occupation was the transportation and distribution of products, the class of merchants. This gave rise to what Bogdanov
termed 'petty-bourgeois society' or 'merchant capitalism', the form of capitalism based on commerce and trade.[75]

The social psychology of the petty-bourgeois period had a transitory character. On the one hand natural fetishism is still retained to a significant degree,
but on the other hand a new special fetishism is formed: commodity fetishism.
This happens because at any given moment the producer of a commodity risks
being un-adapted to the conditions of the market, and in that case his labour
energy, in whole or in part, will be lost. Because of this, the market appears to
the producer as an external force in just the same way as external nature with
its thousands of unexpected dangers appears to primitive man.[76]

Here Bogdanov is neatly bringing together the concept of natural fetishism
with Marx's concept of commodity fetishism. The transition from the one to
the other is presented as an historical evolution. The advantage of Bogdanov's
historical approach to the study of economic science is that he is able to show
how the modern economy is built up layer upon layer from component elements which came into being at different stages of social development. In this
case the understanding of how natural fetishism works provides an insight into
the more complex phenomenon of commodity fetishism.

> The producer of commodities can know nothing of their social value,
> because he is not accustomed to look upon the commodity as a *social
> product*. Observing the mass of occasions of exchange, he constructs the
> concept of value, i.e. in essence the usual price of commodities; but for
> him this is an inexplicable phenomenon. To attribute it to the expendit-
> ure of social-labour energy is impossible for him, first of all because he
> has no conception of the *social character* of labour by which the product
> has been produced, and also because this value appears to him neces-
> sarily in the form of a certain quantity of money rather than as a certain
> quantity of *labour*. But if the perception of the producer of commodities
> is incapable of connecting their value with the relations of human social
> labour, he can only connect it with the commodity itself. And to a superfi-

---

75   Bogdanov 1899, p. 97.
76   Bogdanov 1899, p. 124.

cial view this is quite natural: whoever has a commodity be it the producer or some other person, it does not matter, the commodity is sold for the value inherent in it. Hence there is nothing easier than to conclude that the value, the ability to be sold for a certain sum of money, is a property of the commodity itself, a quality which does not depend on people, on society, but is in general a natural quality of the commodity. Where such a property comes from, what determines its limits, the producer of the commodity does not investigate. For him the exchange-value of an axe is two roubles and no more; it does not depend on anything; it exists in the axe all by itself, just as for the natural fetishist the spirit of the axe is only the axe spirit and nothing else. In this consists the essence of commodity fetishism.[77]

In dealing with the era of industrial capitalism Bogdanov attached special significance to the introduction of machines. He thought of machines as instruments by which the executory labour of a person is replaced by the action of external forces of nature. Machines could take the place of the worker in so far as the worker was a mere executor in the process of production. And the more specialised the machine, the less specialised the worker had to be. Eventually, he thought, machines would achieve such a perfect state of operation that they would not require any input from the workers at all. When that stage had been reached, the labour of the worker at the machine would resemble what was formerly considered to be organising activity. In this way the development of industrial capitalism had the effect of overcoming the age-old division into people who organised and those who carried out orders, at least for the workers.[78]

In Bogdanov's view, in the era of industrial capitalism commodity fetishism remained, but it did not affect every social group in equal measure. It retained its full force only for the entrepreneurial group, whose way of life brought them closest to the process of exchange. On the other hand, for the workers, in whose conditions of life the organisational force of cooperation played an increasing part, and whose place in the division of labour was simple and transparent, there was little place left for fetishism.[79]

In the most recent stage of industrial capitalism, Bogdanov observed, individual enterprises were being merged to form syndicates and trusts to avoid competition. This was a process that had been going on in Russia since the

---

77   Bogdanov 1899, pp. 124–5.
78   Bogdanov 1899, p. 238.
79   Bogdanov 1899, p. 290.

1860s.[80] Significantly, however, Bogdanov did not go on to say that out of these centralising tendencies the basis for a socialist economy would emerge. Although this is implied, it was impossible to make explicit for reasons of censorship. In his pamphlet *On Socialism*, published abroad in 1904, however, Bogdanov was able to make his meaning clear.[81]

7   Agitation

When recalling in 1923 his revolutionary activities in Tula, Bogdanov felt the need for some self-justification, since in almost five years of contact with the workers they had done no more than attend classes in study circles; they had not once gone on strike, and to that extent lagged behind the workers in other industrial centres. The reason, Bogdanov suggested, lay in the special character of the workers in the principal industrial undertaking in Tula, the Armaments Factory. They were, he pointed out, relatively privileged in that they enjoyed higher wages and a shorter working day than was normal in Russia. Their lack of militancy was also, he suggested, due to the fact that industry in Tula was still closely allied with handicraft trades and with the peasant way of life.[82]

The nearest Bogdanov had come to organising a strike was in the autumn of 1897, when a conflict had arisen between management and workers in one of the workshops of the Ammunition Factory. Bogdanov and his associates had formulated the workers' demands in writing and presented them to the management. The employers were so astonished at this untoward occurrence that they immediately conceded what the workers had asked without a single day on strike being necessary.[83]

The note of self-justification in Bogdanov's memoirs was occasioned by the fact that, in keeping with the principle of simply putting himself at the disposal of the workers, even in the case of conflict between them and the employers, he had not used the occasion to encourage them to greater and more extensive forms of opposition. He had not, in the phraseology of the time, progressed 'from propaganda to agitation'. The impression of failure in this respect was experienced more acutely by Skvortsov-Stepanov. In his memoirs he stated:

---

80   Bogdanov 1899, p. 310.
81   Bogdanov 1904c, p. 17.
82   Bogdanov 1923, p. 17.
83   Ibid.

... we did not really engage in mass work. The study circles multiplied and grew. From the Armaments Factory, where we had our base, we only very slowly began to make contacts in the Ammunition Factory, with the Batashev Samovar Factory, with the Bagtsurov Engineering Works, and with the newly built iron foundry on Kosaya Gora. It was only then that things took on the character of mass work. But that happened only in 1900, when I had left Tula, and when the approaching crisis brought about a change in attitude on the part of the working class. But while we were sitting at the Armaments Factory we could not find any way of getting beyond the study circle, purely propagandist type of work.[84]

The question of the transition from propaganda to agitation arose in Tula with special acuteness in the spring of 1897 with the arrival of N.M. Velichkin, who had been involved in the organisation of the Moscow Workers' Union following the arrest of Mitskevich and Vinokurov in December 1894 until his own arrest in July 1896. Velichkin intended to apply in Tula the method of agitation employed by the Moscow Workers' Union. This course of action must certainly have seemed erroneous to Bogdanov. It is clear that he viewed workers' study circles not as a preliminary to mass strike action and thence to more wide-ranging upheavals, but as a first stage in schooling the proletariat in a new world outlook. Retrospectively he saw them as an embryo of a proletarian university. It is not surprising, therefore, that Bogdanov took no part in Velichkin's enterprise. In his memoirs Bogdanov recalled that:

> there were exiled in Tula Nikolai Mikhailovich Velichkin, his sister Klavdia, Mikhail Boikov et al. They began to campaign for immediate and extensive strike action. We considered that conditions were not suitable and favoured a cautious and gradual approach. They consequently acted separately and independently, but were very soon arrested.

In fact, in the aftermath of the Velichkins' and Boikov's abortive attempts at agitation, 73 people, mostly workers, were arrested in August 1897.[85]

---

84   Nevskii 1924, p. 134.
85   Bogdanov 1923, p. 17.

8   Kharkov

From the autumn of 1895 Bogdanov was enrolled in the faculty of medicine at Kharkov University, from which he graduated in 1899. He spent, however, only three to four months of each year in Kharkov, enough to satisfy the requirements of his medical course, but leaving him free most of the time to conduct his teaching in the workers' circles in Tula.[86] Bogdanov's visits to Kharkov brought him into contact with a group of Social-Democrat students at Kharkov University that had been formed in 1892.[87] Among the group were P. Nezhdanov-Cherevanin and B.V. Avilov, the latter having been expelled from Moscow University at the same time as Bogdanov and who was also study-ing medicine at Kharkov University.[88] A third member of the Kharkov group, P. Fomin, came to Tula for a short time, according to Skvortsov-Stepanov, to help the group in Tula to rouse the workers to action, but his efforts met with no success.[89]

At the time the Kharkov Social-Democratic group was formed, Marxists were coming under attack from N.K. Mikhailovsky for insisting that Russia must undergo a capitalist stage. This, to Mikhailovsky, showed that they connived at the development of capitalism and were indifferent to the plight of the victims of the capitalist system. These strictures on Marxism occasioned Plekhanov's pamphlet *The Development of the Monist View of History* (1894).[90] In Kharkov, Nezhdanov and his friends were indignant at Mikhailovsky's accusations and wrote two letters in reply, one in 1893 and one in 1894. The letters denied that the intelligentsia were in any position to halt the inevitable course of economic development, but they did not accept that they were indifferent to people's suf-ferings or that their doctrine of 'economic materialism' lacked a moral dimen-sion.[91] Nezhdanov in fact argued this point at length in a book entitled *Morality*, which was published in 1898.[92]

Bogdanov took no part in this campaign against Mikhailovsky, and the Social-Democratic group in Kharkov was the subject of one of Bogdanov's rare autobiographical asides, recounted in an unusually hostile tone. It is as follows:

---

86   Ibid.
87   Ivashko and Baskov 1980, p. 15.
88   Nevskii 1931, 1, p. 15.
89   Nevskii 1924, p. 134.
90   Plekhanov 1961–81, 1, pp. 542–826.
91   'Dva pis'ma k N.K. Mikhailovskomu' 1924, pp. 106–21.
92   Nezhdanov, 1898.

Fifteen years ago in a certain university town I joined the local 'Marxist' organisation. It consisted of a few dozen intellectuals, and in spite of its terrifying title it was concerned with quite harmless affairs – simply with self-education. Its leaders found the usual Marxism 'vulgar' and set themselves the task of drawing up a programme and building an organisation on a purely moral basis. In several small groups, coordinated by an 'inner circle' and observing the strictest secrecy, furious debates were held on 'freedom of the will', on the absolute principle of morality, on the pre-requisites of perception, and so on. On discovering what kind of questions were being posed, I declared that I considered myself to be a 'vulgar' Marx-ist and that as far as moral principles went I could only see in them social fetishism conditioned by the relations of production. I barely escaped paying dearly for my audacity. My moral comrades met in my absence and discussed whether to expel me from the organisation for immorality. They were tending towards the affirmative, because a person who thought that morality was a fetish was obviously immoral. It was only by a stroke of luck that, having quarrelled with the leaders, I managed to resign from the organisation before the decision was taken. It was only later, from one of the members, that I learnt how near the pleasant prospect had been of receiving the rank and title 'expelled for immorality'.[93]

Bogdanov added that Nezhdanov's book *Morality*, which resulted from the group's discussions and which was a synthesis of the ideas of Lavrov and Kant, had fallen into well-deserved oblivion. His irritation at his treatment by the Kharkov group, however, made Bogdanov's verdict on Nezhdanov's book unduly harsh, as it is a serious discussion of the question of morals and free will and their relationship to Marxism, or 'economic materialism' as it was then widely termed. Some issues Nezhdanov raised would be taken up by Bogdanov. A central one was Nezhdanov's observation that one of the obstacles to the achievement of moral objectives was the modern division of labour, in so far as it confined the personality within the limits of a specialisation, making it alien and incomprehensible to people of other specialisations.[94] This theme, which was a central one to Bogdanov's system, was anticipated by Nezhdanov. It is possible that discussions with the group of intellectuals in Kharkov were a stimulating experience for Bogdanov, and contributed to the direction of his philosophical thought.

---

93   Bogdanov 1911, pp. 81–2.
94   Nezhdanov 1898, pp. 148–9.

It was Bogdanov's association with the Kharkov group which brought his stay in Tula to an end. In the spring of 1899 some of the workers taught in Bogdanov's study circles left to work in Moscow. In June of that year Bogdanov, Skvortsov-Stepanov and a S.I. Stepanov, a worker from the Cartridge Factory, later a prominent Bolshevik, came to Moscow to establish contact with the Moscow Social-Democratic organisation.[95] Some of the Kharkov group, including Nezhdanov and Avilov, were also in the process of transferring their activities to Moscow, where they made contact with the workers from Tula. In the autumn both the workers and Nezhdanov's Moscow group were arrested, and on 4 November Bogdanov was arrested in Tula and sent to the Taganka prison in Moscow. He had expected soon to be released, because there was very little evidence against him. But two of Nezhdanov's associates, one of whom was receiving psychiatric care, were extremely helpful to the police and revealed the various connections of the Moscow organisation. This led to the arrest of Skvortsov-Stepanov in January 1900. Convicted of conducting 'social propaganda among the workers', Bogdanov spent five months in the prison prior to being sent into internal exile.[96]

---

95   Mitskevich 1937, p. 218.
96   Bogdanov 1923, pp. 17–18.

Kaluga

1   Lunacharsky

After spending five months in prison, Bogdanov and those arrested with him were released in May 1900 and sent into the provinces to await their sentences. Bogdanov was not permitted to return to Tula, but was instead sent to Kaluga. He was accompanied by his fiancée Natalia. While the couple had been living in Tula, Natalia had given birth to a son in 1896, but the birth had been a difficult one and the baby did not long survive.[1] The couple had applied to be married while Bogdanov was in prison in Moscow, but this had been refused. They were married in the church of the village of Pokrov on the Kaluga river on 2 July 1900.[2]

In Kaluga Bogdanov found Skvortsov-Stepanov, Bazarov and Avilov, who had also been sent there to await their final sentences. In June Bogdanov and his friends were joined by Anatolii Lunacharsky, who had been arrested in Kiev, and had also been sent to Kaluga while his sentence was being decided.[3] For Bogdanov this was a fateful encounter, because he was to become closely associated with Lunacharsky in the years that followed. There was much he had in common with Lunacharsky, particularly an interest in the philosophy of Ernst Mach and Richard Avenarius.

Lunacharsky is an important figure in Bogdanov's biography for two reasons: one is that over the years the two men collaborated closely, both in political and in intellectual pursuits. The other reason is that, unlike Bogdanov, Lunacharsky never fell foul of the Soviet regime and died of natural causes in 1933. This means that writings by Lunacharsky and about Lunacharsky were much less subject to censorship than sources relating to Bogdanov. Consequently, through Lunacharsky one can gain valuable information about Bogdanov not available elsewhere.

At 25, Lunacharsky was two years younger than Bogdanov. He was born in Poltava in 1875 in the family of a senior civil servant. He went to school in Kiev, where he was a pupil at the First Kiev *gimnaziya*. He did not do particularly well at school, but applied himself with great diligence to studying on his own.

---

1   Klebaner 2000, p. 30.
2   Copy of marriage certificate in the possession of the author.
3   Bogdanov 1923, p. 18.

Besides teaching himself modern languages, music and avidly reading the classics of Russian literature, he studied works of philosophy. He was especially attracted to the works of John Stuart Mill, Charles Darwin and Herbert Spencer.[4]

Through his membership of a study circle organised by the Polish student Józef Moszyński, Lunacharsky was introduced to the writings of radical authors, including Chernyshevsky's *What Is to Be Done?* This led the group to study Chernyshevsky's commentary on John Stuart Mill's textbook on political economy. By the early 1890s Social-Democratic circles had begun to appear in Kiev, and Marxist circles were organised not only by students at the university but also in the city's *gimnazii*. Moszyński's study circle now began to receive Marxist literature, including the works by Plekhanov, *Socialism and the Political Struggle, Our Disagreements* and *The Russian Worker in the Revolutionary Movement*. Lunacharsky read the first volume of Marx's *Das Kapital* in 1893–4 at the age of about 17 or 18.[5] He would have been prepared for it through his previous knowledge of Chernyshevsky's commentary on J.S. Mill, which was much praised by Marx.[6]

The year 1894 saw the publication of two important works of Russian Marxism, Plekhanov's *Monist View of History* and Peter Struve's *Critical Notes*.[7] Both were polemical writings directed against the views of the Narodniki, primarily N.K. Mikhailovsky. Lunacharsky says that when these two works appeared he was already a Social Democrat. He recalls that Struve's book especially made an enormous impression on his friends in Kiev. Struve's views were symptomatic of the way in which Marx's system was viewed in Russia at that time – as mainly an economic doctrine without philosophical underpinnings. In Struve's opinion what the theory of Marx and Engels lacked was a 'purely philosophical basis' and that what it required was a 'reappraisal with the help of the critical philosophy'.[8] Like Struve, Lunacharsky thought that Marxism lacked a philosophical dimension, but whereas Struve proposed to supply this with neo-Kantianism, Lunacharsky favoured the addition of a philosophy from the positivist current. He believed that it was necessary to 'put some serious positive philosophical foundation under the edifice that Marx had created'.[9] He was clear, however, that this philosophical basis would have to be in keeping

---

4   Lunacharskii 1970, p. 550.
5   Lunacharskii 1968, p. 16.
6   Marx 1976, p. 98.
7   Struve 1894.
8   Struve 1894, p. 46.
9   Lunacharskii 1968, p. 18.

with those few statements of a philosophical character that Marx had made in his writings. To this end, while still at school, Lunacharsky, attempted to create an 'emulsion' of Spencer and Marx, though, apparently, not with any great success.[10]

A book which made a deep impression on Lunacharsky was Vladimir Lesevich's *What is Scientific Philosophy?*, published in St Petersburg in 1891.[11] It examined the evolution of Auguste Comte and his school, through the English positivists John Stuart Mill, Alexander Bain and Thomas Huxley to the German positivists Alois Riehl, Ernst Laas, Ernst Mach, Richard Avenarius and Joseph Petztoldt. (Lesevich did not consider Spencer as belonging to the positivist school.) Lesevich gives a very creditable account of his subject, showing the underlying continuities of development in the positivist thinkers. It would demonstrate to Lunacharsky that the school of philosophy that he admired culminated in the work of Mach and Avenarius.

For the purposes of the present study Lesevich's book has a special significance. In it one has a convenient exposition of the philosophy of Mach and Avenarius, and one, moreover, that was endorsed by both Bogdanov and Lunacharsky. Lesevich enables us to reconstruct the philosophy of empiriocriticism in the form that Bogdanov and Lunacharsky became acquainted with it.

Lunacharsky discussed his ideas with other members of the study group, in particular with Nikolai Berdyaev, later to become famous as a religious philosopher, who joined the group in late 1893. The arguments between Lunacharsky and Berdyaev could become very heated. Berdyaev recalls that Lunacharsky refused to accept the independence of truth outside the revolutionary class struggle, and thus the freedom of philosophy in the sphere of perception. Lunacharsky for his part saw in Berdyaev a dangerous individualism, and was not surprised when Berdyaev subsequently abandoned Marxism for religious faith.[12]

Not only did Lunacharsky study Marxist theory, but he became involved in propaganda work among local railway workers in the Kiev suburb of Solomenka. Through his membership of the Marxist circle Lunacharsky got to know the leaders of the Kiev Social-Democratic movement, people like P.L. Tuchapsky and his wife V.G. Krzhyzhanovskaya, and I.A. Sammer.[13] The Social Democrats in Kiev were in touch with the émigré 'Emancipation of Labour' group led

---

10   Ibid.
11   Lunacharskii 1970, p. 550.
12   Berdiaev 1990, p. 113.
13   Lunacharskii 1968, p. 17; Babko and Hlavak 1981, p. 28.

by Plekhanov, Akselrod and Zasulich. Tuchapsky and Berdyaev had visited Plekhanov and Akselrod on trips to Switzerland.[14]

Another Kievan Social Democrat who had been in touch with the Emancipation of Labour group was N.N. Novikov. He was a trained philosopher who had obtained his doctorate from Berne University. Richard Avenarius, the founder of the empiriocriticist school in philosophy, had invited him to remain in Switzerland to work with him, but Novikov had preferred to return to Russia. It was from Novikov that Lunacharsky learnt about Avenarius's ideas. This was an important source, because the account of Avenarius's philosophy in Lesevich's book Lunacharsky described as 'inadequate', because it omitted any discussion of Avenarius's main work *The Critique of Pure Experience*. Lunacharsky became deeply impressed by the philosophy of empiriocriticism[15] and decided that on graduating from the *gimnaziya* he would go to Zurich and become a pupil of Avenarius. Being in Switzerland, moreover, would allow him to further his knowledge of Marxism with Akselrod, to whom he had a letter of introduction. The decision to study abroad was reinforced by the fact that the school authorities had been aware of Lunacharsky's radicalism and in consequence had given him a poor mark for behaviour on his leaving certificate, so that admission to a Russian university would have been difficult.[16]

In the event, Lunacharsky spent less than a year studying at Berne University, but he used the opportunity to acquire knowledge in a number of fields. He attended courses on anatomy, physiology, political economy and jurisprudence. But the highlight of his short university career was provided by the lectures and seminars of Avenarius. Lunacharsky attended Avenarius's course on psychology and his seminars on philosophy and one specially devoted to *The Critique of Pure Experience*. He was later to recall that, despite their brevity, his studies with Avenarius made an impression upon him that was to last for the rest of his life.[17]

Writing in 1907, Lunacharsky explained how his studies of Avenarius's philosophy had inspired both his ideas on aesthetics and religion, and helped him to gain the insight that these two phenomena had a common root in the biological function of making evaluations. He recalled:

> In Avenarius's lectures, work in his seminars I found a definition of the basis of my world-outlook. Especially interesting and important for me

---

14   Berdiaev 1990, p. 120; Kindersley 1962, p. 66.
15   Lunacharskii 1968, p. 19; Tait 1984, p. 20.
16   Lunacharskaia 1979, p. 111; Lunacharskii 1968, p. 19; Lunacharskii 1970, p. 737.
17   Lunacharskii 1968, p. 20.

were those aspects of Richard Avenarius's doctrine which gave the foundation of the biological theory of evaluation. The theory of elements and characters, the law of economy in perception and aesthetics, the theory of the affectual in sex – all this was a revelation to me. The broadest perspectives opened up before me; I anticipated syntheses, filling me with joyful excitement. Had not all evaluations: the crude sensual, the utilitarian, the aesthetic, the ethical – one and the same root? Was not this a variety of biological evaluation – the beginning of which was in the capability of the nerve cell to respond to positive or negative sensations and irritability, and the culmination was in the dualism of good and evil? Did this not open up an aesthetic of the deepest essence of the biological fact of evaluation? And from this point of view approaching my 'faith' in scientific socialism I already anticipated that it was intimately connected at the level of evaluation and the ideal with the whole of the religious development of humanity, that this was the ripe fruit of the whole tree, sprouting entirely from that same root – that of the most pristine – pleasure and pain.[18]

At the time he wrote this passage, which incorporates some of Avenarius's special terminology, Lunacharsky was working on his book *Religion and Socialism*,[19] which caused a sensation when it was published, since it was interpreted as being an attempt to found a socialist religion. But as Lunacharsky makes clear, the inspiration for the work, as for his earlier essay on positivist aesthetics, was the philosophy of Avenarius.[20]

While in Switzerland, Lunacharsky established contact with the émigré members of the Emancipation of Labour group, Akselrod and Plekhanov. Akselrod was the first major Marxist thinker that Lunacharsky had encountered, and Akselrod for his part took a lively interest in Lunacharsky's intellectual development. He dissuaded Lunacharsky from adopting the Spencerian view of society as an evolving organism, but failed completely to shake Lunacharsky's conviction that Avenarius's empiriocriticism was the philosophy most compatible with Marx's system. In later years Lunacharsky would refer to Akselrod as his 'spiritual father' and was pained when he and Akselrod found themselves on opposite sides of the Bolshevik-Menshevik divide.[21]

---

18   Lunacharskii 1970, pp. 550–1.
19   Lunacharskii 1908–11.
20   Lunacharskii 1908–11, 1, p. 10.
21   Lunacharskii 1968, p. 20.

Through Akselrod Lunacharsky was able to meet Plekhanov, to whom he took the opportunity of expounding his idea of combining Marx with Avenarius. Plekhanov's knowledge of Avenarius's philosophy, apparently, was sketchy, but the recommendation he gave to read the works of Fichte and Schelling Lunacharsky found very useful. Plekhanov regarded these philosophers as precursors of Hegel, who in turn was a precursor of Marx, and he recommended them in order that Lunacharsky should view Marx in the same way that he did. But in fact these two great German idealists inspired Lunacharsky to take an entirely different view of Marxism, which later manifested itself in the work *Religion and Socialism*. Plekhanov also recommended the study of the eighteenth-century French materialists, and although Lunacharsky read these, especially Helvétius and Diderot, with some pleasure, they remained marginal to his outlook.[22]

After his stay in Switzerland, Lunacharsky was forced to leave for Nice where his half-brother Platon had become seriously ill and was undergoing medical treatment. His stay in Nice in attendance on his brother gave Lunacharsky the opportunity to meet one of the most distinguished Russian scholars of the day. Along the coast from Nice was Beaulieu, the residence of Maxim Kovalevsky, who had been the professor of State and Constitutional Law at Moscow University until he was dismissed for his liberal views. Kovalevsky had become acquainted with Marx in 1875 and for the next two years had collaborated with him in the study of communal landownership and the origins of the capitalist economy. He was someone with an intimate knowledge of the direction of Marx's thinking, and had supplied Marx with materials for his studies of primitive society, including Morgan's *Ancient Society*, that Engels had used to write the work *Origin of the Family*. Lunacharsky had extensive discussions with Kovalevsky, whose conversation he enjoyed immensely. While in France Lunacharsky was also able to meet such eminent figures in the socialist movement as Jules Guèsde, Paul Lafargue and Jean Jaurès.

Lunacharsky arrived back in Russia with his brother and his wife in the autumn of 1898, bringing with him letters of recommendation from Akselrod to members of the Social-Democrat organisation in Moscow. One of these was to Lenin's sister Anna Elizarova-Ulyanova, and another to a certain A.E. Serebriakova, who was later exposed as a police spy. Lunacharsky was soon arrested and spent six months in prison. After his release he returned to Kiev, where he renewed his acquaintance with the local Social Democrats. In Kiev, while giving a lecture on Ibsen, the flat was raided by the police, who did not

---

22　　Lunacharskii 1968, p. 22.

believe that the meeting was literary and not political, and Lunacharsky once more was placed under arrest.[23]

When Lunacharsky encountered him in Kaluga Bogdanov was studying to elaborate his Marxist outlook and on this Marxist foundation to build an all round scholarly edifice. Lunacharsky joined him in this endeavour, and along with Avilov and Skvortsov-Stepanov formed a study group in which papers on philosophical themes were read and discussed.[24] Lunacharsky recalled

> I think that there were few towns in Russia at that time where one could find such a group of Marxist forces. We had, moreover, a rather original bent. We were all deeply interested in the philosophical side of Marxism and we were anxious to strengthen its epistemological, ethical and aesthetical aspects, independently of Kantianism on the one hand, a tendency which had begun to become noticeable in Germany and in Russia as well (Berdyaev, Bulgakov) and without falling into the narrow French encyclopaedist orthodoxy on which Plekhanov was seeking to base the whole of Marxism on the other.[25]

Meeting Lunacharsky must have seemed an extraordinary stroke of luck to Bogdanov. As an admirer of Avenarius's work, he would be intrigued to make the acquaintance of someone who had actually studied under the philosopher himself. For Bogdanov, Lunacharsky was also a link to the Social-Democratic movement in Western Europe, the milieu to which Akselrod and Plekhanov belonged, and with which Bogdanov would make contact while still in exile in Vologda.

Life in Kaluga, it appears, had its compensations. From Lunacharsky one learns that the 'Marxist forces' were befriended by D.D. Goncharov, a local textile magnate, who was himself a Social Democrat and a follower of Robert Owen. The Goncharov factory was run on the New Lanark lines, with the workers enjoying an 8-hour working day, a profit-sharing scheme and all manner of cultural pursuits. Being a man of sophistication, Goncharov endeavoured to provide at the factory entertainment for his work force which would lack nothing in quality and taste. Therefore, Lunacharsky recalls, the textile factory became a minor Athens where concerts, operas and literary evenings followed one another with bewildering rapidity.[26]

---

23   Lunacharskii 1970, p. 597.
24   Lunacharskii 1968, pp. 248–9.
25   Lunacharskii 1968, p. 26.
26   Lunacharskii 1968, p. 27.

2   Mach

It was from the time of his acquaintance with Lunacharsky that the names of
Ernst Mach and Richard Avenarius began to appear in Bogdanov's writings.
These thinkers would have been the subject of intense discussion between Bogdanov and Lunacharsky, particularly as Lunacharsky had studied under Avenarius and was well acquainted with his works.

At the time Bogdanov and Lunacharsky became acquainted with his ideas
Ernst Mach was a professor of physics at Prague University. He made important contributions to the field of physics and physiological psychology as well
as philosophy. He did not aspire to the designation of philosopher, and thought
of himself primarily as a scientist. As he recalls in his book *The Analysis of Sensations*, his interest in philosophical questions had been awakened when as a
boy of 15 he had read Kant's *Prolegomena to any Future Metaphysics*. In later
years he not only rejected Kant's idea of 'things-in-themselves', but was able to
explain how the illusion of 'things-in-themselves' had been created.[27]

Mach belonged to the generation that was profoundly influenced by the
evolutionary theories of Darwin and Spencer and he saw perception in these
terms. For Mach perception of all kinds, scientific as well as everyday, was the
adaptation of thought to its environment. The conceptions of living beings
were the working hypotheses they had evolved for orientation in their environment. Perception was an interchange between the organism and the environment, the organism striving always to achieve equilibrium between itself and
environmental stimuli.[28]

The other influence that lay at the basis of Mach's philosophy was the theory of the conservation of energy. This went hand in hand with the theory of
evolution, because it stood to reason that the most effective adaptation of an
organism to the environment was one that was most efficient in the expenditure of energy. For Mach, the conservation of energy was his criterion of truth.
The test of a sound theory was that it should adapt itself with the least output
of energy to the present temporary collective state of knowledge.[29]

In Mach's view, once we have discarded all metaphysical assumptions, what
we find as given are combinations or 'complexes' of primary entities that he
terms 'elements'. These elements can be such things as colours, sounds, pressures, spaces, times and so forth, connected with each other in various ways.
Some of these combinations are more durable and permanent than others,

---

27   Mach 1959, p. 30.
28   Mach 1959, p. 71.
29   Mach 1959, p. 32.

and these impress themselves on the memory and find expression in the language. Complexes connected in space and time of colours, sounds, pressures, etc., are the first to show relatively greater permanence and on this account receive special names, and are designated as bodies. But such complexes never have absolute permanence.[30]

The complex of memories, moods and feelings attached to a particular body (the human body) which is referred to as the self or 'I' is one of those of relative permanence. Despite its being preoccupied with this or that matter, or being cheerful or gloomy, sufficient durable features remain for the ego to keep its identity. This complex, like every other, was formed for orientation in the environment. For Mach there was no antithesis between the 'I' and the objective world; both consisted of complexes of elements. In the same way, the distinction between sensations (or phenomena) and things was eliminated; and it was simply a matter of dealing with the relationship between elements, for which this distinction was only an imperfect expression.[31]

What gave rise to the mistaken impression that there was a difference between appearance and reality, that there were 'things-in-themselves', was the possibility mentally to subtract individual elements from the complex without destroying the capacity of the image to stand for the totality. From this procedure it could be imagined that it would be possible to subtract all the elements and have something remaining. From this arose the philosophical conception of a 'thing-in-itself', different from 'appearance' and unknowable.

The complexes can be analysed into 'elements', which are their ultimate component parts, which, Mach thinks, scientists may in the future be able to subdivide further. However, although the exact nature of elements was unclear, what could be known precisely was the relationship of the elements to one another. Elements which were conveyed to the complex of the ego through the medium of the body were regarded by the ego as 'effects' emanating from permanent complexes and were designated as 'sensations'. This procedure, however, according to Mach, deprived the complexes of their sensory content and turned them into mere mental symbols. In this way it was possible to state that 'the world consists only of our sensations' (*Empfindungen*) and that 'we have knowledge *only* of sensations'. This position, however, could only be maintained by ignoring the complexes that had given rise to the sensations and the reciprocal action between them.[32]

---

30   Mach 1900, p. 2.
31   Mach 1900, p. 10.
32   Mach 1900, p. 8; Mach 1959, p. 12; Lesevich 1891, p. 186.

Mach went on to make clear that he did not intend the term 'sensation' to be understood in a purely subjective sense; he conceived of it as having both a physical and a psychical side. As he explained:

> A colour is a physical object as soon as we consider its dependence, for instance, upon its luminous source, upon other colours, upon temperatures, upon spaces and so forth. When we consider, however, its dependence upon the retina ... it is a psychological object, a sensation. What is different in the two domains is not the subject matter, but the direction of the investigation.[33]

In the later editions of *The Analysis of Sensations* Mach felt obliged to insert an explanatory passage to clarify what he meant by 'sensations'.

> In what follows whenever the terms 'sensation', 'sensation complex' are used along with or instead of the expression 'element', 'complex of elements' it must be borne in mind that it is only in the connection and relation in question, only in the given functional dependence that the elements are sensations. In another functional relationship they are at the same time physical objects. The additional term 'sensations' is used for the elements only because most people are much more familiar with the elements in question as sensations (colours, sounds, pressures, spaces, times etc.)[34]

Despite Mach's attempts to clarify his ideas, his laconic mode of expression and the imprecision of his terminology gave rise to misunderstandings of his work, something which he ruefully admitted in the later editions of *The Analysis of Sensations*. As he remarked: 'I have been accused of idealism, Berkleyism, even of materialism and of other "-isms", of all of which I believe myself to be innocent'.[35] One of the main reasons he thought his work had been misunderstood was the avoidance of specialised vocabulary in his exposition. 'I willingly admit', he said, 'that in my distaste for artificial terminology I have perhaps fallen into the opposite extreme to that of Avenarius'.[36] And certainly if Avenarius was misunderstood it was not through the lack of a specialised terminology.

---

33   Mach 1900, p. 13; Mach 1959, pp. 17–8; Lesevich 1891, p. 187.
34   Mach 1903, p. 13.
35   Mach 1959, p. 48.
36   Mach 1959, p. 47.

3   Avenarius

Lesevich had written his book before the appearance of Avenarius's chief work, the *Critique of Pure Experience* (1000-90),[37] so that the account he gave of Aven arius's ideas was based on the earlier publication *Philosophy as Thinking about the World in Terms of the Conservation of Energy: Prolegomena to a Critique of Pure Experience* (1876).[38] However, this much shorter work does present in a concise form the direction of Avenarius's thought and anticipates ideas that would be elaborated at much greater length in the *Critique of Pure Experience*.

As the title implies, like Mach, Avenarius believed that the task of philosophy was to give an account of the given world in accordance with the principle of the conservation of energy. This was necessary because human beings did not perceive the world as it was directly given, but in an anthropomorphic way, attributing qualities to the totality of objective facts which they did not have. This began with the animistic view of the natural world by primitive peoples and was followed by subsequent generations who continued to view the world from an anthropomorphic or a metaphysical perspective. A truly scientific view of reality necessitated the purification of conceptions from the accretions of *a priori* elements in thinking and the adoption of pure experience. According to Avenarius:

> The more conceptual thought is developed to a scientific level, the more decisively ... it excludes everything that is not contained in the given itself. At the present time the purification from the mythological accretion is almost complete; the purification of experience from the anthropomorphic accretion is at least being attempted, whereas the question of the *a priori* forms of thinking ... as a form of accretion, which, in their turn, must also be eliminated in order to arrive at pre-eminently pure experience, this question, to the best of my knowledge, is here being posed and justified for the first time.[39]

On Avenarius's concept of pure experience Lesevich remarks that it is in keeping with the principle of the conservation of energy, because it excludes from thought of the given everything that is not included in it; that is, it refrains

---

37   Avenarius 1888–90.
38   Avenarius 1876.
39   Avenarius 1867, p. 31; Lesevich 1891, pp. 215–16.

from the expenditure on this thought of that portion of energy that the object itself does not demand.[40]

Few works of philosophy can have demanded such an investment of time and concentration on the part of their readers as Avenarius's *Critique of Pure Experience*. The most obvious obstacle to understanding is the strangeness of the terminology that Avenarius employs. In order to avoid using terms that had misleading associations, Avenarius coined his own philosophical vocabulary. He declared that rather than be misunderstood he would prefer not to be understood at all.[41] Besides the unfamiliar language, the work is tersely argued with numbered and cross-referenced sections, interspersed with symbols and algebraic formulae. The *Critique* was the culmination of Avenarius's intellectual creation, and is a work of extreme sophistication, but its inaccessibility deprived it of the attention its author believed it deserved. He was disappointed that very few serious discussions of his work had appeared, especially as he intended his *Critique of Pure Experience* to have applications in psychology, pedagogy, logic, ethics, aesthetics, jurisprudence, political economy and linguistics.[42]

In terms of difficulty Lunacharsky compares Avenarius's *Critique of Pure Experience* to Hegel's *Science of Logic*.[43] In fact the two works are similar in more than this respect and have several key features in common. Both the *Logic* and the *Critique* are progressions which start out from the minimum of presuppositions and culminate in absolute knowledge, the *Logic* in the Absolute Idea, and the *Critique* in the 'perfect constant' in which the 'riddle of the world' is solved. In both of these cases the point of culmination is the place where reality and the human conception of that reality coincide. In Hegel's case it is where the Concept (*Begriff*) becomes 'adequate' to its object; in the case of Avenarius it is where the analytic and the synthetic conceptions of pure experience coincide. In both works the progression is from simpler to ever more complex theoretical categories. In Avenarius these categories are the terms that he has invented to avoid misleading connotations; in Hegel they are the philosophical categories of his day, which he expects his readers to recognise, appreciating how he has incorporated previous philosophical systems into his own. In Hegel's *Logic* the movement from one category to the next is supplied by the dialectical movement of the Concept through the phases of Universality, Particularity and Individuality. In Avenarius there is comparable movement in the three phases

---

40   Lesevich 1891, p. 216.
41   Avenarius 1888–90, 1, p. XVIII.
42   Avenarius 1888–90, 1, p. XIV.
43   Avenarius 1905, p. IV.

of the 'vital series' – from a state of equilibrium through 'vital difference' to a
new state of equilibrium.[44] These points of similarity between the systems of
Hegel and Avenarius are not fortuitous; behind the novelty and strangeness of
Avenarius's terminology he references sometimes explicitly the philosophical heritage of Kant and his successors.

In the *Critique of Pure Experience* Avenarius takes as his starting point the
'natural viewpoint' or 'naive realism', that is, the point of view of the man in the
street. He begins by setting out the assumptions on which his work is premised,
what he calls the empiriocritical axioms. One of these states that scientific
knowledge has no essentially different forms or means than non-scientific
knowledge; that all forms of knowledge are developments of the pre-scientific.
The other presupposition is of the existence of 'the human individual opposite
an environment with multifarious component parts, other human individuals with the multifarious utterances and what is uttered by them having some
dependence on the environment'. He eschews the points of departure adopted
by earlier philosophers, such as 'conscience', 'thought', 'the directly given', or
'the directly known'. These starting points, he argues, are the outcome of theory and are results rather than beginnings. For Avenarius these philosophical
viewpoints are modifications of natural realism.[45]

Avenarius requires one to assume real human beings in a real environment
populated by fellow human beings and their utterances, because his treatment
of experience is not only philosophical in the usual sense, but also physiological
and psychological. Avenarius stresses that when he talks about human beings,
he does not treat them abstractly, as mere ciphers, but as real people with a
physiological make-up, emotions and beliefs, who have a particular ancestry
and who belong to a specific linguistic community.[46]

The standpoint is the point of an observer positioned between the human
individual and the environment, watching the interchange that takes place
between them. Avenarius compares it to a person standing in the market-place
observing both buyers and sellers or an observer in a theatre who looks both at
the stage and the audience.[47]

Avenarius distinguishes two types of experience: the first type is experience
in the broad sense, experience that might include dreams and visions as well as
elements of the environment. Experience in this broad sense Avenarius terms

---

44 This dialectical element in Avenarius's *Kritik der reinen Erfahrung* was noticed by an early
    commentator on the work. See Delacroix 1898, p. 72.
45 Avenarius 1888–90, 1, p. VIII.
46 Avenarius 1888–90, 1, p. 15.
47 Avenarius 1888–90, 1, p. 10.

analytic experience. Experience in the narrow sense, synthetic experience, is defined by Avenarius as 'that content of consciousness (our own or uttered to us) which does not contain in itself anything other than parts of the environment'. It is the objective of the *Critique* to investigate how and under what circumstances these two types of experience might converge.[48]

Avenarius interprets the relationship of consciousness to the environment in terms of biological adaptation. He believes that the activity of the brain should be understood in a way analogous to life in general, as a complex process of self-preservation or adaptation to the environment, as a process of maintaining an equilibrium of the organism in face of the challenges offered by the surroundings. In an evocative passage in the *Critique* Avenarius says that:

> The baby is expelled from its mother's womb, the protective sanctuary, into an environment that is almost absolutely new, strange, and only partially conducive to survival. Now it is abandoned to the changes which grow out of the environment and the transformations the environment undergoes. And it is also at once abandoned to the fates which the typical changes of its own course of development impose upon it.[49]

In other words, Avenarius concludes, 'By the act of birth the System c [the central nervous system J.W.] is removed from an almost ideal environment to one that is non-ideal'.[50] It is then forced to react to the multifarious stimuli that assail it.

The disruption to its equilibrium brought about by the environmental stimuli causes the organism to feel dissatisfaction, either theoretical or practical. In finding a means to overcome this dissatisfaction and return to the preferred state of equilibrium the organism passes through a sequence of states from equilibrium through dissatisfaction to a new equilibrium. This cycle is termed by Avenarius a 'vital series'. The vital series regarded from a physiological point of view Avenarius calls the 'independent vital series'; regarded as a psychical phenomenon he calls it the 'dependent vital series'. By this terminology Avenarius wishes to convey that the psychical processes depend on the physiological ones.

---

48 Avenarius 1888–90, 1, pp. 5–6.
49 Avenarius 1888–90, 1, pp. 63–4.
50 Ibid.

Every reaction the organism has to the environment is the result of the activity of nerve cells, the totality of which constitutes the nervous system. Those cells of the brain which are associated with psychical phenomena Avenarius refers to as the central nervous system, or simply as System C. The most favourable condition for System C, all things being equal, is the absence of any disturbance to its equilibrium. Such a disturbance of the equilibrium of System C Avenarius calls a 'vital difference'.[51]

Since we are dealing with a living system, everything is in a continuous state of motion, so that only a moving equilibrium is possible. Vital differences arise and are resolved continually, but most of these are made by accustomed acts which are almost never accompanied by consciousness. Only the disturbance of an accustomed process serves as the point of departure for a new, unaccustomed, vital difference at the conscious level. The first type of vital difference Avenarius designates as a 'vital difference of the first order'; the second type he calls a 'vital difference of the higher order'. The continual overcoming of vital differences of the higher order by System C has the effect of reducing them to the first order, as what was unfamiliar becomes familiar.

In order to react constantly to external stimuli the brain has to have a reserve of energy available to deploy in any quantity from a potential to a kinetic state. It is structured in such a way as to constitute an organised reserve of such energy. It strives to maintain a balance of the energy it receives from the environment and the energy which it expends in reacting to environmental stimuli. But it must be ready to deal with all possible emergencies that the environment could confront it with. The greater the amount of energy and the better it is organised for deployment, the better its chances of survival will be, and the more effective it will be in effacing vital differences. The reserves of energy must be kept fresh and exercised if it is not to lose its organised character and degenerate into useless ballast.

In elaborating his concept of vital differences Avenarius explains that two types of process take place in the brain: one is the expenditure of the material of the cells through 'work'; the other is the replenishment of the cells through 'nourishment'. The moving equilibrium in the life of the cells is the balance between the expenditure of its chemical composition (i.e. the transformation of its potential, chemical, energy to kinetic energy) and its reconstitution through nourishment. Usually, during the course of the day the balance is towards expenditure, whereas during the night nourishment and reconstitution predominate. The system encounters difficulties if there is an excessive

---

51   Avenarius 1888–90, 1, p. 71.

amount of expenditure of energy, but a surfeit of nourishment is also detrimental. In the latter case some kind of recreational activity would be needed to bring the energy level back into balance.[52]

Having established the nature of the biological and psychical apparatus of experience, Avenarius is in a position to characterise and classify the various types of experience. He is able to do this in great detail with the help of the special terminology which he employs.

Avenarius designates the component parts of the environment 'R values' and the content of statements or 'utterances' about the environment made by people – 'E values'. One could say that the essence of the *Critique* is an examination of how E values relate to R values. In the case of E values Avenarius assumes that when human individuals make statements about the components of the environment they not only apply such expressions as 'green', 'blue', 'cold', 'warm', 'hard', 'soft', but also such epithets as 'pleasant', 'unpleasant', 'beautiful', 'ugly', 'beneficial', 'offensive'. E values of the 'green', 'sweet' etc. type Avenarius calls 'elements'; E values of the 'pleasant', 'unpleasant' etc. type he calls 'characters'. By his concept of 'characters' Avenarius recognises that people do not perceive objects in a uniform way, but have varied approaches to them and evaluations of them. Through characters, experience acquires the additives that prevent it from being pure experience.[53]

If, for example, what is perceived arouses feelings of satisfaction or dissatisfaction, pleasure or pain, Avenarius terms this kind of character 'affectional'. An object perceived may be familiar or unfamiliar, in which case the character would be 'adaptive'; it may arouse greater or lesser interest on the part of the observer giving it a 'prevalential' character. The thing perceived may be something external and material or it may be internal and subjective: in this case the character would be 'positional'. Avenarius examines at some length and further subdivides characters, achieving ever greater precision in his classification of types of experience.

In the elimination of subjective additions to pure experience an important part is played by society and by humanity in general, which Avenarius terms the 'congregal' system, the totality of Systems C. Whereas isolated individuals may continue to colour what they experience with phantoms and superstitions, in society a process of mutual verification takes place, and the wider the community the more effective is this process. By this means the results of individual experience are purified and raised to the level of pure experience.

---

52   Avenarius 1905, p. 43.
53   Avenarius 1905, p. 48.

The truth about the world is the entire organised experience of humanity, the final arbiter to which we resort to judge the validity of any phenomenon or utterance. The process has a historical dimension because in the course of generations the collective experience of humanity is progressively refined to an ever higher state of purity, bringing together analytic and synthetic types of pure experience.[54] The eventual culmination of this social and historical process of purifying experience would be the 'perfect constant',[55] the complete harmonisation of System C with the environment, a state in which all reality would appear logical and comprehensible, and the environment would be an ideal one for humanity.

In 1891 Avenarius published *The Human Conception of the World*[56] to clarify some points that had not been covered in the *Critique of Pure Experience*. It is a relatively short work and contains only a fraction of the special terms that appeared in the *Critique*. In its introductory section Avenarius defines his starting point in natural realism, but this time giving more prominence to the presence of fellow human beings (*Mitmenschen* or M):

> I with all my thoughts and feelings found myself in the midst of an environment. This environment was composed of multifarious component parts which entered into multifarious relationships of dependence with one another. To the environment also belonged *Mitmenschen* with multifarious utterances; and what they said again stood for the most part in a relationship of dependence to the environment. The *Mitmenschen* talked and acted as I did: they answered my questions, as I did theirs ... and so I could not but think that the *Mitmenschen* were beings like me – and that I was a being like them.[57]

The relationship of human individuals to the environment and to one another is basic to the purpose of Avenarius's book, which is to introduce and elaborate on the concept of 'introjection', which involves these relationships.

According to Avenarius, so long as individuals relate to the environment in a purely descriptive way, they treat its component parts as 'things' which belong to the empirical world. But communication with *Mitmenschen* requires that the human individual assume that the *Mitmenschen* see the world in the same way that he does. He therefore attributes to them the same perceptions, feel-

---

54   Avenarius 1888–90, 2, pp. 411–23.
55   Avenarius 1888–90, 2, p. 380.
56   Avenarius 1891.
57   Avenarius 1891, pp. 4–5.

ings and knowledge that he has. By this act of attribution or 'introjection' the individual creates for the *Mitmensch* an inner world distinct from the outer empirical world of the environment. A duplication takes place: on the one hand there is the empirical thing perceived as a component part of the environment, and on the other hand there is the image of the thing as perceived by the *Mitmensch* through introjection.

Though this act of introjection is necessary for communication between human individuals, it impedes the formation of pure experience. As Avenarius points out, through the act of introjection the natural unity of the world is split into two: into an outer world and an inner world, into an Object and a Subject. Clearly, introjection is an extremely useful concept for Avenarius; with it he can explain the dynamics of the division into analytic and synthetic types of experience and related categories, as well as the presuppositions on which previous theories of knowledge were based.

For Avenarius introjection also has an important historical dimension. In primitive cultures not only the *Mitmensch*, but the tree, the river, the stone, the mountain, the sun, the earth, the sky, all were regarded as beings just like people and were credited with having souls or spirits.[58] These spirits, with which the world was filled, were divided, according to human needs, into harmful and useful, bad and good. Through introjection at the stage of primitive animism the content of human utterances (E values) acquired characters.[59] At later historical stages the non-empirical element in primitive animism developed into the various *a priori* components attached to pure experience. In Avenarius's view, the most recent form that introjection had given rise to was idealist philosophy.[60] He believed, however, that historical development would culminate in the elimination of introjection, which would end the separation of the individual and his experience and the duplication of the 'thing'. In this way the natural view of the world would be restored with the assumption that the component part of the environment of one person was exactly the same component for all of them.[61]

---

58   Avenarius 1891, p. 36.
59   Avenarius 1891, p. 37.
60   Avenarius 1891, p. 105.
61   Avenarius 1891, p. 90.

4   Avenarius and Mach

In both the *Critique of Pure Experience* and *The Human Concept of the World*
Avenarius registered his agreement with Ernst Mach.[62] It is possible that the
term Avenarius used to designate the component parts of the environment,
'elements', follows the practice of Mach. In *The Human Concept of the World*
Avenarius adopts what is unmistakably Mach's terminology when he speaks of
'complexes of elements'. Moreover, in exactly the manner of Mach he treats the
'I' as a complex of elements in the same way that a tree could be so described.
He says: 'I experience the tree in just the same sense as I experience the "I" – as
something belonging to an experience; and if I say I experience the tree, that
should only mean: an experience consists of the complex of elements rich in
content "I" and another complex of elements less rich in content "tree"'.[63] Like
Mach, Avenarius treats the elements as objectively existing component parts
of the environment.

In later editions of *The Analysis of Sensations* Mach included a section discussing the relationship of his ideas to those of Avenarius. There he stated that
Avenarius's views had an affinity with his own 'as great as can be imagined
between two individuals who have had different paths of development, who
work in different fields and who are completely independent of one another'.[64]

As for particular points of agreement between himself and Avenarius, Mach
mentioned the economy of thought, as both he and Avenarius interpreted phenomena in the light of the law of the conservation of energy. Another point of
agreement was the adoption of the Darwinian conception of adaptation to the
environment, Mach noting with approval the way Avenarius had shown how
all theoretical and practical activity was determined by changes in the central
nervous system, how Avenarius had based himself on the general assumption
that the central organ was subject to the impulse of self-preservation, a tendency to maintain its equilibrium, not only as a whole but in its parts.[65]

Apart from this, Mach was rather at a loss to say what other points of agreement there were, and he had asked a scholar who had known Avenarius to compare the two viewpoints. The result, which Mach reproduced, was a statement
that the conception of the relation of the physical to the psychical was identical
in both thinkers. Beyond that the statement did little more than expound Avenarius's concept of introjection, of whose use Mach was rather sceptical. Mach's

---

62   Avenarius 1888–90, pp. I, XIII; Avenarius 1891, p. 120.
63   Avenarius 1891, p. 82.
64   Mach 1900, p. 35; Mach 1959, pp. 46–7.
65   Mach 1900, pp. 37–8; Mach 1959, pp. 49–50.

problem was that he was unable to understand Avenarius's *Critique of Pure Experience*; he was defeated by the abstruse terminology. His ideas on what the work contained came from commentaries written by Avenarius's colleagues and pupils. As Mach explained: 'It is asking a lot of an elderly man that in addition to the many languages of peoples he should learn the language of an individual'.[66]

Following the practice of Lenin's *Materialism and Empiriocriticism* of linking the two names 'Mach and Avenarius', the impression has been created of a single (idealist) philosophy which both shared. The implication of this is that an exposition of Mach's ideas – being the more accessible – would apply to Avenarius's views as well. This, however, is far from being the case. Although the philosophical views of Mach and Avenarius coincided in essentials, the systems of the two thinkers were far from co-extensive. In particular Avenarius's *Critique of Pure Experience* contained an elaborate system of ideas that were peculiar to him, and which Bogdanov was to draw upon in several of his writings.

It is also worth noting that Bogdanov and Lunacharsky interpreted Avenarius differently. Of the two, Lunacharsky was the more orthodox follower of Avenarius, Bogdanov being more critical of his conceptions. In his exposition of Avenarius's *Critique of Pure Experience* Lunacharsky notes the various points of difference between Bogdanov and himself on the interpretation of Avenarius's ideas.

An objection that Bogdanov made to Avenarius's *Critique of Pure Experience* in his *Empiriomonism* was of its innate conservatism, that because System C strove to restore the disturbance of equilibrium, this equilibrium was Avenarius's ideal state. As Bogdanov remarked: 'In Avenarius's formula one feels the remnants of a conservative, static, understanding of life, of that which step by step is eliminated in the development of evolutionary thinking'.[67]

This objection, Lunacharsky believed, sprang from Bogdanov's faulty understanding of Avenarius's thought. According to Lunacharsky, what Avenarius was arguing was that with the disturbance of equilibrium the brain tried to restore it, but frequently what was restored was not the former equilibrium, but another, higher state, more complex, more prepared for the next disturbance, and therefore more viable. This process was an integral part of Avenarius's theory of development that Bogdanov had ignored.[68]

---

66   Mach 1900, p. 36.
67   Avenarius 1905, p. 58; Bogdanov 2003, p. 205.
68   Avenarius 1905, pp. 58–9.

The passage about the baby leaving its mother's womb and finding itself transferred from an ideal environment to one that was non-ideal also proved contentious. On this Bogdanov observed: 'Thus, for Avenarius, from the very birth of the baby the "diminution of the conservation of life" begins, which continues right to the onset of death, and fortunately ends there'. To Lunacharsky this remark signified that Bogdanov had missed Avenarius's point entirely. This was, Lunacharsky explained, that in the mother's womb, this protective sanctuary of life, the organism existed in almost ideal conditions, i.e. nothing disturbed the baby's equilibrium. But when it was suddenly propelled into a new environment it was subjected to a thousand hostile influences. In order to survive, the baby's organism had to develop an enormous system of precautionary forms, broaden and enrich its life. It had to adapt itself so that its life would flow smoothly, so that nothing would seem 'secret', 'unexpected' or 'dangerous' to it.[69]

By the growth and development of the brain on the one hand and by the creative transformation of the environment on the other, mankind as a whole progressed towards the ideal equilibrium between its demands and the environment, towards the perfect constant. At some time in the future this ideal relation would be attained between humanity and the environment, such as existed in the mother's womb. At that point, Lunacharsky concluded, 'the whole wide world will become "the sacred sanctuary of the protection of life", but of a life infinitely more complex, because adapted not to the mother's womb, but to the infinity of nature'. This was, he said, a worthy ideal, but one that Bogdanov had overlooked through his careless approach to Avenarius's doctrine of human development.[70]

This was a significant difference of opinion between Lunacharsky and Bogdanov, because it reveals that Lunacharsky believed that Avenarius's philosophy contained a vision of a social ideal. This, however, was not one to which Bogdanov subscribed, because he rejected the idea of an ideal that was fixed, constant; for him the ideal was necessarily a dynamic one, one that changed over time.

Bogdanov also objected to the use of the term 'nourishment'; he thought that instead Avenarius should speak in terms of the assimilation and expenditure of energy. If, he said, Avenarius had not obscured matters by the term 'nourishment', it would have been clear to him that the assimilation of energy in whatever quantity would never be excessive, and that its expenditure would

---

69   Avenarius 1905, pp. 59–60.
70   Avenarius 1905, pp. 61–2.

always diminish viability. To Lunacharsky, however, it seemed that Bogdanov was reasoning abstractly: in the case where the organism was not engaged in any activity, and there was nourishment available, no assimilation would take place. On the other hand, where the organism was engaged in games, sport, artistic creation, etc., the expenditure of energy raised viability, not lowered it.[71]

Bogdanov believed that Avenarius's conception of the affectional was superfluous, since he argued that pleasure was accompanied by the assimilation of energy and pain by its disassimilation. Lunacharsky, however, pointed out that Bogdanov was ignoring the fact that a healthy, fresh person derived pleasure from the expenditure of energy involved in running, jumping, solving riddles and puzzles, activities that for a tired person would be sheer torture. This was an example, Lunacharsky added, that showed that one and the same process could be accompanied by a different affectional. This fact could be easily explained in terms of Avenarius's concept of affectional, but was completely incomprehensible to Bogdanov.[72]

Because he was confining himself to discussing the *Critique of Pure Experience*, Lunacharsky did not mention that Bogdanov did not accept Avenarius's concept of introjection. Bogdanov believed that it was superfluous since the phenomena it explained could be accounted for by other means.[73] He did, however, agree with Avenarius that primitive cultures attributed human characteristics to natural phenomena, and in this practice Bogdanov saw the origins of fetishism, first of all natural fetishism and subsequently the commodity fetishism that was a feature of capitalist society.

Though Bogdanov had particular objections to the way that Avenarius handled his material, there were important areas of common ground between Bogdanov and Avenarius. One was the premiss that a cogent system of thought must incorporate the two great scientific principles of the age: adaptation to the environment and the conservation of energy. The concept of the moving equilibrium was also common to both thinkers, as was the idea of assimilation and disassimilation of energy, though they might disagree on the precise terminology.

Bogdanov accepted Avenarius's idea of universal validity as the criterion of truth. It accorded well with his conception that the individual point of view gave rise to a perverted outlook on the world. He was also to discover that universal validity was the criterion of truth that Marx had adopted in *Das Kapital*.

---

71   Avenarius 1905, p. 58.
72   Avenarius 1905, p. 63.
73   Bogdanov 2003, p. 30.

In important respects too, Avenarius was a predecessor of Bogdanov. His *Critique of Pure Experience* was a system, and although he did not carry it out as he had intended, it would have been a system that embraced several disciplines. The invention of special terminology to characterise particular processes or 'acivities' was also an aspect of Avenarius's work that Bogdanov later took up. It is quite possible to see in the *Critique of Pure Experience* the forerunner of *Tectology*.

CHAPTER 3

Vologda

1 The Exiles

In December 1900 Bogdanov received his sentence. He was to be exiled under open surveillance for three years to the Vologda province. He left Kaluga in February of the following year to begin his period of exile. It had been determined that Bogdanov's place of exile should be Yarensk, a small town located at the north-eastern extremity of the Vologda province. But because Natalia had fallen seriously ill, the couple was permitted to stay over in Vologda until the ice on the river melted and it would be possible to take the steamer to Yarensk. However, by the time the northern rivers had become navigable Bogdanov had managed to extract a further concession from the authorities, and on 16 May he was given permission to spend his term of exile in Vologda.[1]

The town of Vologda was the capital of the Vologda province, one of the most economically backward in the Russian Empire, with a climate more akin to Siberia than the central Russian provinces. It had very little industry and no institutions of higher education, so that it had very few industrial workers and very few students, groups that revolutionaries might hope to propagandise. Its economic backwardness and its great distance from both St Petersburg and Moscow made it a traditional place of residence for political exiles. While something of a backwater, Vologda was at least a substantial town of about seventeen thousand inhabitants with shops, hotels, a theatre and something approaching modern amenities. It may have been thoroughly provincial, but as a place of exile it was infinitely preferable to the tiny isolated settlements, such as Yarensk, that dotted the Vologda province. S.G. Strumilin observed that in comparison with Ust-Systolsk, where he was supposed to serve his sentence, Vologda was a vibrant cultural centre.[2]

What made Vologda especially attractive to political exiles was the company of like-minded people. When Bogdanov arrived, there were about a hundred exiles in Vologda, people who belonged to a variety of political parties, and who were only united in their opposition to the tsarist regime.[3] Just before

---

1   Novoselov 1992, p. 179.
2   Strumilin 1957, p. 143.
3   Drugov 1969, p. 30.

Bogdanov arrived the ranks of the exiles had been swollen by a large contingent from Kiev. The Kiev committee of Social Democrats had played a large part in organising the first Congress of the Russian Social-Democratic Labour Party (RSDLP), which had been held in 1898 in Minsk. Most of the delegates had been arrested, and further mass arrests took place in local Social-Democrat organisations. After a spell of imprisonment, the political prisoners were sent into exile. Among the Social Democrats from Kiev were ones who were well known to Lunacharsky, such people as Tuchapsky, Sammer, P.P. Rumiantsev, Mukalov and Berdyaev. In his memoirs Berdyaev mentions that several of the people in exile in Vologda at that time were later to become famous. These included the future Socialist Revolutionary leader Boris Savinkov, who was accompanied by his wife Vera Glebovna, the daughter of the writer Gleb Uspensky, the 'decadent' novelist Alexander Remizov, the economist Strumilin and the literary historian P.E. Shchegolev.[4] To this can be added the sociologist B.A. Kistiakovsky, who had come to Vologda to join his wife, who had been exiled there for revolutionary activities in Kiev.

Among the exiles there was such an array of talent of various kinds that Remizov called Vologda 'the Athens of the North'.[5] The society of the exiles was sought by people who were not themselves exiles, a case in point being the young Danish businessman Aage Madelung, who aspired to become a Russian novelist, and the medical orderly E.I. Ermolaev, who became an acolyte of Bogdanov and Lunacharsky.[6]

In 1927 Bogdanov was approached by the Lenin Institute for information about the political debates in Vologda in which he had participated. Bogdanov submitted a brief reply which was published in the journal of the Institute *Leninskii sbornik* in 1929. Bogdanov's reply is worth quoting in full because as one of his few autobiographical writings it has an intrinsic interest, and because it provides a very good summary of the salient features of his Vologda exile.

> I arrived there [in Vologda] at the beginning of 1901 and found a few dozen exiles, including a group of people from Kiev, whose chief theoretician was Berdyaev (V.G. Krzhizhanovskaya, P.L. Tuchapsky, B.E. Shen, later N.K. Mukalov etc.) Soon after this S.A. Suvorov, who was working as a statistician, gave a philosophical lecture inspired by critical positivism. Berdyaev opposed and I supported Suvorov. Then I gave a series of lectures on historical materialism (most of which were published in

---

4   Berdiaev 1990, p. 118.
5   Remizov 1986, p. 287.
6   Remizov 1986, pp. 195–236.

journals and later in *From the Psychology of Society*). Berdyaev usually spoke against them; he was then a good speaker (better than we were), but his scientific knowledge did not amount to much, and in philosophy he knew well only the neo-Kantian school (better than we did); he was completely lost with the positivists (he made a fool of himself with Avenarius and Mach). Gradually even the Kievans began to lose faith in him. Even by 1902 the other exiles were firmly on the side of the 'realists', Berdyaev retaining the support of only a few members of Narodnoe pravo (Vera Denish, Neklepaev) and the writer A.M. Remizov. In 1902 Lunacharsky arrived and began to debate with Berdyaev, whom even then he outdid as a speaker. Berdyaev, though, gained the support of the much more learned, though not particularly talented, B.A. Kistiakovsky. The debate was also waged in the pages of journals (*Voprosy filosofii i psikhologii*, Berdyaev's review of my book *A Historical View of Perception*, appeared in the issue for October 1902, and my reply, I think, in December of the same year, or it could have been at the start of the following year, in the 65th issue of that journal). On these articles B.A. Kistiakovsky declared that Berdyaev 'had got into a tangle with Avenarius'. Then the anthology *Problems of Idealism* came out, and we, the Vologda 'realists', in reply organised the anthology *Studies in the Realist World View*. P.P. Rumiantsev, who had arrived to head the Vologda board of statistics, helped us to edit it.

By the end of 1903 Berdyaev's influence among the exiles had evaporated, and the attitude to him of the Social Democrats among them was rather ironic. He no longer delivered lectures, and, making use of his influential connections, departed before his term of exile was completed. By this time the interest in philosophy among the exiles had begun to fade, and had been replaced by the political debate with the Socialist Revolutionaries, in which Savinkov's group was prominent (it included Shchegolev, Budrin, Matsevsky and others). I left early in 1904, my term of exile having come to an end.[7]

Vologda was the place where Bogdanov's father and grandfather had lived, and in the summer of 1902 Bogdanov's parents with their daughters, Maria, Anna and Olga, moved to Vologda from the Yaroslavl province. After being rejected by the 20-year-old Maria, Lunacharsky settled on her 18-year-old sister Anna, whom he married in September.[8]

---

7 Neizvestnyi Bogdanov 1995, 1, pp. 32–3; Leninskii sbornik 1929, 29, p. 333.
8 Letter from V.S. Klebaner to Douglas Huestis dated 31 May 1995; Malinovsky notes.

In order to supplement the small allowance they received from the authorities the exiles tried to find employment locally. Suvorov and Strumilin became
statisticians for the Vologda zemstvo organisation. Bogdanov, making use of
his medical qualifications, successfully applied for a post in the psychiatric
hospital situated in the village of Kuvshinovo, three or four kilometres from
Vologda. In the autumn of 1900 he moved into a house there. Conditions in the
hospital were difficult; for 300 patients there were only two doctors. Bogdanov
depicted conditions in the hospital in his novel *Red Star*. Of the fictional zemstvo psychiatric hospital he relates: 'It was in a wretched condition and always
terribly overcrowded ... the medical staff was undermanned and perpetually
overworked ... Instead of curing the patients, the hospital managed to reduce
many of them to imbecility, while many others, weakened by the lack of fresh
air and proper nutrition, perished from tuberculosis'.[9]

Bogdanov was fortunate to have the assistance of Ermolaev, who had
recently qualified as a medical orderly (*feldsher*). In 1923 Ermolaev published
his memoirs, which contained a sympathetic pen-portrait of Bogdanov, with
whom he had formed a lasting friendship.

According to Ermolaev:

> Bogdanov came to Vologda in 1900 when he was 27 or 28 years of age.
> He was of medium height, broad-shouldered, with fair hair and a reddish
> beard and moustache. Physically quite strong, he lived and dressed simply
> and unpretentiously. He had the face, as he himself put it, of an ordinary
> Russian, of a shop assistant, but an enormous protruding forehead gave
> him a severe appearance, and the firm line of his chin denoted a strength
> of will, mind and purpose. The expression in his grey eyes was usually one
> of seriousness and weariness. He was absent-minded and displayed no
> practical capabilities, though he himself liked to think of himself as adept
> in practical matters. Bogdanov was the first person I had ever come across
> in my life who worked so hard outside his regular hours of employment.
> I had no idea at that time that writing could be a profession. I suppose
> that his motto was, and still is, 'work comes first', i.e. all his life was to
> be ordered to achieve the maximum effort; to eat and to drink only what
> would be good for work; to love or not to love according to whether it was
> conducive or not to working efficiency.[10]

---

9   Bogdanov 1984, p. 125.
10   Ermolaev, 1923, p. 5.

After Lunacharsky arrived in Vologda, Ermolaev acted as his secretary. When in September 1902 Lunacharsky married Bogdanov's sister Anna, Ermolaev acted as his best man, though only after cautioning the groom against marriage, on the grounds that a revolutionary should not be bound by family ties in order to have freedom of action.[11] Lunacharsky, however, was not to be convinced.

Although Remizov was to become famous as a novelist of the 'decadent' school, while in Vologda he had yet to publish anything. He had been arrested for taking part in a demonstration and had been sentenced to three years in Ust-Systolsk in the Vologda province. He was, however, given leave to come to Vologda for treatment for his eye complaint, and, on the strength of a medical certificate signed by Bogdanov, he was allowed to stay for a further month. With further medical certificates Remizov was allowed to stay in Vologda until the end of his exile. Remizov considered himself a Social Democrat, and was familiar with the writings of Plekhanov and Struve, and he says that he had read Bogdanov's *Short Course of Economic Science* while at university.[12]

2   Berdyaev

Nikolai Berdyaev came from an aristocratic Kievan family of French origins. He was a year younger than Bogdanov, and, like him, had been arrested for his part in a student demonstration. He had been educated in Kiev, and had attended the University there. He had joined the same Social-Democratic group as Lunacharsky, and had conducted propaganda among the local workers. Berdyaev was later to make his name as a religious philosopher, but while in Vologda he was still on the route that would lead him from Marxism to religious faith. In his memoirs Berdyaev says of Bogdanov:

> Somewhat curious were my relations with A. Bogdanov (Malinovsky), who later created a whole philosophical system, a synthesis of Marxism with empiriocriticism and empiriomonism. Bogdanov was a very good person, very sincere and selflessly dedicated to his idea, but he was a type of person completely alien to me. At that time I was considered to be an 'idealist' imbued with metaphysical seekings. For Bogdanov this was a completely abnormal phenomenon. He had originally qualified as a psychiatrist. He began to visit me often. I noticed that he systematically put

---

11   Ermolaev 1923, p. 9.
12   Remizov 1986, pp. 194–5.

to me incomprehensible questions: how I felt in the mornings; how did I sleep; what were my reactions to this and that, and so on. It emerged that my inclination towards idealism and metaphysics he considered to be the symptoms of an incipient mental disorder, and he wanted to estab lish how far this malady had progressed. What is interesting, though, is that Bogdanov himself later had a psychiatric disorder and spent some time in a psychiatric hospital. This never happened to me.[13]

Berdyaev is mistaken in thinking that Bogdanov had a psychiatric disorder and spent some time in a psychiatric hospital. During the war Bogdanov suffered from a nervous complaint and was treated for this in a hospital for nervous diseases – an entirely different thing. It is of course possible that Bogdanov was teasing Berdyaev about his alleged mental disorder, because, after all, he took Berdyaev's idealistic views seriously enough to try to refute them. But a significant implication of the story is that Bogdanov visited Berdyaev often, suggesting that personal relations between the two men were good. Berdyaev's biographer confirms that, despite all their differences of opinion and the pub lic polemics, a spirit of solidarity reigned among the Vologda exiles.[14] It is clear that Bogdanov's theoretical understanding was deepened by his discussions with Berdyaev. Berdyaev, like his associates Sergei Bulgakov and Peter Struve, was becoming increasingly disillusioned with the 'dialectical materialism' pro pounded by Plekhanov. His objections to this kind of Marxism were taken up by Bogdanov, who formulated solutions to the problems Berdyaev had raised. In this way Bogdanov arrived at his own particular approaches to aspects of Marxist doctrine, such as the relationship between 'base' and 'superstructure' and the question of socialist ideals. In this respect Berdyaev's intellectual evol ution provides a key to some of Bogdanov's earliest and most characteristic ideas.

By the time he arrived in Vologda Berdyaev had published a major work on Marxist philosophy. This was his critique of Friedrich Lange, the author of *The History of Materialism* published in 1900 in *Die neue Zeit*, the theoretical journal of the German Social Democrats edited by Karl Kautsky.

In defining his standpoint in that article Berdyaev could still say that he 'numbered himself among the most ardent adherents of Marxism', but went on to declare that he belonged to its critical current and that he believed that the doctrine should be subject to a thorough reappraisal that would involve

---

13   Berdiaev 1990, p. 118.
14   Lowrie 1960, p. 59.

the 'purging of Marxism from the Hegelian dialectic and philosophical material-ism'.[15] In the article Berdyaev argued that Bernstein's call in the conclusion of his controversial pamphlet *Die Voraussetzungen des Sozialismus* for a return to Lange was misplaced. Lange had made the mistake of confusing philosophy with psychology and in that way had failed to understand the importance of epistemology. He had not understood that epistemology regarded knowledge not from the psychological, but the logical point of view. Much of Berdyaev's article was devoted to a survey of the recent history of philosophy in Germany, tracing the origins of the 'back to Kant' movement of which Lange was a representative. He showed some sympathy for the French enlighteners of the eighteenth century, but deplored their followers, Büchner and Moleschott, who tried to make philosophy subject to science, a position Berdyaev disagreed with profoundly.

Berdyaev concluded his article by replying to Plekhanov's challenge to suggest any philosophy which could compete with 'dialectical materialism' by declaring that: 'The future does not belong to the subjective idealism of Berkeley, or the absolute idealism of Hegel, or the agnosticism of the neo-Kantians of our days. But it belongs just as little to "dialectical materialism"'.[16]

In 1901 Berdyaev published *Subjectivism and Individualism*, a critical examination of the views of Mikhailovsky; the book had a long introduction by Struve. It was appropriate that Struve should be involved in this publication, because it was to some extent the continuation of the critique of Mikhailovsky's 'subjective sociology' that Struve had undertaken in his *Critical Notes*. But a prominent theme of the book, one developed both by Berdyaev and Struve, was the rejection of the positivist and relativist viewpoint. Here Berdyaev elaborated on the contrast he had drawn in his Friedrich Lange article between psychology and epistemology. Truth, he argued, did not lie in the psychological consciousness, which eternally changed and bred subjectivism, but in the transcendental logical consciousness, which was rooted in the universally obligatory norms of thought and consequently assured objectivity in perception. Theories, he declared, could be relative; truth was always absolute, equal to itself.[17]

In 1901, while in Vologda, Berdyaev published a further article entitled 'The Struggle for Idealism' in the journal *Mir Bozhii*. This was a provocative essay which challenged the basic assumptions of the positivist standpoint. In Berdyaev's view Marxism was in crisis. The doctrine was no longer engaged in the struggle with 'Narodism', but was convulsed by the internal conflict between

---

15   Berdiaev 1900, I, p. 133.
16   Berdiaev 1900, III, p. 207.
17   Berdiaev 1999, pp. 101–6.

orthodox and critical camps. To Berdyaev this was a sign of the spiritual ferment of the times, that the song of positivism, naturalism and hedonism had been sung, and that now was the time to proclaim the struggle for idealism, the struggle for a more joyful and bright world outlook in which the higher and eternal demands of the human soul would receive satisfaction. Berdyaev believed that it was a misapprehension of earlier times that had identified idealism with the forces of reaction. At the present time this mistaken idea impeded the creation of new people for a new society.[18]

Berdyaev conceded that epochs of enlightenment proclaimed materialism, and in those times to be an idealist meant to be a reactionary. In France the materialists of the eighteenth century, in Germany Feuerbach and the Left Hegelians, and in Russia Chernyshevsky and D.I. Pisarev, the homegrown enlighteners, had been justified in directing their materialism against medieval absolutism. But that enlightened era had passed. In the nineteenth century the balance of social forces had changed. The bourgeois era in history had seen a degeneration in the psychological type of human personality by the narrowing of its spiritual horizons. It levelled out distinctive individuality, and stifled the Faustian aspirations to discover the mysteries of existence. The revolutionary materialism of the last century had given way to positivism which impoverished human beings spiritually. It refused to confront the questions that were most vital to human existence.[19]

To Berdyaev the opposition to bourgeois society that emerged in the nineteenth century also had narrow horizons. The ideology of Marxism was arrested at a very low level of philosophical development. Because of the urgency of achieving material gains, the ideology of oppressed producers in the mid-nineteenth century was fatally distracted from the ideal aims of mankind. The aim of human life was interpreted too materialistically. Marxism was poor in its spiritual and cultural content.[20]

Berdyaev considered to be a cardinal error of positivism its rejection of 'metaphysics', anything whose existence and nature was not subject to investigation by scientific means. For Berdyaev this meant the rejection of goodness, morality, beauty, all the most elevated aspects of human life. In this way positivism was demeaning to human existence. And it seemed to him repugnant that all phenomena should be explained in terms of evolution, which had no means of comprehending such things as moral or aesthetic values.

---

18   Berdiaev 1901, p. 3.
19   Berdiaev 1901, pp. 4–5.
20   Berdiaev 1901, pp. 6–7.

Berdyaev, moreover, deplored the positivist vision of the new society coming into being as a result of the social cataclysm, a *Zusammenbruch* that would destroy the old social order. He pointed out that never in the past history of mankind has there been such a means of bringing about a great world-historical idea in a new form of community. Nor was there anything so banal as attaching importance to the speed or the suddenness with which the transition to the new society would take place. In any case, the cataclysm would take place mechanically, in such a way that there was no place for idealism. And the new society that would emerge from this dialectical movement would most probably be as self-satisfied, complacent and philistine as the one it had replaced.[21]

Berdyaev went on to question the Marxist conception of the economic 'base' of society giving rise to its ideological 'superstructure'. 'How can', he asked, 'this economic development *create* ideological development? ... What internal causal link is possible between the economy ... and ideology, whether it be the discovery of a scientific law, the construction of a metaphysical system, the experience of moral ideals or an artistic creation?'[22]

In Berdyaev's view, Marx and Engels only made their contribution to knowledge in the socio-economic sphere; beyond this they added almost nothing to the critical work of the bourgeoisie in its revolutionary struggle with medieval society and its theological world view. The dialectical character of their materialism, borrowed from Hegelian idealism, did not alter the essence of the matter. In their views on the world and life they were materialists and hedonists; their spiritual view was limited. They struggled against idealism because they were in thrall to the misapprehension that idealism was the ideology of reaction.

Berdyaev believed that it was the duty of idealists to insist on moral perfection as the aim of human life. 'Social utilitarianism' in so far as it infringed on Faustian aspirations and demeaned human life he considered to be a reactionary direction in human thought, however democratic the forms in which it might clothe itself.

3   The Debates

The debates that took place among the Vologda exiles were an important part of their social lives. From what Strumilin says, the venue for the debates was the home of Savinkov and his wife Vera Glebovna. He recalls that there one could almost always find Remizov, Shchegolev and one or two others. Quite often the

---

21   Berdiaev 1901, pp. 17–18.
22   Berdiaev 1901, p. 20.

discussion would concern literature, about the latest works of Gorky, Andreev or other writers. Sometimes Berdyaev provoked philosophical debates, as he raised controversial issues by his rejection of Marxism in favour of a new metaphysics. According to Strumilin, Berdyaev was a talented speaker and argued with brilliance and passion, a performance only marred by the nervous tic that afflicted him all his life.[23]

Ermolaev too attended these debates. According to him Bogdanov was among the first to give a paper. He spoke on energeticist method, on perception from the historical point of view and other themes. Kistiakovsky, Berdyaev and Suvorov also gave papers; the audience on such occasions would number about fifty or sixty. A discussion followed almost every paper; those taking the most active part in the discussion were Bogdanov, Suvorov and Berdyaev. Strumilin says that he occasionally spoke too. Ermolaev remarks that as the questions debated at that time were more or less academic, they did not arouse any passions. He adds that he had the impression that most of the subjects discussed were well above the heads of the listeners, although these were on the whole well-educated people.[24]

Even the loyal Ermolaev had to admit that Bogdanov was an ineffective speaker,[25] and that Berdyaev invariably emerged as the victor, as Bogdanov himself recognised. The situation changed in February 1902 when Lunacharsky arrived in Vologda. Lunacharsky was an outstanding orator, and one who had past experience debating with Berdyaev in Kiev. He argued aggressively with Berdyaev, and with some success, deploying his knowledge of Ernst Mach for the purpose. After Lunacharsky's arrival in Vologda Berdyaev's influence among the exiles began to wane, and when Lunacharsky invited Berdyaev to come to his lectures and refute him, Berdyaev declined. Late in 1902 Berdyaev was permitted to leave Vologda first for Zhitomir, and subsequently for his native Kiev.[26]

The fact that Lunacharsky's use of Mach's philosophy against Berdyaev's arguments was effective is symptomatic of the fact that the Marxism Berdyaev was rejecting was the 'dialectical materialism' propounded by Plekhanov and his followers. Neither Bogdanov nor Lunacharsky would be inclined to defend this kind of doctrine against Berdyaev's strictures. Nor would they attempt to explain how the ideology of the 'superstructure' emerged from the economics of the 'base'; their energeticist approach obviated difficulties of this kind. This

23   Strumilin 1957, pp. 139–40.
24   Ermolaev, 1923, p. 5.
25   Ermolaev 1923, p. 6.
26   Lowrie 1960, p. 67.

meant that much of Berdyaev's critique of Marxism missed the point when debating with Bogdanov and Lunacharsky. The main point at issue between the disputants was the positivist standpoint. This was what Bogdanov and Lunacharsky defended with such zeal, bringing to bear on its critic the latest representatives of that positivist school, Mach and Avenarius.

4   What Is Idealism?

Bogdanov published the article 'What is Idealism?' in *Mir Bozhii* in 1901 as a reply to Berdyaev's 'Struggle for Idealism'. A comparison of the two articles reveals why Berdyaev could so decisively best Bogdanov in the debates. This was first of all because the initiative lay with Berdyaev; he had dictated the topic of the discussion by his strictures on the positivist and the Marxist doctrines. Second, much of what Berdyaev said was rhetorical, a clarion call to arms against materialism and positivism, rather than a systematic argument that Bogdanov might have refuted. As Bogdanov remarked: 'Mr Berdyaev has proposed to recognise moral aims for the world process – not on the basis of any arguments founded on facts and logic, but simply *a priori*, on the strength of the fact that the above-mentioned author cannot imagine things being otherwise'.[27] And Bogdanov found it difficult to answer Berdyaev's criticism directly. An effective reply to Berdyaev would have been to argue that his objections to positivism were unjust, because the positivist view of the world provided humanity with just as much spiritual fulfilment as the metaphysical approach did. The obstacle to this strategy was that Comte, the founder of positivism, had believed that a spiritual dimension was exactly what his doctrine lacked, and to fill this void he had instituted a 'religion of humanity' emulating the Catholic Church. Clearly, the direct reply to Berdyaev's argument was not feasible, hence Bogdanov was forced into a more indirect response, based on the resources that positivism had placed at his disposal.

The approach Bogdanov took in 'What is Idealism?' was to deploy some of his characteristic ideas about how societies evolved and how their ideologies developed. He began by posing the question of what is meant by 'progress'. He concedes that this is a controversial concept, because depending on one's point of view different things could count as progress. Through the fragmentation of society and the accumulation of different experience by different people, different individuals and groups have come to view progress entirely differently. A

---

27   Bogdanov 1901, p. 3.

true definition of progress would be one which would not be confined to a particular section of society, but society as a whole; progress would be 'the growth of the fullness and harmony of life'. For Bogdanov progress could only mean social progress.[28]

Bogdanov accepted that the society of the future should not be complacent, and remarked that the image of the future society as depicted by Edward Bellamy in his utopian novel *Looking Backward* was a mistaken vision. This was a self-satisfied society, resting on its laurels, with no incentive to further progress. Bogdanov believed that ideals should not be static, fixed, but in constant development. Bogdanov went on to argue that if ideals were static, if they were regarded as absolutes, such as 'honour', 'duty' or 'justice', they were nothing more than fetishes. Progress with regard to this fetishised ideal could only mean the gradual approach to a fixed point in the future. If this objective were ever reached then progress would have come to an end. In Bogdanov's view, this was the implication of Berdyaev's metaphysical approach to ideals and to progress.[29]

In Bogdanov's argument there was more than a hint of personal affront that he must have experienced in the debates with Berdyaev, because he associated the fetishised view of ideals with what he termed 'intellectual aristocratism'. This phenomenon arose when a person who espoused absolute perception looked on those who propounded relative perception as inferior creatures, as a feudal lord might look upon an insignificant worm. According to Bogdanov, 'this is the tone in which Mr Berdyaev spoke about the evolutionists, positivists etc'.[30] Berdyaev himself confessed that even as a Social Democrat and a revolutionary he never entirely lost the mannerisms of a nobleman.[31]

5   Perception from the Historical Point of View

Bogdanov's major work in the Vologda period was his book *Perception from the Historical Point of View*.[32] In this work, Bogdanov explained, the ideas expounded in *Basic Elements of the Historical View of Nature* were developed in greater detail. He admitted that in some details his views had changed, but that his basic conception remained the same; this was that all modern methods of

---

28   Bogdanov 1906, pp. 10–11.
29   Bogdanov 1906, pp. 21–2.
30   Bogdanov 1906, p. 34.
31   Berdiaev 1990, p. 16.
32   Bogdanov 1901.

scientific explanation could be logically subordinated to the principle of the conservation of energy.[33] *Perception from the Historical Point of View*, however, reflected the two new factors that had influenced Bogdanov's thinking since the publication of *Basic Elements*: the discussions with Lunacharsky on Avenarius's philosophy and the debates with Berdyaev.

Bogdanov begins by arguing that the question of perception can be framed in terms of the expenditure of energy. And here he draws an interesting parallel to illustrate what he means by 'energy' in this connection. Energy, he says, 'is not a means of perception, but just the opposite – it is an abstraction from the different means of perception. Energy is not light, sound, heat etc.; it is the quantitative side of these processes, their measurability and commensurability. It is the same kind of methodological abstraction as the 'abstract labour' of the economists: it is not the labour of the shoemaker, the tailor, the smith, – but the measurability and commensurability of social labour'.[34]

Bogdanov was conscious that in studying the question of perception at that time it would be difficult not to take account of the works of Avenarius, the philosopher who had made such a mark in that field. He did so, however, not to adopt Avenarius's ideas, but to contest them. The point at issue was the effect of an increase of energy in the central nervous apparatus, in Avenarius's terminology 'System C'. According to Avenarius two processes took place in System C: one was the absorption of energy from the environment (nourishment), and the other was the expenditure of energy in the environment (work). For Avenarius the ideal state for System C was equilibrium, and the predominance of either 'nourishment' or 'work' he termed 'vital difference', which was a disturbance of the desired equilibrium.[35]

While sharing the general conception of the perceptive apparatus adapting to its environment much as Avenarius described, Bogdanov had always thought in terms of the increase in energy as the source of pleasure and the decrease in energy as the source of pain. Moreover, he saw the increase in energy as the means by which organisms developed and evolved. Bogdanov believed that there were no grounds for thinking that positive vital difference was detrimental to the survival of System C. In his view Avenarius's equilibrium was a static ideal; it did not cater for the evolution that Darwin had envisaged.[36]

Bogdanov paid considerable attention in his book to outlining the development of various types of awareness, from rudimentary reflexes to human

---

33   Bogdanov 1901, p. IV.
34   Bogdanov 1901, p. 11.
35   Bogdanov 1901, pp. 13–14.
36   Bogdanov 1901, pp. 21–2.

consciousness, which he explained in terms of adaptation of the organism to the environment. Consciousness was the state which enabled this adaptation to take place with the least expenditure of energy. The forms which this consciousness took could also be explained in terms of adaptations to the environment. Thus, in the struggle for survival, the need to generalise from particulars arose at an early stage of human development, as did the opposite necessity, that of distinguishing phenomena from each other. At higher levels these adaptations would appear as the formation of concepts by means of abstraction and the development of language. Bogdanov believed that the early forms of human expression were singing, speech, poetry, and that these forms of expression were differentiated one from another at a comparatively late period.[37]

Adaptation for survival also explained the features of societies, both of humans and of animals. One of the most rudimentary was the herd instinct, which enabled individuals to act in unison. A more advanced type of human collective action was cooperation, the purposeful working association of individuals in the struggle with nature. These forms of cooperation had associated ideological forms which were the indirect adaptation of people to the social struggle with external nature.[38]

In Bogdanov's view, perception was a form of adaptation, and this too developed historically, so that truth could only be relative. Perceptions changed with the succession of types of social cooperation. In patriarchal clan society 'animism' or 'natural fetishism' was the dominant ideology, natural phenomena being credited with human attributes. And because human society was composed of 'organisers', people who gave instructions, and 'executors', those who carried them out, the conclusion was drawn that every action, both in the human and in the natural world, was composed of an organising and an executory element. The conceptions of 'soul' and 'body' arose from the division of society into organisers and the organised.[39]

In a significant passage Bogdanov went on to say that in modern society, along with the division into organisers and executors, one encountered another type of organised cooperation, which he termed 'synthetic'. In democratic organisations the fusion of the organising and the executory roles took place, such that in the labour process the organiser and the executor continually changed places, mutually controlling each other. He continued:

---

37   Bogdanov 1901, pp. 118–25.
38   Bogdanov 1901, p. 137.
39   Bogdanov 1901, pp. 189–90.

For example, when some people get together, on an equal footing, to conduct some business or other, then both in the process of discussion and in
the process of implementation of this business, each of them in turn acts
now in the role of organiser, now in the role of executory. He is the organiser when he gives others orders and advice, how to conduct the business,
when to vote for or against certain actions which others have proposed,
in general, when he influences the general decisions which determine the
course of the business. He is the executor when he participates in the direct collective implementation of the decisions taken, when he submits to
the declared general will.[40]

The importance of this passage is that it contains Bogdanov's conception
of how a democratic organisation ought to function. One can observe from
the kind of business that Bogdanov envisages the organisation as conducting
('when to vote for or against certain actions which others have proposed') that
the organisation he has in mind is a political one. It would have organisers,
but their position would not be permanent; there would be rank-and-file members, but these would in due course become organisers. The implications of this
passage are that Bogdanov believed that a political party should be run on 'synthetic' lines.

In modern, exchange society, Bogdanov explained, the characteristic manifestation of the fetishism was the so-called 'commodity fetishism', the special
form of perception of social relations, characteristic of the anarchist type of
cooperation, a form of perception that had been thoroughly investigated by
Marx. A similar type of metaphysical generalisation, according to Bogdanov,
was the Kantian concept of 'duty', the highest formulation of petty-bourgeois
morality.

Since the anarchist type of cooperation was the outcome of the division
of labour and specialisation into trades and professions, Bogdanov posed the
question whether this kind of specialisation might be overcome. His answer
was that it was possible only by the elaboration of general methods in all
spheres of production. People would be skilled in general methods which could
be applied to the various objects of external nature, but the labour applied
would retain a great measure of homogeneity.[41]

The application of general methods would be characteristic of 'synthetic
cooperation', which Bogdanov believed would be the dominant form of cooper-

40   Bogdanov 1901, pp. 190.
41   Bogdanov 1901, p. 201.

ation in the future, though it had already made its appearance in the present in the form of modern machine production. The machines had taken on the specialisations, requiring the workers only to supervise them. This meant that the activities of the workers had become more of the organising type, the exercise of control and direction, though of machines rather than of people. The earlier two types of labour activity were in this way combined into one.[42]

Although Bogdanov does not draw attention to the fact, the phenomenon of 'synthetic cooperation' appears in two contexts in his book: one concerned with political organisation and the other concerned with the overcoming of specialisation in the economic system of the future. In both cases there is a coalescence of the organising and the executory functions. The implication is that Bogdanov envisaged that a democratic socialist party should function on the same principles as a socialist society. In the case of a political organisation, the directing function should be an attribute of the whole organisation; and in the case of a socialist society, it would be an attribute of the society as a whole. This supposition is confirmed by the article entitled 'Authoritarian Thinking' which Bogdanov published in *Obrazovanie* in 1903. There he explained that if synthetic relations were confined to a small circle of comrades or a utopian commune they would petrify into immobile conservatism, but 'a wide democratically organised party, and even more so, a whole synthetically-organised society in the panoply of its collective experiences cannot but derive continuously newer and newer stimuli to move forward'.[43]

Berdyaev's review of *Perception from the Historical Point of View* appeared in the Russian philosophical journal *Voprosy filosofii i psikhologii* in the autumn of 1902. About Bogdanov's 'pretentious little book' he had very little good to say. In view of the revived interest in idealism, he found it antiquated, unnecessary and irrelevant; in his opinion, it had appeared 40 years too late. He deplored the book's tendency to confuse philosophy with science, and its neglect of the vast literature that had appeared on epistemology over the centuries. He thought Bogdanov presumptuous in considering himself qualified to pontificate on the most complex philosophical, epistemological, psychological and sociological questions simply on the basis that he had undergone a course of natural science and medicine.[44]

Berdyaev thought that Bogdanov's ignorance of epistemology was especially evident in his polemic with Avenarius, whose ideas he had misinterpreted. He had not understood that in the *Critique of Pure Experience* Avenarius was

42   Bogdanov 1901, pp. 201–2.
43   Bogdanov 1906, pp. 128–9.
44   Berdiaev 1902, p. 839.

attempting to provide a general theory of perception, rather than a biological theory. He had taken 'System c' to mean literally the central nervous system, and understood 'nourishment' and 'work' as purely biological concepts. For Berdyaev Avenarius was after all a philosopher; he was concerned with the epistemological questions of the relation of thinking to being, and he intended his terminology to be understood not in terms of biology but of formal logic.[45]

On the question of perception, Berdyaev found Bogdanov too inclined towards positivism to recognise absolute truth. Bogdanov treated truth as relative, and believed the criteria of truth to be adaptation and preservation. Berdyaev, for his part, accused Bogdanov of confusing truth with theory; while a theory might change, truth was always absolute.[46]

To Berdyaev's mind, Bogdanov's basic flaw was that he had a completely erroneous view of what science was, what philosophy was, and what the relationship between them was. Bogdanov seemed to believe that there 'exists some kind of universal science "energetics", and he saw the scientific character of all spheres of knowledge in that they should be subsumed under this universal science. His aim was to include all spheres of scientific perception, including the science of perception itself, into a systematic energeticist world view; for him there exists only the scientific method – the energeticist method, and the ideal of scientific perception (*ideal poznaniia*) expressed in terms of quantitively measured energy'.[47] One must give Berdyaev credit here for his ability to encapsulate so perceptively the intention behind Bogdanov's book. He was surely right in thinking that Bogdanov regarded 'energy' as the factor which united all phenomena into a monist system.

In Berdyaev's judgement, however, Bogdanov's dream of a universal energeticist science was entirely unrealistic. There existed only individual sciences, each with its own objects of study, its own methods, and its own search for the laws governing its particular set of phenomena; in science there prevailed not monism, but pluralism.[48]

Berdyaev thought that the biological and naturalist conception of historical materialism that Bogdanov propounded was completely alien to classical Marxism. But in one respect he was faithful to Marxism, and that was in his rejection of conceptions of morality. For Bogdanov such conceptions were only 'social fetishism'. Berdyaev concluded by saying that while one could not fail to

45   Berdiaev 1902, pp. 841–2.
46   Berdiaev 1902, p. 844.
47   Berdiaev 1902, pp. 847–8.
48   Berdiaev 1902, p. 848.

recognise Bogdanov's sincerity and conviction, it was a pity that the commitment to justice and democracy that he, Berdyaev, shared, was allied to such bad philosophy.

Despite the overwhelmingly negative character of Berdyaev's review, it was nevertheless a serious, and even perceptive, discussion of Bogdanov's ideas. Berdyaev might have disagreed with what Bogdanov had said, but he did so in a reasoned fashion without insults or personal abuse: on the contrary, he paid tribute to Bogdanov's integrity and sincerity. In the light of the opprobrium that was later to be heaped on Bogdanov and his ideas, it is ironic that Bogdanov received better treatment from an ideological opponent than from his fellow Social Democrats.

Bogdanov replied to Berdyaev's review in the following issue of *Voprosy filosofii i psikhologii*. By the simple expedient of quoting from Avenarius's *Critique of Pure Experience* he disproved Berdyaev's contention that Avenarius was a philosopher rather than a natural scientist, and showed that in speaking of System C, Avenarius did indeed mean the central nervous system:

> For our purposes it seemed to me useful perceptually to distinguish from the whole system of central organs this partial system of the nervous apparatus in which are united the changes emanating from the periphery and distributing the changes delivered to the periphery. A more precise anatomical and physiological definition of this partial system I shall leave open – as it would not be sufficiently certain, or in general be accepted – because for our purposes there is no harm in leaving it open. The partial system in question I shall designate simply as System C.
>
> Therefore, for our purposes we can divide the nervous system:
>
> A) System C.
> B) The remaining nervous system.[49]

Since Bogdanov had proved his point with irrefutable documentary evidence, this is probably why Kistiakovsky judged that Berdyaev had 'got into a tangle with Avenarius'. It may have been that Berdyaev had not read the *Critique of Pure Experience*, because although he expressed admiration for Avenarius in his Friedrich Lange article, the references were all to Avenarius's later book *The Human Concept of the World*, whose focus is more on epistemological questions. Bogdanov also disputed Berdyaev's contention that in the sciences there was pluralism rather than monism, by citing recent instances of boundaries

---

49   Bogdanov 1902, pp. 1050–1.

between sciences having broken down and the increasing tendency for disciplines to adopt each other's methodologies.

An interesting aspect of Bogdanov's reply to Berdyaev's review was that it was a rare instance where Bogdanov mentioned the influences on his thinking. In suggesting that Berdyaev's criticism should be directed not at himself, but at the authors of the ideas he objected to, Bogdanov named Simmel, Mach and Avenarius. He said that he followed Wilhelm Ostwald in his conception of energetics and Spencer in his ideas on evolutionism. He concluded by avowing adherence to the positivist school, declaring himself to be 'a rank and file representative of that great and powerful current of life and thought that swept away millions of fetishes ... and gave people genuine freedom of development, and not the illusory freedom of metaphysical flights of fancy'.[50]

Probably Bogdanov was dissatisfied with his reply to Berdyaev in 'What is idealism?' because in the article 'The Development of Life in Nature and Society' he returned to the questions Berdyaev had raised in 'The Struggle for Idealism'. Bogdanov's focus on this occasion was to give his interpretation of how ideology in society related to the technical aspects of production and how he believed the transition to the new society would take place. Altogether this was a more confident performance than 'What is Idealism?' and shows the versatility of Bogdanov's evolutionist approach.

He began by quoting the 'Preface to the *Contribution to the Critique of Political Economy*' which contained Marx's well-known formulation of the base and superstructure of society.[51] Bogdanov conceded that although this formulation was still essentially valid, the concepts Marx had used lacked precision, especially in explaining what the relationship was between the 'economic structure'

---

50   Bogdanov 1902, p. 1059.

51   'In the social production of their lives people enter into definite, necessary relations, which are independent of their will. These are relations of production which correspond to a definite stage in the development of the forces of production. The sum-total of these relations of production form the economic structure of society, the real base, on which there arises a legal and political superstructure, and which corresponds to definite forms of social consciousness. The forms of production of material life determine the social, political and intellectual process of life in general. It is not people's consciousness that determines their being, but, on the contrary, their social being that determines their consciousness. At a certain stage of their development the material forces of production of society come into conflict with the existing relations of production, or to express this in legal terms, with the property relations, within which they have previously functioned. From being forms of development of productive forces these relations become fetters binding these forces. There then comes about an era of social revolution. With the changes in the economic foundation the whole immense superstructure is more slowly or more rapidly transformed'. See Marx 1859, p. v.

of society and the 'legal and political superstructure'. He went on to say that since Marx wrote, much had changed; evolutionary theory had made great strides, such that now the relationship between economics and ideology could be expressed in terms of adaptation.

Bogdanov's argument was that in their struggle for existence, people could not pool their efforts without consciousness. Without consciousness, without perception, there could be no coming together in society. The very concept of society contained the idea of organisation, of the uniting of individuals living together. Thus, for the term 'society' to have any real meaning, it had to imply a particular organising adaptation – the social instinct. In this way the social instinct was inseparable from consciousness, so that, in Bogdanov's words: 'Social being and social consciousness in the exact sense of these words are identical'.[52] He then went on to demonstrate how on the basis of technical progress there developed the complex system of social being, with its varied elements and united whole.[53]

In showing that even at the most rudimentary level a system of social labour implied communication, Bogdanov was supported by the research of Ludwig Noiré on the origins of language. Noiré had found that speech emerged from technical processes, the sounds people made in coordinating their efforts. This allowed Bogdanov to argue that even at the most rudimentary levels of social production some ideological element was involved. This ideological element was organising adaptation in the social-labour struggle for existence.[54]

Although the social instinct might draw people together, the disparity of individuals' experience would lead to conflicts of various kinds arising among them, and to alleviate this problem a series of customs would be enforced to maintain the labour efficiency of the social group. From this line of argument Bogdanov rehearsed his ideas on the evolution of customs, law and morality that he had set out in 'What is Idealism?'

On this occasion, however, Bogdanov took these ideas on law and morality further and deployed them in his response to Berdyaev's strictures on Marxism. He highlighted the dangers of survivals of the past. These inevitably came about because the technical aspects of production always outstripped the layers of ideological adaptation which it had called into being. In advanced societies these ideological adaptations would include such systems as religion, morality and law. The example Bogdanov had in mind was France at the end of the

---

52   Bogdanov 1906, pp. 57–66.
53   Bogdanov 1906, p. 64.
54   Bogdanov 1906, p. 70.

eighteenth century, when the revolution removed the feudal class and freed the bourgeoisie to develop its own system of adaptations.

It seemed to Bogdanov that the way the French revolution had unfolded gave an insight into how the phenomenon of *Zusammenbruch* should be understood. For in no case could there be a moment in which a new technique and a new ideology could be created. Both of these had to subsist ready in the productive-developing class. At the moment of the French *Zusammenbruch* the new bourgeois world outlook and the new bourgeois legal and moral norms already existed; they were only restrained in their manifestations by the ideology of the ruling feudal estate. All the adaptations of the new society were already prepared within the framework of the old one, and all that was needed was the elimination of the old order for the new one to break through. Bogdanov considered that the idea of creating new social forces at a moment of crisis, when the old order had collapsed, was in conflict with the evolutionary point of view. This was not because the evolution had to take place gradually; the speed of the transformation was irrelevant, and in any case 'gradual' was a subjective concept; what was essential to the evolutionist viewpoint was continuity.[55]

This passage contains clear indications of how Bogdanov viewed the transition to the socialist society. The foundations of socialism would be prepared within capitalist society, so that when the time for the *Zusammenbruch* came the adaptations would have already been made and it would only remain to eliminate what had survived of the capitalist system. This was a concept of socialist revolution which saw the construction of socialism as preceding the socialist revolution, not following it, as many of Bogdanov's Social-Democrat contemporaries envisaged.

6 Problems of Idealism and Studies in the Realist World View

In 1902 a collection of essays entitled *Problems of Idealism* (*Problemy idealizma*) was published in Moscow.[56] It reflected the growing attraction of idealist philosophy in intellectual circles, and also the disillusionment in those circles with Marxist and positivist theory. Prominent among the contributors to the volume were figures who had made the transition 'from Marxism to idealism': Sergei Bulgakov, Berdyaev, Struve, Kistiakovsky and S.L. Frank. Berdyaev and Kisti-

55 Bogdanov 1906, p. 107.
56 Problemy idealizma 1902.

akovsky were well known to Bogdanov from their stay in Vologda; Bulgakov, an economist by training, had been an associate of Lunacharsky's in Kiev before he had abandoned Marxism for religion.

The tone of *Problems of Idealism* was set out in the foreword by its editor P.I. Novogrodtsev, who stated that 'the basic problem which in our times leads to the regeneration of idealist philosophy is the moral problem'. He added that 'with regard to those currents who want to know nothing but the principles of experience, we are convinced of their inability to solve this question which is so important and dear to us'.[57]

The contributions to the collection, however, were by no means homogeneous. Only some of the articles took up directly the issues set out in the preface. These included the contributions by Bulgakov, Berdyaev and Novogrodtsev himself. Other contributions to the collection took the form of critical expositions of writers belonging to the Marxist or positivist school, or thinkers who were in some way related to the idealist current. To this category belonged the articles by E.N. Trubetskoi on Marx and Engels, by Kistiakovsky on Mikhailovsky, by A.S. Lappo-Danilevsky on Comte, by Frank on Nietsche and by S.F. Oldenburg on Ernest Renan. The remaining articles were more general disquisitions on philosophy and its history, and included the contributions by S.A. Askoldov, S.N. Trubetskoi and P.G. [Struve].

In the light of the later dominance of Marxism in the intellectual life of the twentieth century, it is remarkable that more articles in *Problems of Idealism* were devoted to combatting positivism than Marxism. There was even more coordination of effort, as the essay on Comte by Lappo was complemented by a substantial study by Kistiakovsky on Mikhailovsky, who had adopted Comte's 'subjective method in sociology'. By contrast only E.N. Trubetskoi's article was exclusively devoted to discussing the philosophical ideas of Marx and Engels. N.A. Rozhkov, who reviewed *Problems of Idealism*, noted that the contributors to the collection focused on the earlier, less sophisticated representatives of both positivism and Marxism, neglecting the more recent developments in these intellectual currents.[58]

This was not entirely true in the case of Berdyaev, whose article showed traces of his encounter with Bogdanov in Vologda. He must have had Bogdanov's ideas in mind when he denounced evolutionism. This doctrine, he claimed, did not raise itself above hedonism; the only difference was that 'evolutionism does not speak of utility and the greatest happiness, but of

---

57   Problemy idealizma 2002, p. VIII.
58   Rozhkov 1903, p. 328.

the greatest adaptability, i.e. something which is completely non-ethical'. And whereas 'the evolutionary theory often successfully explains the historical development of morals, moral concepts and tastes, morals itself eludes it; the moral law is beyond its narrow perceptive field of vision'. And Berdyaev knew that it would annoy Bogdanov when he noted that in his book *Morality*, P. Nezhdanov correctly understood that morals was the 'kind of quality that elevates people'.[59]

As a reply to *Problems of Idealism*, Bogdanov and his friends published a collection of essays of their own. It was entitled *Studies in the Realist World View* and appeared in 1904.[60] Although its contributors referred to *Problems of Idealism*, *Studies in the Realist World View* was not a directly polemical work. It was more conceived as a collection that would demonstrate the breadth and versatility of the positivist school. It had three sections: the first contained philosophical articles by Suvorov, Lunacharsky and Bazarov; the second articles on economic themes by Bogdanov, Finn-Enotaevsky, P.P. Maslov and Rumiantsev; and the third section had two articles on literature by V.M. Shuliatikov and V. Friche, and Bogdanov's article 'Legal Society and Labour Society' which he had contributed under the pseudonym N. Korsak (his wife's surname).

Although Bogdanov did not contribute to the first section of the collection, the articles of Suvorov and Bazarov covered much of the ground that Bogdanov had done in previous articles. Thus, in his essay 'The Basics of the Philosophy of Life', Suvorov explained the energeticist approach to philosophical questions, indicating the contributions made to this approach by Ostwald, Avenarius and Mach. Like Bogdanov, Suvorov followed Noiré in tracing the origins of language to the exclamations accompanying the social-labour acts of primitive people.[61]

Bazarov's article was the most polemical in the collection. It contested the ideas of Berdyaev, Bulgakov and Struve on metaphysics and their Kantian conception of morals. In the case of Berdyaev and Struve this was not only with regard to their essays in *Problems of Idealism*, but in the book *Subjectivism and Individualism* as well. Like Suvorov, Bazarov referred with approval to the works of Ostwald, Avenarius and Mach.

Although both Suvorov and Bazarov repeated philosophical ideas that were characteristic of Bogdanov's works, in neither case were these integrated into an original synthesis. By contrast Lunacharsky's essay 'The Basics of Positivist Aesthetics' was an application of Avenarius's conceptions in the *Critique of Pure Experience* to the theory of aesthetics. For Lunacharsky aesthetics was the

---

59   Problemy idealizma 1902, p. 102.
60   Ocherki realisticheskogo mirovozzreniia 1904.
61   Ocherki realisticheskogo mirovozzreniia 1904, p. 51.

'science of evaluation' which had evolved from the adaptation of the organism to the environment. Particularly useful to Lunacharsky was Avenarius's concept of 'affectional', the character which associated an element with pain or pleasure. This, according to Lunacharsky, was the essential basis of aesthetic emotion.[62] He also believed that the principle of the conservation of energy was an aesthetic principle. As a new departure in positivist theory, Lunacharsky's contribution was the most significant in the philosophical section of the collection.

Bogdanov's article 'Exchange and Technology' was the first one in the section on economic subjects. Whereas Bogdanov's contribution was theoretical, the remaining three by Finn, Maslov and Rumiantsev were mainly factual. Finn wrote on 'Industrial Capitalism in Russia in the Last Decades', Maslov on 'The Agrarian Question' and Rumiantsev on 'The Evolution of the Russian Peasantry'. The third section of the collection contained, apart from Bogdanov's article, one by Shuliatikov entitled 'The Restoration of the Shattered Aesthetic' (on contemporary idealistic trends in Russian literature), and one by Friche entitled 'The Social-Psychological Bases of Naturalistic Impressionism'.

Bogdanov's chapter 'Exchange and Technology' is an essay in Marxist economics, which interprets the process of distribution in capitalist society in the light of the concept of 'social adaptation'. Bogdanov shows that historically the methods of distribution had adapted themselves to the methods of production. Thus, in patriarchal society it was the patriarch who organised the production and distribution of products and decided who was to do what work and what share of the products each member of the community was to receive. In capitalist society the process of distribution was performed by the market. Individuals and production groups which received from the total social product means of production and means of distribution sufficient to fulfil their social function would survive and develop; those who did not would be eliminated by the action of 'natural selection'. Competition dictated that every enterprise had to expand in order to survive. In the system of ruthless competition the strong destroyed the weak, and only by increasing its strength could an enterprise maintain itself.[63]

Bogdanov stressed that the various sectors that composed the capitalist economy did not exist in isolation, but inter-acted with each other, providing each other with materials and articles of consumption. Thus, in capitalist society, any branch of production could expand successfully only in a certain propor-

---

62   Ocherki realisticheskogo mirovozzreniia 1904, p. 62.
63   Ocherki realisticheskogo mirovozzreniia 1904, pp. 280–96.

tionality with the other branches with which it was connected, both with those which served as a market for it, and with those for which it served as a market.[64]

In examining the relationship of competition to the circulation and reproduction of capital, Bogdanov was entering a sphere that Marx had not covered in *Das Kapital*, though he had intended to do so. Consequently, Bogdanov's essay is an original and significant work in the history of Marxist thought. It is also significant historically, because it is the first work in which Bogdanov discusses the need to maintain proportionality between the inter-dependent sectors of an economy in the process of expansion and development. It can be considered as a precursor of his ideas on socialist planning which he formulated in 1921.

The other essay which Bogdanov contributed to the collection under the pseudonym 'N. Korsak' was entitled 'Legal Society and Labour Society'. Although ostensibly a critique of Rudolf Stammler's book *Wirtschaft und Gesellschaft*, it was in fact more conceived as a response to criticisms of historical materialism contained in *Problems of Idealism*, since some of its authors deployed arguments similar to Stammler's. Stammler, as a Kantian, believed that society was necessarily regulated by external norms, and rejected the possibility of a society based exclusively on moral ties between the individuals who composed it.[65]

In countering Stammler's position Bogdanov was able to draw upon conceptions that he had elaborated earlier on the origins of law. Law, he believed, came on the scene when the pristine social unity had been undermined, when the customs that had been obligatory for the whole community were replaced by customary law. So long as the community had remained an integral whole, it followed custom because acting otherwise was inconceivable. Infringers of custom were not punished; they were either driven out or killed as the community might kill a baby born with two heads. The breakdown of the spontaneous system based on custom necessitated the appearance of a type of social adaptation based on external legal norms.[66]

Bogdanov admitted that it was difficult for people who were accustomed to living under a system of external norms to imagine a society which would be governed by free-spontaneous collaboration. But, in Bogdanov's view, this latter type of society would come about through the action of collective experience, as the further development of humanity brought with it a new harmonisation of the experience of different people. The narrowness of specialisation

64   Ocherki realisticheskogo mirovozzreniia 1904, p. 296.
65   Ocherki realisticheskogo mirovozzreniia 1904, p. 558.
66   Ocherki realisticheskogo mirovozzreniia 1904, p. 537.

brought about by the division of labour would gradually disappear and the personality would be re-integrated through increased contact with other people, so that it would become a 'microcosm' of the experience of society as a whole. The normative type of life would give way to a direct free coordination of human labour. The old conservative norms would become as unnecessary as heavy, immobile rails for those who had conquered gravity and were able to fly.[67]

According to Bogdanov, many critics of historical materialism were bemused by the relationship of the 'base' to the 'superstructure' of society. If this was a causal connection, they said, then why was the ideological superstructure not changed directly after the economic base and in proportion to the changes in it? Why should the superstructure be able to 'outlive' the base? This was, in Bogdanov's view, a misunderstanding that could be easily removed, if one recalled that this was a kind of causality that was characteristic of every form of life. Every form of life was conservative and 'outlived' the conditions that had given rise to it. But with time outdated forms would be swept away as the process of adaptation took place.[68]

The most serious contradiction that Stammler found in Marxism was the combination of a social ideal with the idea of historical necessity. Marxists strove to bring about a social ideal that they believed would come about inevitably through historical development. It was as if, Stammler thought, some party had set out as the main point in its programme an eclipse of the moon that astronomers had previously predicted.[69] Stammler considered this dilemma of Marxism unavoidable, and did not think any way round it was possible.

This objection to Marxism had been taken up by several contributors to *Problems of Idealism*, so that it was important that an effective response should be made. Bogdanov was able to do this in a concise and convincing way, drawing on the resources of positivist philosophy. He began by saying that people desired what was pleasant and rejected the unpleasant; people preferred pleasure to pain. It was on this level, that of the will, that people desired an ideal society. Stammler's mistake was to take this expression of will for a theoretical argument.[70]

According to Bogdanov, the position of Marxists was that they aspired to the social ideal because it was pleasant, because it was something desirable. If they then referred to the course of historical development, this was to convey

---

67   Ocherki realisticheskogo mirovozzreniia 1904, p. 564.
68   Ocherki realisticheskogo mirovozzreniia 1904, p. 566.
69   Ocherki realisticheskogo mirovozzreniia 1904, p. 574.
70   Ocherki realisticheskogo mirovozzreniia 1904, p. 576.

the idea that in this aspiration they had a powerful ally on their side, an ally whose voice would eventually decide the matter.[71]

Marxists related to their ideals in a practical way; they acted to bring them about. But what was the point of this effort if historical progress would ensure that they would be realised in any case? An individual's personal actions would not decide the matter, but they would enter into the general sum of causes that would bring the ideal about. One preferred to be a positive force than a negative one, or someone who did nothing. Here Bogdanov introduced his own analogy: it was like seeing a man carrying a heavy burden. One knew he would reach his destination unaided, but one would go to help him nevertheless. Such was the Marxists' practical relation to social development; it lightened the load; it lessened the sacrifices and the suffering.[72]

7   External Relations

Remizov recalls that the exiles in Vologda had extensive connections with the outside world, that every book that was published in Russia was sent to Vologda and found its way to the exiles. He says that the exiles kept abreast of what was happening beyond Vologda through their contacts with sympathetic literary figures. Gorky wrote to them from Arzamas, V.G. Korolenko from Poltava, D.V. Filosofov, A.A. Shakhmatov, Struve, and D.E. Zhukovsky from St Petersburg, and V.Ya. Briusov, J. Baltrušaitis and Leonid Andreev from Moscow. Remizov adds that there was something of a direct line of communication between Vologda and Paris, Zurich and Geneva.[73]

This state of affairs is confirmed by Strumilin in his memoirs. He says that visitors came frequently to Vologda with fresh news from the capital cities and from abroad. He recalls that while he was in prison he had only heard about the appearance of the newspaper *Iskra* in 1900 and the journal *Zaria* in 1901, but he hadn't seen any actual issues of these publications. Nor had he even heard of *Revoliutsionnaia Rossiia*, the paper of the newly-formed Socialist-Revolutionary Party. But in Vologda not only were all of these items available, there was even knowledge of forthcoming publications. The exiles, for example, knew in April 1902 of Struve's *Osvobozhdenie*, the newspaper of the Russian liberals, which began to appear in June of that year.[74]

---

71   Ocherki realisticheskogo mirovozzreniia 1904, p. 577.
72   Ibid.
73   Remizov 1986, pp. 249–50.
74   Strumilin 1957, p. 140.

Bogdanov's correspondence with the editorial board of *Iskra* began in 1901, when he wrote to enquire what he might do to help the newspaper. Bogdanov's letter is not extant, but Nadezhda Krupskaya's reply, as secretary of the *Iskra* editorial board, dated 9 September, has been preserved. In it Krupskaya said that *Iskra* needed money, contacts, correspondence, and literary contributions. She suggested that Bogdanov should make collections of money, send correspondence about the famine, the zemstvo etc. and cuttings from local newspapers. She said it would be very useful if he set out his disagreements with *Iskra*, wrote reviews of this or that article, or contributed articles of his own. Krupskaya also asked him to pass on to *Iskra* any useful contacts that he might have.[75]

Lenin was likely to welcome Bogdanov's collaboration with *Iskra*. He had been impressed by Bogdanov's textbook on economics and in June 1899 he had remarked in a letter to A.N. Potresov that Bogdanov's second book, *Studies in the Historical View of Nature*, had been reviewed unfairly in *Nachalo*. The review had not said anything of substance and only complained that Bogdanov had ignored Kant, but from the reviewer's own words it was evident that Bogdanov had not ignored Kant, but had refuted him.[76] Lenin noted with approval that both of Bogdanov's books had adopted a monist viewpoint. By November 1901, however, the attitude of the *Iskra* editorial board to Bogdanov's work would not have been so positive, because of Plekhanov's emphatic condemnation of it.[77]

At the beginning of 1902, soon after Lunacharsky's arrival in Vologda, some of the exiled Social Democrats established a literary group. The group included Bogdanov, Lunacharsky, Suvorov, Tuchapsky and his wife Krzhyzhanovskaia. Bogdanov was the group's secretary and on its behalf carried on correspondence with the *Iskra* editorial board.[78] At the end of February 1902 the group was visited by Julius Martov's sister Lidia Dan. In her report of her visit she told the editorial board of *Iskra* to expect some correspondence from Vologda with a proposal to supply pamphlets. In the meantime she was forwarding an article from the group on the subject of party organisation, which she was sure that the editorial board would like. Lidia added that the views of the group, at least the ones they had expressed in writing, coincided fully with the views of *Iskra*, and for that reason the group's members could be trusted completely. In

---

75   Perepiska V.I. Lenina i redaktsii gazety "Iskra" s sotsial-demokraticheskimi organizatsiiami v Rossii: 1900–1903 gg. Sbornik dokumentov 1969–70, 1, p. 255.

76   Lenin 1958–65, 46, p. 31.

77   Filosofsko-literaturnoe nasledie G.V. Plekhanova 1973–4, 1, p. 131.

78   Perepiska V.I. Lenina i redaktsii gazety "Iskra" s sotsial-demokraticheskimi organizatsiiami v Rossii: 1900–1903 gg. Sbornik dokumentov 1969–70, 1, p. 560.

particular, they had not been seduced by the ideas of Berdyaev, who was now writing on the subject of ethics.[79] On 3 March Lenin remarked in a letter to Pavel Akselrod that: 'I am told that in Vologda (where Bogdanov and Berdyaev are exiled) the exiles there have lively debates on philosophy and Berdyaev, as the most knowledgeable, is apparently winning'.[80]

On 20 March Bogdanov wrote to the *Iskra* editorial board with the information that there was a group in Vologda which was able and willing to supply a number of pamphlets designed for 'the broad strata of the urban population'. The subjects of the proposed pamphlets would be: militarism, serfdom, autocracy, the church and state, the school and the state, municipal self-government and Leo Tolstoy. It was also proposed to devote a series of pamphlets to the history of Russia and the history of revolutions in Western Europe. There were two conditions attached: one was that the editing of the pamphlets would be carried out in Vologda, and the other was that the text of the pamphlets would not be changed by the *Iskra* editorial board. Appended was a list of books, mainly on the history of the Russian revolutionary movement, that the group in Vologda would like to receive.[81]

The reply that Lenin sent on 6 April was diplomatic, but firm. He appreciated the offer of pamphlets, since *Iskra* needed these badly, but begged the Vologda group not to insist on the stipulation that the pamphlets should be accepted or rejected as they stood, without any corrections. In the case of the article on organisation that Bogdanov had sent, this could not be accepted in its present state, because it contained 'quite inappropriate and tactless remarks, such as "one-man rule" and "dictatorship" by one member of the committee etc'. Yet, Lenin argued, an agreement about such changes, not particularly essential from the author's standpoint (but unquestionably necessary) could be reached without any difficulty. Such an important undertaking should not be impeded by a desire to impose particularly restrictive conditions on the *Iskra* editorial board.[82]

Bogdanov, however, was adamant that the text of the article could not be changed, as, he said, the manuscript the *Iskra* editors had received on technical tasks was the result of practical experience, the author could not possibly agree

---

79   Perepiska V.I. Lenina i redaktsii gazety "Iskra" s sotsial-demokraticheskimi organizatsiiami v Rossii 1900–1903 gg. 1969–71, 1, p. 441.
80   Lenin 1958–65, 46, p. 171.
81   Perepiska V.I. Lenina i redaktsii gazety "Iskra" s sotsial-demokraticheskimi organizatsiiami v Rossii 1900–1903 gg. 1969–71, 1, pp. 444.
82   Perepiska V.I. Lenina i redaktsii gazety "Iskra" s sotsial-demokraticheskimi organizatsiiami v Rossii: 1900–1903 gg. Sbornik dokumentov 1969–70, 1, p. 455.

to any changes in the text, particularly as the editors thought undiplomatic the question of one-man rule, which seemed to the author to be a condition *sine qua non* of a well-run organisation. This was a detail, but a disagreement on this point made one fear for future differences of opinion.[83] On 17 May Krupskaya wrote to Bogdanov to say that the article on 'Technical tasks' was still being considered for publication in *Zaria*, but in the event it did not appear.

We do not have the text of this article of Bogdanov's on the question of party organisation, but from the interchange with Lenin on the contentious phrases it contained, it emerges that Bogdanov thought it essential that a well-run organisation should be characterised by 'one-man rule' and 'the dictatorship of one member of the committee'. In this respect, Bogdanov's ideas were in keeping with *Iskra's* preference for a centralised form of party organisation.

One might have expected, however, that Bogdanov would have opposed the centralising tendency of the *Iskra* group instead of supporting it in the light of his ideas on synthetic organisation. But although Bogdanov clearly thought the synthetic form of cooperation the highest possible, this could not be attained immediately. Experience had shown that centralised leadership in an organisation made for the greatest efficiency. However, he believed that one-man rule was not necessarily authoritarian and incompatible with the synthetic form of cooperation. In the article 'Authoritarian Thinking' (1903) Bogdanov argued that:

> The voluntary subordination of the masses to the ideologue differs from simple authoritarian relations by having within it many elements of synthetic cooperation. A person of the mass both discusses and decides within which limits he will follow the ideologue; he 'carries out' his organising orders only in so far as they express the aspirations and wishes of the man of the masses. He by various ways himself indicates to the ideologue what this latter should give him. He not only subordinates himself to the ideologue, but to a certain degree also *subordinates* him to himself. And the more synthetic elements there are, the more lively the socialising (*obshchenie*) of the ideologues with their followers, the more comradely their mutual connection becomes, the more progressive the psychology of both sides, the more lively will be their cause.[84]

---

83   Perepiska V.I. Lenina i redaktsii gazety "Iskra" s sotsial-demokraticheskimi organizatsiiami v Rossii: 1900–1903 gg. Sbornik dokumentov 1969–70, 1, p. 485.

84   Bogdanov 1906, p. 129.

Bogdanov went on to caution that the more blind subordination comes to the fore, the higher the ideologues rise above the masses, the less influence the followers would be able to exert on the leaders' organising activity, and petrified conservatism would be the result. This is what happened with many religious movements; they succumbed to sectarianism and lapsed into the inevitable authoritarian consequences.[85]

It is possible that in writing about organisational questions Bogdanov had Lenin's pamphlet *What Is to Be Done?* in mind. The work was certainly known in Vologda, and Ermolaev recounts that in 1902–3 there was a large meeting devoted to Lenin's pamphlet. He says that among the speakers were Bogdanov, Lunacharsky and others, and that 'in general the meeting did not come to a unanimous decision'.[86] Unfortunately, Ermolaev does not mention what the attitudes of the participants were to Lenin's work, so we do not know for sure what Bogdanov thought of it at this time.

Krupskaya told Bogdanov that the *Iskra* editors had reluctantly agreed to leave the text of the pamphlets unchanged, and that he could now send the text of the one on militarism.[87] When Strumilin fled from Vologda in June 1902 he took with him a pamphlet written by Bogdanov for publication abroad.[88]

In 1902 much of Bogdanov's efforts were concentrated on editing and publishing *Studies in the Realist World View*. This was no easy matter, because although some of the contributors, such as Lunacharsky and Suvorov, were close at hand in Vologda, others were more remote. Shuliatikov was in prison in Moscow and Bazarov was in exile in Siberia. Bogdanov would have discussed Bazarov's contribution when he visited his friend in October–November 1902.[89] Nor was it possible to receive articles from all of the intended contributors. Through an intermediary Bogdanov had approached Plekhanov and Lenin for contributions, and these had been promised. Lenin would write about the agrarian question, and Plekhanov would write an article against Mach. In fact, Plekhanov had made it a condition of his participation in the project that his contribution should be a refutation of Machist philosophy. Bogdanov's intermediary had accepted this condition unreservedly, and from his correspondence with the *Iskra* editorial board it is clear that in 1902 Bogdanov expected an article from Plekhanov. Having given Plekhanov the deadline of 20 Octo-

---

85   Ibid.
86   Ermolaev 1923, p. 10.
87   Perepiska V.I. Lenina i redaktsii gazety "Iskra" s sotsial-demokraticheskimi organizatsiiami v Rossii: 1900–1903 gg. Sbornik dokumentov 1969–70, 1, p. 545.
88   Strumilin 1957, p. 145. It is not known what this pamphlet could have been.
89   Novoselov 1992, p. 184.

ber, Bogdanov had no choice but to proceed without Plekhanov's article.[90] For some reason neither Plekhanov nor Lenin submitted their promised contributions to the collection.

According to Lenin, at that time Plekhanov regarded Bogdanov as an ally in the struggle against revisionism, but one who had fallen into error by following Ostwald and subsequently Mach.[91] The implication of what Lenin says is that Plekhanov's article would have been a refutation of Bogdanov's philosophical ideas. Yet an article of that kind would not have been in keeping with the character of the collection, which was conceived mainly as a counterblast to *Problems of Idealism*. And if Plekhanov had contributed an article attacking Bogdanov's ideas, Bogdanov would most certainly have replied, probably in the same volume. Perhaps Plekhanov did not contribute his polemical article to the collection because he did not relish the prospect of having his own philosophical conceptions disputed. But the non-appearance of Plekhanov's article can best be understood in retrospect. Plekhanov's promised critique of Bogdanov's ideas was never to materialise, though Bogdanov challenged him repeatedly to produce it. Plekhanov was only ever able to express disapproval of Bogdanov's ideas, but never made the attempt to refute them.

At the beginning of 1903 Bogdanov and Natalia stayed for a time in Moscow, where Natalia underwent a major operation which left her unable to have children. The couple spent the summer of that year at the home of Natalia's sister in the Orel province. Insisting, in the aftermath of her operation, that her husband should have children, Natalia gave her consent to Bogdanov's entering into a relationship with Anfusa Ivanovna Smirnova, whom he had met in Vologda in 1903. Natalia had agreed to this arrangement on condition that Anfusa would not reside in any town where she and Bogdanov were living. Anfusa gave birth to Bogdanov's son Alexander in Paris on 12 July 1909.[92]

---

90 Perepiska V.I. Lenina i redaktsii gazety "Iskra" s sotsial-demokraticheskimi organizatsiiami v Rossii: 1900–1903 gg. Sbornik dokumentov 1969–70, 2, p. 231.
91 Lenin 1958–65, 47, 141–2.
92 Klebaner 2000, p. 30.

The Alliance

1   Pravda

At the beginning of 1904 Bogdanov took up residence in Tver, a town conveniently close to Moscow to which he made frequent visits. Bogdanov joined the Tver committee of the RSDLP which then became one of the main theatres of his political activities. When Bogdanov arrived the committee was deeply involved in the campaign against the war with Japan. They had distributed anti-war leaflets and had brought the workers out on strike from some of the Tver factories. The campaign culminated in a mass demonstration held on 22 February attended by some 200 workers and bearing red banners and slogans such as 'Down with the autocracy!' and 'Down with the war!' The demonstration was intercepted by infantry units, allowing the police to arrest many of the participants. Several members of the Tver committee were imprisoned, including the organisers of the demonstration. For most of 1904, therefore, Bogdanov was in effective control of the Tver RSDLP organisation, and it was he who conducted the correspondence with the party leadership abroad, Lenin and Krupskaya.[1]

In 1904 Bogdanov published a pamphlet to explain the causes of the war to a worker audience. In his view the reason why the tsarist government opened hostilities with the Japanese was, on the one hand, because it was encouraged to do so by the capitalists, who were eager to open new markets in the East, and for this reason came into conflict with the Japanese for domination of Korea. The other motive for the war was the government's desire to quell the social unrest which was becoming increasingly widespread. It was for this reason that the Minister of the Interior Plehve was a strong proponent of the war with Japan.[2]

Bogdanov and his associates on the Tver Committee took the side of the 'majority' at the Second Congress of the RSDLP and were in favour of the kind of centralised party that Lenin advocated for the struggle against the government in the existing conditions in the country. But they also insisted on the right of those who disagreed with the decisions of the congress to express their opin-

---

1   Smirnov 1971, pp. 38–9.
2   Bogdanov 1904a.

ions and have them considered at the following party congress.[3] Like Lenin, the members of the Tver Committee thought that the way to resolve the dispute between the 'majority' and the 'minority' in the party was to hold a new party congress.[4]

From the beginning of 1904 Bogdanov and some of his associates from Volo gda were involved in contributing to a monthly journal entitled *Pravda*. The moving spirit behind the journal was a wealthy railway engineer, V.A. Kozhevnikov. According to the police report compiled in response to his application to publish the journal, Kozhevnikov was 'the son of a professor at Moscow university; he was a graduate of the Institute of Communications Engineering, and he was presently employed by the Moscow-Kazan Railway Company. He was a member of the Russian Society of Dramatic Writers, was in possession of fixed property in Ruzsky uezd, and on the whole was a person of substantial means'. On these grounds it was held that Kozhevnikov might be trusted to extend his activities to the publishing field.[5]

Kozhevnikov was singularly successful in attracting contributors for his journal. The censor was able to note that the pages of the first issue were adorned with the names of the 'young littérateurs', writers, poets and dramatists already known to him from their work in liberal papers. These included Ivan Bunin, N. Teleshov, Stanisław Przebyszewski, V.M. Mikheev, E.N. Chirikov. It was also announced that among future contributors there would be Leonid Andreev, Maxim Gorky and Skitalets (S.G. Petrov). It was indeed from this list of writers that the Moscow censor was able to deduce that *Pravda* was of a 'liberal-oppositionist' character.[6]

Kozhevnikov's success in attracting young and popular figures from the literary world was matched by his being able to secure some highly talented people to comment on current 'social life'. This team comprised Bogdanov, N.A. Rozhkov, Pokrovsky, Skvortsov-Stepanov, Rumiantsev and M.G. Lunts, and they in fact became the editorial board of the journal. Apart from this nucleus, other writers for the journal were V.V. Vorovsky, Friche, Lunacharsky, M.S. Olminsky and Finn-Enotaevsky.

Pravda consisted of the literary section presided over by Ivan Bunin, the philosophical part managed by Bogdanov, and the 'survey' (*obozrenie*) – the province of Rumiantsev, Lunts and Finn-Enotaevsky. It was the first two of these sections which were the most important and which imparted to *Pravda*

---

3   Kak rozhdalas' partiia bol'shevikov 1925, p. 275.
4   Kak rozhdalas' partiia bol'shevikov 1925, p. 309.
5   Lebedev-Polianskii 1926, p. 185.
6   Lebedev-Polianskii 1926, pp. 185–6.

its specific character of a literary-philosophical journal. But what was most striking about *Pravda* was its artistic narrow elongated format and the variety of its typography.

The first issue of the new journal naturally aroused the interest of the censors, who looked upon its appearance with some apprehension, especially since some of the eminent contributors had already achieved notoriety. It is rather curious to note, however, that the theoretical articles of the future luminaries of the Bolshevik party caused considerably less concern than the poems, short stories and plays of the literary figures. It was readily observed that writers such as Lunacharsky, Rozhkov and Bogdanov wrote nothing that was especially inflammatory, that the 'direction of the journal was "realist" and "positivist" and that it was intended to struggle against incipient "idealism" on a purely philosophical and theoretical plane'.[7]

The fictional writers were quite a different matter, however, and several of their contributions were disallowed, though the reasons for this were not invariably political. In April 1904, for example, the Moscow censor prohibited V.V. Brusianin's short story 'On the Field of Life' in view of the fact that it was set in a hospital ward for syphilitic women and the characters were all prostitutes, 'which enabled the author to embellish his story with cynical details relating to promiscuity of the streets and the life in brothels'.[8] Beside this kind of heady fare, the dry treatises of Lunacharsky and Bogdanov were likely to pale into insignificance.

It was in *Pravda* that Bogdanov published one of his most outstanding essays of the period, 'The Integration of Mankind'.[9] This was an almost literary disquisition on the fragmentation of the human psyche brought about by the division of labour in capitalist society. In many respects this essay provides a philosophical dimension to Bogdanov's treatment of social evolution given in *The Short Course of Economic Science*.

As in the *Short Course*, Bogdanov's starting point was a characterisation of primitive society. In his view, at the dawn of human life there was very little difference between the experience of one individual and that of the whole community. The forms of life were simple, elementary, homogeneous. What was accessible to the experience of one was available to them all. The group lived and thought as a whole, with no conception of individuality, or of an 'I' as the special centre of interests and aspirations.

---

7   Lebedev-Polianskii 1926, pp. 187.
8   Lebedev-Polianskii 1926, pp. 189–90.
9   Robert Williams translates the title of this article as the 'collectivizing of man', which gives a misleading impression of what its contents are. See Williams 1986, p. 39.

Despite the absence of social divisions in the primitive collective, Bogdanov cautions against idealising this form of social organisation. The content of such a life was of extreme poverty, and with this poverty came a deep conservatism, since creativity can only emerge where there is a richness of combined exper ience.

For all its immobility, the primitive world had its own powers of development. These were of course spontaneous, biological forces: reproduction, overpopulation, hunger, which brought about change, though its pace was unimaginably slow. The pristine homogeneity of relations within the group disappears step by step. Some, using their accumulated experience, begin to give orders, while others begin to follow them. This difference is destined to increase, as the one who gives orders narrows his sphere of activity and becomes primarily a manager, the organiser of group life. The rest of the group, on the other hand, retain less and less of their personal initiative and become accustomed to subordinate themselves to him, becoming the executors of his orders.[10]

For Bogdanov this separation into people who give orders and those who carry out the orders, those who dominate and those who submit, is the first and the deepest division of mankind. With this division arose the authoritarian form of life. In the course of history this authoritarianism acquired many guises, and at the present time was still the main division in society.

The fragmentation of humanity evokes the fragmentation of the world. The people's thinking ceases to be as one. There emerges the 'I', as the centre of special interests and aspirations. But this 'I' is still at the beginning of its development. The 'I' of the organiser cannot fully separate itself out as an independent entity distinct from the executory. Because it would be impossible to have an organiser without executors and executors without an organiser, the two entities are mutually dependent for their respective existences.[11]

To primitive thought, moreover, authoritarian fragmentation is extended to the whole of nature. The world is seen as a chaos of actions, each one of which divides into two separate elements: into the active-organising will and the passive-executory. In every phenomenon the active will is taken as the determining factor, and the passive force as the thing determined. In human beings this is the 'soul' and the 'body'. And to the primitive mind everything else has the same dichotomy. Stones, plants, animals, lights, all are credited with souls, animism being the universal form of thought at this stage of historical development.[12]

---

10   Bogdanov 1904d, pp. 159–61.
11   Bogdanov 1904d, pp. 166–7.
12   Bogdanov 1904d, pp. 163–4.

In the second phase of humanity's fragmentation the content of experience is divided by specialisation. Here the collective experience is fragmented among individuals, so that each one has access to mainly one of its areas. Thus, the shoemaker only knows his last, the merchant only his shop, the scholar only his folios, the priest his prayers, the philosopher only his syllogisms. For each one the world is confined to lasts, counters, folios and prayers. People's thinking circulates in a closed circle and cannot escape from it. Everyone constructs the world in the image and the likeness of his or her own special experience, so that the possibility for mutual understanding is extremely limited.[13]

In specialised society there emerges the absolute 'I'. This is no longer the relative 'I' corresponding to the authoritarian world, which cannot imagine itself without an executory 'you'. The 'I' of specialised society is the absolute 'I', an entity alien to the consciousness of other 'I's and the whole world. In an evocative passage Bogdanov characterises the view of the world as seen through the prism of the individualist consciousness, the absolute 'I':

> Incarnating the fragmented, contradictory experience, the individualist consciousness necessarily fell prey to the 'vexed questions'. These are the hopeless, pointless questions to which 'the fool has awaited answers' for centuries: What am I? – he asks – and what is this world? Where does it all come from? Why? Why is there so much evil in the world? etc. endlessly.
>
> Look at these questions and you will see that they are the questions of a divided person. They are precisely the questions that the disjointed members of an organism would pose if they could live and ask questions.
>
> What am I? Isn't this the most natural question for some finger of a hand detached from the body? Why am I? Where am I from?
>
> The hopelessness of the questions springs from the fact that there are no answers which could or should be given them which would satisfy the individual consciousness. They are questions which express the torment of a fragmented life – and so long as it remains fragmented there is no answer which can end the pain, because to pain there can be no answer. Here everything is useless: even when developing criticism shows that these questions are wrongly posed, that they have no sense, that they are based on false premises – even then the individual consciousness will not cease to ask them, because criticism has not the power to transform this consciousness in reality, has no power to make fragmented existence whole.[14]

---

13   Bogdanov 1904d, p. 164.
14   Bogdanov 1904d, p. 167.

The dissatisfaction experienced by the fragmented man with his existence engenders in him the desire to become whole. He is impelled to seek ways to accomplish this end, and to begin the long and tortuous process of the integration of mankind. In specialised society the first attempts to unify, to bring together the fragmented experience, are made by philosophy, a discipline concerned with the harmonious integration of the thought of the world. However, this route to the integration of humankind is doomed to failure, because the philosopher himself is a specialist, closed up in his specialisation; he is in the contradictory position of a fragment of existence making pronouncements about the whole.[15]

The most reliable route to the integration of mankind, in Bogdanov's view, appears where the fragmentation of man has reached its extremity. This is the worker in manufacture, who, through the division of labour, spends his entire working life carrying out a single process, such as grinding the points of needles, or punching out the eyes. Workers such as these were reduced to human machines. Their loss of individuality and initiative was so complete that it was possible to replace these workers with machines.

For Bogdanov the appearance on the scene of the worker who operates a machine is a major landmark in the integration of mankind. Like the worker in manufacture, he is an executor, the carrier out of someone else's orders. But he is not only that: he directs and controls the activities of the machine, and to that extent he functions as an organiser, someone who directs and controls the work of others. He deploys the same organising skills, the intelligence, the attention, as the organiser who supervises workers. Thus, in the realm of technology an important step is made towards overcoming the basic authoritarian fragmentation of humanity. This is the emergence of a psychical type who combines the organising and the executory point of view in one directly integral activity.[16]

Moreover, it is a characteristic of capitalist industry that it brings together people in large masses for common labour. The mutual understanding which they develop serves to widen and deepen their experience. And to this mutual understanding there are none of the former barriers erected by specialisation, since machine workers are not the specialised robots of manufacture. Whatever machines the machine workers happen to operate, there is much in the general character and content of their labour that is similar, and this similarity keeps increasing in proportion to the degree the machine approaches perfection to become a completely automatic mechanism. This generality of

15   Bogdanov 1904d, pp. 168–9.
16   Bogdanov 1904d, p. 169.

experience makes for mutual understanding and encourages solidarity among the workers. In this way the second form of fragmentation of humanity, specialisation, is gradually overcome.[17]

On the basis of the commonality of experience gained in machine production, there arise wider forms of social integration. These are group and class consciousness, which broaden the individual experience into that of the group or class. In its turn, group or class consciousness generates new forms and combinations of human integration, such as economic, political, or ideological associations, all of which play a part in bringing about the integration of humankind.

Competition ensures that machines progressively approach their ideal type, the automatic mechanism. This process not only diminishes the significance of specialisation, but also increases the similarity of different forms of labour. In this way the knowledge of general methods replaces the necessity of familiarity with endless details. Consequently, the non-specialist in any given field is able to feel familiar with its general principles, though its many particulars and minutiae are unknown to him. These, on the other hand, may be assimilated as and when they become necessary.

The specialist of the old type becomes redundant. He is incapable of creating anything new in his field, because his methods are stereotyped, and his psyche narrow and impoverished. At best he is suitable for collecting facts, though even here he frequently does more damage than good, because he is not able to orientate himself in these facts, and when he makes generalisations from them these have a scholastic or metaphysical character. The new type of scholar is the antithesis of this type: he is widely educated, monist thinking, socially-vital. He incarnates the conscious, systematic integration of mankind. For Bogdanov, the best example of this kind of person was Karl Marx, the man who first gave a monist understanding of social life and development.[18]

Where does this line of development lead? To the transformation of mankind, to the reintegration of the fragments into a whole person. But this is no return to the primitive type of spontaneous-integral life, where the experience of one and the experience of all coincided. The primitive integrity was based on the limitation of life, and was linked to its extreme conservatism; that new integrity to which the integration of mankind is leading must encompass the great richness of life and give space to its infinite development.

---

17   Bogdanov 1904d, pp. 170–1.
18   Bogdanov 1904d, pp. 171–2.

The integration of mankind implies a new social relationship between people. The growth of mutual understanding breaks down the barriers raised by the old relations of authoritarianism and specialisation. In their place come comradely relations, relations that are inimical to any barriers between people, to any subordination or narrowing of the field of experience, to any fragment- ation of the human personality. This was a stage that in Bogdanov's view man- kind was still to attain, but its silhouette was 'visible on the horizon'.[19]

The conception that the distorted view of the world came from perceiving it from the point of view of an isolated individual and not from the point of view of society as a whole is one that is found in Marx's early writings, par- ticularly in his manuscripts of 1844. It is this conception that lies behind his doctrine of 'commodity fetishism', which attributes properties to things that really belong to the human collective. The congruity of Marx's and Bogdanov's views is explained by the fact that they have a common origin in the current of German thought initiated by Friedrich Schiller's *Philosophical Letters*, which gave currency to the concept of 'reflection'. Bogdanov would have been famil- iar with Schiller's ideas from his reading of Mikhailovsky's essay 'On Progress', if not from the original German sources.[20]

In the June 1904 issue of *Pravda*, Bogdanov published the short essay entitled 'A Philosophical Nightmare', in which he gave his views on the contemporary state of philosophy. The article has a bearing on the section in 'The Integration of Mankind', where Bogdanov recounts how the attempts of philosophers to find unity come to nothing because they are unable to go beyond their own specialist spheres. It begins in an almost flippant tone, Bogdanov describing his struggle to make sense of an abstruse treatise on Kantian philosophy. He believes that his difficulties in comprehension lie with the author's failure to realise that what might be completely clear to him makes no sense to people who are not specialists in the field.

Philosophy, in Bogdanov's opinion, expresses the monist demand of life – the aspiration to connect, to agree, harmoniously to unite the variegated, the diverse, the contradictory and fragmented content of experience. In our times the disharmony of life is terribly strong and is increasing all the time. The differ- entiation of social being and perception has never before been progressing at such a rapid pace. Different interests and aspirations entwine and entangle in a peculiar way and collide so sharply that to make sense of these phenomena, to reconcile at least some of the different points of view on them, has become

---

19   Bogdanov 1904d, p. 175.
20   See White 1998a.

for the individual an almost impossible task. This situation is most agonising for those intermediate social groups which incorporate all the divergent tendencies of developing and decaying life forms, for that 'intelligentsia' which so far has made up the main body of the audience for literature. It is here that the most acute realisation of the 'monist necessity' is juxtaposed with complete absence of hope of bringing it about. 'Preoccupations with philosophy' flare up with great intensity, but on encountering insurmountable tasks they soon degenerate and take on monstrous forms. Being unable to find a unifying point of view on the basis of life itself, people start looking for it outside life. Some have their heads in the beyond, in the world of mysticism and metaphysics, others in the 'logical' world of empty formal abstractions. And, of course, all that goes there is lost to life.[21]

There are other classes, Bogdanov believes, for whom contemporary development presents simpler, clearer and more transparent contradictions: the ways of solving them are indicated by life itself. In such classes the temporary sharpening of philosophical demands does not lead to their distortion, because it finds a solution in healthier means. Philosophy changes its tasks, changes its very self as soon as it forgets that in living experience is its material and its point of departure, that its unchanging aim is the harmonisation of life.[22]

Bogdanov's last contribution to *Pravda* was the article 'The Accursed Questions of Philosophy', which appeared in the December issue. In this article Bogdanov elaborates on the passage in 'The Integration of Mankind' in which he describes how a fragmented individual in specialised society might pose questions such as: What is the essence of man? What is the purpose of life? After analysing how the metaphysical and positivist schools of philosophy approach these questions, Bogdanov concludes that such questions, reflecting the divisions in society, are not capable of being resolved by philosophical methods. But in a society where such divisions have been superseded by the emergence of the proletariat, and where comradely relations prevail, it will be possible to understand the spontaneous forces behind the social process which give rise to the vexed questions, and to bring these forces under human control.[23]

Had he not parted company with *Pravda* at the end of 1904 Bogdanov would probably have published the article 'The Aims and Norms of Life' in it, since it forms one of a cycle of related essays. The article appeared in the journal *Obrazovanie* in July 1905. This article complements both 'The Integration of Mankind' and the *Short Course* by tracing historically the evolution of 'norms',

---

21   Bogdanov 1904, p. 259.
22   Ibid.
23   Bogdanov 1905, pp. 136–68.

that is customs, laws and morals, in society from their origins to their eventual disappearance, with the emergence of comradely relations in socialist society. In this article Bogdanov introduces the concept of 'norms of expediency'.

Although market relations make capitalist society as a whole anarchic, individual firms within it can show a high degree of organisation. As society becomes increasingly organised in this way, the need arises for different kinds of norms. These are what Bogdanov terms 'norms of expediency' (*tselesoobraznost'*). They take the form of 'If you want to do so and so, then you have to act in this way'. And whereas the compulsory norms were categorical and took no account of circumstances, expedient norms are conditional or hypothetical.

Norms of expediency exist at the present time, chiefly in the sphere of science and technology, but in the future, they will replace compulsory norms entirely. In socialist society comradely relations of cooperation and mutual understanding will prevail. In the transition period the state will be employed to effect the transfer to the new economic system. This 'state of the future', like all states, will be an instrument of class domination. But in this case the domination will be of the working class, the class which aspires to eliminate all classes.

In 1905 Bogdanov published a collection of three of his recent articles under the title of *New World*. It comprised 'The Integration of Mankind', 'The Aims and Norms of Life' and 'Accursed Questions of Philosophy'. The three articles, Bogdanov explained, constituted an integral whole, as in them he had attempted to sketch out the development of a new, higher, type of life, as he understood it. 'The Integration of Mankind' was concerned with the future change in the type of human personality – the elimination of the narrowness and lack of fulfilment in human existence that created inequality, disparity and alienation (*psikhicheskoe raz"edinenie*) among people. 'The Aims and Norms of Life' spoke of the changes in the type of social system – the elimination of compulsion in the relations between people. 'Accursed Questions of Philosophy' noted the changes in the types of human perception – the liberation from fetishisms which limited and distorted the perceptual process. In dealing with these questions, Bogdanov stressed that he had tried to follow the direction that Marx had indicated – looking for the lines of development of the 'higher' phenomena, while taking account of the dependence of these on the development of the *basic* conditions of human life.[24]

Bogdanov's association with *Pravda* came to an end in December of 1904. He had disagreements with the publisher over editorial policy; Kozhevnikov did

---

24   Bogdanov 1905, pp. 5–6.

not want to publish one of Finn-Enotaevsky's articles that Bogdanov insisted he accept. As a result Bogdanov and Finn resigned from *Pravda*'s editorial board. Pokrovsky and Rozhkov resigned with them, declaring that they had joined as a group and would leave as a group. After their departure Kozhevnikov invited the Mensheviks to take over the journal, so that during 1905–6 *Pravda* was in Menshevik hands, though the arrangement was not entirely to Kozhevnikov's satisfaction.[25] To fill the vacancy that Bogdanov had left, Kozhevnikov turned to Rosa Luxemburg. In a letter to Leo Jogiches on 21 August 1905 Luxemburg reported: 'I had a visit from Kozhevnikov from Moscow, the publisher of *Pravda*, with the request for my contributions. Finn and Bogdanov have left the journal and the philosophical and scholarly section is headed by Plekhanov. The payment for a ream is 64 roubles. I replied in general terms'.[26] In fact, Luxemburg did not take up Kozhevnikov's offer, perhaps dissuaded by the prospect of working with Plekhanov, whom Jogiches detested.

Although Bogdanov and his associates no longer had *Pravda* as a focus, the group nevertheless retained some cohesion, and continued its group activities. By 1905 it had become extended to form a literary-lecturing group consisting of academics, authors, literary critics and various other intellectuals who at the outset of the revolution toured Moscow and the provinces giving lectures on political themes. According to Rozhkov, until the autumn of 1905 the group had no formal connection with the Social-Democratic Party, though its meetings were attended by V.L. Shantser or other members of the RSDLP Moscow Committee.

According to Skvortsov-Stepanov, the membership of the group was in constant flux, but the permanent core consisted of P.G. Dauge, Lunts, V.Ya. Kanel, D.I. Kursky, N.L. Meshcheriakov, V.A. Obukh, M.A. Silvin (Tagansky), K.N. Levin, Mitskevich, S.Ya. Tseitlin, Shuliatikov, Pokrovsky, Rozhkov and himself. Skvortsov-Stepanov adds that in 1906, following the Fourth Congress, which reunited the two fractions of the party, occasionally meetings of the group would be attended by the Mensheviks V.G. Groman and Bogdanov's bugbear Nezhdanov-Cherevanin. These occasions would invariably give rise to barren discussions, since the views of the two fractions diverged so radically as to preclude any possibility of effective cooperation between them. In spite of the resolutions of the Fourth Congress of the RSDLP, the literary-lecturing group remained purely Bolshevik until its demise in 1908, when prison or exile overtook most of its members.[27]

---

25   White 1974, pp. 198–9.
26   Luxemburg 1971, 2, p. 422.
27   Skvortsov-Stepanov 1925, p. 10.

Between 1905 and 1908 the group's activities included not only lecturing to mass audiences, but the publication of the two symposia of articles: *Tekushchii moment* and *Voprosy dnia* (both in 1905) and a succession of newspapers: *Borba, Svetoch, Svobodnoe slovo, Voprosy dnia* and *Iotina*. Towards the end of its existence it was members of the group, Bogdanov, Skvortsov-Stepanov, Bazarov, Lunts and Silvin, who translated into Russian and edited the three volumes of Marx's *Das Kapital*.[28]

2   Meeting with Lenin

In May 1904 Bogdanov travelled to Geneva to meet the leaders of Russian Social-Democracy abroad.[29] Liadov had come to Tver to inform him about the developments in the party that had taken place in the RSDLP while he had been in exile.[30] The most important of these developments was the Second Congress of the party which was held in July and August of 1903.

Lenin had intended that this Congress would ensure the domination of the supporters of *Iskra* over the 'economists', the Bund and other rival groupings. Initially the *Iskra* group had maintained its cohesion, but tensions began to make themselves felt when the first paragraph of the party's rules was being discussed. Lenin and Martov submitted competing definitions of what a party member was. Lenin's read: 'A member of the Russian Social-Democratic Labour Party is one who accepts its programme and who supports the party both financially and by personal participation in one of the party organisations'. Martov's version departed from Lenin's only in its last phrase, which was: '... by personal work under the control and direction of one of the party organisations'. In the voting Lenin's formulation was narrowly defeated.[31]

Because the Congress dissolved the Union of Russian Social Democrats Abroad, its two delegates left the Congress. The five Bund delegates also left the Congress when their demand for organisational autonomy and recognition as the sole representative of the Jewish proletariat was rejected. This left Lenin's supporters in the majority for the remaining part of the Congress,

---

28   See below.
29   The evidence for this dating comes from the fact that it was in mid-May that Bogdanov is first mentioned in Krupskaya's correpsondence as being in Geneva. (See Plyutto 1998). Valentinov, however, says that Lenin met Bogdanov for the first time in February 1904, before the publication of *One Step Forward, Two Steps Back*. (See Valentinov 1968, p. 233). There is, however, no corroboration of Valentinov's statement.
30   Liadov 1989–91, p. 122.
31   Ascher 1976, pp. 46–7.

at which the composition of the *Iskra* editorial board and the party's Central Committee were to be decided. Lenin argued that in the interests of efficiency the *Iskra* editorial board should be reduced from six members to three, since only Plekhanov, Martov and himself actually performed the function of editors, Potresov, Akselrod and Zasulich being largely inactive. Initially an attempt was made to settle the matter by negotiation, but Martov was prepared to allow only one Leninist among the three members of the Central Committee and insisted on re-electing the old editorial board of *Iskra*, on which his supporters had a two-thirds majority. When the negotiations failed, Lenin used his majority to reduce the editorial board from six persons to three (Lenin, Plekhanov and Martov) and to place his chosen candidates (G.M. Krzhizhanovsky, F.V. Lengnik and V.A. Noskov) on the Central Committee. Martov, however, declined to take his place on the *Iskra* editorial board, he and his followers – the 'people of the minority' – refusing to accept the outcome of the vote.

Martov did not accept his defeat and accused Lenin and his followers, 'the supporters of the majority', of having acted in an underhand way, not in the interests of efficiency, but to control the party organisation. He complained that a 'state of siege' had existed in the party against particular persons and groups, and that, contrary to his expectations, the Congress had not put an end to this state of affairs. Following the Congress Plekhanov and Lenin jointly edited a few numbers of *Iskra*, but as Plekhanov insisted on the return of all the old members of the editorial board, thus putting Lenin in a minority, Lenin resigned from the board. He was, however, able to get himself co-opted on to the Central Committee, from where he waged a campaign against what he considered to be the illegitimately constituted *Iskra* editorial board.

To justify their respective positions both Martov and Lenin produced pamphlets which in their turn served to intensify the polemic. Martov's *Struggle with the State of Siege in the RSDLP* published in 1904 explained that although he had entertained severe doubts about Lenin's plans for party organisation before the Congress, he had not opposed them for the sake of maintaining unity in the *Iskra* camp. He admitted to having overlooked valid criticisms of Lenin's plans emanating from the anti-*Iskra* elements of the Congress. In *One Step Forward, Two Steps Back*, published in the same year, Lenin complained of Martov's inconsistency and bad faith. He maintained that the measures he had proposed at the Congress had been approved beforehand by the members of the *Iskra* editorial board, and that only on the floor of the Congress had Martov raised objections. It seemed to Lenin that the position adopted by Martov was akin to that of the 'economists', who had been defeated at the Congress, and that the campaign against 'economism' by *Iskra* had been in vain.

At the time of Bogdanov's visit to Geneva Lenin was feeling himself increasingly isolated, as Martov and his supporters extended their control of the institutions of the party, including its journal *Iskra*. Liadov reports that what especially depressed Lenin was that he had no newspaper to write for or any means to publish one of his own.[32] This was a serious lack, since it was in journalism that Lenin's aptitudes lay and was the means by which he exercised his political influence. To establish a newspaper he needed funds and also literary talent to provide the material to publish. In this respect, Bogdanov's support was particularly welcome. His involvement in *Pravda* had brought him into contact with the most talented young radical scholars and writers. As Nikolai Valentinov explained, Bogdanov at that time already had a name as a writer; he was very well known among Social Democrats, and had good literary contacts in St Petersburg and Moscow. Moreover, through his friendship with Gorky, Bogdanov had access to considerable funds. To Lenin, who had no important writers among his followers, apart from Vorovsky, Bogdanov was a real find.[33]

Krupskaya wrote to her contact in Tver: 'Bogdanov is a nice and clever chap. It is just a pity that he looks on the cause a bit from the sidelines and doesn't wholly enter into it'.[34] This observation suggests that Bogdanov had communicated to Krupskaya his opinion that the split in the RSDLP was regrettable and unnecessary. He had in fact suggested as much in his article 'The Aims and Norms of Life'. Later, however, Krupskaya was able to note with some satisfaction that Bogdanov had approved of Lenin's pamphlet *One Step Forward, Two Steps Back* and that: 'On the whole Bogdanov is definitely on the side of the majority'. She added that: 'He is terribly sore at Plekhanov, who received him imperiously, like a general, and treated him with every sign of disdain'.[35] According to Liadov, Bogdanov had gone to see the editors of *Iskra*, but had met with a hostile reception. He left with the impression that 'You just can't talk to them'.[36]

In a note to Krupskaya Bogdanov reported: 'Trotsky came to see me. I very much dislike the man; I just can't stand him. He gave me Kautsky's letter to Mandelshtam. I returned the letter with commentaries and with the advice to

32   Liadov 1989–91, p. 122.
33   Valentinov 1968, p. 235.
34   Perepiska V.I. Lenina i rukovodimykh im uchrezhdenii RSDRP s partiinymi organizatsiiami 1903–1905 gg. 1969–77, 2, p. 277.
35   Perepiska V.I. Lenina i rukovodimykh im uchrezhdenii RSDRP s partiinymi organizatsiiami 1903–1905 gg.1969–77, 2, p. 295. That the meeting with Bogdanov was a fraught one for Plekhanov is evidenced by Bonch-Bruevich in his memoirs. See Bonch-Bruevich 1961, 2, p. 354 and Steila 2013, p. 212.
36   Liadov 1956, p. 45.

print the letter in *Iskra*. This would be useful for us, and not for them; if only they do it'.[37] In later years Bogdanov found no reason to revise his opinion of Trotsky, whom he thought conceited. The Kautsky letter Bogdanov refers to had been written in response to the efforts of Mandelshtam (pseudonym Liadov) to justify the position of the 'majority' in the RSDLP to Kautsky, the eminent theoretician of the German Social Democrats.

On Lenin's instructions, Liadov had visited Kautsky in Berlin and had informed him and also Rosa Luxemburg and Leo Jogiches about the divisions that had emerged within the RSDLP at its Second Congress.[38] Liadov suspected that Kautsky and the others had been influenced by the 'minority' supporters, especially by Kautsky's friend Akselrod. Kautsky was reluctant to believe that Akselrod was any kind of opportunist or bourgeois individualist, as Lenin claimed, and thought that Lenin had acted wrongly in excluding Potresov, Akselrod and Zasulich from the editorial board of *Iskra*. Rosa Luxemburg, for her part, could see no principled disagreements in Lenin's dispute with Martov and the adherents of the 'minority'. In an attempt to clarify the issues at stake, Liadov had set out the disagreements between the two sides in an article intended for publication in Kautsky's journal *Die neue Zeit*. Kautsky rejected the article on the grounds that among German workers the desire for unity was so strong that they were unsympathetic towards any Social-Democratic party afflicted by disagreements for which there was no necessity.[39] He did, however, write a letter to Liadov in which he expressed his views on the divisions within the RSDLP as Liadov had described them. On the question of the definition of a party member, Kautsky said that on the basis of his own experience of the German Social-Democratic Party during the period of the Anti-Socialist Law, he favoured Martov's formulation. He deplored Lenin's action in excluding Potresov, Akselrod and Zasulich from the *Iskra* editorial board. Kautsky gave a copy of his letter to Akselrod with permission to publish it if he should think fit. The letter appeared in *Iskra* in May 1904, seemingly with Bogdanov's connivance. The publication gave Bogdanov the chance to reply to it in a short article in *Iskra*.

On the invitation of the editors of *Iskra*, Rosa Luxemburg reviewed Lenin's *One Step Forward, Two Steps Back*. The review, which bore the title of 'Organisational Questions of Social Democracy', was published simultaneously in *Iskra*

---

37   Perepiska V.I. Lenina i rukovodimykh im uchrezhdenii RSDRP s partiinymi organizatsiiami 1903–1905 gg.1969–77, 2, p. 302.

38   Liadov 1956, p. 15.

39   Donald 1993, p. 47.

and *Die neue Zeit*. Bogdanov replied both to Kautsky's letter and Rosa Luxemburg's review in the collection of essays entitled *Our Misunderstandings*.

3   Our Misunderstandings

Our Misunderstandings contained essays by both Bogdanov and Olminsky. As the title suggests, the authors took the view that the positions of the 'majority' and the 'minority' were not so irreconcilable as statements made in the heat of the polemic made it seem. They believed there was no danger of a permanent schism, because the two fractions had more in common than divided them. The attitude of Bogdanov and Olminsky was 'not to blame, not to justify, but to understand'. Nevertheless, while maintaining that both sides were at fault, the drift of the argument, particularly on Bogdanov's part, was that the 'majority' had more right on its side than the 'minority'.

The essay entitled 'At Last!' had been previously published in *Iskra*, seemingly after overcoming some resistance from the new editorial board. In it Bogdanov sought to refute the accusations that had been made against the 'majority' by Plekhanov and Kautsky. In the case of Plekhanov Bogdanov found that the charge of 'Bonapartism' against the 'majority', the urge to dictate to local organisations and even to dissolve them at will, had no foundation in fact.

Bogdanov provided a more detailed refutation of the points made in the letter Kautsky had sent to *Iskra* on the divisions within the RSDLP. He pointed out that Kautsky's reference to advantages of local autonomy enjoyed by the SDP during the operation of the Anti-Socialist Law was misplaced, since the situation in Russia differed markedly from that in Germany. In Russia local autonomy was the rule, whereas centralisation was only in its early stages. In the course of dealing with points that Kautsky made in support of co-option to the party leadership and to *Iskra*, Bogdanov expressed his belief that people in a position of leadership in the party and the members of the editorial board of its central organ ought to be freely elected. The membership of editorial boards, he declared, ought not to be for life or still less hereditary.

Rosa Luxemburg's review of *One Step Forward, Two Steps Back* took issue with two main themes in Lenin's pamphlet: one was the question of centralism, and the other was that of the roots of opportunism in the party. While conceding that centralisation in the RSDLP was highly desirable, Rosa objected to the high degree of centralism that she believed Lenin intended to impose on the party. She thought it deplorable that the Central Committee should be the only thinking element in the party; all other groupings would be its executory limbs. The consequence would be the separation of the organised nucleus of revolutionaries from the rest of the workers. Luxemburg, on the other hand, believed that the Social-Democratic type of socialism could only exist given the existence of a large contingent of workers educated in the political struggle, and the possibility for the workers to develop their own political activity through direct influence on public life. She took exception to Lenin's glorification of the educative influence of the factory, which accustomed the proletariat to discipline and organisation. This idea suggested to Luxemburg that Lenin's conception of socialist organisation was mechanistic, and was comparable to the kind of discipline imposed on the workers by the military and the existing state bureaucracy.

On the subject of the role of intellectuals in the party, Luxemburg disagreed with Lenin's assertion that opportunism sprang from the characteristic leaning of intellectuals towards decentralisation and disorganisation, from their aversion to strict discipline and the kind of 'bureaucracy' which was necessary for the effective functioning of the party. In Luxemburg's view the decentralising and disorganising trends in the party were not to be explained by the intellectual's psychology or his supposed innate instability of character. In Western Europe, she contended, such tendencies were encouraged by the socialist parties' involvement in parliamentary politics and the opportunities this created for careerists. But, in Russia's case, where there was no parliamentary politics, she believed the same tendencies reflected the backward condition of Russian society.

Bogdanov's reply to Rosa Luxemburg was the article 'Rosa Luxemburg against Karl Marx'. He began by saying that he was not responding to Luxemburg on Lenin's behalf, as Lenin was quite capable of doing so for himself; he was answering on behalf of Marx, as what Luxemburg had said was in conflict with Marx's ideas on workers' organisation. In fact, the first line of attack in the article was to quote from Marx's writings and Kautsky's *Erfurt Programme* to show that Luxemburg was out of step with the recognised authorities on the topic under discussion.

The mode of argument that Bogdanov adopted – the appeal to authority – was one he would later condemn as inadmissible. Probably, however, it was less important for Bogdanov to show that Luxemburg was out of step with Marx, than to suggest that his own ideas on workers' organisation did not conflict with what Marx had said on the subject.

In fact, Bogdanov was able to come up with rather few relevant quotations from Marx. He cited a passage from the chapter on 'Primitive Accumulation' in *Das Kapital* where Marx stated that with the concentration of capital in fewer hands came the 'growth of the cooperative form of the labour process', and due to this the working class was 'constantly increasing in numbers, and was trained, united and organised by the very mechanism of the capitalist process of production'.[40] And in the Communist Manifesto Bogdanov found a sentence to the effect that: 'The advance of industry, whose involuntary promoter is the bourgeoisie, replaces the isolation of the labourers, due to competition, by their revolutionary combination, due to association'.[41] While these quotations were certainly to the point, their brevity and paucity could be taken to suggest that they were off the cuff comments by Marx rather than concentrated statements of a well-developed theory of workers' organisation.

A much more substantial quotation, however, came from Kautsky's commentary on the *Erfurt Programme* of the SDP. There Kautsky explained that unlike in handicraft industry, where the worker carried on his trade in isolation, capitalist industry was based on the coordination of labour, on cooperation. Thus, Kautsky concluded, 'the labour itself leads to the consciousness of the power of unity, develops in the workers voluntary discipline, which is the preparatory condition both for every successful struggle against exploitation in capitalist production, and for comradely, socialist production itself'.[42]

The quotations from Marx and Kautsky were a preliminary to Bogdanov's demonstration that the passage from Lenin's *Steps* on the educative influence of the factory that Luxemburg had objected to was in reality in keeping with the ideas of the two authorities. Bogdanov reproduced the passage in question. It read:

> For the factory, which seems only a bogey to some, represents the highest form of capitalist cooperation which has united and disciplined the proletariat, taught it to organise, and placed it at the head of all the other sections of the toiling and exploited population. And Marxism, the ideology of the proletariat trained by capitalism, has been and is teaching unstable intellectuals to distinguish between the factory as a means of exploitation (discipline based on the fear of starvation) and the factory as a means of organisation (discipline based in collective work united by conditions of a technically highly developed form of production). The discipline and organisation which come so hard to the bourgeois intellectual are very easily acquired by the proletariat just because of this factory 'schooling'.[43]

---

40   Marx 1976, p. 929.
41   Marx and Engels 1969, 1, p. 119.
42   Kak rozhdalas' partiia bol'shevikov 1925, p. 169.
43   Kak rozhdalas' partiia bol'shevikov 1925, p. 170.

Having established that Lenin was the disciple of Marx and Kautsky, Bogdanov then argued that Luxemburg's mistake was the failure to distinguish between the exploitative discipline the factory imposed on the workers through fear of starvation and the discipline the workers based on collective work. It was, Bogdanov contended, this latter form of discipline that Lenin had in mind when he spoke of the educative influence of the capitalist factory.

Whereas Luxemburg attributed the resistance to party discipline of intellectuals to the careerism associated with parliamentary activity, or to a stage in the historical development of the party, Bogdanov was more inclined to view the phenomenon as the outcome of intellectual psychology. In Bogdanov's opinion:

> Taking Marxism as our point of departure, we have all become accustomed to think that by his social nature the intellectual is much less inclined towards organisational discipline than the proletarian. The activity of the intellectual in modern society is carried on in an individual form. In this respect he is like the handicraft worker as he is characterised in the above-mentioned *Erfurt Programme*. That discipline of the cooperative form of the labour process of which Marx speaks is alien to him. Therefore, the intellectual needs to make a special effort to overcome the spontaneous antipathy to party discipline, and this antipathy is manifested in the form of displaying anarchistic tendencies. And where life puts forward the demand for centralised organisation, the anarchistic tendency, clashing with this demand, creates organisational opportunism. The Russian intellectual is even less saintly in this respect, because he has had less opportunity to receive an organisational education.[44]

At the root of Bogdanov's disagreement with Luxemburg's account of the origins of the intellectuals' opportunism is the desire to show how differences in the way of life produced the organised worker and the anarchistic intellectual. This was a theme that was central to Bogdanov's thinking at the time, and one that had two important applications in the given context. One of these was to show that the RSDLP was a genuinely workers' party; and the other was to account for the current division of the party into 'majority' and 'minority' fractions.

Whereas Martov had maintained that the composition of the party had a high proportion of intellectuals, Bogdanov insisted that this was not the case.

---

44   Kak rozhdalas' partiia bol'shevikov 1925, p. 171.

He claimed that for every Social-Democrat intellectual there were tens of workers, and not workers who were passive and allowed themselves to be led any-
where the intelligentsia wanted. In fact, Bogdanov pointed out, recently there
had been an exodus of intellectuals from the party, as the Liberal 'Liberation'
organisation had been formed and the Socialist Revolutionary party founded.
Many former 'Marxists' had made their way to these organisations, creating a
shortage of intellectuals to carry out the functions that the workers found difficult. Bogdanov's conclusion was that at the present time the party was not
just 'partly worker' but to a significant degree 'worker' in its composition. Consequently, it rightly called itself a workers' party.[45]

The contrast between the organised workers and the anarchistic intellectuals was employed by Bogdanov in accounting for the division of the party into
'majority' and 'minority' fractions. He pointed out that the dispute was much
less in evidence in the Social-Democratic committees which operated inside
Russia, where the two fractions cooperated closely; the main arena for conflict
was in the institutions of the party which were based abroad. And whereas the
party in Russia consisted mainly of workers, the membership of the émigré
organisations was overwhelmingly intellectuals. Consequently, he argued, it
was no accident that in the émigré section the adherents of the 'minority' predominated, whereas inside Russia it was the supporters of the 'majority' who
were in the ascendency.

As Bogdanov had suggested, Lenin did write a reply to Rosa Luxemburg's
review of *Steps*, though Kautsky rejected it for publication in *Die Neue Zeit*
on the grounds that it was simply about the squabbles in the Russian party,
whereas Luxemburg had dealt with the problem of organisation in a general
way that was of interest to German Social Democrats.[46] Lenin's article, however,
does provide the opportunity to compare the respective approaches of Bogdanov and Lenin to the same challenge. Significantly, there are few points
of similarity. Mainly, Lenin concentrates on correcting errors of fact, denying
views attributed to him by Luxemburg, and referring to the wording of resolutions. His main point is that the 'minority' have acted in defiance of decisions
taken at the Second Congress of the RSDLP. Though Lenin had read *Our Misunderstandings* he does not endorse the points made in it. There is only a fleeting
mention of the discussion on the educative role of the factory,[47] suggesting that
this was something Lenin did not want to develop. On the contrast between
the workers and the intellectuals Lenin only observes: 'Anyone who does not

---

45   Kak rozhdalas' partiia bol'shevikov 1925, pp. 175–6.
46   Donald 1993, p. 58.
47   Lenin 1958–65, 9, pp. 44–5.

wilfully close his eyes to what happened at our Congress is bound to see that our new division into minority and majority is only a variant of the old division into a proletarian-revolutionary and an intellectual-opportunist wing of our party'.[48] Significantly, however, Lenin did not associate, as Bogdanov had done, the proletarian-revolutionary section of the party with the part inside the country, and the intellectual-opportunist part with the part based abroad. He would of course be disinclined to do so, since he himself belonged to the latter group, and indeed had been cited by Olminsky as someone who did not understand how the party operated on the ground.[49]

From *Our Misunderstandings* a number of implications emerge about how Bogdanov saw his defence of Lenin, and, more widely, his adherence to the 'majority' fraction of the RSDLP. First of all, it is plain that Bogdanov was defending the 'majority' position on his own terms; his contribution to 'Our Misunderstandings' is easily recognisable as a continuation of themes he had elaborated previously. Second: he finds himself in alliance with Lenin not because he has been impressed by Lenin's book *What Is to Be Done?* but because he agrees with him that the 'minority' have acted reprehensibly in refusing to abide by the decisions of the Second Congress of the party. From his polemic with Kautsky it is clear than Bogdanov believes that the organisation of the RSDLP should be on democratic principles, that there should be majority rule. Third: at this stage at least, Bogdanov did not see himself as a 'Bolshevik'; he did not think that the divisions between the 'minority' and the 'majority' were insuperable, and he could see no reason why there should not be a united Social-Democratic Labour Party.

4   The Alliance

The main outcome of Bogdanov's trip to Switzerland was the political alliance he formed with Lenin in the summer of 1904. There was, however, a serious obstacle to a meeting of minds between Lenin and Bogdanov. As Valentinov discovered in the spring of 1904, Lenin had no sympathy whatever for the philosophy of Avenarius and Mach, and despite his political differences with him, regarded Plekhanov as the unimpeachable authority on the philosophy of Marx and Engels. Lenin recalls that when he first met Bogdanov they exchanged their recent publications, Lenin presenting Bogdanov with *One Step Forward, Two*

---

48   Lenin 1958–65, 9, pp. 58–9.
49   Kak rozhdalas' partiia bol'shevikov 1925, p. 148.

Steps Back and Bogdanov giving Lenin the first volume of his *Empiriomonism*. Lenin went on to say that 'I at once (in the spring or early summer of 1904) wrote to him in Paris from Geneva that his writings strongly convinced me that his views were wrong and just as strongly convinced me that those of Plekhanov were correct'.[50]

Lenin was prepared to overlook these ideological differences for the sake of the valuable political alliance with Bogdanov. The arrangement was that philosophy would be regarded as a neutral field, and would not be the grounds for conflict between the parties. As Lenin later told Gorky: 'In the summer and autumn of 1904 Bogdanov and I reached a complete agreement as *Bolsheviks*, and formed a tacit bloc, which tacitly ruled out philosophy as a neutral field'. This agreement, he went on to say, lasted throughout the period of the 1905 revolution and enabled Bogdanov and Lenin to cooperate as Bolsheviks.[51]

A plan of action was elaborated by Bogdanov and Lenin at a retreat in the remote village of Puidoux, near the Lac de Bré in Switzerland in August 1904.[52] It was at a juncture when Lenin, Bogdanov and the adherents of the 'majority' had lost hope of being able to convoke a third-party congress through the existing party institutions. The intention was to circumvent these institutions by mobilising the local party committees to demand a new congress. For this purpose a new institution would be created, the Bureau of the Committees of the Majority (BCM), and a new periodical (*Vpered*) established to canvass 'majority' opinion.

Lenin and Bogdanov drew up a document setting out the case for convening a new party congress. Although this document, entitled 'To the Party', appears in Lenin's collected works, Bogdanov must have made a considerable contribution to it. The ideas that appear in it can be found in Bogdanov's writings that preceded the document and in ones that followed it.

'To the Party' began by drawing attention to the growing demands on the Social Democrats presented by the critical economic and political situation within the country, exacerbated by the prospect of a war. It then posed the question: was the party equal to these demands in its present condition? The reply was that any honest person would have to answer in the negative. The split in the party had shaken discipline to its very foundations.

In analysing the causes of the party division, 'To the Party' repeated the explanation given by Bogdanov in his reply to Rosa Luxemburg, that:

---

50   Lenin 1958–65, 47, p. 141.
51   Lenin 1958–65, 47, p. 142.
52   Krupskaia 1989, p. 288.

... opposition cadres have in general been drawn chiefly from those elements in our party which consist primarily of intellectuals. The intelligentsia is always more individualistic than the proletariat, owing to its very conditions of life and work, which do not directly involve a large-scale combination of efforts, do not directly educate it through organised collective labour. The intellectual elements therefore find it harder to adapt themselves to the discipline of party life, and those of them who are not equal to it naturally raise the standard of revolt against the necessary organisational limitations, and elevate their instinctive anarchism to a principle of struggle, misnaming it a desire for 'autonomy', a demand for 'tolerance' etc.[53]

The document went on to reproduce the contrast that Bogdanov had drawn between the party institutions abroad, where the intelligentsia predominated and tended to be supporters of the 'minority', whereas the party committees within Russia were mostly composed of workers and intellectuals who were close to them. These committees were less prone to anarchistic tendencies and were inclined to support the 'majority'.[54]

'To the Party' argued that the way out of the present impasse was the convocation of a new party congress, but it also contained concrete proposals aimed at avoiding splits in the party in the future that would be elaborated by Bogdanov in later party documents. One such proposal was the inclusion in the party rules of guarantees of the rights of any minority, so that any disagreements or complaints that would inevitably arise would be directed into a constitutional channel and a recognised platform for expression for dissident views. Moreover, it was also envisaged that a minority within the party should be allowed one or more writers' groups, with the right to be represented at congresses. The broadest formal guarantees should be given regarding the publication of party literature devoted to criticising the activities of the central party institutions.[55]

Following the negotiations at Lac de Bré, Krupskaya communicated the outcome to Vorovsky: 'Our tactic is this: get a congress, and at it the old *Iskra* current triumphs, with the minority receiving certain guarantees'. Krupskaya stressed that the conference she had just attended was a conspiratorial one and that secrecy was imperative. She was sending Vorovsky a copy of the declaration 'To the Party', which he was to re-publish and distribute. She concluded

---

53   Lenin 1958–65, 9. 15.
54   Ibid.
55   Lenin 1958–65. 9, 19.

by saying that a literary group that would contain Bogdanov and Olminsky was being formed.[56] In her memoirs Krupskaya adds that Bogdanov intended to invite his friends Lunacharsky, Bazarov and Rumiantsev to contribute to the BCM's newspaper, which would be published abroad and would agitate for the summoning of the party congress.[57]

The plan of action drawn up conspiratorially by Lenin, Bogdanov and Olminsky was subsequently given an air of legitimacy at a meeting held in Geneva at the end of September of twenty-two supporters of the 'majority'. At the meeting elections were held for membership of the BCM and for the editorial board of its newspaper *Vpered*. Bogdanov was elected to the BCM and Lenin was elected to his desired position as editor of *Vpered*.[58]

The BCM was to consist of two sections: one operating inside Russia, which would include Bogdanov, Liadov, S.I. Gusev, Rumiantsev, M.M. Litvinov, R.S. Zemliachka, and a foreign centre outside the country whose main element would be the editorial board of *Vpered*, the organ of the BCM, which would include Lenin, Lunacharsky, Olminsky and Vorovsky. The creation of the BCM was a significant landmark in the history of the RSDLP. It was the moment when the 'majority' grouping established its own separate institutions, corresponding to the Central Committee and the central organ of the party as a whole.[59]

According to Liadov there were serious differences of opinion within the BCM. Bogdanov believed in the possibility of working with the Mensheviks and was concerned to find a formula that would ensure that they remained in the RSDLP. By the end of November (beginning of December) 1904, however, Lenin no longer believed in this possibility and was quite prepared to effect a split in the party. He therefore saw no need for diplomacy and thought that if it proved impossible to convene an all-party congress, then an exclusively Bolshevik congress would be entirely acceptable. Bogdanov and Zemliachka urged acting with caution and avoiding an open break with the Central Committee. Other members of the BCM, including Litvinov and Liadov, took Lenin's side.[60]

---

56   Perepiska V.I. Lenina i rukovodimykh im uchrezhdenii RSDRP s partiinymi organizatsiiami 1903–1905 gg. 1969–77, 2, 430–1.
57   Krupskaia 1989, p. 288.
58   Plyutto 1998, p. 466; Lenin 1958–65, 9, p. 560.
59   Khabas 1924, p. 27; Liadov 1956, p. 65.
60   Liadov 1956, pp. 66–7.

5 Pamphlets

Before *Vpered* was launched, the BCM issued a series of pamphlets, the most important of which was *Our Misunderstandings*, which appeared in September 1904, and which made a great impression both abroad and inside Russia.[61] It also included Bogdanov's pamphlet on the causes of the war with Japan mentioned earlier, one entitled *On Socialism* and one on *The Liberals and the Socialists*.

The main argument of the pamphlet *On Socialism* is that in Western countries, where there are civil rights, workers have been able to improve their living standards through the formation of trade unions and by going on strike to force their employers to make concessions. In doing so, Western workers have acquired great strength and experience, and now make confident steps towards socialism. This route is closed to Russian workers because the government will not allow it. There are no civil rights, and if a strike is called, it is broken by the army and the police. Consequently, Bogdanov argues, the chief priority of Russian workers is to unite to fight against the autocracy in order to gain political freedom.[62]

In the pamphlet Bogdanov defines what he considers to be a socialist economic order. This is where the worker should receive the means of livelihood not from the capitalist, but from society. For this it is necessary that all the means of production should be the property of society. This, he says, is the doctrine of socialism.[63] How socialism is achieved, Bogdanov explains, comes through the evolution of modern capitalism itself. Competition forces the capitalists to form bigger and bigger enterprises employing hundreds, thousands, even tens of thousands of workers. The number of enterprises decreases through mergers and the formation of syndicates. Thus, the capitalists, concerned only for their own immediate interests, against their will, prepare the ground for the socialist order, which they, understandably, abhor. As Bogdanov points out, it is easier for the workers to take over a few large firms than a great many small ones. Here Bogdanov makes explicit the implication in his *Short Course of Economic Science* that the formation of syndicates and trusts is a step in the evolution towards a socialist society.

The pamphlet on the liberals and the socialists is interesting because it sets out in a remarkably perceptive way what were to be the social dynamics of

---

61 Liadov 1956, p. 64.
62 Bogdanov 1904c, pp. 17–18.
63 Bogdanov 1904c, p. 13.

the 1905 revolution in Russia. It was written with the possibility in mind that the liberals might become the temporary allies of the working class. In these circumstances, in order to avoid being cruelly deceived, it was advisable to understand what kind of allies the liberals were.[64]

According to Bogdanov, liberalism in Russia had a distinguished past in the person of the Decembrists and their successors, who had campaigned for civil rights and for a democratic constitution in the country. In more recent times the liberalism had fragmented and was no longer a unified doctrine. In Russia there were two main currents. One of these was that of the more enlightened and Westernised landowners, especially those connected with the zemstvo movement, factory owners, bankers etc. Such people had a privileged existence under the present political order, but they had cause to be discontented with the autocratic regime and its bureaucracy, and desired a new ordering of society.[65]

Reforming landowners were unable to run agriculture on Western lines, because the autocracy ruined the peasants with taxes and kept them in ignorance. This prevented the landowners from introducing machinery and new agricultural methods, for which they needed an educated peasantry. Enlightened industrialists and merchants chafed at the rigid oversight which the government exercised over their activities, each of which had to have official approval. These groups represented the moderate right-wing current of the Russian liberalism.[66]

The other current was the more radical one, consisting mostly of the intelligentsia who led a proletarian or semi-proletarian existence. It was made up of lawyers, *littérateurs*, school and university teachers, who were discontented with the restrictions on freedom of expression, press freedom, and freedom to teach.[67]

Both groups wanted more freedom and an end to the autocratic regime, but beyond that there was disagreement between them. The moderates agreed with the radicals that there should be freedom of the person, freedom of conscience, freedom of speech and the press. But they believed that *full* freedom of speech and the press was dangerous, since these freedoms could be used by the workers to campaign for trade unions and strikes. The moderate liberals favoured a constitutional monarchy whose parliament would have a franchise

---

64   Bogdanov 1904b, p. 3.
65   Bogdanov 1904b, pp. 6–7.
66   Bogdanov 1904b, p. 10.
67   Bogdanov 1904b, pp. 11–12.

restricted by a property qualification. They believed that such a parliament would effectively represent their interests.[68]

The radical liberals had no concerns about workers' demands, because their interests would be unaffected by them. Neither would they have any objection to a completely democratic constitution, something which would also be demanded by the workers. This group, Bogdanov warned, could become more or less radical, depending who its allies happened to be at the time, as had been shown by the behaviour of the newspaper *Osvobozhdenie*, which was edited abroad by Struve. It had started out by reflecting the views of the more moderate liberals, but subsequently had been influenced by the radical wing of liberalism and had adopted a more democratic programme with the demand for universal suffrage. Now *Osvobozhdenie* was looking for allies among the socialist groups.[69]

At first sight the radical wing looked like democrats, but they differed from democrats in important ways. A democrat believed in popular sovereignty, and in doing so defended the interests of the lower classes. For the radical intelligentsia, however, democracy was only one point among others in their programme, and far from the dominant one. Moreover, one feature common to all liberals was their hostility to socialism. When there was a danger of socialism the liberals were often prepared to ally with the most reactionary parties, and resort to the most extreme measures.[70]

As Bogdanov pointed out, there was still no liberal party, but there was a wide liberal current in the country: in time a liberal party would be formed, probably not just one, but two: a more moderate and a more radical party, reflecting the two currents in Russian liberalism. As the revolutionary storm approached, all the scattered progressive forces would try to unite, and the programme that was capable of uniting them all was the liberal programme. However, Bogdanov stressed, there could be no merger of the proletarian party with the liberals. Only a temporary alliance was possible. That alliance could only be formalised with a liberal party, when it was eventually constituted. In that case the Social Democrats would insist that the liberals should include in their programme the demand for a democratic constitution based on universal suffrage, with equal, direct and secret ballot. But, Bogdanov concluded, in the last analysis the proletarian party must only rely on itself.[71]

---

68   Bogdanov 1904b, pp. 12–16.
69   Bogdanov 1904b, pp. 17–19.
70   Bogdanov 1904b, pp. 19–23.
71   Bogdanov 1904b, pp. 28–9.

Looking ahead, Bogdanov was right about the emergence of two liberal parties. This occurred in October 1905, when the revolutionary upsurge forced the government to concede a representative institution in the form of the State Duma. The party representing the more moderate current of liberalism, whose membership included the more progressive landowners and industrialists, was the Octobrist party. This took its name from the tsar's manifesto of 17 October 1905, granting civil rights and a representative assembly. The chairman of the party was the Moscow industrialist Alexander Guchkov.[72]

The group associated with *Osvobozhdenie* gave rise to the Constitutional Democrat (Kadet) party led by Paul Miliukov, a professor of history at Moscow University. The party's membership came largely from the professional classes and consisted of teachers, lawyers, writers, clerks and zemstvo employees, etc. It was in essence a party of the intelligentsia. There was no question of the Social Democrats' allying with the Octobrists, but the question did arise of collaboration with the Kadets. The matter became a bone of contention between the two fractions of the RSDLP, Plekhanov and the right wing of the Mensheviks being in favour, while the Bolsheviks, and Bogdanov in particular, were opposed.

6 In St Petersburg

In December 1904 Bogdanov returned to Russia as a member of the Bureau of the Committees of the Majority charged with organising the projected party congress. This proved to be extremely difficult, because of the campaign of obstruction waged by the Menshevik Central Committee of the party, and because the Bureau had very few people it could call upon to do the work. And of the Bureau itself only Bogdanov and Zemliachka were present in St Petersburg; Gusev and Liadov had still to arrive. Bogdanov had, however, secured the promise of financial help from Gorky to hold the congress. In addition, Gorky had promised money to support *Vpered*, if he could be convinced that Lenin would refrain from petty polemics.[73]

Lenin, for his part, wanted Bogdanov to assist with the publication of the newspaper, but in view of the intense campaign of the Mensheviks against the Bureau, Bogdanov refused to leave Russia until Gusev and Liadov arrived. But even when Gusev arrived, Bogdanov was still reluctant to travel abroad. On

72   Ascher 1988, 1, p. 235.
73   Perepiska V.I. Lenina i rukovodimykh im uchrezhdenii RSDRP s partiinymi organizatsiiami 1903–1905 gg. 1969–77, 3, p. 367.

6 January Gusev reported to Lenin: 'I only saw Bogdanov in passing. He doesn't want to hear about going abroad. He said he would go in a month, but I don't really believe it. You just can't talk him round. He is as stubborn as a devil'.[74] Events in St Petersburg within the next few days would put paid to any plans Bogdanov might have had to leave the city and travel abroad.

---

74   Perepiska V.I. Lenina i rukovodimykh im uchrezhdenii RSDRP s partiinymi organizatsiiami 1903–1905 gg. 1969–77, 3, p. 468.

CHAPTER 5

The 1905 Revolution

1   After 9 January

Bogdanov's status as a member of the Bureau of the Committees of the Majority and of the St Petersburg Committee of the party placed him in a leading
position in the 'majority' fraction of the RSDLP in the midst of the upheaval of
the 1905 revolution. With this status came great influence on the formulation of
party policy in the momentous events of 1905. He recalls that 'The tactical leaflets of the Bureau of the Committees of the Majority on armed uprising and on
the convening of the party congress, and the majority of leaflets of the BCM on
other subjects were written by me'.[1] The leaflets Bogdanov refers to chronicle
the episodes of the revolution as they unfolded during the year, and serve as
a valuable source both for those episodes and for the light in which Bogdanov
viewed them.

As the leading Bolshevik in St Petersburg during the 1905 revolution, one
might expect that his name would loom large in histories of the 1905 revolution. In fact it is seldom mentioned. That, of course, is to be expected in studies of the revolution written in the Soviet Union, since Lenin had effectively
made Bogdanov a non-person in 1920 with the republication of his *Materialism and Empiriocriticism*, with its abusive essay on Bogdanov by V.I. Nevsky.
Since Nevsky was one of the principal memoirists and historians of the 1905
revolution, it is natural that his works would omit mention of Bogdanov. Pokrovsky, who, like Nevsky, was a historian who was a participant in the events,
wrote a cogent account of the 1905 revolution in 1925 as a counterblast to Trotsky's book *1905*. Pokrovsky too ignores the part played by Bogdanov in the 1905
revolution, but justifies this by stressing that party history lies outside the scope
of his book.[2] For most of Soviet times Bogdanov, who had been anathematised
by Lenin, could not be mentioned in any historical work.

These considerations did not apply to Western historians of the 1905 revolution, who, moreover, were well aware of the tendentiousness of Soviet historical
writing. The problem for Western scholars has been twofold. While they knew
that Soviet historiography was biased, they didn't know precisely how and

---

1   Neizvestnyi Bogdanov 1995, 1, p. 19.
2   Pokrovsky 1933, 2, p. 106.

where this bias operated. The other difficulty is that the factual material that Western historians have used is derived overwhelmingly from Soviet publications, and with this factual material comes an element of interpretation. Unless one knows how the factual material is slanted, one has to accept it with accompanying interpretation and all. Thus, whereas the foremost Western historian of 1905, Abraham Ascher, is able to note that the part played by Stalin in the 1905 revolution has in the past been much exaggerated by Soviet writers, he overlooks the fact that the role of Bogdanov has been ignored almost completely.[3]

The end of Bogdanov's exile coincided with an upsurge of political activity in the country. The initial challenge to the government came from the zemstvos, the institutions of local self-government which had been established by tsar Alexander II as part of his programme of reform. Although the higher posts in zemstvo organisations were held by members of the local nobility, it was from the intelligentsia that its so-called 'third element', its doctors, teachers, agronomists and statisticians etc., was recruited. Alexander's successors had always been suspicious of the zemstvos and tried to curtail their activities. The effect, however, was to convince many of the zemstvo leaders of the need to replace the autocracy with representative government. The 'Union of Liberation', headed by Struve and P.N. Miliukov, which had been founded by the left-wing zemstvo activists in 1903, soon came to be controlled by the 'third element', which was much more radical than the most liberal of the gentry. In July 1904 the Minister of the Interior, Plehve, an avowed opponent of the zemstvos, was assassinated by a Socialist Revolutionary and replaced by the more enlightened Prince P.D. Sviatopolk-Mirsky, who initiated something of a 'political spring' which allowed a congress of zemstvos to take place.[4]

When the government refused to contemplate the granting of a constitution, the zemstvo liberals initiated a nation-wide 'banqueting campaign', gala dinners to commemorate such events as the fortieth anniversary of Alexander II's reform of the law courts. The banquets served as a convenient platform from which to campaign for constitutional reform. This campaign came at a time when the government had been weakened by its lack of success in the war against Japan for control of Korea. Plehve had been much in favour of a 'little victorious war' as this would strengthen the hand of the regime. The opposite had happened; in August of 1904 the Russian army was driven back from Liaoyang, the first of several major military defeats that were to punctuate the developments of the next few months.[5]

---

3   Ascher 1988, 1, p. 5.
4   Pokrovsky 1933, 2, pp. 102–3.
5   Pokrovsky 1933, 2, p. 102.

The zemstvo campaign for constitutional reform formed the background to the developments in the workers' movement in St Petersburg on the eve of 'Bloody Sunday'. In 1901–3 the chief of the Moscow Okhrana S.V. Zubatov had fostered a system of government-sponsored workers' organisations with the intention of deflecting the workers from political activity against the government to that of pursuing purely economic objectives, such as increasing wages and shortening the working day. Zubatov's methods inspired the young priest Georgii Gapon to obtain Plehve's approval for establishing in the capital a workers' organisation called the 'Assembly of the Russian Factory and Mill Workers of the City of St Petersburg'. It differed from the Zubatov model of workers' organisations by being more independent of the police, whose presence was prohibited at meetings of the 'Assembly'.[6]

What gave Gapon's organisation increased credibility was the presence in it of the former members of the Brusnev organisation A.E. Karelin and his wife V.M. Karelina and a number of their associates. This group of experienced, politically literate workers formed an opposition to Gapon and pushed his organisation in a leftward direction. In particular Karelin wanted Gapon to petition the government in the same way the liberals were doing, but with the demands of the workers. This was something that Gapon at first refused to undertake.[7]

Gapon's hand was forced by the action of the management of the Putilov Works, a major engineering concern in St Petersburg. During Christmas of 1904 it sacked four workers who were members of Gapon's 'Assembly'. Negotiations for the reinstatement of the workers came to nothing, and a strike at the Putilov works was called for 3 January 1905, which soon escalated into a general strike throughout the city. Up to this point the St Petersburg Social Democrats had ignored Gapon's 'Assembly', regarding it as a 'police socialist' Zubatovite organisation; their attention had been focused on the zemstvo liberals. Now, however, they encouraged the workers to prolong the strike and called upon those who had not done so to join it.[8]

When on 6 January the St Petersburg Social Democrats learned that the Gapon organisation intended to organise a procession to the Winter Palace and present a petition to the tsar, they were faced with the dilemma of what their attitude to the procession should be. On the one hand, they did not believe that anything positive could be achieved by petitioning the tsar, but, on the

---

6 Shuster 1976, p. 61.
7 Shuster 1976, pp. 62–3.
8 Shuster 1976, p. 75.

other hand, the petition had a great deal of support among the St Petersburg workers. On the evening of 7 January, Bogdanov, Rumiantsev, Gusev, and other members of the St Petersburg Committee met to discuss the question. It was decided that the Committee members should go on the procession, and, when it was broken up by the authorities, unfurl the RSDLP banners that they would have with them and turn it into a demonstration. When the committee met again on the night of 8 January, there was still a great deal of uncertainty about what the attitude towards the procession should be, but it was felt that the plan of action would be decided by events on the day. It was resolved that if possible all party members should go armed to the procession.[9]

Gapon himself insisted that no arms should be carried on the procession, and in fact the marchers were peaceful and orderly, some of them carrying portraits of the tsar and sacred icons. Although Bogdanov and the other members of the Petersburg Committee had anticipated that the procession might end in violent confrontation with the authorities, they had not foreseen the scale of the massacre on 9 January. When the columns of marchers were stopped by cordons of troops, they nevertheless refused to disperse. The troops opened fire on the columns of the procession, killing at least 130 people and wounding several hundred. The reaction of horror and anger that the atrocity produced spread throughout the country and sparked off the series of events subsequently known as the 1905 revolution.

A crowded and excited meeting of the St Petersburg Committee assembled on the evening of 9 January. Bogdanov and the other committee members exchanged impressions of the day and recounted the episodes they had witnessed. Bogdanov and a student from the technical college edited the first leaflets put out by the Social Democrats in response to the shooting. They reflected the horror and outrage that the scenes of violence had evoked.[10] The leaflet 'To All' declared:

> Comrades! Blood has been spilt; it is flowing in streams. The workers have once more known the tsar's benevolence and mercy. They went to seek truth and received from him bullets. At the Neva Gates, at the Troitsky Bridge, on Nevsky Prospekt – everywhere there are dozens of dead and hundreds of wounded. They were fired on without warning. You know

---

9   Peterburgskii komitet RSDRP. Protokoly i materialy zasedanii Iiul' 1902–fevral' 1917 1986, pp. 123–5.

10   Peterburgskii komitet RSDRP. Protokoly i materialy zasedanii Iiul' 1902–fevral' 1917 1986, p. 127.

what it means to ask the tsar, what it means to place your hopes on him. So you learn to *take by force* what you need; you learn to rely only on yourselves.[11]

The leaflet headed 'To the Workers' highlighted the lesson that 'Bloody Sunday' had taught and made it a turning point in the history of the Russian revolution: 'Now you know that asking the tsar and his government for rights and justice is useless. The tsar filled the streets of Petersburg with your blood. Comrades! with weapons in your hands come and join the RSDLP and its Petersburg Committee'.[12] These leaflets were followed by others appealing to the workers to prolong the strike and to the soldiers to join with the people against the regime, stressing that they themselves were of the people and suffered the same oppression as those whom they were ordered to kill.[13]

The government's realisation that the 9 January massacre had not subdued discontent, but intensified it beyond measure, prompted it to take placatory measures. On 19 January the tsar issued a rescript setting up a 'commission to establish the causes of discontent of the St Petersburg workers and its suburbs and to seek measures to eliminate such in the future'. The commission, chaired by Senator N.V. Shidlovsky, was to be composed of representatives from the government, from the industrialists and from the workers by election.[14]

Bogdanov and other members of the Petersburg Committee saw this as a political manoeuvre to deflect the popular masses from politics, from the revolutionary movement. But as the first institution in the Russian Empire ever to have elected worker representatives, the project developed a considerable momentum, particularly as the rights of the workers in the Shidlovsky Commission were championed by the radical lawyer G.S. Khrustalev-Nosar. The phenomenon of a legal institution with workers' representation posed a serious dilemma for Bogdanov and his associates: whether to boycott it or to participate in it and use it to further the cause of Social-Democracy. It was a question that would be debated at the Third Congress of the party in the spring, and would re-emerge with increased urgency when the elections to the State Duma were held. In the meantime a formula was worked out for dealing with the Shidlovsky Commission: it was that the workers would agree to participate in the Commission if a number of conditions were met, such as the uncensored pub-

11   Listovki Peterburgskikh bol'shevikov, 1902–1920 1939, 1, p. 161.
12   Listovki Peterburgskikh bol'shevikov, 1902–1920 1939, 1, pp. 161–2.
13   Listovki Bol'shevistskikh organizatsii v pervoi Russkoi revoliutsii 1905–1907 gg. 1956, 1, pp. 220, 229.
14   Shuster 1976, p. 101.

lication of the Commission's proceedings, the inviolability of the delegates and the release of people imprisoned after 1 January. Since Shidlovsky could not agree to these conditions, the workers refused to cooperate and the Commission was disbanded. This was an outcome that Bogdanov counted as a success for the Social-Democratic Party.[15]

The onset of the revolution had made new demands on the Social Democrats for which the party was unprepared. Bogdanov made the point forcefully in a leaflet announcing the convocation of a new congress dated 21 January. Recalling the atrocity of 9 January and indicating the general political ferment that engulfed the country, with strikes and demonstrations taking place in all the major population centres in Russia, Bogdanov predicted that a massive uprising was in the offing. He then posed the question: was the party strong enough to carry out this task? His answer was that every honest member of the party was bound to say no. Symptomatic of this state of affairs was that in St Petersburg the leadership of the workers' movement in the January events belonged not to the Social-Democratic Party, but to Gapon, a priest and a group of his followers who had been charmed by his religious-utopian enthusiasm. Moreover, because of the party's divisions and its consequent weakness, the liberal opposition groups refused to recognise Social-Democracy as the legitimate representative of the workers, and aspired to fulfil this role themselves.

In order to prepare the party for the decisive struggle ahead, Bogdanov argued that a congress should be organised as soon as possible. The areas for discussion at the congress, Bogdanov considered, should be the following: 1. questions of the methods of the political struggle; 2. questions of relations with the bourgeois opposition and 3. questions of agreement and negotiation with the national socialist parties: the Jewish Bund, the Polish, Lithuanian, Latvian, Ukrainian, Finnish, Armenian, etc. Social Democrats. The question of including the national parties within the RSDLP was an important one, if the Social Democrats were to coordinate their activities throughout the Russian Empire. The Second Congress had failed to make any headway in this direction as the Bund had walked out of the Congress when it was refused the degree of autonomy it demanded. The implication was that the inclusion of the national parties would depend on the preparedness of the RSDLP to modify its internal organisation to allow the separate identity of the national groups. This requirement was in keeping with how Bogdanov proposed to extend the democratic principle in party organisation.[16]

---

15   Listovki Bol'shevistskikh organizatsii v pervoi Russkoi revoliutsii 1905–1907 gg. 1956, 1, p. 71.

16   Listovki Bol'shevistskikh organizatsii v pervoi Russkoi revoliutsii 1905–1907 gg. 1956, 1, p. 35.

Bogdanov went on to advocate a number of organisational changes to the party. First of all, he thought that the limits of the party should be more strictly defined by adopting Lenin's definition of party membership rather than Martov's. This would mean that a party member would not only have to support the party programme, but also belong to a party organisation. In order to establish party unity Bogdanov suggested that there should be a precise definition of the limits of centralisation and autonomy of particular organisations. While there should be strict centralisation – essential in the conditions of revolutionary struggle – this should 'not be given the naive bureaucratic interpretation of it then put forward by centres who demanded blind subordination in face of its obvious inappropriateness'.[17] Bogdanov stressed, as he had done in his more theoretical writings, that the basis of the party organisation was comradely relations. And, as in *Our Misunderstandings*, he proposed that the party should have only a single directing centre and that that should be in Russia.[18]

A leaflet that Bogdanov issued in early March concerned the relations of the RSDLP with the liberals, with the zemstvo constitutionalists and with the 'Union of Liberation'. He saw a threat from these groups, since they were attempting to take advantage of the divisions within the Social-Democratic camp to assume leadership of the workers' movement. In Bogdanov's view, neither with the zemstvo constitutionalists nor with the 'Union of Liberation' was an alliance possible. He believed it essential to oppose the importation of liberal ideas into the workers' movement, and that the liberal parties must recognise Social-Democracy as the legitimate political representative of the proletariat. He thought that these parties should state openly and clearly what their attitude to the Social-Democrat programme was, and how they regarded each of its individual demands. According to Bogdanov, the slogan of the Social Democrats must be: 'the class purity of the workers' movement'.[19] One can discern in this leaflet on the attitude to the liberals an approach that Bogdanov would later apply to the Soviets. For him the test of what was consistent with the principle of retaining the class purity of the workers' movement was whether it was guided by the Social-Democratic programme. Bogdanov was consistent in applying this test, though even with regard to the liberals it was not without its opponents in the Social-Democrat camp.

---

17   Ibid.
18   Ibid.
19   Listovki Bol'shevistskikh organizatsii v pervoi Russkoi revoliutsii 1905–1907 gg. 1956, 1, p. 49.

Pokrovsky, who was himself a former liberal who had joined the Social Democrats, recalled how he had attended congresses of school teachers in St Petersburg and Moscow in the spring of 1905 but had not been able to make any impression on them because of the inflexible policy adopted by the party leadership. As Pokrovsky explained, 'At that time this was the directive for all professional-political unions: to demand that the congress should accept our programme, and if they refused, to shake the dust from our feet, and leave the congress to the mercy of the Socialist-Revolutionaries and the Liberationists'.[20] In the summer of 1905 while in Geneva, at Lenin's suggestion, Pokrovsky set out his objections to Bogdanov's policy in an article in *Proletarii*. Lenin added a note saying that while he could understand Pokrovsky's point of view, he preferred 'narrow and intolerant distinctness to soft and compliant lack of clarity', that is, he sided with Bogdanov rather than with Pokrovsky.[21]

The Third Congress of the RSDLP took place in London between 25 April and 10 May 1905. The supporters of the party minority declined to take part and held their own separate conference in Geneva. Among the 38 delegates to the London Congress were Lenin, Krupskaya, Bogdanov and his friends Lunacharsky and Rumiantsev. It was during this Congress that the terms 'Bolshevik' and 'Menshevik' began to be used by some of the speakers. Although Soviet accounts of the Congress are at pains to present it as being dominated by Lenin, in fact this was a Congress which approved policies and reforms which had been proposed earlier by Bogdanov. The published proceedings of the Congress show Bogdanov introducing key resolutions, sometimes on his own and sometimes jointly with Lenin.

A crucial issue to be discussed was that of the armed uprising, which was conceived of as a movement on a national scale. Bogdanov saw the point of departure for the armed uprising as the general strike. The logic of the strike would lead to revolutionary action, and this in turn to the armed struggle. The acquisition of arms was consequently of the essence. It was important, moreover, not to allow the workers' revolutionary energy to be dissipated on individual actions. In view of the part played by the troops in the 9 January massacre, Bogdanov argued that special attention should be given to winning over the soldiers to the side of the people.[22] The resolution on the armed uprising adopted by the Congress stated that the proletariat was, by virtue of its position, the foremost and only consistently revolutionary class, and was therefore

---

20   Pokrovskii 1905.
21   Pokrovskii 1905; Lenin 1958–65, 11, p. 177.
22   Tretii s"ezd RSDRP aprel'–mai 1905 goda. Protokoly 1959, pp. 106–14.

called upon to play the leading role in the general democratic revolutionary movement in Russia. It went on to say that the proletariat could only play this role if it was united in a single and independent political force under the banner of the RSDLP.[23]

If the armed uprising succeeded in overthrowing the tsarist government, the Congress believed, the next stage would be a provisional revolutionary government, and according to Lenin, this could only be the democratic dictatorship of the proletariat and the peasantry. The conditions would then be created in which the Social Democrats could campaign for socialism. Plekhanov had accused Lenin of having wanted to take power immediately, and in this way of contradicting what Marx had said on the subject, an accusation that Lenin strenuously denied. In the attempt to cause dissension in the alliance between Lenin and Bogdanov, Plekhanov had implied that Lenin had espoused Bogdanov's philosophy. Lenin took the opportunity to register his disagreement with Bogdanov's ideas, remarking:

> Unable to prove that *Vpered* wants to 'criticise' Marx, Plekhanov drags in Mach and Avenarius by the ears. I cannot for the life of me understand what these writers, for whom I have not the slightest sympathy, have to do with the question of social revolution. They wrote on individual and social organisation of experience, or some such theme, but they never really gave any thought to the democratic dictatorship.[24]

In fact, Lenin's description of the philosophy of Mach and Avenarius can be applied much more accurately to the recently published *Empiriomonism* by Bogdanov.

A significant discussion took place on the question of the participation of the RSDLP in legal organisations. Vorovsky thought that this discussion was superfluous, because the question had only arisen in connection with the Shidlovsky Commission, and this was a unique event. Both Krasin and Rumiantsev thought that this was not the case; the government was likely to propose some sort of parliamentary assembly, so that the issue would emerge in the future – as in fact it did with the State Duma. The Congress thought that in this case policy could not be decided in advance; it would have to be seen what kind of institution it would have to deal with.[25]

---

23   Tretii s"ezd RSDRP aprel'–mai 1905 goda. Protokoly 1959, p. 450.
24   Tretii s"ezd RSDRP aprel'–mai 1905 goda. Protokoly 1959, p. 191.
25   Tretii s"ezd RSDRP aprel'–mai 1905 goda. Protokoly 1959, p. 218.

A resolution which was attributed to Bogdanov and Lenin concerned the relationship between intellectuals and workers and the elective principle in the party. What these two issues seemingly had in common was that they had served as pretexts for criticisms by Martov and his followers. They had accused the 'majority' fraction of consisting mainly of intellectuals and of only giving lip-service to the elective principle. Bogdanov argued that the party should not recognise any distinction of workers and intellectuals; that all were simply party members. He asserted that the party was in fact sympathetic to the democratic principle of organisation, but that the present objective conditions put very narrow limits on the implementation of this principle. He believed that in party organisation the slogan of centralism was insufficient; the slogan of democratism ought to be promoted as well.[26]

A theme that would later be taken up by Bogdanov as a rationale for party schools was voiced by Liadov in describing the part played by intellectuals in the Russian revolutionary movement. He recalled that when Marxism had become fashionable in the 1890s the intellectuals had flocked to join the Social Democrats, but had left the party to join the 'Union of Liberation'; now with the outbreak of the revolution they were returning to the party in droves.[27] Vorovsky predicted that the radical intelligentsia would be reabsorbed into the liberal movement and that there would be a shortage of intellectuals in the RSDLP; for that reason he urged that workers in the party should be given training to enable them to assume leadership roles in local committees.[28]

The Congress amended the party's constitution in the way Bogdanov had suggested, substituting Lenin's definition of a party member for Martov's. The existing system of party organisation with a Central Committee, a Central Organ and a Party Council to arbitrate between them was abolished. Henceforth there would only be a single directing party centre; this would be the Central Committee and it would be located within Russia. It was a change that Bogdanov thought essential to avoid future divisions in the party. Lenin, however, saw no objection to the existing structure, arguing that the problem lay not with the institutions but with the people who composed them. To this argument Bogdanov replied: 'Comrade Lenin has not convinced me. The system of two centres is too favourable a soil for a schism and squabbling ... The question here is not *only* of people, as Lenin thinks, and to reason in this way does not become a Marxist'.[29]

---

26   Tretii s"ezd RSDRP aprel'–mai 1905 goda. Protokoly 1959, p. 254.
27   Tretii s"ezd RSDRP aprel'–mai 1905 goda. Protokoly 1959, p. 257.
28   Tretii s"ezd RSDRP aprel'–mai 1905 goda. Protokoly 1959, p. 260.
29   Tretii s"ezd RSDRP aprel'–mai 1905 goda. Protokoly 1959, p. 285.

The discussion on the need to reunite with the Mensheviks took up the principle set out in 'To the Party': to guarantee the minority, in the words of Avilov, 'the freedom to defend their views and to give assurances that the Menshevik comrades will be accepted in the organisation on the same basis as the Bolsheviks'.[30] It was envisaged that the minority fraction might well become the majority. Lunacharsky compared the process to British parliamentary practice in which the liberals immediately ceded power to the conservatives as soon as the latter gained a majority.[31] From this discussion it emerges that Bogdanov and his associates – if not Lenin – thought of the RSDLP as a single entity in which different groups and individuals would vie for influence and leadership. Thus, when Solomon Schwarz contends that in this period 'The Bolsheviks were increasingly bent on making Social-Democracy a closed organisation of conspirators, of professional revolutionaries keeping an iron hand on any show of activity by the masses',[32] he is expressing a stereotyped interpretation of events. Symptomatically, Schwarz's history of the Russian Revolution of 1905 is Lenin-centred, and makes very little mention of Bogdanov.[33]

Speakers at the Congress were well aware that reunification with the Mensheviks was only one aspect of creating a unified RSDLP. It was also essential to include in the organisation the Jewish Bund and the various national Social-Democratic organisations that had emerged within the Russian Empire. A truly national armed uprising would require their participation and coordination. There was, however, a general reluctance to concede to these organisations the degree of autonomy that the Bund had demanded and been refused at the Second Congress of the RSDLP.[34]

Bogdanov had every reason to be satisfied with the outcome of the Third Congress. It had endorsed the reforms he had thought necessary for adapting the party to the needs of the revolutionary situation in the country. In a leaflet for the workers he summed up what the Congress had achieved:

---

30   Tretii s"ezd RSDRP aprel'–mai 1905 goda. Protokoly 1959, p. 357.
31   Tretii s"ezd RSDRP aprel'–mai 1905 goda. Protokoly 1959, pp. 351, 359.
32   Schwarz 1967, p. 51.
33   Israel Getzler perpetuates the same kind of misapprehension as Solomon Schwartz. In contrasting Martov's idea of 'revolutionary self-government' to 'Leninism', he leaves out of consideration that at the time in question the Bolshevik leader in St Petersburg was not Lenin, but Bogdanov, whom Getzler does not mention as a participant in the 1905 revolution. See Getzler 1967, p. 105.
34   Tretii s"ezd RSDRP aprel'–mai 1905 goda. Protokoly 1959, pp. 365–9.

The Third Congress reforms on the one hand aimed at stricter centralisation towards the development of a cogent and coherent party mechanism, on the other hand – towards increased democratism, to the extension of rights and facilitating the independent activities of the broad mass of party activists. The limits of the party have been given more definition, those recognised as party members are only those who are members of party organisations. Dismantled have been the complicated and cumbersome apparatus of three centres and replaced by one centre with a preponderance of practical people over literary ones and the Russian part over the foreign one.[35]

What had *not* been achieved was the unification of the party, since the Mensheviks had held their own separate gathering, but on this issue Bogdanov was optimistic. He believed that this division had clarified matters: instead of one completely disorganised party there were now two more or less organised ones. In this situation their full unification had become incomparably less difficult and incomparably more probable.[36]

Bogdanov had returned to St Petersburg in time for the celebration of Mayday. The tactics to adopt for this occasion was the subject of controversy between the two fractions of the RSDLP. On the basis of decisions taken at the Third Congress, the Bolsheviks proposed conserving forces for the armed uprising and not dissipating them, so there were to be meetings, a two-day strike, but not street demonstrations. The leaflet Bogdanov issued consequently urged restraint: 'The day of uprising is not far off, but it has still not dawned. The workers and peasants have too few arms, they are still not rallied enough for the struggle'.[37] The Mensheviks, however, proposed something else: 'going on the streets with arms for defence', a 'demonstration with armed resistance'. As a result, there was confusion among the workers, and disappointment that this important date for the labour movement had not been used more effectively through divisions in the RSDLP. In a letter to Lenin, Zemliachka, a member of the St Petersburg Committee, reported that 'Our agitators say that the workers are disappointed that the Petersburg Committee prepared to mark 1 May peacefully and did not distribute arms'.[38]

---

35   Listovki Bol'shevistskikh organizatsii v pervoi Russkoi revoliutsii 1905–1907 gg. 1956, 1, p. 76.

36   Listovki Bol'shevistskikh organizatsii v pervoi Russkoi revoliutsii 1905–1907 gg. 1956, 1, p. 73.

37   Listovki Bol'shevistskikh organizatsii v pervoi Russkoi revoliutsii 1905–1907 gg. 1956, 1, p. 63.

38   Shuster 1976, p. 124.

The destruction of the Baltic fleet by the Japanese in May occasioned Bogdanov to issue a leaflet drawing attention to this disaster for the tsarist regime. Having voiced the opinion that the old order was dying a shameful death, he warned the workers that unless they took power themselves it would be seized by the capitalists and landowners, and it would take another decade of struggle to wrest back the freedom that was rightfully theirs.[39]

The leaflet Bogdanov put out at the end of June was against the background of the strike of textile workers in Ivanovo-Voznesensk, the mutiny on the battleship *Potemkin* and the forthcoming elections to the State Duma. This was a document in which Bogdanov set out his ideas on party organisation, reconciling the need for discipline with his anti-authoritarian principles.

According to Bogdanov the Social-Democratic Party was an organisation that was militant and comradely. It was militant in that it struggled for a social ideal which stood in stark contradiction to the dominant economic and political order. Its comradely character arose from the class ideal which its members shared and consciously and freely recognised as the highest and final goal of their activity.

For Bogdanov, a party which espoused the comradely principle was alien to naked centralisation and blind discipline. These were incompatible with the free and conscious character of the comradely connection; this demanded democratic forms of organisation. He held that an organisation that was not democratic in its form could not attract the sympathy of the masses, or broadly develop within its ranks political, independent activity and initiative.

On the other hand, it was necessary to have a party that was centralised. Centralisation could provide the unity, the decisiveness and the speed of collective action. Hence the need arose for a single directing centre, sufficiently compact and coherent to permit swift discussion of and decision on the urgent political issues of the moment. It had to be a centre connected with the whole mass of party activists, a centre whose decisions were obligatory for all party members. This would be the role that Bogdanov intended the newly-constituted Central Committee to play; local committees would have the same kind of centralised organisation.[40]

But how was it possible to combine in a single party the seemingly mutually contradictory principles of centralism and democracy? Bogdanov was con-

---

39   Listovki Bol'shevistskikh organizatsii v pervoi Russkoi revoliutsii 1905–1907 gg. 1956, 1, p. 66.

40   Listovki Bol'shevistskikh organizatsii v pervoi Russkoi revoliutsii 1905–1907 gg. 1956, 1, pp. 96–7.

vinced that it was possible to construct the party organisations in such a way that without diluting the obligation to follow the decisions of the party centres, these decisions would correspond with the will of the majority of the party. The way to achieve this, Bogdanov argued, was by three types of mechanism: 1. the elective principle; 2. short terms of office; 3. wide transparency (*glasnost'*) in party matters.

In commenting on these three mechanisms, Bogdanov explained that the elective principle consistently carried out at all levels of party organisation by itself was a significant guarantee that those who were entrusted with the practical leadership of the party were in themselves the real expression of the will of the party and that their decisions also corresponded with what had emerged from collective discussion among party members.

If, however, it happened that the choice of party officials had been mistaken, this could be corrected through the second mechanism – the limitation on the terms of office. If the term of office of party officials was limited to a short period then the control of the party over them would take on a very real character. One would not have to wait very long before getting rid of people who were unsuitable and electing replacements who might perform better in the role.

This guarantee was made more effective by the third mechanism, the practice of wide transparency in party affairs. Transparency of this kind would ensure 1) the impossibility for officials to hide the mistakes they had made from the party and so escape responsibility for them; 2) the continued control and pressure on the officials by opinion in the party. Moreover, if the decision-making of officials was open and exposed to free party criticism, this would prevent mistakes from being made, or stop actions being taken which flouted the policies that the party had elaborated.

Bogdanov went on to discuss the guarantees for minorities within the party organisation, clearly with the case of the Mensheviks in mind. He claimed that the implementation of democracy, the rule by the majority, did not imply the suppression of the views of the minority. This minority, moreover, might constitute a considerable proportion of the party, and might well have right on its side. Bogdanov's argument was that those same guarantees which ensured the practical domination by the majority of the party also ensured the ideological independence of the minority. Transparency in party affairs assumed the freedom of the party press, and therefore also the freedom of criticism on the part of the minority. And if through the campaign for the acceptance of its views the minority won over opinion in the party, it then would become the ideological majority of the party, and into its hands very quickly, thanks to the brevity of the period of office of the centres, would pass the leadership of those centres.

It would be a process analogous to the parliamentary succession of power that had been discussed at the Third Congress.[41]

Bogdanov on behalf of the RSDLP Central Committee opened negotiations with the Organising Committee of the Mensheviks to bring about party unity. In an open letter to the Organising Committee he proposed that both parts of the RSDLP could be united on the basis of what had been decided at the Third Congress. Bogdanov stressed again that disagreements between the sections were not so serious as to justify a schism. In reply the Organising Committee put forward a number of demands, among them the demand that both sections should retain their respective central organs – a measure which in Bogdanov's view would preserve the existing split. The Organising Committee's demands were unacceptable to Bogdanov and the Central Committee. The alternative to the Mensheviks accepting unity on the basis of the Third Congress was to hold a special unity congress, though prior to this congress the Mensheviks again set conditions. In Bogdanov's opinion the Menshevik policy remained what it had been before the Third Congress: they preferred schism to unification.[42]

Bogdanov's efforts to unite the party would not have been made any easier by the publication in July of Lenin's pamphlet *Two Tactics of Social Democracy in the Democratic Revolution*. Highlighting the differences in the way the question of the provisional revolutionary government had been treated by the Third Congress and the Geneva Conference, Lenin denounced at inordinate length what he saw as the opportunism of the Mensheviks and their betrayal of the proletarian cause. The differences were summarised by Pokrovsky as: 'Lenin set himself the task of *overthrowing* the tsar; the Mensheviks that of compelling the tsar *to give in*. Lenin regarded the overthrow of tsarism as a task for the workers and *peasants*; the Mensheviks believed that the best way to extract concessions from the tsar was to act in alliance with the *bourgeoisie*'.[43] Lenin characterised the Bolsheviks as the proletarian and revolutionary wing of the party and the Mensheviks as the intellectual and opportunist. Lenin's pamphlet was not a work that saw the Menshevik viewpoint as a legitimate one that might triumph in the party, but more as a mistaken and dangerous doctrine that had to be discredited and eradicated. The picture of the Third Congress that emerges from the pamphlet is of a sectarian and partisan gathering, with

---

41   Listovki Bol'shevistskikh organizatsii v pervoi Russkoi revoliutsii 1905–1907 gg. 1956, 1, pp. 98–104.

42   Listovki Bol'shevistskikh organizatsii v pervoi Russkoi revoliutsii 1905–1907 gg. 1956, 1, pp. 159–60.

43   Pokrovsky 1933, 2, p. 168.

no hint of the resolutions it passed on restoring unity to the party. Like the Menshevik leadership, Lenin too seemed to prefer schism to unification.

In February, in an effort to stem the tide of revolution, the tsar had commissioned Sviatopolk-Mirsky's successor A.G. Bulygin to draw up a scheme for a representative assembly that would take part in discussing legislation. On 6 August the tsar's decree establishing the State Duma and defining the procedure for elections to it was published. In the leaflet issued in response to the announcement Bogdanov indicated a number of objections to the Duma, which he considered to be a counter-revolutionary device. First, there would be no place in the Duma for the workers, since for the urban population there were high property qualifications. Second, the peasants would only have a minimal representation in the Duma through the complicated system of indirect elections, and these indirect elections would prevent the representatives in the Duma from being answerable to the peasant electorate. Third, there was no freedom of speech for candidates to discuss issues with their constituents, and there would be no freedom of expression in the Duma itself because it was forbidden from discussing the basic laws of the Russian Empire. Fourth, the Duma would only have consultative powers; it would only be able to suggest legislation; decisions would be made by the tsar and his State Council. Because of this the power of the autocracy would remain undiminished. Bogdanov concluded by saying that the only genuine form of popular representation would be a constituent assembly elected by universal free, direct and secret ballot. Elections of this kind would be organised by the provisional revolutionary government of the insurgent people.[44] Bogdanov believed that the Bulygin Duma should be boycotted and the elections used for propaganda purposes.

To coordinate its tactics on the Duma with other Social-Democratic groups in the Russian Empire, the Bolshevik Central Committee convened a conference in Riga on 20–2 September. It was attended by representatives of the Jewish Bund (I.L. Aizenshtadt-Yudin), the Latvian Social Democrats, the Polish SDKPiL (Jogiches and Adolf Warski) and the Revolutionary Ukrainian Party. The Bolsheviks were represented by Central Committee member D.S. Postolovsky; a member of the Menshevik Organising Committee (V.A. Gutovsky) was also present as an observer. The resolution on the Duma that the conference adopted developed the points made in the leaflet written by Bogdanov. It drew attention to the restricted nature of the electoral system, the fact that the Duma only had consultative powers and that the elections would take place in

---

44   Listovki Bol'shevistskikh organizatsii v pervoi Russkoi revoliutsii 1905–1907 gg. 1956,1, pp. 142–3.

a situation in which there was no freedom of speech or of the press and where there was no inviolability of the person or the home. The conference endorsed Bogdanov's policy that the Duma should be boycotted and the election campaign used to expose its counter revolutionary purpose and to campaign for the revolutionary overthrow of the autocracy and the convocation of a constituent assembly.[45]

The conference is significant in that it shows that in advance of the formal union established by the Fourth Congress of the RSDLP the national parties collaborated closely with the RSDLP in political campaigns. It also suggests a willingness on Bogdanov's part to involve the national parties in elaborating the policies of the RSDLP.

Some respite was gained by the government by its ending the war with Japan and obtaining relatively lenient terms of peace. It made a significant concession to the opposition on 27 August with a decree restoring university autonomy removed by Alexander III in 1884. It was then possible for meetings attended by thousands of people to be held in the universities. The police were powerless to intervene because they did not have the right to enter the self-governing universities other than by the invitation of the university authorities. The new freedom was used by Bogdanov's friends and associates, some of them former contributors to *Pravda*, such as Skvortsov-Stepanov, Pokrovsky, and Rozhkov, to form a 'literary-lecturing group' which spread Social-Democrat propaganda to audiences in various parts of the country.

In October a strike of the railway workers became a general strike throughout the country, involving white-collar as well as industrial workers. In order to coordinate all the various industries and institutions and organisations taking part in the strike, the need was felt for some unifying centre. The Menshevik Social-Democratic Group took the lead in helping to form this kind of strike committee. Martov, who had recently returned to Russia, saw the new organisation, as he had seen the Shidlovsky Commission, the *Potemkin* mutiny, and the establishment of self-governing centres in the Baltic provinces and the Caucasus, as an embodiment of his conception of 'revolutionary self-government'. As defined in the resolution of the Menshevik conference of May 1905, this was: 'the expediency of a partial, episodic capture of power and the formation of revolutionary communes in this or that town or this or that region for the sole purpose of helping the spread of the rising and the disorganisation of the government'.[46]

---

45   KPSS v rezoliutsiiakh i resheniiakh s"ezdov, konferentsii i plenumov TsK, 1953, 1, 91–4; Najdus 1973, pp. 243–4.

46   Quoted in Getzler 1967, p. 105. In the Menshevik history of the 1905 revolution edited by

The Menshevik Social-Democratic Group decided that the delegates to the strike committee should be elected on the same principle as the elections to the Shidlovsky Commission, that is, one delegate for every 500 workers, though this principle was not strictly adhered to. The first meeting of the committee was on 13 October, when some 35–40 representatives of factories in the Nevsky District assembled in the Technological Institute. By the following day there were 80 delegates and on the 15th there were 226 delegates. By the second half of November there were 562.[47]

Continuity with the Shidlovsky Commission was maintained in the person of the committee's chairman, Khrustalev-Nosar. On 17 October an Executive Committee of 50 was formed on which the two fractions of the RSDLP and the Socialist Revolutionaries were represented; Bogdanov was the representative of the 'majority's' Central Committee. On that day the strike committee became officially known as the Petersburg Soviet, and the first number of its newspaper, the *Bulletin of the Petersburg Soviet* was published. According to Trotsky, the Petersburg Soviet was the greatest workers' organisation that had ever been seen in Russia, and served as a model for similar organisations in Moscow, Odessa and a number of other towns throughout the country.[48] Trotsky was the leading light in the Petersburg Soviet, and, as Pokrovsky observed, whereas Trotsky was a magnificent orator, the Bolsheviks could put up against him only Bogdanov, who had no talent as a public speaker.[49]

Bogdanov and other leading Bolsheviks were concerned that organisations like the Petersburg Soviet, through their lack of political consciousness, might become independent workers' organisations, competing with the RSDLP for support. Bogdanov's opinion was shared by those Mensheviks who had joined with local Bolsheviks to form the St Petersburg Federative Council of the RSDLP in October.[50] The Council issued a resolution which argued that the Soviet was an inferior organisation to the RSDLP. According to the Council:

Martov, the origin of the St Petersburg Soviet is explained in terms of 'revolutionary self-government': 'In the thick of the movement, when Petersburg was filled with the throng of meetings, and it seemed that the existing government had ceased to exist, a section of Social-Democracy (the Petersburg "Group") found the moment suitable to launch among the stirred-up masses the idea of creating a revolutionary self-government, of the type that had been observed, for example, among the peasants of Guria, through elections that the people would organise themselves'. See Maevskii 1910, p. 88.

47   Khrustalev-Nosar 1906, p. 71.
48   Trotsky 1971, p. 104.
49   Pokrovsky 1933, 2, p. 323.
50   Trotsky 1925, p. 278.

Russian Social-Democracy stands at the present moment before the necessity of openly appearing in the capacity of the party of the proletarian masses.

On the way to such an appearance it encounters politically inchoate and immature socialist workers' organisations, formed by the spontaneous-revolutionary movement of the proletariat.

Each of these organisations, representing a certain stage in the political development of the proletariat in so far as it stands outside the ranks of Social-Democracy, objectively faces the danger of retarding the proletariat on a primitive political level, and so subjecting it to the bourgeois parties.

One such organisation is the Petersburg Soviet of Workers' Deputies. The tasks of Social-Democracy in relation to the Soviet consist in prompting it to accept its programme and its tactical leadership.

In the event of refusal on the part of such organisations to accept our party programme and accept any other programme, the Social Democrats must leave them and expose before the proletarian masses their anti-proletarian character.[51]

The idea that the Soviet stood on a lower level organisationally to the RSDLP was widely held among the national parties. The Lithuanian Social Democrat Vincas Kapsukas recalled that all the Social-Democratic parties in Lithuania and Western Belorussia were opposed to the establishment of soviets. Only the Group of the Vilna RSDLP were in favour, and that was for purely Menshevik motives. Other organisations, including the Bund, the Lithuanian Social Democrats and the Polish Socialist Party were firmly against. Their chief argument was that since 90 percent of the workers in that area belonged to political parties they had no need of soviets as an organisation of the broad worker masses. It was a different matter in Russia, where the majority of workers did not belong to any organisation.[52] The Latvian Social Democrat Bruno Kalniņš made the same kind of observation in relation to the Latvian territories. There, he says, no Soviets were formed either in Riga or other Latvian towns. The reason that Soviets were so prevalent in Russia, he believes, was because the RSDLP was still weak and unable to represent the mass of workers. In Latvia, on the other hand, the Latvian Social-Democratic Party had circles in

51   Listovki Bol'shevistskikh organizatsii v pervoi Russkoi revoliutsii 1905–1907 gg. 1956, 1,
      p. 191.
52   Kapsukas 1960–78, 12, p. 566.

all the factories, and these were considered by the workers as their representatives.[53] Khrustalev-Nosar also noted that in Poland and Lithuania the proletariat did not construct mass organisations; the leadership of strikes and workers' demonstrations was in the strong organisational hands of the Bund, the SDK-PiL and the PPS.[54]

At a discussion on a paper by the historian P.O. Gorin on the role of the soviets in the 1905 revolution, held in 1925 and published in the journal *Istorik-marksist* the following year,[55] Bogdanov explained his reasoning for his attitude towards the St Petersburg Soviet in some detail. He was influenced, he recalled, by the fact that the St Petersburg proletariat in the main lacked political consciousness; it after all was fresh from making a procession to the tsar and presenting him with a petition. The workers were, moreover, a scattered and disparate force with differences in attitude between the various trades, such as the textile workers, metal-workers and printers. Serious difficulties were involved in bringing these groups together for concerted action. This was the function that the St Petersburg Soviet managed to perform, and in doing so became an organisation of revolutionary action.

But what the Soviet would become was far from clear at the time of its inception. The Mensheviks looked on the Soviet sometimes as a strike committee and at others as an 'organ of revolutionary self-government'. The Bolsheviks were guided by the resolutions of the Third Congress, which had not foreseen the emergence of an institution such as the Soviet. The chairman of the Soviet, moreover, was the dubious figure of Khrustalev-Nosar, dubious because he had no party affiliation – only later did he declare himself a Menshevik – so that Bogdanov and his associates considered him to be a type similar to Gapon. But there was no denying that Khrustalev-Nosar was influential, because he was a powerful speaker whose words resonated with the mood of the masses, despite the vacuity of their content.[56]

The Bolshevik leadership was of the opinion that the Soviet was a valuable vehicle for mass action, but that it would be difficult for it to perform this function with its present amorphous political complexion. The Soviet contained Bolsheviks, Mensheviks, Socialist Revolutionaries and people of no party affiliation, and was led by the non-party Khrustalev-Nosar. It was accordingly decided to arrange it so that the Soviet adopted a Social-Democratic position, and to do this in conjunction with those Mensheviks in the Federative Council.

---

53   Kalniņš 1972, p. 140.
54   Khrustalev-Nosar' 1906, p. 149.
55   Gorin 1926.
56   Bogdanov 1926, p. 222.

It was decided to adopt the following scheme: to propose to the Soviet, where obviously the majority was Bolshevik and Menshevik, that it adopt the Social-Democrat programme.[57]

When, however, the resolution of the Federative Council was published in the Bolshevik newspaper *Novaia Zhizn*, the group of Socialist Revolutionaries in the Soviet objected that the Soviet had been elected to represent the interests of all workers irrespective of party affiliation and therefore the Soviet had no right to join with any particular party. They pointed out that they had been elected as Socialist Revolutionaries and could not change party allegiance without the consent of their constituents. They also challenged the assumption of the Federative Council that the RSDLP was the sole representative of workers' interests; the Socialist Revolutionaries believed that their claim to represent worker interests was just as valid.[58]

Although the members of the Federative Council reckoned that their resolution could command a majority, they did not present it to the Soviet. They hesitated, fearing that the ultimatum might be rejected or simply not placed on the agenda. At this time the Bolshevik leadership received the news that Lenin was on his way to Russia, so it was decided to await his arrival and consult with him before taking any action.

While in Stockholm on his way to Russia at the beginning of November, Lenin wrote an article for *Novaia Zhizn* in which he accepted that Socialist Revolutionaries were right in saying that the Soviet should not be incorporated into the RSDLP, that it should remain a non-party organisation. He went on to say that the Soviet should be regarded as the embryo of a provisional revolutionary government and ought to proclaim itself as such as soon as possible.[59] Lenin's article, however, was not published in *Novaia Zhizn* and only saw the light of day in 1940.

In his article on the soviets in 1905, P.O. Gorin quotes the memoirs of B.I. Gorev, who was a member of the Petersburg Committee of the RSDLP. Gorev recounts that after his first visit to a session of the Petersburg Soviet, Lenin said that the Soviet was the embryo of that dictatorship of the proletariat and peasantry that he had campaigned for since the spring of 1905. It only needed deputies from the peasants to come and the Soviet would be the organ of the dictatorship of the proletariat and peasantry.[60] It would quickly emerge that the Petersburg Soviet was not constituted in such a manner as to include

57   Gorin 1926, p. 223.
58   Khrustalev-Nosar' 1906, p. 151.
59   Lenin 1958–65, 12, pp. 57–70.
60   Gorin 1926, p. 208.

representatives from the peasantry, so that the role Lenin had envisaged for it at this point in time had to be abandoned.

According to Bogdanov, when Lenin had apprised himself of the situation, he declared: 'This is not at all what you think, these are organs of revolutionary struggle, you have to win them over and not demand now directly that they accept or don't accept our programme; this is the way to create a general-class revolutionary organisation'.[61] Bogdanov adds that this position of Lenin's did not meet any objections; no ultimatum was presented to the Soviet, and there were no walk-outs of Social Democrats. He also points out that Lenin had the advantage of first encountering the Soviet once its character had become clear; if he had known it when it first appeared it is likely that he would have had difficulty in seeing its significance.[62]

In 1925 a former member of the St Petersburg Soviet, D. Sverchkov, published his memoirs of the 1905 revolution. They contained a foreword by Trotsky, which claimed that in opposition to Lenin's attitude towards the Soviet, that of the St Petersburg Bolsheviks had been hostility towards it, influenced by Bogdanov's 'ultimatumist' views. This idea was repeated by Sverchkov in his comment on Gorin's paper.[63] In reply, Bogdanov reminded Sverchkov that the Bolsheviks had not been alone in their sceptical attitude towards the Soviet; so too had the Mensheviks of the Federative Council. Moreover, no ultimatum had been put before the Soviet for the reasons Bogdanov had explained.[64]

Despite Bogdanov's denials and evidence to the contrary in the shape of the resolution of the Federative Council, the idea of purely Bolshevik opposition to the Soviet, tempered by the arrival of Lenin on the scene, is a common theme in literature on the 1905 revolution.[65] It has an interesting evolution driven by the political in-fighting of the 1920s. It is significant that the idea does not feature in Trotsky's book *1905*, which was published in 1922, at a time when Trotsky was still secure in the Soviet leadership. But with the publication of his essay 'Lessons of October' in 1924, aimed at discrediting the then party leadership for its stance in 1917, Trotsky's own past actions and attitudes were re-interpreted in an unfavourable light. The prime example was Pokrovsky's book on the 1905 revolution, which castigated Trotsky for his revolutionary rhetoric, embodied

---

61   Lenin's conception of the soviets was: 'The experience of October–December gave the most instructive indication in their regard. The soviets of workers' deputies are the organs of mass direct struggle. They quickly became under pressure of necessity organs of general revolutionary struggle against the government'. See Lenin 1958–65, 13, p. 320.

62   Bogdanov 1926, pp. 223–4.

63   Gorin 1926, p. 219.

64   Bogdanov 1926, p. 223.

65   See Schwarz 1967, p. 181; Ascher 1988, p. 220; Deutscher 1970, p. 125.

in his theory of 'permanent revolution', contrasted with his opportunistic tactics in the Petersburg Soviet; he had not used his position on the Soviet to launch an armed uprising against the tsarist regime. Trotsky's reply to this charge was contained in his foreword to Sveichkov's book. There he criticised the tactics of the Bolshevik leadership towards the Soviet, and claimed that the party was useless without the guidance of Lenin, whose follower he, Trotsky, professed to be.

When Trotsky came to write his autobiography in 1930, he was able to make explicit the parallel between the haplessness of the Bolsheviks without Lenin both in 1905 and in 1917. He says as follows:

> The part of the Bolshevik Central Committee then in St. Petersburg resolutely opposed an elected non-party organization because it was afraid of competition with the party. At the same time, the Bolshevik workers were entirely free of this fear. The sectarian attitude of the Bolshevik leaders towards the Soviet lasted until Lenin's arrival in Russia in November. One could write an instructive chapter on the leadership of the 'Leninists' without Lenin. The latter towered so high above his nearest disciples that in his presence they felt that there was no need of their solving theoretical and tactical problems independently. When they happened to be separated from Lenin at a critical moment, one is struck by their helplessness. This was the case in the autumn of 1905. It was also the case in the spring of 1917.[66]

Here Trotsky is adjusting the facts in order to make a political point. It misrepresents Bogdanov's attitude to the Soviet and also his attitude towards Lenin, whom he would never have regarded as an 'authority'. Trotsky, on the other hand, is engaged in the exercise of trying to prove that at critical junctures in the Russian revolution his ideas coincided with those of Lenin, as did those of no other Bolshevik. That is, Trotsky's argument takes the cult of Lenin as its starting point. For Bogdanov, however, whether Lenin agreed with him or not on theoretical matters had very little significance.

On the question of the role of the Soviets Bogdanov and Lenin did agree in 1905. Both considered that the Soviets should be regarded as organs of revolutionary struggle. Though Lenin changed his mind on the matter in 1917, Bogdanov continued to regard the Soviets in this same light. As for Trotsky, Ian Thatcher remarks that he did not develop an elaborate and sophisticated theory of the Soviets and their role in the revolution. It was even unclear what rela-

---

66   Trotsky 1930, 1, p. 202.

tionship he thought that the Soviets would have with a constituent assembly, which remained one of his key demands. They did not become a central part of his outlook and thinking.[67]

2   Novaia Zhizn

Under pressure of the general strike, on 17 October the tsarist government issued a manifesto granting fundamental civil liberties: freedoms of speech, the press and assembly and association and amending the law of 6 August by extending the franchise to groups excluded from participation in elections to the State Duma. In reply the Soviet set out its own programme; this included demands for a democratic republic, the convocation of a constituent assembly and an amnesty for political prisoners. Similar demands were made by Bogdanov on behalf of the Central Committee of the RSDLP, though he added the arming of the people and the abolition of the division of the population into estates.[68]

One of the results of the publication of the manifesto of 17 October is that newspapers could now be published without censorship. Bogdanov and his associates took advantage of this new freedom to publish the newspaper *Novaia Zhizn* in St Petersburg, which promoted the cause of the RSDLP majority. It was liberally financed by Gorky, and in order to avoid the lengthy process of applying for a publication licence, it was decided to purchase a newspaper to which a license had already been granted. Such a newspaper was in the possession of a group of 'decadent' writers, including I.L. Minsky, Z.N. Gippius and N.A. Teffi. They had abundant contributors to their newspaper, but no funds. An agreement was made by which Gorky and his associates would have political control of the newspaper but the 'decadents' would be able to publish their writings and the editors would be paid generous salaries.[69] According to Liadov, the editorial offices of *Novaia Zhizn* were in luxuriously-appointed premises on Nevsky Prospekt, with a uniformed commissionaire at the entrance. Liadov records that Bogdanov shared his misgivings about working with Minsky and his friends, but it seemed to him that there was no alternative. Rumiantsev, on the other hand, was enthusiastic about the collaboration with the 'decadents' and about the high salaries to be assigned to the members of the editorial

---

67   Thatcher 2005, pp. 247–8.
68   Listovki Bol'shevistskikh organizatsii v pervoi Russkoi revoliutsii 1905–1907 gg. 1956, 1, p. 184.
69   Liadov 1956, p. 112.

board. In the event, when *Novaia Zhizn* appeared on 27 October it was a great success, achieving a circulation of 80,000 copies, an unprecedented figure for the times.[70]

V.A. Desnitsky recalls the atmosphere in which *Novaia Zhizn* was published:

> After arriving in St Petersburg I met with the comrades of the editorial board of *Novaia Zhizn*, where P.P. Rumiantsev presided and where there was a constant commotion and the newspaper public jostled each other, and there the St Petersburg comrades scurried about on the business of the local organisation. People came here from the provinces too. You could hear the joyful exclamations of people who had met previously only in exile, in prisons and in fleeting encounters at rendezvous in safe houses. The joyful intoxication of a revolutionary spring, of the unexpected 'legalisation' of people, their real names and relationships, made impossible business-like meetings and sessions on the premises of the editorial board.[71]

The necessity of finding a suitable meeting place arose when Lenin arrived in St Petersburg at the beginning of November and questions of tactics had to be discussed. Rumiantsev initially proposed meeting at one of the more expensive restaurants in the capital, and when Bogdanov and Desnitsky expressed surprise at the choice, Rumiantsev assured them that this was the practice of the editorial board of *Nachalo*, the newspaper of the 'minority' group whose leading light was Trotsky. It was decided not to follow this example and the meeting was held at Gorky's flat, with Bogdanov, Lenin, Rumiantsev, Krasin, Gorky, Liadov and Desnitsky in attendance. Lenin insisted that the contract with Minsky and the 'decadents' should be broken, that they should be expelled from the editorial board, and that the editorial board should be taken over entirely by the Social Democrats. It was Lenin's contention that *Novaia Zhizn* was a party organ and there was no room on it, especially in its directing centre, for people who had nothing to do with the party. It was an argument to which Bogdanov offered no opposition, and it fell to Rumiantsev to break the news to the 'decadents'.

On 23 November *Novaia Zhizn* was one of the newspapers that carried the Soviet's 'financial manifesto' urging non-payment of taxes and the withdrawal of gold. The tactic was effective and alarmed the government, especially as the Soviet leaders were preparing for an armed uprising. The government resolved

---

70   Liadov 1956, pp. 112–13.
71   Desnitskii 1940, p. 27.

to take action, and on 26 November Khrustalev-Nosar, the chairman of the Petersburg Soviet, was arrested. The authorities had judged rightly that the revolutionary tide was on the ebb since no wave of strikes accompanied the arrest. Trotsky, Khrustalev's successor as chairman of the Petersburg Soviet, abandoned the call to armed insurrection in his public pronouncements.[72] On 2 December the entire Soviet Executive Committee was arrested, including Bogdanov, who remained in prison until May 1906.

In his memoirs, V.D. Bonch-Bruevich, who was present in St Petersburg during the 1905 revolution, gives his verdict on Bogdanov as a revolutionary leader. He remarks:

> There were times – such as, for example, in 1905 after 9 January – when in Russia the direct leadership of the party belonged entirely to Bogdanov, and his authority among our most active ranks, among the underground members, was really enormous. When I was an illegal activist for six months during 1905 I had the chance to observe him in action as a leader, and his performance in that role was excellent.[73]

While Bogdanov was in prison the tsarist regime began to restore order in the country in a most ruthless fashion. Punitive expeditions were sent into the Baltic provinces to suppress the rebellions there. These acted with great ferocity as they proceeded through the country, shooting from ten to thirty people in each village and flogging hundreds more. The members of peasants' committees and people's militias, and all who were suspected of being agitators were hanged.

In December an attempted armed uprising in Moscow was easily crushed. Despite appeals by the Social Democrats to go over to the side of the people, the soldiers in Moscow showed little inclination to rebellion, and did not scruple to fire on the local inhabitants. Additional troops were dispatched to Moscow from St Petersburg, and from the newly pacified Baltic provinces. Under artillery bombardment even the workers of Presnia, the most militant area of Moscow, were forced to succumb.[74]

Following the suppression of the December uprising, punitive expeditions began in the Russian provinces. Field courts martial were established by the prime minister Peter Stolypin. These meted out summary justice to those found guilty of terrorism or violent political crime. Between their establishment on

---

72   Pokrovsky 1933, 2, pp. 184–5.
73   Bonch-Bruevich 1961, 2, p. 357.
74   Tscherewanin 1908, pp. 96–124.

19 August 1906 and their abolition in April 1907 the field courts imposed over a thousand death sentences.

In order to undermine the peasant commune, as the institution that had organised the peasant movement in the central Russian provinces during the revolution, Stolypin issued a decree on 9 November 1906, giving the peasants the right to leave the commune freely. Every householder who held allotment lands was given the right to demand that his share of the land should be accorded to him as private property. The end result that Stolypin envisaged was the reconstruction of Russian agriculture on the West European model. In the process the peasant solidarity that had sustained peasant uprisings would be diluted if not destroyed. As Bogdanov was to predict, the Stolypin reform ran out of impetus long before it had accomplished its desired result.[75]

3   Revolution and Philosophy

In an article entitled 'Revolution and Philosophy' published in 1906 Bogdanov reflected on what revolution and philosophy had in common. Both were processes by which contradictions were overcome. In the case of the Russian revolution this was the contradiction between the enormous growth of the social division of labour and the development of machine production on the one hand and the stubborn immobility of the semi-feudal state and judiciary, on the other. When the revolutionary storm breaks it destroys everything that stands in the way of the emerging social order. And with the new order a new cycle of historical movement begins which will again culminate in social upheaval. This cycle continues until such time as there erupts the final revolution, in which the antagonistic struggle of classes is replaced by the harmonious development of a system of universal cooperation. For Bogdanov revolution has the function of harmonising human existence.

Like revolution, philosophy too is a means of overcoming contradictions and establishing harmony. The contradiction here was the lack of correspondence between the rational and humane principles which people believed ought to govern their lives and the injustice and inhumanity which characterised actual human relationships. The exploiting classes in society benefited from its irrationality and injustice, whereas, on the side of the exploited classes, the industrial proletariat in its struggle with nature gradually extended the realm of reason and justice in society. The industrial proletariat introduced a new

---

75   Pokrovsky 1933, 2, pp. 279–97.

world outlook which was able to eradicate the contradiction between people's social outlook and their social experience. The contradiction was resolved by Marx's social philosophy, which held that it was not people's consciousness that determined their social being, but their social being that determined their consciousness.[76] This realisation eliminated everything that was absolute in perception. Marx's philosophy eliminated fetishism from perception and made possible an integrated view of the world corresponding to people's actual experience.

Thus, in Bogdanov's view, revolution and philosophy in their respective spheres, in 'practice' and in 'perception', both performed the function of harmonising the developing content of life with its general forms. The inseparable connection between both spheres in the social-labour process created a close dependence in the business of implementing both tasks.[77]

The conception of revolution in this article has close similarities with that in his pre-1905 writings. Revolution is seen as a process of alignment of the political and ideological superstructure with the social base of society. The implication is that this conception of revolution is the one that Bogdanov had in the actual Russian revolution of 1905. The aim of the revolution, in Bogdanov's view, is to eliminate relations of exploitation and replace them with relations of harmony and cooperation. The social class that Bogdanov has designated as the bearer of these new relations, and also of the non-fetishised, integral view of the world, is the industrial proletariat. Given this idea, it is not surprising that Bogdanov should think in terms of preserving the proletarian character of the workers' movement, and that he should try to embody this principle in practical politics.

Implied in this article is that the form relations of cooperation will take in the future society will be of the 'synthetic' type, in which the domination/subordination division will be overcome. Furthermore, Bogdanov believed that the party organisation that brought about synthetic relations should also itself be of a synthetic type. He conceded, though, that in the existing social context the voluntary submission of the party members to the leader would be unavoidable. It is in this light that one should view Bogdanov's efforts in 1905 to make the RSDLP more democratic and its leaders more answerable to the party members. In these respects Bogdanov acted in practice in accordance with what he had advocated in his theoretical writings. Bogdanov the revolutionary was consistent with Bogdanov the philosopher.

---

76   Bogdanov 1906, p. 274.
77   Bogdanov 1906, p. 279.

Empiriomonism

1 Empiriocriticism

Between 1904 and 1906 Bogdanov published a three-volume series of essays under the general title of *Empiriomonism*. Two essays in the first volume, 'The Ideal of Perception'[1] and 'Life and the Psyche',[2] had already appeared in *Voprosy filosofii i psikhologii* in 1903, while Bogdanov was still in Vologda. These essays, however, had more of an abstract character, and had no obvious connection with the polemics that took place there.

At the heart of 'The Ideal of Perception' is the aspiration that Bogdanov had set out in *Perception from the Historical Point of View*: that is, to show that all methods of scientific explanation were logically subordinated to the principle of the conservation of energy.[3] Since the most prominent current of thought among the opponents of this idea was the empiriocritical school of Mach and Avenarius, Bogdanov felt compelled to define his philosophical standpoint in relation to this school. This was, Bogdanov explained, the most modern form of positivism which had been developed on the basis of the latest methods of natural science, on the one hand, and the latest forms of philosophical criticism, on the other. It was gaining an increasing number of adherents among the young representatives of both science and philosophy.[4]

Bogdanov went on to explain that the aim of Mach and Avenarius was to eliminate everything that was not experience from perception. This kind of perception was not just adaptation in general, but social adaptation, something that was emphasised by both thinkers. He quoted Mach as saying that 'Science arose from the needs of practical life ... from technology'. This, Bogdanov insisted, corresponded exactly to the principle of historical materialism, proof that empiriocriticism was a deeply progressive current of thought.[5]

Having set out briefly the ideas of Mach and Avenarius, taking care to emphasise that Mach's 'sensations' should not be regarded as purely subjective entities, Bogdanov stated what he considered to be the advantages of empiri-

1 Bogdanov 1903.
2 Bogdanov 1903a.
3 Bogdanov 1901, p. 4.
4 Bogdanov 2003, p. 5.
5 Bogdanov 2003, p. 6.

ocriticism as a system of philosophy. They were that it was deeply rooted in the discoveries of modern science, that it was distinguished from naive realism by the analytical and critical attitude towards all content of experience, that it was alien to any kind of idealism, that it did not recognise the reality of any ideas that went beyond sensation. Nor had empiriocriticism anything to do with materialism or spiritualism, or with any kind of metaphysics; for it both matter and spirit were only complexes of elements.[6]

Although empiriocriticism had succeeded in resolving everything physical and psychical into complexes of elements, the question still remained whether it had succeeded in constructing a system that was truly monist. Bogdanov thought that it had not; in Avenarius's system, with its dependent and independent series, dualism of the psychical and the physical had only acquired a new form. The task that Bogdanov had set himself was to overcome this kind of dualism and establish a system that would be truly monist.[7]

2   The Meaning of Objectivity

In order to do this, Bogdanov began by defining the characteristics of the physical and the psychical as 'objective' and 'subjective' respectively. He then proceeded to examine what the criteria for objectivity were. It might be said that the criterion of objectivity was something that was constant and stable in our experience. But this would not suffice: the fleeting shape taken on by a cloud at a given moment had to be judged as objective, whereas the more constant and repeated perception of the sun's moving across the sky was a subjective impression.

Another definition of objectivity might be to say that those phenomena on which we could base our actions without encountering contradictions were objective. Physical bodies with their properties were objective, because we, in taking these bodies for reality and using their properties, can do this successfully, without contradiction. But for Bogdanov, this definition too was insufficient, since it applied to individual as opposed to collective experience.

It was possible for individuals in the course of their lives to espouse very subjective views, but because of the narrowness of their range of experience, they would never encounter perceptible contradictions. A peasant who never left his village might imagine that the world was a flat disc, that the sky was

6   Bogdanov 2003, p. 12.
7   Bogdanov 2003, p. 13.

a blue crystal arc, and that the sun was a shining circle that traversed the sky each day. Yet the harmony of his life would not be adversely affected by these subjective views. No doubt drawing on his experience as a psychiatric doctor, Bogdanov also gave the example of paranoids, who constructed unreal worlds inhabited by non-existent people, usually their persecutors. And although such paranoids did not come up against facts which cast doubt on the reality of their constructions, these could hardly be considered objective.[8]

3   Universal Validity

The conclusion Bogdanov arrived at was that the criterion of objectivity could not be in individual experience; this had to lie in the sphere of collective experience. For him what counted as objective were those data of experience which have an identical vital significance for ourselves and for other people. Here Bogdanov introduces his concept of 'universal validity' (*obshcheznachimost'*), the criterion of objectivity.

> We call objective those data of experience which have the same vital significance for us and for other people, those data on which not only we without contradiction build our activity, but on which must, according to our conviction, other people base it too, in order not to encounter contradiction. The objective character of the physical world consists in the fact that it exists not for me personally, but for all, and for all has a definite significance, the same as it has for me. The objectivity of the physical series – this is its universal validity.[9]

Subjective experience, on the other hand, was that which lacked 'universal validity'; it had significance only for one or a number of individuals.

As an illustration of how the collective coordination of experience operated, Bogdanov gave the example of how the abstract concepts of space and time were evolved. The space that is experienced by individuals is always finite and heterogeneous; it differs from place to place and in the manner in which it is perceived. Abstract space, on the other hand, is homogeneous and is infinite in its extent. As Bogdanov showed by reference to the ancient writers such as Aristotle and Epicurus, who did not have the concept, abstract space had come about through historical development.

---

8 Bogdanov 2003, p. 14.
9 Bogdanov 2003, p. 15.

Similarly, with regard to abstract time, this was the product of social evolution. Time as experienced by individuals was heterogeneous; sometimes passing faster, sometimes slower; it also appeared to have finite duration. Primitive peoples were apt to imagine that the sun sometimes speeded up and sometimes slowed down as it moved across the sky. As they were animists, they imagined that natural phenomena acted in the same way as they did themselves. But over considerable time, the effect of the countless 'utterances' (here Bogdanov uses Avenarius's term) of other people in supplementing and coordinating the limited experience of individuals, produced the concept of abstract time, a concept which has universal validity. The conclusion Bogdanov drew from this was that the abstract forms of space and time constituted 'socially-organised experience'.[10]

4   Socially-Organised Experience and Individually-Organised Experience

For Bogdanov 'socially-organised experience' was the ultimate test of objectivity of phenomena. The objectivity of physical bodies we encounter in our experience is established in the final analysis by the mutual checking and coordination of the utterances of different people. The physical world in general is socially-coordinated, socially-harmonised, socially-organised experience. It is inseparable from abstract space and time, the basic forms in which socially-organised experience is expressed.

For Bogdanov, consequently, the physical world consists of socially-organised experience. The realm of the psyche, on the other hand, consists of the inner experiences of a single person, and these do not have universal validity for other people. Psychical experience, however, is not entirely unorganised and chaotic; it possesses a certain coherence, since the elements which compose it, the sensations, impressions, aspirations, etc. are grouped by association into the complex which is designated by the word 'I'. In this way even the psychical experience is organised, though this is not socially, but individually-organised experience

With his conception of socially- and individually-organised experience Bogdanov has departed from Avenarius's presentation of the physical and psychical realms as an independent and a dependent series respectively. Expressed in Avenarius's terms, the contrast Bogdanov draws is between the series depend-

---

10   Bogdanov 2003, pp. 17–20.

ent on the 'congregal' (social) series and the series dependent on the individual System c. He has resolved the problem of duality which he found in Avenarius's system, in that for Bogdanov the difference between the physical and the psychical realms is reduced to the different ways in which experience can be organised: socially and individually.[11]

Having re-formulated the physical-psychical relationship in terms of organisational forms, Bogdanov could then examine the significance of these forms and how they were likely to develop in the future. He could note that there were cases where one could observe a mutual correspondence and harmony between the two types of experience, the physical and the psychical, but in other instances the two were in competition and contradiction. There was harmony when the sensations and perceptions corresponded to the things, so that there was no incongruity between them. Contradiction between the two types of organisation occurred when the sensations and representations did not correspond to the things: when there was an illusion, a misunderstanding, a lapse of memory etc.[12]

Bogdanov explained that dualism occurred not because there were two types of organisation, but because the two types were not united in harmony. The organisation of the cell on the one hand and the organisation of the organism to which it belonged on the other did not constitute a vital dualism; this only arose when the cell began to lead an independent existence, not adapting itself to the organism as a whole. There the absence of harmony would be felt in the reduction of viability either on the part of the cell or of the organism or of both together. Similarly, in experience and perception dualism arose where the individually-organised experience ceased to be an integral part of the socially-organised experience, if the individual experience constituted itself into an independent entity and did not adapt itself harmoniously to the experience that was organised socially.

For Bogdanov, the world of the individual psyche, deprived of wholeness, is turned into a world of contradiction and conflict. Such a person is incapable of coordinating his experience and his actions with the experience and actions of other people, who appear in his consciousness as differently organised entities. He is prey to the contradictions of animism, fetishism and metaphysics. This, for Bogdanov, was precisely the current affliction of the human psyche. The way out of this dualist situation is through the systematic adaptation of individually-organised experience to the socially-organised, so that the former

---

11   Bogdanov 2003, p. 22.
12   Bogdanov 2003, p. 25.

will find a place for itself in the unifying forms of the latter, like a cell in the system of tissues of the organism.[13]

5   Parallelism

Bogdanov now raises the question of in what way perception is capable of carrying out the monist organisation of experience, giving universal reconciliation to its dualist contradictions. To answer this question he examines the connections between the physical and the psychical at the point where they come into closest connection with one another.

Here Bogdanov introduces the principle of 'psycho-physiological parallelism', that is, the idea that there is a constant connection between psychical phenomena and the physiological processes of the nervous system, that a relationship exists in which to each given act of consciousness there is a corresponding change in the nervous system, so that 'parallel' to the series of the facts of consciousness there unfolds a series of simultaneous physiological nervous processes which are in inseparable and constant connection with them.

Bogdanov concedes that this is an idea which is very close to Avenarius's conception of the 'functional dependence' in which the psychical, or 'Series E', stands in relation to the central nervous apparatus, or 'System C'. He emphasises, however, that he has no need for the concept of introjection, which Avenarius finds necessary. Bogdanov, after all, explains distortions of perception by the imperfect coordination of individually-organised and socially organised experience.

The conclusion Bogdanov reaches is that if in its attempt to harmonise experience perception is consistent and faithful to the method it has elaborated, it has to connect the psychical and the neuro-physiological series in a single 'process', as a whole; not psychical and not physiological, but psychophysiological. For Bogdanov the function of perception is the formation of integral complexes, which are not given to it directly, but constructed out of the multiplicity of elements of experience. In relation to physical complexes, this had long since been accomplished in the history of mankind through the application of the law of the conservation of energy; in relation to the psychophysiological it had still to be achieved.[14]

---

13   Bogdanov 2003, pp. 28–33.
14   Bogdanov 2003, p. 30.

According to Bogdanov, perception of the physical world in recent times had become in the highest degree monist. Physical phenomena in all their infinity, complexity and variety had been subsumed in all-embracing formulae, which increasingly harmonised experience. Such formulae as the law of the conservation of energy abstracted from immediate perception and in the process the world of 'elements' gave way to the world of 'relations'. It remained to apply this principle in the realm of psychical experience. It would require that perception abstract from the particular means of perception. The one and the same perceptive whole – the psycho-physiological process – could be apprehended by different means, but for perception they would remain one and the same. The difference of the elements would disappear in the unity of relations, and the unity of perception would be maintained. The difference between 'physical' and 'psychical' would disappear. This single world of experience Bogdanov called 'Empiriomonism'.

Bogdanov concluded the article by explaining why it was that empiriomonism had so far not been achieved. This was because of the fragmented nature of modern society with its domination-subordination divide, the division of labour, class antagonisms, the conflict of interests and competition. When people came into conflict with one another they did not fully coordinate and harmonise their experience. The division of labour, moreover, ensured that one specialist did not understand another. It was an analysis of modern society that Bogdanov would elaborate in 'The Integration of Mankind' and in other works of the period.

6   Life and the Psyche

In the following article, 'Life and the Psyche', Bogdanov elaborated on the arguments he had deployed against the dualist viewpoint, adapting for his purpose some of the terminology used by Avenarius. In examining the way in which perception had evolved he took up Avenarius's example of the child in the womb, where there were no stimuli from the environment. Bogdanov was in agreement with Avenarius that the sum of experience, the richness of impressions, were determined by the relationship of the organism to the environment. Where there was complete equilibrium there were no impressions; it was the difference in the concentration of energy that gave both life and perception. Bogdanov wished to emphasise that these two things were inseparable, and that it was a matter of prejudice to imagine that there could be life without experiences, that impressions were only epiphenomenal to life.

Drawing on Avenarius's idea that there were some elements of the environment that did not attract the attention of the consciousness (*tote Werte*, dead values), and his own experience as a psychiatric practitioner, Bogdanov argued that the distinction between the 'centres of consciousness' and the 'centres of unconscious reaction' was not a valid one. Moreover, a nerve cell was the result of development and differentiation of a cell in the embryo, and the entire phycho-physical organism was the result of the evolution of a single cell of the protozoan type. And development did not create anything new in essence; it only created new and more complex combinations from elements already in existence. Therefore, Bogdanov concluded, where there is a living cell we must accept that it has something in principle in common with our psychical experiences. There could, in other words, be no life without experiences; there could be no purely physiological life.[15]

As far as the inorganic world was concerned, Bogdanov believed that it was only the capacity of the human mind for abstraction that made it possible to view it as 'lifeless'. Yet this was something that contradicted experience, since this inorganic nature was an essential part of human life.[16] In Bogdanov's view, what distinguished inorganic world from living nature was not the material from which it was composed (the same 'elements' which were the elements of experience), but its lack of organisation, or to be more precise, its lower level of organisation.[17]

In Bogdanov's opinion, the materialist viewpoint had come near to scientific truth, but it had not gone far enough. Instead of espousing the two constituent elements of experience, the physical and the psychical, it had posited complexes called 'matter'. Nevertheless, materialism was more objective and positive than the spiritualist current, though insufficiently objective and positive. Here the truth was not in the 'golden mean' between the two warring parties, but in an area outside them both. In Bogdanov's opinion, the progressive thinking of the times had much the same attitude towards the struggle between materialism and spiritualism as to the struggle that was once carried on between Protestantism and Catholicism. Considering one of them to be 'more true' than the other could not be satisfactory.[18]

15   Bogdanov 2003, p. 55.
16   Bogdanov 2003, p. 54.
17   Bogdanov 2003, p. 78.
18   Bogdanov 2003, p. 54.

7   The First Volume of *Empiriomonism*

The articles contained in the first volume of *Empiriomonism* give a full account of Bogdanov's philosophical views at the time of his return from exile in Vologda. They show a high degree of continuity with his two previous books, *Studies in the Historical Viewpoint* and *Perception from a Historical Point of View*, but also the strong influence of the empiriocritics, Avenarius in particular. In the introduction to 'The Ideal of Perception', Bogdanov alludes to what the attraction of Avenarius and Mach was for him. He describes it as the most modern form of positivism incorporating the latest developments in natural science and the latest forms of philosophical criticism. This fusion of natural science and philosophy was characteristic of Bogdanov's own approach, which his training in medicine and the natural sciences made him well qualified to adopt.

Avenarius supplied some of the concepts and vocabulary that Bogdanov would later use to express his own ideas, but these were seldom adopted in their existing form. Avenarius's concepts of 'nourishment' and 'work', for example, became for Bogdanov 'assimilation' and 'disassimilation'. Moreover, Bogdanov did not accept the ideas of Avenarius and Mach uncritically, one important consideration here being that he wanted to modify them to accommodate the energeticist views of Ostwald. However, *Empiriomonism* also shows that Bogdanov was in the process of moving away from the conception that energy was the force that united all phenomena, and approaching the view that the factor common to all types of experience was 'organisation'.

8   Akselrod-Ortodoks's Criticism

The first volume of *Empiriomonism* also has the distinction of being the only one not influenced by the polemic with Plekhanov and his supporters. Soon after its publication in 1904 there appeared an article in *Iskra* by Liubov Akselrod, who wrote under the pseudonym of 'Ortodoks', entitled 'A New Variant of Revisionism'. The article attacked Bogdanov's writings for their allegedly anti-Marxist character.[19] In this it was politically motivated. At the time of the alliance between Lenin and Bogdanov against the Mensheviks, Plekhanov wanted to cause friction between the allies by embarrassing Lenin by his association with the heretical Bogdanov, while at the same time discrediting Bogdanov by emphasising his departures from Marxist orthodoxy.

---

19   Aksel'rod 1904.

Ortodoks accordingly prefaced her article by some reminiscences about how her article had originated. She said that about a year and a half previously she had been approached by Lenin to write a refutation of the criticism of Marx's theory contained in the works of 'Mr (*gospodin*) Bogdanov'. In this connection Lenin had informed her that he had previously approached Plekhanov to write such a refutation, but he had been too preoccupied with party matters to take on the task. Ortodoks had promised Lenin that she would do it at the first opportunity. This episode showed clearly, she said, that Marxists immediately recognised the alien character of the combination of empiriocriticism with the materialist interpretation of history and considered it their party duty to oppose it. However, urgent party work had for a time taken up Ortodoks's attention. It was the appearance of Bogdanov's two books: *Empiriomonism* and the collection of essays *From the Psychology of Society*, that had finally stirred her into action.[20]

The implication of these reminiscences was that at the present time Lenin was allied with a person whose ideas he had previously thought it essential to refute. There was also the suggestion that a salient feature of Bogdanov's works was a criticism of Marx's theory, whereas in fact Marx was seldom mentioned by Bogdanov, and then invariably in positive terms.

In order to avoid possible misunderstandings, Ortodoks defined carefully what the scope of her article was. It was obvious, she said, that within the limits of a newspaper article it would not be possible for her to give a full exposition and substantial critique of empiriomonism; her aim was exclusively to show in general and brief outlines to what extent empiriomonism contradicted the materialist interpretation of history, and 'to what degree the views of Mr Bogdanov, as an adherent of the doctrine, had nothing in common with the theory of Marx and Engels'.[21]

This paragraph is a significant one, because it set a precedent for how Bogdanov's ideas would be subsequently treated by Plekhanov and his followers. On the one hand there would be no meaningful exposition of them, and there would be no substantive critique of them, but on the other there would be the very categorical judgement that they 'had nothing in common with the theory of Marx and Engels'.

Of course, to give a coherent account of Bogdanov's ideas, to examine them critically and to investigate how they related to Marx's system would have been a formidable enterprise. And any such critique would certainly have elicited

---

20   Aksel'rod 1906, p. 171.
21   Aksel'rod 1906, p. 172.

a reply from Bogdanov, which, as his polemic with Berdyaev had shown, was likely to carry the day. It was therefore necessary to contrive a device by which a real discussion of Bogdanov's ideas could be avoided. The method Ortodoks used, which was followed by her successors, was to equate Bogdanov's ideas with the empiriocriticism of Mach and Avenarius. And since Mach and Avenarius were in agreement, it could be claimed that Bogdanov had taken his ideas from Mach. This was convenient, since Mach's formulations lacked the precision of Avenarius's and could be subject to misinterpretation, especially if liberties were taken with the translation of his words.

Ortodoks began by drawing attention to the passage in Bogdanov's article 'The Development of Life in Nature and Society' where he observed that the formulation of historical materialism as it had been presented in Marx's *Zur Kritik der politischen Oekonomie* had become significantly dated and lacked completeness and precision. It did not explain the function of ideology in society and why it was necessary. Since, Ortodoks suggested, Bogdanov proposed to supplement Marx's formulation with empiriomonism, it was necessary to examine the validity of this new 'revision' of Marx's theory.

Ortodoks, however, did not proceed immediately to examine empiriomonism; instead she began to discuss Avenarius's system. This, she said, consisted of two basic principles. The first one was the biological principle of the struggle for survival, the main driving force of perception being the adaptation for this struggle. The second principle was the need to divest all perception from metaphysical and dogmatic presuppositions. The analysis of perception revealed that it consisted of the totality of people's opinions. From the sum of these utterances general scientific experience was constructed. From this Ortodoks concluded that in Avenarius's theory the perceptive real subject had been eliminated from the field of experience.[22]

This was not a summary of Avenarius's views, but a rather garbled account of what Bogdanov had said in his *Empiriomonism*, using Avenarius as a framework. Clearly, Ortodoks did not feel comfortable in the territory of the *Critique of Pure Experience* or *The Human World Outlook*. Her escape route was by the declaration that: 'Avenarius's theory is completely identical in its internal content with the world view of Mach'.[23] According to Ortodoks, the central point of Mach's philosophy, as for Avenarius's, was the critique and rejection of the perceived external object. She demonstrated this with the passage from Mach's *Analysis of Sensations*: 'Thing, body, matter are nothing apart from the sensa-

---

22   Aksel'rod 1906, p. 173.
23   Ibid.

tions of colour, sound etc. apart from the so-called attributes'. This sounded as though Mach's point of view was indeed subjectivist. But in fact, what Mach had written was: 'Thing, body, matter are nothing apart from the combination of elements, of the colours, sounds etc. nothing apart from their so-called attributes'.[24] And since Mach's conception of elements was of something that combined subjectivity and objectivity, Ortodoks's version was a misrepresentation of Mach's position.

This was followed by a second quotation, intended by Ortodoks also to prove Mach's subjectivist approach. This was: 'It is not bodies that cause our sensations, but the totality of elements of our sensations that constitute bodies. If it seems to a physicist that bodies are something stable and real, and sensations are something fleeting and evanescent, he overlooks the fact that all "bodies" are only symbols which are the product of our thinking to designate the totality of our sensations'. In this case what Mach actually said was: 'Bodies do not produce sensations, but complexes of elements (complexes of sensations) constitute bodies. If it appears to the physicist that bodies are stable, real, while "elements" seem fleeting and transient, he overlooks the fact that all "bodies" are only thought symbols for complexes of elements (complexes of sensations)'.[25] Besides distorting Mach's words to get him to say what she wanted him to say, Ortodoks had also omitted to explain the particular way in which Mach used the term 'sensations'.

According to Ortodoks, the quotations she had adduced showed beyond any doubt that for Bogdanov it was not being that determined consciousness, but, on the contrary, consciousness that determined being, an approach that was completely at odds with that of Marx and Engels. She emphasised that Marx and Engels took nature and its processes for a reality that existed outside our consciousness and independent of it. It was a conception that had prompted the founders of scientific socialism to break completely with idealism. To show that Bogdanov did not share the materialist viewpoint of Marx and Engels, Ortodoks quoted Bogdanov as saying:

> Nor has empiriomonism anything to do with either materialism or spiritualism, or with any kind of metaphysics in general: both matter and spirit for it are only complexes of elements (the totality of sensations L.A.). And any kind of 'essence' and any kind of perception beyond experience are terms without content, empty abstractions.[26]

---

24   Mach 1903, p. 5.
25   Mach 1903, p. 23.
26   Aksel'rod 1906, p. 177.

Here too Ortodoks had manipulated the quotation to suit her purposes. In this instance Bogdanov was speaking of empiriocriticism, not empiriomonism, and the editorial insertion of the words 'totality of sensations' served to distort Bogdanov's meaning and misrepresent the arguments of Avenarius and Mach

In Bogdanov's article 'The Development of Life in Nature and Society', Ortodoks seized upon the paragraph which stated that:

> Individual people, even taken as a totality, do not yet constitute society. In the concept of 'society' there is contained the idea of organisation, uniting the vital compatibility of individuals. In this way, in order for the word 'society' to have any sense there has to be a certain organising adaptation. This adaptation is – the social instinct.[27]

While Ortodoks agreed that the word 'society' implied organisation, she objected to the idea that the primary cause of social organisation should be the psychological factor of the social instinct. She went on to say that historical materialism opposed precisely this idealist view of history; that in fact society arose in the course of people's struggle with nature. Here in her support she quoted a passage to this effect taken from the writings of her mentor Plekhanov. She insisted that from the point of view of dialectical materialism, social being was not identical with social consciousness, as Bogdanov had argued.[28]

Ortodoks concluded her article by declaring that idealism in philosophy was the concomitant of social conservatism. She believed Bogdanov to be more an adherent of the subjective method in sociology rather than of historical materialism. She thought his theory of empiriomonism no more than a new variant of the 'critique' of Marx's theory.[29]

Bogdanov did not reply to Ortodoks's cticicisms in any special article of his own, but he did refer to what she had said in footnotes in the third volume of *Empiriomonism* and in later editions of *From the Psychology of Society*. In the case of her calling the social instinct a psychological factor, he pointed out that she had confused psychology with ideology and so had obscured his meaning. Bogdanov offered Ortodoks three pieces of advice: 1. in order to discuss philosophy it was necessary first to find out something about it. 2. To criticise something effectively, one had actually to read it through. 3. One should not distort the ideas of an opponent, because although it wonderfully facilitated

---

27   Bogdanov 1906, p. 66. See above.
28   Aksel'rod 1906, p. 178.
29   Aksel'rod 1906, p. 185.

the task of refutation, such distortions would be discovered when the opponent got round to checking up.[30]

According to Nikolai Valentinov, Martov, as an editor of *Iskra*, had been against publishing Ortodoks's article. He thought it weak in content and unconvincing in its charges against the philosophical trend represented by Bogdanov. Plekhanov, however, had insisted on its publication, and to please him, Akselrod and Zasulich had agreed.[31]

9   The Second Volume of *Empiriomonism*

The second volume of *Empiriomonism* which was published in 1905 appeared too early to make any reference to Ortodoks's article, but it did contain material which could not have pleased Plekhanov. In its first chapter Bogdanov discussed the Kantian 'thing-in-itself' from the point of view of *Empiriomonism*. Since Plekhanov had recently endorsed this Kantian concept, the subject was potentially a sensitive one. However, for Bogdanov the need to examine the significance of the 'thing-in-itself' arose quite independently of any polemical considerations, in the course of introducing the idea of 'substitution'.

Bogdanov explained that he believed Kant's 'thing-in-itself' to be a distant and more abstract development of animism, the practice of primitive peoples to explain natural phenomena by attributing to them 'souls' and human volitions. Avenarius had interpreted animism as a form of 'introjection', the practice of projecting one's own experience into other things or people. For Avenarius the assumption that one could know the feelings and thoughts of other people was one that ran counter to the principle of pure experience. One could only experience other beings through their physical presence and through their utterances, so that the attribution to them of emotions and thoughts that were equivalent to one's own was not something that could be established by experience alone. For Avenarius, therefore, the act of introjection was a violation of the principles of empiriocriticism, and was responsible for the errors in human perception.

Bogdanov, however, thought that the practice of forming assumptions about the psyches of other people was a necessary element in perception. When on the basis of data communicated by other people, one substituted data of feelings and thoughts, this was entirely legitimate. Though the content of the

---

30   Bogdanov 2003, p. 240.
31   Valentinov 1968, p. 230; Steila 2013, p. 213.

substitution might be wrong or mistaken, the act of substitution itself was valid. Substitution was necessary for the eventual discovery of truth through the social coordination and harmonising of experience. Where Avenarius interpreted animism as introjection, a distortion of experience that would be eliminated in the course of human development, Bogdanov thought of it as an early form of 'substitution', a process that would be perfected through social coordination and organisation.[32]

For Bogdanov, however, the concept of substitution functioned as much more than the equivalent of Avenarius's introjection. In keeping with the monist character of his system, he saw it as extending to the most fundamental levels of existence and perception. Developing the idea of psychical and physiological parallelism that he had elaborated in 'The Ideal of Perception', he argued that for every psychical process there was a physiological equivalent. He considered that every physiological process was 'reflected' in a psychical process that could be 'substituted' for it, if the levels of organisation of the two processes were commensurate.[33] He thought of the relationship between psychical process and its physiological equivalent as of one between the 'reflecting' and the 'reflected', a relationship in which the two entities were equally valid. The psychical part was the one which associated, combined and organised, while the physiological part was the one which underwent changes to become part of the organised whole.[34]

For Bogdanov the empiriomonist viewpoint was one comparable to Mach's conception of elements as having both objective and subjective sides, or as Bogdanov would express it, physiological and psychical sides. The elements could be viewed one way or the other, either as psychical or physiological entities. The complexes of these elements could have very different levels of organisation, from inorganic nature to people's experience. And at all of these levels the physiological could be substituted for the psychical and *vice versa*.

The concept of substitution provided Bogdanov with a means of classifying the viewpoints which preceded empiriomonism. Whereas empiriomonism presupposed the equilibrium of the psychical and physiological processes, in other viewpoints some form of substitution had taken place to make either the psychical take the place of the physiological or the physiological – the psychical.[35]

---

32 Bogdanov 2003, pp. 112–13.
33 Bogdanov 2003, p. 120.
34 Bogdanov 2003, p. 123.
35 Bogdanov 2003, p. 129.

To illustrate the forms in which substitution might appear, Bogdanov gave a historical survey of a number of viewpoints. Animism was a case in which the psychical was substituted for the physical, where the complex human psyche was substituted for that of the phenomena of the natural world. It could be manifested in the personification of natural phenomena, pantheism, panpsychism. The reverse of this type of substitution, the substitution of the physical for the psychical, was where the 'soul' was taken to be a simple repetition of the body. Examples of this type of substitution were the materialistic systems of Democritus, Epicurus and Büchner.

A more modern form of philosophical substitution was the substitution of metaphysics for the physical and the psychical. This was the viewpoint which espoused the 'thing-in-itself', an entity distinct from phenomena, but constituting the cause of the phenomena. To this category belonged the epistemological theories of Holbach, the Kantians and Herbert Spencer.

The most recent type of philosophical substitution was that made by the empiriocritics. Their theories were designed to eliminate metaphysics and achieve objectivity by giving a purely descriptive account of phenomena. Their substitution concerned those facts that were not subject to description, and which they classed as 'undefined'. For Bogdanov this was the substitution of the empirically undefined for the physical, unorganised processes. Empiriomonism, on the other hand, regarded 'undefined' complexes as 'unorganised' and saw in this approach a way of investigating the origins of life, both physiological and psychical, by examining how the more organised complexes emerged from the less organised.[36]

10   Plekhanov's 'Thing-in-Itself'

Having elaborated his conception of substitution, Bogdanov returned to the critique of the 'thing-in-itself'. Whereas Kant and Spencer had regarded the 'thing-in-itself' as absolutely unknowable, the modern version of the theory did not take this extreme position. It thought of the 'thing-in-itself' as different in principle from the phenomenon, but 'vaguely perceived' in the phenomena to which it gave rise. Approximately such a viewpoint, Bogdanov contended, was held by 'the French materialists of the eighteenth century and among the recent philosophers by Engels and his Russian follower Plekhanov'.[37]

---

36   Ibid.
37   Bogdanov 2003, p. 130.

This was an argument to which Plekhanov could not but take exception, because it undermined the interpretation of Marxism that he had elaborated over the years, and on which he had built his reputation as a philosopher. To explain why Plekhanov should incorporate the materialists of the eighteenth century and Kant's 'thing-in-itself' into his version of Marxism it is necessary to give a brief account of Plekhanov's attempt to reconstruct the philosophical dimension of Marx's system of thought.

These attempts were no easy matter for Plekhanov, because in the 1880s when he took up the study of Marx, there was very little material available from which to piece together Marx's philosophical ideas. In fact at that time it was widely believed that Marx's economic scheme had no underlying philosophy. Marxism was commonly referred to as an 'economic materialism', and it was considered that the doctrine needed to be supplemented with the philosophical underpinnings it lacked.[38]

The first piece of evidence that came Plekhanov's way which suggested what the philosophy of Marxism might be was an extract from Marx and Engels's book *The Holy Family* that Karl Kautsky published in the journal *Die neue Zeit* in 1885.[39] As the book was long out of print, Kautsky wanted to give readers of the journal the opportunity to acquaint themselves with at least part of it. The extract he chose, though unrepresentative of the book as a whole, was the only one which formed an independent entity. It was entitled 'French Materialism of the Eighteenth Century' and was a short historical sketch of the various currents in French materialism, including those represented by Holbach and Helvétius.

The extract made a strong impression on Plekhanov, and convinced him that eighteenth-century French materialism was a precursor of Marx's philosophy. One of Plekhanov's chief philosophical works was a book published in 1896 entitled *Essays on the History of Materialism*, which consisted of essays on Holbach, Helvétius and Marx.[40] In many of Plekhanov's philosophical writings one finds references to the French materialists of the eighteenth century in connection with Marx's ideas. It is likely that when Lenin visited him in Switzerland in 1895 Plekhanov recommended that he study *The Holy Family*, because the very full notes from it constitute the first item in Lenin's 'Philosophical Notebooks'. The full text of *The Holy Family* was published in 1902 in a collection of Marx and Engels's early works edited by Franz Mehring.[41] The subsidiary status

---

38   Struve 1894, p. 46; Valentinov 1968, p. 156.
39   Marx 1885.
40   Plekhanov 1896.
41   Mehring 1902.

of the chapter on French materialism then became obvious, making it difficult for Plekhanov to maintain that this current of thought was central to the philosophy of Marxism.

The year after the appearance of the extract from *The Holy Family* Engels published a two-part article in *Die neue Zeit* entitled 'Ludwig Feuerbach and the Outcome of Classical German Philosophy'. Ostensibly the review of a book about Feuerbach, the article provided the occasion for Engels to reminisce about how he and Marx had written their early philosophical works, including *The Holy Family*. It was a primary source which indicated that Marx's scheme had Hegelian origins. But Engels was reminiscing at a distance of over forty years from the events in question, and was unable to give an accurate account of what part Hegelian philosophy had played in the formation of Marx's system. Yet despite its subjective character, Engels's 'Ludwig Feuerbach' was to have a profound influence on how Marx's ideas were understood. This applies especially to the distinction Engels drew between the two camps of philosophy: idealism, which believed in the primacy of spirit over nature; and materialism, which maintained the primacy of nature over spirit.

In 1888 Engels published his two *Die neue Zeit* articles as a separate pamphlet, adding as an appendix the notes Marx had made on Feuerbach in 1845 – the famous 'Theses on Feuerbach'. Engels's *Ludwig Feuerbach* was to be an important influence on Plekhanov's conception of Marxist philosophy. In 1892 he published a Russian translation of Engels's pamphlet provided with explanatory notes. In the note which dealt with Engels's rejection of Kant's theory of knowledge, Plekhanov made a concession to Kant by saying that human sensations resembled hieroglyphics, in the sense that they did not resemble the reality that they conveyed, though they did convey faithfully the events themselves and the relations between them. This was an idea that Plekhanov was to disavow in the edition of the pamphlet published in 1905.[42]

In 1889 Lev Tikhomirov, the leader of Narodnaia Volia, defected from the revolutionary camp, explaining his reasons in the pamphlet *Why I Ceased to be a Revolutionary*. This provided the occasion for Plekhanov to add an important feature to his conception of Hegel's philosophy, one which seemed to him to be associated with revolutionary Marxism. Whereas Tikhomirov had come to believe that social change took place gradually, Plekhanov argued that it took place in leaps. He found justification for this in the *Science of Logic*, where Hegel described how changes in quantity led to a change in quality.[43]

---

42   Plekhanov 1956–58, 1, p. 501.
43   Plekhanov 1856–58, 1, pp. 388–9.

Plekhanov's standing as a Marxist theoretician on an international scale was reflected in the publication of his article 'For the Sixtieth Anniversary of Hegel's Death' in *Die neue Zeit* in 1891. The article concentrated mainly on Hegel's *Philosophy of History*, in which Plekhanov could see a parallel with Marx's historical scheme. But it is also significant for introducing the term 'dialectical materialism',[44] a term that neither Marx nor Engels ever used. Plekhanov's standing in the European arena was also enhanced by his defence of revolutionary Marxism against the revisionism of Eduard Bernstein and his followers. It was in the course of defending his conception of 'materialism' in a polemic against Conrad Schmidt, who had criticised it in the pages of *Die neue Zeit*, that Plekhanov had been led to define 'matter' in terms of Kant's 'thing-in-itself'. He had stated that 'along with Kant' he regarded matter as nothing but the totality of 'things-in-themselves', which gave rise to sensations by acting on our sense organs.[45]

This espousal of Kant's 'thing-in-itself' was destined to be at the heart of the polemic that Bogdanov conducted with Plekhanov and Lenin over the next few years. It was to prove the Achilles heel of Plekhanov's interpretation of Marxism and one to which Bogdanov and his associates would repeatedly return.

11   The Fourth Congress

While in prison Bogdanov received news of the collapse of the December uprising in Moscow from a letter from Lenin brought to him by his wife. There too he was able to produce a revised ninth edition of his *Short Course of Economic Science*, and to write the third volume of *Empiriomonism*. Both manuscripts were passed to his wife, with the connivance of the guard who supervised their meetings, and smuggled out of the prison to be published at the end of 1906.[46]

In the Introduction to *Empiriomonism* Bogdanov reflected that for the past eighteen months it had been impossible to do any writing on philosophy because of his participation in the 'historical cyclone' that had shaken the old world. His term in prison, however, now afforded him the leisure to do so. In the past eighteen months the first two volumes of *Empiriomonism* had appeared as well as the two collections of essays *From the Psychology of Society*[47] and *The New World*.[48] These had evoked controversy, though this was less in the

---

44   Plekhanov 1891, pp. 277–8.
45   Plekhanov 1956–58, 2, p. 446.
46   Antonova and Drozdova 1995, 1, p. 22.
47   Bogdanov 1906.
48   Bogdanov 1905.

nature of substantial criticism than repeated expressions of disapproval. Some of these expressions of disapproval were contained in the second edition of Plekhanov's commentary on Engels's pamphlet *Ludwig Feuerbach*, which was published in 1906.[49] Bogdanov would refer to these remarks in his third volume of *Empiriomonism* in the course of his polemic with Plekhanov.

Bogdanov was released from prison on 27 May by decision of special police authority but was subject to open surveillance for three years in the province of Tver. On 4 August of that year by special permission of the Ministry of the Interior he was given leave to travel abroad. He returned to Russia illegally, he and his wife taking up residence in the Finnish village of Kuokkala close to the Russian border. Although part of the Russian Empire, Finland enjoyed a measure of autonomy and the Okhrana had less freedom of movement there. In Kuokkala the Bogdanovs occupied the upper storey of a large uncomfortable summer house, 'Vasa', close to the railway station. It had formerly been a refuge for the Socialist Revolutionaries, who made bombs there, but had subsequently been taken over by Social Democrats; it had been a base for Lenin since the spring. The ground floor was occupied by Lenin, Krupskaya and her mother, and, on occasion, by Lenin's sister Maria. There was considerable two-way traffic between Kuokkala and St Petersburg, as the occupants of Vasa made frequent sorties into the capital, and Vasa was constantly visited by activists from the political organisations operating inside Russia. One visitor to Vasa at this time was Rosa Luxemburg, who had recently been released from prison in Warsaw. She spent August and September in Kuokkala, having extensive discussions with Lenin and Bogdanov on the revolution in Russia, and writing the pamphlet *The Mass Strike*, in which she explained the lessons of the Russian revolution for the German workers' movement.[50]

While Bogdanov was in prison the Fourth Congress of the RSDLP had been held in Stockholm between 23 April–8 May 1906. This formally brought together the two wings of the party into a single organisation. Due to the fact that many local Social-Democratic committees in which the Bolsheviks dominated were in urban areas and subject to oppression by the authorities, they

---

49   Plekhanov's references to Bogdanov were: 'It would be useful for Lenin and the Nietzscheans and the Machists surrounding him to give this some thought. But there are grounds to fear that these 'supermen' have lost the ability to think' (Plekhanov 1956–58, 1, pp. 474). 'That is why a return to Hume is, as Engels justly remarks, a step back compared with materialism. Such a step back, by the way, is made at the present time by the *empiriomonists*, whose philosophy Riehl quite correctly calls a renewal of Hume's philosophy' (Plekhanov 1956–58, 1, p. 488).

50   Plyutto 1998, p. 467; Krupskaia 1989–90, 2, 100; Bol'sheviki. Dokumenty po istorii bol'shevizma s 1903 po 1916 god byvshego Okhrannogo Otdeleniia 1990, p. 393.

were less well represented than the Menshevik organisations, which tended to be outside the main industrial centres. Of the 112 delegates with the right to vote, 62 were Mensheviks and 46 were Bolsheviks, the remainder taking up a centrist position, but in general voting with the Mensheviks.[51]

Bogdanov's absence from the Congress deprived it of a prominent representative of those Bolsheviks who denied that any matter of principle divided the two wings of the party. Lenin, as the principal Bolshevik at the Congress, had a completely different attitude, and made sure that Bolshevik policies on matters discussed were clearly defined and distinct from what the Mensheviks proposed. In the case of agrarian policy, which had arisen as a matter of urgency in view of the wave of peasant rebellion that swept the countryside in 1905, Lenin proposed nationalisation of the land, whereas Maslov and Plekhanov advocated municipalisation, that is, having the confiscated landed estates administered by the zemstvos and democratically elected local authorities. In the debate on the subject it emerged that neither side was entirely united on the issue, and there was support among the Bolsheviks for the policy advanced by Rumiantsev of the confiscation of the landlords' estates and their division among the peasants. The Menshevik majority ensured that the policy of municipalisation was adopted, but with some Bolshevik amendments on the wording of the resolution.[52]

Another contentious issue was the policy to be adopted towards the State Duma. When the Bolsheviks had held a conference in December 1905 in preparation for the Fourth Congress, the electoral law for the first State Duma had just been published. As the revolution was then still in the ascendancy, the conference decided to boycott the Duma and use the election campaign for agitation for an armed uprising. When the Fourth Congress met, it was in the wake of the abortive armed uprising in Moscow and when the elections for the Duma were nearing completion. The newly-formed liberal party, the 'Constitutional Democrats' (Kadets), had emerged as the largest group. As the boycott had not worked, the Mensheviks now proposed that the elections which remained to be held (mainly in the Caucasus) should be sanctioned, and that those Social Democrats who were elected to the Duma should form a special parliamentary group subject to the control of the party Central Committee. Lenin and some other Bolsheviks voted for this motion, which passed, but many others abstained or voted against.[53]

---

51   Lenin 1958–65, 13, p. 5; Solov'ev 1983, pp. 42–3.
52   Schapiro 1970, p. 80.
53   Schapiro 1970, pp. 85–6.

In discussing the question of the armed uprising, the Bolsheviks approved of the general political strike and the December armed uprising in Moscow. The Mensheviks, on the other hand, were less enthusiastic, Plekhanov being of the opinion that the uprising had been a mistake. The resolution on the issue that the Congress adopted recognised the armed uprising as a necessary means of struggle for freedom, one whose preliminary stage was the general strike.[54]

Besides uniting the Bolsheviks and Mensheviks, the Congress brought into the RSDLP three of the national parties, the Bund, Rosa Luxemburg's Social-Democracy of the Kingdom of Poland and Lithuania (SDKPiL) and the Latvian Social-Democratic Party (LSDP).[55] The inclusion of these organisations created a new kind of politics within the RSDLP. Now that decisions on key questions depended on the vote of the national groups, it would be essential to ally with them, to cultivate them and try to influence them. In general the Poles and the Latvians tended to side with the Bolsheviks, while the Mensheviks could mostly count on the Bund as an ally.

In the discussion on the party's constitution, the conference voted to adopt Lenin's definition of what constituted a party member. It also decided to adopt the elective principle in the organisation of the party wherever this was possible, in accordance with the policy Bogdanov had advocated. The resolution referred to his conception of implementing democratic procedures while retaining strict centralisation as 'democratic centralism', though the name of the person who had elaborated the idea was not given a mention.[56]

The preponderance of Mensheviks among the delegates ensured a majority for them on the Central Committee elected at the Congress. There were seven Mensheviks to three Bolsheviks, Desnitsky, Krasin and A.I. Rykov; Rykov was replaced by Bogdanov when he was freed from prison. Subsequently the Central Committee was supplemented by representatives of the national groups which had joined the RSDLP.[57] Mensheviks also predominated on the editorial board of the journal *Sotsial-Demokrat*, which was designated as the Central Organ of the party. This inclined it in due course to become the mouthpiece exclusively of the Menshevik fraction. Although the RSDLP was now formally united, the division into Bolsheviks and Mensheviks persisted. As *Sotsial-*

---

54   KPSS v rezoliutsiiakh i resheniiakh s"ezdov, konferentsii i plenumov TsK, 1953, 1, pp. 107–8.
55   KPSS v rezoliutsiiakh i resheniiakh s"ezdov, konferentsii i plenumov TsK, 1953, 1, pp. 132–5.
56   KPSS v rezoliutsiiakh i resheniiakh s"ezdov, konferentsii i plenumov TsK, 1953, 1, p. 116.
57   The Mensheviks on the Central Committee were: V.N. Rozanov, L.I. Goldman, L.N. Radchenko, L.M. Khinchuk, V.N. Krokhmal, B.A. Bakhmetev and P.N. Kolokolnikov. From the SDKPiL were: A. Warski and F. Dzierżyński; from the Bund were: P.A. Abramovich and A.I. Kremer. From the LSDP was K. Daniševskis. Chetvertyi (ob"edinitel'nyi) s"ezd RSDRP (aprel'–mai) 1906 goda. RSDRP. Protokoly 1959, p. 639.

Demokrat had fallen into Menshevik hands, from August 1906 the Bolsheviks began to issue a journal of their own, *Proletarii*, which served as their fraction's organisational centre.

12 The Third Volume of *Empiriomonism* and the Conflict with Plekhanov

As Bogdanov explained in the Introduction to the third volume of *Empirio-monism*, the episodic character of the criticism of the two earlier volumes had caused him to decide not to answer it piece by piece, but to explain how he had arrived at his philosophical views. The account that Bogdanov produced was not so much an exercise in intellectual autobiography as a demonstration that the views of Plekhanov were ones that he himself had passed through and rejected as inadequate.

Bogdanov recalled that before his contacts with the workers inclined him towards the Marxist viewpoint, he had been engaged in the study of the natural sciences and was an advocate of what he called 'the materialism of the natural scientist'. This was, he said, a somewhat primitive philosophy that had been espoused by the nihilists and others who held extreme ideological views.

According to Bogdanov, in attempting to achieve a strict monism in perception, this natural-science materialism constructed a picture of the world that was composed wholly of a single substance: of 'matter'. The atomistic representation of this matter in its various combinations, in its incessant motion, constituted the entire content of the world, the essence of all experience, both physical and psychical. The unchanging laws of its movement in space and time were the ultimate explanation of everything. To monism was, thus, added the strict tendency of scientific objectivism, and hence the extreme hostility of this philosophy to all fetishes of religious and metaphysical-idealist viewpoints. Such a philosophy, Bogdanov confessed, was not easy to relinquish, and even when one did, one involuntarily continued to maintain a special sympathy for it, and to prefer it to all others.[58]

What Bogdanov was describing here was the kind of materialism that Plekhanov and his followers, including Lenin, professed, based on the concept of 'matter'. Bogdanov argued that this kind of materialism was incompatible with the Marxist viewpoint and had been superseded by it. Marxism regarded the old materialism as a product of human history, one that had developed on

---

58   Bogdanov 2003, pp. 2167.

a material base that changed with the evolution of society. This meant that all ideological forms were transient and consequently they rendered impossible any 'immutable laws' or 'unconditional objective knowledge of the nature of things'.

But, Bogdanov added, not all Marxists were in agreement with his relativist point of view; only a minority of them were. It was, he thought, curious to note the great discrepancy in approach that existed between Engels and his Russian follower Plekhanov. Whereas in his pamphlet *Anti-Dühring* Engels adopted an almost relativist standpoint, Plekhanov spoke in terms of 'objective truths', which once established could never be altered with the further development of perception, but perhaps only given additional confirmation. The example he gave was Marx's theory of money circulation.

Bogdanov explained that he too regarded Marx's theory of money circulation as an objective truth, but only one for our times; it was 'universally valid' for contemporary humanity. But there was no guarantee that this would be the case for succeeding generations. Bogdanov considered Plekhanov mistaken in thinking that there could be super-historical criteria of truth in a world which was in a continuous state of change and development. But he also thought that Engels had made an unwarranted concession to the idea of eternal truths when he had accepted that platitudes like $2 \times 2 = 4$ or that the statement that Napoleon died on 4 May 1821 were always valid. Platitudes of this kind, Bogdanov pointed out, were not truths, but tautologies.[59]

Bogdanov went on to say that having renounced his 'scientist's materialism', he was not tempted to espouse a new form of philosophical materialism, certainly not the type that Plekhanov propounded in Marx's name and with the help of quotations from Holbach. According to Bogdanov, Plekhanov maintained that the basis and essence of materialism was the idea of the primacy of 'nature' to 'spirit'. But, as Bogdanov pointed out, this was a very loose kind of definition of materialism: the concepts of 'nature' and 'spirit' were nebulous, and their antithesis could be understood in a variety of ways, so that it was impossible to construct on that basis the basic characteristics of a world view. As a preliminary it was necessary to give a precise definition of both the concept of 'nature' and of 'spirit', something that Plekhanov had not done.

But, Bogdanov corrected himself, Plekhanov had given definitions of 'spirit' and 'matter' (or 'nature'), but in a rather peculiar manner. Here Bogdanov quoted the passage from Plekhanov's polemic with Conrad Schmidt published

---

59   Bogdanov 2003, pp. 218–20.

in Russian in 1906, in a collection of articles called *Criticism of our Critics*. Plekhanov had stated:

> As opposed to 'spirit', we call 'matter' that which, by *affecting our sense organs, gives rise to some sensation in us*. But what is it that affects our sense organs? To that I reply, along with Kant: *things-in-themselves*. Consequently, *matter is nothing but the totality of things-in-themselves, in so far as the latter are the sources of our sensations*.[60]

This, Bogdanov said, was all the definition of 'matter' that Plekhanov had given. But since 'matter', 'nature' and 'things-in-themselves' remained unknowns, Plekhanov's definition had not said anything meaningful. 'Excuse me!', Bogdanov imagines Plekhanov as objecting, 'we do know a lot about "things-in-themselves". First, they exist, and exist, moreover, outside experience. Second, they are subject to the law of causality – they can "act". Third, the forms and relations of phenomena correspond to the forms and mutual relations of the "things-in-themselves" as hieroglyphics do to the things they designate'.[61]

As for the first two points, Bogdanov dismissed them as having the same lack of content as Plekhanov's original definition of 'matter'. In relation to the third point he pointed out the contradiction that whereas Plekhanov maintained that 'things-in-themselves' had 'form' and 'relations' he denied that they had appearance, though the terms 'form' and 'appearance' were synonymous.[62] There was also the problem of how Plekhanov classified the sense organs, whether they too might be 'things-in-themselves'.

In conclusion, Bogdanov summarised the contradictory nature of Plekhanov's conception of the antithesis between 'matter' and 'spirit'. Plekhanov seemed to be saying that matter is that which, acting on our sense organs, produced sensations (i.e. spirit). As for the 'sense organs', they obviously were to be understood here not as the phenomenon, but as corresponding to the 'thing-in-itself', otherwise they too would be the result of the action of some 'thing-in itself' on another 'thing-in-itself'. Thus, matter is that which acting on matter gives rise to 'spirit'; or – matter is the cause, and spirit is the result; or matter is what is primary in relation to whatever it is that spirit is secondary to. One thus kept returning to the formula that was to be explained with the help of the definitions of 'matter' and 'spirit': the definitions turned out to be simple

---

60   Plekhanov 1956–58, 2, p. 446; Bogdanov 2003, p. 222.
61   Ibid.
62   Bogdanov 2003, p. 223.

repetitions. Was this collection of 'eternal truths' to be recognised as the philosophy of Marxism? Bogdanov asked. His answer was: 'Never! We have to look further than that'.[63]

Having dealt with the 'old materialism' in the person of its representative, Plekhanov, Bogdanov resumed his intellectual autobiography. Following the period in which he had espoused 'scientist's materialism' he had become an enthusiastic follower of Ostwald's theory of energetics. He had, however, encountered a contradiction in Ostwald's chief work *The Philosophy of Nature*. This was that although the author continually stressed that he was using the concept of 'energy' in a methodological sense, to express the relationship between facts of experience, he was apt to lapse into using it in the sense of the substance of experience of the material world. Used in this way energetics did not represent a significant advance on the scientist's materialism. Bogdanov confessed that he too had been guilty of such lapses in his *Studies in the Historical View of Nature*.[64]

About this time too, Bogdanov recalled, he had become acquainted with Kantian philosophy. He had, however, been unable to gain anything of use from it. He thought it naive to believe that something meaningful could be derived from the mere analysis of concepts. He found it impossible to take seriously theories of knowledge formed in this way, without recourse to scientific methods.

Much more useful to Bogdanov was the philosophy of empiriocriticism, with its aim of purging experience from all that was fortuitous, subjective or individual. Bogdanov commended the approach to perception of the empiriociticists, which was to describe the connections of elements and complexes in a precise and systematic way. He emphasised that this school of thought assumed the existence of *Mitmenschen*, so that Plekhanov was quite wrong to accuse it of solipsism.[65]

Bogdanov concluded his intellectual autobiographical sketch, his 'road to empiriomonism', with the observation that the philosophical views he now held were the result of a critical appraisal of the various currents of thought that he had passed through. They had only been given final expression in the present work and also in the collections *From the Psychology of Society* and *New World*, which were published at the same time.

From what he had said, Bogdanov believed that he had the right to consider empiriomonism a philosophical view that was particularly his own and not one

---

63   Bogdanov 2003, p. 223.
64   Bogdanov 2003, p. 223.
65   Bogdanov 2003, p. 225.

that belonged to any of the schools of thought from which material for empiriomonism had been taken. He emphasised that only the social philosophy of
Marx had served as more than material for him; this was at the same time the
regulator and method of his work.[66] He protested that Plekhanov was mistaken
in alluding to him as a 'Machist' or an 'empiriocritic'. He had learned much
from Mach and believed that Plekhanov himself could discover many interesting things from this outstanding scholar and thinker. He cautioned that no one
should be put off reading Mach because Mach was not a Marxist; Plekhanov,
after all, seemed to have found Holbach and Hegel instructive enough, and
they were not Marxists. Bogdanov denied that he was a 'Machist', declaring that
all he had taken from Mach in his general philosophical conceptions was the
neutrality of the elements of experience in relation to the 'physical' and the
'psychical', of the dependence of these characteristics only on the connections
of experience. In view of this, Bogdanov could say that he was less of a 'Machist'
than Plekhanov was a 'Holbachian'. He cautioned that readers of *Empiriomonism* should not be misled by the sympathetic evaluation of empiriocriticism he
had given at the beginning of the first volume into thinking that this represented his own viewpoint. This had only been his starting-point; in the rest of the
work he had shown the shortcomings of the empiriocritics' conceptions.[67]

While having a low opinion of his intellectual abilities, Bogdanov was as-
tounded by Plekhanov's naive faith in his own infallible authority as an interpreter of Marxism. Plekhanov had shown this trait in a passage in *Criticism of
our Critics*, in which he had been dismissive of Bogdanov's ideas. The passage,
which Bogdanov quoted, stated that:

> The relationship of our 'activists' to philosophy has always reminded me
> of the relationship to it of King Friedrich Wilhelm I of Prussia. As we
> know, this wise monarch remained completely indifferent to the philo-
> sophical doctrine of Christian Wolff until it was explained to him that the
> Wolffian doctrine of sufficient cause would cause soldiers to desert the
> army. Then the soldier king ordered the philosopher to leave the Prussian
> kingdom within 24 hours under pain of being hanged. Our 'activists' of
> course would never want to hang anybody for their philosophical beliefs.
> That would be impossible. But our 'activists' are quite prepared to toler-
> ate any given philosophy until it is proved to them that it prevents them
> from achieving their immediate political objectives. Thus, until recently

---

66   Bogdanov 2003, p. 238.
67   Bogdanov 2003, p. 239.

they tolerated Kantianism. Messrs Struve and Bulgakov showed them that Kantianism was not just an abstract theoretical speculation. And now they are up in arms against the 'combination' of Kant with Marx. But no one has yet provided proof with regard to *empiriomonism*. And our 'activists' are ready to accept *Machists* for *Marxists*. In time they will regret it, but by then, I suppose, it will be too late.[68]

Bogdanov interpreted this to mean that Plekhanov thought that he, Bogdanov, as the sole representative of empiriomonism, should be expelled immediately from the Marxist camp. Bogdanov, however, declared that he did not believe that Plekhanov or anyone else possessed the discretionary power to decide on the validity of his views. Arguments had to be presented, and he called upon Plekhanov to do just that.

Bogdanov concluded this literary brush with Plekhanov with a statement of his attitude to criticism that is the very antithesis of what he found in Plekhanov. He said:

> I know how difficult is the cause that I have taken upon myself; I know how short are those ten years of my life that I can devote to it. But it would be impossible for me to decline it, and I have never seen anything personal in this task that life has set me. I am happy to meet any criticism that I may receive from my own current of thought, only if it is criticism, only if it gives material for the elucidation of the truth. If it should happen that this truth should be elucidated at the cost of the destruction of my ideas, I shall be happy to welcome this truth that is new to me ...[69]

This was a laudable stance for Bogdanov to take, and there is no reason to doubt his sincerity in taking it. He was confident that his ideas would stand up to scrutiny, certainly to any that Plekhanov was capable of giving them. But he was prepared to abandon them and adopt other conceptions if they were shown to be wrong by bona fide criticism. Bogdanov's misfortune was that his philosophical ideas were never subjected to this kind of criticism, but only to abuse and denunciation.

Most of the third volume of *Empiriomonism* was devoted to discussing the question of 'social selection', some aspects of which had already been touched upon in earlier works. By 'social selection' Bogdanov meant the influence of the

---

68   Bogdanov 2003, pp. 241–2.
69   Bogdanov 2003, p. 243.

social environment on classes and groups, which, Bogdanov stressed, were not so much aggregations of individuals as systems of relations between people.

As in other spheres, in that of social selection the law of the conservation and transformation of energy operated. Every act of social selection implied an increase or a decrease in the energy of the social complex to which it belonged. In the first case it was a matter of 'positive selection'; in the latter, of 'negative selection'. Although both of these processes were present in the evolution of society, it was the action of positive selection that dominated. For Bogdanov social progress was the development of human cooperation.

In social life, with its enormous complexity, the organising function played an extremely important role. Here Bogdanov distinguished three main types. The first was the most elementary kind: the cries, speech, music that coordinated the efforts of individuals. The second type consisted of perceptive forms, the concepts, judgements and complex combinations that went to form religious doctrines, scientific and philosophical theories that served for the systematic co-ordination of labour on the basis of previous experience. The third type of organising function embraced the normative forms of custom, law, morals and decency. Their role consisted in eliminating the contradictions of life by limiting this or that function that would otherwise lead to social conflict. To these three types of organising function Bogdanov added the forms of art, which he considered to be the means of communicating the direct experience of one person to another.[70]

As in earlier works, Bogdanov explained that society in its historical development became differentiated into classes and groups, the most fundamental of these being the division into those who dominated and those who were subordinate. Referring the reader to what he had written in 'The Integration of Mankind', he predicted that the specialisation brought about by the division of labour would be overcome as the specialisation was transferred from human beings to machines. He also recalled what he had said in *From the Psychology of Society* about the relationship of the 'ideologues' to the 'masses', indicating that he continued to subscribe to his concept of democratic forms of political organisation.[71]

In socialist society all the limitations flowing from privilege or from subordination to the fetish of profit would disappear. There, in a conscious and planned organisation of production, the introduction of every innovation would be judged on the basis of its utility. But even here the relative conser-

---

70   Bogdanov 2003, p. 267.
71   Bogdanov 2003, p. 303.

vatism of ideology would act to limit the adoption of new techniques. In the struggle with the dominant capitalist class ideology, the proletariat would elaborate new norms of behaviour that would have nothing in common with the bourgeois principle of 'legality', and in many cases would contradict it. These proletarian norms would find their ultimate expression in the principle of comradely class solidarity, a principle to which Bogdanov attached particular significance.[72]

Empiriomonism was an important landmark in the evolution of Bogdanov's intellectual biography. It was the fullest and most systematic exposition to date of his philosophical ideas. It was also the most mature, in the sense that it presented in a more considered and polished form ideas and conceptions that had appeared in earlier works such as the *Basic Elements of the Historical View of Nature* and *Perception from a Historical Point of View*. Also, in making clear his relationship to the works of Avenarius and Mach, Bogdanov had shown where his originality as a thinker lay.

The three successive volumes of *Empiriomonism* document how Bogdanov was dragged deeper and deeper into a polemic with Plekhanov and his associates. At that stage, however, his encounter with these critics served to show Bogdanov's superiority over them as a thinker. This was what Plekhanov found unpardonable, and it would account for the animosity which later characterised the 'father' of Russian Marxism's dealings with Bogdanov.

Even in the summer of 1906 Bogdanov had a taste of things to come when he presented Lenin with a copy of the third volume of *Empiriomonism*. After reading it, Lenin became furious, convinced that Bogdanov's ideas were un-Marxist, and sent Bogdanov a letter on philosophy running into three notebooks. In it Lenin declared that he was an ordinary Marxist in philosophy, but that it was precisely Bogdanov's lucid, popular and splendidly written works that had finally convinced him that he, Bogdanov, was essentially wrong and that Plekhanov was right.[73] This letter, ironically called a 'declaration of love' by Lenin, was, according to Valentinov, so thin on philosophical knowledge and so rich in insults that Bogdanov returned it to Lenin, saying that if he wanted to continue maintaining personal relations with him, the letter must be treated as 'unwritten, unsent and unread'.[74] From Valentinov's description of Lenin's letter it must have been a prototype of *Materialism and Empiriocriticism*, Lenin's attempted refutation of Bogdanov's philosophy written two years later.

---

72   Bogdanov 2003, p. 323.
73   Lenin 1958–65, 47, p. 141.
74   Valentinov 1968, pp. 235–6.

Years of Reaction

1 The Fifth Congress

After abortive attempts to hold the Fifth Congress of the RSDLP in Copenhagen and in Malmö, it finally took place in London from 30 April–19 May 1907. This congress was more evenly divided between the two wings of the party than the previous one had been. Of the 303 delegates entitled to vote there were 89 Bolsheviks and 88 Mensheviks. Trotsky represented those members of the RSDLP who did not belong to either fraction. This was the first congress of the RSDLP at which the national parties took part. There were 45 delegates from the SDKPiL, 26 from the Latvian Social-Democratic Party and 55 Bundists.[1] The writer Maxim Gorky attended the congress with his partner Maria Andreeva and it was they who attracted considerable attention from the local press. It was also through Gorky's good offices that the impecunious RSDLP succeeded in receiving a loan of £1,700 from the British industrialist Joseph Fels to hold the congress.[2]

Bogdanov made a substantial and dramatic contribution to the proceedings of the Congress by presenting a counter-report on the activities of the Central Committee to the one that Martov made. He backed up his criticisms of the Central Committee in a pamphlet circulated to the delegates entitled *Did the Party Have a Central Committee in 1906–1907?* It reflected Bogdanov's frustrations at being one of the three Bolshevik members of a Central Committee dominated by 15 Mensheviks. He had found that any initiative emanating from him or his Bolshevik colleagues would run up against the stone wall of Menshevik resistance.[3] He also thought that the policies pursued by the Central Committee's Menshevik majority, in particular the tactics with regard to the

---

1 Solov'ev 1983, pp. 56–8.
2 Gorky had just completed his novel *Mother*, which was set in his native Nizhniy Novgorod, and was based on real characters, workers in the industrial suburb of Sormovo. Some of Gorky's worker acquaintances from Sormovo, Ivan Chugurin, Nikolai Kaiurov and Mitia Pavlov, had been prominent in the 1905 revolution. After the violent suppression of the uprising in Sormovo, the leaders had been forced to flee to different parts of the country. During the war, however, they reconvened in St Petersburg in the 'Sormovo-Nikolaev *zemliachestvo*' and would play an important part in the revolution that overthrew the tsarist regime in February 1917. See White 1979 and White 2011.
3 Protokoly piatogo s"ezda RSDRP 1935, p. 181.

Duma, were in conflict with the decisions recently taken at the Unity Conference in Stockholm. Bogdanov had been responsible for the activities of the Bolshevik deputies to the Second Duma, who had joined the stream of regular visitors to the 'Vasa' in Kuokkala.[4] But in trying to ensure that they followed party policy he was impeded by the attitude of the Central Committee, who were inclined to come to an accommodation with the liberals.

In his report Martov gave an overwhelmingly positive account of what the Central Committee had done since its election at the last Congress. He recounted how, with the arrival of the delegates from the Caucasus, the Central Committee had organised an official Social-Democratic fraction in the Duma under its direction, and how the fraction had exposed the atrocities perpetrated by the government. He described how, when the government dissolved the Duma on 9 July, the Social-Democrat Duma deputies had taken part in the protest meeting in Vyborg, and called for a general strike, though unsuccessfully. When the time came for elections to the Second Duma, the Central Committee was confronted with the task of elaborating an election tactic for the party, and to this end had organised a conference in November. There it had been decided to form an alliance with the Kadets to keep out the more rightist parties. In fact, the Social Democrats had done well in the elections, with 55 deputies in the Duma.

The only things Martov found to criticise in his report were the robberies, referred to by the euphemism 'expropriations', by which money was channelled into the Bolshevik wing of the party, and the fact that the party was an illegal, underground organisation, that was not subject to public accountability. As far as Martov was concerned, the actions of the Central Committee were above reproach.

Bogdanov's version of events was very different from Martov's, and accused the Central Committee of dereliction of its duties in a number of respects. In general, he thought that it was the obligation of the Central Committee to implement the decisions of the Unity Congress, whereas in practice the very opposite had been done, and the decisions had been blatantly flouted.

An example of this cavalier attitude to the Congress's decisions that Bogdanov gave was the actions of the Central Committee and the Duma fraction in connection with the need to issue an appeal to the population on the agrarian question. This arose shortly before the dissolution of the Duma, when the government had published an appeal which offered land to the peasants, provided that landlords agreed and received compensation. In consultation with the

---

4   Krupskaia 1989–90, 2, p. 102.

Central Committee, the Social-Democrat Duma fraction decided to join the Kadet appeal, on condition that it included the principle of 'compulsory alienation of private land'. Crucially, the condition put forward by the Social Democrats did not mention that the alienation should be without compensation (*vykup*). This omission, Bogdanov stressed, was in conflict with the policy laid down at the Fourth Congress.

The tactic of forming an alliance with the Kadets favoured by the Central Committee Mensheviks had no support in the local St Petersburg and Moscow party organisations, where the Bolsheviks were in the majority. To get round this difficulty the Central Committee had engineered a split in the St Petersburg Committee to create a Menshevik-dominated workers' organisation that would give support to the policies of the Central Committee. This tactic was roundly condemned by Bogdanov and his fellow Bolsheviks on the Central Committee, and featured in Bogdanov's report to the Fifth Congress.

A criticism that Bogdanov levelled at the Mensheviks on the Central Committee was their reaction to the government's dissolution of the Duma on 9 July. Bogdanov and the Bolshevik members of the Central Committee wanted to respond to this move by calling for a general strike and demanding the convocation of a constituent assembly. The Mensheviks, however, demanded only that the Duma be reconvened for the convocation of a constituent assembly. Bogdanov and his associates protested that this slogan obliged the party to halt the general strike and the uprising associated with it if the tsar restored the dissolved Duma. In Bogdanov's opinion, moreover, the Menshevik policy on the Duma was in conflict with the resolution of the Fourth Congress, which had spoken of the unsuitability of the Duma for resolving the basic questions of the revolution.[5]

A point of contention between Bogdanov and the Central Committee was its toleration of an article of Plekhanov's in the left-Kadet journal *Tovarishch*, which advocated an alliance with the Kadets in the elections to the Second Duma. In his reply to a reader's question about what in his opinion would be an election platform that would unite the parties of the left and the extreme left, Plekhanov replied: 'A sovereign Duma'. In Bogdanov's view, in this declaration Plekhanov had put forward a slogan that went much further than the decision of the November conference in Tammenfors and was in direct opposition to it. In spite of this, the Central Committee had done nothing to condemn Plekhanov's article or dissociate themselves from it.[6]

---

5 Protokoly piatogo s"ezda RSDRP 1935, p. 118.
6 Protokoly piatogo s"ezda RSDRP 1935, pp. 121, 772.

Bogdanov's conclusion was that 'Neither by its organisation, nor by its composition, nor by its direction, is this the kind of Central Committee we need'.[7] Despite Bogdanov's round condemnation of the Central Committee, the Bolshevik vote of censure was not passed, but neither did the Menshevik vote of confidence in the Central Committee; it was simply resolved to pass on to other business.

In the discussion on the report of the Duma fraction, Bogdanov conceded that the political line followed by the fraction had been on the whole correct, but that this correctness was only approximate and only arrived at by trial and error. In order to avoid such vacillation and hesitancy, he urged that the fraction should be given clear and precise directions by the Central Committee.[8] In its resolution on the Duma the Congress recognised the necessity for the Social-Democrat fraction to conduct its activities under the direction of the party's Central Committee.

In the resolution on its relations with bourgeois parties the Congress judged the Kadet party to be an organisation whose ideals did not go beyond establishing a functioning bourgeois society protected by the monarchy, the police and a bicameral parliamentary system. This being the case, the duty of the Social Democrats was to expose the falsity of the Kadets' claims to promote democracy and to contrast this with the consistent democratism of the proletariat. The resolution reversed the Menshevik policy of cooperation with the Kadet party that Plekhanov had so decisively endorsed.[9]

The Central Committee elected at the Congress reflected the multi-national composition of the RSDLP. It consisted of five Bolsheviks, four Mensheviks, two Poles and a Latvian. Among the Bolshevik members were Rozhkov and I.F. Dubrovinsky, a veteran Social Democrat who had arrived at the Congress on the last day.[10] Neither Bogdanov nor Lenin were full members of the Central Committee; both were candidate members among ten Bolsheviks, eight Mensheviks, four Poles and two Latvians. After the closure of the Congress at the last meeting of the Bolshevik fraction a 'Bolshevik Centre' was established to direct the activities of the fraction, consisting of Lenin, Bogdanov, Krasin, Pokrovsky, Rozhkov, Liadov, V.P. Nogin, G.D. Lindov, Shantser, V.K. Taratuta, G.E. Zinoviev, L.B. Kamenev, Dubrovinsky, Rykov and I.P. Meshkovsky (Goldenberg).[11] Three

---

7   Protokoly piatogo s"ezda RSDRP 1935, p. 125.
8   Protokoly piatogo s"ezda RSDRP 1935, p. 303.
9   KPSS v rezoliutsiiakh i resheniiakh s"ezdov, konferentsii i plenumov TsK 1953, 1, p. 159.
10   Prokof'ev 1969, p. 182.
11   Protokoly soveshchaniia rasshirennoi redaktsii 'Proletariia'. Iiun' 1909 1934, p. IV; Nikolaev-
       skii 1995, p. 14; Yassour 1981, p. 12.

members of the Bolshevik Centre, Bogdanov, Lenin and Dubrovinsky, were elected to the editorial board of *Proletarii*, the newspaper of the Bolshevik fraction.[12]

In defiance of the resolution to discontinue the 'partisan activities' and 'expropriations' under threat of expulsion from the party, the Bolsheviks continued to raise funds by these means, creating a special 'financial-technical commission' for the purpose. Soon after the Fifth Congress, on 13 June 1907, S.A. Ter-Petrosian (Kamo) robbed the State Treasury offices in Tiflis of a sum of 241,000 roubles, of which 23,000 was retained by the local Caucasian organisations, and 218,000 was handed over to Krasin, the Caucasian partisan group's contact within the Bolshevik Centre. The Caucasian group decided to entrust the handling of the Tiflis money to three people within the Bolshevik Centre elected at the London Congress: Krasin, Bogdanov and Lenin. The three agreed to Kamo's request that the existence of this 'private financial group' should be kept secret from the party and from the rest of the Bolshevik fraction. The other stipulation Kamo made was that the money should be used 'in the interests of the Bolshevik current'. It was with this money that the newspaper *Proletarii* was established in emigration in 1908.[13]

2   The Kotka Conference

The Fifth Congress of the RSDLP had taken place on the eve of the dissolution of the Second Duma on 3 June by the Prime Minister Stolypin. The new electoral law which he introduced limited the franchise for workers, peasants and the national minorities, while increasing the representation of the landowners. The result was to produce a Duma dominated by conservatives with which Stolypin was able to coexist and allow to run its full term.

The need to formulate a policy towards the Duma in the new circumstances prompted the Social Democrats to hold a series of meetings to discuss the issue. The first of these was the conference of the St Petersburg City organisation of the RSDLP which met on 8 July in Terijoki in Finland. At the conference Lenin spoke in favour of ending the boycott of the Duma, a position in which he was supported by Dan, the representative of the Mensheviks, and opposed by Kamenev, who favoured a continuation of the boycott. Lenin's persuasive powers were sufficient to swing the Bolshevik delegation over to

---

12   Protokoly piatogo s"ezda RSDRP 1935, p. 786.
13   Neizvestnyi Bogdanov 1995, 2, p. 103.

his point of view and in the voting a resolution to participate in the Duma was carried by 33 votes to 30.[14]

At the end of June Lenin had written an article, 'Against the Boycott', which set out his case not so much for participating in the Duma as for ending the tactic of boycotting it. His reasoning was that the tactic of boycott was the correct one while the revolution was in the ascendancy, as had been the case during the year 1905. But in the subsequent period 1906–7, beginning with the defeat of the December uprising, the revolutionary tide had receded, and in the new circumstances the boycott tactic was no longer appropriate.[15] In quite a lengthy article this is the only substantive point that emerges, and even that lacks conviction. There is no explanation of what is the necessary connection between the decline of the revolutionary movement and the need to participate in the Duma; the point is simply asserted.

A revealing document in his *Collected Works* is a draft speech Lenin wrote for the Bolshevik deputy Grigorii Aleksinsky to give on the agrarian question in the Second Duma in April 1907. It is not simply notes on the subject with points to make, but an entire script complete with rhetorical flourishes.[16] Lenin must have imagined himself delivering the speech as a Duma deputy. In fact, Aleksinsky later recalled that Lenin had actually offered himself for selection by the St. Petersburg Committee of the RSDLP as its candidate in the elections to the Second Duma. In the event Aleksinsky and Dan were chosen.[17]

The conference of the All-Russian Organisation of the RSDLP was held in Kotka, Finland, between 21 and 23 July. It was attended by 26 delegates with voting rights, including nine Bolsheviks, five Mensheviks, five Poles, including Rosa Luxemburg, who had just been released from prison, two Latvians and five Bundists. All of the members of the Bolshevik delegation were in favour of boycotting the Third Duma with the exception of Lenin.

In his speech Bogdanov argued for the boycott of the elections to the Third Duma and of its proceedings. His argument was that all the factors which had brought about the 1905 revolution continued to operate: the disconnect between the political structure of the country and the demands of its economic development, the ruination of the peasantry, the impoverishment of the proletariat, unemployment, all remained as before. Consequently, the objective historical tasks of the revolution had not been carried out, and, at the same time, the forces of the revolution had not been fundamentally weakened. Beneath

---

14   Usyskin 1988. p. 14.
15   Lenin 1958–65, 16, pp. 1–36.
16   Lenin 1958–65, 15, pp. 127–60.
17   Biggart 1989, p. 68.

the outward calm, the economic and political organisations of the proletariat were developing, as was the political consciousness of the peasantry, so that the forces were being gathered for a new and decisive revolutionary struggle.

As evidence for this contention, Bogdanov referred to the fact that people in general were hostile to the elections to the Third Duma, and that the constitutional illusions they had once harboured had dissipated. They were aware that the new electoral law would turn the Duma into a centre for rallying the forces of counter-revolution. In this situation the tactical tasks facing the party in the current bourgeois-democratic revolution were explaining to the masses the need for a popular uprising and the convocation of a constituent assembly, as this was the only means of obtaining land for the peasants and freedom for the entire people. This should be the main focus of party work, and any obstacle to this should be eliminated. In the present situation the party should concentrate on strengthening and extending workers' organisations, consolidating in them the influence of the Social Democrats, and encouraging their agitational and propagandist activities.

Bogdanov argued that ending the boycott of the Third Duma, despite the most revolutionary justifications, would signal to the masses that the present revolution had come to an end, and that it only remained to return to everyday activity for the foreseeable future. He thought that participating in the Third Duma with its reactionary electoral law would not give the party any political benefit, because, in these conditions, there was no possibility of creating a representation worthy of the name and using the Duma as a platform for mass agitation. He called upon the party to boycott the Duma, though taking an active part in the electoral campaign, combining agitation for a boycott with explaining to the masses the essence of the political situation and the tasks of the party.[18]

Lenin spoke in favour of ending the boycott. It was not just a speech which repeated the ground he had covered at Terijoki. The audience he was trying to convince were the other members of the Bolshevik fraction, knowing that it was pointless to try to influence the Mensheviks and Bundists, who were already committed to participation in the Duma. He would of course know what Bogdanov had intended to say, because this would have been talked about at the 'Vasa', where both Lenin and Bogdanov still lived. Lenin's speech was therefore aimed at countering the points Bogdanov had made.

Lenin stated that the boycott tactic had been correct only at the beginning of the general and swift revolutionary upsurge, accompanied by the direct pres-

---

18   KPSS v rezoliutsiiakh i resheniiakh s"ezdov, konferentsii i plenumov TsK 1953, 1, pp. 176–7.

sure on the old regime, or in countering constitutional illusions, as when there had been a boycott of the Bulygin Duma. He claimed that there had been no substantive change in the situation in which the Social Democrats had participated in the Second Duma as a result of the fact that the new electoral law had produced a Duma dominated by the Octobrist rather than the Kadet party. Since the Kadets had always acted in an Octobrist way, there would be no difference in practice. According to Lenin, Stolypin's *coup d'état* of 3 June 1907 was the direct and necessary result of the defeat of the December 1905 uprising in Moscow. The period that followed, 1906–7, had been one in which the reaction advanced and the revolution retreated. In these conditions, to continue with the boycott would be a fetish. Lenin consequently urged that the party participate both in the election campaign and in the Duma itself.

F.I. Dan spoke for the Mensheviks and Bundists, as he had at the Terijoki conference. He argued that the RSDLP ought to take part in the elections to the Duma and in the Duma itself. He believed that the boycott was based on the temporary political apathy of the masses and that its continuation would only increase this passivity; that it helped the reaction to turn the Duma into an instrument for consolidating its power; and that it did nothing to help liberate the masses from the influence of the bourgeois and liberal parties.

When the resolution proposed by Bogdanov was put to the vote it received 9 votes against 15 with two abstentions, all the Bolsheviks voting for it except Lenin and one Latvian Social Democrat. Lenin's resolution got the support of the Polish fraction and one of the Latvians, but not of the Bolsheviks. At this point the Bolsheviks realised that if they continued to support their resolution to boycott the Duma, it was Dan's resolution that would be carried, with its Menshevik-Bundist reasoning behind it. In the circumstances, they decided to take the course of the lesser evil and join with the Poles and the Latvians and vote for Lenin's resolution, which was duly carried. In this way the Bolshevik fraction committed itself, against its will, to participation in the elections and the proceedings of the Third Duma.

The Bolsheviks, however, felt sufficiently aggrieved by the turn of events to sign a declaration making clear that they deplored the decision that had been taken and explaining their reasons for voting for Lenin's resolution. It stated:

> We, members of the conference, have signed a special declaration in favour of the boycott of the Third Duma, and in doing so we divest ourselves before the party of any responsibility for what is, in our opinion, a mistaken decision by the majority of the conference. Not wishing to allow the victory of the opportunist wing of our party to set the tone and content of the forthcoming election campaign, we have found it neces-

sary to vote in favour of that anti-boycottist resolution that seemed, in our opinion, the lesser evil.[19]

The strength of feeling on the issue ensured that there would be considerable antagonism between Lenin and the majority of the members of the Bolshevik fraction, between Lenin and Bogdanov in particular. If not precisely the beginning of the dispute between the two Bolshevik leaders, the Kotka conference was certainly an important landmark in it.

The conference was a defeat for Bogdanov, because his policy on the Duma had been voted down. But although Lenin had had his way on tactics towards the Duma, his standing had been damaged, since he had been unable to command the support of his own fraction. Potentially there was a more serious aspect of the episode: in voting with the Mensheviks against his own fraction, he had shown disloyalty and was exposed to disciplinary measures. Bogdanov would have been within his rights to demand Lenin's expulsion from the Bolshevik fraction. This fact was mentioned by Aleksinsky in a letter to Gorky on 13 January 1909. 'Comrade Lenin', he wrote, 'has diverged from the majority of our fraction on the question of the boycott of the Third Duma. Unfortunately, out of respect for the "leader", the fraction does not apply to him the normal rules of unity and discipline, and allows him to vote at the all-party conference against the fraction'.[20]

Aleksinsky went on to say that Lenin had the choice either of becoming reconciled to the boycottist current in the Bolshevik fraction or bringing the boycottists around to his own point of view. As a true descendant of Napoleon, the latter was Lenin's preferred course. It might be more accurate to say that in this campaign Lenin was the true disciple of Plekhanov. Just as Plekhanov had turned the mainstream of Russian radical opinion into a particular current by giving it the name *Narodnichestvo*, Lenin would give eccentric titles to his opponents such as 'Recallers' (*otzovisty*) and 'Ultimatumists' (*ultimatisty*). The implication was that they were marginal dissidents rather than the majority in the Bolshevik fraction.

A conference was held in Helsinki in November 1907 to determine what the tactics of the Social-Democratic fraction in the Duma should be. A Bolshevik resolution was carried which declared that any cooperation with the Kadets would undermine the class education of the workers in the cause of the revolution.[21] Nevertheless, the performance of the Social-Democratic fraction in the

---

19   KPSS v rezoliutsiiakh i resheniiakh s"ezdov, konferentsii i plenumov TsK 1953, 1, p. 177.
20   Neizvestnyi Bogdanov 1995, 2, p. 243.
21   KPSS v rezoliutsiiakh i resheniiakh s"ezdov, konferentsii i plenumov TsK 1953, 1, p. 183.

Duma served to confirm the forebodings of those who had favoured the boycott, being a continuation of the tendencies that Bogdanov had criticised at the Fifth Congress. The need to form alliances with other opposition groups in the Duma prevented the fraction from following consistent Social-Democratic policies. Moreover, since the Duma fraction was mostly Menshevik in composition, it would not willingly subordinate itself to the demands of the predominantly Bolshevik Central Committee. In March 1908 the St Petersburg Committee of the RSDLP complained that to date the fraction had not done enough to carry out agitation and propaganda for the Social-Democratic Party, and rather than giving support to the party organisation outside the Duma, had made its position more difficult by obscuring the revolutionary stance of the Social-Democracy. The St Petersburg Committee insisted that the fraction should differentiate its position more clearly from the rest of the liberal opposition, and in particular from that of the Kadets.[22] Many members of the Petersburg and Moscow committees felt that if the fraction did not submit to the directives of the Central Committee it should be recalled, a measure that Lenin resisted vehemently.

Since at the end of 1907 there was imminent danger of arrest by the tsarist police, there was a mass exodus of Social Democrats and Socialist Revolutionaries from Russia to find refuge in Western Europe. It was no longer safe for Lenin and Bogdanov to remain in Finland, and Krupskaya recalls how, in preparation for their flight, she and Natalia Bogdanova cleared the Vasa of incriminating papers, covering the snow around the villa with ashes.[23] Early in December the Bolshevik Centre decided that it would be necessary to publish the newspaper *Proletarii* abroad. Lenin, Bogdanov and Dubrovinsky were assigned the task of organising the move. On leaving Finland, Lenin took up residence in Geneva, and Bogdanov first in Paris and subsequently in Geneva. It was in emigration that the most bitter conflicts between Lenin and Bogdanov were to take place.

3   Religion and Socialism

For the sake of his health, Lunacharsky moved to Italy in February 1907, settling in Florence, but was a frequent visitor to Gorky's residence on the island of Capri. It was while in Italy that he completed his major work entitled *Religion and Socialism*, whose first volume was published in St Petersburg in 1908.

---

22   Peterburgskii komitet RSDRP. Protokoly i materialy zasedanii Iiul' 1902–fevral' 1917 1986, p. 339.
23   Krupskaia 1989–90, 2, p. 104.

As Lunacharsky explained in the Foreword, *Religion and Socialism* was a work that was to some extent a continuation of his 1904 essay on positivist aesthetics. The original intention had been to write a history of religion from a materialist point of view. It would have included 'European metaphysics, utopian socialism and, finally, scientific socialism'. The scheme is reminiscent of Comte's stages in human development: the religious, the metaphysical and the scientific or positive. As the materialist history of religion turned out to be over-ambitions, Lunacharsky confined himself to a study of the relations between religion and socialism, defining the place of socialism among other religious systems. In fact, the Comtean type of progression from religious to scientific lies at the root of Lunacharsky's conception of the relationship between religion and socialism.

Lunacharsky, however, does not refer explicitly to Comte. He mentions Josef Dietzgen as a writer who has influenced him, and Marx himself, who had been schooled by the great German idealists, and whose thought he had never looked upon as a 'dry' economic doctrine. But to date, Lunacharsky observed, nobody had sufficiently emphasised the aesthetic and religious significance of the new world outlook and of the workers' movement itself.[24]

As in the essay on positivist aesthetics, the main influence on *Religion and Socialism* is the philosophy of Avenarius. Both works hinge on the idea that human beings not only perceive, but evaluate what they perceive. In this connection Lunacharsky declared that he thought Avenarius's psycho-physical explanation of the emotional colouring people attached to their sensations (affectional) was irrefutable. For Lunacharsky the elemental impulse to prolong those sensations that were beneficial to the organism and to curtail those that were harmful, as an act of self-preservation, was the seed from which there developed the rich variety of feelings, emotions and aspirations. The ultimate outcome of human volition and activity would be, as Avenarius had predicted, the complete harmonisation of the external environment with the processes of the human brain. What we called 'our world' was the relative equilibrium of the 'social brain' and the external forces.

As long as the external world was not in harmony with the human brain, as long as the world had not been 'made cerebral', human beings would always aspire to something better, something higher, for the 'maximum of life'. It was in these aspirations that Lunacharsky saw the essence of religion. For Lunacharsky religion was 'that thinking about the world and that world sensation which psychologically tries to resolve the contrast between the laws of life and

---

24   Lunacharskii 1908–11, 1, pp. 9–10.

the laws of nature'.[25] He saw in these aspirations for a better life a complete continuity between the religious outlook of former times and modern socialism. The kind of process that he envisaged was that 'The mythological creation gives way to metaphysics and finally to exact science, the faith in magic gives way to faith in labour. In place of animism there stands scientific energetics. But has anything changed in the religious essence of the human soul?'[26]

Lunacharsky thought not; human beings still had aspirations and ideals, and in this respect socialists were no different from adherents of religions. Both were able to think and feel about the world in such a way as to resolve for us the contradictions between the laws of life and the laws of nature. Scientific socialism solves these contradictions, putting forward the idea of the victory of life, the taming of elemental forces through reason, by perception and labour, science and technology.[27]

There was a polemical dimension to *Religion and Socialism*, as it was part of Lunacharsky's continuing debate with Berdyaev. It was an answer to Berdyaev's accusation that there was nothing ethical about socialism, since it was the outcome of an impersonal economic process. And it was a response to Berdyaev's charge that socialism was lacking in the higher ideals that were integral to religious faith. In his book Lunacharsky emphasised precisely the idealism of the socialists and the labour movement, and made a point of arguing that the success of socialism was by no means guaranteed.[28]

In his essay 'Atheism' published in the collection *Studies in the Philosophy of Marxism* in 1908, Lunacharsky returned to his definition of religion as the aspiration to resolve the contradiction between the laws of life and the laws of nature. He contrasted the ways in which this question had been approached by old religions and religious philosophical systems and by Marx. Whereas the former had only explained the world, the latter set out to change it.[29] For Lunacharsky the socialist approach to changing the world in the direction of a harmonious human collective, or in Avenarius's term a 'congregal' system, could be described as 'religious atheism'.[30]

In *Religion and Socialism* Lunacharsky had presented a novel interpretation of religion, and at the same time had defended socialism from the strictures of its religious critics. It is an original work that can properly be numbered

---

25   Lunacharskii 1908–11, 1, p. 40.
26   Lunacharskii 1908–11, 1, p. 41.
27   Ibid.
28   Lunacharskii 1908–11, 1, p, 41.
29   Lunacharskii 1908, p. 156.
30   Lunacharskii 1908, pp. 152, 157.

among the most significant in the history of Russian Marxist thought. Yet it is scarcely known, and what is known of it is misleading. One has only to state Lunacharsky's arguments and to understand that he uses the term 'religion' in a very broad sense to know that *Religion and Socialism* is not a work written from a religious point of view. Lunacharsky does not seek to reconcile socialism and religion, or found a new religion of socialism. Yet these have been the common interpretations of the work. The originator of these interpretations was Plekhanov, who reviewed *Religion and Socialism* in 1908 in an article entitled 'On the So-Called Religious Seekings in Russia'.[31]

Plekhanov's review of Lunacharsky's book was not designed to acquaint the reader with its contents, but to discredit it. Although quotations from it were given, these were not in any context, and were only cited so that Plekhanov could take issue with them. The impression given was that Lunacharsky was in fact advocating the belief in God and the religious point of view. In the second volume of *Religion and Socialism*, which was published in 1911, Lunacharsky protested vehemently about the way that Plekhanov had falsified quotations and had misrepresented the content of the work.[32] By that time, however, it was widely believed that Lunacharsky had advocated a kind of socialist religion.

Writing in retrospect in 1914, Bogdanov thought that Lunacharsky had made a serious mistake in presenting his ideas in the context of the development of religion. He conceded that an intelligent reader would be able to understand Lunacharsky's arguments despite the religious terminology in which they were couched. But the common reaction would be to associate the religious terms with the ideological content that they traditionally had possessed. The impression that Lunacharsky was an advocate of a new socialist religion was reinforced by Gorky's writings at the time. In his work *The Confession* he had used the term 'god-building' (*bogostroitel'stvo*) to apply to the collectivist ideal that he and Lunacharsky shared. The term 'god-building' was then used to characterise the philosophical current to which Gorky, Lunacharsky and Bogdanov belonged. Lunacharsky's interest in religion had left him and his associates open to attack by their opponents who did not scruple to misinterpret his intentions.[33]

31   Plekhanov 1956–58, 3, pp. 326–38.
32   Lunacharskii 1908–11, 2, pp. 395–7.
33   Neizvestnyi Bogdanov, 3, pp. 107–9.

4   The Open Letter to Plekhanov

Provoked by the disparaging remarks made on his philosophical ideas by Plekhanov himself or by his followers, without any attempt to confront them systematically, Bogdanov published an open letter to Plekhanov in the September
1907 issue of the journal *Vestnik Zhizni*. In it he said:

> I have followed with great interest the campaign which you, with the sup-
> port of your disciples, have been conducting against *Empiriomonism* for
> the past three years. I expected much from this campaign – I expected to
> find on your part a serious and profound critique, which perhaps would
> be very unpleasant for me personally, but would contribute greatly to the
> elucidation of the truth ... But what happened? You personally confined
> yourself to repeated statements that you are negatively inclined towards
> me and my views. You systematically call me 'Mr [*gospodin*] Bogdanov',
> which, as you well know, is insulting to a comrade, and which, as you also
> well know, you have no right to do. You have brought to the notice of com-
> rades that *Empiriomonism* is not Marxism, but only a variety of bourgeois
> criticism. You have ironically written of my 'profundity', and not ironic-
> ally that you have a 'very low' opinion of my 'philosophical abilities'. You
> have gone so far as to make very transparent hints about how desirable it
> would be, if not to hang me, then at least to 'exile' me beyond the bounds
> of Marxism, and, if I am not mistaken, 'within 24 hours'. You have said
> this very many times, and on every kind of pretext: in the commentaries
> on Engels's popular pamphlet, and in the Introduction to your essays, and
> in your 'diaries', and in articles on tactics, and in the review of Dietzgen's
> book, and even, as I heard, at the Congress. This was very energetic and
> very interesting. But this would also be very convincing ... but one thing
> is missing here – and that is the evidence. It remains unclear and even
> unknown what the 'sufficient grounds' are on which you base your opin-
> ion, which is completely clear in itself and widely popularised by you ...[34]

Of course, Bogdanov was quite right in expecting a serious examination and critique of his work, and justly aggrieved when all that came from Plekhanov were
derogatory remarks and smears. But Bogdanov should not have been surprised
by this. He ought to have been able to interpret Plekhanov's attitude as one
of frustration and despair. There is nothing Plekhanov would have liked better
than to be able to analyse Bogdanov's ideas and refute them systematically and

---

34   Neizvestnyi Bogdanov 1995, 3, pp. 87–8.

convincingly. But Plekhanov did not have that level of ability. It was pointless to demand from him the kind of critique that he was incapable of giving.

5   Materialismus Militans

In response to Bogdanov's 'Open Letter', Plekhanov began to work on a series of three articles in the form of letters with the general heading of 'Materialismus Militans' early in 1908. The first letter was published in the summer of that year in the May–June issues of the Menshevik journal *Golos Sotsial-Demokrata*. The second letter appeared in the same journal in October 1908. Due to a quarrel with the editors of *Golos Sotsial-Demokrata* the third letter did not appear in the journal, but was published, along with the previous two, in a collection of Plekhanov's articles entitled *From Defence to Attack* in 1910. The articles were written in an insulting sardonic tone, larded with literary allusions, designed no doubt to demonstrate the erudition of their author.

Instead of presenting a refutation of Bogdanov's ideas, Plekhanov sought to justify the behaviour that Bogdanov had objected to in his 'Open Letter'. This began with the matter of his addressing Bogdanov by 'Mr' rather than 'comrade'. Here Plekhanov contended that since Bogdanov represented a world outlook diametrically opposed to his own, materialist, outlook, he felt no obligation to address him as 'Comrade'.

Plekhanov made a more substantial point against Bogdanov by quoting the passage from *Empiriomonism* where Bogdanov had criticised the interpretation of the Kantian 'thing-in-itself' adopted by Engels and Plekhanov. Bogdanov had concluded his critique by observing that: 'Such is approximately the standpoint of the French materialists of the eighteenth century and among modern philosophers – Engels and his Russian follower, Plekhanov'.

In this passage Bogdanov had equated the (mistaken) views of Plekhanov and Engels, and Plekhanov was able to seize upon this to argue that Bogdanov rejected Engels's point of view, and since Engels was completely at one with Marx on philosophical matters, it followed that Bogdanov rejected Marx's viewpoint and was a critic of Marx. By equating Plekhanov with Engels on this occasion Bogdanov had given Plekhanov a pretext – a tenuous one to be sure – to argue that an attack on himself was an attack on Marx and Engels. He would claim that the real object of Bogdanov's attacks was Marx and Engels, and that the criticism of himself was only a subterfuge, since Bogdanov lacked the courage to attack Marx and Engels directly.[35]

---

35   Plekhanov 1956–58, 3, p. 204.

Bogdanov regretted bracketing Plekhanov with Engels in this way and so inadvertently providing Plekhanov with a means of implying that he, Bogdanov, was a 'critic of Marx'. Plekhanov claimed that at a recent meeting of Russians in Geneva, when he drew Bogdanov's attention to the passage from *Empiriomonism* in question, Bogdanov rose from his seat and shouted: 'That's what I used to think; now I see I was mistaken'.[36] Writing in 1908, Bogdanov gave a different version of events. Plekhanov, he said, had been one of the first popularisers of Marx's ideas in Russia, and as such he was regarded as the authentic voice of the philosophical views of Marx and Engels. Therefore, when in *Empiriomonism* Bogdanov had criticised Plekhanov's concept of the 'thing-in-itself' he had extended this criticism to Engels in whose name Plekhanov ostensibly spoke. What he had said to Plekhanov at the meeting in Geneva was: 'Then I believed you, but afterwards I checked up on you'. Bogdanov was aghast at the bare-faced way Plekhanov had distorted his words, obscuring the serious accusation that he had made against Plekhanov at the public meeting.[37]

Certainly, in his writings Bogdanov did not repeat the idea that Plekhanov and Engels shared the same mistaken ideas. But this was to little avail, since Plekhanov, and later Lenin, continued to argue that Bogdanov attacked Plekhanov only because he lacked the courage to attack Marx and Engels directly. From what Plekhanov says about the meeting in Geneva, it is clear that the dispute between Bogdanov and Plekhanov was conducted not only on the pages of written publications, but also at open meetings. These were held at the end of 1907 and the first half of 1908 in the Russian émigré communities mainly in Geneva, but also in Berne. They were frequented not only by the local Social Democrats, but also by many visitors from outlying areas who came to listen to the speeches.[38]

Referring to his jibe comparing Bogdanov to the philosopher Christian Wolff, whom Friedrich Wilhelm gave the choice of immediate banishment or being hanged, Plekhanov observed that one could hardly banish Bogdanov from the confines of Marxism, when he was already outside them. He added that the right to be executed was only conferred by talent, and that of this Bogdanov had none, and so from this danger he was quite safe.[39]

Plekhanov denied that he expounded Marx's materialism with the aid of quotations from Holbach.[40] He said that he used Holbach to defend mater-

36   Plekhanov 1956–58, 3, p. 211.
37   Bogdanov 1908b, pp. 20–1.
38   Deborin 1927, p. xiv.
39   Plekhanov 1956–58, 3, pp. 204–8.
40   Plekhanov 1956–58, 3, p. 214.

ialism from the reproaches advanced against it by its opponents, the neo-Kantians in particular, including Bernstein and Conrad Schmidt. This was certainly untrue, since Plekhanov's association of Holbach and other materialists of the eighteenth century with Marx dated from the publication in 1885 of a chapter of Marx and Engels's book The *Holy Family*, while the polemics against Bernstein and Schmidt were a decade later. Franz Mehring's publication of the full version of *The Holy Family* had shown that the chapter on French materialism of the eighteenth century was merely an excursion by Marx on intellectual history and did not represent his views. Nevertheless in 'Materialismus Militans' Plekhanov quoted a passage from *The Holy Family* in which Marx associated materialism with communism and socialism.[41]

It was only in the second letter that Plekhanov got round to answering Bogdanov's substantive point about defining matter in terms of Kant's 'things-in-themselves'. Plekhanov's defence, however, amounted to little more than a re-statement of the position he had adopted. He stated that all 'things-in-themselves' were material in the sense that they aroused in the senses sensations of one kind or another. He believed this had been admitted by Kant himself on the first page of *The Critique of Pure Reason*, but that elsewhere Kant had also maintained that 'things-in-themselves' were unknowable. In this respect Kant had contradicted himself. According to Plekhanov, he had exposed this inconsistency to Kant's followers, arguing that to resolve it they had to choose between the subjective idealist or the materialist interpretation of Kant's thought.[42]

By way of contrast to the materialist interpretation of Kant's 'things-in-themselves', Plekhanov quoted the opinion of Bishop Berkeley, who argued that what people actually perceived was their own ideas and sensations. In his opinion: 'colour, figure, motion, extension are quite known to us as our sensations. But we would entangle ourselves in contradictions if we considered them as signs or images of things existing outside thinking'. Plekhanov went on to contend that Berkeley's point of view was one shared by Ernst Mach, of whom he declared Bogdanov to be a disciple.[43]

Plekhanov was anxious to defend himself against Bogdanov's accusation that he had contradicted himself by saying in his 1906 notes to Engels's *Ludwig Feuerbach* that 'things-in-themselves' had 'form' but did not have 'appearance', since both of these terms were synonymous. Furthermore, the contention that

41   Plekhanov 1956–58, 3, p. 217.
42   Plekhanov 1956–58, 3, p. 227.
43   Plekhanov 1956–58, 3, p. 228.

'things-in-themselves' had these characteristics was in conflict with the conception of them that Plekhanov had expressed in his polemic with Conrad Schmidt, published in the same year. There he had maintained that 'things-in-themselves' simply acted on the sense organs to produce sensations. In his defence Plekhanov explained that his polemic with Schmidt was conducted in 1899, and although he now considered his formulations there unsatisfactory, he had not corrected them, because this had been a polemical article and it would be improper to make alterations to it, since this would be 'like appearing before your adversary with a new weapon while compelling him to fight with his old weapon'. This circumstance, Plekhanov insisted, was something Bogdanov should have borne in mind, and not ignored his 'literary conscience'.[44] In fact, when Bogdanov checked the Russian translation against the German original he discovered that Plekhanov had re-edited his article extensively, and had done exactly what he had declared it unethical to do.[45]

The third letter in the 'Materialismus Militans' series, published in 1910, was the only one in which Plekhanov made some appearance of discussing what Bogdanov had written in *Empiriomonism*. The approach adopted, however, was to take individual statements by Bogdanov and subject them to ridicule. The recurring theme, as in the second letter, was that Bogdanov was a follower of Mach, who in turn was a disciple of Berkeley, and that the logical conclusion of Berkeley's philosophy was solipsism. Hence, Plekhanov argued, Bogdanov's philosophy was one of subjective idealism and had nothing in common with the dialectical materialism of Marx and Engels. This theme was taken up by Lenin in *Materialism and Empiriocriticism* and developed at greater length and in more detail.

A significant fact that emerges from Plekhanov's 'Materialismus Militans', and one which obviously caused Plekhanov considerable annoyance, is that whereas Bogdanov's works sold well and went through several editions, Plekhanov's translation of Engels's *Ludwig Feuerbach* had very poor sales.[46] Neither Plekhanov nor Lenin ever denied that Bogdanov's ideas were popular; that made it all the more imperative that they should be discredited.

In Gorky's view, empiriomonism was the ideology of the RSDLP, and Bogdanov's first duty was to complete his system rather than engage in polemics with his opponents. He feared that Bogdanov was wasting his time in pointless disputes of this kind. Maria Andreeva was of the same opinion; she was surprised that Bogdanov should pay any attention to these critics, since

44   Plekhanov 1956–58, 3, p. 243.
45   Bogdanov 1910a, pp. 208.
46   Plekhanov 1956–58, 3, pp. 219, 299.

they were 'so small, so petty, so impotent'.[47] Despite these entreaties from his friends, Bogdanov went ahead and wrote a reply to the criticisms of Plekhanov and his disciples in a pamphlet entitled *The Adventures of One Philosophical School*.

6   Adventures of One Philosophical School

Bogdanov began his pamphlet with a re-statement of his criticism of Plekhanov's concept of 'matter' as 'thing-in-itself', as stated in the passage from his reply to Conrad Schmidt. Plekhanov's school, Bogdanov said, called itself 'materialist', and its picture of the world was constructed on the idea of 'matter'. But this 'matter' was not matter as it was usually understood, with properties such as colour and temperature; matter was the 'thing-in-itself', the source of sensations.

Plekhanov conceded that 'materialists have never asserted that we know "things-in-themselves"'. But to define what exactly was known of the 'things-in-themselves' had been something of a challenge for Plekhanov. In the 1892 edition of his commentary on Engels's pamphlet on Ludwig Feuerbach, he had speculated that 'our sensations were "hieroglyphs" which bring to our consciousness what is taking place in reality'. But in the 1905 edition of the same pamphlet he admitted that this formulation had been inaccurate, and now said that he agreed with the Russian physiologist Ivan Sechenov, who thought that sense impressions were 'conventional signs' of 'things-in-themselves', but dissented from what he saw as Sechenov's belief that 'things-in-themselves' had 'appearance'. By quoting at length Plekhanov's various attempts to define what people could and could not know of 'things-in-themselves', Bogdanov implied that Plekhanov was tying himself in knots trying to explain something from false premises.

According to Bogdanov, Plekhanov had been so anxious to attribute his concepts of matter and 'things-in-themselves' to Marx and Engels that in his translation of Engels's pamphlet *Ludwig Feuerbach* he had falsified one of the famous 'Theses on Feuerbach'. Instead of Marx's original formulation, 'In practice man must prove the truth, that is, the reality and power, the this-sidedness of his thinking', Plekhanov had rendered the passage as: 'In practice man must prove the truth of his thinking, that is, prove that it has real power and does not stop on this side of phenomena'. By inserting the word 'not', Plekhanov had

---

47   Scherrer 1988, p. 47.

given Marx's words a sense supportive of his own point of view, but completely at odds with the meaning of the original.[48]

An important section of Bogdanov's pamphlet was devoted to the way in which Plekhanov and his school misrepresented the ideas of Mach and Avenarius in order to be able to refute them. The chief method of doing this was to treat the concept of 'experience' in an exclusively subjective and individual sense, as though it was only the totality of sensations. Bogdanov emphasised that for Mach and Avenarius the complexes of elements were neither physical or psychical, but appeared in both physical and psychical groupings. The elements and complexes of this network were closely connected together at many points, called 'I', but such points were not something constant, but constantly appeared, disappeared and changed. This concept of experience espoused by Mach and Avenarius, Bogdanov pointed out, was completely anti-individualist and anti-subjectivist.[49]

He went on to say that any critique of the empiriocriticist school of Mach and Avenarius must take account of this concept of experience as its starting point; it must accept or reject it. Had the philosophical school of Plekhanov and Ortodoks done this? Most certainly not. Instead of this it had done something entirely illegitimate; it had attributed to its opponents its own concept of experience without the slightest attempt to analyse their point of view, without even a passing reference to the real nature of this point of view. Here Bogdanov gave examples from the writings of Plekhanov and Ortodoks, showing that they treated concepts such as 'experience' and 'sensations' in a purely subjective sense, in this way distorting the meaning of the writers they criticised.[50]

Bogdanov concluded his pamphlet by summing up his relationship to the empiriocritics. He thought that they were on the right track, but that their philosophy had its limitations, such as the failure to recognise physical experience as having a collective subject. He outlined once more his conception of 'substitution' which, he thought, gave a better explanation for how people related to each other than the empiriocritics offered.[51] Bogdanov thought it necessary to show how his own philosophy of empiriomonism differed from the philosophy of empiriocriticism, because Plekhanov and his school persistently used the terms interchangeably and implied that Bogdanov was a follower of Mach pure and simple. By doing this they could make for themselves a much

---

48   Bogdanov 1908b, p. 19.
49   Bogdanov 1908b, p. 44.
50   Ibid.
51   Bogdanov 1908b, p. 49.

easier target for their criticisms. But, as Bogdanov pointed out, no attempt was made by his critics to do battle with empiriomonism on a philosophical plane.[52]

Plekhanov did not reply to Bogdanov's *Adventures of One Philosophical School*. In his third letter of 'Materialismus Militans' he said that he had intended to say something about the pamphlet, but could not find the time to do so. But he thought it unnecessary to analyse the pamphlet since in 'Materialismus Militans' he had made clear what he thought of both Bogdanov's philosophical views and those of Bogdanov's teacher Mach. Clearly, the arguments Bogdanov had set out in his pamphlet had failed to make any impression on Plekhanov, or indeed on any members of his philosophical school.[53]

7   Studies in the Philosophy of Marxism

Prior to *The Adventures of One Philosophical School* there had appeared the collection of essays in which Bogdanov was involved, entitled *Studies in the Philosophy of Marxism*. As the foreword of the collection explained, the contributors were not united by adherence to any particular philosophical system; what united them was their belief in socialism and their opposition to the importation into Marxist philosophy of concepts and categories which restricted rather than expanded the spirit of enquiry.[54] In fact the essays covered a variety of topics within the field of socialist theory: Bazarov wrote on 'The Mysticism and Realism of our Times', Lunacharsky on 'Atheism', Ya.A. Berman on 'Dialectics', P.S. Yushkevich on 'Empiriosymbolism', O.I. Gelfond on the philosophy of Joseph Dietzgen and Suvorov on the bases of social philosophy. Some of the essays were openly critical of the Plekhanov school of Marxist philosophy, and mentioned in particular Plekhanov's espousal of the Kantian 'thing-in-itself'. Bazarov, for example, argued that 'Between the materialism of Marx and Engels, on the one hand, and the materialism of Plekhanov and Ortodoks, on the other, there is an enormous difference'.[55] In his essay Lunacharsky made an oblique reference to Plekhanov in his statement that there were two kinds of 'socialist materialism': one was in the tradition of Dietzgen, while the other was the thinly disguised materialism of the eighteenth century.[56]

---

52   Bogdanov 1908b, pp. 56–7.
53   Plekhanov 1956–58, 3, p. 283.
54   Ocherki po filosofii marksizma 1908, p. 2.
55   Ocherki po filosofii marksizma 1908, p. 71.
56   Lunacharskii 1908, p. 145.

Bogdanov's was the most explicitly anti-Plekhanov contribution in the collection. Entitled 'The Land of Idols and the Philosophy of Marxism', it interpreted Plekhanov's concept of 'things-in-themselves' in terms of the evolution of human perception. Bogdanov's contention was that there was an unbroken line of continuity between the animism of primitive peoples, the commodity fetishism of bourgeois society, and the doctrine of 'things-in-themselves' of modern philosophy, the philosophy of Plekhanov and Holbach in particular. He predicted that this fetishism would be finally eliminated with the development of society, the elimination of domination-subordination relationships and advances in science and technology.[57]

Tracing the evolution of the idea of 'things-in-themselves' gave Bogdanov the opportunity to elaborate on his concept of 'universal substitution' and its relationship to Avenarius's 'introjection'. For Bogdanov the prerequisite of 'things-in-themselves' was the doubling of the human being into 'soul' and 'body'. This had been the product of evolution, because for primitive perception there had been no 'things', only actions. At a later stage the actions had crystallised into things, as the primitive dialectic became static. The doubling of the world began with the doubling of human beings. Into the human body a soul was 'introjected', so that for the animist consciousness the body was the passive element, while the soul was the active and moving force. Expressed in social-labour terms, the body was the incarnation of the executory functions, the soul the incarnation of the organising functions.

From what Bogdanov says, it would appear that he thought Avenarius's concept of introjection was valid and useful; he agreed that people 'introjected' their feelings and thoughts into their fellow-creatures. But, in Bogdanov's view, *what* was introjected was substitution, the mutual understanding between human beings that made any cooperation possible. And where Bogdanov disagreed with Avenarius was on how introjection and its accompanying dualism came about; whereas Avenarius saw its origin in logical or general-psychological factors, Bogdanov held it to be in the psychology of the labour process, one characterised by 'subordination' and 'domination'.[58] In this way the concept of substitution was integrated into Bogdanov's existing philosophical system.

The implication of Bogdanov's conceptions of substitution and introjection as being the products of labour relations based on the subordination/domination model is that if this model were to be superseded, then non-substituted

---

57   Bogdanov 1908c, pp. 219–20.
58   Bogdanov 1908c, pp. 223–4.

and non-introjected perception was possible. This would presuppose relations between people in which there were no barriers to a complete mutual understanding. In fact, in the essay 'The Philosophy of the Modern Natural Scientist', written at the same time as 'The Land of Idols and the Philosophy of Marxism', Bogdanov elaborated on his conception of 'comradely cooperation'.

> Comradely cooperation of the proletariat not only liberates perception from the encumbrance of dualist and pluralistic tendencies arising from earlier forms of labour organisation. Moreover, this cooperation in itself also brings with it the direct stimulus to the development of monism. It creates a profound psychological homogeneity between people-comrades, and a close bond between them on the basis of a single common cause, and gives rise to an increasingly full *mutual understanding*. This mutual understanding consists in the fact that people think of their own and other people's experiences in the same way – they think of themselves and others in the same terms; in other words, there is the monist thinking of people about people. It gives natural psychological support and a basis for the general monism of perception; and it emerges in the mentality of the proletariat with the utmost facility and simplicity, as something belonging to it *organically*.[59]

In 'The Land of Idols and the Philosophy of Marxism', Bogdanov went on to demonstrate the impossibility of 'things-in-themselves' in terms of his concept of 'substitution'. While this was a necessary impulse for mutual understanding, cooperation and communication, it was misapplied when extended to inanimate objects, giving rise to the misapprehension that things might have a perception of themselves.[60]

Bogdanov was insistent that the philosophical views of Plekhanov and his 'school' should not be confused with the views of Marx, Engels, Dietzgen and other orthodox Marxists. He thought that the most regrettable aspect of Plekhanov's controversy with Bernstein was 'Plekhanov's claim to be the official philosopher of Marxism, to speak *on behalf* of Marx and Engels, who being already dead cannot put an end to this abuse'. Bogdanov recalled that twice he had challenged Plekhanov to come up with a critique of his philosophical ideas, but so far he had received no reply.[61] In fact, when it came, the reply was not from Plekhanov, but from Lenin.

---

59   Bogdanov 1909a, p. 141.
60   Bogdanov 1908c, pp. 223–4.
61   Bogdanov 1908c, p. 234.

8   Socialist Society

As well as the third volume of *Empiriomonism*, Bogdanov had taken advantage
of his term in prison to write a chapter on 'Socialist Society' for his *Short Course
of Economic Science*. The six editions of the *Short Course* that were published
prior to 1906 concluded with the characterisation of industrial capitalism, any
mention of socialism being likely to fall foul of the censor. But with the relax-
ation of censorship in the 'days of freedom' a section on socialism was now
possible, and Bogdanov took advantage of this to outline his conception of the
society of the future.

Bogdanov looked forward to a time when industrial production would
become fully automated, when the role of workers would be reduced to over-
seeing the functioning of machines. Work at the machine would become much
more of an organising function, and increasingly of an intellectual rather than
of a physical nature. The division of labour would no longer imply specialisation which narrowed and impoverished the psyche of the worker. Now specialisation would be transferred from the workers to the machines. This would
also break down the barriers of communication between people that specialisation had brought about; contacts between people would be broadened and
deepened, furthering cooperation and mutual understanding.

The age-old division into organisers and executors would be overcome, and
labour groupings would become increasingly fluid. Workers would be able to
change jobs easily, going from one machine to another, sometimes in an 'organiser' role and sometimes as an 'executor'. This would be possible because the
anarchy of the market and competition would be eliminated and production
would be organised by society, consciously and in a planned way.[62]

The distribution of products would take place in a rational fashion. There
would be social ownership of the means of production, but each person would
be entitled to 'individual property', and would receive sufficient consumer
goods to satisfy his or her needs. Bogdanov conceded that this operation would
be of enormous complexity, and that the statistical apparatus and information
technology required was far in advance of anything that existed at the present
time.[63]

In terms of social psychology, the socialist society, free of the individualism
engendered by the market and competition, would foster the growth of mutual
sympathy and mutual understanding. From society's mastery over external

---

62   Bogdanov 1906a, pp. 277–81.
63   Bogdanov 1906a, p. 282.

nature and its own nature would come the end of all kinds of fetishism. Peopl
perception would be pure and clear, free of any mysticism or metaphysics. Both
natural fetishism and commodity fetishism would disappear.[64]

The combination of mutual understanding and the absence of fetishism
would create a third element in the psychology of socialist society: this was
the progressive elimination of the remnants of compulsion in social life. These
include what Bogdanov referred to as the 'compulsory norms', the systems of
customs, laws or ethics governing the behaviour of people in society. Since
these were designed to regulate the conflicts which arose between individuals, groups or classes, the absence of these conflicts would render 'compulsory
norms' redundant in a socialist society.[65]

Bogdanov concluded by arguing that the retention in socialist society of a
state structure and a legal framework was unnecessary, even to ensure that
every person ought to perform a certain amount of labour for the social good.
He pointed out that every state structure was an organisation of class domination, and that it would be unnecessary where there were no classes. He believed
that the prevalence of the social sentiment that connected people would be sufficient to ensure that every individual would do what they could for the benefit
of all. Only in the transition period, when traces of the class divisions of the
past remained, was the state form conceivable in the new society. But even this
state would be one of class domination, this time the domination of the proletariat, the class which eliminates the division of society into classes. With the
elimination of that division would come the elimination of the state as well.[66]

Under the heading 'Forces of Development', Bogdanov outlined the future
perspectives of the socialist society. This society would no longer be based on
exchange, but would be a higher type of natural economy; it would be in direct
confrontation with the forces of nature, but no longer as large or small community, but as the whole of humanity. Nor would this society have to wait for
population growth to force the people to further perfect their labour and knowledge; the needs of humanity would grow in the very process of labour and
experience. Each new victory over nature and its mysteries would stimulate
new challenges and fresh discoveries. Power over nature meant the continual
accumulation of the energy of society acquired by it from external nature, and
this energy would seek an outlet and find it in the creation of new forces of
labour and knowledge.[67]

---

64   Bogdanov 1906a, pp. 282–4.
65   Bogdanov 1906a, pp. 283–4.
66   Bogdanov 1906a, p. 284.
67   Bogdanov 1906a, pp. 284–5.

t his ideas on what the future collectivist society would be in the novel *Red Star*. Bogdanov calls *Red Star* a 'utopian' purpose is to set out his conception of an actual socialist ccurate to describe it as an 'Aesopian' novel. The story is set in Russia in the aftermath of the 1905 revolution, when the hero, Leonid, a left-wing Social Democrat, is befriended by Menni, a visitor from Mars, and is taken by him to visit the red planet. The Martians have already established a collectivist society, and the description of its features forms the substance of the novel. Mars plays the same part in Bogdanov's story as the future does in Edward Bellamy's *Looking Backward*.[68]

In *Red Star* Bogdanov is emphatic that his utopia is not a static one, that it could not be accused of being complacent. It was on these grounds that he found Bellamy's social ideal wanting. What Bogdanov says about Bellamy's novel provides an insight into the approach he took in writing *Red Star*. This was as follows:

> Bellamy's society is one that has become petrified in satisfaction and complacency, placidly resting on its laurels following the victories gained by preceding generations over nature, both social and external – such a society does not incorporate any stimulus for further development – it in itself is not progressive. Consequently, Bellamy's utopia in the last analysis is not a progressive ideal, and present-day idealists regard it as a philistine caricature of their own ideals.[69]

From the memoirs of Mitskevich published in 1906 it emerges why Bogdanov was particularly concerned with Bellamy's novel. It had been translated into Russian and was one of the books read in workers' study circles.[70] Since it was from such sources that workers derived their conceptions of the future socialist society, it was important that they should have a novel that gave a more dynamic depiction of the socialist ideal.

In the light of Bogdanov's critique of Bellamy, one knows in advance that a prominent feature of his own novel is going to be a serious challenge posed by the forces of nature to the socialist society of the future. This idea in fact is voiced by one of the characters in *Red Star*:

---

68 Bellamy 1888.
69 Bogdanov 1906, p. 22.
70 Mitskevich 1906, p. 8.

Happy? Peaceful? Where did you get that impression? True, peace reigns among people, but there cannot be peace with the natural elements. Even a victory over such a foe can pose a new threat. During the most recent period of our history we have intensified the exploitation of the planet tenfold, our population is growing, and our needs are increasing even faster. The danger of exhausting our natural resources and energy has repeatedly confronted various branches of our industry.[71]

In other respects *Red Star* follows the template of *Looking Backward* rather closely. In *Looking Backward* the hero, the young American Julian West, falls into a deep hypnosis-induced sleep and wakes up 113 years later in 2000. While he has been asleep the United States has been turned into a socialist utopia in which all the industry has been nationalised and there is a moneyless economy. West is fortunate enough to have the new system explained to him by his host Dr Leete. A romantic element is supplied when West falls in love with Leete's daughter Edith. Towards the end of the novel a note of ambiguity is introduced when West ostensibly wakes up back in the nineteenth century, doubting if he has ever been in the future at all. But this is resolved when it turns out that he has only dreamed about returning to his own times, and that in reality he is still in the future and is able to marry Edith.

In Bogdanov's novel Leonid's trip to Mars plays the same role as Julian West's transference to future times. Leonid, the hero, is befriended by Menni, a Martian who has come to earth to look for suitable humans to take back to Mars to instruct on life there, and to help the Martians better understand life on earth. The main focus of the novel is the description of the collectivist society on Mars. Leonid falls in love with the Martian girl Netti, but because, in a fit of rage, he kills Sterni, her former husband, he is banished to his native Earth. There Leonid suffers hallucinations and is treated in a psychiatric hospital, where he suspects that his visit to Mars has been an illusion. Leonid throws himself into the revolutionary struggle and is severely wounded, but almost on the point of death he is rescued by Netti and transported back to Mars.

In his introduction to the 1929 publication of *Red Star* Boris Legran reminds his readers that in 1908, when *Red Star* was published, Louis Bleriot had still to make his epoch-making flight across the English Channel.[72] Judged against the technological level of the real world, Bogdanov's anticipation in *Red Star* of space travel and other future scientific developments seems truly remark-

---

71   Bogdanov 1979, p. 98.
72   Bogdanov 1979, p. 5.

able. On his trip to Mars Leonid experiences weightlessness, which Bogdanov describes as if he had actually witnessed how human bodies and liquids behave in a spacecraft outside Earth's gravity. On Mars Leonid finds that the Martians are familiar with nuclear energy, anti-matter, synthetic fabrics, 3D films and speech-to-text devices. In the field of medicine they make wide use of blood transfusions, still a recent development in 1908. However, it is not Martian technical achievements that form the centrepiece of Bogdanov's utopia, but the fabric of socialist society, which in his philosophical writings he termed 'comradely cooperation'.

Bogdanov illustrates this cooperation by recounting an episode in which Leonid is operating a machine while working at a Martian factory. When his concentration lapses, he is immediately helped by his fellow-workers. Leonid discovers that the Martian workers do the same for each other as a matter of course. The incident brings home to Leonid that although he has been judged suitable by Menni to be taken to Mars because of his lack of individualism, he is nevertheless much more individualistic than the collectivist Martians.[73]

There are several aspects to Bogdanov's concept of collectivism, reflecting different strands in his thought. One of these is the elimination of the organiser/executor division, that is the distinction between people who organise and those who carry out orders. For Bogdanov this is the earliest and most fundamental social division which afflicted mankind, one which preceded the formation of social classes. It was responsible for authoritarian thinking and for the dualist view of the world that divided phenomena into the physical and the psychical. In socialist society this division is overcome, and the monist view of the world is restored.[74]

Even on the trip to Mars Leonid discovers that Martian society is not authoritarian. Menni is the captain of the spacecraft, but he does not have the power of command. His instructions are followed because he happens to be the most experienced pilot of the spacecraft.[75] On Mars itself the comradely relations prevailed between the individuals, with a directness and absence of formality. Great individuals are not commemorated, only important events.

A second aspect of Bogdanov's concept of collectivism is the elimination of specialisation into trades and professions. The recurrent theme in the analysis of the human predicament that pervades Bogdanov's writings is the fragment-

---

73   Bogdanov 1979, pp. 125–30.
74   Bogdanov 2003, pp. 34–5.
75   Bogdanov 1979, p. 36.

ation of human society brought about through specialisation and the division of labour. The concomitants of this fragmentation are authoritarian relationships and outlooks, fetishism, including commodity fetishism, and the compartmentalisation of experience and knowledge. The obverse side of this analysis is Bogdanov's quest for means to heal these divisions and to re-integrate society, the human personality and the various sciences into a harmonious whole. Bogdanov's vision of the socialist utopia is one in which the fragmentation of all previous forms of social organisation is overcome.

From his earliest works Bogdanov was concerned to find a means by which this fragmentation of society and experience through the division of labour could be rectified. The solution that he proposed was 'the elaboration of general methods in all spheres of production'. With the development of machine industry, in which machines would become more specialised, while the labour of the workers became more homogeneous, the formulation of these general methods would become increasingly feasible. They would break down the barriers between the workers that the division of labour had erected, and foster the development of 'synthetic cooperation' (which Bogdanov later termed 'comradely cooperation').[76] There is thus a close association between 'general methods' and the formation of comradely cooperation among the workers. This close association is carried over into *Red Star*.

In the novel Leonid undergoes training in such general methods when he goes to work at a Martian clothing factory. He has to study the established scientific principles of industrial organisation, as well as the structure of the factory in which he is employed. He has to acquire a general notion of all the machines in use there, and know in detail the one with which he would be working.[77] Leonid works by turns in all sections of the factory, supervising the operation of the various machines.

A third aspect of Bogdanov's concept of collectivism is the absence of any legal or moral compulsion. This is an idea that appears from the earliest of Bogdanov's writings, where he argues that legal or moral norms are fetishes that first appeared in primitive clan society. In capitalist society, which was divided into organisers and the organised, law, morality and manners were framed in the interests of the former, the group responsible for the distribution of the social product.[78] It was Bogdanov's belief that in a socialist society no element of compulsion should determine people's behaviour; what they did should be

---

76   Bogdanov 1901, pp. 201–3.
77   Bogdanov 1979, p. 126.
78   Bogdanov 1899a, pp. 194–7.

entirely voluntary. No formal code of behaviour would be necessary when the relations between people were characterised by comradely cooperation.

Red Star begins with the separation between Leonid and his Earthly girl-friend Anna, arising out of a difference of opinion on morality. While Anna believes that the class ethics of the proletariat would necessarily become the universal moral code, Leonid holds that the proletariat is moving towards the destruction of all morals, and that the comradely feeling uniting people would not develop fully until it had cast off the fetishistic husk of morality.[79]

In respect of the question of morality, *Red Star* goes further than Bogdanov's philosophical writings. Leonid does not recognise fidelity to his partner as an obligation, considering polygamy in principle superior to monogamy, as it provided for both a richer private life and a greater variety of genetic combin-ations. He is supported in these views by Menni, indicating that Leonid's con-ception of morality is generally accepted on Mars. In the course of the novel, Leonid not only forms a relationship with Netti, but also, in her absence, with her friend Enno. From Enno Leonid learns that Netti has been married to two people at the same time. It is clear from the novel that Bogdanov upholds the principle of sexual equality, though this too is not an issue that is prominent in his other writings. One also suspects that in Bogdanov's favourable attitude towards polygamy there is an element of autobiography, bearing in mind his own relationships with Natalia and Anfusa.

In Martian society there is complete equality between the sexes. There is also less physical difference between the sexes than was the case on Earth, and the clothes that men and women wear differ very little. No wonder then that it took some time for Leonid to discover that Netti, the love of his life, was a woman![80] Leonid (and presumably Bogdanov) did not think that there could be love between Martians of the same sex.[81] Leonid is not surprised that Netti has been married before, but is somewhat shocked that she has been married to two men at the same time. Polyandry is possible in Martian society as is polygamy, to which Leonid seems to adjust quickly, as evidenced by his sexual encounter with Enno.[82]

Martian children are brought up collectively in colonies of mixed ages, so that the most varied experience can be passed on. Learning from each other preceded learning from books. Leonid witnesses an incident where a child is chastised for injuring a frog and being told to imagine what pain the frog must

---

79   Bogdanov 1979, p. 15.
80   Bogdanov 1979, p. 120.
81   Bogdanov 1979, p. 123.
82   Bogdanov 1979, p. 134.

have felt. The implication is that on Mars, the fellow-feeling extended not just to people, but to creatures as well.[83]

On Mars any violence was regarded as a symptom of mental illness and treated as such. A feature of Martian hospitals, Leonid discovered, was that they had beautiful rooms set aside for people, especially the old, who had decided to commit suicide to ensure a peaceful and painless death.[84] One means of raising the life expectancy of the Martians was the mutual exchange of blood through transfusions. Both parties received elements which they lacked and in this way their tissues were regenerated. This was one manifestation of the collectivist relationship that existed between the Martians, but that had not been adopted on the individualistic Earth.[85]

Bogdanov does not mention in *Red Star*, though he does in the *Short Course*, that the society of the future has no state structure or other political institutions.[86] These are rendered unnecessary because people's behaviour is regulated by considerations of mutual understanding and sympathy. On Mars there are very few limits to the freedoms Martians enjoy. One of them is the necessity to impose restrictions on patients suffering from nervous disorders. Netti, however, emphasises that the use of such compulsion in these cases is very different from the way it would be applied on Earth. There all practices are codified into laws, regulations and moral codes which dominate people and constantly oppress them. On Mars force did exist, but it was either a symptom of illness or the rational response in a given situation; in neither case was any formal code of law or morals involved.[87] Leonid finds that Mars is so lacking in any restrictions to freedom of any kind that he is surprised to find that Martian poetry observes laws of rhyme and metre.[88]

It is significant that Bogdanov devotes much more space in *Red Star* to discussing the collectivist relations between people than to describing the mechanics of the socialist system. Clearly, for Bogdanov it was the relations between people that was the essential element in his concept of what socialism was. Nevertheless, what he does say about the socialist economy is highly significant as it is practically the only place in pre-revolutionary literature that the subject is touched upon.

---

83   Bogdanov 1979, p. 37.
84   Bogdanov 1979, pp. 105–6.
85   Bogdanov 1979, pp. 107–8.
86   Bogdanov 1906a, p. 284.
87   Bogdanov 1979, p. 104.
88   Bogdanov 1979, pp. 96–7.

Bogdanov had stated in the chapter on Socialist Society in his *Short Course of Economic Science* that the complexity of the organisation of distribution demanded a level of statistical and information technology which was still distant in his own times.[89] The Martians, however, had attained this level. As Menni explained to Leonid:

> The Institute of Statistics has agencies everywhere which keep track of the flow of goods into and out of the stockpiles and monitor the productivity of all enterprises and the changes in the number of workers in them. In that way it can be calculated what and how much must be produced for any given period and the number of man hours required for the task. It then remains for the Institute to calculate the difference between what there is and what there should be, and to make this known to everyone. A flow of volunteers then re-establishes the equilibrium.[90]

To Leonid's inquiry whether there was any restriction on the consumption of goods, Menni informed him that there was none; everyone took whatever was needed in whatever quantities they desired. There was no need for money, documentation or any form of compulsion; all labour was voluntary.

The Martian economic planning system had the necessary flexibility to respond to changed circumstances. As Menni explained, the Institute of Statistics had to be alert to new inventions and changes in environmental conditions that might affect industry. Labour might have to be transferred to different branches of industry, necessitating a re-calculation taking the new factors into account, if not with absolute precision, then at least with an adequate degree of approximation.[91]

In keeping with Bogdanov's conception that the socialist ideal was not static, but dynamic, that there would always be difficulties to overcome, that the struggle against nature would never cease, Mars has to contend with the problem of diminishing natural resources. One possible solution would be the colonisation of Earth. The debate on this subject between Netti and the coldly rational mathematician Sterni gives Bogdanov the opportunity to reflect on two types of socialist revolution: that by which the socialist utopia was achieved on Mars, and the one by which a socialist society might be achieved on Earth.

---

89   Bogdanov 1906a, pp. 281–2.
90   Bogdanov 1979, p. 78.
91   Bogdanov 1979, pp. 78–9.

These two scenarios represent an evolution in Bogdanov's thinking. On his way to Mars in the spacecraft Leonid passes his time profitably by studying Martian history. He discovers that Mars has undergone the same kind of historical evolution as Earth has: from feudalism to capitalism and subsequently to socialism. But because the topography of Mars is more homogeneous than that of Earth, the people were much less divided into separate races, nationalities and linguistic groups than the inhabitants of Earth. As a result, the socialist revolution on Mars had been a relatively peaceful affair. Strikes had been the workers' main weapon, the uprisings that had occurred being restricted to a few, almost exclusively agricultural regions. The possessing classes had bowed before the inevitable, and even when the government had fallen into the hands of the workers' party, had not attempted to assert their interests by force.[92]

The revolution Bogdanov is describing here, in which strikes were the main weapon, was the one in which he himself had been involved in 1905. The difference was that in Russia the ruling classes had not given in so easily, and the revolution had been mercilessly crushed. The implication was that Bogdanov's hopes for a successful outcome of the 1905 revolution had been dashed, because the revolution had taken place in conditions of great social disparity, where class divisions were deep and antagonistic.

The ferocity of the 1905 revolution and the relentlessness of its suppression must have been a rude awakening for Bogdanov, and this is reflected in *Red Star*. In his writings before 1905 the revolution to introduce a socialist society is presented as a fairly smooth and mechanical process – as a realignment of the superstructure of society with its base.[93] But after the experience of the actual revolution his views changed considerably. The opposition to the revolution had been too determined, the radical intelligentsia had deserted when the reaction had begun to triumph, and Bogdanov had found that among the workers authoritarian attitudes were by no means absent.[94] In 1908 Bogdanov was aware that the coming revolutionary upsurge might not be the prelude to the establishment of a society based on comradely cooperation.

This impression is reinforced by the lengthy disquisition on the prospects for a socialist revolution on Earth that Bogdanov puts into the mouth of Sterni, the advocate of colonising the Earth. Sterni is pessimistic about the chances of a successful socialist revolution on Earth in view of the obstacles to it which exist there. Earth is riven by political and social divisions. This means that instead of following a single uniform pattern of development, the struggle for socialism

---

92   Bogdanov 1979, pp. 63–4.
93   Bogdanov 1906, pp. 105–6.
94   Bogdanov 1910a, p. 116; Bogdanov 1990, p. 101.

is split into a variety of autonomous processes in individual societies with distinct political systems, languages and nationalities. In view of this, one had to expect not one, but a number of revolutions taking place in different countries at different times. Sterni could imagine that the individual advanced countries where socialism had triumphed would be like islands in a hostile capitalist and even pre-capitalist sea. In those circumstances, where socialism survived, its character was likely to be distorted by the years of encirclement. This socialism would not be like Martian socialism. Moreover, Sterni pointed out:

> Centuries of national division, a lack of mutual understanding, the brutal and bloody struggle will all have left deep scars on the psychology of liberated Earthly humanity. We do not know how much barbarity and narrow-mindedness the socialists of Earth will bring with them into their new society.[95]

At various junctures in his speech Sterni also drew his audience's attention to the fact that the incessant internal bickering of the peoples of the Earth had led to the development of the psychological peculiarity which they called patriotism. This feature made any co-existence of Martians and Earthlings impossible, and meant that if the colonisation of Earth were to be undertaken, the inhabitants of Earth would have to be annihilated. Fortunately for the Earthlings, Netti presented a convincing argument to counter Sterni's, and it was agreed to attempt the colonisation of Venus rather than Earth.[96]

There are a number of significant things about Sterni's speech. The most striking is that it is remarkably prophetic, something that present-day readers of Red Star can appreciate more than those of 1908. Bogdanov accurately predicted the phenomenon of 'socialism in one country', the hostility towards it, and the attendant barbarities and narrow-mindedness. While later critics of the Soviet state have argued about the precise juncture at which it degenerated, Bogdanov's analysis in Red Star could foresee that the kind of revolution which socialists were trying to bring about would be degenerate from its very inception. Socialism on a world scale, the socialism of comradely cooperation, would not be achieved unless something specific were done to ensure its success.

By the time Bogdanov wrote his article 'Socialism of the Present' in 1910 he had become convinced that the way to eliminate the authoritarian thinking and the narrow-mindedness among the workers was 'to create newer and

---

95   Bogdanov 1979, p. 156.
96   Bogdanov 1979, pp. 157–62.

newer elements of socialism in the proletariat itself, in its internal relations and its everyday conditions of life: to work out a socialist proletarian culture'.[97] That is, he believed that comradely cooperation was not only a characteristic of a socialist society, but also the means by which that society would be achieved. Thus, Bogdanov's concept of 'proletarian culture' was a solution to the problem of carrying out a socialist revolution that he had raised in *Red Star*.[98]

Leonid's return to Earth provides Bogdanov with the opportunity to comment on contemporary political issues. He is predictably dismissive of the State Duma, seeing it as an attempted compromise between the government on the one hand and the landowners and bourgeoisie on the other, 'disguised as a parliamentary comedy' in which 'puppet parliaments were convened and brutally dissolved one after another'. Neither could Bogdanov see any successful outcome for the Stolypin reform, which he viewed as the tsarist regime's attempt to bribe part of the peasantry by selling plots of land to it. This scheme, he said, was implemented on such a petty scale and so idiotically managed that nothing would come of it.

A phenomenon of the post-revolutionary situation that concerned Bogdanov particularly was that the radical intelligentsia, whose participation in the struggle had been limited for the most part to expressions of sympathy, had betrayed the cause almost to a man.[99] This flight of the intelligentsia, combined with his conviction that 'a new upsurge was inevitable and near at hand', convinced Bogdanov that there was an urgent need to train up a cadre of workers to replace the unreliable intelligentsia. This would be the function of the party schools. Though these are not mentioned in the novel, they would occupy much of Bogdanov's attention shortly after it was published.

---

97   Bogdanov 1990, p. 101.
98   See White 2013.
99   Bogdanov 1979, p. 180.

End of an Alliance

1 Ten Questions

Since all of the Bolsheviks at the Kotka conference except Lenin had supported the boycott of the Third Duma, the expectation was that the newspaper *Proletarii*, the mouthpiece of the fraction, would reflect this balance of forces and give prominence to the fraction's boycottist opinion. But since of the newspaper's three editors, two of them, Lenin and Dubrovinsky, were against the boycott, and only Bogdanov was in favour, Lenin used this 'majority' to ensure that a predominance of anti-boycottist material would be published.[1] As far as philosophical disputes were concerned, the line taken by *Proletarii* was one of neutrality. Lenin and Dubrovinsky interpreted this neutrality as the refusal to publish any articles which supported one side or another. Bogdanov, on the other hand, thought that 'neutrality' meant publishing all points of view without fear or favour. Significantly, in March 1909 the Okhrana reported that Krasin had retained the 140,000 roubles from the Tiflis robbery to carry on 'otzovist' propaganda, and even to purchase a printing press for the purpose.[2]

At the beginning of 1908 Gorky submitted an article entitled 'The Destruction of Personality' for publication in *Proletarii*. The article was clearly influenced by Bogdanov's 'The Integration of Mankind'. It traced the evolution of the human personality from the collectivism of primitive society to the fragmentation of the psyche brought about by the division of labour and the conflict of interests in bourgeois society. Gorky tried to show how this process of disintegration was reflected in Russian and world literature.[3]

On 25 February 1908 Lenin wrote to Gorky to explain why his article could not be accepted for publication. This was because, Lenin said, just at a time when differences of opinion on philosophy among the Bolsheviks were threatening to become particularly acute, in his article Gorky was expounding the views of one of the trends. It was essential, however, that *Proletarii* maintain a neutral stance towards all of them, and not give the reader the slightest grounds

1 Lutsenko 2003, p. 29.
2 Bol'sheviki 1990, p. 75.
3 Gorky 1909.

for associating the Bolsheviks, as the revolutionary wing of the RSDLP, with empiriocriticism or empiriomonism.[4]

For his part, Lenin detailed his increasing rejection of Bogdanov's ideas culminating in his vehement reaction to the third part of *Empiriomonism* and the recently published *Studies in the Philosophy of Marxism*.[5] Lenin intimated that he had communicated his impressions of the collection of articles forcefully to Bogdanov in person, and that when he had been presented with a copy of the third volume of *Empiriomonism*, he had written a lengthy refutation of Bogdanov's ideas in a manuscript that he had entitled 'Notes of an Ordinary Marxist on Philosophy', but had not published it. He said that he now intended to take up again the task he had begun in that manuscript, of refuting Bogdanov's ideas in writing. It was in fact about this time that Lenin began to write his book *Materialism and Empiriocriticism*.

Lenin told Gorky that, in his opinion, some sort of fight among the Bolsheviks on the subject of philosophy was now quite unavoidable, but he did not think that this was an issue on which the fraction should split. He stated that the alliance that he had formed with Bogdanov had been stable throughout the revolutionary period, and that the only difference of opinion had been on the boycott of the Third Duma, and this had not led to a split. So, Lenin resolved, when the fight came, it ought to be conducted internally, in such a way that *Proletarii* and the Bolsheviks as a fraction of the party would not be affected by it. He believed this to be quite possible.[6]

In his letter dated 26 February, Bogdanov said that he could see nothing in Gorky's article at odds with revolutionary Marxism, and that if the editors of *Proletarii* interpreted 'neutrality' as weeding out the 'empiriomonist' spirit in articles, then he, as the proponent of that spirit, would be unable to remain a member of the editorial board. His opinion that Gorky's article should be accepted had been voted down by the other two editors. Thereafter Bogdanov had proposed that the editorial board should request Gorky to complete the article so that the finished version could be considered, and suggested that they should arrange a meeting with Gorky and Lunacharsky to discuss jointly the plan of the work.[7] Gorky's 'The Destruction of Personality' was eventually published in a collection entitled *Studies in the Philosophy of Collectivism* along with essays by Bogdanov, Bazarov and Lunacharsky.[8]

---

4   Lenin 1958–65, 47, pp. 141–5.
5   Lenin 1958–65, 47, p. 143.
6   Lenin 1958–65, 47, pp. 144–5.
7   Neizvestnyi Bogdanov 1995, 1, pp. 153–4.
8   Gorky 1909.

When Lenin expressed to Gorky his fear that the Bolshevik fraction of the party would be associated with empiriocriticism and empiriomonism he had grounds for this anxiety. Bogdanov had supplied a foreword to the Russian translation of Mach's *Analysis of Sensations*, in which he had repeated his criticisms of Plekhanov's philosophical ideas, mentioning Plekhanov's belief that Spinoza and Holbach were precursors of Marx and Engels. A German translation of Bogdanov's Introduction was published in *Die neue Zeit*, to celebrate Mach's 70th birthday. The translator of Bogdanov's Introduction prefaced it with an explanatory note, saying that the polemical passages had been removed as being only of interest to Russian readers, and that:

> Russian Social-Democracy takes a very lively interest in Mach, and is unfortunately well on the way to making one's attitude to Mach one of the issues dividing the fractions of the party. The very serious tactical differences between the 'Bolsheviks' and the 'Mensheviks' are aggravated by what is, in our opinion, the completely irrelevant question of whether the Marxist theory of knowledge is compatible with Spinoza and Holbach or with Mach and Avenarius.[9]

The editors of *Die neue Zeit* had obviously assumed that since Plekhanov was a Menshevik and Bogdanov a Bolshevik, the philosophical differences were among those issues that divided the two camps. In this perspective empiriomonism was the philosophy of Bolshevism. It was the association that Lenin hoped to avoid. In response to the comments in *Die neue Zeit*, the editors of *Proletarii* published a statement to the effect that the philosophical controversy was not a fractional one, and in the opinion of the *Proletarii* editorial board should not be so. It added that any attempt to represent the differences of opinion as fractional was deeply mistaken, since both fractions contained adherents of the two philosophical trends.[10]

The Poles shared the Germans' opinion that philosophical questions were an irrelevant distraction from the real functions of a Social-Democratic Party. Thus, when Leo Jogiches came to Geneva at the end of March Lenin cautioned Bogdanov not to mention to him the worsening of philosophical disputes.[11]

On Gorky's invitation, Lenin spent 23–30 April on Capri in the company of Bogdanov, Bazarov, Lunacharsky and many other guests of Gorky. Philosophical differences were discussed, but no meeting of minds took place. Lenin

---

9   Bogdanov 1908, pp. 695–6.
10   Lenin 1958–65, 47, p. 421.
11   Lenin 1958–65, 47, p. 153.

proposed that Bogdanov and his associates should apply themselves to writing a history of the 1905 revolution that would compete with the one presently being produced by the Mensheviks.[12] He would later accuse them of showing no interest in the project.[13]

Gorky and his friends had expected to be joined on Capri by Skvortsov-Stepanov to discuss publishing plans. He was at that time in Germany, and instead of coming to Capri he stayed on in Munich. When Lenin returned to Geneva Skvortsov-Stepanov stayed a week there in his company along with Dubrovinsky and Krupskaya. During that week Skvortsov-Stepanov was won over to Lenin's side, so much so that he would help Lenin with the publication of *Materialism and Empiriocriticism*.[14] This, however, did not prevent Bogdanov from planning an expanded version of his economics textbook to be written jointly with Skvortsov-Stepanov.

By June Lenin had changed his mind about keeping the philosophical dispute out of the public domain. Bogdanov gave a lecture on 'The Adventures of One Philosophical School' in Geneva on 28 June and while in London, working on his book *Materialism and Empiriocriticism*, Lenin sent a series of questions to Dubrovinsky to put to Bogdanov, with the obvious intention of putting Bogdanov on the defensive. The questions avoided mentioning the criticisms Bogdanov had made of Plekhanov in the pamphlet in question, and mainly concentrated on demanding to know whether Bogdanov agreed with various pronouncements that Engels had made in *Anti-Dühring*.[15]

Aleksinsky reported to Gorky what had happened in a letter dated 31 May 1908. Some days, ago, he said, Bogdanov had given a talk on philosophy criticising the Plekhanov school. The talk was excellent, the audience, pleased, listened with great interest. Suddenly, after the meeting was opened to questions, Dubrovinsky, a member of the *Proletarii* editorial board, had got up and made a very unpleasant speech in which he even raised suspicions about the quotations Bogdanov had adduced, hinted at some 'sectional interests' and labelled 'Bogdanov's doctrine' a repetition of Bernsteinism, a bourgeois undermining of Marx and Engels. Moreover, he seized upon a quotation from Lunacharsky's article and made fun of it, calling Lunacharsky a 'priest'. It was something unimaginable, Aleksinsky, remarked, a speech in bad faith against a close comrade-Bolshevik. The Mensheviks were delighted, but the Bolsheviks in the audience were so aghast that they called a meeting of their group in

---

12   See Obshchestvennoe dvizhenie v Rossii v nachale xx-go veka 1910–14.
13   Vladimir Il'ich Lenin, biograficheskaia khronika 1970, 2, p. 406.
14   Podliashuk 1973, pp. 81–2.
15   Lenin 1958–65, 18, pp. 5–6.

Geneva the next day to discuss the question of the 'character of the philosoph-ical polemic'. Aleksinsky concluded by saying that what was most remarkable of all was that Dubrovinsky had referred to the authority of Lenin and said that he had been delegated by him. What was significant in this, Aleksinsky thought, was that the editorial board of *Proletarii* had previously declared itself neut-ral in the philosophical dispute between Bogdanov and Plekhanov. Apparently, this was no longer to be the case.

Aleksinsky and Mikha Tskhakaia wrote to Lenin on behalf of the Geneva Bolsheviks protesting that whereas Bogdanov's lecture had been theoretical and had observed the spirit of neutrality, Dubrovinsky had accused Bogdanov of undermining Marxism for fractional purposes, and had ridiculed an article by Lunacharsky. Quoting from an article by Lenin, Dubrovinsky had implied that Lenin shared his views.[16]

From the beginning of the year, as the only 'boycottist' on the editorial board of *Proletarii*, Bogdanov had volunteered to submit articles criticising the per-formance of the Duma fraction. He had intended to do this in the form of an address to the fraction, pointing out that its tactics had confirmed the boycot-tists' worst fears. Lenin and Dubrovinsky, however, had persuaded him that, in the interests of maintaining the unity of the fraction, it would not be advisable to air material disagreements in the newspaper. Bogdanov had not insisted on writing the articles, though he believed it was less dangerous to discuss dis-agreements than to conceal them.

In this way, the 'boycottist' point of view did not have any exposure on the pages of *Proletarii*, while the shortcomings of the Duma fraction encouraged the opinion among Bolshevik circles that the fraction should be recalled from the Duma. Bogdanov thought that this 'otzovism' was an understandable and legitimate point of view, but he did not share it. He believed that recalling the Social-Democrat fraction from the Duma was impractical. But *Proletarii*'s cam-paign against 'otzovism' had created a situation in which there was no common ground between boycottists and anti-boycottists, and no prospect of reconcil-ing their differences. In these circumstances, Bogdanov believed that it would be advisable for him, as an old boycottist, to show that an intermediate position was possible in discussing this question, and this would prevent the further ali-enation of the two sides. To this end, he and Aleksinsky had written an article in this spirit to be published in *Proletarii* as joint authors.[17]

---

16   Biggart 1981, p. 143.
17   Neizvestnyi Bogdanov 1995, 2, p, 144.

In June 1908 Bogdanov contributed the article 'Boycottists and Recallers', which he had written jointly with Aleksinsky, to *Proletarii*. It set out his position on the RSDLP fraction in the Third Duma in the wake of a conference that had been held in Moscow, at which some devastating criticism of the fraction had been made. This was not, Bogdanov said, a repetition or a continuation of the dispute between the boycottists and the anti-boycottists; this was a new issue concerning whether to continue the existence of the Social-Democratic fraction in the Third Duma, or to try to undo what the party had already done.

Unfortunately, Bogdanov said, the performance of the fraction had confirmed the worst predictions of the boycottists. Although everyone, even the 'otzovists', agreed that there was an urgent need for the 'utilisation of the Duma platform for agitational and organisational purposes', the Duma fraction was failing to provide this adequately. However, Bogdanov insisted, at the present time it would be an enormous mistake to raise the question of withdrawing the fraction from the Duma. Events had a logic of their own, and it was futile to try to force them. The party had created the Duma fraction, and the boycottists, Bogdanov among them, had submitted to the decision of the party majority, and had even taken an active part in supporting the Duma fraction. Once the fraction had been established, one had to reckon with the consequences, of which the main one was that the party was now committed to the fraction and there was no means by which it could divest itself of the responsibility for it.

Bogdanov argued that to recall the Duma fraction the circumstances would have to be very different; there would have to be a 'general upswing of the popular movement', without which the step would simply be impractical. Moreover, the party would have to be unanimous about recalling the fraction, and in the absence of this unanimity the party as a whole would almost certainly split, and there would probably be a split in its left wing. From this point of view the medicine proposed by the 'otzovists' was worse than the disease itself. But what was most needed by the proletariat at this time of an upsurge of mass struggle was unity and unanimity, and these must be preserved come what may.

Despite the shortcomings of the Duma fraction, Bogdanov pointed out, the possibility of its improvement was not out of the question, and the 'otzovists' could not claim that all such possibilties had been exhausted. And so long as these possibilities existed, one should not resort to a tactic so immeasurably final and so immeasurably risky as that of recalling the fraction. Bogdanov emphasised that the ideas he had put forward in the article were not his alone, but also those of Aleksinsky, the former member of the Second Duma.

Bogdanov concluded by saying that personal disagreements were inevitable, and indeed, necessary, for the health of the party. He was pleased to say that so far the Bolshevik fraction to which he belonged had been able to resolve these differences by wide discussion, democratic voting and party discipline, and he hoped that in the interests of the cause that they all served, this would continue to be the case in the future. When he wrote those words Bogdanov would well know that the methods used by his colleagues on the editorial board of *Proletarii* were far from what he described.[18]

Bogdanov's article 'Boycottists and Recallers' was accepted by the editors of *Proletarii*, but with the provisos that it should appear over Bogdanov's name only, and that the article should be accompanied by a note from the editors to the effect that they did not agree with Bogdanov's assessment of the boycott. When the article appeared in print Bogdanov was dismayed to discover that the editorial note did not say that the editors disagreed with Bogdanov, but that Bogdanov agreed with them in essence on the assessment of the boycott. Bogdanov pointed out that he had not been invited to any editorial meeting at which the change was decided, and that readers of the newspaper would assume that since he, Bogdanov, was a member of the editorial board, he would have approved the note.[19]

Bogdanov's demand for the newspaper to print a correction to its note was refused by Lenin and Dubrovinsky, who declared that they had acted entirely correctly in composing the editorial note. Bogdanov, in response to this refusal, on 23 June, wrote to condemn the dishonest means that the editors had employed in silencing their opponents. He accused them of political immaturity of a kind quite inappropriate to the organisation to which they belonged. As he had been excluded from editorial decisions, and in practice excluded from the editorial board, he saw no alternative than to formalise what was in practice the case by his resignation. He requested that the editors make known his resignation in the following issue of *Proletarii*.[20]

The response of Lenin and Dubrovinsky was to ask Taratuta to put to Bogdanov proposals to 'localise' the dispute. These were that Bogdanov could bring up his complaints and grievances at the next meeting of the Bolshevik Centre, but that in the meantime he should not circulate his letter to the *Proletarii* editorial board and should not insist on his resignation being announced in the newspaper. Bogdanov duly agreed to these conditions, saving Lenin and Dubrovinsky from a potentially awkward situation.[21]

Of course, Bogdanov's resignation from the editorial board of *Proletarii* could not be concealed, but Lenin could not give the real reason for this without

---

18   Bogdanov 1908.
19   Neizvestnyi Bogdanov 1995, 2, p. 145.
20   Neizvestnyi Bogdanov 1995, 2, pp. 144–7.
21   Neizvestnyi Bogdanov 1995, 2, p. 144.

revealing his own role in the matter. Thus, when he wrote to Vorovsky on 2 July, he predicted a break between Bogdanov and himself, the reason given was that Bogdanov had taken offence at the trenchant criticism of his philosophical views at the lectures – but not, Lenin added, by the editorial board. When Bogdanov became aware that Lenin was spreading the story that his resignation was the result of philosophical disputes, Bogdanov tried to set the record straight. Thus, on 21 August 1908 he wrote to the Baku organisation of the RSDLP informing them that his resignation from *Proletarii* had absolutely nothing to do with disagreements on philosophy. He informed them too that the matter was to be discussed by a meeting of the Bolshevik Centre, though he doubted whether it would meet.[22]

The Bolshevik Centre did in fact meet, as Bogdanov reported to the Baku committee, on 4 September. The Centre resolved that questions of boycottism and otzovism should be discussed in *Proletarii* to an extent to be decided by the editors, though these latter were enjoined to do this in a way that would not exacerbate disagreements. It was also decided that the philosophical polemic should not appear in the fraction's underground publications, but was permissible in legal ones, but only on condition that the articles of both sides should appear, and only if the polemic was conducted in a comradely manner. All the resolutions were carried unanimously, except the last one, on which Lenin and Dubrovinsky abstained.[23]

In his letter to Vorovsky, Lenin invited him to write for *Proletarii*, with the inducement that his articles would be paid for, and in good time.[24] This was possible because Lenin had recently gained access to a large sum of money which had been bequeathed to the Bolsheviks by Nikolai Shmit, a wealthy supporter. The twenty-three-year-old Nikolai Shmit, a nephew of the textile magnate Savva Morozov, was the owner of a furniture factory in Moscow. Shmit joined the Bolsheviks in 1905 and provided funds for *Novaia Zhizn* and also for arms purchases. His furniture factory, which the police referred to as a 'devil's nest', became a revolutionary stronghold during the December uprising. Shmit was arrested and while in prison was tortured and finally murdered. Before he died, however, Shmit managed to contact friends outside prison and arranged to bequeath a sum of about 200,000 roubles to the Bolsheviks.[25] At a meeting of the Bolshevik Centre on 24–6 August 1908, Lenin succeeded in transferring the management of the Shmit money not to the 'private financial group' of

---

22   Neizvestnyi Bogdanov 1995, 2, pp. 147–8.
23   Neizvestnyi Bogdanov 1995, 2, p. 242.
24   Lenin 1958–65, 47, p. 160.
25   Krupskaia 1989, p. 121.

himself, Bogdanov and Krasin, but to a new 'financial commission' consisting of himself, Zinoviev, Kamenev and Taratuta.[26] The composition of the 'financial commission' ensured that Lenin had complete control of the Shmit money, and had no need for the approval of Bogdanov or Krasin in the way he spent it.

A serious problem with the money from the Tiflis robbery, for which Bogdanov shared responsibility with Krasin and Lenin, was that 100,000 roubles of the 218,000 given to the 'private financial group' were in 500 ruble notes, the numbers of which were known to the police and published in newspapers. These needed to be changed before they could be used. The 'safe' notes were gradually passed to the Bolshevik Centre and thence to the various party organisations. By the end of 1907, however, all of the 118,000 'safe' notes had been spent, and in January 1908 an operation to change the 500 rouble notes organised by M.M. Litvinov ended in the arrest of Bolshevik agents in Munich, Stockholm, Paris and Geneva. The manner in which the arrests had been made suggested that there was a police spy in the Bolshevik organisation. Suspicion fell on Ya.A. Zhitomirsky and Taratuta. Zhitomirsky was later exposed as a police agent, but no evidence was found against Taratuta, though Krasin and Bogdanov continued to distrust him. Early in 1909, soon after the police spy Evno Azev had been exposed by Vladimir Burtsev, Taratuta unexpectedly announced his resignation from the Bolshevik Centre and the Central Committee. In order to secure himself a majority in the Bolshevik Centre in preparation for the split with Bogdanov, Lenin insisted that Taratuta rescind his resignations.[27]

Zinoviev, who had returned from Russia, replaced Dubrovinsky on the *Proletarii* editorial board, and Bogdanov was proposed as an editor, but declined to be considered for the position. He did not want to be exposed to the distrust and irritation that Lenin and Dubrovinsky showed towards him.[28] Bogdanov's proposal that Liadov should replace him on the editorial board was not accepted, and, in the event, it was Kamenev who took his place. In his letter to the Baku Committee, Bogdanov declared himself morally to be completely satisfied with the decisions of the Bolshevik Centre.[29]

In his capacity as an editor of *Proletarii*, Zinoviev wrote to Rosa Luxemburg proposing that she submit an article to the newspaper condemning 'otzovism' and 'ultimatumism'. He assured her that as the leader of the revolutionary wing of Marxism, and as someone who was not directly involved in the fractional

---

26   Nikolaevskii 1995, p. 74.
27   Neizvestnyi Bogdanov 1995, 2, p. 104.
28   Neizvestnyi Bogdanov 1995, 2, p. 148.
29   Neizvestnyi Bogdanov 1995, 2, pp. 242–3.

struggles, her opinion would carry considerable weight.[30] Luxemburg eventually did produce the kind of article Zinoviev wanted. It was entitled 'A Revolutionary Hangover', and was published in *Proletarii* on 8 April 1909,[31] in good time for the meeting of the extended *Proletarii* editorial board that expelled Bogdanov from the Bolshevik Centre.

2   The Paris Conference

The Fifth Conference of the RSDLP met in Paris between 3 and 9 January 1909. It was to be the last one Bogdanov attended before his expulsion from the Bolshevik Centre in June of that year, but the indications are that it went rather well for him. The conference was attended by 16 delegates with voting rights: 5 Bolsheviks (Bogdanov, Lenin, Liadov, A.M. Buiko, N.N. Baturin), 5 Poles (Jogiches, J. Marchlewski, Z. Leder, J. Hanecki, W. Stein-Krajewski), 3 Mensheviks (Akselrod, Dan, N. Ramishvili) and 3 Bundists (A.I. Vainshtein, F.M. Koigen, I.L. Aizenshtadt). Within the Bolshevik delegation Lenin was in a minority as regards attitudes towards the Duma fraction. Whereas he was committed to its continued existence, Liadov and Buiko were 'recallers', while Bogdanov's position was that the fraction should not be recalled, but that its activities should be strictly regulated by the party. Lenin needed the support of the Poles, and offered to pay for their travel to Paris so that he could meet with them before the conference and discuss tactics.[32]

The conference proceedings were never published, though its resolutions appeared in a Soviet collection of documents.[33] Fortunately, however, the newspaper of the SDKPiL *Czerwony Sztandar* carried a concise account of the conference, which indicates the character of the discussions. The account also suggests that the Poles played an important part in the proceedings, and that they tended to support Bogdanov more than they did Lenin.

Lenin spoke on the current political situation and the tasks of the party, though his actual speech has not been preserved. The resolution based on his speech that was adopted had additions by Jogiches and was edited by Marchlewski, Liadov and Aizenshtadt.[34] It did not argue that the revolutionary period

---

30   Najdus 1980, p. 74.

31   Luxemburg 1909.

32   Fal'kovich 1975, p. 85.

33   See KPSS v rezoliutsiiakh i resheniiakh s"ezdov, konferentsii i plenumov TsK 1953, pp. 195–205.

34   Fal'kovich 1975, pp. 85–6.

had come to an end; on the contrary, it stressed that the party's tactics in 1905–7 had been correct and advocated that the party should be strengthened in the way it had been in the revolutionary era. It urged that the party should continue to pursue its unrelenting struggle against the tsarist regime and the reactionary classes as well as against bourgeois liberalism. It did, however, include in the list of tactics for the party to follow 'making use of the Duma and the Duma platform for revolutionary Social-Democratic propaganda and agitation'.[35] The two 'otzovists', Liadov and Buiko, signed a declaration, saying that although they did not agree with this point, they would vote for the resolution as a whole.

The main item for discussion was the performance of the Duma Social-Democratic fraction over the past year. The Mensheviks were against the mistakes of the fraction being discussed for fear of undermining its credibility. The Poles, however, and 'most Bolsheviks' (which presumably included Bogdanov, Liadov and Buiko) were insistent that these should be thoroughly aired and concurred with this demand.[36] A number of instances were listed in which the fraction had departed from the party line, including the failure to criticise the Duma itself for the way in which the votes of the representatives of the workers and peasants were vastly outnumbered by those of the representatives of a small minority of the possessing classes. Lenin was able to alleviate this criticism of the fraction by inserting a clause saying that the blame for its deviations did not rest with it alone, as it had to work in the very difficult situation of a reactionary Duma, but the blame was shared to some extent by all of the party organisations and its Central Committee, which had not yet done all that was necessary and possible to organise the party's work in the Duma on proper lines.[37]

According to the *Czerwony Sztandar* report on the conference, the majority of the delegates were opposed to any attempt to keep the Duma fraction on the desired path 'by means so alien to the spirit of the party' as applying the pressure of an ultimatum, or by the threat of recall, as some of the Bolsheviks (the so-called 'otzovists') were intent on doing. The means of directing the fraction along the right path was to be, on the one hand, giving the fraction clear and well-defined directives, and on the other, calling upon all party organisations to active cooperation with the fraction. The conference intended that the fraction should be guided in the general direction of its activity by the resolutions of the London party congress and also, in particular speeches, by the directives of the Central Committee. In the Duma, it should not confine itself

35   Lenin 1958–65, 17, pp. 325–8.
36   'Ogólnopartijna konferencja' 1909.
37   Lenin 1958–65, 17, p. 334.

to so-called 'positive work', the pursuit of minor reforms, but should, above all, engage in Social-Democratic propaganda and agitation. The resolution went on to detail how the fraction should vote on particular issues that had recently arisen.[38]

In a section of the resolution on the Duma fraction not to be made public it was stated that in cases where the activities of the fraction threatened to harm the interests of the party the Central Committee should not hesitate to use its power of veto over the fraction's decisions. Moreover, if the party's Duma activity did not proceed in the manner that the conference had laid down and that had been approved by the Central Committee, an extraordinary party conference should be convoked to discuss the question of the conditions under which the fraction could continue to exist.[39] The conference's resolution on the Duma was one that, Bogdanov would later state, corresponded to his own position at the time.[40]

Normally an all-party conference would have been followed by a conference of the Bolshevik fraction, but this did not take place as it was cancelled by Lenin and his supporters. In a letter to Gorky dated 13 January 1909, Aleksinsky recounted that he had just returned from Paris, where he had been summoned by Liadov and Desnitsky for the usual Bolshevik conference. This never took place because Lenin, with the connivance of Taratuta, Kamenev and Zinoviev, had aborted it. They were able to do this as they constituted the majority in the Bolshevik Centre, the remaining two members being Bogdanov and Desnitsky. In Aleksinsky's estimation a Napoleonic *coup d'état* had taken place in the Bolshevik fraction with Lenin in the role of Bonaparte. And whereas Napoleon relied on bayonets, Lenin had the Shmit money.[41]

Bogdanov and Desnitsky wrote to the Bolshevik Centre complaining that in defiance of the practice of the Bolshevik fraction to hold its congresses following an all-party congress and its conferences following all-party conferences, this had not been followed in the wake of the recent Paris conference. In the absence of a fraction conference, the Bolshevik Centre proposed having a meeting of the Bolshevik Centre with the Bolshevik delegates to the Paris conference, in which everyone would have the right to vote. In the view of Bogdanov and Desnitsky, it was the aim of the Bolshevik Centre majority to make the Bolshevik Centre a body that was only accountable to itself. They protested against the unconstitutional way the Bolshevik Centre had acted and deman-

38   'Ogólnopartijna konferencja' 1909.
39   KPSS v rezoliutsiiakh i resheniiakh s"ezdov, konferentsii i plenumov TsK 1953, 1, p. 201.
40   Neizvestnyi Bogdanov 1995, 3, p. 70.
41   Neizvestnyi Bogdanov 1995, 2, p. 243.

ded the convocation of a new Bolshevik conference to discuss fractional business, including the present behaviour of the Bolshevik Centre.[42] The protest met with no response and the conference Bogdanov and Desnitsky demanded never came about.

While in Italy making arrangements for a party school, Bogdanov received a letter from Shantser saying that attempts were being made by Lenin to effect a schism in the Bolshevik fraction. He had dispatched N.N. Baturin, one of his followers, to St Petersburg and Moscow to give to the local Social-Democrat organisations an account of the Paris conference from Lenin's point of view. Baturin was to present himself to the organisations as a delegate from the Bolshevik Centre, though in actual fact he had been sent by the inner group of Lenin, Zinoviev and Kamenev. As the Bolshevik Centre's treasurer, Shantser was able to inform Bogdanov that Baturin's trip to Russia was being financed by Bolshevik Centre funds.

On 4 February Bogdanov wrote to the Bolshevik Centre, informing them of the contents of Shantser's letter and setting out what he considered to be the main implications. There was, he stated, a separate organisation within the Bolshevik Centre consisting of Lenin, Zinoviev and Kamenev, an organisation that sent its agents into Russia on special missions using Bolshevik Centre funds. The establishment of this organisation, moreover, was obviously connected with the cancellation of the Bolshevik conference at the beginning of January, since the members of the organisation were the same people who had voted for the cancellation. In view of these developments Bogdanov proposed that the Bolshevik Centre postpone any other, less important, business, until it had addressed the questions to which they had given rise. These were: to explain the emergence and the activities of the new organisation; to prevent the schism in the Bolshevik fraction that had been created by the existence of the new organisation; and to stop attempts to spread the schism to Russian local organisations.[43] Shortly after this Lenin broke off comradely relations with Bogdanov.

On 1 June Bogdanov and Shantser protested to the Bolshevik Centre about the cynical way that Lenin and his allies on the 'finance commission' were deploying the Shmit fortune to influence opinion in Russia in their favour. Following the January party conference, at which the two delegates from the Central Region and one of the two delegates from the St Petersburg Committee had sided with Bogdanov, the finance commission cut the subsidy of the

---

42   Neizvestnyi Bogdanov 1995, 2, pp. 151–3.
43   Neizvestnyi Bogdanov 1995, 2, pp. 154–5.

Central Region by 100 roubles and that to the St Petersburg Committee by 50 roubles a month, although there was by that time no lack of funds.[44]

When the printing press of the Central Region's newspaper *Rabochee znamia* had been confiscated following arrests, the Region requested a grant of 500 roubles for a new printing press. This had been denied, but when the secretary of the Central Region wrote to the Bolshevik Centre with the assurance that the organisation did not support otzovism or ultimatumism, the finance commission restored the subsidy to its previous level, and added 300 roubles for the new printing press. Bogdanov and Shantser considered that in this respect the Bolshevik Centre was acting like an unaccountable clique, but there was little they could do to prevent it.[45]

3 God-Building

In the issue of *Proletarii* for 12 February 1909 Kamenev published an article entitled 'Not on the Same Road'. This was a critique of Lunacharsky's essay on Gorky's story 'The Confession' that had appeared in the collection *Literary Decadence (Literaturnyi raspad)*. Lunacharsky highly approved of Gorky's story, whose hero was Matvei, a 'semi-peasant' who wandered throughout Russia seeking God. From the sages he encountered Matvei learned that: 'God is mankind, the whole socialist mankind ... This god is not yet born, but is being built. And who are the god-builders? Of course, the proletariat ...' This, Lunacharsky said, was the form in which socialist concepts would be available to a person like Matvei. To him, a god-seeker, a 'higher formula' would be understandable. He could be told: 'Do you seek God? God is the humanity of the future; build it together with the humanity of the present, join with its most progressive elements'. This formula, Lunacharsky admitted, was not in the usual Marxist terms, but the essence was the same.[46]

One can see why Lunacharsky should so approve of Gorky's *Confession*; its concept of what religion was corresponded very closely to that propounded in *Religion and Socialism* and the article 'Atheism'. But neither in those works nor in his essay was Lunacharsky appearing in the role of an advocate of religion; his position was that he thought that socialist ideas could be expressed in religious terms to make them more accessible to peasants and semi-peasants,

---

44 Protokoly soveshchaniia rasshirennoi redaktsii 'Proletariia'. Iiun' 1909 1934, pp. 165–7.
45 Ibid.
46 Lunacharskii 1909, pp. 92–3.

like the hero of Gorky's story. It was to this idea that Kamenev took exception. In his opinion, what was being offered to this section of the population was not proletarian socialism, but medieval, peasant socialism. Instead of criticising this type of socialism, Lunacharsky was acting as an apologist for it. Kamenev thought that it was sheer opportunism to adapt proletarian ideology to make it more accessible to non-proletarians. Socialism, adapted to the religious psyche of semi-peasants and intended to facilitate their understanding, was comparable to adapting socialist politics in order not to frighten the liberal bourgeoisie. Despite Lunacharsky's good intentions, Kamenev contended, Lunacharsky's presentation of socialism would simply complicate the critical work of proletarian socialism, especially in Russia.[47]

Originally the editorial board of *Proletarii* had been against publishing Kamenev's article, but on Lenin's insistence this decision was reversed.[48] On learning of this from Shantser, Bogdanov wrote a letter of protest to the editorial board. In it he objected that the decision to publish Kamenev's article infringed the resolution of the Bolshevik Centre that no polemic on philosophical questions should appear in the illegal publications of the fraction, and stated that such polemics were permissible only under conditions of formal equality of the sides in *legal* publications, as, for example, *Literaturnyi raspad*.

Bogdanov went on to say that any attempt to get round this resolution by claiming that philosophical neutrality was not being infringed, since this was a struggle against *religion*, was an obvious subterfuge. No one in the Bolshevik fraction, he believed, would be so naive as to confuse the *philosophical* use by Dietzgen, Lunacharsky and some other writers of terms of a religious origin with *religion* in the historical and political sense of this word. The complete artificiality of this argument was clear from the very fact that it has not occurred to anybody on the editorial board of *Proleterii* to apply it until now, whereas Lunacharsky had previously published a number of articles in which religious terminology had been employed more obviously than in the one to which Kamenev had claimed to have taken such exception.[49]

As Krasin suspected that Taratuta was responsible for the arrest of the Bolshevik agents who were attempting to change the 500 rouble notes from the Tiflis robbery, he decided to move the money which was kept in Paris to another location which would be unknown to Taratuta. Both Taratuta and Zhitomirsky would have been aware of the reason for the measure, but Lenin suspected that the money was being moved to be at Bogdanov's disposal when the split

47 Kamenev 2003, p. 292.
48 Protokoly soveshchaniia rasshirennoi redaktsii 'Proletariia'. Iiun' 1909 1934, p. 272.
49 Protokoly soveshchaniia rasshirennoi redaktsii 'Proletariia'. Iiun' 1909 1934, p. 271.

occurred. He accordingly ordered Zhitomirsky to demand that he be given the banknotes immediately. Krasin, with Bogdanov's support, explained to Lenin that he had no right to do this, as he was only one of a college of three, and in a letter to Lenin Krasin explained his real motives for moving the money, though not accusing Taratuta directly. Nevertheless, egged on by Zhitomirsky, Lenin broke the agreement with the Caucasian group and made a complaint against Bogdanov and Krasin to the Bolshevik Centre.

Lenin was not present at the meeting of the Bolshevik Centre on 23 February, and Krasin was not in Paris at the time. Bogdanov abstained from voting on principle, leaving Lenin's supporters, Zinoviev, Kamenev and Taratuta, against Shantser. In the resolution that was carried all Lenin's accusations against Bogdanov were upheld. The Bolshevik Centre judged Bogdanov and Krasin to have secretly seized the Tiflis money and refused to hand it over to Zhitomirsky. They contended that the 'college of three' had ceased to exist in 1907, when the management of the money was handed over to the Bolshevik Centre as a whole. They maintained that Bogdanov and his associates were preparing a split in the Bolshevik fraction, and to this end were waging a campaign of slander against their opponents, thus undermining any possibility for joint action. Other reproaches against Bogdanov were his disagreement concerning 'otzovism' and 'ultimatumism' as well as his threat of schism over Kamenev's article in *Proletarii* against 'god-building'. The Bolshevik Centre's resolution demanded that Bogdanov and Krasin return the money and restore normal relations in the Centre. If these demands were not met within a week, the Bolshevik Centre would convoke a more extended meeting of the Bolshevik Centre with members presently in Russia, with a view either to receiving an undertaking from Krasin and Bogdanov that they would cease their divisive and defamatory actions or to expelling them from the Bolshevik Centre. Bogdanov wrote in reply saying that he did not consider the resolution taken by three members of the Bolshevik Centre as legitimate, and that the matter which had given rise to it was not one that was within the competence of the extended editorial board of *Proletarii* to decide.[50]

In the spring of 1909 Bogdanov was occupied organising the party school for workers. The idea for the school had originated with the group of Geneva Social Democrats to which Aleksinsky belonged. In September 1908 the group had presented the *Proletarii* editorial board with a draft of the scheme, but lack of commitment by the board prevented the scheme from getting off the ground. But a new stimulus to organise a party school came from workers' reports to

---

50   Neizvestnyi Bogdanov 1995, 2, p. 122.

a conference of the RSDLP held in Paris in December 1908. This was that with the defeat of the 1905 revolution there had been an exodus from the ranks of the party, both of workers and more especially of intellectual elements. The exodus of the latter was especially felt in all party organisations, because they had acted as party secretaries, treasurers, *littérateurs*, propagandists and agitators. With their departure these functions had been taken over by the workers themselves, but the workers felt the need to acquire more knowledge and training to carry out these essential party tasks.[51]

Bogdanov took up this cause with enthusiasm, because it was entirely in keeping with his view that it was essential to prepare the workers for the next revolutionary upsurge, which must inevitably come. Conversely, it was contrary to the opinion held by Lenin and the editorial board of *Proletarii* that the revolutionary tide had subsided and that the chief focus of the party should be on parliamentary tactics. It was through this conflict of political perspectives that the project of training some workers in a school for agitators and propagandists generated such bitter controversy. The school was also being organised at a time when Bogdanov was suspected of plotting to establish a new Social-Democratic fraction to rival the Bolsheviks, and it was believed that the party school would be a convenient platform from which to launch it.[52]

There was a precedent for organising party schools, as the German Social-Democratic Party had done so since 1906, Rosa Luxemburg giving lectures on political economy. In a letter to Jogiches of February 1908, Luxemburg recommended that in organising a party school the Russians could do no better than get in touch with the person who was in charge of the workers' courses in Berlin.[53] Presumably Jogiches passed on this recommendation to Aleksinsky's group in Geneva.

Having read Aleksinsky's draft project and bearing in mind the reports from the workers' conference, Bogdanov, Gorky and N.E. Vilonov, decided to set up a school for party activists on Capri, where both Gorky and Vilonov lived. Vilonov was a worker Bolshevik, a professional revolutionary who had been active in several Russian towns, enduring terms of prison and exile as a result. Suffering from tuberculosis, he had been given permission to go abroad, and at the end of 1908 he had settled on Capri, where he became friendly with Gorky, Lunacharsky and Bogdanov.[54]

51   Bogdanov 1910, p. 1.
52   Livshits 1924, p. 35.
53   Luxemburg 1971, 3, p. 1.
54   Livshits 1924, p. 36.

Vilonov composed an appeal addressed to party committees in Russia asking them to send workers to the school. Bogdanov, to whom the appeal was sent for approval, found it satisfactory and passed it on to the editorial board of *Proletaru* for publication. The editorial board, however, did not print the document. Knowing that behind its author was the group composed of Bogdanov, Lunacharsky and Gorky, the editors were not inclined to give the party school project any encouragement. They made it known to Vilonov that if there were funds for a party school the *Proletarii* editorial board would be prepared to organise one, though not on Capri, but in Paris.[55]

Meeting this obstruction, Vilonov got in touch with the local party committees directly, beginning with the Moscow Committee. This measure was contested vehemently by the *Proletarii* editorial board, who wrote to the Moscow Committee informing it that the organisers of the proposed school had close connections with those elements in the party who propounded the doctrine of 'god-building'. This agitation was effective, as the Moscow Committee declined to give its approval to the establishment of the Capri school. At the end of June Vilonov went in person to Russia in an attempt to neutralise the campaign of vilification against his project and to expedite the selection of students by the party committees. A sticking-point that Vilonov encountered was that the workers wanted the school to be organised officially by the Bolshevik Centre rather than the informal grouping to which Vilonov belonged. This problem was not resolved even by the time the school began to function.

In the meantime, Gorky and Bogdanov had been busy raising funds for the school. They did not use any of the Tiflis raid money, but sought contributions from wealthy individuals that Gorky or Bogdanov knew. These included the singer F.I. Chaliapin, the playwright and novelist A.V. Amfiteatrov and the ship-builder V.M. Kamensky, as well as Gorky's partner, the actress Maria Andreeva.[56] The organisation of the Capri school was well under way when the meeting of the extended editorial board of *Proletarii* was held which expelled Bogdanov from the Bolshevik Centre.

4 The Extended Editorial Board of *Proletarii*

The Bolshevik Centre in the guise of the extended editorial board of *Proletarii* met in Paris between 21 and 30 June 1909. Those who took part in the sessions

---

55 Livshits 1924, pp. 37, 42.
56 Rogachevskii 1994, p. 666.

were the members of the Bolshevik Centre who had been elected at the meeting of the Bolshevik fraction that had been held directly after the Fifth Congress
of the RSDLP. These were: Lenin, Bogdanov, Shantser, Taratuta, Zinoviev, Kamenev, Dubrovinsky, Rykov and Meshkovsky. To these were added representatives
from the regions: Shuliatikov (Moscow region), M.P. Tomsky (St Petersburg)
and N.A. Skrypnik (Urals). Krupskaya and A.I. Liubimov took the minutes of
the meetings, a rather onerous task, as it happened, since the participants in
the meetings were anxious that the damaging admissions of their opponents
should be recorded. Bogdanov was considerably outnumbered by Lenin supporters, his only ally being Shantser and, intermittently, Shuliatikov. Krasin did
not attend any of the sessions, though he was in Paris at the time; he seems to
have been occupied with making arrangements for the party school on Capri.
Pokrovsky had intended to attend, but, due to a misunderstanding, had arrived
in Paris in April, and as he could not afford to stay there until June, had returned
to Moscow. Other members of the Bolshevik Centre who might have supported
Bogdanov, such as Rozhkov, were at that time in prison or in Siberian exile.[57]

Bogdanov was clearly in no doubt that the purpose of the meeting was to
expel Krasin and himself from the Bolshevik Centre and that the result was a
foregone conclusion. To get things over with, he demanded that this matter
should be discussed first, but was over-ruled, and the prepared agenda was
adhered to. This had obviously been carefully worked out, because the sessions covered such topics as 'otzovism' and 'ultimatumism', 'god-building', the
party school on Capri, and in general any topic on which Bogdanov was vulner-
able and could be criticised. The main speakers in these sessions were one or
another of Lenin's supporters, so that Lenin himself never had to make the running. Bogdanov, on the other hand, was placed permanently on the defensive.

The first session was devoted to a discussion on whether it was desirable
to call for the convocation of a congress or a conference of the Bolshevik fraction. This was an important question to decide, because, whatever the outcome
of the meeting of the Bolshevik Centre, it could be overturned by a congress
or conference of the Bolshevik fraction. Bogdanov thought that this was what
would happen, because he believed that although Lenin's supporters might be
in a majority in emigration, in Russia they were in a minority, so that, in Bogdanov's words, the Leninists were generals without an army.[58] This, however,
was a matter of dispute, Meshkovsky alleging that 'otzovism' was in decline
among the workers in Russia.[59]

---

57   Gukovskii 1968, p. 130; Rozhkov 2010, p. 16; Nikolaevskii 1995, p. 67.
58   Protokoly soveshchaniia rasshirennoi redaktsii 'Proletariia'. Iiun' 1909 1934, p. 13.
59   Protokoly soveshchaniia rasshirennoi redaktsii 'Proletariia'. Iiun' 1909 1934, p. 29.

The Leninists were adamant that a purely Bolshevik congress should not be held, as this would split the Social-Democratic Party. There was even a reluctance on their part to hold a conference of the Bolshevik fraction. In Bogdanov's view, this reluctance was because the Leninists did not trust a conference and preferred to decide matters 'within their own family circle'.[60] Nevertheless, the meeting resolved to hold a conference of the Bolshevik fraction at the same time as the regular all-party conference. The Bolsheviks on the Central Committee would be urged to call such a conference within the next two or three months.[61]

The following session was devoted to the condemnation of 'otzovism ultimatumism'. The main speaker was Zinoviev, who was able to cite Rosa Luxemburg in support of his views on the evidence of the article she had published in *Proletarii*. He argued that 'otzovism' and 'ultimatumism' were the same thing, and declared that he did not want the Bolshevik current to be confused with these two new currents. To this Bogdanov observed that after the Kotka conference, to speak of 'ultimatumism' as a new current was highly misleading. He said that Zinoviev was distorting what 'ultimatumism' was; it was not about issuing ultimatums, but about maintaining the independence of the party position with regard to the Duma fraction. Moreover, Zinoviev was concealing the true purpose of the resolution he was proposing; he did not have the courage to say plainly: 'We are with Plekhanov, and you can go to the devil'.[62]

The resolution that was carried, despite the efforts of Bogdanov and Shantser, declared that Bolshevism as a distinct current within the RSDLP had nothing in common with 'otzovism' and 'ultimatumism'. It called upon the Bolshevik fraction to conduct the most resolute struggle against these deviations from the path of revolutionary Marxism.[63]

In the course of this discussion on 'otzovism' and 'ultimatumism' Dubrovinsky formulated a significant point of doctrine. This was that since a fraction within a political party represented an ideological current, 'You cannot remain in the fraction if you don't recognise its ideological current'.[64] This was the first time that the Bolshevik fraction had demanded ideological conformity, something previously unheard of, and with ominous implications. This must have been a doctrine agreed among the Leninists, for, at the following session, on 'god-building', it was referred to again, this time by Kamenev. In denoun-

---

60   Protokoly soveshchaniia rasshirennoi redaktsii 'Proletariia'. Iiun' 1909 1934, p. 15.
61   Protokoly soveshchaniia rasshirennoi redaktsii 'Proletariia'. Iiun' 1909 1934, p. 10.
62   Protokoly soveshchaniia rasshirennoi redaktsii 'Proletariia'. Iiun' 1909 1934, pp. 19–26.
63   Protokoly soveshchaniia rasshirennoi redaktsii 'Proletariia'. Iiun' 1909 1934, p. 22.
64   Protokoly soveshchaniia rasshirennoi redaktsii 'Proletariia'. Iiun' 1909 1934, p. 33.

cing Lunacharsky's ideas on religion, he regretted that they could not expel him from the Social-Democratic Party, but they could expel him 'from that ideological unity in which we find ourselves'.[65] The doctrine was the opposite of the one Lunacharsky was fond of citing, first formulated by August Bebel: 'We have no dogma, so we have no heretics'.[66]

The session on 'god-building' was a particularly uncomfortable one for Bogdanov, because Lunacharsky's ideas on the relationship of socialism to religion found no sympathisers among any of the participants. Even Shantser, who took Bogdanov's side on most important issues, was vocal in his rejection of the association of socialism with religion. He had submitted an article to *Proletarii* arguing as much, but had withdrawn it on Bogdanov's insistence.[67] Bogdanov admitted that Lunacharsky's use of religious terminology had been foolish, but predicted (wrongly as it turned out) that he would give up using it in the future. However, Bogdanov added that the resolution on 'god-building' was motivated not so much by antipathy to religion, which he himself had in greater measure than the proposers of the resolution, but the desire to sharpen disagreements within Bolshevism in order to consolidate the split in the Bolshevik current.[68]

One resolution that was passed condemned 'god-building' as a current of thought which undermined the basic principles of Marxism and impeded the work of the Social Democrats in educating the worker masses. A second resolution declared that Bogdanov's contention that Kamenev's article in *Proletarii* infringed the decision of the editorial board not to publish philosophical articles in the illegal journal was unfounded because the struggle against all forms of religious consciousness and religious sentiments, whatever their origin, was one of the basic functions of the newspaper. The resolution regarded Bogdanov's protest as an attempt to cover up the 'god-building' propaganda among the Social Democrats and to prevent *Proletarii* from carrying out one of its functions.[69]

The fourth session of the conference was devoted to the question of the party school on Capri. Rykov, who was the main speaker for the session, accused the organisers of using the school as a forum at which to launch a new fraction which would secede from the Bolsheviks. He claimed that the sponsors of the school, acting over the heads of the party centres, had contacted numerous committees in Russia, organised an independent fund and collections, and

65   Protokoly soveshchaniia rasshirennoi redaktsii 'Proletariia'. Iiun' 1909 1934, p. 40.
66   Protokoly soveshchaniia rasshirennoi redaktsii 'Proletariia'. Iiun' 1909 1934, p. 155.
67   K istorii otzovizma, 1924, pp. 202–7.
68   Protokoly soveshchaniia rasshirennoi redaktsii 'Proletariia'. Iiun' 1909 1934, p. 45.
69   Protokoly soveshchaniia rasshirennoi redaktsii 'Proletariia'. Iiun' 1909 1934, pp. 41–2.

were appointing their own organisers, without even informing the editorial board of *Proletarii* or the leadership of the Social-Democratic Party.

To this Bogdanov replied that the organisers of the school had not sought the approval of the Bolshevik Centre because of the in-fighting. He denied that the school was a centre of 'god-building', because Lunacharsky was only one of the lecturers, and as for the 'otzovists', there was only one 'otzovist' in the school, and that was Gorky.[70] Nevertheless the meeting passed a resolution saying that, since the aims of the school were not ones common to the Bolshevik fraction as a whole, as an ideological current in the party, but were the individual aims of a group with a separate ideology and policy, the extended editorial board of *Proletarii* declared that the Bolshevik fraction was not prepared to take any responsibility for this school.

Dubrovinsky was the main speaker at the fifth session of the conference. He advocated an alliance between the Bolshevik fraction and those of the Mensheviks who had opposed the liquidation of the underground party organisation, whose leading representative was Plekhanov, and a resolution was passed in this spirit. He referred to Plekhanov as 'one of the best representatives of orthodox and revolutionary Marxism', something that Bogdanov found ironic in view of the fact that not so long ago Plekhanov had been classed as the leader of the opportunists.[71]

It was at this session that Lenin felt himself compelled to reply to Bogdanov's accusations that he had betrayed Bolshevism and had adopted a quasi-Menshevik position. Lenin challenged Bogdanov to put his accusations in writing, so that they could be rebutted in public. He said that he had made this challenge as far back as August of 1908, but that Bogdanov had not taken him up on it.[72] Bogdanov's reply was that while he might commit his objections to paper, Lenin and his associates were in a position to deny them publication in *Proletarii*. He added that he had considered setting up his own newspaper, but had rejected the idea out of party loyalty.[73]

The sixth session of the conference was the last one that Bogdanov attended. It was on the unity of the Bolshevik fraction, and seems to have been designed specially to engineer Bogdanov's expulsion. Rykov proposed a motion that all members of the Bolshevik Centre should submit to its decisions. Bogdanov protested that the resolution was illegitimate because only the decisions of the Bolshevik fraction as a whole could bind the members of the Bolshevik

---

70   Protokoly soveshchaniia rasshirennoi redaktsii 'Proletariia'. Iiun' 1909 1934, p. 58.
71   Protokoly soveshchaniia rasshirennoi redaktsii 'Proletariia'. Iiun' 1909 1934, p. 62.
72   Protokoly soveshchaniia rasshirennoi redaktsii 'Proletariia'. Iiun' 1909 1934, p. 66.
73   Protokoly soveshchaniia rasshirennoi redaktsii 'Proletariia'. Iiun' 1909 1934, p. 72.

Centre. The conference thereupon adopted a resolution to the effect that since Bogdanov did not share the unanimity on principles and tactics of the other ten members of the extended editorial board of *Proletarii*, and since there had lately been actions by Bogdanov tending to violate the organisational unity of the Bolshevik fraction, and since Bogdanov had refused to abide by its decisions, the extended editorial board of *Proletarii* henceforth disclaimed any responsibility for Bogdanov's political actions.[74]

On the following day Bogdanov wrote to his friends on Capri declaring: 'The fight ended yesterday, very favourably for me: I have already been excluded from the Bolshevik Centre'.[75] In this reaction there was no doubt an element of relief that he was free from the internal tensions of the Bolshevik Centre, and satisfaction that the Centre had acted illegitimately and would have to answer for its behaviour to a party congress or conference.

In Bogdanov's absence the conference had six more sessions, discussing a number of organisational questions. It emerges from these discussions that the Bolshevik Centre subsidised local party committees in Russia as well as the national groups, the Poles, Latvians and the Bund. It was decided, however, to end these subsidies, and instead advance funds for particular purposes.[76] The money saved would be used to support legal publications, including a popular newspaper to replace *Proletarii*, one to report the activities of the Duma fraction. To conceal his connections with expropriations, Lenin was authorised to destroy the correspondence between himself and Krasin.[77] A resolution was passed which stipulated that any member of the Bolshevik Centre who had not taken part in its activities for more than six months would no longer be regarded as belonging to the Centre.[78]

On learning of Bogdanov's expulsion, Krasin wrote an angry letter to the Bolshevik Centre, deploring its treatment of a comrade who was 'one of the most prominent theoreticians and writers of revolutionary Social-Democracy'. He demanded that the Centre reconsider its decision and reinstate Bogdanov. Until they did so, he declared, he would consider the Centre's meeting one of private individuals. Krasin himself was not expelled from the Bolshevik Centre, but he had nothing further to do with it, as an act of solidarity with Bogdanov.[79]

---

74   Protokoly soveshchaniia rasshirennoi redaktsii 'Proletariia'. Iiun' 1909 1934, p. 76.
75   Bailes 1967, p. 123.
76   Protokoly soveshchaniia rasshirennoi redaktsii 'Proletariia'. Iiun' 1909 1934, p. 130.
77   Protokoly soveshchaniia rasshirennoi redaktsii 'Proletariia'. Iiun' 1909 1934, p. 126.
78   Protokoly soveshchaniia rasshirennoi redaktsii 'Proletariia'. Iiun' 1909 1934, p. 136.
79   Lutsenko 2003, p. 40. Krasin ceased to take any part in political activities until February 1918, when, at Trotsky's invitation, he joined the Russian delegation to the Brest-Litovsk

On 16 July Bogdanov and Krasin, in association with Shantser and Pokrovsky, circulated *A Report to the Comrade Bolsheviks of the Expelled Members of the Expanded Editorial Board of Proletarii*, a pamphlet analysing the factors that had brought about the expulsion of Bogdanov and Krasin from the Bolshevik Centre. The authors began by reviewing the situation in Russia since the defeat of the armed insurrection in Moscow in December 1905. They argued that although for the moment the reaction had triumphed, the country had not ceased to be revolutionary; a new revolutionary wave was inevitable. That being the case, what the situation demanded was that the Social-Democratic Party should be strengthened. The illegal and conspiratorial character of the party should be retained in preparation for the new revolutionary upsurge.[80]

There was also a need for the broadening and deepening of socialist propaganda, and for this there should be a party school to train workers in propaganda methods. This was especially urgent, since following the defeat of the revolution the intelligentsia had deserted the party organisations, leaving the functions they had previously carried out to the workers. The party schools would give the workers the mental disciplines that the intellectuals had acquired in school.[81]

The experience of the 1905 revolution had shown that although disorganised and demoralised, the tsarist regime nevertheless had a preponderance of military expertise. There was a need for propaganda in the army and a need to ensure that uprisings in the armed forces should not be isolated and therefore ineffective.[82]

The authors emphasised that the Bolsheviks should make use of all the legal possibilities that were open to them, such as, for example, work in the trade unions. But this should not imply the abandonment of the party's illegal activities. And it was in this light that the authors viewed the experience of participation in the Duma over the past few years. In general, they thought that this participation had been of dubious value, and they emphasised that it should not be of primary and fundamental importance in the life of the party; it did not merit the overwhelming and decisive significance it had been accorded. It was this question of Duma participation, the authors stated, that was at the root of the present schism in the Bolshevik fraction.[83]

peace negotiations. Thereafter he served as a Soviet diplomat in London until his death in November 1926. See Glenny 1970, p. 221.

80   Protokoly soveshchaniia rasshirennoi redaktsii 'Proletariia'. Iiun' 1909 1934, pp. 171–4.
81   Protokoly soveshchaniia rasshirennoi redaktsii 'Proletariia'. Iiun' 1909 1934, p. 175.
82   Protokoly soveshchaniia rasshirennoi redaktsii 'Proletariia'. Iiun' 1909 1934, pp. 176–7.
83   Protokoly soveshchaniia rasshirennoi redaktsii 'Proletariia'. Iiun' 1909 1934, pp. 177–9.

At the Kotka conference in 1907, they recalled, only Lenin was in favour of participation in the Duma, but the Bolshevik contingent was out-voted. Those who supported a boycott of the Duma, thinking it only a practical question rather than one of principle, duly submitted to the party decision, and took an active part in the elections. Because the Duma fraction was unsuccessful, an 'otzovist' current began to emerge among the former boycottists. The authors did not share the otzovists' point of view, but thought they had a perfect right to express it, and cautioned against turning this into a matter of principle. But those who aspired, consciously or unconsciously, to turn the Duma activity into the main focus of party life, who could dream of broad parliamentary activity in present-day Russia, who conducted a frenzied struggle against the 'otzovists', these people were determined to make this a matter of principle.[84]

The pro-Duma current among the Bolsheviks had adopted the quasi-Menshevik standpoint of 'parliamentarianism at any price'. The logical conclusion was a split in the Bolshevik fraction, and this was implemented in the Extended Editorial Board of *Proletarii*'s resolution of 22 June, which stated that 'Bolshevism as a particular current has nothing in common with "ultimatumism" and "otzovism"'.[85]

A measure the authors had advocated to strengthen local party organisations was to encourage the publication of regional newspapers that would be more attuned to local conditions than a newspaper published in emigration. However, this idea had been rejected in favour of having a single popular newspaper printed abroad. The authors believed that this decision had nothing to do with strengthening local party organisations, but would give the editors control over what was published and ensure that the pro-Duma line would be reliably disseminated.[86]

As for the necessity to deepen and widen socialist propaganda, in the whole sixteen months of life in emigration not a single propagandist book or pamphlet had been published, though plenty of literary talent and monetary resources were available. Yet when some comrades took the initiative to organise a party school, then no energy was spared in opposing the project. The organisers were accused of acting in secret, but in fact they had asked for cooperation from the editorial board of *Proletarii*, only for the request to be ignored.[87]

---

84   Protokoly soveshchaniia rasshirennoi redaktsii 'Proletariia'. Iiun' 1909 1934, pp. 177–80.
85   Protokoly soveshchaniia rasshirennoi redaktsii 'Proletariia'. Iiun' 1909 1934, p. 181.
86   Protokoly soveshchaniia rasshirennoi redaktsii 'Proletariia'. Iiun' 1909 1934, p. 182.
87   Protokoly soveshchaniia rasshirennoi redaktsii 'Proletariia'. Iiun' 1909 1934, p. 182.

The authors suspected that a new grouping of party forces was in the offing, a new fraction of the centre. It was noticeable that the boundary between
the pro-Duma Bolsheviks and the left wing of the Mensheviks was becoming
increasingly blurred, so that the *Proletarii* editorial board's announcement of a
split with all the 'left Bolsheviks' removed the last obstacle to their unification.
Plekhanov, for his part, had been making signs that he might be prepared to
countenance such an alliance. The recognition of Duma activity as a central
and basic one would serve as a unifying principle of the two groupings.[88]

However, the authors reasoned, the idea of a 'central' fraction which would
lead the whole party by divesting itself of the left wing of the Bolsheviks and
the right wing of the Mensheviks was illusory. In reality there were only two
basic currents in the party: the revolutionary and the opportunist. This fundamental divide was concealed by the conditions of the present reaction when
there was little scope for political action, but when the situation changed, the
incompatibility of the new alliance would be exposed, and there would be a
need for a fresh alignment of forces, a difficult and painful manoeuvre.[89]

This, the authors concluded, was, in broad terms, how the expulsions from
the Bolshevik fraction came about. They had not described in detail the course
of the in-fighting involved, but would be prepared to document it if any competent authority should demand it. They insisted that only a party congress or a
conference with enhanced powers was competent to decide on what happened
in the Bolshevik fraction, on any schism in it, certainly not the *Proletarii* editorial board. The authors declared that they regarded Bogdanov's expulsion as
illegal, since he had been elected to the Bolshevik Centre at the Fifth Congress
of the RSDLP.[90]

Simultaneous with Bogdanov and Krasin's report, Lenin published his
account of the proceedings of the extended editorial board in *Proletarii*. This
reproduced the resolutions of the conference and justified Bogdanov's expulsion from the Bolshevik Centre on the grounds that between Bogdanov and the
rest of the conference participants there was lacking that unanimity of opinion
which was a basic condition for the existence of a fraction within the party. To
Bogdanov's accusation that the line adopted by the conference was a betrayal
of Bolshevism and an adoption of the Menshevik point of view, Lenin had the
reply that Bogdanov should say this openly, in the press, so that the falsity of
his claims could be exposed.[91]

---

88   Protokoly soveshchaniia rasshirennoi redaktsii 'Proletariia'. Iiun' 1909 1934, p. 183.
89   Protokoly soveshchaniia rasshirennoi redaktsii 'Proletariia'. Iiun' 1909 1934, pp. 184–5.
90   Protokoly soveshchaniia rasshirennoi redaktsii 'Proletariia'. Iiun' 1909 1934, p. 185.
91   Lenin 1958–65, 19, p. 10.

Bogdanov was at this time in correspondence with Rosa Luxemburg on the subject of having her textbook on political economy published in Russian translation by his publishers Charushnikov and Dorovatsky. In his letter of 23 July he told her that as she had probably seen Lenin's account of the split in the Bolshevik fraction in *Proletarii*, he would send her a copy of the report that he and Krasin had written of the episode.[92] Luxemburg replied that she had not seen the copy of *Proletarii* in question, but that if the split had been on account of 'Machism', 'you, Messrs. Bolsheviks, ought to be shot'.[93]

On 10 August, having received the copy of *Proletarii*, Luxemburg wrote to Jogiches that she did not know what the attitude of the SDKPiL to the schism would be, but she herself considered it to be Tatar-Mongol savagery. Nevertheless, she thought that it would be difficult for the Polish party to do anything constructive in the situation. Any action against the Bolsheviks would only strengthen the Mensheviks, who were the patrons of the PPS, the rival Polish party to the SDKPiL.[94] Jogiches, who looked after more practical matters, would be influenced by the consideration that opposing the Lenin fraction would jeopardise the subsidies that accrued to the SDKPiL from the Shmit inheritance.[95]

On 22 August there appeared in *Vorwärts* an anonymous article written by Karl Radek, 'Questions of Tactics in Russian Social-Democracy', which gave a positive presentation of the proceedings of the Extended Editorial Board of *Proletarii*. Bogdanov wrote to Luxemburg in protest,[96] and received in reply a letter from Jogisches assuring him that Radek had acted independently, without the knowledge of the Polish leadership. Although, Jogiches stressed, the Poles did not sympathise with the policies of 'otzovism' and 'ultimatumism', they considered the conference that had expelled Bogdanov 'a crude and complete mockery of the party as a centre'. That meeting had shown that in spite of the resolutions of the Stockholm and Helsinki party conferences the Bolsheviks had continued and were still continuing to exist as a fraction, as 'a party within a party'. In a jibe which suggested that he shared Lenin's suspicion that the organisation of the Capri party school would form the nucleus of a new fraction within the RSDLP, Jogiches remarked that in this situation he would not be surprised if now a third fraction would appear with a Central Committee that would call itself 'the College of Lecturers of the Workers' School' or something

---

92   Neizvestnyi Bogdanov 1995, 1, p. 164.
93   Luxemburg 1971, 3, p. 40.
94   Luxemburg 1971, 3, pp. 46–7.
95   Nikolaevskii 1995, p. 80.
96   Luxemburg 1971, 3, p. 66.

of the kind. Jogiches concluded by saying that he thought Bogdanov's criticism of *Proletarii*, that it had grown closer to the Mensheviks, unjust; he welcomed this evolution, as it led to greater unity of the party.[97]

Bogdanov replied saying that he was glad to know that Radek's article did not represent the official views of the SDKPiL, though nevertheless there was a danger that this is how it would be widely viewed. He rejected Jogiches's reproach that he did not want to collaborate with the Mensheviks. He declared that he had nothing against working with the Mensheviks, but not if this implied the coming together of a Leninist and a Plekhanovite fraction. He told Jogiches that he found it repugnant that the money bequeathed to the Bolsheviks by Shmit, who had perished in the Moscow uprising, should 'be allocated and utilised in the struggle against Bolshevism by the very same Plekhanov who at the graveside of the Moscow fighters had declared "We should not have recourse to arms"'. Bogdanov also declared that he had no intention of replacing the existing Central Committee with a new fractional centre; he intended to keep to the Bolshevik tradition of exerting ideological influence, but doing this within the party structure. He made it clear that neither he nor Shantser had any intention of resigning from the party Central Committee.[98]

This interchange between Bogdanov and the Poles was significant in two respects. For one thing, it shows that although on his expulsion from the Bolshevik Centre Bogdanov might have tried to form a rival fraction, he did not follow this course. It is also a stage on the way to the Tenth Party Plenum in January 1910, at which all fractions in the RSDLP were formally dissolved.

5   *Materialism and Empiriocriticism*

Lenin spent nine months working on *Materialism and Empiriocriticism*, mainly in the Geneva libraries, but in order to extend his range of sources he went in May 1908 to London where he worked for about a month in the library of the British Museum. (It was while on this study trip that he sent the list of questions for Dubrovinsky to ask at Bogdanov's lecture.) The list of sources quoted or mentioned in the book exceeds 200 titles. Lenin had difficulty in finding a publisher for the work, although he was prepared to forego any royalties and to make any concessions required for the censor. His main concern was that it should be published quickly. With the help of his sister Anna Ulyanova and

---

97   Protokoly soveshchaniia rasshirennoi redaktsii 'Proletariia'. Iiun' 1909 1934, pp. 261–3.
98   Neizvestnyi Bogdanov 1995, 2, pp. 186–7.

Skvortsov-Stepanov, a publisher was found in the shape of the Socialist Revolutionary firm 'Zveno' in Moscow. The publisher insisted, however, that the personal abuse that abounded in the book should be toned down, a demand supported by Skvortsov-Stepanov and Anna Ulyanova. Skvortsov-Stepanov found the gratuitous attacks on his former associates Bogdanov and Bazarov unacceptable and demanded that they be removed, a demand that Lenin acceded to with reluctance. Lenin's *Materialism and Empiriocriticism* finally appeared in Moscow in May 1909.[99]

From reading *Materialism and Empiriocriticism* one can see that it is written with two main objectives in mind: one is to defend Plekhanov, and the other is to discredit Bogdanov and Plekhanov's other critics. It is Lenin's silence on Bogdanov's critique of Plekhanov that makes *Materialism and Empiriocriticism* such an enigmatic book. However, placed in context, it is clear that Lenin's real concern is to defend Plekhanov against the attacks of Bogdanov and his associates in *Studies in the Philosophy of Marxism*. In particular he wants somehow to rescue Plekhanov from the gaffe of having stated that he agreed with Kant on the question of 'things-in-themselves'. Lenin, however, never states this aim explicitly, and never in the course of the entire work does he quote what Plekhanov actually said. The implication is that to have done so would have been detrimental to the case Lenin wished to make. Instead, he refers, when necessary, to Plekhanov's statement obliquely, as when he says, for example:

> Our Machists have written so much about the 'thing-in-itself' that if all their writings were to be collected they would make a mountain of printed matter. The 'thing-in-itself' is a veritable *bête noire* for Bogdanov and Valentinov, Bazarov and Chernov, Berman and Yushkevich. There is no abuse they have not hurled at it, there is no ridicule they have not showered on it ... All the would-be Marxists among the Machists are combating Plekhanov's 'thing-in-itself'; they accuse Plekhanov of having become entangled and straying into Kantianism, and of having forsaken Engels.[100]

The implication here is that the preoccupation with the 'thing-in-itself' is an irrational obsession on the part of Plekhanov's opponents, rather than a devastating piece of evidence against him.

---

99   Ul'ianova 1989–90, 1, p. 105.
100   Lenin 1958–65, 18, p. 97.

Lenin had to deploy a good deal of ingenuity to counter these attacks on Plekhanov. Accordingly, he resorted to two types of argument. The first of these was that Bogdanov, Bazarov and the others had only seized upon Plekhanov as a tactic; that what they wanted to attack, but were afraid to do so, was Engels and his materialist standpoint. Thus, according to Lenin:

> Machist would-be Marxists have diplomatically set Engels aside, have completely ignored Feuerbach and are circling exclusively around Plekhanov. It is indeed circling around one spot, tedious and petty, pecking and cavilling at a disciple of Engels, while a frank examination of the views of the teacher himself is cravenly avoided.[101]

The other argument Lenin deployed was more convoluted, and was, in its way, a kind of justification for Plekhanov's espousal of Kant's 'thing-in-itself'. According to Lenin, the principal feature of Kant's philosophy was the reconciliation of materialism with idealism, a compromise between the two opposing currents. Thus, when Kant assumed that something outside us, a 'thing-in-itself', corresponded to our ideas, he was a materialist; when he declared this 'thing-in-itself' to be unknowable, he was an idealist. It was Lenin's contention that the 'Machists' criticised Kant for being too much of a materialist, while Marxists like Plekhanov criticised him for not being materialist enough. The 'Machists' criticised Kant from the right, the materialists from the left. In this way Lenin could argue that there was a materialist 'thing-in-itself' that Plekhanov was quite right to uphold, that is, a reality that existed independently of our senses, something that Lenin accused the 'Machists' of denying.[102]

In response to Bogdanov's accusation that Plekhanov had deliberately mistranslated Marx's thesis on Feuerbach so that it would conform with his own conception of 'hieroglyphics' and 'things-in-themselves', Lenin asserted, rather lamely, that the passage in question was not a translation, but a 'free paraphrase'.[103] Nevertheless, he made clear that he did not agree with Plekhanov's conception of 'hieroglyphics', since it was not endorsed by Engels, who had spoken neither of symbols nor of hieroglyphs, but of 'copies', 'photographs', 'images' and 'mirror-reflections' of things.[104] Suspecting that Bogdanov might dismiss the procedure of using Engels's utterances as a criterion of truth to be 'authoritarian thinking', Lenin cautioned:

---

101   Lenin 1958–65, 18, p. 98.
102   Lenin 1958–65, 18, p. 205.
103   Lenin 1958–65, 18, p. 104.
104   Lenin 1958–65, 18, p. 244.

And do not complain, Machist gentlemen, that I refer to 'authorities'; your outcry against the authorities is simply a screen for the fact that for the socialist authorities (Marx, Engels, Lafargue, Mehring, Kautsky) you are substituting bourgeois authorities (Mach, Petzoldt, Avenarius and the immanentists). You would do better not to raise the question of 'authorities' and 'authoritarianism'.[105]

Like Plekhanov's 'Materialismus militans' and Ortodoks's *Iskra* article before it, Lenin's *Materialism and Empiriocriticism* did not undertake a systematic refutation of Bogdanov's ideas or those of the other contributors to *Studies in the Philosophy of Marxism*, whom he insisted on referring to indiscriminately as 'Machists'. Lenin's strategy was not to refute the ideas of his opponents, but to discredit them by attaching to them the label 'idealist'. Here Lenin took up Plekhanov's ploy of claiming that the ideas of Bogdanov and other contributors to the collection were simply variants of Bishop Berkeley's philosophy, and that they were inconsistent with the propositions Engels had enunciated in *Ludwig Feuerbach* and *Anti-Dühring*. For this purpose it was enough for Lenin to reproduce those fragments of the writings of his opponents that he could claim were evidence of idealism or that he could in some way hold up to ridicule.

Predictably, Lenin seized upon the passage in *The Analysis of Sensations* where Mach had left himself open to misinterpretation: the statement that 'we have knowledge *only* of sensations'. This was held up as proof of Mach's denial of an objective reality and his intellectual kinship with Berkeley.[106] Lenin, however, omitted to explain that Mach used the term 'sensation' in the sense of an element that had both a physical and a psychical side.

By claiming that Bogdanov was a 'Machist' it was then a matter of showing the weakness of Mach's position to undermine that of Bogdanov. But there were one or two instances where Lenin did feel he was on safe enough ground to criticise Bogdanov's ideas directly. One was on the issue of eternal and absolute truths. Bogdanov had repeatedly insisted that no such things existed, but Lenin cited the example that Engels had given in *Anti-Dühring* of an indisputable truth. This was that Napoleon had died on 5 May 1821. According to Lenin, in the third volume of *Empiriomonism* Bogdanov had evaded the issue by claiming that the statement was not a real truth, but a platitude.[107]

Another direct criticism of Bogdanov was in a section of *Materialism and Empiriocriticism* entitled 'How Bogdanov corrects and "develops" Marx'. Here

---

105   Lenin 1958–65, 18, p. 263.
106   Lenin 1958–65, 18, p. 37.
107   Lenin 1958–65, 18, p. 133.

Lenin, following Ortodoks, quoted the passage from the essay 'The Development of Life in Nature and Society', where Bogdanov had argued that Marx's
formulation of the relationship between 'base' and 'superstructure' could be
made more precise, that 'Social being and social consciousness in the exact
sense of these words is identical'.[108] Lenin contended that this statement was
not correct, that 'social being' and 'social consciousness' could not be identical.
He believed that in this case Bogdanov had transformed Marx's materialist formulation into one of idealism, and pointed out that this criticism of Bogdanov's
re-formulation of Marx had already been made in an article by Ortodoks.
Bogdanov had not answered Ortodoks's criticism, but had only complained
about being misquoted. Lenin went on to accuse Bogdanov of not really being
engaged in a Marxist enquiry, but simply re-packaging results already obtained
in biological and energeticist terminology, the whole exercise being worthless
from beginning to end.[109]

6   The Fall of the Great Fetish

Bogdanov's reply to *Materialism and Empiriocriticism* was a work in two parts
published in 1910, one part entitled *The Fall of the Great Fetish* (*The Contemporary Crisis in Ideology*), and the other *Faith and Science*. In the first section
of the work Bogdanov recapitulated his scheme of intellectual development,
tracing the emergence of fetishism, authoritarian thinking, and their eventual
supersession with the emergence of a collectivist outlook. In *Faith and Science*,
he confronted Lenin's *Materialism and Empiriocriticism* directly, answering systematically the points it had raised.

   Since Lenin had criticised Bogdanov's formulation that 'social being and
social consciousness are identical', *The Fall of the Great Fetish* began by setting
out systematically and in detail Ludwig Noiré's theory that the origins of language lay in the exclamations made by people in the course of their work to
coordinate the efforts of the collective. Bogdanov had first deployed Noiré's
work to counter Berdyaev's contention that Marx's idea of 'base' and 'superstructure' was unconvincing. This was a very convenient theory for Bogdanov,
because it presented speech as an essential component of the production process, making it possible to argue that social being and social consciousness were
identical.

---

108   Bogdanov 1906, p. 57.
109   Lenin 1958–65, 18, pp. 342–51.

Noiré is one of the few writers that Bogdanov mentions by name and always with the epithet 'genius'. It is also remarkable that although Noiré was the author of works aiming at monism and re-stating the philosophy of nature to accommodate Darwin's theory of evolution, Bogdanov never mentioned these works, though they were close to his own area of interest, and though he must have been familiar with them.[110] It was Noiré's work on the origin of language that was important to Bogdanov, as it supplied him with an essential component of his system.

For the most part *The Fall of the Great Fetish* goes over familiar ground, recapitulating topics dealt with in earlier works. It traces the rise of bourgeois individualism, 'the great fetish', which occupies the whole historical period between primitive communism and socialism, and argues that this is about to be replaced by a new era of 'comradely cooperation'. This broad perspective provides the context in which the phenomenon of 'leadership' is discussed. Clearly, Bogdanov has Lenin in mind, though this is not stated explicitly. The work is in some respects a continuation of Bogdanov's 1903 article 'Authoritarian Thinking', in which he argued that the leadership of a single person, an 'ideologue', was not necessarily authoritarian and incompatible with the 'synthetic' form of cooperation. There he had cautioned that the higher the ideologues rose above the masses, the less influence the followers would be able to exert on their leaders, and petrified conservatism would be the result. By the time he wrote *The Fall of the Great Fetish*, Bogdanov had experienced in practice how leaders behaved, and found that the dangers he had indicated were fully justified. By that time too, he had abandoned the term 'synthetic cooperation' for the term 'comradely cooperation', though the content remained the same.

In writing about the phenomenon of leadership of the working class, Bogdanov obviously had Lenin's *What Is to Be Done?* in mind, particularly those passages which state that 'the history of all countries shows that the working class, exclusively by its own efforts, is able to develop only trade-union consciousness', that Social-Democratic consciousness could only be brought to the working class from outside, 'by the educated representatives of the propertied classes, by intellectuals'.[111] While agreeing with Lenin on the basic facts, Bogdanov's interpretation of them differed considerably from Lenin's.

Bogdanov accepts that the intelligentsia played an important part in the workers' movement. He says that the very basis of proletarian thought and pro-

---

110   See Noiré 1874 and Noiré 1875.
111   Lenin 1958–65, 6, p. 30.

letarian ideals was originally formulated by intellectuals. They were able to do this better than the working classes themselves, because they had better access to all the earlier discoveries of science and culture, on which the development of a higher type of ideology had to rely. They were also able to devote a greater amount of time to intellectual activities than workers, who were engaged in production. In sum, 'The proletariat needed associates, and they found them among the best representatives of the old classes'.[112] The difference between Lenin and Bogdanov is that whereas Lenin regarded the limitation of working-class consciousness to trade-unionism and its consequent reliance on intellectuals as a law of society, Bogdanov saw the working class's need for associates from the intelligentsia as an empirical historical fact. For Bogdanov the working class did not have a limited consciousness, only a lack of opportunity.

Though there were benefits to be gained from the assistance the intellectuals gave to the working-class movement, there were also considerable dangers, as Bogdanov was at pains to emphasise. Once a person was designated as a leader, and in this way distinguished from the rest of the collective, there was the danger of an authoritarian relationship. The specialised organiser was not wholly a comrade. Even if he had no formal personal 'power', even if all the comrades followed his directions voluntarily, and even if they could hold him to account, there was still the serious possibility of a drift towards authoritarianism. The danger was especially great where the level of collective consciousness in the organisation was not high, and where the role of the 'authority' was filled by an outsider from an environment where authoritarianism was prevalent.

In an organisation in which the sense of collectivity was poorly developed, there was a strong likelihood that ideological leaders would be looked up to as 'authorities' in the traditional sense, and regarded as people of a *higher* type, whose words always had the force of truth. It was easy, moreover, for leaders from outside the working class, who were to a lesser degree than the workers imbued with a sense of comradely relations, to think of themselves as innately superior to the workers, as they carried this attitude with them from their former way of life. Bogdanov thought that incomer leaders almost always brought with them an authoritarian relation to the working masses. But there were some rare exceptions:

> Only such intellectual giants as Marx himself, and perhaps a few other people with an exclusively pure soul, while remaining leaders, are capable of developing and preserving in themselves genuinely comradely

---

112   Bogdanov 1910a, p. 115.

relations to all other members of the collective which has adopted them, their psychological make-up completely corresponding to the tendencies of proletarian-class life and development.[113]

Bogdanov does not give examples of the few other people besides Marx who were able to preserve comradely relations with other members of the collective, while occupying positions of leadership. Perhaps modesty forbade, but Bogdanov would certainly have numbered himself in this exclusive category. Perhaps more to the point in the given context, he would have excluded Lenin from it.

Bogdanov went on to say that at the present time more and more leader-ideologues were emerging from among the workers themselves. Although these people were less prone to authoritarian tendencies than their colleagues from the 'intelligentsia', they were by no means immune. Bogdanov had encountered working-class leaders who had come to the fore during the revolutionary upsurge of 1905–6, and he had been struck by how spoilt they were by authoritarian conceit and ambition. Nevertheless, he said, the phenomenon was much more common among the intelligentsia than among the workers.[114]

In *Faith and Science* Bogdanov raised more explicitly the subject of Lenin's attitude towards the workers in *What Is to Be Done?* when he recalled:

> Once Lenin in *What Is to Be Done?* made a slip of the tongue, saying that the working class was incapable, independently, without the help of the socialist intelligentsia, to raise themselves above the ideas of trade-unionism and come to the socialist ideal. The phrase was uttered quite by chance in the heat of a polemic with the 'economists', and had no connection with the basic views of the author. This did not prevent Menshevik writers in the course of three years from concentrating their triumphant polemic on the above phrase of Lenin's, by which he had allegedly once and for all shown the anti-proletarian character of Bolshevism.[115]

It is unlikely that Bogdanov really believed that Lenin's pronouncement was a 'slip of the tongue', but by saying this he registered his own opinion that the idea was too absurd to be taken seriously.

As Lenin had anticipated, in his analysis of *Materialism and Empiriocriticism* Bogdanov took up the question of how Lenin used pronouncements by Marx

---

113   Bogdanov 1910a, p. 116.
114   Ibid.
115   Bogdanov 1910a, p. 193.

and Engels as the ultimate criteria of truth. He did this by asking the question whether Lenin's thought could be characterised as authoritarian. His answer was that it could, since, in Bogdanov's view, where there was faith there was authority. In this case, Lenin's faith was embodied in ideas espoused some where and at some time by Marx and Engels. He regarded Marx and Engels as prophets of absolute truth. And it was perfectly understandable that as prophets they ought not and could not say anything that was untrue. It was notable that Lenin never disagreed with Marx or Engels in any way.[116] Thus, Bogdanov's objection to Lenin's method of argumentation was not that he used Marx and Engels, but the *way* in which he used them. The ideas of Marx and Engels might be right or they might be wrong, so that it was quite improper to use their writings as the arbiter of absolute truth.

However, in the course of his analysis of Lenin's book Bogdanov was pleased to be able to quote Marx in support of his own concept of social validity as criterion for objectivity that he had expounded in *Empiriomonism*. He quoted the passage from *Das Kapital* which said that 'The categories of bourgeois economics consist precisely of forms of this kind. They are forms of thought which are socially valid, and therefore objective (*gesellschaftlich gültig, also objektive*) ...' According to Bogdanov, the passage showed that on this question Marx was a strict 'empiriomonist', adding that in order to defend Marx's philosophy, it was desirable to know what Marx's philosophy was.[117]

For Bogdanov, Lenin's main misapprehension was that there was such a thing as absolute and eternal truths, whereas in fact all truths were relative and ephemeral. As an example of an absolute and eternal truth Lenin had cited the one used by Engels in his book *Anti-Dühring*, namely the statement that Napoleon had died on 5 May 1821. He had put it to Bogdanov that 'If you cannot assert that the proposition "Napoleon died on 5 May 1821" is false or inexact, you acknowledge that it is true. If you do not assert that it may be refuted in the future, you acknowledge this truth to be eternal'.[118] Bogdanov replied to this by arguing that as the personality changed at different periods in a lifetime, the term 'Napoleon' was not an absolute. Moreover, physiologically, death was an imprecise term, and was changing with the development of medical science. Also, the date of Napoleon's demise would vary depending on the system of chronology used, e.g. the Julian or the Gregorian calendar.[119]

---

116   Bogdanov 1910a, p. 160.
117   Bogdanov 1910a, pp. 188–9.
118   Lenin 1958–65, 18, p. 133.
119   Bogdanov 1910a, pp. 153–4.

As Bogdanov pointed out, two-thirds of Lenin's book was devoted to accusing the 'Machists' of idealism. But the argument used to do this was illegitimate; it consisted in the 'substitution of concepts'. Thus, according to Lenin, the 'Machists' subsumed all reality under 'elements of experience'. What were those elements? They were colour, form, time, scent, hardness etc. But Hume had considered all of them to be 'sensations'. Hence 'elements' were the same as 'sensations'. But Berkeley called the same colour, form etc. 'ideas', therefore Machism was nothing but the purest idealism.

Another of Lenin's illegitimate methods of argument that Bogdanov pointed out was that of shifting his critique from the strongest representatives of the empiriocriticist school to the weakest, and so attacking the softest possible targets. Thus, since Mach had recommended Cornelius, Lenin concentrated his criticism on Cornelius rather than Mach. On this method, Bogdanov remarked: 'If A recommends B, then why criticise A when you can criticise B? And if B happens to recommend C, then it is even better to blame A for the behaviour of C, and so forth. This chain of "protection" could be extended to infinity'.[120]

An aspect of *Materialism and Empiriocriticism* that Bogdanov especially deplored was that despite the superficiality of the knowledge it contained, it had an extremely impressive scholarly apparatus. There were a myriad of footnotes and references to a multiplicity of works quoted. This, Bogdanov thought, was intended to overawe the reader and to create the impression that a writer of such erudition must be believed, that he was an authority on the subject. But Lenin's method of exposition was inherently unsound: nothing could be learned from the collection of quotations taken from different schools and times, presented out of context and with no coherent analysis of the ideas contained in them. Bogdanov added that Lenin's economic works were quite different; there he knew what he was talking about, and there was no posturing with pseudo-erudition and no pompous tone.[121]

Although ostensibly devoted to an analysis of *Materialism and Empiriocriticism*, Bogdanov paid a substantial amount of attention in *Faith and Science* to Plekhanov, Lenin's chief influence in ideology. According to Bogdanov, Plekhanov considered himself to be a follower of Spinoza, since he held the view that all material phenomena were inseparably connected to the psychical, that the psyche was an attribute of matter in general. Bogdanov pointed out that this was a mistaken interpretation of Spinoza's ideas, and that Plekhanov had not only attributed it to himself, but to Marx and Engels as well.[122]

---

120   Bogdanov 1910a, pp. 169–70.
121   Bogdanov 1910a, pp. 197–202.
122   Bogdanov 1910a, pp. 206–7.

Lenin did not reply to *The Fall of the Great Fetish* and *Faith and Science*. At the time Bogdanov wondered what kind of response he would make, as did other people. In 1910 one of Bogdanov's acquaintances from the Caucasus asked Lenin if he would be publishing a rebuttal of Bogdanov's criticisms of his *Materialism and Empiriocriticism* in the near future. Lenin's answer to the question was: 'Am I obliged to reply to everything?'[123] In retrospect Lenin's decision not to reply to Bogdanov was a wise one. A reply would have elicited more criticism from Bogdanov and would have drawn attention to *Faith and Science*. With the passage of time few people knew that Bogdanov had made a very effective reply to *Materialism and Empiriocriticism*. Paradoxically, however, *Materialism and Empiriocriticism* was for many years the main work that kept Bogdanov's name alive, albeit in a way that distorted the nature of his philosophical ideas.

---

123   Neizvestnyi Bogdanov 1995, 3, p. 163.

Vpered

1   Party Schools

At the beginning of August 1909, the First Higher Social-Democratic Propagandist and Agitational School began to function with 15 workers from Russia, with an additional 12 émigré workers living on Capri who planned to return to Russia and engage in party work. The lecturers were Bogdanov, Lunacharsky, Liadov, Gorky, Aleksinsky and Desnitsky. The school was organised on democratic lines with a School Council consisting of the students and lecturers, each with a vote, and an Executive Commission of three students and two lecturers to carry on the day-to-day running of the school. Prompted by Vilonov, the School Council passed a resolution declaring that it had nothing against the ideological leadership of the School by the Bolshevik Centre, and invited the Centre to participate in the school by contributing literary forces and financial support.

The School Council sent invitations to give courses in the school to a number of prominent figures in the workers' movement including Lenin, and the Bolshevik Centre members Dubrovinsky and M.K. Vladimirov, Pokrovsky, Trotsky, Plekhanov, D.B. Ryazanov, Martov, Kautsky and Rosa Luxemburg. The response to these invitations was mixed, only Pokrovsky agreeing to attend, the rest declining with various degrees of courtesy. Kautsky sent a polite letter saying that he had no time to come, and that in any case he was a writer rather than a speaker, and had little talent for teaching. Nevertheless he thought the programme of studies excellent and wished the organisers of the school success in their endeavour.[1]

Rosa Luxemburg's reply was that she could not spare the time, but in a letter to Jogiches she revealed that the real reason was more complex. She might have liked to go to Capri for a week or two, she confessed, but she was not sure to what extent this would conflict with party-political considerations, 'in view of the hostility between the Capri-Colony and Lenin'. Although she was reluctant to alienate Bogdanov, who was trying to find a Russian publisher for her economics textbook at that time, Luxemburg decided not to risk antagonising Lenin by attending the Capri school.[2]

---

1   Livshits 1924, pp. 33–55.
2   Luxemburg 1971, 3, p. 48.

Martov said that in principle he was willing to come, but did not have enough money for the fare to Capri. Trotsky, who had learned about the school from Vilonov, entered into correspondence with Gorky about the curriculum, thinking it too broad. Though at first Trotsky expressed willingness to participate, he subsequently changed his mind, probably under pressure from the Leninists.[3] Plekhanov did not bother to reply, and Ryazanov replied with a refusal.[4]

Lenin declined the students' invitation to lecture in the school, informing them that it was the centre of a new ideological fraction and that the lecturers at it were 'otzovists' and 'god-builders'. He suggested that the students should come to Paris, where he and his associates would gladly give them lectures on a variety of topics. When the students replied asking why Lenin thought the school fractional, they received a long letter explaining that the anti-Marxist views of the lecturers made it impossible for the school to be other than fractional.

The programme of studies at the Capri school, designed to last four months, was drawn up at an early meeting of the School Council. It consisted of the following courses:

> Political Economy taught by Bogdanov.
> History of the RSDLP – Liadov.
> History of Russia – Pokrovsky.
> The agrarian programme – S. Volsky.
> Trade unions and finances – Aleksinsky.
> History of Russian literature – Gorky.

Besides being given lectures on Marxist theory, the students were trained in public speaking, the conduct of meetings, and the techniques of newspaper printing. The students' day consisted of a period of preparation for the lectures, the lectures themselves, and a session at which the lecturers could be asked questions about the content of the lecture they had given. Following this, the students would demonstrate the extent to which they had assimilated the material by filling in questionnaires on the given topic. Bogdanov provided model answers for the questions he asked, and this gave rise to his book *Political Economy in Questions and Answers*.[5]

V.M. Kosarev, one of the students at the Capri school, recalls the impression that Bogdanov made.

---

3   Bailes 1967, pp. 126–8.
4   Bogdanov 1910, pp. 6–8.
5   Kosarev 1922, pp. 66–7.

A.A. Bogdanov was listened to with enormous interest. He described in a masterful, sometimes even in an artistic, way the epochs of human economic relations. We read together the first chapters of Marx's *Das Kapital*. He had a good knowledge of the history of philosophy, natural science and mathematics. In a word, he was a great scholar in the full sense of the word. It must be added that he was a very good and responsive comrade. He was simple and very attentive. His wife, Natalia Bogdanovna, like a good mother, looked after us while we were studying.[6]

Kosarev also had warm words to say about his other lecturers, Lunacharsky, Gorky and Pokrovsky.[7]

Although most of the students were in sympathy with Bogdanov and his associates, a minority were Leninists, causing tension between the two groups. In October there arrived on Capri the issue of *Proletarii* with Lenin's reply to Bogdanov and Krasin's joint *Report to the Comrade Bolsheviks of the Expelled Members of the Expanded Editorial Board of Proletarii*. This was a long article written in a mocking tone, ridiculing the arguments that Bogdanov and Krasin had put forward in their *Report*. Lenin denied espousing the policy of 'parliamentarianism at any price', and insisted that in the present political circumstances the use of the parliamentary tactic was the right one to adopt. He accused Bogdanov of hypocrisy in establishing a party school while in fact continuing to form a new political fraction whose ideological inspiration was 'otzovism' and 'god-building'.[8]

Some of the students asked Bogdanov how he proposed to reply to this attack, and in response to this Bogdanov drafted an article which he entitled 'Do Not Obscure Matters', which he read to the students in the free time after the studies had finished for the day. In the article Bogdanov contended that in the heat of the polemics that raged around the Capri school, the real issues were being obscured. The chief one of these was the controversy about the perspectives for the coming revolution. Lenin's basic premiss – which he did not state openly – was that the time-scale was very long, 'if not geological time' then at least beyond the lifetime of the present political generation. This was the premiss which made rational the tactics that Lenin advocated: the priority to be given to participation in the Duma and the use made of other legal openings, such as the trade unions and the cooperatives.

---

6   Kosarev 1922, p. 71.
7   Ibid.
8   Lenin 1958–65, 19, pp. 74–108.

Bogdanov, on the other hand, started from the assumption that the present generation would see the next revolutionary upsurge, that the present time was one between two revolutions. In this case the tactics to be followed were preparation for the coming revolutionary struggle, strengthening the party locally and training up activists to be propagandists of Social-Democracy.

As for the motivation of Lenin and his followers, Bogdanov suggested that this was the conscious aspiration of a handful of party *intelligenty* to retain for themselves a monopoly on the leadership, afraid as they were of competition from the fresh forces emerging from the proletariat itself. This kind of attitude, Bogdanov maintained, was incompatible with the spirit of Bolshevism.

For Bogdanov, Bolshevism was not simply a political phenomenon, but a social-cultural one. Bolshevism was the first doctrine to set itself the objective of achieving the political hegemony of the proletariat over the bourgeois classes in the bourgeois-democratic revolution. But for those who understood the inseparability of politics from other aspects of the ideological life of society it would seem anomalous that while the proletariat was recognised as being capable of achieving political hegemony, it was thought unable to establish hegemony in the general-cultural sphere. This was the hidden premiss of Bolshevism, the idea that it was possible to create, in the here and now, within the confines of the present society, great proletarian culture, stronger and more cogent than that of the declining bourgeois classes. Bogdanov emphasised the point about proletarian culture by modifying a famous dictum of Marx: 'We, the old Bolsheviks, take up the old slogan "The emancipation of the workers must be the affair of the workers themselves", and we say: Yes! Primarily political and cultural emancipation for the struggle for complete freedom, for the socialist ideal'.[9]

Some of the students found the article insufficient. In their view, the ideological disorder which reigned in the party made it essential to work out a platform with a thorough analysis of the present situation and the tasks of the party, a platform that would be accessible to the widest strata of the organised workers and would be able to serve as a guide to the party activists. Those students who were basically in sympathy with the lecturers at the school proposed that they should begin immediately to collectively elaborate such a platform.[10]

Five students who declared themselves to be 'Leninists' protested against the drawing up of a platform, asserting that this would impede their studies, and that they did not have the right to work out any platforms whatsoever,

---

9   Bogdanov 1909c, pp. 1–5.
10   Bogdanov 1910, p. 19.

not being delegated to do this by their organisations. The lecturers replied that their objections were unfounded, since work on the platform would be outside school hours and not on the school premises.[11]

Vilonov had not been at the meeting at which Bogdanov read his article, but when he heard of what had been said he became convinced that what *Proletarii* had said was true: that the school was being used as a base from which to launch a new political fraction in opposition to the Bolshevik Centre. At a fraught meeting with the lecturers Vilonov gave a critical evaluation of Bogdanov's article, and declared his solidarity with the editorial board of *Proletarii*.

Vilonov and the five 'Leninist' students wrote a letter to *Proletarii* protesting against the behaviour of the lecturers at the Capri school. It stated that in the school there were secret groupings of 'Bogdanovists' and that while studying in the school there was no chance of ignoring this fact, when each day that went by a most furious polemic took place. They did not want to serve as a screen for the formation of a new ideological centre with a platform elaborated in a spirit of militancy.[12]

The letter appeared in a supplement to *Proletarii* which arrived on Capri in November. It was accompanied by a triumphant commentary by Lenin, who could claim that his accusations that the Capri school was a cover for the creation of a new fraction had been fully justified. At an extraordinary session of the School Council the five 'Leninist' students were asked to clarify their attitude towards the school. They responded in a document which stated that the responsibility for the conclusions made by the editorial board of *Proletarii* from their letters did not lie with them, that they were answerable to the party only for the information they had provided. They added that they had never complained of any fractionalism in the lectures themselves; that, on the contrary, they recognised the knowledge they had received from the lectures at the school as useful and necessary. The School Council decided that as the five 'Leninists' had directed their efforts to disrupting the school and sending letters to the Bolshevik Centre containing a number of falsehoods about the school, they, along with Vilonov, should be expelled.[13]

The five expelled students and Vilonov then set out for Paris, where they were warmly received by Lenin and the other editors of *Proletarii*, by whom they were given a short series of lectures. Lenin spoke on the Stolypin reform, Dubrovinsky on organisational questions in the party, Zinoviev on the trade-union movement, Kamenev on the Social-Democratic Party in the 1905 revolu-

---

11   Ibid.
12   Bogdanov 1910, p. 20.
13   Bogdanov 1910, pp. 20–2.

tion and Vladimirov on the national question. The five students and Vilonov contributed to a supplement of *Proletarii* containing a 'Report on the Capri School' which denounced the lecturers for turning the school into the nucleus of a new fraction. At the end of the lecture course in Paris all six returned to Russia in December.[14]

A description of the schism at the Capri school by the five expelled students was published in an offprint of *Proletarii* and also in the October–November issue of *Sotsial-Demokrat*, the central organ of the party. Bogdanov sent a reply to *Sotsial-Demokrat*, but this was not published. Bogdanov wanted to send a letter of protest from the Capri school, but the School Council was reluctant to do so, being in awe of the party leadership. In despair at this capitulation to authoritarian thinking, Bogdanov sent the Council an emotional letter of resignation. In it he said:

> The faithlessness of Vilonov, an intelligent and talented worker and comrade, and those five, dealt the first blow to my faith. But I decided, no matter, many are called, but few are chosen. But then this …
>
> During the first discussion of an answer to the Central Organ I was deeply shaken by the thought that passed through my head during the debates to the effect that the Central Organ signifies 'a higher party institution' that one must not deal with as other institutions, that one is forbidden to point out frankly and directly to the party its impermissible form of activity, which is debasing the party. But the final decision almost satisfied me: an ultimatum to the effect that *if a definite and satisfactory answer is not received*, then the party will be told everything.
>
> And now an answer has been received – *indefinite, unsatisfactory*, treacherous. What happened to the categorical promise, made in writing by the School Council to act decisively *in such an event*? You reneged on it.[15]

The School Council refused to accept Bogdanov's resignation, and he, along with the other lecturers and some of the students, got down to drafting a programme for the group that was to bear the name 'Vpered' (Forward).

By December the course of studies on Capri had been completed, and the students were invited to Paris, where they were given the same series of lectures as were given to the expelled five. On arrival, the group of students had inquired

---

14   Livshits 1924, p. 70.
15   Quoted in Bailes 1967, p. 131.

whether the studies would be organised on the same democratic principles as on Capri. They were told that there would be no such 'self-government'; that they were there to learn. One of the students, Kosarev, noticed that Lenin's lecture on Stolypin was only a pretext. His real objective was to win over at least some of this contingent of students from Bogdanov. In this attempt he analysed the platform that the Capri group had drawn up, arguing that the points it made were untenable and inappropriate for the existing political situation. For the most part, however, the students remained unconvinced by Lenin's critique.[16]

After three weeks of study in Paris the Capri students made their way back to Russia. Not long after, however, most of them were arrested, some being sentenced to long terms of imprisonment. In the short term the purpose of the Capri school might have been frustrated, but later, in Soviet times, several of its graduates were to fill important positions in the party and the government.[17]

2   The Translation of Marx's *Das Kapital*

At the same time as the conflicts within the Bolshevik fraction were taking place, Bogdanov was involved in a project to translate and publish the three volumes of Marx's *Das Kapital*. The project had been initiated in the spring of 1906 by N.S. Klestov (Angarsky), a Social Democrat who had just escaped from Omsk, where he had been imprisoned for revolutionary activities. Klestov had been successful in finding a financial backer for the project in the person of G.A. Blumenberg, a merchant and paper manufacturer. As translators Klestov recruited Skvortsov-Stepanov and Bazarov. Klestov wrote to Lenin in Finland, proposing that he become general editor, a proposal that Lenin accepted. In November 1906 the newspaper of the Moscow Bolsheviks *Voprosy dnia* announced that a Moscow firm was publishing the translation of the three volumes of Marx's *Das Kapital*, editied by Bazarov and Skvortsov-Stepanov, with Lenin as general editor.[18]

The translation, which was of the fifth German edition of *Das Kapital* (1903), began with volume II, of which Lenin edited the first chapter, before giving up the work for lack of time. The obvious candidate to take over was Bogdanov, but Blumenberg was reluctant to accept him, objecting that: 'We need circula-

16   Kosarev 1922, p. 73.
17   Livshits 1924, p. 73.
18   Saralieva 1970, pp. 120–1.

tion. All the newspapers write about Lenin: he has a name'.[19] With Lenin gone the new translation of Marx's work became increasingly associated with the Moscow literary-lecturing group, headed by Shantser. Not only did Bogdanov become general editor, but the group supplied two of the main translators for volumes II and III of *Das Kapital*, which were published in 1907, M.A. Silvin and M.G. Lunts.

The problem of establishing a uniformity of style between translators persuaded Skvortsov-Stepanov to use, as far as possible, a single translator, Bazarov, for volume I. This was published in 1909 with a Foreword, presumably written by Bogdanov as general editor. The Foreword was mainly concerned with justifying the translation of the German term *Wert* (value) by the Russian word '*stoimost*'' rather than by '*tsennost*''. This was not such an esoteric question as might appear at first sight, because the concept of 'value' was a pivotal one in Marx's argument in *Das Kapital*, and how it was to be translated had an important bearing on the way one interpreted Marx's ideas.

The question also had a long history in the development of Marxism in Russia. Nikolai Sieber, whose 1871 dissertation first introduced Marx's economic ideas to the Russian reading public, translated *Wert* by *tsennost*', following the way in which classical economists like Ricardo had been translated. However, the first translator of Marx's *Das Kapital* into Russian, G.A. Lopatin, had broken with this practice and translated *Wert* as *stoimost*', as he believed it better conveyed the sense of Marx's argument. Lopatin had in fact met Marx in London and discussed the problem of *Das Kapital*'s peculiar terminology with him. The other translators of the first volume of *Das Kapital*, N.F. Danielson and N.N. Liubavin, had followed Lopatin's example and translated *Wert* by *stoimost*'. When the Russian translation of the first volume of *Das Kapital* was published in 1872, Marx, who could read Russian fluently by that time, declared it 'masterly'. In the 1880s and 1890s it became customary for Russian Marxists to use the word *stoimost*' when referring to Marx's theory of value.

In 1896 two members of a Social-Democratic circle in Minsk, E.A. Gurvich and L.M. Zak, completed a translation of the fourth edition of the first volume of *Das Kapital*. In order to get their work published they sought the help of Struve, who acted as general editor for the translation and supplied it with a Foreword. The main change that Struve made to the translation, against the wishes of the translators, was to substitute the term *tsennost*' for *stoimost*', and in the Foreword Struve gave his justification for doing so.

---

19   Saralieva 1970, p. 122.

This was that in *tsennost'* was contained the idea of 'evaluation': the individual or the social evaluation of economic good, and also the individual or the social evaluation of the urgency of usage. Besides this, *tsennost'* expressed social evaluation from the point of view of the expenditure of labour, which, according to Marx's teaching, was a category common to all socio-economic formations, in which the acquisition of benefits was determined principally by the expenditure of labour. On the other hand, the Russian word *stoimost'*, in its common everyday usage, meant the expenditure on production or the costs of production in an economy based on exchange, i.e. in a money economy or even in a capitalist economy. The usual sense of this Russian word was thus no wider than that of the English 'cost' or the German *'Kosten'*.

Bogdanov's Foreword was aimed principally at refuting Struve's case for replacing *stoimost'* with *tsennost'*, which he saw in the context of the campaign of Russian revisionism of the 1890s to combat the 'petrified dogmas' of the orthodox Marxists. As for the contention that *stoimost'* meant no more than the English 'costs' or the German *'Kosten'*, Bogdanov pointed out that on the few occasions that Marx used the English term 'cost' he regarded it not as a separate economic category, but simply as a synonym for *Wert*, which implied that *stoimost'* was a suitable translation of *Wert*.[20]

Bogdanov explained that in Russian there is no word which exactly corresponded to the sense of the German *Wert*. But in the present case it was not necessary that the Russian term should be equivalent to the word *Wert* in all possible areas and applications. It was only a matter of the most convenient rendering of *Wert* in the given specific area, in the political economy of Marx. Therefore, the question was: what more corresponds to the spirit of Marx's economic doctrine: the psychological interpretation of *Wert* (*Wert* as *tsennost'*, the object of subjective evaluation) or its objective interpretation (*Wert* as *stoimost'*, the result of particular expenditures)?[21]

In all the three volumes of *Das Kapital*, Bogdanov declared, there was not even a hint of the phenomenon of 'evaluation' as a problem of political economy. But, on the other hand, in the very first chapter of the first volume it is made clear that it is necessary to abstract from any form of evaluation in order to arrive at an economic analysis of the commodity. Thus, the methodological elimination of the category of *tsennost'*, the abstraction from it, is for Marx the necessary condition of correctly posing the problem. The fact was that if one used the concept of *tsennost'*, as the supporters of the psychological

---

20   Bogdanov 1909d, pp. IV–V.
21   Bogdanov 1909d, p. VI

current insisted, it served not to illuminate Marx's thought, but to obscure the starting-point of his doctrine. This is what Struve's Foreword had done, and indirectly shown that *tsennost'* was completely unsuitable to convey the term *Wert* in Marx's usage.[22]

Bogdanov himself had not always been so consistent in his usage of the term *stoimost'* for *Wert*. In his *Short Course of Economic Science* he often uses *tsennost*. One may speculate that he may have had an authoritative confirmation for his choice of *stoimost'*. In his memoirs of the Capri party school in 1909, one of the students, Kosarev, recalls that Lopatin, the first translator of *Das Kapital*, who was living on the island at that time, told the participants of the school about his personal acquaintance with Karl Marx.[23] It would be natural for Bogdanov to broach the subject with him of how he came to choose *stoimost'* over *tsennost'* in his translation.

3   The Platform of Vpered

The desire to reply to the campaign of vilification conducted by Lenin on the pages of *Proletarii* and, more recently, of *Sotsial-Demokrat* must have been a powerful motive for Bogdanov's formation of the Vpered group. *Sotsial-Demokrat* would not publish his rebuttals, and *Proletarii* most assuredly would not. Trotsky's newspaper *Pravda*, published in Vienna, had at first seemed a promising outlet, but had taken a hostile approach to the Capri school to please Lenin in return for financial subsidies.[24] The solution was to launch a newspaper of one's own, but representing what? The answer that Bogdanov came up with was the literary group Vpered.

The Platform of the Vpered group that the lecturers and students of the Capri school drew up is a remarkable document for the depth of its analysis of the economic and political situation of Russia at the time, for the cogency of its arguments and for its prophetic insights. The continuity of the Platform with 'Do not Obscure Matters' and other of his works is evidence of Bogdanov's hand in composing the document. In particular, the Platform develops the concept of proletarian culture that had first made its appearance in 'Do not Obscure Matters'.

The Platform begins by surveying the parlous state of the party in the aftermath of the 1905 revolution: the catastrophic loss of membership through

---

22   Bogdanov 1909d, p. x.
23   Kosarev 1922, p. 67.
24   Bailes 1967, p. 129.

arrests and banishments, the mass desertion of the intelligentsia, the sever-
ing of links between local committees, the sparsity of local newspapers and
the cessation of propagandist activity in trade unions and the army. There
were, however, grounds for optimism: a nucleus of dedicated worker-activists
remained who had taken over the functions of the intellectuals who had left
the party. A large proportion of local party publications which had recently
appeared had been put out by the workers themselves, though the lack of the
necessary skills and knowledge to do this was strongly felt.

According to the Platform, the regeneration of the party was threatened by
the recent split in Bolshevism. If this split had not yet in fact taken place, it
had been at least officially proclaimed. And since Bolshevism was the unifying
factor in party work as a whole, the split meant destroying the unity of that
work. In view of the critical state the party found itself in, the supporters of the
Platform declared that they had decided to form themselves into an ideological group, whose main task was to campaign for the restoration of Bolshevik
unity.[25]

A prominent element in the Platform was the analysis of the contemporary
Russian economy and its dynamics of development. Capitalism had taken root
in Russia, but its further development was impeded by the restrictive policies
of the autocracy. Its need for a thriving internal market was frustrated by the
agrarian policies of the tsarist regime, which kept the peasantry impoverished
and indebted. The policies of privatising communal land pursued by the Prime
Minister Stolypin would not improve this situation, because its application
would be limited to the western areas of the country where the commune
was already weak, and it would also create new tensions among the peasantry
between those who separated out of the commune and those who remained
within it. This was an accurate prediction about how the Stolypin reform would
be implemented in the years before 1914 and about its implications for the peasant movement in 1917, in which separators were forcibly brought back into the
commune.[26]

Capitalism also needed an external market to thrive, but although the government had expanded into territories in Central Asia and the Far East, it had
suffered a crushing defeat at the hands of the Japanese and an end was put to
colonial seizures. Instead of expanding, foreign markets were contracted and
the enormous expenditure on an unsuccessful war further weakened the home
market by reducing the purchasing power of the people.

---

25   Neizvestnyi Bogdanov 1995, 2, pp. 37–8.
26   Neizvestnyi Bogdanov 1995, 2, p. 39.

In the international arena the competition of different countries for markets had led to extreme tensions, and there was reason to expect the outbreak of war in the near future. The whole of Europe was divided into two hostile military camps, one led by England and the other by Germany. Russia would be drawn into the war, though it was unclear on which side it would fight.

The argument in the Platform was that the economic and social factors that had given rise to the revolution of 1905 were still present, and had if anything become more pronounced. Consequently, Bogdanov could predict that: 'A new revolutionary crisis is inevitable. We do not know when it will come, but we, the present party activists, will take part in it. We have to be ready'.[27]

The following section of the Platform surveyed the history of Bolshevism from its inception to the present point in time. The Platform argued that Bolshevism implied a socialist consciousness that went further than simply a struggle in the spheres of economics and politics; it was in life as a whole. As in *The Fall of the Great Fetish*, Bogdanov made the point that the proletariat and its ally, the socialist intelligentsia, had emerged from the old peasant and bourgeois world, and without themselves being aware of it, had kept many of the habits and attitudes of that world and brought them into their revolutionary practice. The individualism of many party activists, their personal ambition, their desire to distinguish themselves, their rejection of comradely discipline, their intolerance of comradely criticism, were all detrimental to the workers' movement. In these circumstances differences of opinion led to fruitless internal squabbles. Clearly, here Bogdanov had Lenin in mind, and the implication is that Lenin had not taken kindly to Bogdanov's 'comradely criticism', and had not hidden his aversion to it.

The Platform went on to say that no less harm was caused by the widespread practice among party activists of putting their trust in authorities, uncritically accepting the opinions of this or that recognised leader without putting them to any test of reliability. This kind of deference belonged to a former era, and the Platform urged Bolsheviks to campaign against such survivals of the past.

Closely associated with the campaign against authoritarian thinking was the concept of 'proletarian culture' that Bogdanov was to develop in later works of the period. His argument was that:

> The bourgeois world, having its well elaborated culture, had left its mark on modern science, art and philosophy, and through them it imperceptibly schools us in its direction, at the same time as the class struggle and

---

27   Neizvestnyi Bogdanov 1995, 2, p. 52.

our social ideal pulls us in the opposite direction. We cannot break completely with this culture that has come about through history, because from it we can and must derive powerful weapons for the struggle against that same old world. To accept it as it is would mean to preserve in oneself that very past against which the struggle is conducted.

There is only one way out: using the previous, bourgeois culture, to create, and oppose to it, and spread among the masses a new proletarian culture, strengthen genuine comradely relations in the proletarian environment, elaborate a proletarian philosophy, direct art towards proletarian aspirations and experience. Only in this way can there be achieved an all-round socialist education, which will eliminate the countless contradictions of our life and work, and increase manyfold our strength in the struggle, and at the same time bring us closer to the ideal of socialism, elaborating more and more its elements in the present time.[28]

This task of cultural creativity was one which was to be undertaken by the revolutionary wing of the party. The creativity that the proletariat had shown in economic and political organisation was proof that it was capable too of creativity in the cultural sphere.

In the section on the 'Organisational Question' the Platform observed that from 1906 the party had been run according to the principles of democratic centralism, but that since 1907, when the reaction became consolidated in the country, democratic centralism had fallen into abeyance. The Platform deplored the existence of fractions in the party which had become laws unto themselves. Of course it was natural that there should be different ideological currents within the party; this was a sign of its vitality. These currents might find expression in the form of literary groupings or clusters of kindred spirits at congresses and conferences. But the formation of fractions was a different matter; these were 'parties within a party', which undermined the effectiveness of the organisation as a whole, and even impeded the formation of ideological currents themselves. The Platform required that the fractions should in reality only be ideological and literary centres.[29]

The Platform recognised that the unification of the fractions could only be effected by a party congress. But a congress which took place in the current disorganised state of the party would be unlikely to meet the demands placed upon it. When there had not been a conference for eleven months, or even a

---

28   Neizvestnyi Bogdanov 1995, 2, p. 56.
29   Neizvestnyi Bogdanov 1995, 2, pp. 58–9.

full meeting of the Central Committee, convoking a congress in the near future would be impossible. There would have to be preparatory work done in the localities.[30]

A special section of the Platform was devoted to the question of participation in the State Duma. It summarised the attitudes adopted by the Social Democrats to the three Dumas, setting out Lenin's viewpoint objectively and almost sympathetically. This was, the Platform said, a point of view held by some former anti-boycottists, who considered that the question of the party's participation in the Third Duma was no longer a secondary and purely practical one, but one of principle. The long period of reaction, which had severely limited the possibilities for illegal work, had enormously increased the importance of Duma work and made it of top priority. Disagreements in relation to the Duma fraction they therefore considered fundamental, and found collaboration with those who disagreed with them on this question impossible.

The Platform, however, believed this point of view mistaken, since the experience of the past two years had shown the futility of giving the Duma such an overwhelming significance. In the judgement of the Platform the lessons of these years of reaction had shown that the highest priority should have been given to local work in re-establishing the organisation, in broadening and deepening propaganda, in strengthening influence among the workers on the basis of the direct needs and demands of the proletariat etc. Only by doing this would it be possible to make the best use of the platform provided by the Duma.

Much of the Platform was devoted to particular and detailed measures to be taken to make the agitational and propagandist functions of the party more effective and to extend the influence of the party to wider sections of the population. It was urged that Social-Democratic propaganda should be conducted in the trade unions, the army and among rural proletarians and peasants. To promulgate its views the Vpered group proposed to publish a number of pamphlets based on its Platform and a newspaper aimed at a mass audience.[31]

4   The Tenth Plenum of the Central Committee

Bogdanov's efforts to canvass the support of the SDKPiL against Lenin and his supporters paid off when in January 1910 a Plenum of the Central Committee was held in Paris at the insistence of Jogiches and Warski. It lasted from

---

30   Neizvestnyi Bogdanov 1995, 2, p. 59.
31   Neizvestnyi Bogdanov 1995, 2, p. 76.

15 January to 5 February, and from Lenin's point of view it was 'three weeks of hell'. Present were the 14 voting members of the Central Committee (four Bolsheviks: Dubrovinsky, Meshkovsky, Zinoviev, V.P. Nogin; four Mensheviks: A.S. Martynov, B.I. Goldman, N. Zhordania, N. Ramishvili; two SDKPiL: Jogiches, Warski; two Bundists: Koigen, Aizenshtadt; one SDLK: M. Ozoliņš and one Vperedist: Shantser) plus representatives of the various socialist publications: Lenin, Kamenev, Martov and Trotsky. Bogdanov attended as a candidate member of the Central Committee.[32]

This promised to be an awkward moment for Lenin. The existence of the Bolshevik Centre was unconstitutional, let alone Bogdanov's expulsion from it. He had also been the recipient of funds that had come from expropriations, which was a serious breach of party discipline, and his appropriation of the entire Shmit legacy was of dubious legality, since it was arguably bequeathed to the party as a whole and not just to the Bolshevik fraction. However, it was the influence that Lenin had acquired through the Shmit fortune that allowed him to emerge from the Tenth Plenum with only a mild rebuke, and that was for his complicity in expropriations, not for his expulsion of Bogdanov from the Bolshevik Centre.

The Poles had initially condemned Bogdanov's expulsion, but this resulted in a reduction of their subsidy from the Bolshevik Centre, so that they subsequently started to approve the split in the Bolshevik ranks in their publications. Bogdanov believed that the SDKPiL as a whole was unaware of the subsidy from the Bolsheviks. The ones in the know were Jogiches and Warski, the SDKPiL representatives at the Tenth Plenum.[33]

The measure that the Plenum took to avoid past breaches of discipline was the abolition of all fractions within the party. Lenin agreed to dissolve the Bolshevik Centre and to cease publication of its newspaper *Proletarii*. The Mensheviks were expected to follow suit and to end the publication of their paper *Golos Sotsial-Demokrata*. The Bolsheviks also handed over at least part of the Shmit inheritance to the three trustees Karl Kautsky, Franz Mehring and Clara Zetkin. The understanding was that if the Mensheviks failed to dissolve their fraction and *Golos Sotsial-Demokrata*, the Bolsheviks would demand the return of their money.

It is likely that by handing over the Shmit money Lenin bought himself a much easier passage with the Plenum than he would have had otherwise. He also was able to extract the concession of a resolution condemning both 'liquid-

---

32   Najdus 1980, pp. 85–6; Khalipov 1982, p. 81.
33   Neizvestnyi Bogdanov 1995, 2, p. 106.

ationism' (the call for the underground party organisation to be abolished and political activity to be entirely legal) and 'otzovism', which served as a justification of his past behaviour and a preliminary to joining forces with Plekhanov. A more important prize for Lenin was the place on the editorial board of the party's official newspaper, *Sotsial-Demokrat*, amply compensating him for the loss of *Proletarii* as a mouthpiece. With his allies Zinoviev and Warski Lenin had a majority on the editorial board and could determine the content of the newspaper.

The Plenum also accommodated Lenin by depriving Bogdanov of his place on the Central Committee.[34] But there were also some small gains for Bogdanov at the Plenum. The Central Committee recognised Vpered as a literary and publishing group, though it was envisaged that the party as a whole should take over these activities, making the existence of a separate group unnecessary.[35] The Central Committee also recognised the value of the party school that had been held on Capri, but acceded to Lenin's insistence that future schools should not be organised by the Vpered group alone. Accordingly, a committee of nine people was appointed consisting of two Bolsheviks (Leninists), two Mensheviks, two members of the Vpered group, and a representative of each of the nationalities: a Pole, a Latvian and a Bundist. It was intended that Bogdanov and his associates would refrain from establishing a separate school and would participate in the one organised by the Central Committee, in which they would find sufficient outlet for their teaching and lecturing skills. The party school would function under the auspices of a newly formed Foreign Bureau of the Central Committee, which would dispense the funds necessary for organising the school.[36]

Following the Plenum Jogiches remarked with some satisfaction that 'The Bolsheviks as a party within a party (as a separate organisation) have suffered outright defeat, as has Lenin's very narrow conception of intra-party objectives'. Rosa Luxemburg was convinced that finally the unification of the Russian fractions had been achieved, but other observers, like Feliks Dzierżyński and Karl Kautsky, were more sceptical, believing that the compromise would be of short duration. In the event the pessimists proved right; Lenin was soon able to extricate himself from the stipulations of the Tenth Plenum, helped in this by the alleged intransigence of the Mensheviks.[37]

---

34   Neizvestnyi Bogdanov 1995, 2, p. 107.
35   KPSS v rezoliutsiiakh i resheniiakh s"ezdov, konferentsii i plenumov TsK, 1953, 1, p. 241.
36   KPSS v rezoliutsiiakh i resheniiakh s"ezdov, konferentsii i plenumov TsK, 1953, 1, p. 240.
37   Najdus 1980, p. 88; Kochanski 1971, p. 380.

On the face of it Bogdanov ought to have been satisfied with the party unity that the Tenth Plenum had brought about, since it was something he had long campaigned for. But in fact he was bitterly disappointed, because Bolshevism, which had been the spirit of Social-Democracy, no longer existed as an ideological current within the party. In a pamphlet entitled *To Comrade Bolsheviks!* he castigated Lenin and his followers for abandoning the traditions of Bolshevism while claiming to defend them. They had dissolved the fraction without asking the opinion of its members by convoking a conference or congress to discuss the matter. The Lenin clique was too anxious to retain its privileged and irresponsible position to risk consultation with the fraction as a whole. It was for this reason too that they expelled those members of the Bolshevik Centre who would stand in its way. The Leninists were able to exert their influence on the party because they controlled its finances. And although they were in possession of enormous monetary resources, they had not put out a single agitational or propagandist leaflet. Nor did they give money to the party school but tried to deprive the school of the autonomy that its students enjoyed. Bogdanov, on behalf of the Vpered group, called upon comrades in Russia to organise in the near future a Bolshevik conference that would restore the spirit of Bolshevism to the party.[38]

5   The Bologna Party School

With the Central Committee's recognition of Vpered as a literary group and its admission that the party schools performed a useful function, Bogdanov felt that he had won a moral victory.[39] But the strains of the Capri school had taken their toll. By the spring of 1910 relations between Bogdanov and Lunacharsky on the one hand and Gorky on the other were deteriorating, exacerbated by the intrigues of Gorky's partner Maria Andreeva. Andreeva conducted a correspondence with Lenin separate from Gorky's and aided and abetted Lenin's aim of ending the friendship between Bogdanov and Gorky.[40] Andreeva thought that Bogdanov and Lunacharsky were bad influences on Gorky, because they distracted him from writing literary works, which was where his talent lay, towards politics and philosophy, for which he had no special aptitude. In a letter to Bogdanov Andreeva deplored the fact that Gorky had broken off his literary work to contribute to *Novaia Zhizn* and that political considerations had led

---

38   Neizvestnyi Bogdanov 1995, 2, pp. 77–83.
39   Rogachevskii 1994, p. 671.
40   Rogachevskii 1994, pp. 667–8.

him to write *Mother*, which was lacklustre from a literary point of view. Gorky had countless philosophical plans and projects with which he intended to help Bogdanov's campaign, but these took a long time to come to fruition. To make Gorky publish these thoughts and feelings, not in his accustomed literary form, but as an article in a philosophical collection, would be to lose for Gorky's readers something that was irreplaceable.[41]

Lenin got his sister to spread rumours that there had been a split between Gorky and Bogdanov, and Bogdanov wrote to Gorky asking him why he did not quell them. Gorky wrote to Bogdanov in reply at the end of 1910 saying: 'As you know, I respect you both as a thinker and a revolutionary, but I shall not reply to your letters: they are too severe, written as though you were a sergeant and I was a simple private in your squad'.[42] In a letter to Aleksinsky Gorky wrote:

> It seems to me that he [Bogdanov] does not have the temperament of a revolutionary, but that he is a maker of systems. The inclination towards synthesis is strongly developed in him, and like all people of this kind he is a conservative and a despot. As far as other people are concerned – he despises them all, because he thinks himself incomparably more intelligent and significant than them, hence his arrogant attitude towards them. But he has talent. I am sure that he will accomplish much.[43]

The loss of Gorky's friendship was a serious one for Bogdanov, as it was through Gorky that Bogdanov enjoyed the goodwill of wealthy patrons like Amfiteatrov, and these were not prepared to finance enterprises in which Gorky was not involved.[44] For this reason Bogdanov found it difficult to cover the expenses of the party school in Bologna.

Preparations for the second party school began even before the school on Capri ended, since it was decided that the success of that school justified the organisation of a new one. But the organisers found that their functions had been taken over by the School Committee set up by the Tenth Plenum of the Central Committee, on which they had two representatives. Very soon, however, the two representatives of the Vpered group, Pokrovsky and Aleksinsky, resigned from the School Committee on the grounds that it did not countenance the kind of autonomy that the Capri school had enjoyed. Nor did they think that the Central Committee was serious about organising a party

---

41   Haupt and Scherrer 1978, pp. 325–6.
42   Haupt and Scherrer 1978, p. 330.
43   Ibid.
44   Rogachevskii 1994, pp. 675–6.

school, since it had only assigned the meagre sum of 1,500 francs to the project. Following the departure of their two representatives from the Central Committee's School Committee, the Vpered group prepared to establish a second party school independently, collecting funds for the purpose and putting out an appeal to the workers in local party committees, explaining why they had ceased to cooperate with the Central Committee's School Committee.[45]

Bologna was chosen for the location of the school, because the organisers could count on the cooperation of the socialist municipal authorities there, in particular in curbing the activities of the Okhrana. The school was considered to be a section of the Bologna Garibaldi People's University. It opened on 21 November 1910 with four lecturers (Lunacharsky, Liadov, Bogdanov and Savelev) and 17 students representing local committees in Russia, and private students, among whom were Natalia Bogdanova and Anna Lunacharskaya. As was the practice with the Capri School, the School Council of lecturers and students decided whom to invite to teach at the school. On this occasion there was greater success in getting the acceptance of people who did not belong to the Vpered group, notably Trotsky and Alexandra Kollontai. The courses and lecturers were as follows:

> Political Economy – Bogdanov.
> History of the workers' movement and socialism in the West: in France, England and Germany – Lunacharsky; in Austria – Trotsky; in Finland – A. Kollontai.
> History of the workers' movement and socialism in Russia – Liadov.
> History of Russia: the pre-Petrine period – I.M. Kheraskov; from Peter I to the liberation of the peasants – Pokrovsky.
> Survey of political parties in Russia – Aleksinsky.
> The agrarian question – Maslov.
> The basics of state law – V.P. Menzhinsky.
> History of social outlooks – Bogdanov.
> International politics – M.P. Pavlovich (Volonter).
> History of Russian literature – Lunacharsky.
> The present situation – Volsky.[46]

As Kautsky had previously declined to lecture at the school he was not sent an invitation, but Liadov sent him a letter informing him about the school

---

45   Bogdanov 1911a, pp. 3–4.
46   Bogdanov 1911a, p. 13.

and its programme of study. Kautsky replied in a long letter, which compli-
mented the organisers on the excellence of their programme, but added a long
harangue, much in the Leninist spirit, about not underestimating the importance of parliamentary activities or engagement in legal possibilities. As before,
Ryazanov refused to participate in teaching, and Plekhanov didn't reply to the
invitation. Rosa Luxemburg too did not reply to the invitation to lecture at
Bologna.[47] Gorky sent a letter in which he explained that his health and the
pressure of his literary activities prevented his participation in the activities of
the school.

Lenin turned down his invitation to lecture at the Bologna school, contending that the Platform drawn up by the lecturers and students at the Capri school
was incompatible with Marxist philosophy, politics and the tactical aims of the
party, and accusing the organisers of the Bologna school of undermining the
efforts of the School Committee that had been set up by the Plenum of the
Central Committee. He invited the students at Bologna to come to Paris, where
he would be happy to provide them with a series of lectures on tactics, the
situation in the party and the agrarian question.[48] The Bologna School Council replied that if the Foreign Bureau of the Central Committee were to send
an official invitation to hear lectures in Paris the Council would have nothing
against this, but that the cost of travelling from Bologna to Paris would have to
be met by the Central Committee's Foreign Bureau.[49]

With the help of one of the students, Lenin attempted to disrupt the school,
and tried to discredit it by hinting to the editors of the Menshevik publication
Golos Sotsial-Demokrata, including Martov and Dan, who particularly abhorred
expropriations, that this is how it was financed. In reply to a letter from Dan,
inquiring if this was indeed the case, Bogdanov and Lunacharsky wrote to give
their assurances that the story was a fabrication.[50]

Lenin's letter to the students of the Bologna school was followed by one from
the Central Committee's School Committee offering to organise in Paris a series
of lectures given by Plekhanov, Lenin and other prominent party theoreticians.
The Council of the Bologna school replied, as it had to Lenin, that it had nothing against the proposal if the expenses of travelling to Paris were met. After
a long pause the School Committee replied with the undertaking to meet the
travel expenses of the students who had come from Russia, but not those of
the private students. With this letter was enclosed a programme of courses to

47   Bogdanov 1911a, pp. 14–15.
48   Lenin 1958–65, 48, pp. 5–6.
49   Bogdanov 1911a, pp. 25–6.
50   Livshits 1926, pp. 128–30.

be delivered in Paris, a programme that was to form the basis of the programme of lectures for the party school held in Longjumeau near Paris in the summer of 1911.[51]

In March 1911, when the course of studies had been completed in Bologna, all of the students, both those who would return to Russia and private students, set off for Paris for the supplementary lectures. On arrival, the Bologna contingent demanded organisational autonomy, including the right to invite lecturers, the cost of the journey from Bologna to Paris and living expenses for the stay in Paris, including those of the private students. All of the demands were turned down by the School Committee. In response the students complained about the School Committee to the Foreign Bureau of the Central Committee and threatened to put their case before the international proletariat. The School Committee then relented, and the students were paid their expenses, whereupon they set out for Russia. While the conflict with the School Committee was proceeding Martov and Dan had the opportunity of lecturing to the students on the Menshevik position on the current situation.[52] As in the case of the Capri students, on their return to Russia most of those from the school in Bologna were arrested and were unable to carry out the functions that the school had intended to fit them for.

6   Longjumeau

Despite the protestations to the contrary by Semashko, who compiled the report of its proceedings, the school at Longjumeau was largely a Bolshevik affair, since a majority of the lecturers and also of the students were Bolsheviks. Lenin played a prominent part in the teaching, giving lectures on political economy and the theory and practice of socialism in Russia. He was supported by Zinoviev, who lectured on the history of the RSDLP, and Kamenev, on the political parties in Russia. The political orientation of the school was underlined by Semashko's lectures on Parliamentarianism and the Social-Democratic fraction of the Duma.[53]

Some members of the Vpered group had been invited to lecture at Longjumeau. Lunacharsky had accepted the invitation and lectured on the history of Russian art. Pokrovsky, on the other hand, refused on principle to participate. Gorky replied to his invitation with the same excuses as he had made to the

51   Amiantov and Iunitskaia 1962, p. 52.
52   Bogdanov 1911a, pp. 30–1.
53   Amiantov and Iunitskaia 1962, p. 43.

Bologna school: that he was too unwell and that he had insufficient time. Rosa Luxemburg wished the school well, but regretted that she was unable to teach at it, because her time was taken up with the Reichstag elections. To this party school Plekhanov agreed to give a series of lectures on historical materialism, but in the event was unable to leave his home in Geneva.[54]

Plekhanov did, however, meet with a group of the Longjumeau students in Geneva after the school had ended. He lectured to them on the theory of perception and historical materialism, and also discussed political questions. One of the students, I.D. Chugurin, a friend of Maxim Gorky's from Nizhnii Novgorod, asked Plekhanov about a possible alliance with Lenin against the 'liquidators'. Plekhanov answered that an alliance with Lenin was impossible, because Lenin chased everyone he did not agree with out of the party.[55]

Plekhanov's words were prophetic, because Lenin's main purpose in organising the party school in Longjumeau was to garner support for the conference he was to convene in Prague in January 1912. He was largely successful in this, because, of the eighteen delegates at the conference who had evaded arrest, eight had been at Longjumeau. Chugurin had been invited, but refused to take part. The conference declared that the Mensheviks 'had placed themselves outside the party' and went on to elect new party institutions which were all controlled by Lenin's supporters.[56] The Prague conference marks the culmination of the process by which Lenin gained complete control of the Bolshevik organisation, and was the logical outcome of his campaign begun against Bogdanov in 1908. Lenin may have emerged victorious, but the organisation he now controlled had been reduced to an insignificant clique. It would have disappeared into obscurity and taken Lenin with it had it not been for the outbreak of war in 1914.

7   Cultural Tasks of Our Times

Bogdanov's book *Cultural Tasks of Our Times*, published in 1911, shows the influence of the polemic with Lenin and the experience of the party schools on Capri and in Bologna. It takes up the subject of proletarian culture that Bogdanov had mentioned in the Platform of the Vpered group and elaborates this within the framework of his existing historical conceptions of the evolution

---

54   Amiantov and Iunitskaia 1962, pp. 43–4.
55   White 2011, p. 17.
56   Elwood 1966, p. 390.

of class ideologies. There is much in *Cultural Tasks* that is familiar from Bogdanov's earlier works, but, as the title implies, the focus on this occasion is on the practical implications of the theoretical arguments.

Bogdanov begins his book with a definition of what he means by 'culture', which is much broader than the conventional understanding of the term. For Bogdanov, culture was the whole sum of acquisitions, material and non-material, that had been made by humanity through the labour process, which had raised its level, enriched its life, and given it power over the elemental forces of nature and over itself. This included the various tools, applied by people in their common struggle for existence as means of their cooperation; the language, which united people in their activity by means of mutual understanding; the whole of perception, incorporated in accumulated experience of their past; art, which connected the multifarious experiences of people in a single mood; and customs and moral, legal, and political institutions, incorporating the social life of people in particular, well-defined forms. All these phenomena, Bogdanov held, could be legitimately regarded as elements in human culture. For the purposes of his book, however, Bogdanov discussed culture in a way that was closer to the usual sense. He dealt with the elements that could be designated as 'spiritual culture': world-outlook, artistic creation, ethical, political relations etc., elements that could be designated as 'ideology'.[57]

Looked at historically, human culture had undergone a process of fragmentation. Originally, in primitive society, the same culture had been shared by everyone, but with social development and the emergence of classes the pristine unity had been lost and culture had become specific to the various classes in society. Each class has its own world-outlook distinct from other classes, other values and norms of human behaviour. Bogdanov traced the origins of culture from the emergence of speech. In this connection he again referred to Noiré's theory of the origins of language in work cries and songs which coordinated the efforts of individuals. In the act of speech one person *adapted* himself to another person. This was a process of organisation, in that it was the adaptation of some life processes to others.[58]

Bogdanov regarded art as having the same origins as speech and perception; it was a means by which people coordinated and systematised their experience. In its initial form, poetry was not distinguished from perception, the religious myth representing its chief form. These myths played the same part in educating people as did the philosophy of modern times. The *Mahabharata* for the

---

57   Bogdanov 1911, p. 3.
58   Bogdanov 1911, pp. 9–10.

Indians, the poems of Homer for the Greeks and the Bible for the Jews, were
the encyclopaedias of life; they presented to the individual the life of his native collective, sketched out for him the human relations and the phenomena
of nature as they were experienced and understood by his society.[59]

The polemical edge of *Cultural Tasks of Our Times* was directed against those
who maintained that the workers had no time, energy and resources to create
their own culture, pointing out that the pioneers of socialist ideas were people
from outside the working class, intellectuals and children of the bourgeoisie,
like Marx, Engels and Lassalle. Strange as it may seem, Bogdanov remarked,
such views had supporters among those who sympathised with the working
class, even those who participated in its organisations. But they showed a very
low estimation of the cultural-creative capabilities of the working class, and
from this came the extreme theoretical conservatism of people like Plekhanov
and Lenin. These views, Bogdanov considered, could not count as a slander on
the working class, because they were so obviously untrue; they were the hope-
less dream of those who felt threatened and disturbed by the process of the
organisation of the new social forces taking place before their eyes.[60]

Unlike Lenin, who saw the organisation of the working class as a distinct
theoretical sphere, Bogdanov held that the cultural principles of the working
class were identical to the principles of its organisation, that comradely cooperation was for the working class its particular form of organisation. Whereas
bourgeois culture was individualistic, proletarian culture was collectivist, anti-
individualist and anti-authoritarian. That, however, did not mean that the
working class was immune from the influence of individualistic bourgeois culture, which was apt to manifest itself in the cult of 'leaderism' in the labour
movement.[61]

In their political and economic struggle the workers needed knowledge, but
not in the fragmented form in which they found it in individualised bourgeois
society. To be useful it had to be integrated and, in Bogdanov's term, 'democratised'. The task of democratising knowledge was not the same as providing
a good popular exposition of the existing corpus of scientific facts such as they
were, with division according to discipline. It was a matter of systematising
afresh the content of the various fields of acquired scientific experience and
overcoming not only the specific terminology of the specialised fields, but also
the division into disciplines itself, in order to present the available scientific

---

59   Bogdanov 1911, p. 14.
60   Bogdanov 1911, p. 42.
61   Bogdanov 1911, p. 52.

knowledge in an integrated and systematic form. In setting out these requirements for the democratisation of knowledge, Bogdanov stated, he had arrived
at the idea of a new kind of encyclopaedia, a Proletarian Encyclopaedia.[62]

The precedent for such an encyclopaedia was the one compiled in France
in the eighteenth century by Diderot and d'Alembert, which had reflected the
individualist culture of bourgeois society. Whereas the entries of this and other
existing encyclopaedias were written by individual scholars within their particular disciplines, without any regard for the overall coherence of the work, the
new proletarian encyclopaedia would integrate knowledge and break down the
barriers between disciplines. Subjects would be treated in their historical and
social context and in relation to each other. Bogdanov's correspondence with
Gorky shows that work on such an encyclopaedia had been already begun,
but the cooling of relations between the two men would obviously jeopardise progress on the encyclopaedia, which did not in fact materialise. However,
the way in which the encyclopaedia proposed to integrate the various forms of
knowledge was taken up in *Tectology*, which Bogdanov began to work on at this
time.[63]

Closely associated with the idea of a new encyclopaedia was that of a proletarian university. Its aim would be, within the existing society, to prepare cadres
of conscious representatives of the society of the future, people who would be
equipped to bring about the great transformations to come. The new university
would not be for boys fresh from school, but for mature workers with experience in the sphere of labour and social struggle. The teaching in the university
would not be run on the authoritarian lines of conventional universities, but on
the principle of comradely cooperation; the students would be the comrades of
their teachers, and would not learn passively, but would continually question
what they were being taught.[64]

Here Bogdanov was able to assure his readers that this kind of relationship
between teachers and students was possible, based on his own experience. He
recalled how he had taught political economy to young workers in Tula, and,
although they were not the kind of elite workers who would study at the Proletarian University, they were by no means passive recipients of knowledge. To a
significant extent they had determined how the course was taught. It was out of
this course, Bogdanov recalled, that his first book, the *Short Course of Economic
Science*, had emerged.[65]

---

62   Bogdanov 1911, p. 57.
63   Bogdanov 1911, pp. 58–9; Neizvestnyi Bogdanov 1995, 1, p. 157.
64   Bogdanov 1911, pp. 69–71.
65   Bogdanov 1911, pp. 71–2.

A more recent experience of non-authoritarian teaching had been the party schools on Capri and in Bologna. These were closer to Bogdanov's conception of the proletarian university, and, indeed, had shown the need for such a university. It had been found that the three months the schools lasted was insufficient time to impart to the students all the information that they required. From this Bogdanov concluded that a course of study at the Proletarian University would last for two years, about half of the period of study at a conventional university.[66]

In keeping with his broad conception of what constituted culture, Bogdanov included in *Cultural Tasks of our Times* a discussion of morality, emphasising, as he had done elsewhere, that proletarian morality would be free of any element of compulsion, and that conventional morality, manners and legal norms were forms of fetishism. He recalled that while a student in Kharkov, these views had almost led to his expulsion from the Marxist circle there for 'immorality'. But, Bogdanov argued, the proletariat did not need the sanction of any higher authority; it did not need the internal 'voice of duty'. With comradely cooperation norms of utility for the collective would prevail.[67]

Cultural Tasks of Our Times is a work that reflects the aftermath of the conflict with Lenin and Bogdanov's expulsion from the Bolshevik Centre. The book is, in its way, a reaction to Lenin's behaviour in the episode. The lesson Bogdanov took from it was that even at the heart of what he had conceived to be the most essentially proletarian organisation, the Bolshevik fraction, there were modes of thinking and behaviour that were more characteristic of the enemies of the proletariat. He now voiced an opinion that he must have had for some time: that Lenin's view of workers' organisation was patronising and arrogant. In response to this Bogdanov was prompted to formulate his own view of workers' organisation. This was that the workers' culture and workers' organisation was the same thing; it was comradely cooperation, a concept to which Bogdanov would continually add concrete content.

The arguments advanced in *Cultural Tasks of Our Times* were put more concisely and more forcefully in the article entitled 'Socialism of the Present' that Bogdanov contributed to *Vpered*, the journal of the Vpered group, in 1911. In it Bogdanov re-states his view that a socialist society is one in which the whole of production is organised on the basis of comradely cooperation, and from this flow all the other features of socialism, such as the abolition of private property, the elimination of classes, and a distribution of products such that every person

66   Bogdanov 1911, p. 73.
67   Bogdanov 1911, pp. 81–5.

would be able to achieve their full potential in following their vocation. But this would only be possible when the working class had finally achieved its victory and had the opportunity to organise the whole of society. Until that time there could be no gradual elimination of classes, gradual transition to social property of the means of production, or the planned distribution of the social product. But the element of socialism that could develop within the existing capitalist society was socialism's most essential element – comradely cooperation. In Bogdanov's view, this was the prototype of socialism, its real beginning. The more it grew and developed within the narrow confines of the old society, the more acute would be its contradictions with them. These contradictions would culminate in a series of revolutions that would lead to the establishment of a socialist society.[68]

It was completely natural that the proletariat would want to live in its own way and not in the manner that the old society had imposed upon it, that it would want to develop its own forms of human relations and express them in its own social ideal. This being the case, it followed that the struggle for socialism would not be reduced simply to the war against capitalism; it would also be for the creation of newer and newer elements of socialism in the proletariat itself, in its internal relations, in its everyday living conditions, that is, it would be the '*elaboration of a socialist proletarian culture*'.[69]

For Bogdanov, therefore, the campaign to foster a proletarian culture, to cultivate comradely cooperation, was a means of laying the foundations of a socialist society within the confines of the existing capitalist system. In this way the ideal of socialism became the means of achieving it. As he had indicated in *Cultural Tasks of Our Times*, comradely cooperation was the form of organisation characteristic of the proletariat.

Bogdanov called upon socialists to further the development of genuinely comradely relations in all the everyday practice of the proletariat. This was essential, since even in proletarian organisations one could observe the continued existence of relations between people which had nothing in common with socialism: the struggle of ambitions, the authoritarian pretensions of 'leaders', the unconscious deference of their followers, the resistance to comradely discipline and the intrusion of personal interests and motives into the collective cause, etc. All these phenomena were unavoidable in the initial stages of the workers' movement, considering that the proletariat had not come into the world as a well-established class, but had been composed from the urban poor,

---

68   Bogdanov 1990, p. 100.
69   Bogdanov 1990, p. 101.

the peasantry and small proprietors, all of whom were accustomed to living by private, individual, interests and subordinating themselves to despotic authorities. Besides that, the workers' organisations attracted to themselves some non-proletarian elements from the radical intelligentsia and petty bourgeoisie, who also found it difficult to assimilate the spirit of comradely cooperation. Bogdanov believed that it was essential to campaign against any manifestations of individualism, ideological slavery or ideological haughtiness, explaining their absolute incompatibility with proletarian socialism.

In the article 'Socialism of the Present', Bogdanov drew attention to the urgent need for change in the family life of the proletariat. There, the despotic relationship of the husband to the wife, the demand for unquestioning obedience of the children to the parents, were attributes of the traditional structure of the family. He considered that the slavery of women impeded the increasing power of the working class by depriving its ranks of female comrades, while the slavery of children harmed the socialist upbringing of future activists. It consequently behoved socialists to campaign energetically, by word and by example, against any remnants of family slavery, and not to think the matter unimportant or relegate it to the status of private affairs.[70]

As in *Cultural Tasks of Our Times*, Bogdanov contended that socialism also demanded a new science and a new philosophy. These were disciplines that consisted in collecting human experience and organising it in a systematic way. But proletarian experience was different from that of the old classes, and earlier experience was insufficient for the proletariat. It had fallen to Marx to lay the foundations of a new social science and a new historical philosophy. It was possible to think that all sciences and the *whole of* philosophy would receive at the hands of the proletariat a new look, because other conditions of life give rise to other means of perceiving and understanding nature.

The failing of present-day science and philosophy was that they were characterised by their disjointed character; they were fragmented into a mass of details and particulars, so that study of each branch of knowledge would take a whole human life to master. Scholars had a faulty understanding of each other, because none could see beyond the boundaries of their specialisation.

According to Bogdanov:

> The proletariat needs a science in its life and struggle, but not the one which is accessible to people only in fragments and leads to mutual misunderstanding between them. In comradely relations the most import-

---

70   Bogdanov 1990, pp. 101–2.

ant thing is, on the contrary, the complete understanding of each other. The working out of socialist knowledge must therefore aspire to simplification and unification of science, to finding those general methods of investigation, which would give the key to the most varied specialisations, and would allow the rapid mastery of them – as the worker in machine production, who knows by experience the general features and general methods of his technique, can comparatively easily transfer from one specialisation to another.[71]

This specification had appeared in *Cultural Tasks of our Times* in relation to Bogdanov's idea for a Proletarian Encyclopaedia. No particular embodiment for it was mentioned in 'Socialism of the Present', but shortly it would find its expression in 'tectology', the universal science of organisation.

In Bogdanov's view, art, like science, served to bring together human experience, though it organised its material not in abstract concepts, but in living images. For this reason, art was more accessible to the masses than science, more democratic in its character. The proletariat needed its own, socialist art, imbued with its feelings, its aspirations, its ideals. Already one could discern the first steps in the creation of this kind of art, and being the first steps these were also the most difficult. But, Bogdanov cautioned, it would be naive to think that within the present capitalist order the proletariat had succeeded to the full measure of elaborating its socialist culture; this was a cause that could not be accomplished quickly because of the enormity of the undertaking, and the greatness of the obstacles in its path.[72]

'Socialism of the Present' is an article that provides a clear indication of the direction of Bogdanov's thinking at the time, and how the elements within it related to each other. Proletarian culture, or comradely cooperation, was central; this was both the essence of socialism and the means by which socialism would be achieved. This had been confirmed by his experience of the 1905 revolution and his subsequent conflict with Lenin, whose ideas on party organisation he viewed as profoundly mistaken and injurious to the proletarian cause.

For Bogdanov proletarian culture was anti-individualist, anti-authoritarian and its outlook on the world was not the fragmented view brought about by the division of labour and specialisation. Proletarian science would integrate the scattered disciplines and discover general methods which would be applicable to several branches of knowledge. This approach to knowledge would be

---

71   Bogdanov 1990, p. 102.
72   Bogdanov 1990, p. 103.

the inspiration for tectology. It emerges from 'Socialism of the Present' that in Bogdanov's mind proletarian culture and tectology, the universal science of organisation, were inseparable.

8 The Course of Political Economy

Despite Skvortsov-Stepanov's defection to Lenin, Bogdanov nevertheless continued to collaborate with him on a major publication project that had been agreed in 1908. This was the *Course of Political Economy*, whose first volume appeared in St Petersburg in 1910 and whose last came out in Soviet times. It was conceived as being an expanded version of Bogdanov's *Short Course of Economic Science*, which had proven its popularity by going through several editions. In all these editions, however, its character as an outline had remained, suggesting the possibility of treating the topics it covered at greater length. In fact, as the Foreword to the *Course of Political Economy* explained, the arrangement of the material followed that of the *Short Course* closely, the historical approach being retained, the difference being that whereas the *Short Course* aimed at popularisation, the *Course of Political Economy* was concerned with systematisation.[73]

The agreed division of labour between the two authors was that Skvortsov-Stepanov would write the historical parts and Bogdanov would contribute the chapters concerned with ideology. This meant that most of the writing would be done by Skvortsov-Stepanov, who would accordingly receive a greater share of the royalties.[74] It promised to be an easy work to complete, because it was going over familiar ground, with, in the first volume at least, very little that was original.

The *Course of Political Economy* was more explicit than the *Short Course* had been on the methodology it adopted. It declared itself to belong to the school of Marx, and saw its task as to organise a coherent and objective picture of development, observing a historical perspective. In this there could be no thought of separating the economic element from the general categories of social phenomena. However, unlike the approach of Marx himself, who examined the inter-relationship of the categories of political economy, this was not the method adopted by Bogdanov and Skvortsov-Stepanov. They explained that despite the tradition of commencing the study of political economy with the analysis of economic categories such as 'exchange', 'value', 'capital', etc. they

---

73   Bogdanov and Stepanov 1910–25, 1, p. xi.
74   Neizvestnyi Bogdanov 1995, 1, p. 159.

would approach these as they arose historically, from their simple, embryonic condition to their final stages of development. The advantage of this method was that it would avoid the common error of economists and sociologists of applying modern concepts to primitive conditions, to which they were anachronistic.[75]

The correspondence between Bogdanov and Skvortsov-Stepanov reveals how their historical approach to Marx's economics was arrived at. In a letter to Skvortsov-Stepanov of December 1909 Bogdanov expressed the opinion that there would be very little use in expounding the chapters of *Das Kapital* in Marx's own words, because here one would be in competition with Marx himself and to some extent with Kautsky. He supposed that the readers of his book would be the same ones who would read *Das Kapital*, and there would be little point in repeating for them Marx's grotesque-philosophical (*utrirovanno-filosofskoe*), Hegelian exposition. It would be much better to reveal the historical content of the chapters in question. In particular, the scholasticism of the first chapter of *Das Kapital* obviously needed to be translated into the language of the rest of humanity, into the language of history.[76]

Bogdanov was not the first to make the case for translating Marx's Hegelian exposition into more accessible historical terms. This had been done by the pioneer of Marxism in Russia, Nikolai Sieber. In an article published in 1874 Sieber had pointed out that the barrier to people's comprehending Marx's ideas had been the obscurity of the language used, 'by the difficult, and, if the truth be told, somewhat scholastic language in which a considerable part of the book is written ... and by the ponderous argumentation encased in the impenetrable armour of Hegelian contradictions'.[77] The article in question had been read by Marx, and he had raised no objection to what Sieber had said about his exposition. In fact, Sieber was the commentator whom Marx most commended for having thoroughly understood his economic ideas. Sieber's book, *David Ricardo and Karl Marx*,[78] with which Bogdanov and Skvortsov-Stepanov would have been conversant, was an exposition of *Das Kapital* stripped of its Hegelian terminology and re-cast in historical terms.

In his correspondence with Skvortsov-Stepanov, Bogdanov was insistent that the topic of socialism merited special treatment, preferably in a separate chapter.[79] The second volume of the work, written entirely by Bogdanov, did

---

75   Bogdanov and Stepanov 1910–25, 1, p. 17.
76   Neizvestnyi Bogdanov 1995, 1, p. 168.
77   Ziber 1874, pp. 43–4.
78   See Ziber 1885.
79   Neizvestnyi Bogdanov 1995, 1, p. 168.

contain a lengthy section on 'The Collectivist Order'. In it Bogdanov elaborated on the ideas he had put forward in *Red Star* and his *Short Course of Economic Science* on what the future socialist society would be like. He emphasised, for example, that socialism would embrace the whole of humanity, and that consequently there would be a need for a universal language.[80] However, due to disagreements between Bogdanov and Skvortsov-Stepanov on the subject of imperialism, the second volume of the *Course of Economic Science* appeared only in 1918.

9   Engineer Menni

In 1912 Bogdanov published a second novel set on Mars entitled *Engineer Menni*. But unlike in *Red Star*, the action of *Engineer Menni* takes place in its pre-socialist historical past, an era corresponding to Earth in Bogdanov's day. In this respect, the setting on Mars is not intended to give a vision of the socialist future, but to show the timelessness of the action. Mars has undergone its bourgeois revolution, but Menni, the hero, is descended from feudal nobility. His outlook is thoroughly individualist, but he is a person of enormous integrity and completely incorruptible. He is a gifted engineer and is placed in control of the project to construct irrigation canals to bring water to the arid Martian deserts.

The project of course involves enormous amounts of money, of which Menni is in charge. A consortium of capitalists wishes to gain control of the financial management of the project in order to increase their profits. Menni plays into their hands by alienating the workers' trade unions. He will not recognise the unions as the legitimate representatives of the workers, because he maintains that the contract of employment is between him and the individual workers. In this way Menni shows that his way of thinking is characteristic of the individualist, bourgeois society.

By fomenting labour unrest and strikes, which hold up work on the canals, the leaders of the consortium try to gain Menni's connivance in diverting the project's finances. He refuses, and kills his assistant who has betrayed him, for which he is imprisoned. The capitalist consortium then takes over the running of the project and they give full rein to their corrupt methods. Wages are claimed for fictitious workers; low-grade explosives to blast the rocks are supplied, but high-grade explosives are charged for. When fatalities are

---

80   Bogdanov and Stepanov 1910–25, 2, pp. 198–9.

caused by the deficient explosives, people are paid large sums to keep quiet about the frauds perpetrated.

Shortly before Menni's prison sentence is about to end, the fraud of the capitalist consortium is exposed by a young socialist, Netti, who turns out to be Menni's son. The fraudsters are caught and punished, and some of the embezzled money is returned. Menni is put back in charge of the project from his prison cell, with Netti as his deputy. Long interchanges take place between Menni and Netti, presenting the logic of their respective outlooks. Netti argues the collectivist case that the trade unions represent the class interests of the workers.

During his discussions with Menni, Netti expounds his theory of the vampires. Although he does not say so explicitly, Bogdanov probably regarded it as the reverse side of the dynamic view of ideals that shapes *Red Star*. If one has ideals that are not dynamic, but fixed, so that once achieved they are held on to tenaciously, they will increasingly be at odds with the rest of existence, which will continue its infinite process of change. The attempt to conserve what one holds most dear by resisting change is both self-defeating and destructive to the rest of humanity, and accordingly Bogdanov designates it as a kind of vampirism.

In *Empiriomonism* Bogdanov had expounded this conception in regard to social or national groups and to ideas.[81] Now he applied it to human beings. The theory was that during their working lives people contribute more to society than they take out. But with age, instead of being net contributors to society, they take more out of it than they give, so that the balance is negative. In this parasitic existence, such people sink their fangs into life and try to turn it back to the past, to the time when they were still productive members of society, and by so doing stand in the way of progress. Menni fears that when he comes out of prison he will become such a vampire and commits suicide on the eve of his release.

The bright spot in the novel is the Epilogue, in which Netti, having given up engineering, devotes himself to transforming science so as to make it accessible to the working class. It was while engaged in compiling a 'Workers' Encyclopaedia' that Netti made his greatest discovery and laid the foundations of a universal science of organisation. This was what Bogdanov was working on at the time, a science to which he would give the name 'tectology'. Its essence is summed up in Netti's conclusion that:

---

81   Bogdanov 2003, p. 258.

No matter how different the various elements of the universe are – may they be electrons, atoms, things, people, ideas, planets, stars – and no matter how different outwardly their combinations seem to be, it is nevertheless possible to establish a small number of general methods by which any of these elements are connected together, both in the spontaneous processes of nature and in human activity.[82]

In *Red Star* it is easy to see what Bogdanov wanted to convey to his readers, but this is not the case in *Engineer Menni*. Partly he wishes to show the contrast of outlooks between the individualistic Menni and his collectivist son, Netti. But the main theme of the novel is Menni's extraordinary integrity. He refuses to be entangled in corruption, though this would make his life infinitely easier. He will not become a vampire, though to escape this state he has to kill himself. He will not accept clemency from the judges or early release from prison when this is offered, as this will compromise his sense of justice. Bogdanov makes him the son of a feudal noble to signify that Menni has something of the nobility of a past age. Despite his individualism and his feudal background, Menni is a hero that Bogdanov admires and identifies with. The time at which the novel was written was a difficult one for Bogdanov, further complicated by his own adherence to principle even when this demanded personal sacrifices. In this respect *Engineer Menni* contains many autobiographical elements.

10   **The Fate of Vpered**

The Tenth Plenum of the Central Committee of the RSDLP had established the Vpered group as a legitimate entity within the party structure. It included some of the most prominent and talented members of the party and it could easily vie with the rump of the Bolshevik fraction that Lenin now led. The point was not lost on Lenin. On 25 February 1911 Lenin wrote to Rykov: 'The Vperedists are very strong. They have a school = a conference = agents. We (and the Central Committee) *have not*. They have money, some 80,000 roubles. Do you think they will give it to you?? Are you really so naive??'[83]

In fact, the situation within the Vpered group was not so favourable as Lenin imagined. Through a contact in America it had been possible to exchange some of the large-denomination banknotes and finance three issues of the publica-

---

82   Bogdanov 1979, p. 156.
83   Lenin 1958–65, 48, p. 20.

tion *Vpered*. But the influx of the money caused friction within the group. Some of the members, Aleksinsky in particular, wanted the group to be able to discuss the money and how it should be used; Bogdanov, on the other hand, felt honour-bound to keep the matter confidential, since these were the terms on which he had been entrusted with the money by the group from the Caucasus that had expropriated it. He considered that it was the Caucasians who had the first call on the money, and, in fact, considerable sums of it were expended in the attempt to free some of them from prison.[84]

Nor was the Vpered group united ideologically, the opposition to Bogdanov's ideas on proletarian culture being especially pronounced. Bogdanov's article 'Socialism of the Present' was followed in the same issue of *Vpered* by a critique written by Volsky entitled 'On Proletarian Culture'. Volsky considered that Bogdanov's conception of the proletariat and its life under capitalism was too idealised and took too little account of the hardship and squalor in which Russian workers lived. He maintained that the comradely cooperation that Bogdanov valued so highly was forced upon the workers by economic necessity. Conditions were not improved by the introduction of machines into the factories; rather the effect was to make them unemployed. It was not a vision of an ideal but hatred of the capitalist system that inclined the workers towards socialism. And if a new science, art and philosophy did emerge, it would be in a socialist revolution, not through the dissemination of a proletarian culture.[85]

Pokrovsky was also critical of Bogdanov's conception of proletarian culture. In November 1910 he wrote to Bogdanov protesting that 'If in the Platform [of the Vpered group – J.W.] there were incautious expressions such as "proletarian science" and elements of socialism in the present, now there appears an article specially devoted to this, where the same unfortunate expressions are repeated in a widely disseminated way and with deadly clarity'. In other letters Pokrovsky described Bogdanov's article 'Socialism of the Present' as 'revisionist'. On the insistence of Pokrovsky, Aleksinsky and Menzhinsky, the Vpered group adopted a resolution declaring that 'proletarian culture and science' were not the views of the journal's editorial board. This, however, did not prevent Pokrovsky from resigning from the group in May 1911.[86]

Aleksinsky attacked the idea of proletarian culture in a review of Bogdanov's *Cultural Tasks of Our Times* published in the journal *Sovremennyi mir* in 1911. He denounced Bogdanov's conception of the gradual accumulation of elements of proletarian culture as 'Kulturträger-Bernsteinism'. Like Volsky, Aleksinsky

---

84 Neizvestnyi Bogdanov 1995, 2, p. 108.
85 Vol'skii 1911, pp. 71–82.
86 Kin 1929, pp. 388–9.

thought that the proletariat did not have the means to create its own culture since it was limited by the conditions of its relations of production and its class position. The tone of Aleksinsky's article, Bogdanov later remarked, was not designed to convince, but to insult [87]

Aleksinsky proved to be an extremely disruptive influence in the Paris section of the Vpered group. When Lunacharsky left the group in 1913, he explained his departure with reference to the behaviour of Aleksinsky, adding that it was this which had caused the earlier resignations of Bogdanov, Pokrovsky, Menzhinsky, F.I. Kalinin and a number of others.[88] Bogdanov says that he left the group in the spring of 1911 when it abandoned cultural-propagandist activities in favour of politics in the émigré spirit. He took no further part in politics and devoted himself entirely to writing.[89]

11   Pravda Articles

In the spring of 1912 the Bolsheviks in St Petersburg began the publication of a legal newspaper for workers called *Pravda*. Although a Bolshevik publication, the newspaper at its inception was not narrowly fractional in its content, as it aimed to attract the support of workers in all sections of the RSDLP. This was made clear in the editorial written by Stalin, which stated that:

> We by no means seek to hide the disagreements that exist among the Social-Democratic workers. Moreover, we believe that a strong and full life of the movement is inconceivable without disagreements ... But that does not mean that the points of disagreement are greater than those of agreement. Far from it! ... Therefore *Pravda* will call first and foremost and mainly for the unity of the proletariat's class struggle and for unity come what may.[90]

Given the avowedly non-fractional stance of the newspaper, one can understand why Bogdanov would have no qualms about contributing to it. Bogdanov's relations with the *Pravda* editorial board in this period were generally amicable, especially as the newspaper had favourably reviewed the novel *Engineer Menni*. In the spring of 1913 he submitted a series of articles to *Pravda*

87   Neizvestnyi Bogdanov 1995, 3, pp. 165–73.
88   Ostroukhova 1925, p. 213.
89   Neizvestnyi Bogdanov 1995, 1, p. 19.
90   'Nashi tseli' 1912. p. 1; Petriakov 1956, p. 3.

entitled 'From the Lexicon of Foreign Words'. The series consisted of short, factual articles, such as one might find in an encyclopaedia, on the terms 'Programme', 'Class', 'Party', 'The Taylor System', 'Tactics' and 'Politics'.

Bogdanov expanded his article on 'The Taylor System' into a separate pamphlet, probably because of the important bearing it had on his ideas on the liberating potential of machines on the working class. He thought that the Taylor system, which tried to make workers more efficient by simplifying their movements, had good and bad points. The system was useful because it had the capability of raising the productivity of labour, which would benefit society as a whole, and for that reason workers should not struggle against the introduction of machinery, even though in the short term it was against their interests. However, Taylor's concern with increasing the intensity of labour could only benefit the capitalists and harm the workers by wearing them out. In any case, machine production required not unthinking workers, but ones who were intelligent and educated to be capable machine operators. Bogdanov concluded that 'The machine needs a real person, not a Taylorist living machine'.[91]

The next article in the series, 'Ideology', contained more of Bogdanov's characteristic ideas, including an oblique reference to proletarian culture.[92] The editors thought it somewhat heretical, and though they did not publish it, encouraged Bogdanov to continue his contributions to the newspaper.[93]

Lenin, who was at this time in Krakow, fretted about the non-partisan attitude of *Pravda*'s editorial board, on which were Stalin, Olminsky and Ya.M. Sverdlov. He urged a more energetic campaign against the 'liquidators', and in April 1913 he himself contributed a series of articles outlining the history of the 'liquidationist' current. In the second of the articles Lenin claimed that the Vpered group had advocated abandoning Social-Democratic activity in the Duma and the utilisation of legal possibilities. Bogdanov contested this in a letter published in *Pravda* in which, with quotations from the Platform of Vpered, he demonstrated that Lenin's accusations were untrue.[94] Lenin wrote a furious letter to the *Pravda* editorial board on 16 June deploring its decision to publish Bogdanov's letter with what he called its 'distortions of party history'. On Lenin's insistence, Bogdanov's name was removed from the list of *Pravda*'s contributors, along with those of Lunacharsky, Bazarov, Kalinin and Aleksinsky.[95]

---

91   Bogdanov 1913, p. 14.
92   Neizvestnyi Bogdanov 1995, 3, p. 58.
93   Neizvestnyi Bogdanov 1995, 3, p. 103.
94   Neizvestnyi Bogdanov 1995, 2, pp. 257–8.
95   Neizvestnyi Bogdanov 1995, 3, p. 103.

Bogdanov protested to the *Pravda* editorial board, and was informed that his exclusion was not on the initiative of any of its members. From this he concluded that the driving force behind the move had been Lenin and his supporters Zinovlev and Kamenev. As *Pravda* was closed to him, Bogdanov put his case in an article published in *Novaia rabochaia gazeta* in January 1914. Lenin replied in the same month with a letter in *Pravda*, claiming that the real reason for Bogdanov's exclusion from the newspaper was that as a proponent of bourgeois-idealist views against the materialism of Marx and Engels, he had launched a campaign against Marxist philosophy in his article on 'Ideology'.[96]

At the beginning of 1914 a group of 'Left Bolsheviks' from Tiflis wrote to *Pravda* enquiring why Bogdanov was no longer a contributor to the newspaper. Lenin replied that the cause was not, as the group implied, one of personal spite, but the fact that in a workers' publication which took a consistent Marxist standpoint, it was inappropriate to have as a contributor someone like Bogdanov who was not a Marxist. Lenin reminded the group that as far back as May 1909 a delegate meeting of Bolsheviks, after a long and detailed discussion, had divested itself of all responsibility for Bogdanov's literary-political activities. Orthodox Marxists were convinced that the sum of Bogdanov's literary activities amounted to attempts to instil into the consciousness of the proletariat the touched-up idealistic conceptions of bourgeois philosophers. With Aleksinsky in mind, Lenin pointed out that Bogdanov's theories had been opposed, not only by his 'fractional' opponents, but also by his former colleagues in his political group.

But, Lenin conceded, *Pravda* had published several of Bogdanov's articles. His explanation was that this was a mistake inevitable in such a new undertaking as the publication of the first workers' newspaper. The editors who were in charge at the time had hoped that in the popular articles which Bogdanov submitted the factual content would outweigh the specific features of Bogdanov's theories. But this was not to be: after the first articles, which were more or less neutral, Bogdanov sent in an article on 'Ideology' in which he obviously attempted to transform the workers' newspaper into an instrument for the propaganda, not of Marxism, but of his own empiriomonism.[97]

With this prohibition on contributions to *Pravda* a final door had been slammed in Bogdanov's face. He saw it as the point at which Plekhanov's dearest wish had been realised: to expel him completely from the Marxist camp. Bogdanov could only marvel at the vindictiveness and cynicism with

---

96   Lenin 1958–65, 24, p. 307.
97   Lenin 1958–65, 24, pp. 338–41.

which the campaign against him had been conducted. But although excluded from the political arena, he was still able to continue his academic work, and in fact the period leading up to the First World War was the time that he made his most notable contributions to the field of socialist ideas.

Tectology

1 The Secret of Science

In 1913 Bogdanov published the first part of *Tectology, The Universal Science of Organisation*. This work marked the culmination of all his earlier development, and it occupied him for much of his later life. A second part of the work appeared in 1917, and was serialised in 1919–21 in the journal of the Proletkult, *Proletarskaia Kultura*. A shortened version of *Tectology* was published in Samara in 1921, and a longer one containing all three parts in Berlin in 1922. A German translation of parts one and two appeared in Berlin in 1928, and in the following year a second edition of Part Three was published in Moscow shortly after the author's death.[1] However, from an article entitled 'The Secret of Science', written in 1913 but only published in 1918, one can see that even before the war Bogdanov had at least the contours of the complete work in mind, as the article refers to topics that are covered in later parts of *Tectology*.[2]

The need for a universal science of organisation emerges from the theme in Bogdanov's writings of the fragmentation of society and of the human psyche caused by the division of labour. Specialisation had caused people to have different experiences and to become incomprehensible to one another. The antidote to this fragmentation would be an integrated approach to the world that would bridge the gulf between the various specialisations.

As early as 1901, in *Perception from the Historical Point of View*, Bogdanov had argued that there was need for 'general methods in production' which would eliminate specialisation, and allow workers to perform a variety of different operations.[3] In *Red Star* he had described how before going to work at the Martian factory the hero Leonid had undergone training in general methods so that he is able to work in all sections of the factory. In his article 'Socialism of the Present', published in *Vpered* in 1910, Bogdanov had contended that: 'The working out of socialist knowledge must ... aspire to the simplification and unification of science, to finding the general methods of investigation, which would give the key to the most varied specialisations and would allow the rapid

---

1 Biggart 1998, pp. 333–43.
2 Bogdanov 1918e.
3 Bogdanov 1901, p. 201.

mastery of them'.[4] When Bogdanov published *Engineer Menni* in 1912 he could give a precise definition of what his science of general methods would consist in. It would involve discovering the small number of general methods by which any of the elements in the universe were combined, whether these were the spontaneous processes of nature or of human activity.[5]

When Bogdanov wrote 'The Secret of Science', his conception of a science of general methods had changed somewhat; it was no longer focused on making factory workers more versatile, but on a much wider set of organisational tasks which required urgent attention. One of these had been brought about by the recent spread of machine production in industry. It had led to the creation of enterprises with a workforce of thousands if not tens of thousands of workers of different kinds, using specialised implements, materials and machines of different degrees of complexity.

A second organisational task was in science, where the accumulation of experience ensured that most of its multifarious branches suffered from a surfeit of factual information, the collection of raw material overwhelming the specialists themselves. A third task for organisational science was in the economic sphere. There the anarchy of production with its conflicts and interweaving interests was such a chaos of contradictions that it was impossible to orientate oneself in it. All these areas needed to be systematised, coordinated, *organised*, and not only in part, but as a whole, on the scale of an entire social process.[6]

These were the areas in which Bogdanov thought that the application of a universal science of organisation was necessary in 1913. But the outbreak of war in the following year added infinitely more weight to Bogdanov's case, and in subsequent editions of *Tectology* it is the war and its consequences that eclipses all of Bogdanov's other justifications for his science of organisation.

It is in 'The Secret of Science' more than in *Tectology* itself that Bogdanov sets out the main premise of his science of organisation, which is that the organisation is an activity that can be applied not only to living beings, but to non-living beings as well; that everything organises. He does this by presenting a number of parallel cases where human practice has in some way emulated nature. He cites the case of a sail, designed to propel sailing vessels by harnessing the power of the wind and the same mechanism applied by airborne seeds. In nature one found numerous examples of the protection of plastic living fibres, fluids or semi-fluids, using the method of an external skeleton. These included

---

4   Bogdanov 1990, p. 102.
5   Bogdanov 1979, p. 156.
6   Bogdanov 1918e, pp. 92–3.

the shell on a snail, chitin covering on insects, the skin on mammals, and above all the skull to protect the brain. This was in essence the method used by people when they made different vessels, crockery, boxes etc. The societies of humans and ants both engaged in herding, the humans of cows and the ants of aphides. The sexual organs of a flower and a woman had many parallels in their respective structures.[7]

These coincidences, Bogdanov argued, could not be due to imitation or to a common origin. What united them was the organising activity, something common to both living and non-living things. The definition that he gave of organisation was 'a whole that is greater than the sum of its parts'. Organising activity was always directed towards formation of some kind of system from parts or *elements*. Whatever any particular case might be, one characteristic always remained the same: that what was being organised was a given *activity*, a given *resistance*.[8]

Bogdanov went on to explain that a resistance was simply an activity from another point of view. If one fought against an enemy, the enemy was the resistance to be overcome; from the point of view of the enemy it was the other way round. Activity and resistance were not two entities, but two inter-related sides of the same phenomenon. Everything that was accessible to our experience, to our efforts and to our perception, was activity-resistance. If something else existed that did not have this character, it would not produce any effect on our senses, would not offer any resistance to our movements. Consequently, it could not enter into our experience and would forever remain unknown to us, inaccessible.[9]

If one approached the question of organisation in this way, Bogdanov argued, then the concept was universally applicable at all levels of being, not simply in the sphere of life: everywhere there were combinations of activities and resistances. It followed that absolute non-organisation was impossible in experience; for if it existed we could know nothing of it. The entire world consisted of an organising process, an infinitely developing series of complexes of different forms and levels of organisation in their mutual relations, in their struggle or their unification. All of these, however remote from each other they were qualitatively and quantitatively, could be subsumed under the same organisational methods, the same organisational forms.[10]

---

7   Bogdanov 1918e, pp. 72–6.
8   Bogdanov 1918e, p. 79.
9   Bogdanov 1918e, pp. 79–80.
10   Bogdanov 1918e, pp. 89–90.

2   Tectology as Science

Bogdanov gave his science of organisation the name 'tektologiia', a term that
he had borrowed from the naturalist Ernst Haeckel, though Haeckel had used
it only to refer to the activities of human beings. Unlike in 'The Secret of Science', in *Tectology* Bogdanov did not go into the philosophical implications
of his idea of universal organisation. He confined himself to the contention
that the concept of organisation was applicable not only to living, but also
to non-living nature, that everything was organised, and that the absence of
organisation was equivalent to non-being. 'Science', he declared, 'is now breaking down the impassable barriers between living and non-living nature and
filling in the chasm between them'. According to Bogdanov, Nature was the first
and the greatest organiser, in comparison with which humanity was a mere
novice.[11]

Bogdanov was at pains to stress that the monist system of tectology was not
a philosophical, but a scientific one; tectology was not a philosophy, but a science. The difference was that philosophical systems were merely theoretical,
whereas tectology, as a science, had practical applications. Philosophy, in particular Hegel's system, was seen by Bogdanov as a precursor of tectology, but
Hegel did not think of his system as having a practical application. Even materialist dialectics remained merely at the level of explaining the world. Only with
Marx did dialectics take on a practical character.[12]

Bogdanov did not discuss the question of the relationship between tectology and his own earlier philosophical writings. From a reading of *Tectology*,
this turns out to be a rather intimate one. As was mentioned above, the idea
for such a science of general methods emerged from a series of earlier works.
And it is clear that, although presented in a novel form, Bogdanov did not abandon ideas that he had elaborated during his philosophical phase. But he did
not only re-formulate his own philosophical ideas into tectological forms; he
re-formulated other people's ideas too, in order to demonstrate that everything
could be accounted for in organisational terms.

With its examples taken from a great variety of sciences, *Tectology* was a
work that could only have been written by a person with Bogdanov's breadth
of knowledge. One finds in it references to physics, chemistry, mathematics,
psychology, sociology, mechanics, linguistics, medicine, theology, geology etc.
Some of the examples are autobiographical, taken from Bogdanov's experi-

---

11   Bogdanov 1989, 1, pp. 71–2.
12   Bogdanov 1989, 1, pp. 47–8.

ences in the Bolshevik fraction of the RSDLP. There are also many references to military affairs, suggesting that his experience in the army was an instructive, as well as a traumatic one for him.

Because the essence and the attraction of *Tectology* is in the variety and richness of the examples that Bogdanov marshals from a myriad of fields of knowledge to instruct and delight his readers, it is a work that defies summary. What is given below is a survey of the work's architecture, with a particular regard to the place of the various structural elements in Bogdanov's intellectual development.

In tracing the origins of tectology Bogdanov recounted not how he himself had come to elaborate the system, but how it had emerged historically from earlier forms of perception, from the animism of primitive peoples, through the various systems of philosophy, including those of Hegel and Herbert Spencer, culminating in the emergence of the industrial proletariat with its demand for a monistic type of world view. The division of labour and specialisation had impeded the emergence of a universal science, but since specialisation had been transferred from the worker to the machine, it was now possible to formulate a universal science of organisation. Indeed, the great social crisis brought about by the war had demonstrated an urgent need for a science of organisation, as the proletariat had to organise its forces in time of revolution.[13]

From the earliest historical times the existence of unifying organisational forms had been illustrated in 'popular tectology' by common sayings and the prevalence of metaphors. But, on the other hand, these common forms had also been obscured by the use of specialised language. Through the division of labour and specialisation the various trades and professions had applied their particular terminology to what was in essence the same operation. In *Tectology* Bogdanov overcame this difficulty by the coinage of special terms to denote the various organisational forms. In this respect Bogdanov followed the example of Avenarius in his *Critique of Pure Experience*.

In an echo of Mach and Avenarius's usage, Bogdanov called a unit of organisation a 'complex', and its component parts 'elements'. Depending on what was the subject of study anything might be a complex or an element. In an almost poetic passage, Bogdanov illustrated the relativity of his terms and simultaneously the breadth of vision of tectology:

> Gigantic suns and nebulae have to be taken as elements of star systems; enterprises or people as elements of society; cells as elements of an organ-

---

13   Bogdanov 1989, 1, p. 109.

ism; molecules or atoms or electrons as elements of a physical body, depending on the question at hand; ideas and concepts as elements of theoretical systems; representations and voluntary impulses as elements of psychical associations, etc.[14]

In *Tectology* Bogdanov elaborated on his definition of organisation given in 'The Secret of Science' as constituting 'a whole which is greater than the sum of its parts'. There he held that a complex which was greater than the sum of its elements was organised; conversely, a complex which was less than the sum of its elements was disorganised. Neutral complexes were those which occupied an intermediate position between these two states, the point of equilibrium between organisation and disorganisation. The elements which constituted the complexes were activity-resistance of all possible types, so that the theme of activity-resistance pervaded the whole of the work.[15]

There was, Bogdanov maintained, a close relationship between mathematics and tectology. The laws of mathematics did not refer to any particular phenomena, as laws of other special sciences did, but to all and any phenomenon, and only from the point of view of their magnitudes. In this respect, mathematics was as universal as tectology. The method of both disciplines was to abstract from the concrete world. The difference was that mathematics dealt with complexes whose sum was equal to their parts, that is with neutral complexes, ones in which the organising and disorganising forces were equally balanced. Although from the point of mathematics all complexes were identical, in experience one did not encounter two complexes which were the same.

3   Organising Methods

Having described the general characteristics of tectology as a universal science of organisation, Bogdanov proceeded to survey the basic mechanisms of organisation, of which he noted six. These were: 'conjunction', 'ingression', 'linkage', 'disingression', 'boundary', and 'crises c and d'. These were concepts that served in the creation of a great variety of organisational forms. They would be supplemented by mechanisms concerned with determining whether and to what extent these organisational forms survived and consolidated themselves or declined and were absorbed into the environment.[16]

---

14   Bogdanov 1989, 1, 119–20.
15   Bogdanov 1989, 1, p. 125.
16   Bogdanov 1989, 1, p. 188.

The first and predominating of the organisational forms described by Bogdanov was 'conjunction'. This, as all the tectological concepts, was to be understood broadly, as the joining of complexes. As Bogdanov explained:

> Conjunction is cooperation or any other social contact, such as speech and the connection of concepts into ideas, the meeting of images and aspirations in the field of consciousness, the fusion of metals, the electrical discharge between two bodies, an exchange of commodities between enterprises, and an exchange of ray energy between heavenly bodies. Conjunction connects our brain with the most distant star when we see it through a telescope, and with the smallest bacteria which we see in the microscope. Conjunction is the assimilation of nourishment which sustains an organism and of poison which destroys it, the tender embraces of lovers and the furious engagement of enemies, the congress of workers of the same trade and the close skirmishing of opposing military detachments.[17]

As Bogdanov's examples suggest, the act of conjunction could have both beneficial and harmful effects on an organism. He stresses that there can never be any completely harmonious unification of complexes, that there is always some degree of mutual resistance. An illustration of this would be of two workers cooperating together, partially assisting each other and partially hindering each other's efforts.[18]

According to Bogdanov, what held connected complexes together was some element or elements that they had in common, some linkage between them, forming a 'chain connection'. This could appear in a variety of forms. The linkage in a chain was that part of one link which lay inside the other. The linkage of two associated images in consciousness was their common feature: the linkage of cooperatively organized efforts was their common purpose.

The linkages of elements in a complex implied the 'entry' of elements of one complex into another, and *vice versa*. For that reason, systems which were formed from complexes bound together by a linkage Bogdanov termed 'ingressive'. The act of ingression was the introduction of some intermediate cohesive factor between the separate complexes. This could be the glue which stuck two pieces of wood together or the weld joining two pieces of metal. In the realm of perception the ingression linking the common elements of given com-

---

17   Bogdanov 1989, 1, p. 144.
18   Bogdanov 1989, 1, p. 145.

plexes would be a 'generalisation', the factor which all of the given concepts had in common. In a prophetic example, Bogdanov alluded to the possibility of coordinating the efforts of two workers who happened to be at the opposite sides of the earth: it was only necessary to introduce between them a sufficient number of telegraphic stations and lines.[19]

For Bogdanov, the principal type of organisational relationship is ingression. Correspondingly, the principal type of disorganisational form he termed 'disingression', that is, negative ingression. Whereas in ingression the activities which were not previously connected are joined together, creating a linkage of the conjugating complexes, in disingression the complexes are separated, either partially, creating a 'partial disingression', or wholly, creating a 'complete disingression'. In the latter case a 'tectological boundary' is established between the two complexes. But, as Bogdanov emphasises, there are not and cannot be complexes which are completely isolated; each is surrounded by an environment, by other organised complexes and other activities.[20] Bogdanov was also insistent that the act of conjunction was primary and necessarily preceded any act of disingression. A saw, for example, had to be applied to the piece of wood through conjunction, before the act of cutting (disingression) could be performed.[21]

Drawing on his war experiences, Bogdanov gave an example of a tectological boundary, which at the same time gave an illustration of conjunction and linkage:

> A vivid illustration of a tectological boundary and also the changes in it is the front line. It passes through the points where the antagonistic efforts of two armies are held in mutual balance, and for as long as they are so held. As soon as this balance is disturbed, as happens with an attack by one side, the front line disappears; this gives rise to conjugating processes – battles and skirmishes in which elements of both sides intermingle in various combinations and interactions. Subsequently, military activities may again come to a balance along a new front line; or conjunction may spread further and further and culminate in the creation of a linkage, embodied in a peace agreement or a relationship of conquest and subordination.[22]

---

19   Bogdanov 1989, 1, pp. 155–60.
20   Bogdanov 1989, 1, p. 164.
21   Bogdanov 1989, 1, pp. 142–3.
22   Bogdanov 1989, 1, p. 165.

With the processes of conjunction and disingression Bogdanov associated two types of crises: the first type, a conjunctive or joining one, he denoted as 'crises C'; the second, disjunctive or separating variety of crises, he denoted as 'crises D'. As an example of the crisis C Bogdanov gave the case of two drops of water fusing to form a single drop. Crisis D was represented by a single drop of water dividing into two separate drops. The divisions brought about by crisis D, Bogdanov argued, were not necessarily destructive, because the division of the drop of water could take on the nature of 'propagation', as the daughter drops might also achieve the same threshold sizes.[23] In the first part of *Tectology* Bogdanov merely outlined his conceptions of crises C and D; in the third part he would develop them substantially in propounding his conception of revolution and in his critique of the dialectical method.

4   Regulative Mechanisms

Having set out the basic concepts of the tectological method, Bogdanov proceeded to characterise the mechanisms which regulated the various tectological forms and determined whether they would be conserved, consolidated, diffused, or destroyed. The first of these mechanisms was 'selection', of which there were two types: 'conservative' and 'progressive'. In this section of *Tectology* Bogdanov is on familiar territory, because in his earlier writings he had spoken about the interchange of both living beings and inanimate objects with their environment and the process of their adaptation to it.

Bogdanov introduces the tectological concept of selection by saying that everything that comes about is faced with the dilemma: conservation or destruction. Both of these possibilities have laws which govern them, so that frequently one can predict the fate of a particular form. The laws which determine the conservation or the destruction of forms are the first scheme of the universal regulatory mechanism. Bogdanov designates it by the name it has been given in biology: 'selection' (*otbor* or *podbor*). He sees no need to distinguish between 'natural' and 'artificial' selection, because for tectology the distinction is inessential.

By conservative selection Bogdanov had in mind that process of selection which determined the conservation or destruction of organisational forms. The example he gave was that of a country in which the climate became colder and where only some of the living forms in it were successful in adapting to

---

23   Bogdanov 1989, 1, p. 162.

the new conditions. Selection had the effect of a sieve in sifting out beings or things according to set criteria. A party programme acted as a kind of sieve by attracting only the people who supported it into an organisation. Sifting out the agent which killed syphilis from the ones that did not was the method of finding a cure for the disease.[24]

Because tectology was concerned only with activities, and activities implied change, it followed that a simple and pure 'conservation' of forms which kept them in a static state was out of the question. Conservation was always the result of a process by which changes were counter-balanced by equal and opposite changes; this was what Bogdanov termed the 'dynamic equilibrium' of change.

Bogdanov describes the process of dynamic equilibrium in a passage reminiscent of Avenarius's *Critique of Pure Experience*. He says:

> In its life activity, the organism is constantly expending, losing, giving up to its environment, its activities in the form of the substance of its tissues or the energy of its organs. This does not prevent its remaining – approximately or practically – 'the same', i.e. it is conserved. In exchange for what it has lost it just as constantly takes in, assimilates, from the environment, the elements of its activities in the form of nourishment, energy, external impressions, etc.[25]

The maintenance of the dynamic equilibrium depended on keeping in balance the processes of assimilation and disassimilation.[26]

For Bogdanov, complete conservation was unattainable, and approximate conservation implied only small changes in the direction of the dominance of assimilation over disassimilation, or *vice versa*. But over time, perhaps over a considerable length of time, these minute changes could lead to the development of the given complex. A drop of water could increase its volume; a living cell could thrive in a favourable environment which provided it with a prevalence of nourishment over the expenditure of its substance.

As Bogdanov admitted, the treatment of selection in terms of dynamic equilibrium and deviations from it had taken him some way from the primary meaning of the term. But, he argued, this scheme was broader and deeper; it covered both the progressive development of complexes and their relative downfall; it resolved the processes of conservation and destruction into their

---

24   Bogdanov 1989, 1, p. 193.
25   Bogdanov 1989, 1, pp. 197–8.
26   Bogdanov 1989, 1, p. 199.

elements. The most expedient way of expressing it was with the term 'progressive selection': positive, when the sum of activities of a complex grew, when
assimilation prevailed over disassimilation, and negative, when the sum of
activities was diminished, when disassimilation prevailed over assimilation.[27]

Under positive selection a complex becomes less regular and geometrically
more elaborate. On the other hand, its resistance to division lessens, and with
continued growth it will divide under its own weight. This indicates the growing complexity and heterogeneity of the internal relationships of the complex.
As the complex acquires new elements its heterogeneity increases and with it
its instability.

Under negative selection the form of a complex becomes geometrically simpler and more regular, and its resistance to division becomes relatively greater.
This indicates the simplification of the inner structure and increase in its
homogeneity, a tendency opposite to positive selection. This is to be expected,
since under the impact of the environment it is first of all those elements which
are less firmly bound which detach themselves from the whole. Together with
the reduction in the number of bonds the increased homogeneity ensures the
simplification of the complex's structure.[28]

Having discussed the two types of selection, Bogdanov pointed out that
the regulating mechanism was not something separate from the formulating
mechanism, that a thorough analysis would show that any process of positive
or negative selection could be resolved into a number of elementary changes,
such as conjunctions with ingressions and disingressions arising from them. In
essence, formulating and regulating were two different points of view in the
tectological investigation, both of which were necessary and complemented
each other. The survey of both processes served as a preliminary to an examination of the actual organisational processes.[29]

5   The Stability of Forms

The first aspect of the organisational process that Bogdanov turned his attention to was the question of the stability of the forms. Here, taking as his example
a drop of water in an atmosphere saturated with vapour and one in an unsat-
urated atmosphere, he could show that the drop which assimilated moisture
was more stable than the one that did not. The implication was that positive

27   Bogdanov 1989, 1, p. 202.
28   Bogdanov 1989, 1, pp. 202–3.
29   Bogdanov 1989, 1, p. 206.

selection led to a growth in the stability of complexes, while negative selection did the opposite.[30] However, positive selection could lead to the given complex becoming more complex and more heterogeneous, which was a factor leading to instability. Over time, the accumulation of internal instability would lead to a 'crisis'.[31]

The stability of a complex as a whole in regard to its particular environment depended on how stable the constituent parts of that complex were in relation to the stresses put upon them. It was consequently necessary to examine the relationship between the stability of these separate parts and the total system which they went to form.

The example Bogdanov gave of this was of a chain from which a weight was suspended. When the weight was increased beyond a certain point the chain would break at its weakest link. The structural stability of the whole was determined by the least stable of its parts. This scheme applied not only to mechanical systems, but to all systems, physical, psychical and social etc. If an organisation of people, such as an army, was to overcome destructive influences, then its stability would depend on the least stable of its units; and in exactly the same way, a logical chain of proof would collapse if one of its links did not stand up to criticism.[32]

This 'law of the leasts' had a great number of important practical consequences. A squadron could only sail as fast as its slowest ship; an experienced leader who on a single issue lost concentration for a moment could cause untold disaster to his organisation. If there was a political party consisting of a bloc of two fractions, one progressive and one conservative, the party programme and tactics would be decided by the conservative fraction. Although the advanced group might to a great extent 'lead' the backward one, in the sense that it would be the one to put forward slogans and nominate leaders etc., the actual limit to the effectiveness of slogans and leadership was determined by what the backward part of the organisation could go along with. In the same way, a military detachment consisting of infantry and cavalry would break up, if the cavalry did not limit itself to the speed of the infantry.[33]

At the time he was working on *Tectology*, Bogdanov had fresh in his mind some of the worst instances of the law of the leasts, taken from the war and the revolution that followed it. Millions of people, he observed, belonging to the most cultured nations and the most advanced classes in society had rushed to

---

30   Bogdanov 1989, 1, p. 206.
31   Bogdanov 1989, 1, p. 212.
32   Bogdanov 1989, 1, p. 216.
33   Bogdanov 1989, 1, pp. 216–22.

exterminate each other with the same zoological cruelty as their savage ancest-
ors had done. London and Paris, the great centres of world culture, had witnessed the same kind of patriotic massacres as had the semi-Asiatic Moscow.
The officer gentlemen of liberal England had shot Russian revolutionary prisoners of war in concert with the generals of despotic tsarist Russia.[34]

For Bogdanov, atrocities were not the prerogative of any particular nation. In
his view, modern individuals, taken separately, were not homogeneous wholes.
Their psycho-motor systems contained a gradation of layers: from inferior to
superior, from the animal instincts of the cave dweller to the pure social idealism found in different forms in the various classes of society. But when an
external force was directed towards the inferior complexes of their psycho-
motor systems, even people whose baser reactions were a small part of their
overall make-up would be as destructive as those in whom the inferior instincts
were a major part of their character. This 'levelling down' is most often manifested in the herd actions of a crowd, where the baser instincts predominate and
where cruelties are perpetrated even by people who only have the rudiments
of a zoological heredity. In a crowd too people who are normally courageous
succumb to panic and behave like cowards

Bogdanov saw the danger that the law of the leasts might come to dominate
humanity if it was not brought under control. There was, he believed, a problem for tectology to solve: how to master the law in the cultural sphere in order
to avoid equalisation according to the lowest common denominator, so that
humanity's major achievements should not be lost to the survivals of barbarity
which threatened to overwhelm them?[35]

The structural stability of a system could also be considered from the point
of view of the extent of its contacts with its environment. A system might be
'diffused' and branch out, having many points of contact with the environment,
or it might have fewer points of contact and display a 'compact' structure. From
the examples Bogdanov adduced he concluded that, as far as the preservation and development of complexes was concerned, under negative selection a
compact structure was to be preferred, and under positive selection a diffused
structure.

State structures could be viewed in diffuse and compact terms. The govern-
mental structures of Switzerland, the USA, and England, with their internal
wide local self-governments and external colonial-federative connections, was
possible only because of exceptionally favourable conditions. On the other

---

34   Bogdanov 1989, 1, p. 241.
35   Bogdanov 1989, 1. p. 242.

hand, states that developed during long periods of war and which were surrounded by enemies could exist only on a centralist basis; such were the Eastern
despotisms, Russia and France.[36]

The recent history of Russian political parties could also be seen in the light
of diffuse-compact structural types. According to Bogdanov, in the period of
reaction the relationships between central and local organisations which had
a diffuse structure were inevitably broken, and the party was turned into a number of scattered groups. Where unity was maintained, it was only the unity of
the programme or dogma, which became more stringent. This was also a kind
of compactness, but an ideological compactness.[37]

Bogdanov concluded his survey of the stability of forms by showing that Le
Châtelier's Law of Equilibrium, formulated for physical and chemical systems,
had a universal application and should be considered as a principle of tectology. The law was as follows. When a system at equilibrium is subjected to an
action which changes any of the conditions of equilibrium, then in it will arise
processes which counteract this change.[38]

Most of the examples Bogdanov gave to illustrate the workings of Le Châtelier's Law came from physics or chemistry, but he did give a few examples of its
application to the human personality. One of them echoed what he had said
regarding family life in *Cultural Tasks*. This was that 'A man, who tends towards
equilibrium in some aspects of his life, can be positively or negatively unbal-
anced in the others: a "citizen" or even a "revolutionary" in political life, can be
a "philistine" in his family relationships, or, for example, a "philistine" in all his
contacts with society and a "petty tyrant" in his own home etc'.[39]

6 Divergence and Convergence of Forms

In the second part of *Tectology* Bogdanov examined the various ways in which
complexes related to each other. He explained that in experience one did not
meet two absolutely identical complexes. The differences in practice could be
minuscule, but with detailed investigation they could be found. One could not
find two identical leaves or two identical drops of water. This applied not only
to real complexes, but to ideal ones as well; no two ideas, even in the mind of a
single person, were ever the same. Moreover, the environment in which com-

36   Bogdanov 1989, 1, p. 245.
37   Ibid.
38   Bogdanov 1989, 1, p. 249.
39   Bogdanov 1989, 1. p. 256.

plexes existed was constantly changing. The differences between complexes might grow, causing them to diverge, but convergence of complexes was also possible.[40]

Sometimes the difference in complexes was made deliberately, as in the case of horticulture or bird rearing, in the practice of artificial selection. Social systems provided another example of the divergence of complexes, when after generations of accumulated differences clan communities disintegrated, giving rise to various tribes and peoples. A similar process took place in dialects and languages; these grew increasingly divergent with the dispersion of the population over wide areas.

In keeping with Herbert Spencer's conception that progress implied the increase in heterogeneity, Bogdanov held that systemic differentiation was essential in the development of any complex organism. A plant shoot differentiated into a root and leaves; the cells in the human body were specialised; and in human society progress came through the division of labour and the emergence of specialised occupations.[41]

There were, however, limits to the process of systemic differentiation. A point would be reached when the parts of the whole became 'too different' from each other, and it would no longer be possible to coordinate them the precise way required for the continued stability of the system. The result would be the disorganisation and eventual death of the organism. This 'contradiction of systemic divergence' was the way that Bogdanov explained the ageing process.[42]

The differentiation of the social division of labour, Bogdanov held, would follow a similar course. It had been responsible for enormously raising the productivity of the efforts of mankind; but it had also led to disintegration of the originally integral communities into separate households, which were only connected through market relations. And since the market was dominated by struggle and competition, rather than cooperation, it encouraged the proliferation of disproportions and disingressions. The culmination of this process had been the collapse of finance capitalism, the gigantic crisis of the World War and revolutions that had emerged from it.[43]

In a reference to the divisions within the RSDLP that led to the formation of the Bolshevik and Menshevik fractions, Bogdanov observed that it was interesting to see how the schism of political organisations developed. At the moment of the rift itself the differences were barely perceptible even to the

---

40   Bogdanov 1989, 2, p. 5.
41   Bogdanov 1989, 2, pp. 14–16.
42   Bogdanov 1989, 2, p. 24.
43   Bogdanov 1989, 2, pp. 26–7.

participants themselves: one side attributed negative features to the other. But after the division, when some time had elapsed, significant and serious differences appeared: tactical, programmatic and theoretical. These continued to grow; and with them the need for actions that would bring the two sides together again.[44]

However, under the heading of 'counter-differentiation', with Lenin's union with the Plekhanov group of the Mensheviks in mind, Bogdanov went on to say that:

> With the merger of political parties or fractions, to avoid internal conflict, some programmatic and tactical elements are sacrificed. In the same way, having become superfluous or inconvenient, some individual organs, posts or special centres are got rid of. Usually too, some members of the organisation, who are unhappy with the merger or who can be an obstacle to its implementation, are thrown out.[45]

Here, in tectological terms, Bogdanov characterised his own expulsion from the Bolshevik Centre.

The term 'counter-differentiation' referred to the kind of mergers and unions that took place to counteract the effects of the law of differentiation. Here Bogdanov referred to the benefit of mixed marriages between races, the success of the English language as a merger of Germanic and Romance elements, and the advantages of the mule as the offspring of a horse and a donkey.

He also classified Marxian scientific socialism as the result of counter-differentiation. This was a union of the utopian ideal of 'communism' with the workers' movement. In Marx's synthesis the workers' movement was freed from its hostility to machine technology, professional-guild narrowness, and the crudely materialist character of its aims. The ideal of communism, on the other hand, was freed from moral and philanthropic overtones and from its connection with religion. The resulting Marxist synthesis was more coherent and viable.[46]

A special case of the workings of counter-differentiation in psychology which Bogdanov called 'the bifurcation and restoration of the unity of personality' was Shakespeare's portrayal of Hamlet. For Bogdanov Hamlet was a striking example of a system differentiation of the human psyche. Hamlet is the son of a warrior king and descendant of the Norman Vikings. His upbringing

---

44   Bogdanov 1989, 2, p. 11.
45   Bogdanov 1989, 2, p. 48.
46   Bogdanov 1989, 2, p. 51.

was that of a warrior, but his education had made him an aesthete. He communicated with actors and his love for Ophelia had made him a poet. Although the play ended with the hero's death, Bogdanov argued that by that point Hamlet no longer had internal struggles and doubts; the two sides of his character had been finally reconciled.[47]

Under the heading of 'Contradictions in Systemic Divergence' Bogdanov had explained the ageing process in terms of the excessive differentiation of cells within the human body. Because it embraced the entire structure of the organism rather than any particular part of it, he saw old age as a tectological disease. If ageing was brought about by differentiation, then the cure must be in some measure one that would ensure counter-differentiation in the organism. This was the role Bogdanov attributed to blood transfusion, whose significance for the furtherance of comradely cooperation he had alluded to in his novel *Red Star*.

For Bogdanov, blood transfusion was a method by means of which the conjunctive renewal of living cells could be achieved. With modern scientific technology, it was quite possible to have a straight, direct conjunction of those tissues of various organisms which had a liquid form, i.e., blood and lymph. These were the tissues which composed the internal conjunctive environment of the organism and maintained its chemical unity. It was a matter of performing a simultaneous interchange of blood between a young and an old individual, with neither of them sustaining a quantitative loss of blood.[48]

'Convergence of forms' has a different organisational significance from counter-differentiation and also a different origin. Bogdanov likens the convergence of forms to the process of metal casting, in which a mould produces casts of the same shape. This could be generalised to give a definition of convergence of forms: convergence is the result of similarly directed selection on the part of a similar environment. The difference from counter-differentiation is that in counter-differentiation the divergence or its negative consequences are negated by the direct conjunction of the diverging forms themselves; in the convergence of forms no such conjunction takes place; the similarity of the complexes is determined only by their relationships to the environment.[49]

The role of 'mould' for the converging forms could be performed by any environment. Thus, mammals, such as dolphins and whales, having moved from dry land into water, acquired many features common with fish. The necessity to overcome the mechanical resistance of water to movement had ensured

---

47   Bogdanov 1989, 2, p. 65.
48   Bogdanov 1989, 2, p. 85.
49   Bogdanov 1989, 2. pp. 89–90.

that, by natural selection, the external body form of these mammals replicated the shape earlier arrived at by the selection process of fish under the same
environmental conditions.[50]

Bogdanov was able to provide various examples of convergence of forms
from the natural world, such as the analogous structures of the atom and of
planetary systems, the hand of a human being and the foreleg of a horse, the
fluctuations of light and of electro-magnetism. In posing the question of the
origin of this tectological unity, Bogdanov suggested that with the advance in
science some common origin of the similarities, though a remote one, might
be discovered.[51]

In the convergence of forms the environment acted on the complex like a
mould on a casting, but there were also cases where two complexes determined each other mutually. This happened when a living organism ingested food
from the environment, but its protoplasm remained unchanged, unaffected by
the food. The merger of the food with the protoplasm did not result in the
counter-differentiation that might have been expected. In order to explain this
phenomenon Bogdanov introduced two new tectological concepts: the 'regulator' and the 'bi-regulator'.

A regulator was a device which served to maintain some process at a definite level, such as that on a steam boiler designed to prevent the emergence of
excessive steam which could cause it to explode. A bi-regulator was a derivative
of a regulator, but more complex. In it the regulator and the complex regulated
had a mutual action, such that, for example, it could be so arranged that the
speed of motion and the pressure of steam in a steam engine could mutually
regulate each other. If the steam pressure rose above a certain level then the
speed also increased, and the mechanism which monitored speed would then
decrease the pressure, and *vice versa*. The bi-regulator was a system for which
there was no need for an external regulator, because the system regulated itself.
And if living protoplasm could be shown to be a chemical bi-regulator, this
would account for the fact that the materials entering it cannot change its composition, but conform to the composition of the protoplasm.[52]

In his book *The Science of Social Consciousness* Bogdanov gives as an example
of the bi-regulator the self-steering mechanism of a torpedo. He also makes
clear there the ideological significance that the bi-regulators had for him. With
self-regulating mechanisms of this kind the level of labour that would be

---

50   Bogdanov 1989, 2, p. 90.
51   Bogdanov 1989, 2, p. 62.
52   Bogdanov 1989, 2, pp. 95–7.

needed to supervise them would be of a very high order, ensuring that the workers involved would have the skills presently possessed by qualified engineers.[53]

There were two organisational forms that Bogdanov thought particularly important because of their prevalence and the tectological role that they played. These were 'egression' and 'degression', the first concentrating activities for their maximum accumulation within a system, and the second fixing activities and securing them in a given form, thus ensuring the maximum strength of the system. The first could be described as 'centralist' and the second as 'skeletal', both in broad senses of the terms.

'Egression', which could be translated as 'going out of the ordinary', signified a complex that had a dominating influence on other complexes, such as the Sun in the planetary system, the leader in a group of people, or a generalising concept among more particular concepts. Its distinction from other complexes was an 'egressive difference', and the complex itself, in relation to other complexes, was an 'egressive centre'.[54]

The most obvious example of egression was the relationship of the brain to the sensory organs and other nerve centres of the body. This was the most extreme level of egression so far known, but every centralist organisation of people displayed essentially the same kind of relationship, though to a lesser extent. The head of a community did not usually carry out any physical work, but through verbal contact he stimulated and directed the activity of the other members of the group just as the brain through innervation stimulated and directed the physical activity of the muscles.[55]

In tracing the origins of egression, Bogdanov explained that in contemporary organisations of people an egression, if not of power, then at least of leadership, was extremely common. There were, however, grounds for supposing that in primitive tribal groups such egression did not exist; methods of struggle for survival were so simple and instinctive that each member of the community knew as much as any other member. The homogeneity of the group, however, was never complete, since within it there were differences in ability. That member of the community who surpassed all the others in the skills of survival would provide an example or instruction for others. In time the egressive difference between the man who had mastered better the collective experience and the rest of the collective increased through the workings of the tectological law of divergence. In this way Bogdanov explained the emergence of leadership and

53   Bogdanov 1914, p. 180.
54   Bogdanov 1989, 2, pp. 100–1.
55   Bogdanov 1989, 2, p. 103.

power from within an egalitarian community. Or, in other words, he had re-
cast his existing conception of the domination/subordination relationship in
a tectological framework.[56]

Bogdanov held that the egressive type of organisation was the dominant one
in social life for a whole historical era. Drawing on his own recent experience,
he added that in revolutionary eras one could observe the evolution of organisations with barely perceptible authoritarian tendencies into ones with highly
developed egression, with strict authoritarian discipline and 'firm rule'.[57]

There were, however, important limits to egression. A despot could control his ministers, but he could not control the humble peasant, because the
peasant was too far from the concentration of power. The same loss of control
would occur if the difference between the organisers and the executors became
too great. The two types would understand each other less and less, and so
'mistakes' would creep in. A recent example from the war was the alienation
between the soldiers and their officers that led to a breakdown in discipline.[58]

From the organisational point of view a single centre was effective, while
two centres were not. In the history of Russian Social-Democracy there was
an example of infringement of this principle, which led to many harmful consequences. At the congress in 1903 the party leadership set up two centres: the
editorial board of the central organ and the Central Committee. The result was
competition and conflict between the two centres. It was a mistake that could
have been avoided since the people involved had before them the example of
feudalism with the struggle between the spiritual and the temporal spheres.[59]

For Bogdanov, an important feature of complexes was their organisational
'plasticity'. By plasticity he meant the mobile and flexible character of a complex's connections, the facility with which it could re-group its elements. This
quality had a tremendous significance for organisational development. The
more plastic the complex, the greater the number of combinations that it could
form in changing conditions, the richer would be the material for selection, and
the more rapidly and completely it could adapt to these conditions.

However, the plasticity of complexes also was a cause of their vulnerabil-
ity. The mobility of their elements permitted the relatively easy destruction of
connections among them. The complexity of their internal equilibriums also
meant their relative instability. A vivid illustration of this was the human brain,
the most highly organised of all biological complexes, the most intricate, the

---

56   Bogdanov 1989, 2, pp. 104–5.
57   Bogdanov 1989, 2, p. 108.
58   Bogdanov 1989, 2, p. 117.
59   Bogdanov 1989, 2, p. 123.

most plastic, but also the most tender. It could be disorganised by the most insignificant harmful influences, once they gained access to it.

Correspondingly, plastic complexes were protected by the mechanism of a relatively rigid external 'skeletal' form. To indicate that the phenomenon was found at all levels of organisation, intellectual as well as physical, Bogdanov termed it 'degression'. The literal meaning of the word was 'going down', but, Bogdanov stressed, degression was an organisational form of great positive significance: degression made the higher development of plastic forms possible, securing their activities, and protecting tender combinations from their rough environment. Degression would refer to such things as clothing, dwellings, and vessels for liquids etc.[60]

There was a negative side to degression, arising from the fact that although skeletons protected plasticity and flexibility, they also, at a certain level, impeded its growth and development. An especially important case in the sphere of social degression was that of ideology. Bogdanov thought that the phrase 'ossified dogma', when applied to religious, scientific, legal, political and social doctrines, was aptly borrowed from the physiology of the skeleton; its tectological role in obstructing progress was exactly like that of a skeleton.[61]

Rules, regulations, official programmes, and technical or tactical directives, etc., were examples of 'skeletal' forms. In Bogdanov's opinion these should be formulated with a sufficient degree of flexibility to allow for the subsequent growth and development of the organisation. Usually this was not done, the framers of the regulations or programmes only having regard to the present situation. Bogdanov believed that had the rigid constitution of the RSDLP been framed with more elasticity at its first congress, the internal disagreements of 1904–6 would have been avoided.[62]

Bogdanov concluded the second part of *Tectology* by returning to the topic of selection, this time in complex systems, such as a society, an organism, a scientific or philosophical doctrine or a cosmic body. He thought it important to do so, because the mechanism of selection was universal; it operated everywhere and at every moment, so that every event, every change could be regarded from the point of view of the conservation or proliferation of some activities and the weakening and breaking of others in this or that complex or system. The factor, the catalyst for selection, was always the 'environment' in the broadest sense of the term.

---

60   Bogdanov 1989, 2, p. 130.
61   Bogdanov 1989, 2, p. 137.
62   Bogdanov 1989, 2, p. 144.

Because more elaborate complexes could be broken down into smaller, simpler complexes, each with its particular relationships to the other complexes and to the environment, this gave rise to the phenomenon of 'chain selection'. Since the factor of selection was environmental, its transformatory influence was felt first and foremost on the boundary 'layer' of the system that must adapt to the environment. This first series of changes acted on the second layer, and then on the third, progressing to the elements which were tectologically innermost and only indirectly experiencing the influences from outside the system.[63]

It was possible to consider human society in terms of the layering of activities. The boundary layer was the one whose activities came directly into contact with nature and the struggle with it in the form of labour. It was here that the primary processes of selection and adaptation went on, through the application of technical means and methods. The next 'layer' of society consisted of the interactions and mutual relations of people in the social-labour process, in production relations, which constituted the realm of the 'economy'. In other words, the development of economic forms was determined by technical ones.

The high plasticity and complexity of both of these forms created the necessity for their organisational consolidation, their social degression. This was the realm of ideology, which went to constitute the third layer, or, in Marx's terminology, the 'superstructure', which was determined by the first and second layers. As Bogdanov pointed out, the issue of 'base' and 'superstructure' that had caused such controversy for historical materialism was explained easily by tectological methods.[64]

7   Crises C and D

In the third part of *Tectology* Bogdanov returned to the question of crises, one that he had touched upon earlier in his survey of tectological forms. There he had distinguished two types of crisis: crisis C, which was conjunctive, and crisis D, which was disjunctive. Crises, however, had to be treated as complex phenomena, since they involved tectological concepts from lower levels, and since crises were in fact chains of elementary crises of both types. Crises were the means by which Bogdanov could explain the disturbance of continuity. He did

---

63   Bogdanov 1989, 2, pp. 152–3.
64   Bogdanov 1989, 2, p. 154.

this by regarding crises as a disruption of one equilibrium and at the same time the transition to a new one. In other words, Bogdanov envisaged the existence of not one continuity, but two.

In the case of crisis C the complexes coming together could result in an explosion, as with the combination of certain chemicals. The clash of two armies was also a crisis C, but if one of the armies should retreat while retaining its fighting capacity, this was termed by Bogdanov a 'fading crisis'. Social revolutions could also proceed along the lines of 'fading crises', as in England, when the feudal order was replaced by the capitalist one. Then the course of history unfolded in a series of fading crises, each of them tending towards an equilibrium of old and new forms. Although in the English revolution the explosive type of crisis made an appearance at the beginning, it was not so prominent as in revolutions in other countries.[65]

In discussing crisis D, that of disjunction, Bogdanov examined the stability of complexes which had divided. Following Avenarius, he gave the example of the human organism, which, while it was in its mother's womb, had the best environment possible, but following birth and the separation from its mother, found itself in a most unfavourable environment. Thereafter the human organism achieved equilibrium with its environment only for part of its life, during the period of maturity and propagation.[66]

Bogdanov emphasised that for tectology the concept of crisis was universal; it was simply a special point of view applicable to everything that occurred in experience. For only changes occurred, and any change could be considered from the point of view of the difference in form between its initial and final point.[67]

Analysing the way in which complexes at any level of organisation, such as new social, political or ideological groupings, were formed, served to illustrate the operation of what Bogdanov termed the 'tectological act'. This began with crisis C, in which linkages were formed; it then progressed through crises D, with differentiation and the separation of functions; the final phase was that of systemic consolidation through counter-differentiation; this last phase was on the basis of crises C with secondary crises D.[68]

The triad of the organisational act inevitably called for comparison with the triad of dialectics, and this prompted Bogdanov to elaborate on the critique

65   Bogdanov 1989, 2, p. 233.
66   Bogdanov 1989, 2, pp. 241–2.
67   Bogdanov 1989, 2, p. 254.
68   Bogdanov 1989, 2, p. 260.

of dialectics that he had first made in 1899 in his *Basic Elements of the Histor-ical View of Nature*. There he had objected that dialectics was only applicable to living nature and that 'development in contradictions' also had a limited application.[69] Now, from the point of view of tectology, he was able to present a more detailed examination of the limitations of the Marxist dialectics of the kind that Plekhanov and his followers propounded.

He began by recapitulating the 'Marxist' concept of dialectics with its three-stage progression through 'thesis,' 'antithesis' and 'synthesis' or the 'negation of the negation'. He went on to reproduce the concrete illustration that Engels had given of the process in *Anti-Duhring*. This was of a grain of barley, the thesis, which 'negated' itself with germination and passed into its antithesis – the whole plant. The plant in turn 'negated' itself by the creation of seeds, and passed into a synthesis, formally similar to the thesis, but enriched in content, the end result being a plurality of barley grains.

Bogdanov then demonstrated how these events were interpreted tectologic-ally. In terms of organisation, the grain of barley could not be considered stat-ically, outside its relationship with its environment. Its contact with the activ-ities of the soil constituted the primary conjunctive phase, which stimulated a series of systemic differentiations, which included the inevitable destabil-ising actions in the form of partial destruction, disease, etc. After differentiation came the consolidating tendency – counter-differentiation on the one hand, and separating disingressions on the other. This tendency culminated in the ripening of the seed, which to the greatest extent furthered the activities of the plant and fixed the results of its development in new seeds, which would be the carriers of both heredity and the acquisition of a newly experienced cycle. However, it was also possible for the cycle to end in the disintegration of the plant into an inorganic equilibrium.[70]

Such a scheme, Bogdanov argued, was universal; it embraced any tectolo-gical act as a whole, even in its smallest detail. Admittedly, like any tectological scheme, it was in essence formal. Nevertheless, in contrast to the old dialect-ical triad, it showed the direction and linkages in organisational changes and, consequently, the ways to look for them.

In the concluding section of *Tectology* Bogdanov examined the question of the relationship of complexes of different ages. Any complex developing sys-tem represented a chain of groupings which were different in their age on the one hand, and in their connectedness and stability on the other. Historically,

---

69   Bogdanov 1899a, p. 18.
70   Bogdanov 1989, 2, p. 268.

this represented a series of sequential layers, some layers being created earlier while others were later 'superimposed' on earlier ones.

As an example of this temporal layering of complexes Bogdanov gave the fact that with the failure of memory in old age, recent memories were forgotten, whereas those of the past remained relatively fresh. The situation facing the RSDLP in the aftermath of the 1905 revolution also provided an example of such a phenomenon. For when the party was subjected to decomposition in the unfavourable environment of a blind reaction, the process of decline was generally felt first of all by the most recently formed layers – the newest members of the party and the newest party cells; these separated first. With a forced review of party doctrines, the most recent and the least established doctrinal elements were those to be discarded first, tactics showing less durability than the party programme.

Connected with the same scheme of historical layers was still another law, so far formulated only for biology. This was that the evolution of an individual repeats that of its species. In the psychology of the child could be discerned many features characteristic of primitive peoples, such as the lack of individuality and the presence of naive communism. Only later did a consciousness of the 'I' emerge, signalling the start of the individualistic phase. Still later, in mature years, the phase of social idealism, the spirit of collectivism, emerged. Such, in general, Bogdanov concluded, has been the historical path of mankind to date.[71]

8   Tectology and General System Theory

Tectology is a work of considerable length (531 pages in the 1922 edition), most of which is taken up with examples. At first sight it is a diffuse work, but that impression belies its sophisticated structure. The organisational forms that Bogdanov unfolds, conjunction, linkage, ingression etc. form a progression of complexity, so that the later ones, such as crises c and d and chain selection, contain in themselves simpler organisational forms that have been met with earlier. The examples that Bogdanov provides to illustrate his organisational forms also have a progression. In this case they begin with concrete cases taken from everyday life, such as drops of dew on a leaf, and become increasingly abstract, so that they embrace phenomena in politics or ideology.

---

71   Bogdanov 1989, 2, p. 286.

Although *Tectology* is not in itself a philosophical work, there are philosophical assumptions behind it. The way Bogdanov treats the elements that make up complexes as activity-resistance is a very elegant solution to the problem of avoiding the dualism of subjectivity-objectivity, physical-psychical. It is an advance on both Mach's concept of elements and on Avenarius's idea of a dependent and an independent series. It has the advantage that it can be interpreted in terms of labour and of organisation. At levels higher than the element the theme of activity-resistance is repeated throughout the exposition of *Tectology*. It is noticeable that every organisational activity has its corresponding resistance. Thus, ingression-disingression, differentiation-counter-differentiation, diffuse-compact etc. By these pairs of opposites, Bogdanov wishes to imply that at every level of organisation the principle of activity-resistance operates.

Inevitably, *Tectology* is a book of its time, so that some of the scientific ideas it contains have become obsolete in the light of subsequent scientific discoveries in genetics, astronomy, particle physics, etc. These, however, are not fatal to Bogdanov's work, as other examples can easily be substituted. Similarly, one could supplement the examples Bogdanov has given in politics and history with ones taken from more recent events. In fact the nature of the work is such that it invites new additions and the discovery of fresh applications for the organisational forms. This has been done by Takhtadzhan in his book *Principia Tektologica*, published in 1989.[72] This is an exposition of *Tectology* with examples taken both from Bogdanov's original work, and from other sources.

It is more in the organisational forms that tectology's strength lies, in their appropriateness and applicability. In this respect Bogdanov has been singularly successful. Although the names he has given to the forms are often invented, the forms themselves are by no means contrived. They are, for the most part, based on everyday relationships and associations that are naturally made. Bogdanov has taken clues from common metaphors and folk wisdom.

The most compelling argument in favour of the viability of Bogdanov's scheme of organisational forms is that, quite independently, after the Second World War, Ludwig von Bertalanffy formulated what became General System Theory, which to a significant degree replicated Bogdanov's organisational science. That this coincidence came about without any direct influence by Bogdanov, is a ringing endorsement of Bogdanov's conception of a 'convergence of forms'; the environment in this instance would be the inter-disciplinary approach to knowledge.

---

72   Takhtadzhan 1989.

The similarities between tectology and General System Theory were noticed at the beginning of the 1960s in the Soviet Union by scholars such as Takhtad-zhan, and in the West by Sergei Utechin and George Gorelik. Bogdanov's son Alexander pointed out that in the guise of the bi-regulator, his father had dis-covered the important cybernetic concept of 'feedback'.[73] In Gorelik's judge-ment, a comparison between General System Theory and tectology would be in favour of the latter. He says: 'While tectology contains and integrates ideas later developed and popularized by general systems theory and cybernetics, its universal scope and method make it something more than either of them taken separately or simply added together'.[74]

Bertalanffy's rationale for General System Theory could have been written by Bogdanov. It is that modern science has become characterised by the mass of data, the complexity of techniques, and the theoretical structures within every field. Thus, science is split into innumerable disciplines continually creating sub-disciplines. In consequence, the physicist, the biologist, the psychologist and the social scientist are, so to speak, encapsulated in their private universes, so that communication between them is well-nigh impossible.

There was consequently a need for a new science that would transcend the various disciplines. This was possible, because independently of each other and unknown to each other the same problems and concepts had emerged; tech-niques had appeared in one discipline that were applicable in others. Math-ematics need not be the only technique that was applicable to all kinds of phenomena; so too could be the approach that regarded phenomena as sys-tems. A General System Theory would be a 'logico-mathematical discipline'.[75]

Not only was Bertalanffy's rationale for General System Theory remarkably similar to Bogdanov's for tectology, but the terminology used was identical. Like Bogdanov, Bertalanffy spoke in terms of systems, of complexes of elements. For Bertalanffy, as for Bogdanov, the mark of a system was that its whole was greater than the sum of its parts. For Bertalanffy the characteristic feature of what he termed 'open systems' was that they interacted with the environment, an essential feature of the complexes in tectology. Both Bertalanffy and Bogdanov thought of the state of rest as a dynamic equilibrium, and both incorporated Le Châtelier's principle into their concepts of how equilibria functioned.

Bertalanffy's approach to what in *Tectology* Bogdanov calls 'organisational forms' diverges somewhat from Bogdanov's. These forms Bertalanffy refers to as 'isomorphisms', and he has a hierarchy of these. At the first level there are

---

73   Malinovskii 200, pp. 47–9; Bogdanov's Tektology 1996, p. xvii.
74   Gorelik 1983, p. 43.
75   Bertalanffy 1968, p. 36.

analogies, superficial similarities, such as when the growth of an organism is compared to the growth of a crystal or an osmotic cell. For Bogdanov, of course, types of growth would be the same organisational form.

Bertalanffy's second level of isomorphism, which he terms 'homologies', is more instructive, as it provides an interesting insight into how *Tectology* related to Bogdanov's concept of substitution. Homologies are cases which serve as conceptual models in science, such as the case in physics where the flow of heat is interpreted as a flow of a liquid, in general the transfer of the originally hydrodynamic concept of gradient to electrical, chemical and other spheres. Although there is no heat substance, the model of the fluid enables the formulation of laws for heat which are formally correct.

In the section devoted to substitution in *The Philosophy of Living Experience* Bogdanov recounted how scientists had formed a kinetic theory of gases by mentally replacing the bodies being studied by the mechanical movements of solid, extremely small, molecules of gas. They found that they could explain the movements of gases using methods that had previously developed in the field of mechanics. By a series of examples, Bogdanov showed how the development of science proceeded by making increasingly detailed and accurate substitutions, going further and further into the depths of the phenomena studied.[76]

Both Bertalanffy and Bogdanov are talking about the same thing, though in slightly different contexts. Bertalanffy has brought what Bogdanov calls 'substitution' into the heart of his system theory. Bogdanov does not do this explicitly in *Tectology*, but one can see that the concepts of substitution and organisational forms are interdependent. The existence of organisational forms that embrace different types of phenomena and processes makes substitution possible. But on the other hand, it is the practice of substitution, the particularly human practice of experiencing the world in symbolic forms, that requires and reveals the existence of organisational forms.

Bertalanffy discusses in some detail the philosophical implications of explaining one phenomenon in terms of another, arguing in particular that language, historical and cultural presuppositions have a profound effect on the way the scientific view of the world had evolved. In this sense he believes that man creates his own universe. One finds the same conception in Bogdanov, repeatedly expressed in his *Philosophy of Living Experience*. There, for example, he argues against Berdyaev, who had claimed that after the death of all the worlds the square on the hypotenuse of a right-angled triangle would still equal the sum of the squares on the other two sides. Bogdanov answered this by

---

76   Bogdanov 1920a, pp. 234–5.

pointing out that Berdyaev had overlooked the fact that Pythagoras' theorem necessarily presupposes the measurement of lines and angles with fixed, exact units of measurement, and that there cannot be measurement without people to do the measurement, or exact units of measure without people who work them out.[77]

There are important differences between Bogdanov's tectology and Bertalanffy's General System Theory. One of these is Bertalanffy's fundamental distinction between open systems which interrelated with the environment and closed systems, like cybernetics, which did not. For Bogdanov this distinction did not exist; all systems were 'open'; they all interrelated with the environment. The only difference concerned the time-scales. Whereas in some cases, the interaction was instantaneous, in others it might take millenia.

In General System Theory mathematics plays a much bigger part than in tectology. Bertalanffy is eager to express all relations in mathematical formulae, and his text is replete with equations and graphs to illustrate his arguments. However, the observation that digestion was impossible to model mathematically because it never reached a state of equilibrium suggests that Bertalanffy agreed with Bogdanov that mathematics was a science of neutral complexes.[78]

Because of its proposition that there are no identical complexes, tectology is much more aware of the limitations of quantification. Bogdanov questions, for example, whether two women and two unicellular embryos at the initial stage of development within their organisms can really be considered as four persons.[79] Elsewhere he remarks that the number of residents of a town can be determined with complete accuracy; but that is only because we arbitrarily take as identical units for our counting complexes that we know to be not only heterogeneous but even incommensurate: the personality of a mature adult, the impersonal being of a newly-born baby, the disintegrating person of an old man in his dotage, the thinker of genius, the idiot, the athlete, the dwarf etc.[80]

Bogdanov's tectology could not be described, as Bertalanffy defines General System Theory, as a 'logico-mathematical discipline'. Bogdanov does not think

---

77   Bogdanov 1920a, pp. 63–4.
78   Bertalanffy 1968, p. 142.
79   Bogdanov 1989, 1, p. 123.
80   Bogdanov 1989, 1, p. 183. Bogdanov's contemporary Bertrand Russell says much the same thing: 'When actual objects are counted, or when Geometry and Dynamics are applied to actual space or actual matter, or when, in any other way, mathematical reasoning is applied to what exists, the reasoning employed has a form not dependent upon the objects to which it is applied being just those objects that they are, but only upon their having certain general properties'. See Russell 1903, p. vii.

that the real world is amenable to description entirely in terms of mathematics or logic. Logic and mathematics are abstractions from reality, and we do not, and never shall, live in an environment that is so absolutely comprehensible as Avenarius's 'perfect constant'. For Bogdanov every form of organisation presupposes an area of disorganisation or resistance, and it is this sphere that is the permanent challenge to human ingenuity.

For, looked at differently, it is in the sphere of disorganisation and resistance that the opportunities to organise the elements differently lie, to devise alternative organisational forms that will be more expedient for the tasks that confront mankind. It is the existence of this sphere that makes it possible to devise alternative approaches to science that will be better adapted to the interests of the working class than the ones that presently exist. Tectology is a dynamic science, one that is in keeping with Bogdanov's conception of the dynamic social ideal.

Another difference between tectology and General System Theory is that in Bogdanov's work the organisational forms are well developed and are richly illustrated by concrete examples, whereas Bertalanffy's theory treats the subject of system mainly at a general level. The set of concepts he offers, and believes to be 'remarkably complete', are 'wholeness', 'sum', 'centralisation', 'differentiation', 'leading part', 'closed and open system', 'finality', 'equifinality', 'growth in time', 'relative growth', and 'competition'. In other words, the principles of system science that Bertalanffy suggests are only a fraction of those to be found in *Tectology*.

The lack of development of Bertalanffy's General System Theory can probably be attributed to the conditions in which it emerged. Bertalanffy recalls that in contrast to the 1930s, when he first came up with the concept of General System Theory, the period after the Second World War saw an upsurge of interest in model building and abstract generalisation. A number of scientists had followed the same lines of thought as Bertalanffy, and General System Theory was no longer a personal idiosyncrasy, but a trend in modern thinking.[81] Different people developed various aspects of what is in tectology individual organisational forms. The most obvious example of this is the development of the mechanism that Bogdanov calls the 'bi-regulator' into the discipline of cybernetics by Eric Ashby. Bertalanffy in General System Theory also refers to the book by K.E. Boulding, *The Organizational Revolution*, which argued that there was an optimum size to which organisations could grow, beyond which they would become inefficient through the over-extension of their lines of commu-

---

81   Bertalanffy 1968, p. 96.

nication.[82] This, of course, was a phenomenon already covered by Bogdanov in *Tectology* under the heading 'The Limits of Egression'.

The development of system theory by Bertalanffy and others has vindicated both Bogdanov's conception of a universal science of organisation and his ideas of individual organisational forms. But whereas tectology presents its material as a coherent and integrated whole, Western system theory is scattered and fragmented in the works of numerous writers and practitioners. In a passage in *General System Theory* that Bogdanov would no doubt have seen as highly ironic, Bertalanffy surveyed the general trend in the organisational outlook on the world. This trend, he said, was marked by the emergence of a bundle of new disciplines such as cybernetics, information theory, General System Theory, theories of games, of decision, of queuing and others; in practical application, systems analysis, systems engineering, mathematical techniques and aims.[83] In other words, the fragmentation of knowledge that Bogdanov had set out to overcome was being perpetuated in the West by offshoots of General System Theory, which was also designed to overcome the fragmentation of knowledge into separate disciplines.

Comparisons between tectology and General System Theory are instructive in bringing out the more comprehensive nature of Bogdanov's work. Bogdanov is able to countenance a greater range of phenomena and situations than Bertalanffy. Bogdanov is justly seen as a pioneer in the field of systems thinking, and it is this more than anything else that has stimulated a revived interest in Bogdanov's ideas after a long period of oblivion. A result of this, however, has been to place the ideas of *Tectology* in the context of a later epoch, rather than in the context of Bogdanov's own times. After all, Bogdanov could not possibly have seen himself as a precursor of Bertalanffy; but he did think of himself as someone who had improved upon Hegel's system, which he regarded as a forerunner of his own. To see *Tectology* in the light of what had gone before rather than what came after, it is worth surveying briefly the relationship of *Tectology* to Hegelian philosophy.

There are features that Bogdanov's and Hegel's systems have in common. Like *Tectology*, Hegel's system is multi-disciplinary; it aims to bring together Logic, the natural sciences, politics and society in an all-embracing whole. Running through the entire edifice is the unifying movement of the Concept. This, in tectological terms, would be Hegel's 'organisational form'. The limitation of Hegel's method is that this is his *only* organisational form. By way of contrast,

---

82   Bertalanffy 1968, p. 47.
83   Bertalanffy 1968, p. 96.

tectology has a whole panoply of organisational forms, which, if need be, could be modified or increased; it is an extremely flexible system that envisages an infinitely varied and changing world.

A great advantage that Bogdanov had over Hegel was that he could incorporate Darwin's theory of natural selection. Hegel, on the other hand, belonged to the pre-Darwinian age, and he could treat 'nature' as a synonym for 'essence', something that did not change. After Darwin this was no longer possible, and Hegel's followers struggled to bring *Naturphilosophie* into line with this important development in science. The Darwinian concepts of selection and adaptation to an environment are central to tectology. Bogdanov's originality was to see that these concepts were universal and applied to both living and non-living nature.

There is also a fundamental point of difference between tectology and the Hegelian system on the question of historical progress. For Hegel history has a definite direction, which will culminate in the triumph of reason and freedom. Bogdanov could offer no such certainty; history would not deliver up anything without effort. Progress was the preponderance of organisation over the forces of disruption, and regression was also possible. Progress cannot be taken for granted; humanity will have to take some firm action to ensure that things are organised.

By publishing a serialised version of *Tectology* in the Proletkult journal *Proletarskaia Kultura* and in an abridged book form through the Proletkult in Samara,[84] Bogdanov obviously tried to interest Russian workers in his ideas. But whatever impact they might have had among individual workers, tectology did not become the basis for a proletarian science that Bogdanov had hoped. This is hardly surprising. A more erudite book it would be hard to imagine. To appreciate it fully one would have to have at least some knowledge of physics, chemistry and biology, but an acquaintance with economics, astronomy and linguistics would not go amiss. In other words, readers would have to already possess the kind of knowledge in which *Tectology* was intended to school them.

---

84   Bogdanov 1921. There is an excellent English translation of this edition by George Gorelik. See Bogdanov 1984.

The Philosophy of Living Experience

1 Philosophy in Tectological Perspective

Shortly after the appearance of the first part of *Tectology* Bogdanov published the popular survey of the history of philosophy entitled *The Philosophy of Living Experience*. Much of the content of this book had already appeared elsewhere, so that it is a kind of compilation of Bogdanov's most characteristic ideas. In that respect K.M. Jensen's commentary on the book serves as an introduction to Bogdanov's philosophical ideas as a whole.[1] But although the themes in *The Philosophy of Living Experience* are familiar they are presented there in a particular and novel way: what Jensen has missed is that they have been re-cast in the light of *Tectology*, or more precisely, the philosophical presuppositions of tectology. In *Tectology* Bogdanov treats the unity of the physical and psychical realms as the interchange of activity and resistance, or as the combination of organisation and disorganisation. *The Philosophy of Living Experience* looks back over the history of philosophy and judges to what extent thinkers of the past have contributed to this point of view. Bogdanov is also concerned to show the social context from which the various schools of philosophy emerged.

In the introductory chapter Bogdanov begins his history of philosophy by answering the question: what existed before the appearance of philosophy? Predictably, he refers to Noiré's theory of the origin of language, but here stresses the organising function of language: 'Labour interjections, in contrast to cries of emotion, not only could, but necessarily *had to change* and develop with progress and the increasing complexity of production. They *organised* production, served as a means of systematically uniting the efforts, helping to establish the rhythm of common action'.[2]

Much of the introductory section is devoted to the evolution of the concept of causality, which Bogdanov explains as a reflection of the way society organised its labour relations in different historical eras. Originally, people found the connection of cause and effect ready made in their social environment, in the labour relations of the patriarchal commune. With the emergence of a partic-

---

1 Jensen 1978.
2 Bogdanov 1920a, p. 18.

ular manager or organiser, who would show others what they needed to do and issue instructions, primitive society became authoritarian. When faced with a permanent relationship between two processes, one following the other, a person inevitably explained it in authoritarian terms: as an act of an organising will and an act of implementation. Bogdanov illustrates this with a line taken from the Estonian national epic *Kalevi-poeg*: 'The wind orders the leaves to rustle'.[3]

Authoritarian causality gave rise to the first genuine worldviews. They were characterised by an animistic and religious nature, and encouraged the dualistic conception of a body and a soul. The emancipation of causality from its religious associations was facilitated by the growth of exchange relations and dependence on the market. How commodities were exchanged and for what price lay beyond human control. It was not possible to see the living economic connection between people, and instead people thought of causality in terms of an abstract necessity, and no longer as a concrete relationship of collaboration in an authoritarian community. Like the older form of causality, however, the new one was transferred from the economic realm to all other spheres of experience.

Unlike the authoritarian concept of causality, which presupposed a first cause in the shape of an ultimate authority, the organiser, the new abstract one had no such supposition, and the chain of causes and effects could be followed to infinity. For that reason, the abstract form of causality was incomparably more progressive than the authoritarian one, though the old authoritarian conception continued to linger on.

In the first chapter entitled 'What is Materialism?' Bogdanov begins by equating labour with organisation by saying that: 'All types of labour boil down to humanity's changing the inter-relationships of some elements of nature, rearranging them, establishing between them new mutual relationships etc ... Consequently, labour in general organises the world for mankind'. Continuing in the tectological vein, Bogdanov went on to argue that 'Labour is effort, that is, it necessarily overcomes some kind of resistance; otherwise it would not be labour. Nature, as the object of all the efforts of humanity, is the world of resistance or, what is the same thing, the kingdom of matter'.[4] Repeating a metaphor he had used in *Tectology*, he emphasised that:

> There cannot be activity without the matter which it overcomes; one cannot conceive of matter without the activity directed upon it; the one and

---

3   Bogdanov 1920a, p. 22.
4   Bogdanov 1920a, p. 45.

the other are relative. In the collision of two activities each of them is matter from the point of view of the other. So in the battle of two armies each regards the other exclusively as a material barrier which has to be overcome.[5]

In accordance with his criterion of objectivity, Bogdanov stressed that the idea of 'matter' was correlated with social labour and expressed resistance encountered not merely by individual activity but by social activity. Images in dreams might seem to provide the greatest possible resistance to individual efforts to struggle against them, but they did not present any kind of opposition from the perspective of the collective, and therefore they were characterised as non-material.

In the process of organising the world for its own purposes, humanity comes up against the materiality of nature – that is, against nature's resistance to organising activity, or labour. In this circumstance is based one of the main traditions of philosophical thought, materialism, which holds that 'everything is matter'. Because consistent materialism substituted matter, the side of resistance for the organising side of human labour, Bogdanov described it as a substitution. In the same way, the idealist viewpoint, which held that 'everything is spirit' and explained things in terms of activity, organisation, was also a type of substitution. However, of the two substitutions Bogdanov found the materialist one closer to his own point of view.

Bogdanov conceded that his conception of materialism would not be universally accepted; Plekhanov's school would certainly dispute it. As he observed:

> Here in Russia there are some moderate materialists, comprising something of a school, headed by Plekhanov. Several times I asked them to explain what matter is which they say is the foundation of everything. After prolonged failure I got the following answer: and this is really what it is literally: matter is matter, and being primary, cannot be defined. When I expressed doubt that thinking people would be satisfied with such an explanation, since it lacked any sense or content, my interlocutor supplemented his answer with a whole series of epithets which are scarcely acceptable in society, addressed, however, only to my modest self, and not to the question.[6]

---

5   Bogdanov 1920a, p. 65.
6   Bogdanov 1920a, p. 56.

One of the misconceptions of Plekhanov and his school was the belief in absolute truth. However, since in experience everything was relative, depended on conditions and was determined by something else, there could be nothing that was absolute. For Bogdanov, the concept of 'the absolute' was a fetish of perception, which he compared to Marx's idea of commodity fetishism.

The corollary was that if people lived in collectives and were always conscious of being a member of a collective, then no fetishism could enter their conceptions of matter. But with the disintegration of collectives people's view of the world had fragmented. In modern society individuals in their personal experience only encountered an extremely small part of the kingdom of matter, and viewed the world from an individualist point of view.

In the chapter on 'The materialism of the ancient world' Bogdanov reviewed the contribution of the Greek philosophers to philosophical thought that had a bearing on the views that he now held. Thales had espoused a monist theory that had much in common with materialism and was based on an original universal substitution. This was that everything was water. Anaximedes propounded a similar theory, also based on a substitution: that everything was ultimately composed of air.

Bogdanov attributed special importance to Democritus, who had an atomic theory of the universe. Greek atomism, Bogdanov believed, had its origins in the technical-labour process. Labour involved the breaking of things down into their constituent parts and reassembling them in a different form. In this way 'analysis' and 'synthesis' were of the essence of labour activity in general. People were organised in this way too: in creating an army individuals were taken out of their accustomed groupings and organised in military formations. Thinking was also an organising activity: it dealt with complexes of experience by the same methods as in production. Atomism was a particular case of intellectually breaking the world down into elements and then systematically combining them to reconstruct a perceptive picture of the world.

In later times, following the development of exchange relations and the appearance of economic individualism, people began to think of themselves as atoms. The most prominent example of this approach was Leibnitz's theory of monads, each of which acted as an autonomous unit, independently of other individuals.

For Democritus atoms were governed by natural necessity; because they were of different kinds and fell at different speeds, they readily combined, in this way forming the universe. Epicurus, on the other hand, believed that atoms were homogeneous and fell at the same speed, obliging him to suppose that they combined together by means of deviations from their perpendicular fall, though the reason for this deviation he could not explain.

Empedocles was able to provide a theory that accounted for the way in which atoms could combine to form the material world. He held that life was created by the opposing forces of love and hate; love brought elements together and combined them, hate separated and dispersed them. According to Bogdanov, in modern philosophical language, the two forces would be called 'attraction' and 'repulsion'. By their action all kinds of combinations were generated, but the majority of them were insubstantial, unstable and inexpedient and so were unable to survive. The combinations that survived were those that were harmonious, elegant and expedient. Thus, without any conscious intention on the part of nature, forms were elaborated that were adapted for life.[7]

This idea, Bogdanov pointed out, was the first germ of what would become Darwin's theory of natural selection. He believed that the Greeks, like Darwin, had taken the idea from their social environment. But whereas Darwin's social environment had been capitalist production, for the Greeks it had been their encounter with communities of primitive peoples, which they plundered. These communities were much less capable of resisting attack than the Greek colonial organisations.[8] Of course, Empedocles' conception did not just anticipate Darwin; it also anticipated Bogdanov's concept of 'selection' as it appeared in *Tectology*.

Bogdanov found Greek sensualism also to have given rise to ideas that reappeared in more recent philosophical systems. The sensualists saw the world in terms of their own personal experience, rather than as members of the human community. The Sophist Protagoras coined the phrase: 'Man is the measure of all things', which Bogdanov re-stated as 'all things are relative to human beings'. This, he maintained, was the formula for the *relativism* of knowledge. Protagoras also held that no truth was universally obligatory for all people. This, according to Bogdanov, was the formula of *scepticism*, the denial of objectivity in perception, which was to play a major part in later philosophical thought.[9]

2   The Materialism of Modern Times

Bogdanov began his survey of the materialism of modern times with an account of Francis Bacon's contribution to the progress of philosophy. He expressed approval of Bacon's insistence that induction was the only rational

---

7   Bogdanov 1920a, p. 86.
8   Bogdanov 1920a, p. 88.
9   Bogdanov 1920a, p. 95.

method for the study of nature, that one must ascend from the observation of separate facts to ever broader generalisations. One can see in this endorsement the recognition that Bacon was a pioneer of the philosophy of 'pure experience'. He also advocated the elimination from thinking of 'idols', or, in Bogdanov's terminology, 'fetishes'. Another point in Bacon's favour was that he conducted research into the most varied fields of experience, and considered it possible and necessary to apply the same methods to the knowledge of people and society.

For Bogdanov Hobbes expressed the spirit of the merchant capitalist era when a new technology based on precise measurement and numerical computation was coming into being. Consequently, his materialism was of an abstractly geometrical character; his entire methodology boiled down to mathematics, to geometrical construction and to computation. It was in this abstract light that he viewed the particles that made up physical bodies. Although a defender of absolute monarchy, Hobbes's philosophy was anti-religious, and so facilitated the development of atheism.[10]

Bogdanov could also regard Locke as a forerunner of the doctrine of 'pure experience'. In his campaign against the doctrine of innate ideas, Locke had argued that in its pristine state the psyche was a 'tabula rasa', like a blank sheet of paper on which nothing had yet been written. The entire content of the psyche was obtained through external sensations and consisted, on one hand, of perceptions, and on the other hand of reflections relating to those perceptions, that is, the thinking that processes them. Locke's sensualism was based on an individualist understanding of experience; he overlooked completely the social character of thinking.[11]

Like Locke, though more thoroughly and fully, Hume had analysed indiviual-psychical experience to which he had reduced all experience in general. For Bogdanov's purpose there were two points in Hume's work that were of interest: one was his treatment of the 'I', the other was his explanation of causality.

On the first point, in his *Treatise of Human Nature*, Hume had humorously refuted those philosophers who supposed that human beings perceived their 'I' as a special, constant reality identical with themselves. He argued that in experience one found no such thing; that what was experienced was a bundle of sensations, but nothing that could be called an 'I'. As far as causality was concerned, Hume saw this only as an accustomed series of perceptions. If event A was invariably followed by event B, there was no reason to suppose that they were connected by objective necessity. The conviction that such a necessity existed only arose through their constant conjunction.

---

10   Bogdanov 1920a, pp. 115, 134.
11   Bogdanov 1920a, pp. 119–20, 134.

One can see why Bogdanov should think these two aspects of Hume's philosophy significant. The reduction of the 'I' to a collection of sensations was an idea central to Mach's, and later to his own, ideas of perception. And Hume's concept of causality was consistent with the method of pure experience.

The flourishing of English materialism in the seventeenth century encouraged the development of French materialism in the eighteenth. For Bogdanov the most important feature of French materialism was its systematising character, which was embodied in the two great works of the age: The *Great Encyclopaedia* and the *System of Nature*. Systematising was necessary, because of the educating and propagandising role that these works were intended to play. This was to unite the social forces in France under the new worldview of the bourgeoisie. While it was impossible to create a political organisation strong enough to defeat the feudal classes and the state machinery that supported them, it was feasible to undermine the ideological doctrines supporting the old regime. This could be done with a system, a complete and coherent worldview, that could discredit the authoritarian tradition that had been built up over the centuries. Obviously what Bogdanov has in mind here is a French revolutionary prototype of his own conception of proletarian culture.

In view of the fact that Holbach, the main author of the *System of Nature*, was held by Plekhanov to propound a materialism that was the forerunner of Marx's dialectical materialism, Bogdanov did not miss the opportunity to imply that Holbach's materialism was not as consistent as Plekhanov made out. There were, he said, sceptical nuances in the *System of Nature* that under other conditions could have led the way to faith. Thus, the authors held that the essence of matter is unknown and is not even knowable. All that is known are the sensations generated by matter, the results of its actions on the sensory organs. In itself, however, matter remains beyond perception. Having located matter in the realm of 'things-in-themselves', Bogdanov argued, the way had been left open for some kind of religiously tinged abstraction to find a place for itself. This is what Immanuel Kant had done in similar circumstances. For him, the unknowable 'things-in-themselves' turned out to be an arena hospitable to faith, and, by means of practical reason, he brought into that arena the image of God, the immortality of the soul, and free will. Once something is acknowledged to be in principle inaccessible to experience, by the same token it is acknowledged that it is accessible only to faith.[12] In this passage Bogdanov contrives implicitly to attack not only Plekhanov's espousal of Holbach, but also his agreement with Kant's doctrine of 'things-in-themselves'.

---

12   Bogdanov 1920a, p. 129.

In the chapter on empiriocriticism Bogdanov elaborated on the commentary he had given earlier on that school of thought in *Empiriomonism*, though
this time with the insights he had gained from working on *Tectology*. This is
noticeable in the way he finds the empiriocritics' concept of elements deficient. This deficiency was that they were immobile, static, and alien to change;
in other words, the empiriocritics had not treated elements as activities, and
for that reason he thought them insufficient to express reality.

In the tradition of Bacon, the empiriocritics sought to remove from perception all the sources of misrepresentation of experience, such as adding to it
something that was not given in it. This was necessary in order to arrive at the
reliable knowledge that would be given by pure experience. Like Hume, the
empiriocritics rejected the notion of causality, but went even further by arguing
that explanations should be abandoned in favour of pure description: that it
was legitimate to pose the question 'how?' but not 'why?' It was also a contention of the empiriocritics that they had avoided the distortion of materialist
substitution in their approach, since they regarded the elements of experience
as fusions of both psychical and physical series.

Bogdanov contested the claim of the empiriocriticist school that it had been
able to avoid both materialist and idealist forms of substitution. He pointed
out that Avenarius's *Critique of Pure Experience* was based on the idea that
changes in the psychical, 'dependent series' involved corresponding changes
in the physical, 'independent series' or the nervous-physiological system. How,
Bogdanov inquired, did this differ from materialist substitution? It was only
in the form of expression, in the reluctance of the empiriocritics to admit
that changes in the psyche were brought about by, or were to be explained by,
changes in the nervous system. Hence, Bogdanov contended, empiriocriticism
ought to be regarded as an extension of materialism.

In Bogdanov's view, the idea of pure description was sheer utopia, the essence of which was that it was a passive, or in Marx's expression, a 'contemplative' view of experience. Perception organised experience, whereas pure
description had the aim of slavishly subordinating itself to experience, to
reflect it. In organising experience into a coherent whole perception inevitably
transformed and supplemented it to some extent, otherwise it could never master it. Bogdanov here gave as an example Newton's theory of gravity. This, he
said, could be a great truth, although in nature there was probably not a single
movement that completely conformed to Newton's scheme. Similarly, not one
chemical formula was a pure copy of any actually occurring chemical reaction.
In general, not one abstraction of perception was any kind of concrete reality.[13]

---

13   Bogdanov 1920a, p. 150.

The principle of pure description was related to that of the economy of thought: that one must eliminate from perception all that was superfluous so that one could assimilate experience with the minimum of energy. But, Bogdanov argued, economy need not mean the simple reduction of expenditure. Mankind in its historical development had constantly increased the sum of its labour, its efforts, and this had been more than requited by the results. The victory over nature was not to be achieved by small savings in energy, but by putting it to the greatest productive use.[14]

Bogdanov then turned his attention to Avenarius's 'first empiriocritical axiom', with which he had begun his *Critique of Pure Experience*. This was that originally man found himself in a particular environment consisting of different parts, among which were fellow-men with their utterances, which he understood as relating to the parts of the environment. Could one really consider, Bogdanov asked, such a view of the world as 'original', when the history of culture unambiguously showed how impossible this characterisation was?

To be aware of oneself and one's fellow men presupposed the concept of an 'I' distinct from other people. It also presupposed the abstraction of 'man' from particular living people. But to attribute these ideas to primitive man was deeply mistaken; he had not yet separated himself as an independent entity, as a special 'I' from that close tribal group to which he belonged. Primitive man 'originally finds himself' in this group, the community united by blood, and not simply in a particular environment, but in a desperate, exhausting struggle with the environment.

Things were no better with Avenarius's concept of 'utterances' relating to particular parts of the environment. Recalling Noiré's theory of the origins of language, Bogdanov stated that the first human utterances did not relate to the environment, but to the common working activities of the group, and were not individual, but collective. Consequently, the conception of the primitive state of the world presented by Avenarius and his school was factually incorrect and highly anachronistic.[15]

Bogdanov's overall conception of empiriocriticism, which he formulated in the tectological terms of 'activity' and 'resistance', was that the idea of pure experience to which people brought nothing of themselves was a fetishised abstraction. The essence of experience was *labour*; experience arose where human effort overcame the spontaneous resistance of nature. It was the relationship of human activity with nature, but this activity was not personal, but

---

14   Bogdanov 1920a, p. 152.
15   Bogdanov 1920a, pp. 152–3.

collective, something inaccessible to the consciousness of the individualist. Consequently, 'pure experience' without any 'additions' was just as impossible as resistance without the effort to which it related.[16]

The title of the chapter 'Dialectical Materialism' implies that Bogdanov took the term that Plekhanov had coined as the way that Marx and Engels genuinely designated their system. This was no doubt a tribute to Plekhanov's persuasiveness. However, the title suited Bogdanov's purposes, because the chapter is a critique of the Hegelian tradition in philosophy to which Plekhanov belonged.

To Bogdanov dialectics was nothing other than an organisational process going on by means of contradictions, or, what was the same thing, by means of a struggle of different tendencies. He found the origins of this approach in the philosophical thought of Anaximander and especially of Heraclitus the Obscure. After Heraclitus the dialectical scheme was encountered, sometimes in a disguised form, in the majority of thinkers of ancient and modern times. But the dialectical viewpoint in which this scheme was all-embracing was to be found in the philosophy of the German idealists: Fichte, Schelling and especially Hegel.

Bogdanov's treatment of the German idealists is remarkably cursory, considering that in many respects they anticipated the multi-disciplinary system of tectology. Although he notes that Schelling constructed a scheme of nature that displayed a progression of forms from inorganic matter, through light, electricity and chemical affinities right up to the living individual, he does not remark on how close this comes to his own methods in *Tectology*. He omits to mention too Schelling's insistence on an active as opposed to a static approach to knowledge.

Bogdanov is more appreciative of Hegel's system, but he does not elaborate on the way Hegel succeeded in incorporating the very different spheres of logic, natural science and political philosophy under the unifying principle of the movement of the Concept. This movement of the Concept is what Hegel understood by 'dialectics'. Bogdanov mentions that Hegel's Concept 'is not what we usually understand by the term', and attributes this strange use of terminology to Hegel's idealist substitution. He recognises that the 'development of concepts' is dialectics, but instead of mentioning the phases Universality, Particularity and Individuality, which Hegel actually used, he states that the phases are Thesis, Antithesis and Synthesis. This terminology was not used by Hegel, but it was commonly attributed to him, probably through the equation of Hegelian dialectics with its Greek antecedents.[17]

---

16   Bogdanov 1920a, pp. 164–5.
17   Bogdanov 1920a, pp. 178–9.

With Engels in mind, Bogdanov observed that some writers had tried to separate Hegel's dialectics from his idealist system, recognising the former and rejecting the latter. This he considered to be a mistaken distinction; Hegel's dialectics was idealist, and could not have been otherwise: the model for it had been the process of discussion and contemplation belonging to the sphere of ideology.[18]

Although Marx called his doctrine 'materialism', Bogdanov pointed out, its central concept was not 'matter', but practice, activity, living labour: this was an *active* view of the world. The method by which it is constructed Marx called materialist dialectics in contrast to the idealist dialectics of Hegel. Both one and the other defined dialectics as *development through contradictions*; but whereas for Hegel it was a matter of contradictions of the internal development of concepts, for Marx the contradictions are of real life, of the struggle of real forces.

In Bogdanov's view Marx's dialectics retained many features of Hegel's, especially the scheme of the 'triad'. The whole structure of *Das Kapital* is suffused with the triad; the main one summing up the course of social development as a whole. The 'thesis' is the link of the producers with the means of production; the 'antithesis' is the expropriation of the producers with the transition to large-scale production in capitalism; the 'synthesis' is the expropriation of the expropriators, the restoration of the link of the producers with the means of production, of the transfer of these latter into the hands of the whole society, the socialist organisation. The development of exchange and capitalism was set out also in a number of similar triadic schemes.

Comparing Marx's dialectics as an organising process with his own tectological approach, Bogdanov posed the question of how far the two methods coincided. He had to admit that they were not quite the same, because Hegel and Marx spoke in terms of development rather than organisation. However, Bogdanov found that 'development' was a rather imprecise term, and that both Hegel and Marx had failed to achieve complete clarity because of their reliance on a method that could produce vague or contradictory results.[19]

This brought Bogdanov to an examination of *Anti-Dühring*, in which Engels had defended materialist dialectics. Taking the reader through the examples Engels gives from mathematics and the natural sciences, including that of the grain of barley, Bogdanov shows that the way in which Engels uses the terms 'negation' and 'synthesis' are arbitrary and subjective. Hegel could apply his dia-

---

18   Bogdanov 1920a, p. 181.
19   Bogdanov 1920a, p. 189.

lectical formula with conviction, because he was dealing in mental constructs, whereas Marx and Engels professed to be dealing with the real world.[20]

Bogdanov then turned his attention to the Plekhanov school of dialecticians. There was, he said, a very curious position adopted by a group of Russian writers, who purport to be firm supporters of dialectical materialism and even guardians of its traditions: Plekhanov, Ortodoks, Lenin and a few others. In its essential points they radically depart from Marx's doctrine and return to the materialism of the eighteenth century. This, on the one hand, is the conception of matter as the 'thing-in-itself', and, on the other hand, as the conception of the absolute nature of truth.[21]

Bogdanov concluded his disquisition on dialectics with the position he had first enunciated in his earliest writings, re-cast in the tectological mould. This was that dialectics was an organisational process, carried on by means of a struggle of opposites. As soon as one took this into account it became clear that dialectics was not at all something universal, but a particular case of organising processes, which could also proceed by other means.[22]

3   Empiriomonism

The chapter on Empirionism is not a summary of his book with that title, but an elaboration of some of the arguments that Bogdanov put forward there, now informed by conceptions of tectology. In the section on 'Labour Causality' the idea of activity-resistance has been applied to the question of cause and effect. In the socialist collective based on comradely cooperation, the old fetishistic and authoritarian notions of causality will be surpassed by the new conception that the forces of nature will be harnessed to overcome the resistance of nature, so that cause and consequence will be the same.

In the light of tectology the conceptions of what the elements of experience were could be made more precise. Whereas the empiriocritics had conceived elements as static entities, Bogdanov argued that all elements, such as colours, shapes and sounds, had to be arrived at as a result of some labour activity either in the present or in the past – that they were crystallised labour activity.

In a section discussing the criteria for the objectivity of experience Bogdanov re-stated his contention that objective experience was experience that was

---

20   Bogdanov 1920a, pp. 192–8.
21   Bogdanov 1920a, p. 202.
22   Bogdanov 1920a, p. 204.

socially valid. He was able to show by quotations from the *Theses on Feuerbach* and *Das Kapital* that this idea was shared by Marx. It was, he said, ironic that people like Plekhanov who claimed to be followers of Marx should reject the idea. To Plekhanov's contention that the laws of gravity existed before human ity, Bogdanov pointed out that if one ignored the 'social practice' of measurement, the establishment of units of measures, calculations, etc., nothing of the law of gravity would remain. Therefore, if it was said that the law of gravity operated before there were human beings, this is not the same as saying that it was independent of human beings.[23]

The idea that people's thinking was a reflection of their relations of production was a doctrine that Bogdanov called 'sociomorphism': he believed it to be universal. The original identity of social practice and thinking can be traced to the beginning of language and the work exclamations of primitive peoples. In later times productive relations had continued to provide a model for the ideology of the day, be it authoritarian or individualistic. From this Bogdanov could conclude that sociomorphism was a necessary and universal law of the organisation of experience. It could be formulated in the following way: thought takes its form in the last analysis from social practice; or, the connection of elements of experience in perception has at its basis the inter-relationship of the elements of social activity in the labour process.[24]

In a section devoted to substitution, Bogdanov brought this concept into closer alignment with those in *Tectology*. The premiss of substitution was that in the attempt to make sense of the enormous quantity and variety of the material presented by experience with its contradictions and resistances, perception actively changed and replaced the available elements and combinations.

By a series of examples Bogdanov showed how the development of science proceeded by making increasingly detailed and accurate substitutions, going further and further into the depths of the phenomena studied. As substitutions became more sophisticated they embraced content that was more involved and richer, but less definite and organised. Bogdanov explained this by saying that since knowledge was the product of effort, the result of the struggle with nature, it was like the production of all other products: success demanded the richest possible material to work on and the lowest possible resistance to its processing. Substitution sought to replace less content with more content, so that the material for processing would be richer. At the same time the more

---

23   Bogdanov 1920a, pp. 220–3.
24   Bogdanov 1920a, p. 229.

stable and more coherently organised complexes were replaced by less stable and less organised ones that would offer less resistance for the productive activity of thought.[25]

The picture of the world presented by empiriomonism was one of an ascending scale of organisation. At its lowest level it was a chaotic mass of elements with infinitely little organisation. Above this came the level of inorganic matter in which the organisation of elements was already present, but in primitive and lower forms. These elements possessed more or less stability and displayed some resistance to the environment, but no more. They did not show any tendency to overcome the environment, to master its material, or to progress at its expense.

At the next level came life, which in turn had various levels of organisation, from simple cells to the human organism. The highest level of all was the human collective. In the human collective, in labour and in perception, humanity worked out its own 'reality', its own objective experience, in strict conformity with the laws governing that experience, and with its coherent organisation.

Empiriomonism, Bogdanov held, was the social-labour view of the world. It was characterised by the features he had set out, i.e. the labour view of causality, the criterion of objectivity as being socially valid, the elimination of abstract fetishism, the doctrine of sociomorphism of thought, and the theory of universal substitution.

4   The Science of the Future

In the last chapter of *The Philosophy of Living Experience* Bogdanov rehearses the arguments in favour of developing a universal science of organisation. In speaking of specialisation he stresses its positive side, saying that specialisation is an essential stage in the development of labour and of perception. As a result of it, in each sphere of experience a growing quantity of material can accumulate and methods can attain an inconceivably higher level of perfection and precision. However, specialisation stands in contradiction to the unifying tendency in perception; it rends experience into fragments and each of these organises itself independently. This gives rise to two undesirable consequences: the excessive accumulation of material and to the diversity of the means of perception.

---

25   Bogdanov 1920a, pp. 234–5.

Philosophy is the attempt to bring together the experience that has been disjointed and scattered by specialisation. But philosophy is incapable of performing this function because it is itself the product of fragmented human practicoi it cannot work miracloo. The oituation, however, io changod by the emergence of machine industry. Since the workers now supervise the activities of the machines, the difference between the worker and the engineer disappears. The division of labour ceases to be the division of the person, and becomes simply the division of effort directed towards different objects. The effort itself remains essentially homogeneous. Overcoming specialisation by bringing the various fields of knowledge together is one of the most important requirements of the new proletarian culture. The activity of workers will be increasingly of an organisational nature, and this demands the unification of the whole of humanity's organisational experience in a special general science of organisation. Philosophy, Bogdanov declared, was in its last days; even *Empiriomonism* was no longer a philosophical work, but a transitional form on the way to the new organisational science. By the time *The Philosophy of Living Experience* was published the first volume of *Tectology* had already appeared.[26]

It is worth remarking on some peculiarities of the way Bogdanov arranges his material in *The Philosophy of Living Experience*. The two chapters 'The Materialism of the Ancient World' and 'Modern Materialism' follow quite closely the corresponding sections of Friedrich Lange's *History of Materialism*. As Lange's book was published in 1873, one does not know if he would have agreed with Bogdanov in including the empiriocritics in the materialist current. However, the book by Lesevich, *What is Scientific Philosophy?* places Mach and Avenarius squarely within the Positivist tradition of Auguste Comte. Bogdanov himself in *Empiriomonism* describes the philosophy of Mach and Avenarius as the 'latest form of positivism'. In *The Philosophy of Living Experience*, however, these thinkers had become materialists, and indeed criticised for their espousal of 'materialist substitution'.

Probably Bogdanov's arrangement is partly defensive and partly offensive. Placing the empiriocritics in the materialist camp was no doubt in response to Lenin's condemnation of them, and, by association, Bogdanov himself, as idealists. But Bogdanov was also following an offensive tactic by arguing that both Marx and himself subscribed to an active concept of materialism, whereas Plekhanov, Lenin and their associates were materialists only of the contemplative type.

---

26   Bogdanov 1920a, pp. 248–55.

5   A Decade of Excommunication from Marxism

In response to his exclusion from *Pravda* in the spring of 1914, Bogdanov wrote a pamphlet which he intended to publish legally in the autumn of that year.[27] It was entitled 'A Decade of Excommunication from Marxism: A Jubilee Symposium (1904–1914)'. The title alluded to the quasi-religious attitudes that his opponents had to Marxism, and the way that they treated his writings as some kind of heresy. The decade in question marked the period from the first attack on *Empiriomonism* by Ortodoks in 1904 to the latest condemnation of his system in 1914. The pamphlet was aimed at a worker audience, and the exposition was in the 'democratic' style that Bogdanov had used for his popular textbooks. In places the pamphlet presented in democratic form material that had previously appeared in other works, such as *The Adventures of One Philosophical School*, *The Fall of the Great Fetish*, *Cultural Tasks of Our Times* and *The Philosophy of Living Experience*; the influence of *Tectology* is also in evidence.

The pamphlet did not appear in 1914 as intended because of the severe censorship restrictions imposed by the tsarist government after the outbreak of the First World War; and publication would have been impossible in Soviet times, also for reasons of censorship. It first saw the light of day in 1995 as one of the volumes in the collection of Bogdanov's unpublished writings, *The Unknown Bogdanov*. Although it did not have the role intended for it, the work is a valuable source for Bogdanov's intellectual biography, and it gives a bird's eye view of his system of thought in the period prior to the First World War and the Russian revolution.

'A Decade of Excommunication from Marxism' is structured to resemble the kind of proceedings that would be applied to religious heretics. The first chapter, entitled 'What it is That the Excommunication is From' is composed of Bogdanov's own interpretation of Marxism, stressing its openness and flexibility. There then follows a chapter on 'The Crimes of the Excommunicate', in which Bogdanov outlines in 'democratic' language the main points of his system. The third chapter is on 'The Course of the Excommunications', which is divided into two phases: the Plekhanov phase and the Lenin phase. This chapter gives an account of Bogdanov's polemics, first with Plekhanov and then with Lenin. The fourth chapter, 'Fellow Excommunicates', discusses the activities of Lunacharsky, Gorky and of the Vpered group as a whole. In the fifth chapter, 'The Excommunicators' Bogdanov gives characterisations of Plekhanov, Lenin, Aleksinsky and minor figures who have condemned his work.

---

27   Neizvestnyi Bogdanov 1995, 2, p. 241.

The chapter on 'The Crimes of the Excommunicate' is significant because in it Bogdanov was stating what he thought was most important in his system to communicate to his worker audience. In it the ideas of his earlier works were refined and crystallised. Although he still referred to his system as 'empirio-monism' and regarded what he is defending as philosophy, the content of this philosophy has been deeply influenced by *Tectology*. Now the monist principle of empiriomonism is said to be the organisational one. For Bogdanov the world of experience consists of elements which always appear in combinations. As in *Tectology*, it is stated that these combinations could be the solar system or a single atom. Bogdanov also here re-stated his conception that there was no such thing as complete disorganisation accessible to our experience; if such existed we could know nothing of it, because it would show no resistance to our efforts.[28] Later in the chapter Bogdanov informed his readers that he had progressed from *Empiriomonism* to founding a science of organisation.[29]

The most recent and ultimate crime for which Bogdanov had been excommunicated from Marxism was his article on 'Ideology', which he reproduced in his pamphlet. He introduced it by saying that although Marxists were familiar with the idea that ideology was the superstructure over the base of economic forms, they had not attempted to explain what the objective significance of ideology was. This, however, could be done simply from the organisational point of view. This was what the article Bogdanov submitted to *Pravda* had set out to do.

In the article Bogdanov explained that ideology included a number of different phenomena: these were 1) speech, 2) knowledge, 3) art, 4) customs, laws, moral precepts. What they all had in common was that they were varieties of social consciousness. The function of social consciousness was to organise the life of society. Ideally, ideology should be an integral whole; but it could not be if the social organism was divided. Ancient clan communities had been integral and their ideology had been likewise, though in an undeveloped, naive and often religious form. Modern society was divided into classes which organised themselves one against the other, and the same happened with ideology, with social consciousness.

Not only was the everyday knowledge of the worker and the capitalist different; neither was scientific knowledge the same for both. Each, for example, had a different view of political economy. Art, which reflected life and col-

---

28   Neizvestnyi Bogdanov 1995, 3, p. 30.
29   Neizvestnyi Bogdanov 1995, 3, p. 39.

lated experience, and also expressed people's general attitudes, could not be the same for the different classes. Existing art was overwhelmingly bourgeois, whereas proletarian art was still in its infancy. Bourgeois heroes were individuals, whereas the heroes of the proletariat were the masses, organisations. Even language was not the same for all classes of society; words had different connotations for the bourgeoisie and the proletariat.

The lesson Bogdanov drew from this was that the ideology of a class was its class consciousness. It was always formed gradually, imperceptibly, by the thought of the masses and the conscious efforts of ideologues. As long as a class had not formed its own ideology, it would be subjected to the ideology of other, older classes. This weakens and retards the organisation of the young class, because class consciousness is its means of organisation. The clearer the ideology of a class becomes, the more completely and effectively that class can create its own place in life, its own aims, its own ways, its distinctiveness and its contradictions with other classes. The closer its internal cohesion becomes, the more considerable its social strength will be; the self-consciousness of a class is the basis of its organisational potential.[30]

Bogdanov may have implied that his article on 'Ideology' was uncontroversial, but it embodied ideas that were peculiar to himself, and indeed that had split the Vpered group; they were the argumentation behind the conception of proletarian culture. Lenin was right that the article was different in kind from the factual ones that preceded it in *Pravda*, but it could only be classed as 'heretical' from the point of view of his own understanding of Marxism.

Bogdanov devotes much of his attention in 'A Decade of Excommunication' to the characters and behaviour of his principal excommunicators: Plekhanov and Lenin. Much of what he says about Plekhanov replicates passages in *The Adventures of One Philosophical School*, and as he had not crossed swords with Plekhanov since that work was published, there was nothing of substance to add.

With Lenin the position was entirely different: the conflict with Lenin was still in progress, and was the occasion for Bogdanov's writing the pamphlet. Accordingly, the circumstances surrounding the rejection of the 'Ideology' article and his exclusion from *Pravda* were chronicled in some detail. More interesting, however, was Bogdanov's estimation of Lenin as a Marxist theoretician, in the light of all that he now knew of his former political associate. In his view, Lenin's claim to be an ultra-orthodox Marxist was illusory; in fact, his ideas were vague and eclectic, adhering stubbornly to the outmoded ideas of Plekhanov.

30　Neizvestnyi Bogdanov 1995, 3, pp. 55–8.

As long as he was studying specific concrete phenomena, like the class composition and character of some political party, he was competent enough. But when it was a matter of general-theoretical questions, such as the origins of religion, or the origins of socialism, he was at a loss.

Bogdanov gave as an example of Lenin's ineptitude in explaining the origins of religion a passage from *Materialism and Empiriocriticism* which asserted that religion had been invented by priests.[31] His example of Lenin's theoretical deficiency in explaining the origins of socialism was the passage from *What Is to Be Done?* where it was stated that the working class on its own could rise no higher than trade-unionism; it could acquire the socialist ideal only from the radically-thinking intelligentsia. Bogdanov thought that the same type of misconception was in evidence in both cases; in the first the priests had thought up the wrong ideology; in the second they had come up with the right one.[32]

The innovation of 'A Decade of Excommunication' in its treatment of Lenin is the interpretation of his behaviour in tectological terms. Bogdanov recalled that in *Tectology* he had pointed out that from an organisational viewpoint the decision in 1903 to create two centres of power in the party, the Central Committee and the central organ, had ensured that disagreements between the two would necessarily lead to a schism. This blunder, Bogdanov told his readers, was a vivid illustration of how necessary a science of organisation, a tectology, was.[33]

Seen from a tectological perspective, Lenin's attempt in 1909 to split the Bolshevik fraction and ally with Plekhanov's supporters among the Mensheviks was doomed to failure. The manoeuvre involved the Leninists getting rid of the left wing of the Bolsheviks, while Plekhanov detached his group from the 'liquidationist' right wing of the Mensheviks. The Leninist Bolsheviks and the 'party Mensheviks' would then be required to form a coherent centre organisation. However the two fractions had become so distant that the desired merger was impossible, and the organisation collapsed at its point of least resistance. No centre grouping of Lenin's and Plekhanov's forces gelled, and instead of two fractions there were now four.[34] Despite this failure, Lenin remained non-

---

31 The passage in question is: 'beings outside time and space, as invented by the priests and maintained by the imagination of the ignorant and downtrodden mass of humanity, are disordered fantasies, the artifices of philosophical idealism, rotten products of a rotten social system'. See Lenin 1958–65, 18, p. 193.

32 Neizvestnyi Bogdanov 1995, 3, pp. 155–6.

33 Neizvestnyi Bogdanov 1995, 3, 149.

34 Neizvestnyi Bogdanov 1995, 3, pp. 161–2.

plussed. He seemed to Bogdanov like a chess player whose strategy had been unsuccessful and had lost the game, but now calmly returned to the board to deploy his pawns in a better way.

6   Reaction to the War

Although his article on 'Ideology' had been rejected by the editorial board of *Pravda*, Bogdanov made sure the ideas in it reached the public by publishing an expanded version of them in book form: *The Science of Social Consciousness. A Short Course of Ideological Science in Questions and Answers*. The question and answer format of the book suggests its origins in the lectures Bogdanov gave to the party schools, but the content reflects Bogdanov's current preoccupation with the question of ideology. It shows, moreover, the influence of both *Tectology* and *The Philosophy of Living Experience* as well as the article on 'Ideology'. It is Bogdanov's fullest and most systematic treatment of the subject.

Like the article on 'Ideology', *The Science of Social Consciousness* equates ideology with social consciousness. Bogdanov considers that ideology is a means of organising society, production, classes, in general any social forces of elements; without ideology this kind of organisation would be impossible.[35] Ideology could also be referred to as 'culture' or 'intellectual culture', indicating the breadth of its sphere of operation.[36]

Ideology is constantly changing, since it is a means of adaptation. The beginnings of ideology are in language, which, as Noiré discovered, arose from the exclamations of people's labour efforts. From language there came concepts, ideas and ideological forms. Here again, one sees the importance of Noiré's explanation of the origin of language for Bogdanov; it links together in an unbroken sequence production and language, and by extension production and ideology. From this Bogdanov can make the case that ideology has a key role in the way production is organised and how society is ordered. For Bogdanov the place where production and ideology meet is technology, on which, in turn, economics is based. Bogdanov's argument is that: 'If speech arose from social labour and thought from speech, then it is obvious that the whole of ideology, the whole of intellectual culture came from the technical process, from material culture or, in other words, social consciousness from production'.[37]

---

35   Bogdanov 1914, p. 7.
36   Bogdanov 1914, p. 10.
37   Bogdanov 1914, p. 45.

Having shown the origins of ideology or social consciousness and its place in the structure of society, Bogdanov devoted most of his attention to examining how it had evolved historically. He distinguished four periods in the historical development of ideology: 1) the era of primitive culture, 2) the era of author itarian culture, 3) the era of individual culture, and 4) the era of collectivist culture.[38]

Much of the material Bogdanov used in the historical treatment of ideology had appeared previously in other works, especially in *The Philosophy of Living Experience*. But although not entirely novel, it is the last section of the work which is of most interest, because it shows how Bogdanov saw the emerging socialist order shortly before the outbreak of the First World War and the Russian revolution it would bring in its wake.

He thought that at the first stages of comradely cooperation some passivity would still remain in the working class. This would manifest itself in the weakness of initiative of the mass members of an organisation, insufficient control over elected comrades, leaders, etc. The very conditions of class struggle would dilute comradely discipline with elements of authoritarian discipline. The necessity for centralised unity of action and swift decision-making would compel everyone to submit to the orders of a few without criticism or discussion, to have faith in their competence.

To the question: would compulsion remain in developed social collectivism, Bogdanov's answer was reminiscent of what he had said in *Red Star*. It was that compulsion would continue only as long as the social struggle went on; it should die out naturally, and social norms would be understood simply as norms of organisational utility. There would still be people who infringed these norms, but these would not be representatives of hostile social forces, but people with psychological conditions. Force could be applied to them, but without hostility, as to patients in a psychiatric hospital.[39]

Bogdanov was no pacifist, and clearly he expected that the collectivist society that he envisaged could not be achieved without some measure of bloodshed. But he could not have imagined the cost in human life that was to be claimed by the events that were about to unfold with the outbreak of the First World War.

38   Bogdanov 1914, p. 34.
39   Bogdanov 1914, p. 197.

War and Revolution

1   Bogdanov in the War

Taking advantage of the amnesty granted in 1913 to mark the 300th anniversary of the Romanov dynasty, Bogdanov returned to Russia and settled in Moscow. Soon after the war broke out, he was called up and assigned to the 221st Roslavl-sky Infantry Regiment in the Second Army as a junior doctor.[1]

As one can deduce from the references to military manoeuvres in *Tectology*, the kind of war Bogdanov experienced was not one of attrition, bogged down for long periods in trenches, but of continuous advances and retreats. Two Russian armies operated in East Prussia: the First Army under General Rennenkampf and the Second Army under General Samsonov, in which Bogdanov served.

In response to appeals from the Allies to create a diversion on the Eastern front to retard the swift German advance through Belgium and France, the Russian High Command launched an offensive in East Prussia. Rennenkampf was at first successful, inflicting heavy casualties on the German Eighth Army and forcing it to retreat beyond the Vistula. Instead of pursuing the Germans and consolidating his victory, Rennenkampf hesitated, allowing them to re-group.

Under the impression that the Germans were still in full flight, Samsonov directred his forces towards the Vistula to cut off their retreat. However, the new German commanders, Hindenburg and Ludendorff, put into operation a manoeuvre that was directed against Samsonov's forces. Leaving a thin screen of cavalry to occupy Rennenkampf, the Germans encircled the Russian Second Army at Tannenberg, the battle raging between 29 and 30 August. The Russians were crushingly defeated and Samsonov committed suicide shortly afterwards.[2] Bogdanov luckily avoided this encirclement because he was on a short official visit to Moscow to accompany an officer who was seriously wounded.[3]

While in Moscow, Bogdanov took the opportunity to visit Anfusa Smirnova and his son Alexander, to whom he recounted his experiences of army life. He thought the officers foolish and was shocked by the primitiveness of the soldiers. He was taken aback by the fact that his batmen used to eat sweets

---

1   Rogachevskii 1995, p. 105; Biggart, Gloveli and Yassour 1998, p. 292.
2   Zaionchkovskii 2002, pp. 137–89; Rostunov 1976, pp. 118–25.
3   Rogachevskii 1995, p. 106.

together with the wrapper. Once during an offensive the troops destroyed a hospital abandoned by the Germans with all the equipment and medicine in it.[4] Bogdanov himself referred to this incident in 1925, recalling that:

> At the front I was a witness to how the young soldiers, with the collusion of most of the officers, and with enormous expenditure of energy, destroyed, and with fierce delight, defiled in every way all the gentry's and peasants' houses, the shops, the hospitals, all the useful and comfortable amenities, as a result of which they themselves had to make do with quartering in nothing but sheds and pigsties.[5]

This was a low cultural level that Bogdanov had never encountered before, and it shaped his conception of the 'logic of the barracks' that appeared in some of his wartime writings.

Bogdanov must have re-joined his unit just at the tail-end of the battle at Tannenberg. This emerges from a letter he wrote to Klestov, the moving spirit behind the Russian translation of *Das Kapital*, dated 20 October 1914. There he says: 'This is what I can tell you about myself: I was on the march, on the offensive, then – in retreat, as and when necessary ... I had my baptism of fire on 30 August, my name-day; as a name-day gift the Germans captured my luggage: they have bizarre customs. I was recommended for an award for the retreat; well, actually, not for the retreat itself, but because I retreated not on my own, but accompanied by a transport, the head physician of which had been taken prisoner'.[6]

In this somewhat diffident way, Bogdanov conveys to Klestov that he had been recommended for a decoration for leading a medical convoy out of the line of fire, in the absence of his senior officer. Although Bogdanov was twice recommended for a decoration for his courage under fire, he did not receive it, and presumably it was not a matter he would wish to pursue.[7]

In his letter to Klestov on 25 December Bogdanov reported:

> I am writing to you again from the so-called 'front-line', although, to tell you the truth, life has been quite peaceful here for about a month and a half. We and the Germans would sit opposite each other, somebody would open fire from time to time to clear either our, or their, conscience, and

4   Rogachevskii 1995, p. 106.
5   Bogdanov 1925a, 10, p. 85.
6   Rogachevskii 1995, p. 106.
7   Biggart, Gloveli and Yassour 1998, pp. 292–3.

then there would be quiet again: there are one or two wounded a day, with a few dead. However, there was violent fighting, and more than enough work, at the end of October ... There are a lot of interesting things for a writer on social themes here, but a pen fails to reproduce all the colours. If I see you, I'll tell you.[8]

Bogdanov confessed to Klestov that the conditions at the front were undermining his health. Initially, he said, he had treated military service as a welcome distraction from his writing, which had 'overstrained his brains', as well it might, bearing in mind the considerable literary output of 1913. But latterly it had proved to be 'a source of an annoying weariness'. Finally, Bogdanov contracted a nervous disease involving skin eruptions, requiring intensive treatment in a Moscow clinic specialising in nervous disorders. He never returned to the front, but was kept in the rear as a junior house surgeon at the 153rd Joint Evacuation Hospital in Moscow. In the summer of 1916 he became a medical inspector for the prisoner of war camps in the Moscow region. Bogdanov was only demobilised from the army after the Bolsheviks came to power, in the spring of 1918.[9]

At the end of 1915 Anfusa Smirnova died in Barnaul where she had been living with her sister. One of Anfusa's last acts was to give the young Alexander into the care of her friend Lidia Pavlova. Lidia and Alexander returned to Moscow, where Bogdanov regularly visited them and provided for them materially in conditions that would become increasingly difficult.[10]

2 The Science of Social Consciousness

Despite Bogdanov's being something of a war hero, he profoundly disapproved of the war. His son Alexander told Andrei Rogachevskii that Bogdanov had experienced only two periods of serious depression: after the break with Lenin and after the outbreak of the First World War.[11] His dismay at the events of 1914 is understandable. His writings of the period reflect the bitter disappointment at the behaviour of the working classes of both the belligerent and the non-belligerent countries who succumbed to the patriotic fervour and sided with their governments in support of the war effort. He was especially irked by

---

8   Rogachevskii 1995, p. 107.

9   Rogachevskii 1995, pp. 107–8; Plyutto 1998, p. 475; Krementsov 2011, p. 53.

10   Klebaner 200, p. 31.

11   Rogachevskii 1995, p. 107.

the participation in anti-German riots of the workers in the Presnia district of Moscow, who had been among the most militant in the 1905 revolution.[12]

Bogdanov was also disillusioned by the attitude of the socialist parties of the Second International, who had resolved in 1912 to do everything in their power to prevent the occurrence of war, and if it should nevertheless break out, to make use of the opportunity to hasten the end of the capitalist system. In the event the German Social Democrats voted for war credits, precipitating a crisis in the International from which it never recovered.

Of the Russian socialist parties, none voted for war credits, and some socialist deputies in the Duma were exiled to Siberia as a result. Nevertheless, among the various socialist currents there was a considerable range of opinion on what the attitude towards the war ought to be. At the extreme right of the socialist spectrum was Plekhanov, who considered the war against Germany to be an entirely just one and called upon the workers of the Allied Powers to support the war in the interests of peace and progress. This opinion was shared by Bogdanov's former ally, Aleksinsky, who had also become a fervent advocate of the war against Germany. The majority of Russian socialists took a 'defencist' position, believing that the war on Russia's part was not one of aggression or conquest, but simply to defend the country from German attack. Among the minority of Russian socialists who took an 'internationalist' or anti-war stance were Martov, Akselrod, Trotsky, Lunacharsky, Lenin and Bogdanov. There were, however, divisions within the internationalist camp about how the war should be ended. Lenin belonged to the 'defeatist' current, who believed that Russia should withdraw from the war unilaterally, even if it meant defeat by Germany; Trotsky on the other hand argued that this would be disastrous for the prospects of a revolution in Russia, and that the war had to be ended by a general peace.[13]

Bogdanov's place in this spectrum had a certain ambiguity. He was an internationalist who desired an end to the war as soon as possible, but he did not demand Russia's immediate withdrawal from hostilities. One must suppose that his desire to end the war was tempered by the realisation that the collapse of the Russian front would be accompanied by enormous casualties among the soldiers, whose lives, as a doctor, he had tried to save. In a pamphlet published in 1917 Bogdanov explained that the struggle for peace should be conducted by legal means where these were available. He continued:

---

12   Bogdanov 1990, p. 354.
13   Thatcher 2003, pp. 74–5.

For this objective we propose nothing should be done that would weaken our front or disrupt the work of the rear. We, of course, fought and worked for the needs of the war, by force of necessity, not recognising the war and not believing in the fraudulent phrases of all governments about defending truth and justice. We fought and worked for the war because we could not prevent its breaking out, and we could not break away from state conditions which bound us, and also because from the victory of the enemy we can expect nothing good for our country or for humanity in general.[14]

In the edition of *The Science of Social Consciousness* published in 1914 Bogdanov added a chapter entitled 'Social Consciousness in the World War', in which he analysed the causes of the war and the reasons for capitulation of international socialism to the nationalism and militarism which accompanied it. In analysing both of these aspects of the war Bogdanov employed the organisational approach.

For Bogdanov the war was a crisis caused by the disturbance of the equilibrium of two forces: the force of bonding, which arose from the common interests of the various countries in exchange and trade, and the force of pressure, which came about through the competition for markets. The forces for bonding grew during peace time with the development of the international exchange of commodities, with the parties involved acting as suppliers and customers for each other's goods. But with the precipitous advances in technology the scale of production grew rapidly, causing an increase in the forces of pressure, as the various capitalist states competed to find new outlets for their commodities.[15]

Just as in peacetime the competition between individual enterprises could lead to crises of over-production, so the international anarchy manifested in the struggle for markets stimulated states to develop their organising force, military power, which had inevitably led to the world military crisis. This too was a kind of over-production: in this case an over-production of state-organised human force.

But how could one explain the ideological about-turn of the German working class on the outbreak of the war? For Bogdanov this was an object lesson in the organising role of ideology. Ideological forms, like any other organisational forms, only operated within the limits to which they had been worked out and no further. At the start of the war the collective-labour ideology was

14   Bogdanov 1917c, p. 9.
15   Bogdanov 1914, p. 201.

far from being a complete, systematic, culture; it only existed in embryo, only in scattered parts, and not as an integral living whole.[16]

In this situation it was only to be expected that when confronted by the unprecedented challenge of the world military crisis the working class was caught completely unprepared. Its embryonic and fragmentary culture was unequal to the task. And since there was no culture of its own that could guide it, the working class had to resort to someone else's. This was bourgeois culture with its economic anarchy, nationalism and militarism.

In the case of the German working class, it took part in the war not as a forced labourer, but as a devoted servant. Besides his body, the German worker gave his ideological soul, which had not even been demanded. He felt solidarity with the German capitalists, and the conflict of his interests with the working classes of other countries. He reconciled both of these positions with his conscience.[17]

A prominent feature of wartime ideology in comparison with peacetime was the enormous development of authoritarian elements. There was nothing surprising in this. The main social functions were transferred to the army, an organisation constructed on the authoritarian model. The army itself expanded several-fold, swallowing up the best forces in society, subordinating them to itself. It compelled all other organisations, productive, political and even cultural, to conform to its authoritarian character.[18]

Bogdanov considered the organisational process at work during the war to be that of 'negative selection'. This was the process of retrenchment, one which increased the simplicity and cohesion of the whole in order to enhance its chances of survival. Because this was a process which eliminated the weakest elements in the system, it could result eventually in the re-emergence of the system in a stronger and more resilient form, as could be observed in a patient who had recovered from an illness.

But, Bogdanov added ominously, not every illness leads to regeneration, and not every war gives a stimulus to progress. The question was how great the loss of forces was and at what level would the destruction stop. The growth of simplicity and cohesion could take place at the cost of lowering the very type of organisation and reducing it to a less advanced cultural level.[19]

---

16   Bogdanov 1914, p. 208.
17   Bogdanov 1914, p. 209.
18   Bogdanov 1914, p. 212.
19   Bogdanov 1914, pp. 214–16.

3   World Crises Peaceful and Military

In an article 'World Crises Peaceful and Military', serialised in Gorky's journal *Letopis* during the summer of 1916, Bogdanov elaborated on what he had said in the final chapter of *The Science of Social Consciousness* on the causes of the war and the reasons for the failure of socialist internationalism to prevent it. In it Bogdanov returned to examining the disruption of the equilibrium of forces that precipitated the military crisis of 1914.

There were, he considered, three different forces involved. The first was of the economic bonds, the mutual relations between buyers and sellers. These bonds increased as international trade broadened and deepened. This growth necessarily slowed down as the world market was saturated and its extension to non-capitalist countries was completed, and the stage of constant distribution between states was reached.

The second of the purely economic forces was that of pressure, arising from the competition between different capitalist nation states for an increased share of the world market. The growth of the forces of pressure would necessarily accelerate as the world market approached saturation point. If the growth of the force of bonds slowed down and the growth of the force of pressure accelerated, then the difference between them would rapidly lessen. However, the catastrophe would not come when the two forces were exactly equal, but earlier, due to the operation of the third force, that of the military.[20]

The military force also grew parallel with the increase in world competition between states. When the other two forces approached equilibrium the build up of military force would upset the balance and precipitate a military crisis. This sequence of events, according to Bogdanov, explained why the driving force of the crisis was the military element and why the war was unexpected by the capitalists of all countries, since the predominance of the economic forces was that of bonds.

For Bogdanov the war was a spontaneous phenomenon, comparable to the kind of crises of over-production that occurred during peacetime; it happened independently of the personalities involved, whether of Kaiser Wilhelm or Franz-Ferdinand's assassin Gavrilo Princip. Nor had it anything to do with 'principles', ideas or 'law and morality'. Whereas in peacetime crises had their origin in the over-production of commodities, the world war was a crisis of over-production of organised human forces, a phenomenon characteristic of the capitalist state, in the form of militarism. The war would not end until this kind

---

20   Bogdanov 1916, 5, pp. 115–17.

of over-production, which had accumulated in the nation states of the world system, had been eliminated.[21]

How was it possible, Bogdanov inquired, for the war to continue for so long? Economists had predicted that the war could not last for more than a few months. The answer was that militarism had created an enormous consumer market, so that it facilitated the movement of capital, which to a certain extent countered the over-production of goods. Initially the war had caused economic decline in the countries connected with it, but latterly the military market had come into play. It increased its demand tenfold, and so compensated the national capitals for the loss of their markets. Those branches of industry connected with military demand found that their profits had returned to long-forgotten levels.[22]

As in the final chapter of *The Science of Social Consciousness*, Bogdanov devoted considerable attention in the article to the question of proletarian culture. It was paradoxical, he said, that although one associated the bourgeoisie with individualism and anarchy, and the proletariat with organisation and discipline, in fact the bourgeoisie had a much higher level of organisation than the proletariat. This was shown by the fact that the bourgeoisie maintained a dominant position in society, and in particular this level of organisation had been decisively demonstrated in the summer of 1914, when the Socialist International had collapsed and the workers had followed the bourgeoisie in supporting the war. According to Bogdanov, this was because bourgeois culture was well established, while that of the proletariat was only in its infancy.[23]

Bogdanov held that the organised nature of human collectives was determined by all the things that give them unity in the practical direction of thoughts and attitudes. This, moreover, was not done only by formal organisations. The organising form was much wider and more general, and without it those organisations would not even be possible. This was the whole intellectual culture of the collectives: the combination of its customs, morals, laws, its science and its art. All this was combined in the world-outlook specific to the given collective.[24]

Bogdanov invited his readers to compare this colossal, all-encompassing culture of the bourgeois classes that had been formed in the course of centur-

21   Bogdanov 1916, 4, p. 153.
22   Bogdanov 1916, 5, p. 122.
23   Bogdanov 1916, 4, p. 135.
24   Bogdanov 1916, 4, p. 136.

ies with the diffuse, inchoate elements of the new collectivist culture of the working classes. It was clear that in any competition the bourgeois culture was bound to prevail. And it was precisely this, Bogdanov averred, that had happened on the outbreak of the war. For, he said:

> When the great crisis broke out, the weakness of the new shoots of culture was immediately revealed, their inability to play an independent role. The old bourgeois-state culture almost without opposition carried the day, uniting its forces with nationalist-patriotic slogans. The internationalism of the working classes at once disintegrated because it existed only as a feeling or an attitude of the masses; it could only be a real force to be reckoned with if it were the incarnation of a particular and integral class culture.[25]

The implication of this was that what was needed was to inculcate in the working class its own proletarian culture.

4   Disagreement with Skvortsov-Stepanov

One finds the same explanation of the outbreak of the World War in terms of bonds and pressure in the second volume of *The Course of Political Economy*. An introductory note to the volume states that it was written entirely by Bogdanov, though edited by both authors. A further note at the end states that there would have been a chapter on 'The Most Recent Prototypes of Collectivism' written by Bogdanov, but it was omitted because of disagreements between the authors. The title suggests that the content of the chapter would have been something similar to Bogdanov's essay in the journal *Vpered*, 'Socialism of the Present,' an argument in favour of proletarian culture. Presumably the theme had been as unwelcome to Skvortsov-Stepanov as it had been to Pokrovsky, Volsky and other members of the Vpered group.

This, however, was not the only disagreement between Bogdanov and Skvortsov-Stepanov, or even the most serious one. The volume would have contained a chapter by Skvortsov-Stepanov on 'Imperialism', but this had been rejected by Bogdanov. This is not surprising, since Skvortsov-Stepanov's chapter would have been completely at odds with the entire direction of Bogdanov's thinking.

---

25   Ibid.

The inspiration for Skvortsov-Stepanov's chapter was Rudolf Hilferding's book *Finance Capital* (*Das Finanzkapital*) that had been published in 1910, and had become extremely influential on socialists at the time of the First World War. Skvortsov-Stepanov had been much impressed by Hilferding's work and published a Russian translation of *Finance Capital* in 1912. Hilferding conceived his book as an extension of Marx's analysis of capitalism to recent economic developments. These developments included the emergence of industrial trusts, cartels and syndicates which limited the play of free-market competition and tended towards monopoly; the erection of high tariff barriers; the export of capital to undeveloped countries, and increasing rivalry among the capitalist nations to secure spheres of influence in different parts of the world.

Hilferding believed that the factor which explained these phenomena was the emergence of finance capital as a driving force behind recent economic developments. It was industry's need for credit that had given the banks such importance in the economies of capitalist countries, and it was this which had caused industrial and finance capital to coalesce. Any firm that had a guaranteed source of credit had an enormous advantage over the isolated entrepreneur. It was therefore more capable of withstanding crises than its competitors. In the modern world the successful company was one which was linked to finance capital.

Whereas formerly capital had demanded free trade and non-intervention from the state, finance capital sought to dominate markets, and called upon the state to erect tariff barriers to protect its monopolies. When tariff barriers were raised in other countries, finance capital replied by exporting capital in order to set up production behind them. In less developed countries too labour was cheap, and so could be employed to produce values, and thereby counter the tendency of the rate of profit to fall.

The export of capital, in Hilferding's view, was an important factor in equalising the level of economic development throughout the world. It was one of the positive features in the recent evolution of capital with which he was especially concerned. For him, it appeared that modern capitalism was evolving in a direction that would make the emergence of socialism a distinct possibility. The concentration of the economy had put its central control within easy reach. The fact that industry was dominated by the banks meant that a central bank could exercise control over the whole of social production.[26] In Germany, for example, taking possession of the six large Berlin banks would mean taking possession of the most important branches of larger-scale industry, and

---

26   Hilferding 1923, p. 218.

would greatly facilitate the initial phases of socialist policy.[27] The extension of the sphere of finance capital also implied that when the socialist revolution came it would be on an international scale. According to Hilferding, 'The proletariat must see that the imperialist policy generates revolution ... and with it the conditions for the victory of socialism'. He predicted that 'the dictatorship of the magnates of capital will finally be transformed into the dictatorship of the proletariat'.[28]

In Hilferding's view, finance capital had been singularly successful in winning over the support of most classes in society. This, moreover, applied to the working class, among whom there had emerged a new group, of highly skilled and well-paid salaried workers, whose careers depended on subservience to finance capital. It was the members of this group that most easily became infected with the ideology of imperialism.[29]

Skvortsov-Stepanov's chapter followed Hilferding's line of reasoning fairly closely. Thus, according to Skvortsov-Stepanov, one of the most characteristic features of recent economic development was the rise of protectionism. Whereas tariff barriers had originally been designed to protect infant industries, they were now employed by highly developed industrial powers to keep prices high and overcome competitors. This had been accompanied by the steady elimination of free competition and the growth of cartels and monopolies.[30]

High prices imposed limits on the home market, so that in order to expand its activities capital was forced to 'emigrate'. The emigration of capital could take place in the form of commodities, but the possibilities for expansion were increased if capital was exported to backward countries as loan capital. The loans would then extend exchange relations in that country, and this in turn would stimulate the demand for fresh loans and increase the capacity of the market for European goods. The emigration of capital was facilitated by the close alliance in recent times of industry with the banks, a phenomenon that Hilferding had termed 'finance capital'.[31]

Capital was especially attracted to those economically backward countries that were politically weak. These could be turned into colonies of the economically developed country. Political control over a territory was an effective means of exploiting it while excluding competitors from among other industri-

27   Hilferding 1923, p. 473.
28   Hilferding 1923, pp. 471, 477.
29   Hilferding 1923, pp. 444–7.
30   Skvortsov-Stepanov 1930, p. 261.
31   Skvortsov-Stepanov 1930, p. 272.

ally developed nations. There was, however, competition among these nations for the possession of colonial territories, leading to the threat of armed conflict.[32]

Skvortsov-Stepanov echoed Hilferding's idea that imperialism produced its own social basis of support in the mass of functionaries and officials it generated as a result of imperialist activity. It was from among these that the ideologists of imperialism came, people who presented the appetites of finance capital in a quasi-philosophical gloss. Usually this took the form of emphasising the national identity of the imperialist power and ascribing to it a historical mission of conquest and domination.[33]

In Skvortsov-Stepanov's view, imperialism in the long term undermined its own foundations. In emigrating to backward countries, European capital gave them a stimulus to economic development, so eliminating the difference in economic level that had originally prompted capital to emigrate. The receipt of loans and the introduction of industry encouraged the growth of an indigenous bourgeoisie in the colonial country. And with this came the beginnings of a popular movement from which there emerged the modern proletarian struggle, the soil for which was prepared by the emigration of European industry.[34]

There were two aspects of Hilferding's work – repeated by Skvortsov-Stepanov – that Bogdanov took issue with. The first of these was that finance capital, by subordinating the branches of industry to itself, was preparing the way for a future, centrally-directed socialist economy. In Bogdanov's view, the control exercised by the central banks over industry was by no means as decisive as Hilferding maintained. The banks in practice seldom intervened in the running of the economic units under their control, and that intervention was mostly indirect, through concealed economic pressure. 'However great', Bogdanov concluded, 'the economic power of finance capital, and however broad its field of operation, its real organising function is less profound, the bond of its systems less close and firm than even in the lowest forms of cartels and syndicates. This bond is reminiscent of the vassal-suzerain relationship of loosely-connected feudal groupings'.[35] The implication was that capitalism would not so conveniently provide the economic base for socialism.

The second point of contention, and one that was to increase in importance with the onset of the Great War, was Hilferding's conception of a social basis

---

32   Skvortsov-Stepanov 1930, pp. 274–9.

33   Skvortsov-Stepanov 1930, p. 280.

34   Skvortsov-Stepanov 1930, p. 283.

35   Bogdanov and Stepanov 1910–25, 2, p. 142.

of support for the policies of imperialism among the more highly paid wage-earners and salaried employees. Skvortsov-Stepanov fully concurred with this view, and the conception of the treachery of the 'workers' aristocracy' was to become a mainstream feature of Russian Social-Democratic thinking before and during the World War. Bogdanov, however, rejected the theory completely, believing that the capitulation of the workers to the capitalists was due to the immaturity of proletarian culture.

5   Bukharin

Skortsov-Stepanov's chapter on 'Imperialism' was published in the Leninist journal *Prosveshchenie*, signifying an endorsement of the ideas it contained by the Leninist camp. In fact, Bogdanov's disagreement with Skvortsov-Stepanov did not remain a purely personal one. It marked the beginning of a new ideological divide between Bogdanov and the rest of the Bolshevik fraction on the related questions of finance capital and the prospects for a socialist revolution in Russia.

Bukharin's article 'The World Economy and Imperialism' appeared in the Bolshevik journal *Kommunist* in 1915. In it, like Hilferding, Bukharin argued that recent developments in the world economy were laying the foundations of the socialist order on a world scale. He was of the opinion that: 'The growth of the world market proceeds apace, tying up various sections of the world economy into one strong knot, bringing ever closer to each other hitherto "nationally" and economically isolated regions, creating an ever broader base for the world socialist economy'.[36] He believed that the process of centralisation of the economy had created a strong tendency towards 'transforming the entire national economy into a single gigantic combined enterprise ... an enterprise which monopolises the national market and forms the prerequisite for an organised socialist economy'.[37]

Later Bukharin expanded his article into a pamphlet which was first published in 1917. It was in this version of his work that he included a section devoted to Hilferding's conception of the support given to finance capital by a privileged stratum of the working class. It was the collaboration of this stratum with the bourgeoisie that Bukharin thought explained the collapse of the Second International. Lenin wrote an Introduction to Bukharin's pamph-

---

36   Bukharin 1915, p. 11.
37   Bukharin 1915, p. 23.

let, dated December 1915. He did not dissent from any of Bukharin's arguments, but thought Kautsky mistaken in believing that the formation of a single world trust was possible. Lenin believed that before this happened imperialism would explode and capitalism would turn into its opposite [38]

In 1916 Lenin wrote his book *Imperialism the Highest Stage of Capitalism*. The main feature which distinguished it from the works of Skvortsov-Stepanov and Bukharin was its polemic with Kautsky. Whereas Kautsky thought that it was industrial capital that was the driving force behind imperialism, Lenin argued that it was finance capital. Like Skvortsov-Stepanov and Bukharin, Lenin agreed with Hilferding that in recent years free competition had given way to monopoly and that this had brought with it the socialisation of production, a step in the transition towards socialism.[39]

Lenin explained the failure of the international labour movement to oppose the current war in the same terms as Hilferding, Skvortsov-Stepanov and Bukharin. This was that the receipt of high monopoly profits by the capitalists enabled them to pay relatively generous wages to a minority of the workforce, and so gain the support of this privileged stratum or 'labour aristocracy'. It was, he thought, this group which fostered opportunism within the working-class movement, an opportunism that found its most characteristic incarnation in the leadership of the Second International.[40]

These were the ideas with which Lenin and the Bolsheviks went into the revolution in 1917 and which guided them on their accession to power. Hilferding encouraged them in the belief that by gaining possession of the banks they would be able to exert control over the economy as a whole. This belief is reflected in Lenin's writings on the eve of the conquest of power in October when he stressed: 'Without big banks socialism would be impossible. The big banks are the "state apparatus" which we need to bring about socialism, and which we take ready-made from capitalism'.[41] Events after the Bolsheviks came to power would show how far this was true.

6   Will It Be Tomorrow?

Bogdanov intended to follow up his article on world crises with another entitled 'Will it be Tomorrow?', but the editors of *Letopis* rejected it, and it was

---

38   Lenin 1958–65, 27, pp. 93–8; Bukharin 1972, pp. 9–14.
39   Lenin 1958–65, 27, p. 320.
40   Lenin 1958–65, 27, pp. 423–4.
41   Lenin 1958–65, 34, p. 307.

only published in 1918. 'Will it be Tomorrow?' was directed against those among the left, internationalist wing of the Social Democrats who believed that the present crisis was one of the transition from capitalism to socialism and would culminate in a socialist revolution. As in his article on world crises, Bogdanov took up the question of the behaviour of the workers on the outbreak of the war in 1914. In this essay Bogdanov explicitly dismissed the theories that the workers had been deceived into support for the war, or that they had done so through the influence of the petty-bourgeois fellow-travellers of the movement. Their views were coloured by the remnants of petty-bourgeois peasant thinking with its primitive nationalism. He reiterated that the workers had been overwhelmed by traditional patterns of thought, because their own, comradely-collectivist, culture still existed only in embryo. When the catastrophe of the war unfolded they had been powerless before it, 'like a child transfixed before an unknown and terrifying spectacle'.[42] The proletarian modes of thought were still not sufficiently generalised and systematised to embrace the entirety of life, and be able to respond to the most unexpected crises, even those on an international scale.

In the article Bogdanov was also concerned to show that the socialists who thought that the transition from capitalism to socialism was being prepared by current economic developments were deeply mistaken. He dismissed the idea that the German war economy provided a model for a managed socialist economy and emphasised that the apparatus for the distribution of products that would replace the market in a planned economy would be of enormous complexity. It would require prodigious statistical information about the goods produced and their consumption. The mechanisms, moreover, would be on an international scale.[43]

The problem was not only an economic, but an ideological one. The elaboration of new mechanisms would require new, socialist, ways of thinking. The sciences would have to be transformed from their existing individualist and authoritarian approaches to ones which reflected the spirit of labour collectivism. Bogdanov went on to argue that as long as the proletariat did not have these necessary organisational tools it would be utopian to embark on the adventure of a transition to socialism that the 'maximalists' advocated.[44]

---

42   Bogdanov 1990, p. 307.
43   Bogdanov 1990, pp. 307, 31.
44   Bogdanov 1990, p. 315.

7   The February Revolution

During the war years Lenin was preparing for further conflicts with Bogdanov, or with the 'Machists', as he referred to Bogdanov and his associates. A stimulus to renew his philosophical studies was the publication in 1913 of a four-volume collection of the correspondence between Marx and Engels. Lenin made a summary of the letters, noting passages that might be of use in supporting his ideas.

In those cases where Marx or Engels referred favourably to an author or discussed his work, Lenin followed up the references and himself read and made notes from the books they mentioned. In this way Lenin was led to read and summarise the works of Hegel, Lassalle, and Clausewitz. In 1929 these notes were published under the heading 'Philosophical Notebooks', but without the extracts from the Marx-Engels correspondence that had prompted them. The impression was thereby given that at the start of the war, in response to the collapse of the Second International, Lenin had made an intensive study of Hegel in order to restore the dialectical content to revolutionary Marxism that had been suppressed by the opportunist leaders of the international socialist movement. In fact, Lenin did not have the creativity that this interpretation implies, and treated the Marx-Engels correspondence as holy writ, just as Bogdanov had described. The main lesson that Lenin was able to draw from his 'Philosophical Notebooks' was that Plekhanov had been insufficiently assiduous in his campaign against the 'Machists'.[45]

When in January 1917 Lenin gave a lecture on the anniversary of Bloody Sunday, he still thought of the coming revolution as a long-term prospect, supposing that people of his generation would not live to see its decisive battles.[46] When the revolution that brought an end to the tsarist regime erupted in the following month it had nothing to do with the Bolshevik Duma fraction to which he had attached such significance, and which had caused such bitter controversy. Because none of the Bolshevik leaders were present in Petrograd at the time, the ideologists of the Soviet regime later declared it to be a 'spontaneous' uprising. But from the memoirs of participants and the documents they produced at the time, it emerges that from 23 February the group of former Sormovo workers, friends of Gorky's, who had come through the 1905 revolution, and whose 'Sormovo-Nikolaev *zemliachestvo*' now formed the nucleus of the Vyborg District Committee of the RSDLP, were active in organising anti-war and anti-government demonstrations and engaging in street battles with the

---

45   On this see White 2015.
46   Lenin 1958–65, 30, p. 328.

police. The group was preparing to establish a Provisional Revolutionary Government at the Finland Station, but at the point when the troops had come over to the side of the insurgents, on 27 February, the movement was taken over by Menshevik defencists, who established the Petrograd Soviet. This then became the rallying point for the insurgent forces. One of the most politically experienced of the former Sormovo workers, Ivan Chugurin, had been a student at the party school in Longjumeau. Although the Longjumeau school was not one that Bogdanov was involved in, Chugurin's participation in the February revolution went some way towards vindicating the value of party schools that Bogdanov had defended.[47]

8   Bogdanov in 1917

In Petrograd by 1 March the tsar had abdicated and there had come into being, besides the Soviet of Workers' Deputies, the Provisional Government, headed by Prince Lvov and composed mainly of Duma deputies from the Kadet and Octobrist parties. These included Miliukov, Guchkov and M.I. Tereshchenko, with the addition of the Socialist Revolutionary lawyer Alexander Kerensky as Minister of Justice. The Menshevik leadership of the Petrograd Soviet allowed the Provisional Government to take power, on the understanding that it would follow a democratic programme that was acceptable to the Soviet. In this way there was established the sharing of power between the Provisional Government and the Petrograd Soviet that was known by contemporaries as 'dual power'.

In Moscow, where Bogdanov was living, events followed a similar course to those in the capital. On 28 February Skvortsov-Stepanov, Olminsky and Smidovich met with other members of the Moscow Committee of the RSDLP and together set about establishing the Moscow Soviet of Workers' Deputies. Its chairman was the Menshevik L.M. Khinchuk and the vice-chairman the Bolshevik Smidovich. Skvortsov-Stepanov became the editor of the Soviet's publication, *Izvestiia Moskovskogo Soveta Rabochikh Deputatov*, to which Bogdanov contributed several articles, some of which appeared in the pamphlet *Lessons of the First Steps of the Revolution*, which was published in the first half of 1917. Bogdanov's writings of this period show the light in which he viewed the various issues that emerged after the fall of the tsarist regime.[48]

---

47   See White 1979 and White 2011.
48   Skvortsov-Stepanov 1970, pp. 210–12; Burdzhalov 1971, pp. 59–60, 79; Koenker 1981, pp. 102–3.

Bogdanov thought it right that the Petrograd Soviet should cede power to the Provisional Government on condition that the Provisional Government follow the revolutionary-democratic programme that the Soviet had proposed. In this way the Soviet would have its policies implemented without incurring the hostility of the liberals, as happened in 1905, and was a cause of the failure of that revolution. He only regretted that representatives of the Soviet had not participated in the Provisional Government, whose only socialist member, Kerensky, had joined on his own initiative. Bogdanov welcomed the formation of the coalition government after the April Crisis, when Miliukov had sent a note to the Allies, affirming that Russia would continue to pursue the war to a decisive victory.[49] Bogdanov believed that had there been a socialist contingent already in the government, Miliukov's action could have been prevented.[50]

One of the first acts of the Petrograd Soviet had been to issue an appeal calling upon the peoples of Europe to work together to bring about an end to the war. While approving of this gesture, Bogdanov thought it had a serious deficiency that would prevent its having the desired effect. This was that it addressed itself in particular to the 'proletarians of the Austro-German coalition', appealing to them to 'throw off the yoke of semi-autocratic rule, as the Russian people have cast off the tsar's autocracy'.[51] It was unfair, Bogdanov thought, to single out the Germans, implying that they alone were responsible for the war, when in fact it had been caused by the struggle of the capitalist powers for markets. In his view, the governments of Britain and France were just as deserving to be overthrown as that of Germany.[52]

Accordingly, on behalf of the Moscow Soviet, Bogdanov drafted an appeal which was more even-handed towards the proletariats of the belligerent and neutral countries. In it he deplored the fact that the workers were divided into two camps, each bent on the other's destruction, that they had 'torn up the red banner of international brotherhood of workers, and in its place unfurled the state banners of the ruling classes'. As to the nature of the war, Bogdanov explained:

> The world war emerged from the struggle of gigantic national capitals for domination on the world market. Governments, the lackeys of these capitals – are the representatives of their power over the peoples – they are all equally to blame for the catastrophe, whoever began it. They all forged

---

49   Browder and Kerensky 1961, 2, p. 1098.
50   Bogdanov 1917b, pp. 2–4.
51   See Browder and Kerensky 1961, 2, pp. 1077–8.
52   Bogdanov 1917b, pp. 16–18.

the devilish machine of militarism, which could not but explode; they all stoked the flame of blind hatred of nations. Their phrases about the struggle for right, justice and freedom are a cynical lie. Did the tsarist government fight for the freedom of Poland and the Jewish people? Did the Austrian government fight for the rights of the Balkan peoples? Did the British government campaign for justice for Ireland, or the Germans for it for Alsace-Lorraine? Annexations and indemnities, the robbery of the weakest – those are the aims of the war.[53]

In addressing himself to the new Provisional Government, Bogdanov called upon it to make a complete break with the past:

> And we say to our Provisional Government, which has emerged from the revolution: 'If you do not want to inherit fully the share of blame of the overthrown government for the world catastrophe, you must take upon yourself immediately the initiative of negotiations for peace! A government, unconnected with the past, emerging from the revolution, more than any other is called upon to undertake this great cause; and if you are found wanting, then so much greater the responsibility that falls upon you!'[54]

In concluding his appeal, Bogdanov expressed the hope that workers of other belligerent countries would follow the example of Russia by breaking their chains and effecting a change of regime. If they did so, he stressed that the workers of other countries were obligated to prevent these revolutions being crushed by enemy invasions.[55]

Soon after the February revolution Bogdanov published a pamphlet, *The Tasks of the Workers in the Revolution*, which aimed to orientate the workers in the new situation. The advice he gave to the workers came under four heads: 1) The Constituent Assembly; 2) The struggle for peace; 3) The 8-hour working day; 4) Whence came revolution and what are the tasks of the workers now?

Bogdanov began by explaining what the Constituent Assembly was: that it was not simply a Duma, not a parliament that engaged in legislative work, where there already existed a well-established regime with a recognised government; the Constituent Assembly laid down the foundations of this regime. Bogdanov stressed that the existing arrangements were provisional ones, that

---

53   Neizvestnyi Bogdanov 1995, 1, p. 80.
54   Neizvestnyi Bogdanov 1995, 1, pp. 80–1.
55   Neizvestnyi Bogdanov 1995, 1, p. 81.

the new was mixed up with the old. The new government that had emerged from the revolution ought to be revolutionary, but it was not. Most of its members were liberals, and represented not the working class, but capital.

Bogdanov advocated that the outcome of the Constituent Assembly should be the establishment of a democratic republic. The Provisional Government had promised to see that the war was not used as a pretext for not calling the Constituent Assembly, and the workers had to see to it that it kept its word. To be effective the Constituent Assembly had to represent all the people, and for this the voting had to be by universal, equal, direct and secret ballot.

It was essential, Bogdanov insisted, that the army should take part in these elections. The soldiers were workers and peasants in uniform. It should be possible to devise a means by which the army could participate in the elections, while still maintaining military discipline. The soldier-citizen should not be deprived of this basic civil right.

In Bogdanov's view the practice of democracy required a measure of economic equality. He therefore proposed that the Constituent Assembly should incorporate in the new order those conditions which would allow working people genuinely to make use of their civic freedom. The workers should be granted an 8-hour working day, state insurance against unemployment and a legally established minimum wage. All land should be transferred to the peasants. As a measure to benefit the people as a whole, the burden of taxation should be transferred from the poorer to the better-off classes.

Under the heading of 'The Struggle for Peace' Bogdanov reproduced the explanation for the war that he had argued at length in his article in *Letopis*: the competition of national capitals for the world market. He deplored the enormous loss of life that the war had cost. At the present time there had been no progress in the hostilities; it had become a war of attrition with no hope of a victorious conclusion. The only result could be ruin for both sides. The belligerents were all defeated, so that the only winners were America and Japan. In this situation it was essential to conduct a struggle for peace by legal means while legal means are still available. Here Bogdanov made his plea that while agitating for peace, nothing should be done to weaken the front or disrupt the work of the rear. To do otherwise could only lead to more loss of life and economic disruption.

Bogdanov wrote his pamphlet soon after 10 March, when a delegation from the Petrograd Soviet had reached agreement with the Petrograd Society of Factory Owners on the introduction of an eight-hour working day in factories belonging to the Society. The agreement was considered to be temporary until a decision for the whole country was made. Bogdanov was entirely in favour of the introduction of an eight-hour working day, but thought that the agreement reached in Petrograd was deficient, in that it still envisaged overtime working, something of which he strongly disapproved.

The most interesting section of Bogdanov's pamphlet is where he explains the origin of the present revolution and the tasks of the workers in it, because of the consistency it shows with earlier writings on revolutionary perspectives. For Bogdanov the 1917 revolution was the continuation of the revolution of 1905 that had suffered a setback and remained unfinished.[56]

The causes of the 1905 revolution, Bogdanov explained, had been that the old landowner and bureaucratic state had long ago become a serious obstacle to Russia's economic development, the growth of its productive forces. It smothered the proletariat and impoverished the peasantry, kept the masses in ignorance, and, although it protected the bourgeoisie with high tariff barriers, it had not allowed it to conduct its own affairs. It had restricted the development of capitalism and held back economic progress.

The 1905 revolution failed because the forces of the new order were not yet sufficiently prepared and organised, and the forces of the old were insufficiently undermined. The peasantry poorly supported the proletariat, which led the movement, and the bourgeoisie, alarmed by the workers' and peasants' revolution, hurriedly made terms with the landowners and bureaucrats, gaining pitiful concessions for themselves alone, in the semi-constitution of 3 June. The present revolution, the continuation of 1905, was a democratic revolution; it could and must culminate in a democratic republic.[57]

In outlining the dynamics of the February revolution, Bogdanov's interpretation coincided with those who had actually taken part in it, such as Chugurin, V.N. Kaiurov and A.G. Shliapnikov; he had no illusion that it was 'spontaneous'. According to Bogdanov, 'The workers began the revolution, going out on to the streets from the factories and workshops; it was developed and given its victory by the soldiers – the same workers and peasants in military uniform. The bourgeoisie followed the revolution, and gave it new representatives of power'. Bogdanov warned that the Provisional Government was not to be trusted, because its members were not democrats and came from the conservative Fourth Duma.[58]

From the vantage point of the spring of 1917 it seemed to Bogdanov that two great dangers threatened the revolution: one was that the prolonged war would lead to the complete exhaustion of the country; the other was that there would be a break-down of ties and mutual understanding between the revolutionary

---

56   Bogdanov 1917c, p. 15.
57   Bogdanov 1917c, p. 17.
58   Ibid.

people in the rear and the national army at the front. He believed that the plan of the reaction consisted precisely in creating dissension between the army and the workers, to convince the army that the workers, who were against the war, were indifferent to the fate of the army, although he did not think this plan would succeed.[59]

Bogdanov reminded his readers that the aim of the working class was not just civic freedoms, but socialism. To this end, the working class must demand the immediate convocation of the Constituent Assembly, an end to the war and the eight-hour working day. It should help the peasants take the land, but in doing so should prevent excesses. To replace the disbanded tsarist police force the workers should form a people's militia. The attitude of the working class to the Provisional Government should depend on how that government related to the revolution: it could be support while it carried out a democratic programme, but insistent pressure upon it when it departed from this programme, and direct and decisive struggle against it if it betrayed its obligations and went against the revolution. At present the pressure on the government came through the Soviets, but even if the socialists entered the government, this situation would not change; vigilance and pressure would still be required from the workers.[60]

9   What Is It That We Have Overthrown?

In April Gorky got together the finances to launch the newspaper *Novaia Zhizn*, whose main contributors, Bazarov, Avilov and Desnitsky, had been involved in the 1905 *Novaia Zhizn*. The newspaper was not formally attached to any Social-Democratic fraction, but welcomed contributions from supporters of the various RSDLP fractions and from writers who did not belong to any. Bogdanov naturally gravitated towards *Novaia Zhizn* because of its non-aligned status, and because it was run by his long-term friends and associates. In June Bogdanov contributed to *Novaia Zhizn* his article 'What Is It that We Have Overthrown?' which was occasioned by Lenin's return to Petrograd in April, and the promulgation of his 'April Theses'.

Roman Malinovsky had been exposed as a police spy, and Plekhanov's newspaper *Edinstvo* had used the revelation to attack the Bolsheviks by claiming that Bolshevik policy in the preceding year had been determined by the police

---

59   Bogdanov 1917c, pp. 17–8.
60   Bogdanov 1917c, pp. 18–22.

spy. Meshkovsky, who replied on behalf of the Bolsheviks, insisted that the Bolshevik line had always been determined by Lenin, and that this line had always been followed exactly by the secret agents who worked for the police department. Bogdanov, for his part, thought it immaterial who it was that laid down the line of a particular political grouping. What he found objectionable was that any individual should be in a position to determine the attitudes of any group of people.

It was objectionable on two counts. On the one hand, however talented an individual might be, his experience was limited and he was subject to all the usual human frailties. The fate of the collective which he led was thus built on a precarious foundation. On the other hand, a human collective that was led in an authoritarian way would inevitably try to impose this authoritarian model on the rest of society. In Bogdanov's words:

> Every organisation, on achieving a position of decisive influence in the life and ordering of society, quite inevitably, irrespective of the formal tenets of its programme, attempts to impose on society its own type of structure, the one with which it is most familiar and the one to which it is most accustomed. Every collective re-creates, as far as it can, the whole social environment after its own image and in its own likeness. And if this structure is of the authoritarian type, based on the domination-submission model, albeit in the intellectual spheres, it will inevitably give rise to authoritarian tendencies in the ordering of society itself, however democratic, communist etc. the programme of the organisation might be.[61]

It seemed to Bogdanov, therefore, that although tsarism had been overthrown, the authoritarian principles which it embodied were still intact. They lived on in the way political parties of both right and left subjected themselves to the dictates of a leader.

In order to illustrate the dangers of authoritarianism for the still politically unstable and culturally weak democracy in Russia, Bogdanov sketched out the development of authoritarianism within Bolshevism. He said he chose this example because it was the one most familiar to him, and because he considered it to be a typical one. In its early days, in the period 1904–7, Bolshevism was decidedly democratic, not only in its programme, but in the attitudes that permeated the organisation. Lenin was the most experienced and influential political figure in the organisation, but no one would have thought of waiting

---

61   Bogdanov 1917.

to hear Lenin's opinion before forming one's own. Moreover, often on important questions Lenin had found himself in a minority and had to put into effect the collective decision which he had voted against.

Things began to change with the victory of the reaction after the defeat of the 1905 revolution in Russia. The Bolshevik organisation was weakened, and the will of most of its members was broken. Lenin and his entourage at that time underwent a significant turn to the right. They effected a union with the Mensheviks, despite the opposition of local organisations in Russia. This was a victory for the principle of leadership, causing it to become entrenched. It was precisely from this time that many Bolsheviks began to refer to themselves as 'Lenininst', a title that had formerly been used by their opponents in polemics against them.[62]

Bogdanov went on to say that although the union with the Mensheviks lasted for only a few months, it was followed by a number of instances where Lenin was able to lay down the line in the teeth of opposition from members of his own party fraction. The latest example of Lenin's authoritarianism was in April of the present year, when he returned from abroad and in his 'April Theses' demanded a complete break with the policies currently being pursued by the Bolsheviks in Russia. In Bogdanov's view, if an ordinary party member had done this, he would have been brushed aside, but because it was the leader who made these demands the treatment was quite different; a veritable earthquake took place. In Bogdanov's opinion, 'the basic feature of the authoritarian way of thinking consists precisely in the acceptance of a qualitative difference between the ruler and the ruled'.[63]

The conclusion that Bogdanov drew from this was that although the fall of the tsarist regime had overthrown authoritarianism politically, authoritarian attitudes continued to survive culturally. And they did so among the most progressive elements of the population, let alone among the unenlightened masses. What it would take to eliminate them, Bogdanov stated, was a 'cultural revolution', a term which he introduced for the first time.[64]

Bogdanov went on to argue, as he had done in his 1914 and 1916 writings, that the war had taught socialists a great lesson. Why, he asked, had it been able to destroy the international brotherhood of the workers so easily? Why did most of the proletariat and its ideologists in the belligerent countries submit so blindly to the leadership of the bourgeoisie? This was, he said, because the socialist way of thinking existed only in an embryonic form, and was powerless

---

62   Ibid.
63   Ibid.
64   Ibid.

to cope with the new challenges confronting it on a global scale. The socialist as a cultural type was and remained essentially bourgeois. The proletariat was still a long way from having elaborated its own particular modes of thought. In Russia, Bogdanov believed, even the democratic cultural type was a stage that still had to be reached. For that reason, he concluded: 'We must have a cultural revolution'.[65]

10   The Commune State

The policy that Lenin urged on the Bolsheviks on his return to Russia prompted Bogdanov to publish a critique of the 'April Theses' in *Izvestiia Moskovskogo Soveta Rabochikh Deputatov* entitled 'The Commune-State'. This article is in its way a sequel to 'What Is It that We have Overthrown?' and lays bare the ineptitude of Lenin's contribution to revolutionary theory in 1917.

In his 'April Theses' Lenin had advocated that the Bolsheviks demand a 'commune state' as the form of political structure in the period of transition from the bourgeois order to socialism. The model he had in mind was the Paris Commune of 1871, which would be 'not the usual parliamentary bourgeois state, but a state without a standing army, without a police opposed to the people, without an officialdom placed above the people'. In place of this he called for 'a republic of Soviets of Workers', Agricultural Labourers' and Peasants' Deputies throughout the country, from top to bottom'. On this idea, Bogdanov remarked that such a 'commune' differed greatly from the Paris one; the Paris Commune had had a system of representatives who were not elected by separate curia of workers, soldiers and peasants, but chosen directly by the population as a whole.

Bogdanov thought that Lenin's version of the commune state was unfeasible. Like other members of the *Novaia Zhizn* group, he held that the Soviets were organs of revolutionary struggle, a means of furthering the revolution, but were unsuitable as permanent organs of government. Soviets were not elected on a uniform basis, and the proportion of delegates to electors varied widely throughout the country. Some towns had one delegate for every fifty inhabitants, others had one for every hundred, others again for every two hundred and so on. This did not matter in the revolution, but as a permanent state organisation this was obviously less suitable than a parliamentary democratic republic.[66]

---

65   Ibid.
66   Bogdanov 1990, p. 345.

If the different classes were represented in different hierarchies of Soviets with no overall institution, they would relate to each other like countries in international law. Because of the disparity of interests, disagreements between worker Soviets and peasant Soviets must inevitably arise. An increase in workers' wages, for example, would result in rising prices for goods bought by peasants. With no higher instance to appeal to, the Soviets were left to resolve their differences by themselves. According to Bogdanov, there had already been a confrontation of Soviets in Ekaterinburg. The incident had ended peaceably, but one could imagine that under different circumstances the outcome would not have been so favourable. This was understandable, Bogdanov considered, because the nature of Soviets was that they were organs of revolutionary struggle, and their way of resolving conflicts was by armed force.[67]

Bogdanov pointed out that Lenin would be more consistent if he were to argue, as Trotsky had done in 1905, that the Russian revolution would be a permanent one and give rise to socialism. In that case the Soviets would continue to be organs of revolutionary struggle and not permanent state institutions. But in his 'April Theses' Lenin had specifically ruled this out. In this judgement Bogdanov considered Lenin to be entirely right; the present revolution was a democratic one, and there were good reasons why the progression to socialism was precluded. The peasants would not tolerate a long period of revolutionary ferment; they wanted to be given the land and thereafter to be left in peace.

There were people who did think that the Russian revolution could be a permanent one. They conceded that socialism was unattainable by Russia alone, but believed that the workers of Western Europe would turn from the struggle for peace to the overthrow of capitalism, and would then come to the help of the Russians in accelerating their progress to socialism. Bogdanov thought it would require a strong exercise of faith to believe that the European workers, the majority of whom had meekly followed the capitalists, and even after three years of war were still doing so at tremendous cost, would all of a sudden decide to reconstruct society on a new basis. But even if they were to do so, many years would lie between the democratic and the socialist stages of the revolution in Russia. It was inevitable that in this prolonged period there would be relapses into reaction, and when these occurred conflicts of interest would come to the fore. With a democratic republic these conflicts could be resolved by parliamentary means, the weaker side succumbing, but with the chance of becoming the stronger side some time in the future. With a republic of Soviets this way

---

67   Bogdanov 1990, p. 346.

was closed, so that the reaction had every chance of developing into a civil war, with enormous losses of human life.[68]

Another impracticality of Lenin's programme was in his idea that 'The salaries of all officials, all of whom are elective and subject to recall at any time, [should not] exceed the average wage of a competent worker'. To Bogdanov this went against elementary economic sense. Work such as that of an organiser, which was prolonged, intensive and complex, demanded a great expenditure of energy from the human organism. It would therefore need a corresponding assimilation of energy, that is more plentiful and more complex consumption. If a commissar or a minister exhausted his mental and nervous energy in his post, so as to be incapacitated for several years, and received the same 200–300 roubles as a competent turner, what turner would want to be a minister? Bogdanov was of the opinion that Lenin's communism was of an infantile, pre-scientific kind. If everyone was to be paid the same the end result would be that the most demanding and responsible posts would be held either by the children of the bourgeoisie, who had an alternative income, or by intriguers who did not scruple to supplement their incomes by corruption.[69]

The idea that officials should be subject to recall at any time conjured up to Bogdanov the situation where, in a given region, where the Bolsheviks held the majority, Bolshevik delegates would be elected. If then the Mensheviks came to be in the majority, they would recall all the Bolshevik delegates irrespective of whether they had done well in their posts or not.[70]

To Bogdanov, Lenin's programme was an extreme example of maximalist thinking. It lacked any organisational analysis, but was inspired by the faith that somehow the revolution would deliver up the desired results. Bogdanov did not have long to wait to see that nothing in Lenin's 'April Theses' was actually implemented, and the revolution in fact took a very baleful turn. The absence of any mechanism to resolve the clash of interests was to be an important factor in the outbreak of the civil war in 1918.

11   On Party Unity

In company with the *Novaia Zhizn* group as a whole, Bogdanov believed that in the present revolutionary situation it was necessary to re-unite the various fractions of the RSDLP. Obviously, this would greatly strengthen the party, and

---

68   Bogdanov 1990, p. 347.
69   Bogdanov 1990, p. 348.
70   Ibid.

would enable it to give direction to the workings of the Soviets, rather than simply follow the vagaries of the prevailing moods within them, as happened at the present time. Although a united Social-Democratic Party would help remedy this situation, there were vested interests in maintaining the existing divisions. In each of the separated fractions the role of leader was dominant, so that he was able to lay down the line in the given organisation without resistance or counter-balances. In a united party, on the other hand, leaders would have to argue their case, counter criticism from opponents, and find themselves on many occasions in a small minority.

One of the worst results of the divisions in the RSDLP was that when the respective fractions recruited workers to their ranks, they did so in a polemical way, inculcating into the recruits the mistakes of the Bolsheviks if they were Mensheviks, and the mistakes of the Mensheviks if they were Bolsheviks. Workers therefore became Bolsheviks or Mensheviks before they became Social Democrats, knowing all the subtleties of the disputes, but not knowing the basics of the economic and historical doctrine of Social-Democracy.

Nevertheless, Bogdanov believed that unity was possible. After all, there was no need to unite everyone. A political party was an organisation for action, not an organisation of opinion. Opinions were taken into account in so far as they determined a given course of action. But where there were significant differences of opinion on the course of action to be taken, this would not matter so long as democratic discipline was maintained, and the minority refrained from action that had been rejected by the majority, limiting oneself, in Lenin's phrase, to 'patient explanation and propaganda'.[71]

In this article Bogdanov provided an explanation for many of Lenin's actions in 1917. It was clearly Lenin that Bogdanov had in mind when he spoke of the leader who 'laid down the line', and to do that he had to maintain the Bolshevik fraction as a separate entity. The 'maximalism' of the 'April Theses' enabled him to do this, and it was in all probability this consideration that determined their character. And bearing in mind Lenin's behaviour after the Kotka conference, maintaining democratic discipline was not something that Lenin could be relied upon to do.

According to Skvortsov-Stepanov, the break with Lenin and its aftermath in emigration was still very fresh in Bogdanov's mind – as indeed his writings in 1917 suggest. Nevertheless, Skvortsov-Stepanov states, Bogdanov did not give any credence to the accusations raised against Lenin by the right-wing parties that the mode of his return to Russia in the sealed train showed that he was a

---

71   Bogdanov 1917a.

German agent. Nor did it enter Bogdanov's head that Lenin had accepted German money.[72] He recognised the accusation as one designed to discredit the parties of the left. The same accusation had been made in 1905, he recalled, but then it was of accepting money from the Japanese or from the British.[73]

What Bogdanov was doing during the first half of 1917 emerges from a letter he wrote to the editorial board of *Novaia Zhizn* dated 30 May 1917. He explains that he is kept very busy, first of all by his military duties, which involve visiting German prisoner-of-war camps. Then there are his literary activities: his contributions to *Izvestiia Moskovskogo Soveta Rabochikh Deputatov* and *Novaia Zhizn* plus propagandist pamphlets, such as *The Tasks of the Workers in the Revolution*, which had gone through three editions. In addition to these, he is occupied with his life's work – writing *Tectology*. On 5 June Bogdanov wrote to P.I. Lebedev-Poliansky informing him that he was about to leave for a four-day inspection of prisoner-of-war camps in the Vladimir province. When he returned he would be giving a series of four three-hour lectures to an audience of 500 trainee propagandists attached to the Soviet of Soldiers' Deputies.[74]

12   Questions of Socialism

Although Bogdanov shared the opinions of his friends on *Novaia Zhizn* on the role of the Soviets and the need for party unity, he parted company with them on the significance of the war economy, on 'state capitalism'. In November 1917 he published a collection of his recent writings entitled *Questions of Socialism* that included an article entitled 'War Communism and State Capitalism', in which he contested the idea, put forward by Bazarov, that the measures of state regulation necessitated by the war could be regarded as a transition stage to a socialist society.

According to Bogdanov, the army in general, in peace and in wartime, is an enormous consumer commune with an authoritarian structure. A mass of people live at the expense of the state, distributing amongst themselves goods from the producing apparatus, which they consume uniformly. In peace time the commune is a small part of society as a whole, and has no great influence upon it. In war time, however, the commune grows in extent and in importance for the country. Its influence on society in terms of structure and culture

---

72   Skvortsov-Stepanov 1970, pp. 239–40.
73   Bogdanov 1917b, p. 21.
74   Neizvestnyi Bogdanov, 1, pp. 187–8. Unlike in Petrograd, in Moscow the Soviet of Soldiers' Deputies was separate from the Soviet of Workers' Deputies.

increases enormously. The character of this influence is determined by two distinctive features of the military apparatus: its authoritarian structure and its consumer communism.[75]

As it was obvious that in wartime countries experienced an expansion of authoritarianism, Bogdanov did not consider it necessary to dwell on this topic. His main interest in the article was to examine the dynamics of the military consumer commune in wartime conditions, its gradual extension from the army to the rest of society.

The first stage in the process was the maintenance of soldiers' families by the state, so that millions of people were either wholly or partly supported at state expense. This was quite irrespective of any function they might perform in production. And it was not as if they were state employees; they were supported simply because they had the right to have their needs supplied. This was an extension of the soldiers' commune in the country.[76]

The destructive course of the war extended the consumer commune even further. The shortage of goods was exacerbated by the uneven way they were distributed, hence a rationing system was introduced. This gave the purchaser the right to buy a given quantity of goods, but that did not guarantee that the goods in question would be available and at a price that could be afforded. The solution was to control prices and the supply of goods, leading to a further extension of consumer communism and restrictions on the private ownership of goods.

With continuing economic decline the regulation of the supply of goods turned out to be futile without regulation of their production, because capitalists had no incentive to produce rationed goods, from which they could not gain any profit. The state was forced to exercise control over branches of production and the quantities of that production, and consequently over the distribution of raw materials, implements and the labour force. While the state control of supplies could lead to the merger of whole sectors into syndicates, the regulation of production could necessitate the compulsory formation of trusts, the merger of whole sectors into corporate organisations with the complete loss of independence for individual enterprises.[77]

This, Bogdanov explained, was how 'state capitalism' came about. Its point of departure was military consumer communism, and its driving force was the progressive decline of the economy. Its organising method was rationing and

75   Bogdanov 1990, p. 335.
76   Bogdanov 1990, p. 336.
77   Bogdanov 1990, p. 337.

restrictions enforced by authoritarian-compulsory means. To understand this system it was essential to bear in mind that it arose out of consumption, and through supply had entered the sphere of production. This sequence of events was the exact opposite of the normal course of development. There it was the development of production which determined changes in the forms of distribution and consumption. In tectological terms, normal growth was one of progressive changes in the social organism. In 'state capitalism' the processes were of decline, destruction, simplification, i.e. these were regressive phenomena.

This did not mean, however, that the changes wrought in the social forces by regression were unnecessary or harmful; on the contrary, since they regulated the process of decline by retarding and alleviating its course, they were essential adaptations to the circumstances. But the character of these adaptations, and in particular their relationship to socialism, could not be rightly understood if one lost sight of their origin.[78]

In *Novaia Zhizn* Bazarov had argued that state capitalism was a transitional form between capitalism and socialism, an idea that Bogdanov disagreed with strongly. He pointed out that there was an enormous difference between socialism, which was primarily a new form of cooperation, and war communism, which was a special form of social consumption, an authoritarian-regulated organisation of mass parasitism and annihilation. If state capitalism really was the first stage of a socialist revolution then it would be the outcome of the progressive driving forces of capitalism, of the culmination of the class struggle of the proletariat. In actual fact, state capitalism embodied class cooperation of nations for the purpose of destruction. There would be no socialist revolution in Europe or Russia, but that did not mean that there could not be revolutions to restore or to establish democratic regimes, eliminate national oppression, restore the economic and cultural bonds between countries and cancel oppressive debts.[79]

Bogdanov devoted much attention in his article to considering what features of war communism were likely to remain after the end of the war. As it happened, in Russia the World War shaded into the Civil War, which lasted until 1921, so that war communism had a greater longevity than Bogdanov might have expected. And in fact the features of the economic system which was in force in Soviet Russia between 1918 and 1921 are remarkably accurately described in Bogdanov's article; the essence of that system was precisely that it

---

78   Bogdanov 1990, pp. 337–8.
79   Bogdanov 1990, pp. 338–43.

was an attempt to manage scarce resources in a spiral of economic decline. Bogdanov himself took pride in his analysis of war communism, giving it a special mention in a lecture in the Socialist Academy in 1922 and in the autobiographical sketch which he wrote in 1925.[80]

The final essay in *Questions of Socialism*, 'The Ideal and the Way', was reminiscent of Bogdanov's *Vpered* article 'Socialism of the Present', in that it stressed that the ideal of socialism was embodied not only at the end of the road, but at every step of the way. According to Bogdanov, in the old way of understanding things, socialism triumphed and then was implemented; before the victory it was not a reality; it did not exist; it was only a 'final objective'. This, in Bogdanov's view, was a mistaken idea, because socialism was a world system of comradely cooperation between people who were not separated by private property, competition, exploitation or class struggle, people who dominated nature and consciously and systematically strengthened their mutual relations. This was exactly what the proletariat was in the process of doing.

Bearing in mind this understanding of what socialism was, Bogdanov rejected any suggestion that the present war communism bore any resemblance to it. He did so in a rather emotional passage:

> We are asked now to 'recognise' future socialism in a repulsive caricature of it born of the war and the old order. We do not agree to do this. Fortunately for us, our socialism is beautiful at all stages of its historical incarnation. It does not hide itself under the mask of a vampire and you do not need any special efforts to recognise it in its deepening divide from the old world, among the tragic situations of the epoch.[81]

From this concept of socialism, Bogdanov believed, what had to be done was to continue the previous struggle and organisation, consciously to collect, nurture and systematise the growing shoots of the new culture, the elements of socialism in the present.[82]

Bukharin reviewed Bogdanov's pamphlet *Questions of Socialism* in the issue of the 'Left Communist' journal *Kommunist* for May 1918. Bukharin began by paying tribute to Bogdanov, the controversial author of *Empiriomonism*, as an interesting and original thinker, whose views on the origin of religion had received support from specialist historians and ethnographers. He did not feel

80   Bogdanov 1922a, p. 147; Neizvestnyi Bogdanov 1995, 1, p. 19.
81   Bogdanov 1990, p. 350.
82   Bogdanov 1990, pp. 349–50.

able, however, to recommend the present pamphlet to his readers. He believed it to be an attack on the Bolshevik party, a critique which was conducted from the point of view of 'opportunist culturalism'.

According to Bukharin, Bogdanov's basic idea was that the socialist transformation of society and the socialist revolution should be undertaken according to an organisational plan worked out in advance. First, the working class would create its own science, elaborate its scientific methods in all spheres of knowledge, construct for this purpose workers' universities, write a proletarian encyclopaedia etc. and then make an 'organisational plan' to decide the 'world organisational tasks'. When all this was done, only then would it be possible to achieve socialism. To do otherwise would be 'maximalism' and utopia.[83]

In Bukharin's opinion, Bogdanov's mistake was not that he regarded ideology as a force in transforming society, but the fact that he viewed the social-historical process as a rational one, something for which one could set out a detailed plan that could then be carried out. Bukharin's greatest objection to the way Bogdanov presented the socialist revolution was in the sequence and the timing of the various phases: 1) the realisation of the class socialist order within the framework of capitalism; 2) its culmination in the socialist revolution, which for the first time would establish 'the class socialist order' (the 'dictatorship of the proletariat' in Bukharin's terminology); this socialist revolution does not complete, but commences the socialist development; 3) the period of the dying away of the dictatorship and the state and the transformation of the 'class social order' into a 'general-human' one. This final period can arrive only after the decisive and final victory of the workers. In Bukharin's view, this order of things simply postponed the workers' victory and in this respect was an opportunist theory.

Bukharin was in agreement with Bogdanov on the subject of state capitalism. He thought that Bogdanov was right to criticise Bazarov's idea that the war economies of Germany, Britain and other countries were the precursors of socialism. But Bukharin did not concur with Bogdanov in explaining the collapse of the Second International by the remnants in the working class of bourgeois-peasant thinking. In accord with Hilferding, Bukharin attributed the collapse to what he called 'worker imperialism'.

With regard to Bogdanov's critique of Lenin's conception of the commune state, Bukharin commented that this was a case where Bogdanov did not under-

---

83   Kommunist: Ezhenedel'nyi zhurnal ekonomiki, politiki i obshchestvennosti: organ Moskovskogo Oblastnogo Biuro RKP (bol'shevikov) 1990, p. 173.

stand the significance of the epoch of the dictatorship of the proletariat. On this point, he thought that the best answer that could be given to Bogdanov was that which would be given by life itself.[84] In the event, 'life itself' did not come up with the answer that Bukharin expected.

On 25 October 1917, without a great deal of resistance, the Bolsheviks were able to come to power and form their Council of People's Commissars headed by Lenin.[85] In the new government Lunacharsky became the Commissar for Education with Pokrovsky as his deputy. Lunacharsky wrote to Bogdanov proposing that he too should accept a post in the newly-formed People's Commissariat for Education (Narkompros).

Since Bogdanov regarded the accession to power of the Bolsheviks, not as the socialist revolution that Lenin claimed it to be, but merely as a war communist one,[86] it is not surprising that he refused Lunacharsky's offer. His letter to Lunacharsky, dated 19 November, is couched in tectological terms, and reflects Bogdanov's preoccupation at the time with the question of war communism.

After summarising what he had said in *Questions of Socialism* about the development of war communism, Bogdanov went on to observe that the atmosphere of war communism had given rise to the maximalism of *Novaia Zhizn* and to that of Lunacharsky himself. It had also deeply affected the Bolshevik party. The party had won the support of the soldiers because of its promise of peace, and as a result had been transformed from a workers' party into a workers' and soldiers' party.

The consequence of this was that, following the tectological law of the leasts, where a system consisted of parts with higher and lower levels of organisation, its relationship with the environment was determined by those with the lowest levels of organisation. Here Bogdanov gave as examples a chain which was only as strong as its weakest link and the speed of a squadron that was only as fast as its slowest ship. The position of a party composed of contingents from different classes would be determined by the most backward wing. A workers' and soldiers' party was objectively simply a soldiers' one. And it was striking to what degree the Bolsheviks had been transformed in this way; they had assimilated the logic of the barracks, all its methods, all of its specific culture and its ideals. Bogdanov explained that the logic of the barracks, in contrast to the

---

84   Kommunist: Ezhenedel'nyi zhurnal ekonomiki, politiki i obshchestvennosti: organ Moskovskogo Oblastnogo Biuro RKP (bol'shevikov) 1990, p. 175.

85   Bogdanov stated in 1922: 'I know how the Bolsheviks felt when power fell into their hands. The first sentiment was something like perplexity'. See Bogdanov 1922a, p. 147.

86   Bogdanov 1990, p. 348.

logic of the factory, was that it regarded every question as one of force rather than one of organised experience and labour. To the mentality of the barracks it was simply a matter of smashing the bourgeoisie and seizing political power and that would be socialism; compromises would seem pointless if one had the stronger hand.

As an example of how the spirit of war communism permeated the Bolshevik party Bogdanov indicated how this affected himself personally. He explained to Lunacharsky, that even if he wanted to take up Lunacharsky's offer of a post in the Council of People's Commissars, he would be unable to do so for material considerations. It would be a post that would demand all his time and effort, but the payment would be 'no higher than that of a skilled worker'. That would be entirely insufficient to maintain two families and to publish the second volume of *Tectology* at his own expense, since no publisher would take it on.

This problem would not occur to people from the barracks, because they were not involved in production; all they would know is the ration. Had Lenin and Trotsky not read Marx to know that the value of labour power was determined by the normal level of consumption connected with the carrying out of the given function. Of course they knew, but they had consciously broken with the logic of socialism for the logic of war communism.

The barracks atmosphere which prevailed in the new Soviet government was not one in which Bogdanov believed he would be able to live and work. For him comradely relations were the principle of the new culture. He had made great personal sacrifices for the sake of comradely relations, so that in this he would not change.

Bogdanov declared that anyone who thought that a soldiers' uprising was the way to begin the implementation of the socialist ideal had broken with worker socialism and gone the way of military-consumer communism. That person had taken a caricature of decline for the ideal of life and beauty. He did not mind if this course was taken by the 'rude chess player Lenin or the narcissistic Trotsky', but he thought it sad that Lunacharsky should have done so.

In Russia, in Bogdanov's opinion, the soldier-communist revolution was something more opposed to socialism than related to it. The demagogic-military dictatorship was in principle unstable; it was impossible to 'sit on bayonets'. The worker-soldier party would have to split. Then a new workers' party, or the remainder of it that survived the soldiers' bullets and bayonets, would demand its own ideology and its own ideologists. It was for that future, Bogdanov said, that he would work. It was necessary that proletarian culture should cease to be simply a topic for discussion, but should have a definite concrete content. One had to work out what its principles were, establish its criteria, formulate its logic, so that one could always decide what was proletarian culture and what was not. This, Bogdanov, stated, would be his objective, for as long as it took to accomplish it.[87]

This passage is highly significant, because it establishes what Bogdanov envisaged the proletarian culture movement as being. Obviously, it emerged as a critique of war communism and state capitalism and their influence on working class consciousness. It was a continuation of the conception of proletarian culture that Bogdanov had first enunciated in 1907. Bogdanov did not think of the proletarian culture movement as existing comfortably within the Soviet regime. He saw this as a caricature of socialism, and regarded the development of proletarian culture as a step towards a genuine socialist revolution. Bogdanov, however, was unable to make the connection between the concepts of war communism and proletarian culture explicit because of the strict censorship imposed by the Soviet regime.

Some of the ideas in the letter to Lunacharsky reappeared nine weeks later in an article entitled 'The Fortunes of the Workers' Party in the Present Revolution' in an issue of *Novaia Zhizn* that came out just before the dissolution of the Constituent Assembly. In the article Bogdanov attempted to analyse the way in which the Bolshevik Party had evolved since taking power in October 1917.

Bogdanov's starting point was a comparison between the revolutions of 1905 and 1917. Although both involved the proletariat and the peasantry, the revolution of 1917 differed from 1905 in that it took place in the unprecedented conditions of the World War, thus ensuring a major role in it for the soldiers, the peasants in uniform. The widespread desire for peace in 1917 had brought a mass influx of both workers and soldiers into the Bolshevik party, the party which promised peace. The change in the membership meant that the Bolsheviks were no longer the party of the workers, but of the workers and soldiers.[88]

Because Bogdanov considered that the continuation of the war would have meant the irreversible economic and cultural decline of Russia, he viewed the seizure of power by the Bolsheviks and their conclusion of peace as historically inevitable. He saw the seizure not as a conspiracy, but as the eruption of spontaneous forces brought about by the ruinous continuation of the war. It was this that had brought the Bolsheviks to power.

The fact that the Bolsheviks were a workers' and soldiers' party had determined how the party had behaved on coming to power. Since the party was made up of two class cohorts with different levels of culture, the law of the leasts

---

87   Bogdanov 1990, p. 355.
88   Bogdanov 1918f.

ensured that the political standpoint of the whole party, its programme, tactics and methods, would be dictated by the group with the lower cultural level. Consequently, for all practical purposes, the worker-soldier party was simply a soldiers' party.

Whereas the working class viewed political activities in terms of labour and skill, the soldiery saw them in terms of physical force, as an offensive. This was evidenced by the way the Bolsheviks attempted to take over the banking system. This, as Bogdanov explained, was an enormously complex mechanism, beyond the comprehension of even most economists. The crude methods employed in nationalising the banks destroyed the networks of deposits and debt on which they were based and made them unworkable.[89]

The existing legal system was approached in the same military fashion. Instead of dismissing leading figures and replacing old laws by new ones, dealing with political opponents by special tribunals, the entire legal structure was destroyed and replaced by a hastily constructed new one. According to Bogdanov, the military approach was also employed in the question of the workers' control over production. In Lenin's decree of 14 November 1917 factory committees were entrusted with control over production, the purchase and sale of goods and raw materials, their safe-keeping and the finances of the enterprises. However, decisions concerning the expansion or contraction of production required an understanding of the operation of credit, something of which the workers had no experience.[90]

Bogdanov considered that egalitarianism was an attitude characteristic of war communism rather than of worker socialism. It was military egalitarianism that determined the mistaken attitude of the Bolsheviks to the technical intelligentsia, in particular, to civil servants and the officer corps. As in his letter to Lunacharsky, Bogdanov pointed out that this policy conflicted with Marx's teaching that the value of labour power was determined by the values that would satisfy the basic needs of the worker and restore his full working capacity. The needs of a skilled worker were higher than those of an unskilled labourer, and by the same token the wages of a skilled organising intellectual or military officer should be even higher. Otherwise the maximum labouring capacity would not be restored and the net loss would be far greater than any savings in wages. If military commanders were elected, Bogdanov argued, the kind of people who would be chosen would be skilled agitators who could appeal to the crowd rather than a person with knowledge and judgement.

---

89   Ibid.
90   Ibid.

Bogdanov concluded by echoing what he had said in his letter to Lunacharsky, that in time the two components of Bolshevism, the workers and the soldiers, would separate. Then a new workers' party would emerge, which would then be joined by the Social Democratic intelligentsia whose ideals remained intact and had not been contaminated by the attitudes of war communism. Bogdanov hoped that this separation would take place as soon and as peacefully as possible.[91]

------

91   Ibid.

Proletkult

1   *Proletarskaia Kultura*

Even before the Bolsheviks took power Lunacharsky had chaired a conference of cultural and educational societies in Petrograd that took place on 16–19 October. It was from this conference that the organisation later known as Proletkult emerged. Lunacharsky's conception of what Proletkult was, however, was not as well defined as Bogdanov's. He thought of Proletkult as the proletariat's organisation in the cultural sphere in the same way as the party was its organisation in the political sphere and the trade unions in the sphere of economics.[1] However, Bogdanov's preparations to give the Proletkult movement definition were already well ahead. As early as May of 1917 he had been collaborating with Lebedev-Poliansky to publish a journal entitled *Proletarskaia Kultura* which would perform this function.[2] When its first issue finally appeared in July 1918 it was as the Organ of the Central Committee of the All-Russian Council of Proletkult, published by the State Publishing House.

The first opportunity that Bogdanov had to give definition to the Proletkult movement was his editorial article in the first issue of *Proletarskaia Kultura*. In this unsigned editorial he re-stated the idea, first expressed in his 1914 and 1916 writings on the collapse of the Second International, that the necessity for a proletarian culture had been highlighted by the response of the workers to the outbreak of the war in 1914. According to Bogdanov, when the world war broke out:

> The majority of workers even in the most advanced countries followed the bourgeoisie of their own free will, recognising its national interests as being higher than their class interests, concluded peace and an alliance with their own capitalists, so that together they might wipe out their enemies – their own comrades of yesterday and tomorrow. Both the thought and the feeling of the workers turned out to be unreliable and unstable. Why? Because they came up against a new and unprecedentedly difficult question, and they did not have at their disposal a

---

1   Lunacharskii 1963–7, 7, pp. 205, 650.
2   Neizvestnyi Bogdanov 1995, 1, p. 186.

sufficiently profound and integrated education to resolve it firmly and decisively, in their own way, from the point of view of their own task and their own ideal. Not being strong enough to resolve it in this way, the working class subordinated itself to an alien solution, that which was foisted upon it by the whole of the surrounding environment the capitalist world.[3]

The solution that Bogdanov proposed to this problem was the inculcation into the working class of an autonomous proletarian culture. He explained that: 'To give a class an all round education, unequivocally directing the collective will and thinking can only be done by elaborating an autonomous intellectual culture. The bourgeois classes have it – therein lay their strength; the proletariat lacked it – therein lay its weakness'.[4]

Bogdanov went on to caution against the wholesale rejection of bourgeois culture. This had to be assimilated in such a way that it became an instrument in the hands of the proletariat. In older cultures there were elements that were useful to the proletariat, but there were also others that were harmful. This being the case, the proletariat had to learn to distinguish what was beneficial from what was harmful and alien to it in the heritage of the past. For this purpose the proletariat had to develop an independent critical approach to the products of earlier cultures.[5]

Two of Bogdanov's contributions to *Proletarskaia Kultura* during 1918 were concerned with the criteria to be employed by the proletariat in evaluating bourgeois art, and in creating works of art of its own. The first article, entitled 'On the Artistic Inheritance', was published in *Proletarskaia Kultura* No. 2. In it Bogdanov declared that two great tasks confronted the proletariat: one of these was to produce its own artistic creations, and the other was to accept its inheritance, to take possession of the great storehouse of art that had been created in the past, to appropriate all that was great and beautiful in it, without being affected by the spirit of the bourgeois and feudal societies that was contained within it. This second task, Bogdanov considered, was no less difficult than the first one.

Bogdanov likened the approach of the proletarian critic towards the art of the past to the approaches that might be taken to the study of Buddhism. First, there was the attitude of the religious person. He would be critical of Buddhism from the point of view of his own Christian beliefs, would seek to show the

---

3   Bogdanov 1918g, p. 1.
4   Ibid.
5   Ibid.

falsehood of its doctrines, and would be unable to see in them any kind of truth whether poetic or about life. A free-thinker, on the other hand, who regarded all religions as popular poetic creations, would also be critical of Buddhism, but he would appreciate the beauty and depth of its teachings that had made it attractive to millions of people. A free-thinker would derive more from the study of Buddhism than a Christian scholar, because he was not burdened by considerations of its being heresy and in conflict with Christian teachings. A strict atheist would see in all religions nothing but superstition and deceit. He was the mirror-image of the Christian scholar. He had risen above religion sufficiently high to reject it, but not high enough to understand it.

Of the three approaches to religion, Bogdanov thought that the one most appropriate was the free-thinker. This was an approach that could evaluate the subject dispassionately. He was free from religious consciousness in general, and was able to campaign against it wherever it clouded people's thinking and sapped their will. But at the same time he was capable of making all religions a valuable cultural inheritance for himself and for others.

Bogdanov argued that the proletariat should not simply adopt the culture of the past as it stood. Nor should it reject that culture entirely in the manner in which the naive atheist rejected the religious heritage; the proletariat's attitude to the culture of the bourgeois and feudal past should be analogous to the approach of the free-thinker to religion. With this approach the proletariat would be able to master this culture without submitting to it, making it an instrument in the construction of the new life and a weapon in the struggle against the old society from which that culture came.[6]

Bogdanov then posed the question: could and should the whole world of religious creation become the cultural inheritance for the working class, against which every religion to date had clearly served as a means of enslavement? What would be the use of such a heritage, and what could be done with it?

The answer Bogdanov gave to his question was that this inheritance was very important and valuable for the working class. The critique of religion would allow the proletariat to understand its authoritarian nature. For although the authoritarian world had outlived itself, it had not died; its remains were to be encountered all around, sometimes openly, but more often in a disguised and unexpected form. To defeat such an enemy one had to understand it profoundly and seriously.

It was not enough to refute religious doctrines, although to do this the worker was better prepared than the severe but naive atheist who rebuts them by

---

6 Bogdanov 1918b, p. 6.

logical deductions or – here a reference to Lenin – childish assertions that 'religion was invented by priests to deceive the people'. Much more important was the fact that mastering the religious heritage made it possible to evaluate correctly the significance of authoritarian elements of the present society, their mutual connection and their relation to social development. In the new world the figures of authority were the party leaders, and one had to understand the importance of exercising collective control over them.[7]

As an example of a work of art which had a lasting significance Bogdanov chose Shakespeare's *Hamlet*. In the autumn of 1918, with the Soviet state convulsed by civil war, he gave a new dimension to his understanding of Hamlet's personality as the synthesis of the aesthete and the warrior. In this case it was the proletarian idealist or, even more so, the collective psyche of the working class that was in the tragic situation of Hamlet with his divided soul. For, as Bogdanov explained, the ideal it cherished was brotherhood, a harmonious life for the whole of humanity, but this was far from being achieved in the present environment, when the proletariat was involved in a cruel struggle for survival. As Bogdanov pointed out, the enormous significance of this drama for the proletariat did not require proof.[8]

In the following issue of *Proletarskaia Kultura* Bogdanov discussed the criteria for evaluating proletarian art. He began this in a tectological way by stating that the creation of new images by the artist was like the process of natural selection; some of them were adapted to their environment, some were not. Criticism was a means of sifting out the more from the less stable images. In this way proletarian criticism had the role of a regulator, controlling the development of proletarian art.

The first task was to define the boundaries of proletarian art and distinguish it from the art of other classes. In Bogdanov's view, what distinguished proletarian art was that its central value was collectivism, comradely cooperation. By contrast, peasants were individualists, as was reflected in the work of the peasant poets, Nikolai Kliuev and Sergei Esenin. They gloried in religious imagery, were nostalgic about the past and extolled leaders of the spontaneous forces of the people, such as Stenka Razin. All of these features were alien to the socialist consciousness of the proletariat. Nonetheless, poetry of this kind found its way into workers' newspapers and anthologies and was analysed by critics as workers' poetry.[9]

---

7 Bogdanov 1918b, p. 8.
8 Bogdanov 1918b, p. 11.
9 Bogdanov 1918c, p. 13.

Another source of confusion was the influence of the soldiery to which the proletariat was subjected during the war and revolution. The soldiers were mostly by origin peasants who had been torn from production and lived in masses in conditions of consumer communism. They were either being trained in the business of destruction or were carrying it out. The soldiers were much less conscious and much more selfish than the workers with whom they were allied. The soldiers' influence on more impressionable proletarian poets was to deprive their work of the nobility of tone that was obligatory for the ideals of the class to which they belonged, and to infect it with hatred towards individual representatives of the bourgeoisie. This feeling was understandable in life, but impermissible in literature. There were excesses, such as mocking the defeated enemies, extolling lynchings, and even sadistic delight in gouging out the entrails of the bourgeoisie, sentiments that had nothing in common with the ideology of the working class.[10]

Here Bogdanov defined what he thought the attitude of the proletariat towards violence ought to be in the present civil war situation. This was that the proletariat must of course take up arms when its freedom, its development, its ideals were threatened, but it rightly struggled against that spontaneity that any armed conflict gave rise to. The ferocity that this conflict evoked in the human soul could, of course, temporarily dominate the psyche of the fighters, but it was alien and hostile to proletarian culture, which permitted only the severity that was necessary. The spirit of real strength was nobility, and the labour collective was real strength. Reading Bogdanov's words, one is conscious that their realism came from someone who had seen at first hand the kind of emotions that were evoked in military encounters.[11]

Another line of demarcation that Bogdanov sought to draw was that between proletarian culture and the socialism of the intelligentsia. Here the fusion of the two was natural and easy due to the similarity of the respective ideals. The labouring intelligentsia had its origins in the bourgeoisie, whose principle was individualism, and the very character of intellectual labour retained this tendency: in the labour of the scholar, the artist or the writer no direct cooperation was felt, so that the role of the collective did not enter their field of vision. In cases where cooperation should occur, this was generally of an authoritarian kind, in which the *intelligent* appeared in the role of a manager or the organiser of labour, as an engineer in the factory, a doctor in a hospital etc. Even when an *intelligent* espoused the socialist ideal, the individu-

---

10   Bogdanov 1918c, p. 15.
11   Ibid.

alist and authoritarian strands were retained in his artistic creation. Examples of this were the dramas of Emile Verhaeren and the sculptures of Constantin Meunier.[12]

As regards the content of proletarian art, Bogdanov's impression was that to date this had been dominated by agitational calls to the class struggle, celebration of the proletariat's victories, and denunciation of capitalism and its agents; all else had been drowned by these themes. Proletarian art, however, demanded that all aspects of life should be treated.

Agitational considerations had determined that capitalists and their associates from the bourgeois intelligentsia should be portrayed as being evil, cruel, despicable characters. Such an approach was naive and in conflict with the collectivist mode of thought. The point was not in the personality traits of this or that bourgeois, and revolutionary efforts should not be directed against an individual person. What was being opposed was a social system and the collectives who were connected with it and gave it their protection. The capitalist personally could be an honourable man, but in so far as he was a representative of his class, his actions and thoughts would necessarily be determined by his social position. And here Bogdanov offered a piece of advice that gives an insight into his own approach to his adversaries. 'For victory over the old world it is more useful to understand it in its best representatives and in its highest manifestations, than to imagine that there all people are evil and act out of base motives'.[13]

Also out of agitational considerations, Bogdanov observed, a theory had emerged that proletarian art should be cheerful and enthusiastic. This theory had acquired a considerable following, especially among the younger and less experienced proletarian poets. Bogdanov, however, thought that the range of emotions embodied in proletarian art should not be artificially limited in this way; art ought to be first and foremost sincere and true. He reproduced some lines from a cheerful and enthusiastic poem published in May of 1918, commenting that at that very time the German invasion was under way, and there was fierce fighting in the Ukraine, the Caucasus, Finland and the Baltic region. The country was exhausted, starving and in a state of economic collapse. Certainly despair was unworthy of warriors, but even more unworthy was to present things through rose-coloured spectacles; it was a retreat from reality, a false mask covering that same despair.[14]

---

12   Bogdanov 1918c, pp. 15–16.
13   Bogdanov 1918c, p. 17.
14   Bogdanov 1918c, p. 18.

Bogdanov advocated that in artistic technique the proletariat should learn from its predecessors. But in this there was a temptation to take as a model the latest thing that old art had produced. This, however, was to be resisted. The art which arose out of a society that had lost its vitality was art that was distorted and decadent. One could observe this in the last decades with the collapse of bourgeois culture: the main artistic currents had been the decadent ones of 'modernism' and 'futurism'. One should learn artistic technique not from the organisers of decadence, but from the great masters who had appeared during the flowering of the now defunct classes, from the revolutionary romantics and the classics of different times.

It was sad, Bogdanov remarked, to see a proletarian poet, who was searching for the best artistic forms, thinking he had found them in the work of the affected intellectual commercial artist V.V. Mayakovsky or Igor Severianin, 'the ideologist of the gigolos and courtesans, the talented incarnation of varnished banality'. Much better models were the simple, clear and pure forms of the great masters such as Pushkin, Lermontov, Gogol, Nekrasov and Tolstoy. Of more recent writers Bogdanov was only able to recommend Gorky unreservedly.[15]

Bogdanov deplored the fact that the present cruel and coarse times, the era of world militarism, prompted artists to employ cruel and coarse imagery. An egregious example of this was V. Kirillov's attempt to express his readiness to struggle against the old world to the bitter end, prepared to make any sacrifice, however terrible and difficult it might be, when he threatened:

> For the sake of our Tomorrow – we shall burn Raphael
> We will destroy museums, we shall trample the flowers of art.

This, in Bogdanov's view, was a symbol in the spirit of the soldier and not of the worker. The soldier could and should shell Rheims Cathedral if an enemy observation post was or was suspected to be located there, but what compelled the poet to choose this Hindenburg image? A poet might express regret for such a cruel necessity, but he should not glory in it.[16]

For Bogdanov criticism was the regulator of the life of art, not only from the side of its creation, but also from the side of its reception. It was the interpreter of art for the broad masses. It showed people what they could derive from art for the arranging of their lives, both internal and external. In following this course criticism might itself in time become an art form.

---

15   Bogdanov 1918c, p. 19.
16   Bogdanov 1918c, p. 21.

In the essay 'What is Proletarian Poetry?' published in the first issue of *Proletarskaia Kultura* Bogdanov showed how the concepts he had developed in *Cultural Tasks, The Science of Social Consciousness* and related works could be applied to literary theory. His explanation of the origins of poetry was a variant of the way he accounted for the beginnings of speech, religion and ideology. This was that the labour exclamations that gave rise to human speech and later, the war chants before battle, were mechanisms to organise social activity. Initially, words signified the various types of human activity, but it was only by these words that people could communicate to each other about the phenomena of external nature and its elemental forces. It was through talking about natural phenomena as if they were persons that nature was personified, and in this way the 'basic metaphor' was born. This personification of nature still remained a principal method in poetry.[17]

Following Herder, Bogdanov held that in primitive times, poetry was indistinguishable from religion and science. Scientific ideas were presented in the form of myths, as the deeds of heroic individuals. These myths were a means of organising people socially, and had the educational purpose of introducing young people into the norms of the community to which they belonged.

Bogdanov believed that in class society all poetry had a class character: aristocratic-landowner, bourgeois or proletarian. He stressed, however, that by this he did not imply that poetry simply defended class interests, though this in a few instances might be the case. What he meant was that the poet invariably adopted the point of view of the class to which he belonged; he saw the world through its eyes, thought and felt as it thought and felt.

As an example of the aristocratic-landowner poetry, Bogdanov gave the lyrics of Afanasy Fet. In Fet the class point of view was reflected in the complete absence of material or economic concerns, something only possible for the nobility. The way Fet could understand and convey the phenomena of nature marked him as someone who was at home in the countryside. There was also a refinement and delicacy of feeling that implied that the class to which the poet belonged had sensibilities that were unique and should be preserved. In this way, Bogdanov remarked, the landowning class, although in decline, indicated that it was not going to give up its privileged position without a fight.[18]

Bogdanov was aware that poetry could have a mixed class content. Nekrasov, for example, was a poet from the landowning class who was an ardent defender of the peasantry. But while he had a deep sympathy for the peasants

---

17   Bogdanov 1918, p. 21.
18   Bogdanov 1918, p. 15.

and understanding of their way of life, his poetry was an expression of the aspirations, thoughts and feelings of the urban intelligentsia, with which Nekrasov was closely connected. Nekrasov's poetry, consequently, had a mixed class character, a feature that was common in recent times to democratic poetry. This bore the stamp of worker-peasants or of the worker-peasant-intelligentsia. But, Bogdanov argued, the proletariat did not need a mixed, but a pure proletarian class poetry.[19]

In Bogdanov's view what essentially distinguished the proletarian from other democratic elements was his special type of labour and cooperation. In these, deep divisions that had plagued society in former times had been overcome. The deepest of these divisions has been the one between the organiser and the executor, the beginning of power and subordination, in which one person became a higher being to another, and the feeling of deference was born. Thus, the poetry of the feudal era reflected the authoritarian spirit. This was found in such works as the book of Genesis among the Jews, the Illiad and the Odyssey among the Greeks and the *Mahabharata* among the Indians. The aim of these narratives about the activities of gods, heroes, kings, leaders etc. was to instil and reinforce a feeling of reverence and obedience.[20]

The other type of division was specialisation, in which every person had his own little world and knew only things connected with their particular profession or trade. This division generated the individualism of the bourgeois world. In bourgeois poetry it was the individual personality that was the centre of attention: its struggle for happiness, its creativity, its victories, its defeats etc. This was the basic content not only of bourgeois poetry, but also of the novel and the drama. Because bourgeois society preserved many elements of authoritarian collaboration, of authority and subordination, bourgeois poetry still retained elements of authoritarian consciousness.

Since proletarians engaged in machine production, in which specialisation was transferred from the worker to the machine, the fragmentation caused by the division of labour was overcome. And because, as the operator of a machine, the worker united in himself the roles of organiser and executor, the reflection of this distinction too had disappeared from proletarian poetry. The characteristic of proletarian poetry was that it embodied the spirit of comradely cooperation.[21]

As an example of what proletarian poetry was not, Bogdanov cited verses which extolled a political leader, presumably Lenin. This, Bogdanov explained,

---

19   Ibid.
20   Bogdanov 1918, p. 17.
21   Bogdanov 1918, p. 18.

was alien to the spirit of proletarian poetry, because it was inspired by deference, an authoritarian attitude that was more suited to poetry of the feudal
period. This position echoed what Bogdanov had said in *Red Star*; there the
Martians did not commemorate people, but events. If leaders were to be
lauded, Bogdanov insisted, it should be as people who expressed *general* aims,
the *general* will of the collective, as the representatives of its *general* forces.
Despite Bogdanov's opposition to monuments celebrating people, or perhaps –
who knows – because of it, Lenin at that very time was insisting on the speedy
erection of monuments commemorating eminent figures of the revolutionary
movement.[22]

Bogdanov was able to mention two works, one called 'Whistles' by A.K. Gas-
tev and another titled 'To a New Comrade' by A.I. Mashirov-Samobytnik, as
examples of what proletarian poetry should be. He indicated the qualities in
them that he thought admirable. Both of them dealt with themes from factory life, and portrayed the generosity, solidarity and selflessness of the workers.
Samobytnik's poem also had a nostalgia for the country life that workers had
left behind when coming to live in the city.[23]

Bogdanov stressed that proletarian poetry was still in embryo, since proletarian consciousness was still in its early stages. But even when it reached maturity the proletariat would still have recourse to the best things in the poetry
of the feudal and bourgeois worlds. It must acquire this inheritance in such
a manner as not to submit to the spirit of the past which reigned in them, but
to assimilate them critically and creatively, so that the proletariat might have a
poetry that was indisputably its own.[24]

An essay that paralleled 'What is Proletarian Poetry?' was 'Science and the
Working Class', which Bogdanov published in the collection *The Socialism of
Science*. As was the case with the essay on poetry, Bogdanov had abundant
material for 'Science and the Working Class' in several of his earlier works, such
as *The Philosophy of Living Experience* and *The Science of Social Consciousness*.

Bogdanov defined science as 'the organised experience of human society'.
As the experience was acquired through labour, a more precise definition of
science was 'organised social-labour experience'.[25]

An important element in Bogdanov's argument was that in class society, science necessarily had a class character. He asserted this with reference to the
historical development of science. In ancient Egypt and Babylon the priests,

---

22   Bogdanov 1918, p. 19.
23   Bogdanov 1918, pp. 20–1.
24   Bogdanov 1918, p. 22.
25   Bogdanov 1918e, pp. 5–6.

the intelligentsia of the day, had possessed a monopoly on knowledge and kept it secret from the mass of people. In this way, science was a means of domination.[26]

In more recent times, science had become a commodity to be bought and sold. It was taught in universities and was only accessible to the children of the wealthy. It was made unnecessarily complicated by the mode of explanation and the specialised terminology used, in this way putting it out of the reach of ordinary people.[27] Besides being an instrument of domination, science had another function, that is, as an offensive weapon. The bourgeoisie had used this weapon against feudalism, and with it were able to organise their victory in the social struggle.[28] In its turn the proletariat needed its science to replace that of the older classes. Thus, it was necessary for the proletariat to master science, not after the socialist revolution, but before it and for it. Gradually, this enterprise was being undertaken.

How could a proletarian science be formed? Marx had already shown this in the field of political economy. It was a matter of changing the viewpoint. The revolution Marx had wrought in economics was similar to the one Copernicus had brought about in astronomy. Copernicus had understood that the sun and not the earth was the centre of the universe; Marx had conceived of economics not from the viewpoint of the employer, but of those who produced, of the working class.[29]

Bogdanov emphasised the immensity of the tasks that proletarian science would have to solve. As he observed:

> We now know – and the war has shown this especially clearly – that socialism cannot be established in any separate country; it must embrace all countries, or at least, such a union of countries which could manage all production independently, not depending on the importation of materials from backward states and not being in danger from their armed forces – such a massive scale of planned organisation has the working class to create.[30]

The introduction of socialism on a world scale could only be done in a scientific way. But this was impossible with the fragmented state of existing science.

---

26 Bogdanov 1918e, p. 9.
27 Bogdanov 1918e, pp. 9–10.
28 Bogdanov 1918e, p. 13.
29 Bogdanov 1918e, p. 17.
30 Bogdanov 1918e, pp. 24–5.

There was need for a universal organisational science that the bourgeois world had been incapable of creating.[31]

In Bogdanov's view, science needed not only to be democratised, but also socialised, that is, spread throughout the masses. The proletariat must do this by means of a class socialist-propagandist organisation – a Workers' University. This would be a university in the original sense of the word: a collectivity, an institution of mutually related teaching and learning, an institution based on comradely cooperation.[32]

2   Methods of Labour and Methods of Perception

In an article published in *Proletarskaia Kultura* entitled 'Methods of Labour and Methods of Perception', Bogdanov explained the methods of induction and deduction and also demonstrated how major advances in science were prompted by the needs of everyday life. But the chief interest of the article is that in it Bogdanov developed his ideas on the origins of human speech. This was a pivotal part of his system, because for him speech was a rudimentary form of ideology which emerged out of production in the form of labour exclamations. In this way he could argue that production and ideology were intimately connected. Hitherto he had supported this position with reference to the research of Ludwig Noiré, but in 'Methods of Labour and Methods of Perception' he reinforced this by argumentation of his own.

Bogdanov's starting point was that the activity and resistance of the environment which every organism encountered were infinitely varied and never repeated themselves. If the organism had to react differently in every single case, and the reaction was only valid for a single occasion, no organism could adapt to its environment. It followed that generalisation was a capacity that organisms had at the level of reflexes, and constituted an important economy of effort. Because the organism was an integrated whole, the reflex involved different organs of the body. The reflex could be accompanied by a cry. This, according to Bogdanov, was a factor of enormous importance.

A mother hears the cry of her baby and comes to its aid. She knows the baby is in distress because the cry is an expression of pain. If the baby was alone in the world, the cry would not only be superfluous, but a dangerous waste of energy, but in the embryonic social system of 'mother-baby' this part of the

---

31   Bogdanov 1918e, pp. 26–7.
32   Bogdanov 1918e, p. 33.

reflex is transformed into a very useful adaptation. The cry of pain is comprehensible to the mother, and also to every other person, because all of them are equally part of the reflex evoked by a strong and harmful stimulus.[33] In Bogdanov's view, the reflex of this kind was a practical generalisation. It was one expressed and understood, but it could not be considered as a form of perception, because it did not meet the criterion of being universally valid. It was, however, a prototype of a perceptual generalisation.[34]

In the struggle with nature man adapts himself to its conditions not only by spontaneous reflexes, but by conscious-expedient efforts, actively changing these conditions; he is a labouring being. Labour efforts are distinguished by two features: their social nature and their plasticity. In labour a person is connected with other people as a member of a collective. Only in a collective does he deploy sufficient strength to change the conditions of the external environment; taken singly he would be powerless before the elements. Even if he managed to subsist, it would be passively, by adapting himself to them, like any animal; he would not be able to develop a labour consciousness. This, moreover, is inseparably connected to the changeability of the efforts themselves, with their 'plasticity'. As labour changes the existing conditions, so further efforts have to 'reckon' with changes that have been made. If, for example, a tree has been chopped sufficiently for it to fall, it requires not further chopping, but a push in the right direction.[35]

Labour gives rise to a new stage in the development of sociability. The labour act, like the reflex, from which it was produced, due to the same interconnectedness of an organism, is accompanied by a corresponding sound: the labour exclamation. These labour exclamations, Bogdanov maintained, were the original roots of human speech. Each of them was understood by all the members of the collective, who could associate it with the labour act to which it referred. Here, then, was the solution to the riddle of the origins of language, as given by Noiré, 'the Marxist of comparative philology who had no conception of Marxism'. The word-concept developed out of labour, the plasticity of labour determining the plasticity of the word, and by the same token the development of speech, beginning from a few primitive roots to that incomparable wealth which characterises the languages of civilised peoples.[36]

---

33   Bogdanov 1918a, p. 5.
34   Ibid.
35   Ibid.
36   Ibid.

3   The First Conference of Proletkult

Between 1 and 20 September 1918 there was held in Moscow the First All-Russian Conference of Proletarian Cultural and Educational Organisations, attended by 330 delegates and 234 guests. There would have been more attendees had not the Conference taken place at an inauspicious moment in the life of the young Soviet state. The Czechoslovaks had cut off contact with Samara, the Urals and Siberia. On 30 August, after a meeting at the Mikhelson factory in Moscow, Lenin had been subject to an assassination attempt by the Socialist Revolutionary Dora Kaplan. He had survived, but was severely wounded. On the same day Socialist Revolutionaries assassinated two commissars of the Petrograd Soviet, M.S. Uritsky and V. Volodarsky. Rumours circulated that the White armies were advancing on Moscow. In response, the Soviet state unleashed a wave of terror, taking hostages from the families of the Moscow and Petrograd middle classes and carrying out reprisals for any Communists killed.

In sympathy with Lenin, Lebedev-Poliansky wrote a lengthy tribute to Lenin as a leading article in the September issue of *Proletarskaia Kultura*, comparing him to an experienced captain steering the red ship of revolution towards socialism.[37] Commenting on the draft of the article in a note to Lebedev-Poliansky and Kalinin, Bogdanov remarked that there was much in the article that he, 'as an anti-maximalist', could not agree with, but that the characterisation of Lenin as a representative of the practical line in communism he thought correct. However, Bogdanov suggested that at the end of the article Lebedev-Poliansky should delete the phrase: 'Let our enemies know that in the struggle with them we shall be merciless'. He explained that he didn't want to defend counter-revolutionaries, but such words should not appear in a journal of culture, 'especially at the given moment, when they smelt of fresh blood from the mass shootings'.[38]

Despite the dire military and political situation, delegates had managed to come from almost all localities to attend the Proletkult conference. At the conference there were sessions on such topics as the attitude of the proletariat to science, art, on cultural and educational tasks of the trade unions and workers' cooperatives, on the Workers' University, proletarian clubs, work among the youth and other matters. On each of the questions discussed resolutions were passed. The Conference adopted a constitution, determined the composition

37   Lebedev-Polianskii 1918a, pp. 1–3.
38   Neizvestnyi Bogdanov 1995, 1, p. 194.

of the All-Russian Proletkult Council and its Central Committee, elected representatives to the college of Narkompros's Department of Proletarian Culture and also the editorial board of the journal *Proletarskaia Kultura*. At the conference Bogdanov was elected as a member of the Proletkult Central Committee and a member of the editorial board of the journal *Proletarskaia Kultura*.

Lenin, was unable to attend, but sent his greetings to the Proletkult conference. According to Krupskaya, who gave a paper on education at it, her husband thought that the deficiency of Proletkult was that it had very little to do with helping the workers becoming involved in the running of the state through the Soviets.[39] It was in this direction that Lenin wanted to steer the conference, and his message to it was:

> All our success has been due to the fact that the workers understood and got down to *running* the state, through their Soviets.
>
> But the workers still have not sufficiently understood this and often are too shy to put forward workers for *running* the state.
>
> Struggle for this, comrades! Let the proletarian cultural and educational organisations help this. In this is the guarantee of further successes and the final victory of the socialist revolution.[40]

This was not, however, the utilitarian direction which the conference took. One of its resolutions stated that: 'The cultural and educational movement among the proletariat must have an autonomous place beside the political and economic movements'. Another resolution held that 'the content of the new culture must be based upon social labour and comradely cooperation'.[41]

On the face of it, Bogdanov did not play a particularly prominent part in the conference. The opening address was made by Lebedev-Poliansky, and in the absence of Lunacharsky, Pokrovsky spoke on behalf of the Commissariat of Education. However, the ideas expressed by these speakers were very close to Bogdanov's own. Lebedev-Poliansky, for example, echoed Bogdanov's belief that: 'While bourgeois culture is exclusively anarchic and individualist, the culture of the proletariat is strictly monist, and develops its science and art on the basis of collective labour'.[42]

---

39   Krupskaia 1989, p. 317.
40   Proletarskaia kul'tura 1918, 5, p. 27; Lenin 1958–65, 37, p. 87.
41   Protokoly pervoi vserossiiskoi konferentsii proletarskikh kul'turno-prosvetitel'nykh organizatsii 1918, p. 30.
42   Protokoly pervoi vserossiiskoi konferentsii proletarskikh kul'turno-prosvetitel'nykh organizatsii 1918, p. 5.

In his speech Pokrovsky observed that the present time was not conducive to peaceful cultural and educational work. Soviet Russia was undergoing difficult times, hemmed in by the forces of counter-revolution, who were supported by the Czechoslovaks. However, the socialist revolution had not ended; the next stage would be world revolution. It was a situation akin to France in 1793–4.[43]

Like Bogdanov, Pokrovsky held that the transition from the capitalist to the socialist order was first and foremost a grandiose organisational task. In order to carry out this task, an organisational apparatus was necessary. In bourgeois society this organisational apparatus would have been formed from the ranks of the intelligentsia, but in the aftermath of the October Revolution the Russian intelligentsia had not rallied to the support of the Soviet regime; on the contrary, it had obstructed it wherever possible. For Pokrovsky the remedy was clear: since the old organisational apparatus had refused to work, it was necessary to create a new one, a new proletarian intelligentsia. Pokrovsky clearly saw an important practical role for Proletkult, as the provider of a new cohort of intellectuals who would willingly serve the new order.

Pokrovsky declared that, like Proletkult, the Commissariat of Education considered itself to be a proletarian organisation, but recognised Proletkult as the senior partner, since its antecedents went back to the workers' study circles of the previous century. He recalled with some pride his own participation in the party schools of Capri and Bologna, which, he said, had encouraged him to write a textbook on Russian history for the kind of student who attended the party schools.[44]

In his speech on 'The Revolution and Cultural Tasks of the Proletariat' Lebedev-Poliansky defined what he thought the relationship of Proletkult to Narkompros was. He denied that the two institutions were in competition; on the contrary, they supplemented each other's functions. Proletkult's relationship to Narkompros was like that of a laboratory to a well-equipped factory. In the laboratory intensive creative work was carried on with the aim of improving production. By its direct contact with the masses, Proletkult would bring together their creativity and put this at the disposal of Narkompros, which would disseminate these proletarian achievements among the wider public. In coordinating its activities with Narkompros, Proletkult did not regard

---

43   Protokoly pervoi vserossiiskoi konferentsii proletarskikh kul'turno-prosvetitel'nykh organizatsii 1918, p. 7.

44   Protokoly pervoi vserossiiskoi konferentsii proletarskikh kul'turno-prosvetitel'nykh organizatsii 1918, p. 12.

itself as subordinating a lower institution to a higher one, but as engaging in friendly free cooperation.[45]

In the discussion on Lebedev-Poliansky's speech one of the delegates proposed substituting the word 'communist' for 'collectivist'. Bogdanov resisted this, arguing that historically 'communism' expressed more the commonality of consumption than the collectivity of production; the word 'collectivist' implied the comradeship that was the basis of proletarian relations. At the vote the amendment fell.[46]

In his speech 'Science and the Proletariat' Bogdanov went over some familiar ground. He deplored the fact that the development of bourgeois science had been one of increasing specialisation and the compartmentalisation of knowledge. Every specialist created his own language, incomprehensible for the scholars in other disciplines, let alone for the broad masses. The development of machine production, however, had created the conditions for overcoming the harmful aspects of specialisation.

In bourgeois society knowledge had become a commodity, too expensive for workers to afford. Those workers who did succeed in acquiring an education became divorced from their proletarian roots, and became influenced by bourgeois culture.

Throughout history science had been employed as a means of social organisation. In different epochs science had been understood in different ways and had been in the hands of different classes. From this point of view it would not be paradoxical to say that since there had been a feudal geometry and a bourgeois geometry, there was now a need for a proletarian geometry.[47] In fact, in 1920, Bogdanov set out the principles of such a geometry, whose possibility emerged from the tectological approach to the sciences.[48]

The new proletarian science would be taught in a Workers' University. This would be different from a modern bourgeois university, which is based on authority, on intellectual power, on a strict separation of the undisputed preceptors and passive students, obediently assimilating the intellectual riches from their tutors. In a proletarian university there were no 'students', but comradeship and cooperation, people working together in the spirit of free critical

---

45 Protokoly pervoi vserossiiskoi konferentsii proletarskikh kul'turno-prosvetitel'nykh organizatsii 1918, pp. 20–1.

46 Protokoly pervoi vserossiiskoi konferentsii proletarskikh kul'turno-prosvetitel'nykh organizatsii 1918, p. 30.

47 Protokoly pervoi vserossiiskoi konferentsii proletarskikh kul'turno-prosvetitel'nykh organizatsii 1918, pp. 31–4.

48 See Bogdanov 2003a, pp. 122–5.

thought. Bogdanov insisted that he knew this was possible since he himself had taught in workers' schools at Capri and Bologna, which were organised on a comradely basis, and they had been successful.[49]

Lunacharsky had intended to present a paper to the Conference on 'The Proletariat and Art', but was unable to do so, since he had been called away to Petrograd. It fell to Bogdanov to present a paper on the subject in his stead. For the most part this contained themes that he had treated more extensively in his articles in *Proletarskaia Kultura*. He rebutted the idea that art was simply a decoration of life, arguing that it was an effective means of social organisation. It introduced new members into the community, fitting them for their future roles in society. And, whereas bourgeois art was individualist, the kind of art needed by the proletariat was collectivist, one that reared people in the spirit of solidarity and comradely cooperation.[50]

The November issue of *Proletarskaia Kultura* carried an account of the Proletkult conference.[51] Commenting on the draft to Lebedev-Poliansky and Kalinin, Bogdanov said that he agreed with most of it, but was insistent that the editors should omit the effusive commentary on the greetings Lenin had sent to the conference. Of course, the conference could be pleased to have official sanction, but to enthuse over greetings from this or that comrade reminded one yet again of the need to struggle against the spirit of authoritarianism. 'And of course we all know that in this matter Lenin is least of all an authority. In the good sense of this word – in the sense of being competent'.[52]

Although most of Bogdanov's attention was paid to higher education and to the education of workers, he did have ideas on the education of children. In a lecture given to a conference of teachers in Moscow in May 1918 on the subject of 'The Ideal of Education', Bogdanov explained what the comradely collectivist approach to child education would be. In doing so, he took the opportunity to dispel some misconceptions about the implications of collectivism. In accordance with his general conceptions of the evolution of society and ideology, Bogdanov sketched out the various phases that education had undergone in social evolution, its primitive, feudal, bourgeois and proletarian stages.

In primitive society, when social roles were undifferentiated, education was not a separate function. With the emergence of authoritarian patriarchal and

49   Protokoly pervoi vserossiiskoi konferentsii proletarskikh kul'turno-prosvetitel'nykh organizatsii 1918, pp. 34–6.

50   Protokoly pervoi vserossiiskoi konferentsii proletarskikh kul'turno-prosvetitel'nykh organizatsii 1918, pp. 72–7.

51   Kunavin 1918.

52   Neizvestnyi Bogdanov 1995, 1, p. 195.

feudal societies, education was the inculcation of the discipline of subordination, so that the division into organisers and executors was maintained. Individualist bourgeois education was designed to produce autonomous individuals and specialists in different spheres of activity.

In collectivist socialist society education changed its character and direction. It no longer had to produce specialists, or, more exactly, not *only* specialists, but people who had general knowledge and who were versed in general methods of labour. Bogdanov emphasised that in a collectivist society individualism would not be suppressed. His argument was that:

> The idea that collectivism is incompatible with, or has no need for, personal autonomy, is absurd. In the collective each person supplements the others, and in this is the essence of his role. But he can only supplement the others in so far as he differs from them, in so far as he is original, in so far as he is autonomous. It is clear that the point of this autonomy is not the defence of individual interests, but consists in fostering initiative, criticism, originality – in general the development of individual capabilities.[53]

Producing such individuals would be the job of teachers in the socialist society. It would be a complex and responsible role for them to fulfil as organisers of society, but it would be extremely rewarding.

4   Elements of Proletarian Culture

In the spring of 1919 Bogdanov gave a series of lectures to the Moscow Proletkult entitled 'Elements of Proletarian Culture in the Development of the Working Class', which were published in book form in 1920. In part these lectures summarised what he had said previously about comradely cooperation and the overcoming of fetishes, but they also elaborate some implications of collectivist proletarian culture that had not appeared in Bogdanov's earlier works.

In his sketch of the origins of the modern industrial proletariat Bogdanov makes it clear that its antecedents in the de-classed petty proprietors were individualist and authoritarian in outlook, and that the collectivism of the working class is acquired only gradually over a prolonged period of time. Just how far the working class had to go in creating its own collectivist culture was shown by its

---

53   Bogdanov 1924a, p. 236.

behaviour at the beginning of the war, when nine-tenths of workers had been strike-breakers and had supported the war effort, not through compulsion, but as a matter of conscience.[54]

Bogdanov considered trade unions to be comradely organisations, but that they were understood in an individualist way. The objectives of trade unions were not in the collective, but in the individual. Workers joined them as individuals to pursue their individual interests. If they discovered that their interests were better served elsewhere, they could leave the union if and when they so desired.[55]

For Bogdanov trade unions were a stage in the development of 'democratic' consciousness. In the democratic consciousness there was an awareness of the need for combined action, but there was no sense of collectivism, in which there would be an internal unity of purpose. This lack of unity of purpose was reflected in the way questions were decided by the democratic consciousness: by putting matters to a vote. What was voting? It was a process in which people were considered as equal homogeneous units. This would seem to be entirely proper, but in practice it meant that each person was transformed into an abstract integer. The side that had more of these abstract units was held to be in the right, and the minority was required to subordinate themselves to the majority or go elsewhere. This, in Bogdanov's view, was an authoritarian procedure. Moreover, history had shown that in most cases the minority was right, and the majority wrong. Very often the majority were the representatives of conservatism, of tradition, of the past, and the minority – representatives of the future.[56]

In this connection Bogdanov recalled a discussion with fellow Social Democrats in 1907 in which he had argued that although they campaigned for democracy, they were not democrats. What kind of democrats could they be, he asked, when among the population as a whole the proletariat was a small minority. And of the proletariat those workers who were in any way conscious was a small number. And those who could be classed as revolutionary constituted only a small fraction of those conscious workers. Thus, the Social Democrats were always in a minority, and a minority to the third or fourth degree.[57]

Bogdanov did not believe that matters could be settled by a majority of votes. If a collective was a genuine whole, the question would be resolved unanimously. But was this possible? An example was science. In science what was the

---

54   Bogdanov 1920, p. 81.
55   Bogdanov 1920, pp. 62, 75.
56   Bogdanov 1920, p. 75.
57   Ibid.

case was not decided by vote. If there had been a vote on whether the earth revolved around the sun, this position would have been lost. At the start of the war most proletarians decided to end the class struggle. Was it necessary to submit to this decision? Of course not.

Taking up an idea that he had put forward in *The Philosophy of Living Experience*, Bogdanov pointed out that in the age of Copernicus everybody had believed that the sun went round the earth. Only Copernicus came up with the idea that the earth revolved around the sun. But who genuinely expressed the experience of the collective? Copernicus could draw upon the astronomical tables that the Spanish King Alfonso had ordered be compiled for the purpose of navigation. In this way Copernicus had at his disposal experience gained by other people.[58]

For Bogdanov the transition from democratic consciousness to collectivist consciousness consisted in people ceasing to be abstract integers and becoming inseparable elements in a single whole. It was not a matter of the minority subordinating itself to the majority, but of its complete agreement with the majority. Bogdanov stated that when he had to depict the social ideal in *Red Star*, he deliberately avoided any mention of voting in it, since this would imply that the masses consisted of disparate elements.[59]

In terms of the dynamics of collectivism, and in speaking of a future collectivist society, Bogdanov was no doubt right in his critique of democracy. But in the context of 1919 his arguments brought him perilously close to those that Lenin and Bukharin would deploy in defence of their ruthless suppression of dissent in the next two years. They could claim that the Communist Party represented the objective, long-term interests of the working class, as opposed to the empirical demands of actual workers in the present situation. A majority vote was at least something objective, something verifiable, whereas the collective experience was more insubstantial and open to subjectivity. Who is to decide what the collective experience is?

Bogdanov does not explain here in detail how it is that collective experience can be expressed in the opinion of a single person, in this case Copernicus. But this is a question he has already elaborated on in his concept of 'universal validity'. Here he is applying in the political sphere his ideas on the theory of knowledge. These, however, are ideas that he cannot speak about, because of the popular character of his lectures, and also because philosophy is something that he has ostensibly abandoned.

---

58   Bogdanov 1920, pp. 77–8.
59   Bogdanov 1920, p. 79.

The final lecture of the series is devoted to 'The Socialist Ideal', and in this Bogdanov develops the approach to the subject first set out in the *Vpered* article 'Socialism of the Present'. In keeping with the historical treatment of the emergence of the proletariat through different historical epochs, Bogdanov presents a picture of a progressively unfolding proletarian, and ultimately all-human, culture. A significant element in his argument is that the human collective was always present in all the forms of social and economic organisation, even in those that were fragmented due to the division of labour. According to Bogdanov:

> We call proletarian culture class culture. It is of course class culture because it is worked out by a particular class, and is formed in its struggle with other classes. But is this culture only a class one? Look at its elements. It is collective-labouring. But was not the life of humanity always collective-labouring? Yes, in fact it was never otherwise. Humanity has always lived and developed by the force of collective labour. Of course, labour did not cease to be collective just because it was scattered among many economies, and because people, giving to each other, distributing the products of this labour, entered into a struggle with each other in the market. It remains, nevertheless, that people always worked and still work for each other, and consequently, work for the collective. The collective-labour sense of life has been veiled, hidden from people by the apparent fragmentation of the collective and the apparent struggle; but only veiled, obscured. In the proletariat these obscured, concealed conditions are removed, like a kind of outer covering being torn open, and what is revealed? Humanity in general; what there always was in humanity, but which was just not realised.[60]

Hence, Bogdanov concluded, all the elements of the proletarian culture that had been explained had a general-humanity character, although by necessity they had been wrapped in a class husk. The argument here is similar to Marx's in the *Grundrisse*, that 'private interest is already a socially determined interest, which can be achieved only within the conditions laid down by society'.[61]

---

60   Bogdanov 1920, p. 89.
61   Marx 1973, p. 156.

5   The Proletarian University

A significant article by Bogdanov in November 1918 in the fifth issue of *Proletarskaia Kultura* was 'The Proletarian University'. In this essay he put forward the case for establishing a new Proletarian University rather than reforming the universities already in existence. Bogdanov contended that the new type of university would not subject its students to passive learning, as traditional universities did, but engender in them the capacity to learn in a critical way.[62] The new university, moreover, would be an 'integrated system of cultural-educational institutions, built on comradely cooperation of teachers and students'.[63] Much of the article was autobiographical, Bogdanov recounting how his experiences of teaching workers at various junctures in his revolutionary career had led him to elaborate the principles which would guide the running of the Proletarian University.

The first of these experiences, which had influenced him profoundly, was in Tula, where he had been banished in 1895. This was an episode that he had first mentioned in the book *Cultural Tasks of our Times*, but because of its being a legal publication and subject to censorship, he had not been able to be completely explicit. In his 1918 account he was able to say that when he had arrived in Tula he had been a member of the revolutionary organisation People's Will. He was also able to name his associates, Bazarov and Skvortsov-Stepanov, with whom he had taught political economy in a workers' circle founded by Ivan Savelev. Bogdanov stressed that he had found that his audience did not simply listen to him passively, but questioned him, engaged him in discussion, and forced him to go far beyond the subject of his lectures. Bogdanov found that his audience wanted him to bring together, like links in one complex chain of development, technical and economic phenomena along with the forms of spiritual culture that arose from them. This had led Bogdanov to put together his own textbook on political economy, which did adopt the method demanded by the workers, the *Short Course of Economic Science*, which went through many editions.

The second formative influence on Bogdanov's approach to teaching was his experience of organising the two party schools, one on Capri in 1909 and one in Bologna a year later. Both had shown the value of involving the students in drawing up the programme of study, and of encouraging them to question their lecturers rather than accepting passively what they had to say. Bogdanov

---

62   Bogdanov 1918d, p. 15.
63   Bogdanov 1918d, p. 9.

referred indirectly to the fact that the Capri school had been to some extent undermined by the criticisms of Lenin and his adherents. But from this circumstance too Bogdanov drew the conclusion that a critical approach was the antidote to fractional disputes. For, Bogdanov contended, 'it is no secret for anyone how much harm is caused by the individualism of very many activists, their personal ambition, their aspiration to prominence, their aversion to comradely criticism ... No less harm is caused ... by the habit of blindly believing certain authorities, relying on the opinion of this or that recognised leader, without weighing it up, and ignoring any doubts about their rightness.'[64] In the reference to 'leaders' there is a distinct echo of Bogdanov's earlier essay 'What is it that we have overthrown?'

The article 'The Proletarian University' also indicated that Bogdanov envisaged that the new university would undertake the compilation of a Workers' Encyclopaedia which would, in an orderly, simple and clear way, set out the methods and achievements of science from a proletarian point of view. It would be the counterpart of the *Encyclopaedia* compiled by d'Alembert, Diderot and others during the French revolution to set out the foundations of the new bourgeois culture.[65]

According to Bogdanov, an attempt had been made in the spring of 1918 to establish a Proletarian University in Moscow. The attempt, however, had failed, because the project had been undertaken in haste by a small group of people. The programme of lectures was ill thought out, and the students had not been able to contribute anything to the running of the University. Very few of the students, moreover, had been proletarians; most of them had been intellectuals employed in Soviet institutions.

A Proletarian University was ceremonially opened in Moscow on 23 March 1919. Lebedev-Poliansky chaired the meeting, which was attended by a large audience of workers and Red Army men. Pokrovsky addressed the meeting on behalf of Narkompros, saying that besides its role as a disseminator of higher learning among the workers and peasants, the Proletarian University also had an important political part to play in training instructors for the Red Army, for whom a great need was felt.

Bukharin also addressed the meeting as a delegate to the Eighth Congress of the Russian Communist Party. He remarked that the Proletarian University was a necessary institution to remedy the shortage of cultural forces which dogged all the best Soviet initiatives. He believed that 'proletarian culture is the main

---

64   Bogdanov 1918d, p. 13.
65   Bogdanov 1918d, p. 9.

lever of the proletarian revolution, and the proletarian revolution is the main lever of proletarian culture'.

There were also speeches in support of the Proletarian University from representatives of the Austrian and American Communist Parties, as well as from representatives of Soviet institutions. Significantly, however, there was no speech by Bogdanov, the main proponent of the idea of a Proletarian University. As in the case of the Proletkult, Bogdanov preferred to keep in the background.[66]

However, at the Congress of Extramural Education in May 1919, Bogdanov reported on the Proletarian University's progress so far. According to Bogdanov:

> The Proletarian University by its idea is a class institution. The Proletarian University devotes itself completely to the elaboration and development of proletarian science, and its work has in part the character of a laboratory experiment.
>
> All the work is conducted on the basis of practical activities, seminars and excursions. Lectures are given as an introduction to practical activities.
>
> In the university there are 450 delegates, mostly from Soviet institutions, and primarily coming from the workers and peasants, with an insignificant number from the working intelligentsia.[67]

N.V. Roginsky, the President of the Proletarian University, in response to Bogdanov's report, expressed the opinion that the courses taught and the professors were not appropriate to a Proletarian University. By way of contrast, he praised the approach taken by the Central School of Soviet and Party Work, established on Sverdlov's initiative in 1918 for the training of Communist organisers and propagandists. In the summer of 1919 the Proletarian University was merged with the Central School of Soviet and Party Work, the new institution being called the Sverdlov Communist University. Under its rector, V.I. Nevsky, the Sverdlov University did not offer the kind of broad education that Bogdanov envisaged for the Proletarian University, but specialised in equipping party activists with the practical skills they required to become Soviet functionaries. With the Civil War still in a critical phase, Lenin's government did not see the point of Bogdanov's Proletarian Universities or of a 'Workers' Encyclopaedia'.[68]

---

66   Izvestiia, 25 March 1919.
67   Izvestiia, 17 May 1919.
68   Fitzpatrick 1970, pp. 101–3; Read 1990, pp. 139–40.

An institution that was related to the Proletarian University did get off the ground. This was the Socialist Academy of Social Sciences (SAON) founded in October 1918. Bogdanov envisaged the Socialist Academy as an institution in which graduates of the Proletarian Universities could continue their studies, and where lecturers for the Proletarian Universities could be trained.[69] Bogdanov was a founder member of the Academy, along with Lunacharsky, Pokrovsky and Skvortsov-Stepanov.

SAON was conceived as a free society of people having the aim of studying and teaching social studies from the point of view of scientific socialism. Initially membership of SAON was not limited to Communists, but included Socialist Revolutionaries as well. Its first constitution stated that the principles on which SAON operated must have a genuinely collectivist nature, and that its work must not bear a personal, individualist, but a comradely, cooperative character. There were no hierarchies; staff and students were held to be equally called to the construction of new social thought. SAON also aimed to be internationalist, and sought the participation of scholars from outside Russia. SAON was divided into two sections: one concerned with research, and the other with teaching. In May 1919 along with Bukharin, Vorovsky, Pokrovsky and Ryazanov, Bogdanov was elected to the Presidium of SAON.[70]

The main attention in this first period of its existence was concentrated on the teaching side. There were no formal entrance qualification to study at SAON; it accepted all applicants over the age of 16. Its first intake was of 1,870 students, of whom 70 percent were male, though only a small minority could be classed as proletarians; most were Soviet officials. The disillusion on learning the statistics of the composition of the student body prompted the decision to abandon the idea of opening a university section attached to SAON, since non-proletarian students would be adequately served by universities of the normal type.

In November 1919 SAON was reorganised to give more prominence to its research function. It was divided into a number of 'cabinets' or subject areas, each supervised by a commission of members of the Academy. Bogdanov headed the section on the history of ideology, Pokrovsky on history of the Russian revolutionary movement, F.A. Rothstein on foreign policy and Sh.M. Dvolaitsky on economics.[71]

In 1919 Bogdanov brought out a new edition of his textbook *A Short Course of Economic Science*, this time with Dvolaitsky, an economics graduate from Tartu

69   Bogdanov 1918d, pp. 22, 33.
70   Vestnik Sotsialisticheskoi Akademii 1922, 1, pp. 13–37.
71   Vestnik Sotsialisticheskoi Akademii 1922, 1, p. 35.

University, as co-author. According to Bogdanov, Dvolaitsky's contributions were to the last part of the course: the sections on the circulation of money, taxation, finance capital and the fundamental conditions for the collapse of capitalism. However, the overall approach to the subject was not noticeably altered. This edition of Bogdanov's book was issued in English translation in 1923, J. Fineberg, its translator, noting that 'it serves today as a textbook in hundreds, if not thousands, of party schools and study circles now functioning in Soviet Russia, training the future administrators of the Workers' Republic'. There was no suggestion that Bogdanov's book was in any way heretical. On the contrary, Fineberg stated that 'Comrade Bogdanov's book is a comprehensive and popular introduction to the study of the profound and enthralling principles of Marxian philosophy. In fact, it is a textbook on Marxism'.[72]

6   The Workers' Encyclopaedia

The fate of the Workers' Encyclopaedia gives an indication of the deep divergence between Bogdanov's conception of proletarian culture and the actual Proletkult movement. This was explained in the introductory article written by Yu.K. Milonov to Bogdanov's *Studies in Universal Organisational Science*, a short version of *Tectology*, published in Samara in 1921.[73] Milonov was secretary of the Saratov party organisation, a post he retained though he was an adherent of the 'Workers' Opposition'. He had been the moving force behind the creation of a Proletarian University in Saratov,[74] and, as his article shows, he had assimilated Bogdanov's ideas on proletarian culture.

Milonov deplored the fact that to date no progress had been made on the Workers' Encyclopaedia by the Proletkultists. This, he said, was due to the fact that although proletarian culture consisted of proletarian art and proletarian science, rank-and-file Proletkultists regarded it as exclusively art and ignored proletarian science completely. To see how art had usurped the place of science, according to Milonov, it was sufficient to observe the difference between the content of the leading Proletkult journal, *Proletarskaia Kultura*, and the actual activities of local Proletkults.

The point of a Workers' Encyclopaedia, in Milonov's view, was that it would systematically expound the whole range of knowledge as it appeared to the proletariat, encompassing both art and science. Every previous great transforma-

---

72   Bogdanov 1923, p. vi.
73   Bogdanov 1921.
74   http://gubernya63.ru/Lichnost-v-istorii/ruc/milonov.html.

tion of society had seen the appearance of its corresponding encyclopaedia. The Pentateuch of the Bible had reflected the transition from nomadic herding to settled agriculture, from the clan commune to the village community. The French Encyclopaedia had presaged the emergence of the bourgeoisie in the French revolution.

In Russia the need for a Workers' Encyclopaedia was a matter of urgency at the present time. The proletariat had seized power in the country with the help of its petty-bourgeois ally the peasantry. But as the proletariat came to rule on its own and to undertake the task of social transformation, it was increasingly handicapped by its lack of organising ability. It had the help of the bourgeois intelligentsia, the 'bourgeois specialists', but these also presented a danger. The workers were likely to succumb to the influence of these representatives of bourgeois culture who encouraged the growth of bureaucratism and anarchism. For Milonov, it was due to the bourgeois intelligentsia that the Soviet State was beset with bureaucratism and departmentalism. In the conditions of war communism and state capitalism, when the proletariat was forced to cooperate with the old industrial and commercial bourgeoisie, the need to strengthen proletarian consciousness through a Workers' Encyclopaedia was undeniable.

In concluding his introductory article, Milonov explained that Bogdanov's Universal Science of Organisation was itself part of the Workers' Encyclopaedia. Moreover, using its methodology was a means by which further works contributing to the Workers' Encyclopedia could be produced. He also explained that the practical purpose of Bogdanov's *Studies in Universal Organisational Science* was to change the direction of the Proletkults' activities, turning them away from purely artistic endeavours to scientific and scholarly ones, and in particular to the creation of a Workers' Encyclopaedia.[75]

Milonov's article is instructive in indicating why Bogdanov should publish this abridged version of *Tectology* before the publication of the full work in 1922. It is also instructive for the insight it gives into how Bogdanov saw the relationship of *Tectology* to the Workers' Encyclopaedia, that he continued to view *Tectology*, as he had in *Cultural Tasks of Our Times*, as an integral part of the Workers' Encyclopaedia.

One is also indebted to Milonov for indicating that the creation of the Workers' Encyclopaedia was by no means a harmless exercise, that it had political implications. The strengthening of the workers' organisational consciousness through the Encyclopaedia was intended to counteract the influence of the 'bourgeois specialists' and the bureaucratism and compartmentalism that this

---

75   Milonov 1921, pp. III–XXIV.

had engendered in the Soviet State. This kind of critique was not made by Bogdanov himself, but Milonov's presentation of Bogdanov's concept of the Workers' Encyclopaedia showed how close this came to the platform of the 'Workers'
Opposition' and other dissident movements of the time. Since by 1921 official
campaigns against the 'Workers' Opposition' and Bogdanov himself were well
under way, it was unlikely that further progress would be made on the Workers'
Encyclopaedia.

7   International Proletkult

It was logical that there should be an international dimension to Proletkult,
since the war had revealed the lack of an independent standpoint of the working class in all the countries involved. The international aspirations of the Proletkult were mentioned in the very first issue of *Proletarskaia Kultura*.[76] The
second issue contained an article by Lebedev-Poliansky which discussed the
eclipse of socialism by nationalism during the war and explained it in the same
terms as Bogdanov had, accounting for the domination of the proletariat by
bourgeois culture. According to Lebedev-Poliansky: 'The strength and depth of
the nationalist tendencies within bourgeois culture is shown by the fact that
during the world slaughter the best representatives of international socialism
took the side of the imperialist bandits who had brought it about'. Symptomatically, for Lebedev-Poliansky there was no suggestion of betrayal by the 'best
representatives of international socialism'; they, like everyone else, had been
'caught up in the web of the nationalist-individualist world-view'.[77]

During the First Conference of Proletkult in September 1918 several delegates had called for the creation of an international Proletkult organisation.[78] In
Proletarskaia Kultura in February 1919 V. Kerzhentsev recommended the establishment of an International Proletkult in order to create a proletarian culture
on the international scale that it required.[79] It was not until the summer of
1920, during the Second Congress of the Communist International, that Bogdanov himself set out Proletkult's international aims. He stressed that every
new development in the field of proletarian culture must immediately be communicated to the world proletariat as a whole. He envisaged that in the near

76   Polianskii and Kalinin 1918, p. 27.
77   Lebedev-Polianskii 1918, p. 2.
78   Protokoly pervoi vserossiiskoi konferentsii proletarskikh kul'turno-prosvetitel'nykh or-
     ganizatsii 1918, pp. 14–16.
79   Kerzhentsev 1919, pp. 1–3.

future the question would arise of an international congress of Proletkults. In the meantime he urged the cultivation of links with workers in different countries through the exchange of literature, information and delegates.[80]

As a first step in this direction the two delegates to the Comintern Congress from the British Socialist Party, Tom Quelch and William MacLaine, had been prevailed upon to contribute articles to *Proletarskaia Kultura* on workers' education in Britain.[81] In addition to Quelch and MacLaine, delegates to the Congress from Belgium, France, Germany, Switzerland, Italy, Norway, the USA (John Reed) and Soviet Russia were elected members of an International Provisional Bureau of Proletkult.[82] The Executive Committee of the Provisional Bureau issued an appeal dated 10 August 1920 to the proletariat of all countries to join with their Russian brethren in the struggle not only for political and economic, but for cultural liberation. The appeal contained some themes that were familiar in Bogdanov's writings, such as the idea that: 'In the struggle for the new culture the proletariat will necessarily take possession of the spiritual inheritance of the past, but it will subject it to its criticism. It will not accept this inheritance as a pupil, but as a creator who has been called upon to build a new culture and new collective labour on the basis of the economic realisation of communism'.[83] The Bogdanov influence was unlikely to endear the emergence of an international Proletkult to Lenin, and it is at this time that a new offensive against Bogdanov was launched.

---

80   Bogdanov 1920b, pp. 3–6.
81   Quelch 1920, pp. 52–5; MacLaine 1920, pp. 55–7.
82   Gorbunov 1974, p. 129.
83   Ästhetik und Kommunikation 1972, pp. 92–3.

The Final Decade

1   Bogdanov's Influence

During the period of the Civil War, between 1918 and 1920, Bogdanov's influence in Soviet Russia reached its height. Although he was not part of the government, and was not a member of the ruling Bolshevik party, he had considerable standing as the most eminent socialist theoretician in the country. His ideas inspired Proletkult, a powerful organisation that rivalled the Commissariat of Education, and whose branches spread throughout the Soviet republic. In the Civil War Proletkult had contributed to the war effort by giving lectures and theatre performances for the Red Army.

In the early 1920s it was Bogdanov's writings that were the standard works on socialist and Marxist theory, and they were widely studied in Soviet educational institutions. Judging by the number of editions, one can observe that his most popular books in the period were: the *Short Course of Economic Science*, *Introduction to Political Economy*, *The Philosophy of Living Experience*, and *The Science of Social Consciousness*. *Red Star* and *Engineer Menni* were republished in 1918. Their reviewer in *Proletarskaia Kultura*, S. Dolynkov, mentioned that he had read the novel *Red Star* when it first came out in November 1907 (sic). It was interesting to note, he said, that 'many of us completely missed the author's main idea about an organised society and about the principles of this organisation'.[1] Dolynkov certainly did not leave his readers in any doubt about what the present significance of Bogdanov's novel was, stating that this was the kind of society to which workers should aspire. Dolynkov drew attention in particular to Bogdanov's concept of distribution on Mars:

> The Institute of Statistics calculates the movement of products in the stockpiles, the productivity of all the enterprises and the changes in the number of workers in them. In that way it can calculate what and how much must be produced for any given period and the number of man hours required for the task.
>
> The difference is communicated to everyone. A flow of volunteers then re-establishes the equilibrium. The visitor from Earth asked in amaze-

---

1   Proletarskaia kul'tura 1918, 3, p. 31.

ment: Can it be that consumption is not limited in any way? – and received the answer. Not at all; everyone takes whatever they need and as much as they want.[2]

The nearest parallel with these passages in Bogdanov's novel are to be found in the commentary on the programme of the Russian Communist Party published in 1919. The commentary, entitled *The ABC of Communism*, written by Nikolai Bukharin and Evgenii Preobrazhensky, describes the communist system of distribution in the following way:

> Products are ... neither bought nor sold. They are simply stored in communal warehouses, and are subsequently delivered to those who need them. In such conditions, money will no longer be required ... The main direction will be entrusted to various kinds of book-keeping offices or statistical bureau. There, from day to day, account will be kept of production and all its needs; there also it will be decided whither workers must be sent, whence they must be taken, and how much work there is to be done.[3]

The similarity between the two works is not fortuitous, since Bukharin was an admirer of Bogdanov's book. It is remarkable, however, to reflect that the best vision of a socialist economy that was available to the Bolsheviks in the revolutionary era was one that was taken from Bogdanov's novel. This fact also suggests an important reason why Bogdanov could not but be influential in the post-revolutionary period: he was the only one among the Russian Social Democrats who had thought systematically about what the socialist society would be like. In all Russian Social-Democratic literature there is nothing comparable to Bogdanov's *Red Star* or the sections on collectivist society in his economics textbooks.

Lenin had come to power with the theory of socialism that had been provided by Hilferding. Accordingly, the Bolsheviks had attempted to take over the banking system with which to control the whole national economy, but had found it much more difficult than anticipated. Although the State Bank was taken over relatively early, the Soviet government was confronted by obstruction and sabotage directed by the private bank proprietors, who organised a strike by their employees. Attempts to utilise the banking system as a mechan-

---

2 Proletarskaia kul'tura 1918, 3, p. 32.
3 Bukharin and Preobrazhensky 1969, p. 118.

ism of economic accounting failed miserably. By the time the decree nationalising the private banks was promulgated on 14 December 1917, the economic
accounting objective had been tacitly abandoned, and the main objective
was to break the strike.[4] Spearheading this campaign was the 'All-Russian
Extraordinary Commission for the Struggle against Counter-Revolution and
Sabotage' – the notorious Cheka, headed by Feliks Dzierżyński.[5] It had been
intended that the Cheka should be a temporary institution, only in existence
until the crisis had been overcome. In fact, under different names, it was to
become a permanent fixture of Soviet life. When Bogdanov was arrested by the
security police force in 1923, it had become known as the State Political Admin-
istration (GPU).

In his book *Economics of the Transition Period*, published in 1920, Bukharin
alluded to Hilferding's idea that the seizure of the six leading banks would
give the proletariat command over the whole of industry. He went on to state
that: 'It has been shown empirically that nothing of the kind occurs'. The
reason it did not occur was the one Bogdanov had given, namely: 'Because
the banks "controlled" industry on the basis of credit-financial relations. The
type of bonds here were exactly of the type of credit bonds that were severed
when the proletariat seized the banks'.[6] Bukharin, of course, did not point it
out explicitly, but what his statement meant was that the theory Lenin had
propounded as making a socialist revolution possible had been shown to be
unworkable. Lenin would certainly be aware that Bogdanov had predicted as
much.

Bogdanov in fact pointed this out in a lecture given in April 1921, in which he
told his audience that:

> Finance capital transformed the economic organisation of society much
> less profoundly than Hilferding and others supposed. Enterprises, united
> together in enormous conglomerations of several dozen concerns, subor-
> dinated to their power the whole of the capitalist world. But they only to
> a very small extent organised it. To regard a concern as a planned organ-
> ised system would be naive in the extreme, a misapprehension of what
> organisation is.[7]

---

4 Philips Price 1921, pp. 209–11.
5 Lenin 1958–65, 35, pp. 156–8.
6 Bukharin 1990, p. 117.
7 Neizvestnyi Bogdanov 1995, 1, p. 94.

He repeated the analogy he had used in his *Course of Political Economy*, when he had compared a financial centre's control over individual enterprises to a feudal lord over his vassals.[8]

Bukharin was someone who was profoundly influenced by Bogdanov. His *Economics of the Transition Period* was referred to by Bogdanov as a work which had adopted the tectological method.[9] It was certainly regarded in that light by Lenin, who deplored Bukharin's use of Bogdanov's terminology. Bukharin's book *Historical Materialism*, published in 1921, drew upon a wide range of works by Bogdanov.[10]

In January 1921 Bogdanov gave a lecture entitled 'The Organisational Principles of a Unified Economic Plan' to the first congress of the Scientific Organisation of Labour. It was a significant one, because in it he formulated the principles of Soviet economic planning. Bogdanov's definition of a planned economy was one in which all its parts are systematically coordinated on the basis of a unified and methodically worked out economic plan. In this way the economy as a whole would be treated as a system in the tectological sense. The essence of this approach was expressed in the two propositions:

1) Every organised whole is a system of activities, unfolding in a particular environment and in constant interaction with it. Thus, society is a system of human activities in the natural environment and in a process of struggle against its resistances.

2) Every part of an organised system exists in a particular functional relationship to the whole. Thus, in society every branch of the economy, every enterprise, every worker fulfils its own particular function.[11]

These propositions were the points of departure for establishing the equilibrium of the system and its further development. In this Bogdanov stressed that equilibrium came first and development second.

The equilibrium of the economic system depended on there being a balance between production and distribution. Since production provided all the products for distribution, and distribution in its turn served to support production, it was possible to define the conditions for equilibrium, namely: the equilibrium of the social economy is possible where each one of its elements by means of distribution receives all the necessary means to fulfil its social-productive functions. Thus, the worker should be given the means of consump-

---

8   Ibid.; Bogdanov and Stepanov 1910–25, 2, p. 142.
9   Bogdanov 1989, 1, p. 61.
10   See Bukharin 1965.
11   Bogdanov 1989, 1, p. 274.

tion sufficient to maintain his normal labour power; the enterprise should be given the materials, fuel, implements etc. in sufficient quantity for continued production.

Seen from the organisational viewpoint, the inter-relationships of the branches of industry were functionally linked between themselves in a chain connection. Some branches provided others with the necessary means of production, including even those who produced objects of consumption, and by doing so, provided for all others the means to renew labour power.

From the chain connection there emerged directly a particular proportionality of the branches of production as the necessary conditions of the equilibrium of the economic system: all of them must be mutually sufficient, otherwise the equilibrium would be disrupted and would to some extent bring about the disorganisation of the whole. The economy as a totality was an integrated chain mechanism, the first link of which was the production of the basic means of production, and the last link of which was the production of articles of consumption, which supported the life and the labour energy of society.

Having explained how the equilibrium of the economic system was achieved, Bogdanov then proceeded to show how the expansion of its different branches was also dependent on the maintenance of proportionality between them. If, for example, the production of iron is expanded by five percent then all the branches depending on it in chain connection together can expand by no more than five percent, otherwise there would be no demand for iron by them; and if they expand by less than five percent then some of the iron produced will be surplus to requirement. In the same way, sectors supplying the means for the production of iron, obviously, must provide five percent more than previously, i.e. must themselves expand by five percent.

As a result of the inter-dependence of the sectors of the economy, the expansion of the economic system as a whole is subject to the law of the leasts, making the expansion depend on the rate of development of its most backward parts. If, say, for a new cycle of production, some of the necessary elements can be obtained in a quantity that is increased by only two percent over the previous one, but other elements can grow by 4%, 6%, 9%, in such a case even the expansion of the other branches can only take place successfully within the limits of two percent. If they exceed this rate, it will be to no purpose, and will probably cause a bottleneck.[12]

As to the steps that should be taken to begin the process of socialist economic planning, Bogdanov believed that it was essential to make a scientific-

12   Bogdanov 1989, 1, p. 275.

statistical calculation of the proportions of the different links of the economic whole. Ideally this calculation would be made in peacetime, when it would simply be a matter of recording the existing relations which were observed in the productive system prior to the revolution. But in the present catastrophic conditions, when the very composition of society, its internal dynamics and, consequently, also the character and the sum of its needs had changed, the calculation of necessity had to be done afresh. Since the whole purpose of the social economy was primarily the satisfaction of human needs (and then their development), the point of departure of the calculation must be precisely these needs, the final link in the chain mechanism, to which the other links must adapt themselves.[13]

The statistical calculation would be conducted in the following way. One would do a survey of the population, taking account of the quantity of available labour power, its skills and the numbers of those unfit to work. The normal living budgets of the population would be ascertained on the basis of previous experience, physiology and statistics. From this it could be established that for a fixed period of production the renewal of all this labour power and the non-working elements, including the training of future workers, demands in total such and such quantities of particular items of consumption.

The production of these items of consumption presupposes certain expenditures of certain materials, fuel, implements and other means of production. But for the production of these means in their turn there is the requirement for certain other means, and so on. The entire process results in a chain connection of the various types of production. In this way a 'norm of equilibrium' will be defined that acts as the starting point for all further economic developments.[14]

Since the transition to a planned organisation of the economy was being carried out in the wake of a severe economic catastrophe, an urgent task would be to restore equilibrium to the system. Here, obviously, one was dealing primarily with the regeneration of production. According to the law of the leasts the most constraining role in the process of reconstruction would be played by the most backward sectors of production. These branches would be prioritised by having directed into them labour power and appropriate resources from the sectors that were least backward. In this way all the sectors in turn would be raised to the level that would restore equilibrium to the whole. Sectors would be prioritised in an order of expediency since, for example, it would be wrong

---

13   Bogdanov 1989, 1, p. 276.
14   Bogdanov 1989, 1, p. 277.

to raise transport to its normal scale immediately, when its capacity need not be used for an extended period through the weakness of other branches of the economy.

Until the systematic organisation of production was on a world scale – Bogdanov still hoped for this in 1921 – it might be necessary to enter into barter agreements with other societies, even those of a capitalist type, to make good shortages. For this purpose relative surplus in some sectors could be used as a means of settling accounts. Under conditions of extreme devastation it might be impossible to get a relative surplus in any sector, in which case one could temporarily lease some of the system's unexploited natural resources in the form of concessions to foreign capital.

Bogdanov recognised that a special difficulty in the construction of the economic plan for Soviet Russia was the contrast between the almost entirely state-controlled industry and the agricultural sector with its 20 million small peasant farms. He thought that it would be impossible to include the whole of this agricultural sector in the economic plan, but equally he believed it would be wrong to consider it as something akin to a foreign state, with which one had to barter. It was the source of the industrial sector's food and to some extent its labour power, so that its needs had to be taken into account and included in the general plan, otherwise all the calculations would be undermined.

Bogdanov concluded his lecture by insisting that the difficult and complex task of drawing up a unified economic plan was possible by the application of the tectological method, but only by the tectological method.[15] However, in his lecture one can recognise not only Bogdanov's tectological concepts, but also the way he envisaged the organisation of a socialist society in his previous economic writings. The concept of proportionality had first appeared in his article 'Exchange and Technology' published in the collection *Studies in the Realist World View* in 1903. The state of equilibrium in Bogdanov's lecture, in which all the sectors of the economic system interact and renew themselves, corresponds to Marx's 'reproduction'. What Bogdanov terms the development of the state of equilibrium is for Marx 'expanded reproduction'. Bogdanov's scheme also incorporates Marx's division of the economic system into 'departments', one of which makes producer goods and the other articles of consumption. Bogdanov's presentation of the two sectors in terms of tectological chain links is the equivalent of Marx's reproduction schemes in the second volume of *Das Kapital*.

---

15   Bogdanov 1989, 1, pp. 277–8.

A particular case of equilibrium in economics that attracted Bogdanov's attention was the renewal of the expenditures of workers' labour power. This was a law of equilibrium implied in Marx's theory that the value of labour power was determined by the value of a worker's normal means of consumption. This meant that a worker should receive in the form of wages the quantity of means of consumption necessary to maintain his labour power and the lives of the members of his family. This was the abstract law, but in the anarchy of capitalism the quantity of wages fluctuated above and below this necessary level, so that some workers were unable to recover their living expenditures, while others enjoyed surpluses that inclined them towards parasitism.[16]

In primitive communities, Bogdanov explained, the law of labour expenditures was implemented in a relatively planned way, the patriarch or the organiser of production supplying each group of workers who were assigned a special task with the technical means to carry it out and also the necessary means of consumption to support their labour power. In the society of the future the same operation would be accomplished on a gigantic scale, with scientific planning.[17] The needs of a worker were highly varied. Besides food with sufficient calories to replace the energy expended in labour, there were a number of necessary material requirements. Without adequate housing, clothing and cultural amenities the worker could not function efficiently. Some types of labour were highly skilled, demanding intense concentration or creativity. People who occupied responsible positions on which a great deal depended, such as the organisers of production, needed to be freed from the distractions of communal living and be paid accordingly. The idea that everyone should be paid the same, Bogdanov argued, was not genuine equality, since some occupations were more demanding in mental labour expenditures than others.

It is significant that although in his writings in general Bogdanov took the side of the executor against the organiser, he thought that the organiser merited his relatively privileged position. It is interesting to reflect that in the concept of an equilibrium between the expenditure of energy and its replacement there is not only the evident influence of Marx's theory of value, but also an echo of Avenarius's *Critique of Pure Experience*.

In 1920 the Central Statistical Board drew up a balance-sheet for the Soviet economy for the period 1923–4 of the type Bogdanov had suggested. The authors of the work subscribed fully to the theory of equilibrium propounded by Bogdanov. As Andrei Belykh has pointed out, recognition of the necessity of an

---

16   Bogdanov 1989, 1, p. 261.
17   Bogdanov 1989, 1, p. 262.

economic equilibrium was typical of Soviet economists of the 1920s. Bukharin argued this case most forcefully in his 1928 article 'Notes of an Economist', where the equilibrium that was under discussion was that between the industrial and the agricultural sectors of the economy. He maintained that:

> In the transition period ... classes still exist, nevertheless the society of the transition period has a certain *unity*, though a contradictory one. Therefore, even for this society ... one can construct, on analogy with the second volume of *Das Kapital*, a 'reproduction scheme', i.e. establish the conditions of a sound combination of the different spheres of production and the different spheres of production among themselves, or, in other words, the conditions for a *moving economic equilibrium*. In essence this is what constitutes the task of drawing up a national economic plan.[18]

Like Bogdanov, Bukharin thought in terms of the interchange between the sectors of the economy defined through 'labour expenditures'. It is also noteworthy that he argued the case in terminology taken from *Tectology*, as when he declared:

> One thing is clear, that if any sector of production does not receive back its costs of production plus a certain additional sum, corresponding to the part of the surplus labour, and its ability to serve as some of its expanded reproduction, it will either stay the same or it will regress.[19]

As Belykh indicates, the consensus on the need to maintain an equilibrium in the Soviet economy and promote the balanced growth of its sectors was to be broken in 1929, when Stalin embarked upon his 'great turn' and began a campaign against the 'Rightists' in the party.[20]

2   Oppositions

The Red victory in the Civil War had come at enormous cost in human life. Economically, the country was devastated, both its agriculture and its industry in ruins. In 1920 the system of compulsory grain requisitions was still in force,

---

18   Bukharin 1990, pp. 395–6.
19   Bukharin 1990, p. 405.
20   Belykh 1990, p. 576.

causing deprivation to the peasantry without yet feeding adequately the diminishing urban population. The militarisation of the Soviet state had encouraged centralisation of power and the suppression of popular initiative. The restrictions on press freedom and other civil rights that had been introduced by the Bolsheviks on their accession to power as temporary measures had become permanent. Sympathetic socialist visitors to Soviet Russia in 1920 such as Alexander Berkman, Emma Goldman and Bertrand Russell,[21] who had expected to find there the makings of a socialist society, were quickly disillusioned by the reality that confronted them, and which they documented in contemporary accounts.

While the Red Army was still quelling peasant revolts up and down the country, a number of opposition movements emerged during the course of 1920. One of these was the 'Workers' Opposition', which called for greater rights for the trade unions in the running of the economy. The theoretical case of the 'Workers' Opposition' was made by Alexandra Kollontai, who called for a return to the elective principle, freedom of expression and the elimination of bureaucracy by making all officials answerable to the public at large.[22] 'Democratic Centralists' argued that since coming to power the Bolshevik party had betrayed its own ideals. They opposed the bureaucratic centralism of Lenin's Central Committee and insisted that every important question should be discussed by the party rank and file before decisions were taken.[23]

The most serious opposition movement, however, was that by the sailors at the Kronstadt naval base on the Gulf of Finland at the beginning of 1921. It was a dangerous rebellion since the sailors were an armed force and located near Petrograd, where they were likely to attract wide support among the workers. The demands of the sailors included ones that could be classed as basic human rights: democratically elected Soviets, freedom of speech and the press for workers, peasants and left socialist parties, the release of political prisoners from socialist parties. The response of the Soviet government was to storm the Kronstadt fortress, imprison the sailors on the mainland, and shoot them in batches over the next few months.[24]

The feature that the opposition movements had in common was that the demands they put forward were for the democratic forms that the Bolshevik party itself professed to subscribe to. But in the situation following the Civil War the call for democracy was a threat to the very existence of the Bolshevik

---

21   Berkman 1925; Goldman 1925; Russell 1920.
22   Kollontai 1977, pp. 159–200.
23   Daniels 1960, pp. 113–15.
24   Serge 1963, pp. 115–31.

regime. Bogdanov himself took no part in any opposition movement, but the anti-authoritarian spirit which suffused his writings, which were still being published, was a standing reproach to Lenin's government. There was an echo of this in Kollontai's pamphlet *The Workers' Opposition*,[25] and the very concept of 'democratic centralism' owed its existence to Bogdanov. Also important politically was what Bogdanov's writings did not say. Nowhere did Bogdanov endorse Lenin's use of the term 'the dictatorship of the proletariat', the formula by which the Bolsheviks justified their resort to force against the people. Its absence in Bogdanov's writings implied his refusal to accept the Bolshevik regime's legitimacy.

In the circumstances, it is understandable that Bogdanov's ideas would have the potential to inspire democratic opposition to the Soviet regime. This danger was noted by Bukharin in an article in *Pravda* on 22 November 1921. He said that on the eve of the opening of the Second Congress of Proletkult a number of party members had circulated a programme entitled 'We are Collectivists'. In this programme the 'Collectivists' said that they had no intention of forming a new fraction, but of establishing themselves in leading positions in the trade unions and the Proletkults. The group said it 'rejected the religious philosophy of Lenin and Plekhanov, but were Marxists of the school whose leader is Bogdanov'. Bukharin's objection to the 'Collectivists'' programme was that it encouraged people to follow Bogdanov's example and stand aside from the difficult tasks confronting the Soviet regime, avoid getting their hands dirty, and wait until such times as the ruling party split and when a genuine proletarian revolution was on the horizon. On Bogdanov's attitude, Bukharin remarked that there was nothing worse than a proud monk who retreated from the world.[26]

Bogdanov replied to Bukharin in an open letter stating that all he knew of the 'Collectivists' was what Bukharin had written in his *Pravda* article. In the letter Bogdanov clarified his own position towards the Soviet regime. He said that although he disagreed with the Bolshevik party's analysis of the situation, he recognised the objective necessity of its policies. He denied that he had

---

25   Kollontai writes: 'Bureaucracy is not a product of our misery as comrade Zinoviev tries to convince us. Neither is it a reflection of "blind subordination" to superiors, generated by militarism, as others assert'. See Kollontai 1977, p. 191.

26   Bukharin 1921. In a letter to the Politburo of 2 December 1921 Lenin wrote: 'Now having read the Platform 'We are Collectivists (Vperedists, Bogdanovists, Proletkultists etc.)' I have finally come to the conclusion that it would doubtless be useful for us to *print* it as a pamphlet with 2–3 thousand copies with a thorough analysis, with the addition of an article on Bogdanov's political speeches in 1917 etc'. See Lenin 1958–65, 44, p. 266.

ever advocated in any of his writings that one should 'decline from participation in the most difficult work and struggles'. Bukharin's impression that he
did not want to get his hands dirty was from what had been said in jest in
private conversation, but not to be taken seriously. He added that he did not
consider the work that Bukharin was involved in 'dirty', but tragic; the blood
and dirt that had been involved in the revolution was excessive, but it was not
individuals that were to blame, but the backwardness of the country. Bogdanov
reassured Bukharin that the Bolsheviks would be unlikely to lose their heads or
their power. The danger was that what would be lost was the idealism that had
inspired Bukharin in the past.[27]

3   Lenin's Offensive against Bogdanov

In May 1920, on perusing Bogdanov's *Short Course of Economic Science*, Lenin
commented in his notes: 'It seems that there is no mention here of the "dictatorship of the proletariat"?!!? And the "State Publishing House"!! lets it be published?'[28] Bogdanov's remissness on this account was not Lenin's only cause
for annoyance with him at this time. Although Bogdanov was not a member
of the Provisional International Bureau of Proletkult, his influence could be
observed on its ideological orientation. And the same 14 August 1920 issue of
Izvestiia that reported the formation of the Provisional International Bureau
contained the information that the Russian Proletkult contained no fewer than
400,000 members, of whom 80,000 were actively participating in studio work.
Bogdanov was a major figure in a mass autonomous movement which was in
the process of acquiring an international dimension. It must have seemed to
Lenin that it was high time to clip Bogdanov's wings.

On 17 August 1920, during a meeting of Sovnarkom, Lenin enquired of Pokrovsky:

1) What is the legal status of the Proletkult? 2) Who is in charge of it? and
3) How are they appointed? 4) What else is there of importance to be known
about the status and role of the Proletkult and the results of its work?

On 24 August Pokrovsky informed Lenin that Proletkult was an autonomous
organisation working under the supervision of Narkompros and subsidised by
the latter. Commenting on Pokrovsky's report, Lenin showed scepticism that
the supervision that Narkompros exercised over Proletkult was effective, and

27   Neizvestnyi Bogdanov 1995, 1, pp. 206, 240.

28   Genkina 1969, p. 436.

began to take measures to control Proletkult more directly. His method was to isolate Bogdanov from Proletkult by showing that the theory of proletarian culture was organically connected with his idealist theory of empiriomonism. The other line of attack was to draw Proletkult into the state structure and force Narkompros to curb the activities of Proletkult.

By 2 September Lenin had launched his campaign against Bogdanov with the publication of a new edition of *Materialism and Empiriocriticism*. For this Lenin commissioned V.I. Nevsky to write a foreword, whose basic message was that Lenin's work was still valid, because, despite its appearance of novelty, *Tectology* embodied the same idealist principles as *Empiriomonism* and other of Bogdanov's writings that Lenin had criticised in the first edition of his book.

Nevsky entitled his foreword 'Dialectical Materialism and the Philosophy of Dead Reaction'. He justified his excursion into philosophy by pointing out the danger of Bogdanov and his followers who attempted to assure the working class that the philosophy of a dead, decaying reaction was the last word in science. Under cover of a new set of terms, Bogdanov was continuing to propound the philosophy of idealism, inspired by Mach and Avenarius, that permeated his prolific writings.

Nevsky recalled Engels's division of schools of philosophy into two camps: materialists, who recognised the primacy of matter, and idealists, who recognised the primacy of spirit. Using this criterion, he found Bogdanov's definition of the physical world as 'socially organised experience' to belong to the idealist camp. The same was true of Bogdanov's definition of matter as 'resistance to collective labour efforts'. Further evidence of idealism was found in Bogdanov's pronouncements on the inadequacy of the dialectical method of Hegel and Marx.[29]

With regard to *Tectology*, Nevsky seized upon the fact that in this work Bogdanov continued to make use of the idealist terms 'complexes' and 'elements'. Nevertheless, he could not avoid noticing that *Tectology* employed a great many new terms. On these he remarked: 'Bogdanov himself, who likes to protest against the barbarous terminology of the bourgeois sciences, piles up scores of new terms. One will find all sorts of names and wonder where on earth he got them from'. Nevsky found that these terms confused the exposition of the metaphysical system and added to its obscurity.[30]

Like previous critics of Bogdanov's ideas, Nevsky avoided giving a cogent account of what these ideas were. In this case, like others, the excuse was the

---

29   Nevskii 1931, p. 319.
30   Nevskii 1931, p. 322.

limitations of the task in hand. These were that 'We are not engaged in a critical review of Bogdanov's works. We are only making a few remarks in view of the appearance of the book *Materialism and Empiriocriticism*. It is, therefore, impossible for us to expound in detail either the content of all the works of our philosopher, or his philosophy'. Nevsky explained that his purpose was to illustrate by two or three references to his fundamental propositions that Bogdanov's philosophy rested on such idealistic foundations as the denial of matter, of the external world, and the recognition of the primacy of spirit rather than matter.[31] Nevsky's approach, in fact, was another example of what Bogdanov had termed a 'polemic on credit'.

No doubt prompted by Lenin, Nevsky concluded his foreword on philosophical matters with the remark that in all his books Bogdanov had made no mention of production and the system of management during the dictatorship of the proletariat, just as there was no word about the dictatorship itself.[32] Possibly in response to criticism of this kind, the edition of the *Short Course* that Bogdanov had written in collaboration with Dvolaitsky did have a mention of the 'dictatorship of the proletariat'. But the term was not attributed to either Marx or to Lenin, but, somewhat mischievously, to the now discredited Hilferding.[33]

In 1930 the journal *Leninskii sbornik* published an exchange of notes between Bukharin and Lenin on the subject of Nevsky's article. The exchange began with Bukharin's comment that:

> Earlier, Bogdanov's point of view was that of *philosophy*. Now he annihilates philosophy (I speak not of the truth or otherwise of his viewpoint, but of the character of these views). *Tectology* is, according to Bogdanov, a *replacement* for philosophy. It *excludes* epistemology. The line of his argument is:
> 1. Everything can be regarded as systems, i.e. elements in a particular type of connection.
> 2. If this is the case, one can draw from this some general laws.
> 3. The philosophy becomes redundant and is replaced by universal organisational *science*.
> This way of posing the question is on a *different* level from the empiriomonist one. You can disagree with it, but it has to be understood. And Nevsky does not have this minimum requirement.

---

31   Ibid.
32   Nevskii 1931, p. 324.
33   Bogdanov 1923, p. 371.

Lenin's reply was: 'Bogdanov has deceived you by changing (*verkleidet*) and trying to shift the old dispute. And you have fallen for it!' To this Bukharin answered: 'But this is exactly what you have to *prove*. In my opinion, in *essence* here, really there is no philosophy and tectology is something different from empiriomonism. It is not so easy to deceive me in such things'.[34]

The exchange of views shows that Bukharin had a profound understanding of *Tectology*, and that he was well aware that in order to refute it or to show its kinship to *Empiriomonism*, it was necessary that its arguments be expounded. Lenin, however, was not interested in giving Bogdanov's work even this kind of exposure; he simply wanted it condemned. We only have this revealing document because its publication was designed to discredit Bukharin as part of Stalin's campaign against the 'Rightists'. It demonstrated that in 1920 Bukharin had taken the side of Bogdanov against Lenin, and that he had defended a doctrine that Lenin had placed beyond the pale. Neither in 1930 nor in 1920 were ideas discussed and evaluated on their merits.

When, in 1922, Bogdanov was invited to reply to Nevsky's article, he used the opportunity to present a summary of the main ideas in *Tectology*, and the weaknesses of Plekhanov's approach to philosophy. With regard to Nevsky's criticism of his ideas, Bogdanov thought that there was no need to enter into any detailed polemic. When his opponents accused him of idealism on the grounds that in his organisational analysis he used the terms 'elements' and 'complexes', he could only smile; any kind of science which analysed phenomena was likely to break them up into 'elements' and then examine them in their inter-connections as 'complexes'.[35] As for the reproach that in his books there was no mention of the forms of society in the transitional period, Bogdanov replied that in the period in question, 1918–21, when the latest editions of his textbooks had been published, there had been no accepted views on this subject, though in the present year (1922) there now were.[36]

The second prong of Lenin's offensive against Bogdanov was to subordinate the Proletkult organisation to Narkompros, and, in this way, to bring it into the Soviet state structure. Lenin intended that this should be done at the First Proletkult Congress which was to take place between 5–12 October 1920. This, however, turned out to be more difficult than Lenin had expected. On 7 October he instructed Lunacharsky to announce to the Congress on the following day that Proletkult would come under the control of Narkompros and be regarded as one of its institutions. However, from the report of Lunacharsky's

---

34   Leninskii sbornik 1930, 12, pp. 384–5.
35   Neizvestnyi Bogdanov 1995, 1, p. 118.
36   Ibid.

speech at the Congress in *Izvestiia* Lenin discovered that Lunacharsky had said the very opposite of what Lenin had instructed, and had defended Proletkult's autonomy. In view of this Lenin drafted a resolution, 'On Proletarian Culture', to be discussed in the Politburo on 10 October and to be immediately presented to the Congress. It rejected the idea of autonomy for Proletkult and demanded its subordination to the Soviet state, to Narkompros in particular and to the Communist Party which would define its tasks as part of the dictatorship of the proletariat.[37]

Lenin had no trouble defining what he wanted the outcome to be, but a resolution of this kind demanded justification for the desired course of action. This involved the denial of a specifically proletarian culture and the associated assertion that Marxism did not 'reject the most valuable achievements of the bourgeois era'. Bukharin, however, did not accept what seemed to him Lenin's uncritical adoption of bourgeois culture in his draft resolution, and proposed to alter it accordingly. Lebedev-Poliansky, who attended the meeting, insisted on inserting into the resolution a clause declaring that 'The Proletkults preserve the basic principles of their structure as class proletarian organisations', which undermined the spirit of Lenin's resolution.

The following meeting of the Politburo on 11 October took place with a number of Proletkultists in attendance, whom Lenin managed to win over to acceptance of his resolution. On this occasion too Bukharin expressed his reservations to Lenin, but was nevertheless delegated to announce the decision to the Communist fraction of the Proletkult Congress. The Politburo's resolution was adopted by the fraction and subsequently, after heated debate, by the Proletkult Congress.[38]

There was a further complication for Lenin, however, when the Communist fraction of the Proletkult Congress passed a resolution saying that although the fraction submitted to the decision of the Central Committee as a matter of party discipline, it thought it necessary to inform the Central Committee of its firm and sincere belief that the merger of the Proletkults with Narkompros was at the present time premature, and requested that the implementation of the decision be postponed until the next party congress. This resolution forced the Politburo to return on 14 October to the question of the Proletkult and subsequently to take the matter to a plenary meeting of the Central Committee on 10 November. The Plenum discussion centred round the forms of Proletkult's merger with Narkompros, but other aspects of Proletkult, including its inter-

37   Lenin 1958–65, 41, pp. 336–7.
38   Smirnov 1969, p. 80.

national dimension, were also considered. It was thought that in the purely artistic sphere Proletkult should remain autonomous, and that the supervision of Narkompros should only be exercised in clear cases of bourgeois deviation. For the rest, it was decided to draft a letter on behalf of the Central Committee on the merger of Proletkult with Narkompros and to instruct party members on the Executive Committee of the Comintern to dissolve the International Proletkult at a convenient moment.[39]

The Central Committee's letter 'On the Proletkults' was published on the front page of *Pravda* on 1 December 1920. The announcement of the merger of Proletkult with Narkompros provided the occasion for the anonymous authors of the letter (Zinoviev, with the participation of Lenin and Krupskaya) to denounce 'proletarian culture' and its proponents.[40] Although no names were mentioned, it was clear that Lenin and Krupskaya had Bogdanov in mind. Prominent in the letter was Krupskaya's scheme of the history of Proletkult and its autonomy. Proletkult, the letter claimed, emerged prior to the October revolution. It proclaimed itself to be an independent workers' organisation, independent of Kerensky's Ministry of Education. The October revolution changed this perspective, but the Proletkult organisation continued to be independent, but now independent of Soviet power. It was this kind of independence that attracted to Proletkult alien, petty-bourgeois, elements who often seized the leadership of Proletkult. There were futurists, decadents, adherents of an idealist philosophy alien to Marxism and losers from the ranks of the bourgeois journalism and philosophy who tried to make their influence felt in the affairs of Proletkult. Under the guise of 'proletarian culture' the workers were served up bourgeois views and philosophies (Machism). In the realm of art they were given nonsensical perverted conceptions (futurism).

The letter contained the historical explanation of the origins of the anti-Marxist conceptions that were manifested in 'proletarian culture' that would be repeated in subsequent Soviet historiography. This was that during the reaction following the defeat of the 1905 revolution the Social-Democratic intelligentsia had resorted to 'god-building' and all kinds of idealist philosophy. Now these intellectual elements were trying to smuggle in these reactionary conceptions under the guise of proletarian culture. These same elements were now trying to present the decision of the Central Committee on the merger of Proletkult with Narkompros as a move to deprive the workers of their artistic creativity.

---

39   Smirnov 1969, pp. 81–2.
40   Gorsen and Knödler-Bunte 1974, p. 81.

This, however, was not the case, and here the letter set out the Central Committee's policy on the mild supervision to be exercised in matters of purely artistic activities.

The contents of the letter make it clear that the subordination of Proletkult to Narkompros was an integral part of Lenin's campaign against Bogdanov and was organically connected with Nevsky's Foreword to *Materialism and Empiriocriticism*, although on the face of it Lenin was connected with neither. The denunciatory part of the letter was an element introduced after it had been discussed by the Central Committee, and had not been part of the negotiations that had been conducted with the representatives of Proletkult.

The letter gave encouragement to Bogdanov's opponents within the Proletkult Central Committee. In her memoirs a Central Committee member, Anna Dodonova, records that after reading the letter she became convinced that the disfavour that Proletkult was in with Lenin was due to the ideological influence of Bogdanov and his close associate Lebedev-Poliansky. She thought that it was thanks to Lebedev-Poliansky that *Proletarskaia Kultura* had become a tribune of the Bogdanovists. Consequently, it would be desirable for the Proletkult to change its leadership, though she expected resistance to this from the provincial Proletkults, since Bogdanov and Lebedev-Poliansky were influential in these circles. In fact, when the Proletkult Central Committee met on 16 December 1920 to discuss the letter on the Proletkults and its implications, there was a deep division of opinion on whether there was a need for the organisation to change direction.[41]

The Presidium of Proletkult replied to the party Central Committee's letter with one entitled 'A Necessary Clarification'. It was intended for publication in *Pravda*, but this was not allowed. The letter argued that the attitude of Proletkult to the Communist Party could be seen from the fact that at the recent Congress no less than three-quarters of the delegates were Communists, and that out of the 30 members of the Central Committee 29 belonged to the party, 17 of them being workers. The 30th member of the Central Committee was Bogdanov, a pioneer of proletarian culture who throughout the whole revolution had been on the side of the Communist Party. His books were published by the State Publishing House and by the party Central Committee. He was a professor at the Sverdlov Communist University. In view of this it was obvious that there were no aspirations for 'independence' from Soviet power.

As for the ruling organs of Proletkult, they were elected at congresses and consisted overwhelmingly of Communists. The Presidium of Proletkult did not understand what anti-Marxist group of intellectuals had taken over the affairs

---

41   Dodonova 1967, p. 491.

of Proletkult that the Central Committee's letter referred to. The Presidium objected that matters were mentioned in the Central Committee's letter that had not been broached before and were based on false information. The alleged influence of Machism and the philosophy of 'god-building' and futurism in art was based on such false information. In fact, the Proletkult opposed futurism in its publications. It was an external current, because futurism did not exist inside Proletkult. Neither had Proletkult concerned itself with Machism and 'god-building', these older philosophical currents being outside its field of vision. Moreover, in his writings Bogdanov had classed Machism as the ideology of democratic engineers and professors, not of proletarians. And certainly there was a time when Lunacharsky was reproached for his 'god-building', but that question had long been resolved, and, with the full approval of the party, for the past three years he had stood at the head of Narkompros. If any of these currents should ever re-appear, the Presidium undertook to oppose them decisively.[42]

The Presidium then sent a delegation to Lenin consisting of N. Nikitin, F. Blagonravov, V.F. Pletnev and F. Volgin to discuss the reorganisation of Proletkult. According to Volgin, Lenin heard them out, but it was clear that his mind was already made up on the matter.[43] Blagonravov and S.S. Krivtsov resigned from the Central Committee of Proletkult in protest. At the Plenum of the Proletkult Central Committee on 20 December Lebedev-Poliansky resigned as chairman, demanding that his reasons for resignation be published in *Proletarskaia Kultura*, but this was refused. He was replaced by Pletnev, whose candidature had been approved by the Communist Party fraction.[44]

The re-issue of Lenin's *Materialism and Empiriocriticism* with Nevsky's foreword had its effect. It encouraged a vigorous anti-Bogdanov campaign in the press. In the autumn of 1921 Bogdanov had to resign from the Central Committee of Proletkult. In this connection Bogdanov once remarked to Dvolaitsky that half of the journal *Pod znamenem marksizma* was directed against Bogdanovism. Dvolaitsky, who was connected with the journal, corrected him, saying: 'Not half of it; the whole of it'.[45] This was something of an exaggeration. The journal did have anti-Bogdanov articles, but its main focus was on the endorsement of Plekhanov as a Marxist theoretician, showing that the current of thought which he represented was to be adopted as Soviet orthodoxy.[46]

42   Gorsen and Knödler-Bunte 1974, pp. 169–70.
43   Kim 1972, pp. 284–5.
44   Gorbunov 1974, pp. 160–2.
45   Neizvestnyi Bogdanov 1995, 1, p. 39.
46   Hänggi 1984, pp. 78–279.

The adoption of Plekhanov as the approved interpreter of Marxist theory was encouraged by Lenin as a means of countering Bogdanov's influence. During the debate on the trade unions in January 1921 Lenin had remarked: 'Let me add in parenthesis for the benefit of young party members that it is *impossible* to become a conscious, *genuine* communist without studying – and I mean studying – everything that Plekhanov has written on philosophy, because nothing better exists in the international literature on Marxism'. He expressed the hope that the edition of Plekhanov's Collected Works, then in progress, would contain a special volume or volumes of Plekhanov's philosophical articles to be included in a series of standard textbooks on communism. (In April 1922 Lenin commissioned Kamenev to compile just such a volume.)[47] He urged that the Soviet state should demand that professors of philosophy have a knowledge of Plekhanov's exposition of Marxist philosophy and ability to impart it to their students.[48] Apparently, such professors were not in abundance in 1921, so that the followers of Plekhanov, A. Deborin and Ortodoks, were invited to lecture at the Sverdlov University, despite the fact that both of them had been Mensheviks.[49] In the article 'The Significance of Militant Materialism' published in the journal *Pod znamenem marksizma*, Lenin again endorsed Plekhanov as a Marxist theoretician and gave his support to Plekhanov's version of Marxism as Hegelian dialectics interpreted in a materialistic way.[50]

The effect of Lenin's establishment of a Plekhanovite-Hegelian orthodox version of Marxism was to reinforce the impression that Bogdanov's ideas were heretical. It opened up Bogdanov personally to all kinds of abuse. His attempts to reply to the smears were not printed, and in any case there were so many it would have been impossible to answer them all. Around Bogdanov there was created a poisonous, hostile atmosphere. In these circumstances he saw that his continued participation in Proletkult could compromise the organisation and accordingly resigned from it in the autumn of 1921. He left it, he says, reluctantly, using Bukharin's metaphor, for the 'monk's cell' of the Socialist Academy.[51]

In December 1921, along with Krasin, Bogdanov was sent to London as an economist by the People's Commissariat of Foreign Trade.[52] Also in the capacity as an economic advisor to the Soviet government, he was commissioned to

---

47   Lenin 1958–65, 45, p. 166.
48   Lenin 1958–65, 42, p. 290.
49   Iakhot 1981, pp. 10–1.
50   Lenin 1958–65, 45, pp. 24–30.
51   Neizvestnyi Bogdanov 1995, 1, p. 49.
52   Plyutto 1998, p. 476.

write an analysis of the Versailles Treaty for the Soviet delegation to the Genoa Conference in April 1922. For this purpose he read the book by John Maynard Keynes, *The Economic Consequences of the Peace*. It was while in London that Bogdanov discovered that Keynes's brother Geoffrey, who had served as a military surgeon during the Great War, had written a book on blood transfusion. This book, along with other literature on the subject, was acquired by Bogdanov, who, with a few interested medical colleagues, began to experiment with the techniques it described on his return to Russia.[53]

Bogdanov's report on the Versailles Treaty formed the basis of a lecture he gave in the Socialist Academy on 14 September 1922. This contrasted two types of imperialism, the more liberal American type, represented by the idealism of Woodrow Wilson, and the predatory European type, represented by Cecil Rhodes and Joseph Chamberlain. Bogdanov saw the Versailles Treaty as a peculiar combination of these two ideological currents. The discourse of Versailles might have been inspired by Wilson, but the practice was of a short-sighted predatory kind, demanding exorbitant reparations from Germany and imposing humiliating peace conditions that Bogdanov thought would create enmity for future generations. He thought that the framers of the Versailles peace had performed very badly in the tasks that faced them of bringing normality to the post-war world. These included ending war communism, restoring international economic bonds, the reconstruction of a normal money circulation and system of credit, and eliminating military dictatorships. In the course of the discussion on the lecture Bogdanov remarked: 'Comrades, in December 1917 I gave a public lecture in which I said that we had war communism. This was printed in January 1918. But in the official literature the term was used in April 1921'.[54] Here Bogdanov was referring to Lenin's article 'On the Tax in Kind', in which the term 'war communism' appeared in quotation marks, but with no indication of what its source might be.[55]

At the end of December 1922 Bogdanov gave a lecture on the effects of the New Economic Policy on proletarian culture in the club of Moscow University. No record was published of the lecture, but it provided the occasion for Ya.A. Yakovlev to publish a condemnatory article in *Pravda* on 4 January 1923 entitled 'Menshevism in Proletkult Garb'.[56] The immediate cause for Yakovlev's ire was Bogdanov's alleged view that the Russian Communist Party was con-

---

53   Krementsov 2011, p. 57.
54   Bogdanov 1922a, p. 147.
55   Lenin 1958–65, 43, p. 243.
56   Iakovlev 1923a.

ducting a 'bourgeois policy' in economics, an idea that was characteristic of the émigré Menshevik journal *Sotsialisticheskii vestnik*. Besides this, the article reviewed the various episodes over the years in which Bogdanov had slighted or opposed the Communist Party. Yakovlev mentioned Bogdanov's expulsion from the editorial board of *Proletarii* in 1909, his refusal to recognise the legitimacy of the 1912 party conference at which Lenin had expelled the 'liquidators', and the refusal to recognise the October revolution as anything but a workers' and soldiers' rebellion. Bogdanov's attempt to rebut Yakovlev's allegations was printed in *Pravda*, but together with Yakovlev's replies to the points Bogdanov had made, suggesting that Yakovlev had had official backing for his article.[57]

Yakovlev published his article again in 1923 as the Introduction to a volume entitled *Against A. Bogdanov*, containing Plekhanov's 'Materialismus militans' and the last (sixth) chapter of Lenin's *Materialism and Empiriocriticism*. The need to re-publish these works, Yakovlev explained, was that 'the conditions of the New Economic Policy were inevitably accompanied by the resurgence both of various idealist currents and attempts to organise anti-revolutionary groups under the flag of bourgeois idealism'.[58] The implication of Yakovlev's introduction, backed by the authority of Lenin and Plekhanov, was that Bogdanov's ideas were not just wrong, but posed an actual threat to the Soviet regime. This idea was underlined in Yakovlev's statement that 'Bogdanov is trying to organise a struggle against the Communist Party utilising the idea of proletarian culture and unified organisational science. He criticises the position of the Communist Party and the Soviet government in the sphere of cultural construction as it were from the left, at the same time organising a political struggle against the Communist Party from the right, from the point of view of the capitalists'.[59]

4   Bogdanov's Arrest

Bogdanov was arrested on the night of 8 September 1923 on the orders of the GPU, for reasons that were not revealed to him. He was put in the Lubianka prison, sharing a cell with a prisoner charged with a criminal offence. Despite his protests, he was kept for five days without books, without writing materi-

---

57   Bogdanov 1923b.
58   Iakovlev 1923, p. 3.
59   Iakovlev 1923, p. 7.

als, without exercise, and without any interrogation. At the end of five days the conditions began to improve to approximately what they were in Kresty prison, when he was last there in 1905–6.

On Thursday 13 September, during his first interrogation, Bogdanov discovered that he was suspected of having organisational and ideological connections with the group Workers' Truth. He was given three issues of the group's publication *Rabochaia pravda*, of which previously he had only seen one. Back in May Bogdanov had heard rumours that the people who were conducting a literary campaign against him wanted to connect him with 'Workers' Truth'.

Workers' Truth was a small splinter group that had come into existence despite the prohibition on fractions adopted by the Tenth Party Congress in 1921. It held that the revolution had not brought any benefit to the working class, and that the class that had been brought to power was the 'technical intelligentsia'. The Communist Party, after becoming the ruling party, the party of the organisers and leaders of the state apparatus and the capitalist-based economic life, had lost its ties with the proletariat. Workers' Truth called for the creation of a new Workers' Party to fight for the democratic conditions under which the workers could defend their interests.[60]

Rabochaia pravda No. 2 contained an article signed 'Leonid', a pseudonym taken from the name of Bogdanov's hero in *Red Star*. Parts of other articles were written in Bogdanov's terminology, or incorporated passages taken from some of his writings. It was easy for Bogdanov to show that he was not the author of any of the articles, but some inexperienced writer who imitated his style. The investigators, nevertheless, insisted that Bogdanov was responsible for Workers' Truth, since they were obvious 'Bogdanovists'. Bogdanov replied that he was no more responsible for Workers' Truth than Plekhanov or Lenin were for their theoretical followers, or Marx for Menshevism or the founders of Menshevism for the 'maximalist' position of Trotsky, Dan and Martynov in 1905.

Bogdanov insisted that Feliks Dzierżyński, the head of the GPU, interrogate him, since Dzierżyński knew him personally. When Dzierżyński did so, it emerged that he had the same distorted conception of Bogdanov's ideas as his investigators had. Dzierżyński told him: 'If you think that our revolution is one of advanced capitalism, then you are our enemy, because that undermines us and gives support to our enemies'. Bogdanov explained that he never had such an opinion, and after an hour's conversation Dzierżyński's attitude changed completely. Bogdanov wrote a lengthy report on his views and enclosed a copy of the latest edition of his *Introductory Course of Political Economy* with the

---

60   Daniels 1960, p. 161.

chapter on the Russian revolution and war communism. Dzierżyński promised that Bogdanov would be released within a week and allowed Natalia to
visit him.

At the second visit Natalia came very agitated, reporting that there was
evidence against Bogdanov coming from someone claiming to have seen and
heard him speak at a conference of Worker's Truth. This, however, was not put
to Bogdanov himself, and after a further delay he was released from prison
on 13 October.[61] On his five weeks in a GPU prison he observed in his autobiography: 'Although I had finally given up politics, it had not given up me,
as my arrest in September–October 1923 has shown'.[62] Victor Serge had no
doubt about what was responsible for Bogdanov's imprisonment. In speaking of Lenin's Bonapartist inclinations, he remarked: 'He has Bogdanov, his old
friend and comrade, jailed because this outstanding intellectual confronts him
with embarrassing objections'.[63]

5   The Communist Academy

Following his resignation from Proletkult the institutional refuge remaining
to Bogdanov was the Socialist Academy, renamed in 1924 as the Communist
Academy. This was the 'monk's cell' to which he retreated. Most of his last works
were published in the Academy's journal, *Vestnik Sotsialisticheskoi Akademii*
(from 1924 *Vestnik Kommunisticheskoi Akademii*). But even though Bogdanov
tried to divorce himself from public life and devote himself entirely to scholarship, the attacks on him were unrelenting.

On 6 November 1923 Bogdanov wrote to the Presidium of the Socialist
Academy that an anonymous review in *Pod znamenem marksizma* had accused
him of being 'an opportunist in theory and a renegade in politics'. This, Bogdanov complained, was not only a lie and a slander against himself, but also
an insult to the Socialist Academy that twice elected an opportunist and a
renegade to its Presidium. It was ironic, Bogdanov observed, that these accusations were made in a journal that had devoted two of its issues to Plekhanov
and had not once applied the epithet of 'renegade' to him. And Plekhanov
was the leader of the group around the newspaper *Edinstvo*, which in 1917 had
campaigned against the Bolsheviks with every means possible, including the
accusation that Lenin was in the pay of the Germans. Bogdanov gave a short

61   Neizvestnyi Bogdanov 1995, 1, pp. 34–57.
62   Neizvestnyi Bogdanov 1995, 1, p. 19.
63   Serge 1963, p. 134.

account of his revolutionary career as evidence that there were no grounds for the anonymous reviewer's accusations, and demanded that the Academy defend the honour of one of its members and its own integrity.[64]

On the following day Bogdanov wrote to Preobrazhensky as a member of the Academy's Presidium pointing out the discrimination practised against him in the institution. He was not invited to give lectures; some of his articles could not be printed in the Academy's journal out of political-tactical considerations; he could not attend certain of the Academy's functions. Nevertheless a person had the right to human rights, including that of self-defence. His letter asking for the Academy's protection was just such an act of self-defence, in the most basic sense of the term. Bogdanov was apprehensive that the sycophantic attacks on him were the prelude to more drastic treatment. He feared that following the three years of slander that had culminated in his recent imprisonment, some agent of the GPU might think it his communist duty to arrest him under some pretext or other.

There was a reason, Bogdanov reminded Preobrazhensky, why the Socialist Academy should act in an honourable way. This was because:

> Our revolution – although it is not what we thought it to be, and what it is even now thought to be – is nevertheless a great revolution and a stage in world history. And I am often amazed when I see how little other people, who have been carried to the highest positions by it – how little they think that they are acting before the eyes of history, that they will be studied by it, judged by it, dispassionately and mercilessly. Yes, it will be forced to study much, both great and sometimes small. Even the most petty sycophant, who would be able to reckon, by his silent insignificance, on complete oblivion – even he will appear in someone else's biography.[65]

That would have been true had not the sycophants also been in charge of the history of the revolution.

The historiography of the revolutionary era in Russia constituted one essential facet of the campaign against Bogdanov. It is this which can explain how it could be that a figure so prominent in the history of the Russian revolutionary movement and in the history of Russian socialist thought could have left so little trace in historical works on these subject areas. Bogdanov's apparent obscurity is a consequence of the pervasive Lenin-centred approach adopted

---

64   Neizvestnyi Bogdanov 1995, 1, pp. 213–15.
65   Neizvestnyi Bogdanov 1995, 1, p. 217.

in both Soviet and Western historiography. This approach to the history of the revolutionary era was institutionalised by the creation in the summer of 1920 of the Commission for the History of the Russian Communist Party and the October Revolution (Istpart) under the chairmanship of Olminsky. From its inception Istpart was a political and ideological organisation rather than a scholarly one. Its function was to present the interpretation of the history of the Bolshevik party and the process that had brought it to power that was favoured by Lenin and his associates. It extolled those figures who occupied positions of leadership in the party and ignored or denounced those who were perceived as political or ideological enemies.[66]

It was not simply a case of Bogdanov's being ignored by Soviet historiography; the historical context in which he had operated in the Russian revolutionary movement was also presented in such a way that his absence from the historical record would not be apparent. The method that Istpart used to achieve the Lenin-centred presentation of history is well illustrated in the memoirs of the Soviet historian K.A. Ostroukhova, where she recalls her attempts to write a series of articles on Lenin's campaign against the boycott of the Second and Third Dumas. According to Ostroukhova:

> I was worried about my ability to expound these complex themes correctly. M.S. Olminsky gave me advice: first of all study Lenin's works, his pronouncements on the question of intra-party struggle in these years ... I remember that in writing the article 'Social-Democracy and the Elections to the Third State Duma' I took my guidance chiefly from Lenin's article 'Against the Boycott'.[67]

By structuring historical events around Lenin's writings in the way Ostroukhova describes, one would naturally produce an account in which events appeared to vindicate Lenin's viewpoint, or in which only events that supported Lenin's interpretation of events would appear. Bogdanov was inevitably a major casualty in this approach to historical writing.

One party historian was Emelian Yaroslavsky, who had twice written in *Pravda* accusing Bogdanov of having views similar to the Mensheviks on the grounds that his ideas had inspired the Workers' Truth group. In an open letter to Yaroslavsky dated 19 December 1923 Bogdanov pointed out the illogicality of this position. It was like saying that Marx was responsible for the Mensheviks

---

66   See White 1985.
67   Ostroukhova 1967, pp. 94–5.

and every other current of opinion, however wrong-headed, that claimed to be his follower. Bogdanov illustrated the inconsistency of Yaroslavsky's reasoning by two propositions: (1) If the supporters of *our* theory succumb to opportunism, it is not our theory that is to blame. (2) If the followers of Bogdanov's theory 'go astray', it is Bogdanov's theory that is to blame.

This was, in Bogdanov's opinion, 'Hottentot' logic,[68] and his last articles published in *Vestnik Kommunisticheskoi Akademii* were devoted to explaining the phenomenon of this kind of illogicality.

If the persecution of Bogdanov had been driven by Lenin's personal antipathy towards him, one might have expected that this would be alleviated following Lenin's death in January 1924. This, however, was not the case, since Lenin's successors decided that the accepted doctrine of the Soviet state would be 'Leninism', a new stage in Marxism. One of the main activities of the Socialist Academy during 1924, one in which Bogdanov did not participate, was to work out what should constitute 'Leninism' and how it should be propagated. The works of Plekhanov ceased to be criteria of orthodox Marxism and were replaced by those of Lenin. Quotations from Lenin now became the infallible arbiters of the truth. This ensured that one of the essential components of 'Leninism' was antipathy towards Bogdanov and his ideas.

It is important to note that the officially accepted 'Leninism' involved some re-working of Lenin's actual conceptions. The problem was that, in 1917, Lenin had subscribed to the now discredited Hilferding theory that by taking over the banks one could control the economy of the country. Experience had shown this to be illusory, as Bukharin had pointed out in his book *Economics of the Transition Period*, reproducing Bogdanov's reasons for why this was the case. Bukharin's book also contained a tectological explanation for why a revolution should break out in Russia rather than in one of the advanced countries. This arose from the inter-dependence of the individual capitalist states, so that they formed a chain-like connection between the parts of the world economy. When the equilibrium of this system was disturbed by the World War, it would lead to a general collapse. And, according to Bukharin, it stood to reason that 'the collapse was bound to begin with those links which were the weakest in terms of capitalist organisation'.[69]

Lenin was not enamoured with Bogdanov's influence on Bukharin's work, and objected in particular to Bukharin's theory that the chain of imperialism broke at its weakest link. In a marginal note he commented: 'Untrue: with the

---

68   Neizvestnyi Bogdanov 1995, 1, pp. 218–22.
69   Bukharin 1990, p. 200.

moderately weak. Without a certain level of capitalism nothing would have happened here in Russia'.[70] Since it was inspired by Bogdanov, it is unsurprising that Lenin did not agree with Bukharin's application of the law of the leasts. But after Lenin's death, when Stalin felt obliged to credit Lenin with a theory of proletarian revolution, he could hardly say, as was the case, that in 1917 Lenin had subscribed to Hilferding's theory of how the banks could be used to control the economy, but that experience had shown this to be illusory. Instead, Stalin maintained that Lenin's theory of revolution had been that 'the front of capital would be breached where the chain of imperialism was weakest, for the proletarian revolution consisted in this breaking of the chain of imperialism at its weakest point'.[71] Stalin, of course, would know that Bogdanov's theory of the weakest link was the last thing that Lenin would want to be associated with, but Stalin no doubt savoured the irony.

In September 1924 Bogdanov felt impelled to respond to an article that had appeared in the journal *Kommunist*, signed by a certain Petrov. This had been critical of the way Bogdanov had expounded economics historically in his books on the subject. There had been previous critics who had objected that Bogdanov's works treated not political economy but economic history, but Petrov had gone beyond the bounds of scholarly criticism, saying that Bogdanov's historical approach to economics was revisionist and counter-revolutionary. Bogdanov thought it pointless to enter into a polemic with Petrov, since he wanted to be left alone to get on with his academic pursuits. But he had the means at his disposal to silence Petrov, making use of the burgeoning cult of Lenin. He quoted at some length the review of the *Short Course of Economic Science* that Lenin had published in *Mir Bozhii* in 1898 and which praised in particular the historical mode of exposition.

On what Lenin had said Bogdanov commented that there was no mention in it of any 'harmful tendency' hidden behind the historical method of exposition, nor any suggestion that it was not political economy but economic history. What Lenin had said was that 'this was exactly how political economy should be expounded'.

In contrast to Lenin, who had approved of Bogdanov's historical approach, Bogdanov said that he could not recall a single Menshevik or revisionist who had. On the contrary, his method was opposed by economists from a wide range of currents. These economists included Bukharin, Hilferding, the Menshevik theoretician I. Rubin, M.I. Tugan-Baranovsky and almost all bourgeois econom-

---

70   Lenin 1929, p. 397.
71   Stalin 1948–53, 6, p. 97.

ists. Bogdanov added that it was natural for bourgeois economists to reduce political economy to the theory of capitalism, because they regarded capitalism as the single normal system, and all previous forms as capitalism in embryo. And for them there could be nothing higher than capitalism.[72]

Bogdanov's listing of Bukharin among the economists who opposed him suggests that he knew or suspected that the campaign against the historical approach came from him. This was borne out during the course of the discussion on the lecture Skvortsov-Stepanov gave to the Communist Academy on 31 January 1925 on the subject of 'What is Political Economy?' In the discussion on this lecture Bukharin contended that political economy was the theory of capitalist society, and that categories such as value, wages, profit, capital, rent, etc., were all categories of an exchange economy. Marx's analysis in *Das Kapital*, therefore, only applied to capitalist society, not to either pre- or post-capitalist formations. Bukharin criticised the approach taken by Bogdanov and Skvortsov-Stepanov in their historical treatment of political economy, with its implication that the category of value existed before capitalism. Bukharin put it to Skvortsov-Stepanov:

> When you expound pre-exchange social formations or when Bogdanov does this in *Red Star*, do you use the categories of capitalist society? Of course not. Because the basic economic category of capitalism, value, has no perceptive meaning whatever. But if in the planned society there is no category of value, then there are no wages, no profit, no rent i.e. none of the usual categories of theoretical economy.[73]

Skvortsov-Stepanov's lecture marks the end of the historical approach taken to economics by both himself and Bogdanov. No more editions of the *Short Course* were published, and the *Course of Political Economy* was discontinued in 1925. That his lecture would not prevent this from happening, because the decisions had already been taken, was probably plain to Skvortsov-Stepanov. Neverthess, the lecture made an impressive case, given as it was by the translator of Marx's *Das Kapital* into Russian, someone with an extensive knowledge of Marx's works. The thrust of Skvortsov-Stepanov's argument was to show by means of quotations from their writings that the approach of Marx, Engels and Lenin to economics was not only abstract but also historical.

---

72   Bogdanov 1924, pp. 399–400.
73   Vestnik Kommunisticheskoi Akademii 1925, 11, p. 301.

In addition to Marx's *The Poverty of Philosophy* and Engels's *Anti-Dühring* Skvortsov-Stepanov deployed a quotation from Marx's 'German Ideology' that had been recently published by Ryazanov's Institute of Marx and Engels. The quotation was:

> Communism is for us not a *state of affairs* which is to be established, as an *ideal* to which reality will have to adjust itself. We call communism the real movement which abolishes the present state of things. The conditions of this movement result from the premises now in existence.[74]

According to Skvortsov-Stepanov, this was Lenin's view of communism. But, as Skvortsov-Stepanov was well aware, it was much closer to Bogdanov's conception of socialism that had been expounded in his article in *Vpered*, 'Socialism of the Present'.

Skvortsov-Stepanov's task would have been much simplified if he had been able to draw on the still unpublished manuscripts of Marx's earlier works, such as the *Grundrisse*, with its lengthy section on pre-capitalist social formations, or on his later drafts on Russian post-reform economic development. He had, however, recognised the significance of Marx's letter to Engels of 1868 which marked the end of Marx's use of a Hegelian framework for *Das Kapital* and the beginning of his sociological and historical treatment of the question of the circulation and reproduction of capital. In this letter Marx first expressed his interest in the history of primitive village communities, including the Russian peasant commune, of which he made an extensive study.

In keeping with the spirit of the times, Skvortsov-Stepanov spoke of Lenin as an equal of Marx as a theoretician. This allowed him to use Lenin's authority to add force to one of the most telling points he made in his lecture. Following Bogdanov, Skvortsov-Stepanov cited Lenin's review of Bogdanov's *Short Course*, which wholeheartedly endorsed the historical approach that the author had taken. The calculation here, as in Bogdanov's case, was that the Lenin cult could be used in a good cause.

Skvortsov-Stepanov had presented his audience with a paradox that their formulaic way of thinking had made unsolvable: if Lenin was always right, and Bogdanov was always wrong, how could it be that Lenin could endorse Bogdanov's book? A great deal of ingenuity was employed in the attempt to explain away Lenin's enthusiastic endorsement of Bogdanov's historical approach. The first attempt was by Preobrazhensky, whose explanation was that in 1898 when Lenin's review was written Marxists were struggling against the 'Narodniki' and

---

74   Skvortsov-Stepanov 1925, p. 17.

the autocracy and felt duty bound to defend Bogdanov's book.[75] Osinsky had a different, more convoluted, explanation. This was that when Lenin wrote his review Bogdanov was a Marxist. Now he was not, and this meant that one had to reconsider the book in the light of Bogdanov's later position.[76]

In his contribution to the discussion on Skvortsov-Stepanov's lecture Bogdanov argued that in both natural and exchange economies society produced a product and society consumed a product. Producing a product cost labour, that is, the product had social-labour value. If in a socialist society there could be no values, then it would be unable to organise itself, to calculate its demands and its production. This was in accordance with Marx's idea that the basis of production and distribution in collectivist society was labour time.

Bogdanov pointed out that in all societies a product cost labour, that is, had value. This was something that Bukharin and his supporters denied and regarded as heresy, even though it was stated plainly in Marx's *Das Kapital*. Bogdanov stressed that he did not attach great importance to having Marx's opinion on his side, but he did want to point out that when a great doctrine became an object of faith, as in the case of Marxism, people ceased to know it and understand it. This was, in Bogdanov's view, the tragic fate that had overtaken Marxism.[77]

Although Bogdanov supported Skvortsov-Stepanov in his defence of the historical approach to political economy, he did not approve of the kind of arguments Skvortsov-Stepanov had deployed in doing so. Skvortsov-Stepanov had to a great extent built his case on texts from Marx and Engels, as though they were the final arbiters of truth. Moreover, he had adopted to some degree the 'strategical' approach of his opponents, pandering to political expediency. But he conceded that in this respect Skvortsov-Stepanov was less a 'strategist' than Bukharin, whose conceptions of what Marxism was could change by the day in response to the political situation.[78]

A year later Bogdanov returned to the subject of labour value in his commentary on the lecture Preobrazhensky gave on 21 January 1926 on 'The Law of Value in the Soviet Economy'.[79] Preobrazhensky's view was that in the Soviet

---

75   Vestnik Kommunisticheskoi Akademii 1925, 11, p. 310.
76   Vestnik Kommunisticheskoi Akademii 1925, 11, p. 315. Neither of these explanations satisfied the authors of the entry on Bogdanov in the *Great Soviet Encyclopedia* in 1930. Their theory was that the popularised form of Bogdanov's book had concealed the heresy of its content. See Sol'tsnev and Karev 1930.
77   Bogdanov 1925, p. 302.
78   Bogdanov 1925, p. 306.
79   For the term 'value' Preobrazhenskii uses the Russian word *tsennost'*, whereas Bogdanov continues to use the word *stoimost'*.

Union the law of value, the characteristic feature of the capitalist economy, would, in the course of industrialisation, give way to the law of 'primitive socialist accumulation'. Bukharin, on the other hand, feared that the 'pumping over' of resources from the agricultural sector to state industry would upset the equilibrium of the economy and destroy the worker-peasant alliance that assured stability under the NEP. Bogdanov's objection was that Preobrazhensky did not understand what the concept 'value' meant.

In Bogdanov's view, whenever Preobrazhensky spoke of the law of value one could substitute for this term 'the law of the free play of supply and demand'. This was not the same, because the law of free play of supply and demand was only the spontaneous form of the law of value's manifestation. What was missing was the labour element. In the case of the confrontation between the state sector and the private sector of the economy, the state in its own interests gave the seller the means to reproduce and expand its resources in plant and labour, just like a capitalist enterprise in equilibrium with the market would.

In this light, the difference between Marx's and Preobrazhensky's conceptions of the law of value became apparent. With Preobrazhensky the social-labour element disappeared from the law of value. And this omission was not accidental, because Preobrazhensky contended that political economy was the science of capitalism; for socialism another science was needed, and in the present transition period – another one still. Bogdanov denied holding any brief for political economy; the very name of this science was bourgeois. But if another science was needed, it should be a more generalising science. Preobrazhensky here guessed that he had tectology in mind, something that Bogdnov did not deny.[80]

Bogdanov recalled that in the previous year Skvortsov-Stepanov had made the case for the historical approach to political economy, and in doing so had adduced many texts from Marx which clearly expressed the historical view of political economy, and in which it was obvious that Marx regarded the science as relating to different social formations. In the discussion Skvortsov-Stepanov's opponents did not even attempt to explain these texts, but in the prevailing intellectual climate simply ignored them. And in Bogdanov's view Preobrazhensky was acting in exactly this way by regarding the law of labour value simply as the law of free supply and demand.

Bogdanov ended his contribution to the discussion by characterising the kind of mentality that had become current in the Communist Academy, and which he contrasted with his own attitude:

---

80   Bogdanov 1926a, p. 214.

There are heretics (I am one of them). Heretics are characterised by the fact that they say: 'Here is a doctrine. Here is what I disagree with in this doctrine'. But there are many people who *always* agree with their author-ity; they interpret it, transform it, and in this way always appear in agree-ment with it. That is not the way heretics behave, but priests. That is how your teacher Plekhanov behaved. When one of Marx's propositions did not suit him, he in a translation inserted the word 'not' and in this form used it in a scholarly polemic.[81]

Bogdanov deplored the fact that Marx was being treated like a religious author-ity and distorted in that fashion, his ideas being adapted to suit the needs of the moment. This had been the fate of Marx's historicism and now was to be that of the social-labour factor in his economic conceptions. To Bogdanov the process had all the signs of being a scientific reaction.[82]

In the lecture 'The Doctrine of Reflexes and the Riddle of Primitive Think-ing', Bogdanov returned to the theme he had raised in the *Proletarskaia Kul-tura* article 'Methods of Labour and Methods of Perception', namely the con-nection of work exclamations with reflexes. In this respect he was elaborat-ing on Noiré's theory of the origin of language by giving it a more substan-tial grounding in physiology. As he explained, there was no need to expound Noiré's theory in detail, since he had done so on numerous previous occasions; what was important was to impart to this theory the clarity and conviction that was possible when interpreted from the point of view of reflexes. Noiré himself had been unable to do this since he had not been versed in psycho-physiology.[83]

Much of the lecture, however, was devoted to the characteristic of primitive thought that Bogdanov termed 'alogism', that is, the irrational belief that one could exercise power over something through one of its parts, by its depiction, or its name or symbol. It was the attitude that gave rise to voodoo, to impreca-tions, love potions and curses. One might have expected that in this connection Bogdanov would have compared 'alogism' to the concept of substitution that he had elaborated earlier, but no such connection was made. In this lecture Bogdanov was more concerned to analyse irrational and superstitious attitudes than rational thought processes. This is presumably because he was encoun-tering ever more manifestations of irrationality in the intellectual climate of

---

81   Bogdanov 1926a, p. 216.
82   Ibid.
83   Bogdanov 1925a, p. 71.

the times. It was in this connection that he recalled how in 1914 the soldiers in his unit had destroyed all the buildings in a village simply because they had belonged to Germans. This was, he said, 'the logic of equating the bear with its abandoned lair'. He remarked that there came forms of alogism were used in the most widespread forms of polemic at the present time.[84] He might have added that many of these polemics were against himself.

On 14 May 1927 Bogdanov delivered a lecture entitled 'The Limits of Scientific Reasoning' in the Communist Academy. It was the last one that he would give, and its theme was appropriate as a valedictory speech. His argument was that whereas reasoning was a valuable and powerful means of perception, it could also be the source of error. This was especially true of reasoning *a priori*, which, Bogdanov noticed, had of late become prevalent in Soviet publications and academic activities.

Bogdanov cautioned that words did not have a fixed meaning. People might use the same word in their discourse, but the meaning they attached to that word could differ widely. In some respects this was a useful phenomenon, because it could lead to new connections being made, resulting in scientific discoveries. This was the case with Copernicus's discovery that the earth revolved around the sun. If the word 'revolves' had had a strictly fixed meaning, it could not have been applied in the way Copernicus had done.[85]

It followed that when one used a scientific term one should not harbour any illusion that the thought expressed was unambiguous. Every concept, even those used constantly in scientific discourse, had a variety of meanings. If, for instance, one took the term 'matter' in its purely scientific sense, this concept could be defined in different ways, depending whether one was speaking of mechanics, electro-magnetism, atomic structure or energetics, etc. Bogdanov reckoned that in all there were five or six concepts of 'matter', all scientific to a sufficient degree.

If one considered 'matter' in a philosophical sense, there were even more potential meanings. The present philosophical school of Plekhanov recognised that the word had two meanings: the whole of being and the nature of physical phenomena. Words in common use like 'thing' as in 'thing-in-itself' and 'quality' were also cases in point. Bogdanov considered that when people used these words without analysis they were engaging in a kind of verbal sport, because they meant different things. On the question of 'things-in-themselves', Bogdanov recalled: 'In the past (I with sadness now remember) I myself participated in disputes about it, wrote whole articles on this question. But that was a long time ago, now I would consider it in the highest degree useless to quarrel about such things'.[86]

The word 'prove', it appeared, also meant different things to different people. To Bogdanov it meant that when he asserted something he would support it with facts, and in this way prove what he had said. He adduced facts, he systematised and he verified; that to him was 'proof'. But when his opponents disagreed with what he said, they would present him with quotations, such as what Marx said in 1866, what Plekhanov said in 1906, what Deborin said in 1926 and so on. This to them was 'proof' that what Bogdanov had said was wrong. Clearly for the two sides the word 'proof' had a completely different meaning. There was a similar difference in usage between Bogdanov and his opponents about the words 'polemic' and 'refute'.[87]

Since no individual word was unambiguous in its meaning, it followed that reasoning in, say, ten logical steps would have little chance of producing any meaningful result. An example of this was Hegel's system, which did not maintain the same meaning for the concepts it embodied.

For Bogdanov, all philosophical systems were enormous chains of reasoning, with very few experiments and a very narrow basis of data. They had no scientific value, but they did have value of a different kind. They were monist utopias, which presented an ideal of all the fields of knowledge encompassed in a coherent whole. This was something to strive towards. Spinoza's philosophical system was just such a utopia, though, in Plekhanov's interpretation, Spinoza's concept of 'substance' was a pseudonym for 'matter' in Plekhanov's understanding of it.[88]

Bogdanov's lecture was given a hostile reception by his audience, which is not surprising, since it was in essence a criticism of their way of thinking. He was in effect saying to them: 'You use terms like "matter", but you don't know what you are talking about. You use quotations against me, but they are neither here nor there; if you want to refute me, you have to do it with facts and arguments'.

In his concluding remarks Bogdanov observed that the discussion had been an illustration of what he had been talking about in his lecture. He had been talking about one thing, but the discussion had been about another. Every one of his propositions had been replaced with another. Every concept that he had

---

86   Bogdanov 1927, p. 258.
87   Bogdanov 1927, p. 253.
88   Bogdanov 1927, p. 260.

introduced, carefully explained and defined, had been substituted for another, not necessarily deliberately, but because every individual had a different fund of experience.

Bogdanov declared that he had a great deal of sympathy for Spinoza, because Spinoza was a man who was not afraid to stand up to everyone else, and was not understood by his own generation.[89] The members of the Communist Academy must have realised that in these words Bogdanov also had himself in mind. They were a fitting epitaph with which to end his final lecture in the Academy.

6   Blood Transfusion

Bogdanov's resignation from the Proletkult organisation and the restrictions put on his writing and publishing left him with medical research as his main sphere of activity. This had been given a stimulus by his acquisition of Geoffrey Keynes's book *Blood Transfusion* during his trip to London in 1921–2. Although there was a considerable body of literature on various aspects of blood transfusion, Keynes's book was the first to provide 'a connected account of the whole subject and of the problems arising from it, together with practical instructions for performing transfusions'.[90] In 1922, when the book was published, blood transfusion was a relatively novel clinical procedure. It emerges from Keynes's history of blood transfusion that when Bogdanov mentioned it in *Red Star* in 1908 the classification of blood groups had just been discovered, and in 1913, when the first part of *Tectology* was published, the technique of preventing transfused blood from clotting was still being perfected. It was only during the Great War that blood transfusion was widely practised, but only after 1917, when the British Army Medical Corps was reinforced by officers from the USA. It was then that knowledge of blood transfusion began to spread throughout the Allied armies. These developments gave Bogdanov the chance to test whether his theories about the exchange of blood had any basis in fact.

Keynes could offer no clues as to any rejuvenation effects that blood transfusion might have, since most of his experience of the procedure had been in treating war wounds. The areas in which he thought blood transfusions were appropriate were in treating anaemia (both acute and of slow onset), haemorrhage, or what he called 'cases of general toxaemia', in which new blood was

89   Bogdanov 1927, p. 283.
90   Keynes 1922, p. iv.

given on account of its therapeutic properties or to dilute the circulating toxins. As treatment for cases involving anemia and haemorrhage Keynes could say that blood transfusion was 'now very firmly established', but for general toxaemia the procedure was 'still in its experimental stage'. Bogdanov's interest of course lay in an area beyond even that of toxaemia.

A significant chapter in Keynes's book is the one on the dangers of blood transfusion. According to Keynes, at the beginning of the twentieth century, with the discovery of blood groups, it was thought that all danger had disappeared. Now the pendulum was swinging back with the realisation that the elimination of danger was more complex than previously thought. There were, in Keynes's view, two main sources of danger: that of introducing into the recipient a disease carried by the donor, and that due to the inherent properties of the donor's blood which might interact in a serious manner with the blood of the recipient. With regard to the first danger, among the diseases that had been communicated through blood transfusion, Keynes mentioned malaria and syphilis. Although tuberculosis and gonorrhoea might be present in a donor, it was unlikely that these diseases would be transferred. As regards the second danger, Keynes warned that even after the discovery of blood groups fatalities had still occurred due to the incompatibility of bloods.[91]

On his return to Russia Bogdanov brought with him from England literature on blood transfusion and the necessary equipment for performing the operation, including serum for testing blood groups, needles to insert into veins and a solution of paraffin wax in ether to prevent the transfused blood from clotting. Bogdanov gathered together a group of associates who shared his interest in blood transfusion. At the core of this group was Bogdanov's wife Natalia, his school friend from Tula Ivan Sobolev, who had served with the Red Army as a doctor, and Semen Maloletkov, a doctor whom Bogdanov had met during his time on the North-West front.[92]

Initially they formed a study group, meeting at Maloletkov's flat where they experimented with determining to which blood groups they belonged. The group was an informal one, and, considering the suspicion with which the Soviet authorities looked on initiatives from below, might have been regarded as conspiratorial. In fact, when he was arrested in 1923 Bogdanov assumed that the existence of his 'physiological collectivism' group was the cause, particularly as Maloletkov's flat was searched at the same time.[93]

91   Keynes 1922, pp. 67–9.
92   Belova 1974, p. 30.
93   Neizvestnyi Bogdanov 1995, 1, p. 34.

In the course of 1923–4 some experimental blood transfusions were carried out between members of the group, including Bogdanov himself and Natalia. Sobolev recruited his colleague D.A. Gudim-Levkovich to assist in carrying out the operations, which were performed in the hospital of a local medical practice. He also used his contacts to bring into the group younger people with whom the established members of the group could exchange blood.[94] The results of these experiments were recorded in Bogdanov's book *The Struggle for Viability*, published in 1927.

Krasin, who visited Bogdanov and Natalia in December 1925, was impressed by the visible improvement in their health as a result of the blood exchanges. At that time Krasin suffered from acute anemia, and tried to persuade Bogdanov to perform a blood transfusion on him. Bogdanov was at first reluctant to do so, advising Krasin to go to Paris or London, where the science of blood transfusion was more advanced than in Russia. But, having again consulted Keynes's book, and found reassurance that 60 percent of blood transfusions to treat anemia were successful, Bogdanov agreed to carry out the operation. It was a success, and Krasin's health improved immediately. He left for a holiday in the south of France before taking up the post of Soviet ambassador to Britain.[95]

If the 'physiological collectivist' group wanted to build on its success in blood transfusions and expand its activities, it was essential to find financial backing. Moreover, Bogdanov would realise that the group could not long remain autonomous; it needed to have some kind of official recognition. In 1925 Bogdanov submitted a proposal to found an institute for blood transfusion, a proposal that was supported by the Commissar for Health Nikolai Semashko. Bogdanov's proposal was approved by the Communist Party's Central Committee and on 26 February 1926 the Council of Labour and Defence passed a resolution signed by V.V. Kuibyshev to form the proposed institute. In March 1926 Semashko, on behalf of the Commissariat of Health (Narkomzdrav), issued an edict setting up a research institute of haematology and blood transfusion, with Bogdanov appointed as Director. The new Institute was given a modest budget and rather grand premises in the house of a former merchant, in which Bogdanov and Natalia had an apartment.

This was not only the first institute of its kind in Soviet Russia, but in the world. To be made its Director, enjoying the support of Stalin, Bukharin and Semashko, gave Bogdanov a certain status, and must have gone some way to dispelling the shadow that had hung over him since his arrest in 1923. The Insti-

---

94   Sobolev 1992, p. 221.
95   Krementsov 2011, pp. 60–1.

tute held out a long-awaited opportunity for Bogdanov to test his theories of blood transfusion in practice. For 19 years, he declared, since the publication of *Red Star*, he had tried to persuade scientists who had the technical means at their disposal to experiment with blood exchanges, but without success. Now he himself had these technical means and the power to deploy them in the investigation of 'physiological collectivism'.[96]

Initially the Soviet medical establishment, out of innate conservatism, was hostile to the new Institute and dismissive of its Director, who, although he had medical qualifications, had very little clinical experience. Another source of annoyance was that Bogdanov obviously looked on the Institute as the extension of his 'physiological collectivism' group, so that leading positions in it were held by Maloletkov, Sobolev and Gudim-Levkovich, none of whom were considered by the medical establishment as eminent physicians. Considerable friction resulted, but this was ameliorated by the intervention of Semashko's Commissariat.[97]

7   The Struggle for Viability

Since one of the aims of the Institute was the publication of scientific and popular literature on blood transfusion, in 1927 Bogdanov published a book to serve as a general introduction to a series of other works on the subject. This was *The Struggle for Viability*, which was intended not only for doctors, but for readers who had 'some education in the natural sciences'. *The Struggle for Viability* is a unique work, because it is not only theoretical, but also a text in which Bogdanov relates the concepts of tectology to actual medical practice.

At the outset Bogdanov made it plain that his book was not about 'rejuvenation', which, he said, was an imprecise and outdated term, something like the 'philosopher's stone' or the 'elixir of life'. The return to youth, he argued, was neither possible or even desirable, because many advantages were gained with age. Among them were immunities to such diseases as tuberculosis, which was a scourge of the young. It was impossible to say that all the advantages lay with youth and all the disadvantages with age.

Whereas earlier in his writings Bogdanov had exhibited some abhorrence to age, and even thought of it in terms of vampirism, in *The Struggle for Viability* he saw it in a much more positive light. In one place he declares that 'elderly

96   Bogdanov 2001, p. 189.
97   Belova 1974, p. 46; Neizvestnyi Bogdanov 1995, 1, p. 137.

humans do more than just "eat up the future" of youth. They are socially useful as preservers of experience, teachers of children, advisers of adults, and,
to a considerable degree, organisers of life'.[98] Bogdanov thought that with a
healthy lifestyle, diet, environment, the avoidance of stress, tobacco and nar-
cotics, people could lead full lives well into old age. In the future it might be
possible to extend the life-span considerably, and it was finding ways of doing
this that Bogdanov discussed in his book.

In many ways *The Struggle for Viability* is an extension of *Tectology*, and this is
most pronounced where Bogdanov describes how the human body functions.
This is in terms of assimilation and disassimilation, the bi-regulator, skeletal
structures, differentiation and counter-differentiation, the convergence of
forms and the law of the leasts. But beyond this there are distinct echoes of
Bogdanov's writings on the planned economy. Bogdanov's definition of a normally functioning body is one in which 'each individual system works exactly
so as to give the other individual systems just what they need from it'.[99] And in
several places he speaks of the body as a factory, though one 'with wider, finer,
and stricter division of functions than the most highly organised of contemporary enterprises'.[100]

The analogy of the factory helps Bogdanov explain the processes that cause
the infirmities associated with ageing. It would be like the case in which a factory was working at less than full capacity for the lack of a single element of
production, perhaps a small one, such as the inadequate delivery of lubricating
grease. In the same way the lack of sex hormone could cause the vital activity
throughout the body to decline, since, by the law of the leasts, in the intercon-
nected chain of individual body systems viability is determined by the vital
power of the weakest of them.[101]

As in *Tectology*, the *Struggle for Viability* also attributed age-related deteri-
oration to the action of differentiation and specialisation. Although specialisation had an enormous positive significance, it also had its negative side,
which became more pronounced as the process progressed. The more the parts
of a whole diverged from each other, the more difficult it was to support the
coordination of their functions, the harmony of their inter-relationships.[102]

Another kind of specialisation was in society, such as that associated with
the division of labour, the pursuit of records in sport, mental exertion and

---

98   Bogdanov 2001, p. 111.
99   Bogdanov 2001, p. 59.
100   Bogdanov 2001, p. 86.
101   Bogdanov 2001, pp. 85–6.
102   Bogdanov 2001, p. 80.

excessive sexual activity. This kind of specialisation, which encouraged a one-sided and disproportionate development of the body, was harmful and caused its degeneration.[103] The implication was that in a collectivist society these disproportions would be overcome, and people would live longer and more harmonious lives.

As to what could be done to prevent ageing, Bogdanov gave a summary of methods that had been employed to date. The biologist Ilya Mechnikov had considered that the flora of the large intestine were responsible for toxins in the body. To counteract these he recommended adding sour milk to the diet. Charles Brown-Séquard had attempted to combat ageing by the application of extracts from animals' sex glands. Eugen Steinach had followed Brown-Séquard's lead and looked for ways to reinforce the sex hormone function. He did this by tying off the spermatic ducts, so that only seminal fluid and not spermatozoa was secreted. By this method he had managed to prolong the life of rats. The approach of Serge Voronoff had been to transplant animal testicles, and by this method he had succeeded in adding some years to the life of rams. Although the human subject of his experiments, a 74-year-old English civil servant, appeared to be rejuvenated, he died within three years of his transplant operation. Although Bogdanov did not reject these various methods out of hand, since they might after all contain an element of truth, there was none of them that he thought worth adopting.

Bogdanov looked to the means nature employed to prolong life. The example he took was that of the paramecium, a slipper-shaped single-celled organism living in a fresh water environment. Its usual way of reproducing was by cell division, but after some dozens of generations, in order to avoid dying out, it would fuse with another paramecium, forming a single organism. This process was referred to by biologists as 'conjugation', and Bogdanov interpreted this in the tectological sense, arguing that fusion increased the total sum of elements of the vital structure, thus augmenting the sum of activities that it could oppose to the environment. The new cell would be much stronger than either of the original two cells in conflict with a possible enemy, or an encounter with toxins in the environment. However, as in *Tectology*, Bogdanov stressed that with conjugation a certain amount of disorganisation was inevitable.[104]

Of course conjugation was not a method of reproduction open to more complex organisms, and certainly not to human beings. But there were certain tissues in the human body that, due to their semi-liquid, colloidal composition,

---

103 Bogdanov 2001, pp. 86, 92–8.
104 Bogdanov 2001, pp. 135, 142.

did have a certain resemblance to a culture of unicellular organisms, and these were the lymph and the blood.[105] This made them suitable for the conjugation method.

Blood differed from all other tissues and organs of the body in that it was a truly universal tissue in which there was something of all other tissues, and it in turn influenced the composition of all other tissues. The entire structure of the body found its reflection in the blood as in no other system. It was also highly individual, as it was as difficult to find two people with identical blood as it was to find a pair of physical doubles. One aspect of this individuality was the differences in clotting properties of blood, on which the division into blood groups was based. If some useful properties of the blood acquired by one person, such as immunities or protective adaptations, could be transmitted to another by means of transfusion, this would have an enormous significance in the struggle for viability.

In his survey of the development of blood transfusion to date Bogdanov drew on the historical chapter of Geoffrey Keynes's book. Mainly this concerned the search for a suitable means of preventing blood clotting during transfusion. Bogdanov argued that the best way to do this was by the addition of sodium citrate to the transfused blood, though he felt impelled to defend this method against writers who had found objections to it. The other aspect of Bogdanov's historical survey was to review the kind of cases where blood transfusions had been successfully carried out. These included the treatment of trauma, shock, anaemia and toxins of the blood. However, these transfusions had only been unidirectional, from donor to recipient, not the exchange of blood between two persons, a procedure that Bogdanov called 'physiological collectivism', and was one that he had first described in his novel *Red Star*.[106]

It was experiments in blood exchange that Bogdanov and his circle had carried out during 1924–5. They were particularly interested to see if immunity to disease could be transferred by transfusion. Bogdanov believed that the immunities acquired with age were particularly valuable to the young, for example, the increased resistance to tuberculosis. A total of 11 people, four elderly and seven young, participated in the experiments, young people being paired with the elderly for blood exchanges.

Because Bogdanov regarded blood as being peculiar to the individual, and influenced by their mode of life, the medical profiles of all the participants were recorded along with the results of the transfusions. Since Bogdanov was one

---

105   Bogdanov 2001, p. 142.
106   Bogdanov 2001, p. 160.

of the participants in the experiments, he recorded what he thought were the relevant facts of his medical history. He described himself as a literary man aged 50 when the experiments began, who had been active in revolutionary work in underground conditions. Pronounced burnout of the nervous system, and marked arteriosclerosis of the blood vessels, enlargement of the heart and widening of the aorta, greatly weakened his work capacity. His general status was significantly worse than it had been earlier. By nature he was a strong-willed, optimistic type. He had taken part in six procedures, but in one of them he had only given blood and in two he had only received it. Bogdanov reported that as a result of the transfusions both his physical and mental states had improved noticeably.[107] He admitted that the experiments had not been conclusive enough for theoretical pronouncements and predictions. Nevertheless, he believed that he had shown that there was 'something there to study'.[108]

As to the future likely applications of blood transfusions, Bogdanov thought it would be quite unfeasible to use them to treat conditions such as tuberculosis or malaria. Much more promising would be the transmission of immunities to various illnesses, particularly by matching up elderly and young 'companions'. There was also the possibility that exchanges of blood could be used to even out hormonal imbalances, such as between pubescent girls and menopausal women.

8   A Martyr to Science

In the first year of its operation the Institute carried out blood transfusions of two types. The main type was the unidirectional one that had become standard in Western medicine. Quite often this was used to treat the debility caused by over-work, the so-called 'Soviet burnout'. The other type was the bi-directional exchange of blood between young and old. Several such transfusions had been carried out, and all with encouraging results. It was noted that the blood of older people did not cause younger ones to age, but to experience an improvement in general health and nervous states. It was still unknown whether the blood of elderly people could increase the resistance of the young to tuberculosis, as might be supposed on theoretical grounds.[109]

In March 1928 a group of students from Moscow University learned about the benefits of blood transfusions from a newspaper article written by Bog-

---

107   Bogdanov 2001, pp. 175–6.
108   Bogdanov 2001, p. 189.
109   Bogdanov 2001, p. 258.

danov, and some of them came to the Institute hoping to improve their health through the exchange of blood. On 19 March blood tests and blood groupings were carried out on two students of the physics and mathematics faculty, the 21-year-old geophysics student Lev Ilich Koldomasov and his roommate. When, however, Koldomasov was found to have tuberculosis of the lungs and a latent form of malaria that he had contracted in Georgia in 1924, he was refused the operation.[110]

On the following day, Bogdanov contacted Koldomasov and invited him to come to the Institute. There he explained that as an elderly person he had acquired an immunity to tuberculosis of the lungs, which through an exchange of blood might be transferred to Koldomasov. Both he and Koldomasov shared the same AB blood group. Koldomasov readily agreed to this and on 24 March the operation was duly carried out, nearly a litre of Koldomasov's blood being transfused to Bogdanov, Koldomasov receiving a similar amount of blood from Bogdanov.[111]

Three hours after the transfusion Bogdanov had chills, fever and intestinal distress. On the following day he developed jaundice, a swollen belly and enlarged liver, and by the third day there was evidence of internal intoxication. After about a week he seemed somewhat better, and joked to the doctors that now that he was on the mend they would no doubt be taking the credit for his recovery.[112] But the kidney failure worsened, skin haemorrhages appeared, and he had a seizure. In the second week Bogdanov's heart began to fail and he died on 7 April at 8.55 p.m. During the 15 days of painful illness and the prospect of death Bogdanov had shown great courage and composure, keeping a journal to record his condition for as long as he could.[113]

Koldomasov also suffered an adverse reaction to the transfusion. He experienced fever, vomiting, diarrhoea and severe pain throughout his body. Within a few days, however, he felt better, and after remaining at the Institute until the end of March had a two months' stay at a sanatorium, during which his lung lesions completely cleared. In a letter to Bogdanov's son Alexander in August 1973, Koldomasov attributed his cure to the blood exchange he had had with Bogdanov.[114]

In his report on Bogdanov's death published in both *Pravda* and *Izvestiia* on 8 April, Semashko gave prominence to the fact that Bogdanov had infused the

---

110   Konchalovskii 1928, p. XVIII.
111   Konchalovskii 1928, p. XIV.
112   Konchalovskii 1928, p. XVI.
113   Konchalovskii 1928, p. XVII.
114   Letter from L.I. Koldomasov to A.A. Malinovsky dated 10 August 1973.

blood of a malarial sufferer, a procedure that was known to lead to the destruction of red blood cells, but that Bogdanov had gone ahead with the operation as an experiment.[115] However, Bogdanov's colleague, Professor Konchalovsky, who carried out the autopsy, found that there were no grounds for this supposition. Koldomasov had no signs of active malaria, all the tests for it being negative. In Konchalovsky's judgement, Bogdanov's death was caused by the toxicity of kidney failure, in turn caused by blood destruction from incompatible blood. He pointed out that although Bogdanov's and Koldomasov's blood groups were the same, individual peculiarities sometimes led to incompatibility despite such matching.[116]

Bogdanov's illness and death have been researched in detail from a modern medical point of view by Professor Douglas Huestis. Like Konchalovsky, Huestis rejects the malaria explanation for the massive breakdown of red blood cells that Bogdanov suffered, and thinks Konchalovsky's supposition that the infusion of incompatible blood was correct. In 1928 there were incompatibilities undetectable using the cross-matching techniques of the time. A person's blood plasma could have powerful antibodies, such as those of the Rhesus system, which were not discovered until new techniques were applied in the 1940s. Huestis believes that this kind of incompatibility was responsible for Bogdanov's death. He finds that all the symptoms displayed by Bogdanov and Koldomasov are consistent with this explanation. Koldomasov survived because his tuberculosis and his malaria were both inactive, and through the resilience of youth, but the poor state of Bogdanov's constitution, weakened by previous transfusions, had left him unable to survive a medical catastrophe.[117]

It is ironic that what defeated Bogdanov was not the known risks of Koldomasov's tuberculosis and malaria, but blood incompatibilities that he could not possibly have known about. Bogdanov had not, as Semashko surmised, paid the price of a miscalculation, but had been the victim of a tragic accident that could not have been foreseen.

Could Bogdanov's death have been suicide? There is no escaping the fact that in exchanging blood with a former malaria sufferer, Bogdanov was taking a risk, and the possibility of suicide may have passed through Semashko's mind, since he pointed out that Bogdanov did not inform his wife or responsible workers at the Institute about what he intended to do. There are other considerations that might point to suicide. In *Red Star* some of the older Martians, who preferred not to await a natural end to their lives, came to the dying

---

115   Semashko 1928.
116   Konchalovskii 1928, pp. XIX, XXIV.
117   Huestis 1996; Huestis 1997; Huestis 2001.

room to commit suicide in pleasant surroundings. In *Engineer Menni*, the hero, feeling himself at odds with the times, and unwilling to become a vampire by clinging on to the old ways, ends his life. In an intellectual environment dominated by sycophants where he was routinely insulted and denounced, Bogdanov would certainly have had a sense that the Soviet system had left him behind. And can one believe that Bogdanov, the great organiser, who railed against leaving anything to chance, would not organise something as important as his own death?

Suicide is unlikely for a number of reasons. Although in his earlier writings Bogdanov had shown an abhorrence of age and the infirmities that went with it, and this is reflected in *Red Star*, by the time he wrote *The Struggle for Viability*, this is no longer in evidence. Along with the rejection of 'rejuvenation' as a feasible objective comes the appreciation of the advantages of age. Old blood forms an essential element in the 'physiological collectivist' transfusions. Bogdanov participates in them precisely in his capacity as an older person.

Although Bogdanov must have felt a deep sense of injustice and frustration at the irrational spirit of the times and how he and his work were treated by the Soviet regime, there is nothing to suggest that he suffered any serious psychological damage by it. He was a person of strong will, and he never doubted for a moment that he was in the right. He caricatured his detractors in erudite academic papers delivered to the Communist Academy and saw himself as a kind of Spinoza, who was a thinker before his time. Moreover, through the difficult times of the early 1920s he had the moral support of his 'physiological collectivist' team.

Nor can there be any doubt that Bogdanov wanted and expected the blood exchange with Koldomasov to succeed. It was one of the series of experiments that he 'had waited 19 years' to carry out. It was of the type that Bogdanov had championed, of the pairing of a young and an old participant so that immunities could be communicated. By virtue of his age Bogdanov believed that he had immunity to tuberculosis, and he must also have assumed either that he had acquired resistance to malaria or that Koldomasov's malaria was sufficiently inactive to pose no danger. Moreover, the Institute's record in blood transfusion to date had been remarkably successful, and Bogdanov had the right to expect that the exchange of blood with Koldomasov would have proceeded in the same manner.

9   Obituaries

The obituaries that appeared immediately after Bogdanov's death were influenced by the manner in which Semashko had presented it in his report, as the tragic outcome of a risky experiment on himself carried out in the cause of science. Consequently, at the time of his death Bogdanov was held in high esteem. Nevertheless, no one was allowed to forget that his ideas were non-Marxist and that he and the Bolshevik party had parted company.

The most sympathetic obituary was the one by Bukharin in *Pravda* for 8 April. Its opening words set the tone for other obituaries to follow. They were 'Bogdanov has died a martyr. He fell victim to an unsuccessful extraordinarily bold and risky scientific experiment carried out on his own organism'. Bukharin credited Bogdanov with playing an enormous part in the development of the Bolshevik party and of social thought in Russia. Many Marxists of the younger generation had been reared on his *Short Course of Economic Science* and had been enthralled by his articles. For a considerable time he had been one of the greatest theoreticians of Marxism.

Bogdanov's alleged heresies were dealt with cursorily by Bukharin. Everybody knew, he said, about Bogdanov's departure from the political stances of Bolshevism and from some basic positions of Marxism in general. But his greatest anti-materialist and anti-dialectical mistakes had been overcome both inside the party and among its followers. However, Bukharin continued, 'we, his present ideological opponents, must recognise the enormous scale of the deceased's thought, his completely exceptional education, the boldness of his generalising mind. Bogdanov was a man of the greatest scale, with the most multi-sided, truly encyclopaedic, knowledge: doctor, mathematician, philosopher, economist. He followed literally all the branches of science'.

In his funeral eulogy, Bukharin was less restrained and let his admiration for Bogdanov show through the official doctrines, and give the deceased his due as an original thinker of international standing. Bukharin declared:

> I came here *despite* our disagreement to bid farewell to a man, an intellectual figure who cannot be measured by ordinary standards. Yes, he was unorthodox. Yes, from our point of view, he was a 'heretic'. But in the realm of thought he was no mere *artisan*; he was its greatest *artist*. In the bold flights of his intellectual fantasy, in the strict and clear directness of his extraordinarily logical mind, in the rare harmony and internal elegance of his theoretical constructions, despite the non-dialectical nature and abstract schematism of his ideas, Bogdanov was undoubtedly one of the greatest and most original thinkers of our time. He charmed and

captivated with his passion for theoretical monism, with his theoretical attempts to introduce a great plan into the whole system of human knowledge ... In the person of Alexander Alexandrovich, there has departed from us one who, by his encyclopaedic knowledge, occupied a unique place, not only on the territory of our Union, but also among the greatest minds of all countries.[118]

Bukharin also paid tribute to Bogdanov as a revolutionary, when he had fought along with Lenin for the founding of Bolshevik fraction, later to become the Communist Party, and when he had taken part in the heroic and bloody battles of the 1905 revolution that were so artistically described in the final pages of Red Star. Through his writings Bogdanov had exerted a tremendous influence on a whole generation of Russian Social Democrats and many of them owed to him their first steps as revolutionaries.[119]

Lunacharsky's obituary in Pravda took the form of a psychological sketch of Bogdanov, to whom, he said, he had been close in his best years, between 23 and 37. Lunacharsky had been a witness and a participant in Bogdanov's intellectual development, so his assessment of the deceased had a particular value. It is significant that while Lunacharsky agreed with Bukharin about Bogdanov's intellectual powers, he also gave prominence to Bogdanov's strong will.

According to Lunacharsky, in his youth Bogdanov had been an instinctive revolutionary before he became a Marxist. Having adopted Marxism, he regarded it as a scientific discovery on a par with those of Copernicus and Darwin, and had an unshakable faith in its universal applicability. He set out to extend the Marxist outlook to all areas of knowledge. To do this he set about acquiring expertise in a wide range of disciplines, studying at university, reading a great many books in different languages and carrying out independent experiments. In the course of his whole later life he constantly added to the exceptionally rich and varied store of his personal knowledge.

Lunacharsky conceded that at times such universalism might border on dilettantism, but this was not the case with Bogdanov, who abhorred dilettantism. Whatever Bogdanov studied, be it medicine, natural science, mathematics, political economy, sociology or philosophy, he always studied it thoroughly and in depth. Bogdanov's talent was the ability to deploy his enormous knowledge in constructing and expounding schemes of thought. The most characteristic feature of Bogdanov's mind was the compulsion to reduce the great multiplicity

---

118   Bukharin 1928a, p. IX.
119   Bukharin 1928a, pp, X–XI.

of being to a number of repeating varieties of a few basic laws. This feature was one which Lunacharsky regarded as a weakness, because it gave rise to schematism.

In Lunacharsky's view it was Bogdanov's schematism that had made it possible for Lenin to defeat him. For whereas Lenin had a feeling for actual life, Bogdanov felt much less the pulse of reality, which led him to pursue policies that Lenin had abandoned as a tactical retreat. Lenin's ousting of Bogdanov, who had been one of the most influential leaders of the party, was the cause of his further political collapse, his abandonment of politics and the shrinking of his philosophical influence.[120]

Pokrovsky's obituary in *Vestnik Kommunisticheskoi Akademii* took the form of a biographical sketch of the deceased. Despite, or perhaps because of, his often heretical past, Pokrovsky adopted an orthodox Leninist point of view, interpreting Bogdanov's conflicts with Lenin as 'mistakes'. However, Pokrovsky did not deny Bogdanov's greatness as a thinker, or his contribution to the revolutionary movement. According to Pokrovsky:

> In Alexander Alexandrovich Bogdanov we have lost one of the most genuinely brilliant, historical figures on our cultural front. The further we go from the pre-revolutionary epoch, of the years 1905–1917, the more clearly the change in Bogdanov's significance appears. History recruited him for politics; his personal inclinations made him a philosopher. In both these fields he suffered defeat. But as one of the cultural heroes who died at his post, he will remain in the memory of many generations, perhaps he will remain there for ever.[121]

Also, according to Pokrovsky, Bogdanov was 'without doubt one of the greatest philosophers to appear in our literature'.[122]

In one respect, Pokrovsky's Leninist approach worked in favour of Bogdanov. In speaking of Bogdanov's book *Short Course of Economic Science* Pokrovsky must have annoyed the economists of the Communist Academy by citing Lenin's favourable opinion of the book that they had tried to suppress or explain away. He quoted Lenin as saying that it was 'a remarkable phenomenon in our economic literature', that it was 'the best work of its kind' and that it 'held consistently to historical materialism'. He said that the book had taught a whole generation, and had only recently become out of date.[123]

---

120   Lunacharskii 1928.
121   Pokrovskii 1928, p. V.
122   Pokrovskii 1928, p. VI.
123   Ibid.

Whereas, in Pokrovsky's view, the *Short Course* had emerged from Bogdanov's contact with the workers, his *Empiriomonism* was the product of an intellectual milieu, and was inspired by People's Will rather than Marxism. It was, despite Bogdanov's assurances to the contrary, a work that was imbued not with collectivism, but individualism. However, Pokrovsky concluded, Bogdanov had found himself a worthy death, a death from a risky scientific experiment. He had, as Bukharin expressed it, become a martyr, and in the halo of martyrdom his political mistakes had long become past history.[124]

Skvortsov-Stepanov's obituary in *Izvestiia* made practically no mention of Bogdanov as a thinker and none as a pioneer of blood transfusion, being mainly concerned with his political views and activities, beginning with his exile in Tula. As might be expected from his paper on 'What is Political Economy?', Skvortsov-Stepanov mentioned that Lenin had thought highly of Bogdanov's *Short Course of Economic Science*, but most of the obituary was devoted to ways in which Bogdanov had admired and supported Lenin. As to Bogdanov's qualities, in Skvortsov-Stepanov's view: 'A clear head, a revolutionary temperament, great dedication to the cause, great organisational abilities, a great master of conspiracy and a multi-faceted education, all this secured for him a completely exclusive position in the ranks of our party'.

Among Bogdanov's failings, in the eyes of Skvortsov-Stepanov, was a purely Menshevik evaluation of the proletarian dictatorship. In the question of socialist construction he was very close to the opposition, but at the same time he thought that only the majority of the Central Committee was capable of running the state and leading the proletariat. He consequently wished for the victory of the ruling group and welcomed the defeat of the opposition. However, Skvortsov-Stepanov conceded, it was not possible to be definite about Bogdanov's views, because in general, he declined to be drawn into conversation on political subjects.[125]

One can well imagine that in the climate of suspicion that prevailed in the late 1920s Bogdanov would be reluctant to make any pronouncements on politics that might be used against him. One can imagine too that he would have sympathy for the Left Opposition's call for increased democracy, at least within the confines of the party. But he may not have sympathised with the Opposition's economic platform calling for an increased pace of industrialisation, as this would have disrupted the equilibrium of the economy, as Bukharin argued.

---

124   Pokrovskii 1928, p. x.
125   Skvortsov-Stepanov 1928.

At the time of his death, wreathed in the halo of martyrdom, Bogdanov's reputation was very high. One important sign of this was that the Institute of Blood Transfusion was re-named the Bogdanov Institute. And whereas in February 1928 Bogdanov had been complaining to the publishers Moskovskii Rabochii about their refusal to re-issue *Red Star*, in the following year the novel was re-published with a preface by Boris Legran.[126]

This interlude in the attacks on Bogdanov was to be of short duration. They began again with increased intensity as Stalin launched his campaign against the 'Rightists', Bukharin and his group, who tried to resist the 'extraordinary measures' that were being employed against the peasants to ensure deliveries of grain. Stalin refused to believe that the problem could be solved by adjusting agricultural prices to give the peasants the incentive to sell their grain. He saw it as part of a class struggle, and was intent on forcibly collectivising Soviet agriculture. The policy would be a break with the economic orthodoxy on which NEP was based, but Stalin was not to be deterred. At the First Conference of Agrarian Marxists held in December 1929 Stalin told his audience:

> You know, of course, that the so-called theory of 'equilibrium' between the sectors of our national economy is still current among communists. This theory, of course, has nothing in common with Marxism. Nevertheless, it is a theory that is being spread by a number of people in the camp of the Rightists.[127]

Stalin argued that maintaining an equilibrium between large-scale socialist industry and the small-scale capitalist agricultural sector would never result in socialism. Objectively, the theory of equilibrium served to defend individual farming and to supply the kulaks with an ideological weapon to use in their struggle against collective farms. It was only by the introduction of collective and state farms, moreover, that the Marxist theory of expanded reproduction could be implemented. Hence the country was faced with a choice of going backwards to capitalism or forward to socialism through the collectivisation of agriculture. The theory of equilibrium was an attempt to find a third way between capitalism and socialism, but as no such third way existed, the theory was utopian and anti-Marxist.[128]

As the theory of equilibrium had originated with Bogdanov, whom Lenin had castigated as an anti-Marxist, this source of Bukharin's inspiration could be

---

126   Biggart, Gloveli and Yassour 1998, pp. 128–9.
127   Trudy pervoi Vsesoiuznoi konferentsii agrarnikov-marksistov 1930, p. 434.
128   Trudy pervoi Vsesoiuznoi konferentsii agrarnikov-marksistov 1930, p. 435.

used against him. The more Bogdanov could be portrayed as a Menshevik, an idealist and anti-Leninist, the more effective association with him would be in discrediting Bukharin. This campaign was the occasion for *Leninskii sbornik* to publish Lenin's notes on Bukharin's book *Economics of the Transition Period*, in which Lenin deplored Bukharin's Bogdanovist terminology, and the exchange of notes between Lenin and Bukharin on the subject of Nevsky's introduction to Lenin's *Materialism and Empiriocriticism*. This latter document contained the damning evidence of Bukharin defending Bogdanov against Lenin.

Since the rationale for one of Stalin's key policies was bound up with the defeat of Bukharin and the discrediting of his concept of equilibrium, Bogdanov's reputation suffered accordingly during the Stalin era. When Bogdanov was mentioned at all, it was in a condemnatory way. In the *Short Dictionary of Philosophy* published in 1954, for example, the entry on 'Bogdanov' reads:

> Bogdanov's 'Science of Organisation' sees the driving force of development, not in the class struggle, but in the establishment of an 'equilibrium' between society and nature, in the 'organisation' of productive forces. It regards the productive forces as being outside the relations of production, as pure technology. Bukharin and other enemies of the people made use of Bogdanov's 'Science of Organisation' in their struggle against the construction of socialism in the USSR.[129]

This was the attitude to Bogdanov that prevailed in the Soviet Union until the 1970s. The story of how he was rehabilitated has been told elsewhere,[130] and the rewarding task of unearthing the great treasury of his ideas continues until the present day.

---

129   Rozental'and Iudin 1954, p. 54.
130   Biggart 1998.

Bogdanov in Retrospect

Bogdanov's obituaries go some way to making an assessment of his significance in the various fields in which he was involved. But because of political considerations of the time, they could not do so objectively. Moreover, they could not foresee the developments that would take place between 1928 and the present day that would affect his assessment profoundly. The Soviet system has come and gone, leaving behind the authoritarian rule that Bogdanov predicted. Consequently, the perspective of his contemporaries, that Bogdanov was a lone heretic in a pro-Leninist consensus, has to be abandoned. And as a result, Bogdanov's historical significance at the present time is immeasurably greater than that envisaged by his contemporaries at the time of his death.

In assessing Bogdanov as a thinker a key question is the nature of his Marxism. A common reproach against Bogdanov by Lenin, Plekhanov and their followers was that he was not a Marxist. Even Bukharin, who judged Bogdanov to be 'one of the greatest and most original thinkers of our time', modifies this verdict by saying that Bogdanov was a 'heretic'. What was Bogdanov's relationship to Marx? This is a question that we are in a better position to answer than Bogdanov's contemporaries, who had much fewer of Marx's writings available to them.

In the light of Marx's own intellectual development, one can say that Bogdanov's procedure of 'democratising' *Das Kapital* by removing from it the Hegelian dimension was entirely in line with Marx's thinking. In 1868, shortly after the first volume of *Das Kapital* was published, Marx came to the conclusion that the Hegelian framework he had used was inappropriate, and in subsequent editions of *Das Kapital*, Volume I, he progressively eliminated it.[1] Nikolai Sieber, whose commentaries on *Das Kapital* Marx highly approved of, explicitly stated that his objective was to present Marx's economic ideas in a form that would be free from 'the impenetrable armour of Hegelian contradictions'.[2]

An important element in Marx's thinking that Bogdanov adopted and developed was the idea of the collective subject, which is treated most fully in Marx's 'Economic and Philosophical Manuscripts of 1844' and 'The German Ideology'.

---

1   See White 1996, pp. 204–10.
2   Sieber 1874, p. 44.

It is the conception that the world as it truly exists can only be apprehended from the point of view of the human collective. The viewpoint of the isolated individual, on the other hand, is necessarily distorted. Following earlier German thinkers, Schiller, Schelling and Hegel, Marx called this distorted view of the world 'reflection' in his early writings, but in *Das Kapital* he refers to it as 'fetishism', as in the term 'commodity fetishism'. This is exactly the sense in which Bogdanov uses the concept of fetishism in his writings, and is the foundation of his theory of perception.

In 'The German Ideology' Marx and Engels attribute the fragmentation of the human individual in capitalist society to the division of labour, just as Bogdanov does. And they envisage that in a communist society – which Bogdanov would term a 'collectivist' society – nobody is confined to any particular activity, but can become accomplished in any sphere they choose: 'to do one thing today and another tomorrow, to hunt in the morning, fish in the afternoon, rear cattle in the evening, criticise after dinner, as one chooses, without ever becoming a hunter, fisherman, shepherd or a critic'.[3]

Like Marx, Bogdanov thinks of socialism not as a particular system of economics, but as a relationship between people, the emergence of the human collective. That is why for both Marx and Bogdanov socialism is not 'a state of affairs to be established', but an ongoing process which is taking place at the present time and will continue to develop in the future.

A point on which Bogdanov apparently diverged from Marx was on the issue of 'base' and 'superstructure', Bogdanov attributing an element of ideology to the base in the form of the origin of language. One can argue, however, that Bogdanov's interpretation of Marx's formulation was entirely legitimate. The section of *The Critique of Political Economy* that was to elaborate on the concepts of base and superstructure remained in manuscript and was not included in any published version of *Das Kapital*. Marx had discovered that the assumptions behind the concepts were invalid, since the action of the circulation and reproduction of capital did not necessarily transform existing social institutions to make them conform to capitalist relations. Bogdanov's interpretation gave cogency to Marx's formulation which it lacked. Moreover, Bogdanov could explain how capital could transform pre-capitalist institutions in a much simpler way – by adaptation to the environment.[4]

If Bogdanov's critics had taken the time and effort to compare Bogdanov's ideas with those of Marx, especially with Marx's early writings, they would

---

3   Marx and Engels 1969, pp. 35–6.
4   On this see White 1996, pp. 172–3.

have found that, far from being a heretic, Bogdanov represented the mainstream of Marx's thought and had highlighted some of its main themes. The corollary would have been that it was Plekhanov and his followers who had diverged from the essential content of Marx's project. The history of Marxism in the Soviet Union demonstrated the truth of Bogdanov's contention that when people did not understand what Marxism was about they could only cling on to individual texts and treat them like holy writ.

Bogdanov's *Tectology* is the pinnacle of his intellectual achievement. It is rightly regarded as a precursor of system theory, but the work is diminished by regarding it only in this light. Tectology is the answer to the fragmentation of the human personality by the division of labour that is a constant theme in Bogdanov's writings. In tectology the vast disparities in human experience accumulated during the course of previous history are reintegrated into a single whole. It is the fulfilment of the promise held out in the essay 'The Integration of Mankind' to overcome fragmentation both of the human psyche and the society which it inhabits.

Tectology also has its practical origins in Bogdanov's attempt to democratise knowledge and make it accessible to the working class. It is the final elaboration of the intention to devise general methods that would provide workers with the skills they needed to overcome the limitations of a particular trade or profession. Tectology would be the science of socialist society, because it transcended the division into specialities that was characteristic of class societies and would enable people to engage in the activities of their choice, exactly in the manner described in 'The German Ideology'.

Despite Bogdanov's protestations to the contrary, *Tectology* is a profoundly philosophical work. It deals in a novel way with the issues that earlier thinkers had raised, in particular the question of the limitations of rationality. Kant and his successors had suspected that people saw rationality in the world because they imposed on it the logical operations with which the human mind functioned. But by and large he focused on the rational element in human existence. Bogdanov approaches this problem quite differently. For Bogdanov, it is because we continually encounter the resistance of the irrational, the unorganised, phenomena in existence that we can be sure that the world we inhabit is real and not a figment of our imaginations. But what is resistance and unorganisation for us is the organisation and rationality of our environment or of the beings within it.

Although it contains ideas from *Empiriomonism* and other early philosophical works, *Tectology* is by no means simply a re-statement of earlier conceptions in a different form. These earlier writings only speak of the need to overcome specialisation and of the necessity for a universal science of organisation.

Tectology is that new science, and it answers the requirements that Bogdanov had previously set out.

For Bogdanov an important feature of tectology was that it should be able to account for the kind of dialectical changes that Plekhanov had characterised by the term 'dialectical leaps' and that Engels had described in *Anti-Dühring* with the example of the growth of a grain of barley. In demonstrating that these changes are explicable in tectological terms, Bogdanov wishes to imply that his method is more flexible and more adaptable than Hegelian dialectics, and at the same time he is intent on showing the limitations of Plekhanov's version of Marxism.

The conflict with Lenin dominates much of Bogdanov's political career. The Russian Bogdanov scholar A.L. Takhtadzhan writes that it never ceases to amaze him that a cultured and humane person like Bogdanov should be for so many years the political associate of such a sinister character as Lenin.[5] In other words, for Takhtadzhan the question is not what brought an end to the association between Bogdanov and Lenin, but how it could ever have come about in the first place. That is a useful way to look at the question of the relationship between Bogdanov and Lenin, because it raises some fundamental issues.

Bogdanov's relationship with Lenin brought him a great deal of grief during his lifetime, and after his death prevented his contribution to Russia's cultural heritage being appreciated. Might Bogdanov not have devoted himself entirely to academic pursuits? After all, he became a revolutionary in an accidental way when he was arrested as a student. But Bogdanov clearly did not want to be only a scholar; he wanted not just to champion the oppressed classes in his writings, but actually to become involved in their revolutionary struggle. Teaching in workers' study circles gave him great satisfaction, and, moreover, involvement in the revolutionary movement stimulated his theoretical works, first his *Short Course*, and later his works of socialist theory. These were always produced with a view to practice. Up to the 1905 revolution his membership of the Bolshevik fraction gave Bogdanov scope for engaging in revolutionary politics. He became a prominent member of the Bolshevik fraction, but he could never think of himself as a revolutionary 'leader'. Leadership, or any kind of authority, was anathema to Bogdanov, and he bent his efforts to eliminating it from the Bolshevik fraction. Even during the 1905 revolution he was drawing up guidelines to ensure that party leaders were elected for a finite period, were subject to scrutiny and were answerable to their electors.

---

5 Takhtadzhan 1998, p. 9.

Lenin's perspective was very different. He did want to be a revolutionary leader and he did crave power and authority. The kind of organisation he favoured was of like-minded people in which he would be the acknowledged head. From Lenin's point of view Bogdanov was an obstacle to his aspirations. Bogdanov had a claim to influence the direction that the Bolshevik fraction took, because he had rescued it from oblivion in 1904. Moreover, in a Marxist party the legitimation of leadership was the mastery of socialist theory, and this Bogdanov had in abundant measure. He was coming to be thought of as the leading theoretician of Russian Social-Democracy. By comparison, Lenin's contribution to theory was modest. It was contained in his pamphlet *What Is to Be Done?*: the idea that the workers' socialist consciousness had to be brought to them from outside, by the intelligentsia. This idea was so alien to Bogdanov's way of thinking that the price Lenin paid for Bogdanov's help in reviving the Bolshevik fraction was that this idea should be abandoned. Lenin's subsequent pamphlet *One Step Forward Two Steps Back* accommodated Bogdanov's conceptions of proletarian consciousness, and when these were attacked by Rosa Luxemburg, it was appropriate that Bogdanov should come to their defence.

What Lenin did excel at was political manoeuvring and in-fighting, and by this means he was able to remove Bogdanov from the Bolshevik Centre in 1909. But even outside the Bolshevik fraction, and later outside the RSDLP, Bogdanov still posed a threat to Lenin. In October 1917 Lenin seized power with the assumption that Hilferding's analysis of finance capital was correct, and that seizure of the banks would give the Bolsheviks control of the economy, which would lead to the emergence of a socialist system. Bogdanov, who had always contested this idea, was proved right by events. The seizure of the banks did not give control of the Russian economy, because, as Bogdanov had indicated, their influence over industry had never been as dominant as Hilferding had imagined. It could have been extremely damaging to Lenin's standing if it had emerged that the Bolshevik revolution had been carried out on false premises. Lenin's sensitivity on the matter caused Hilferding to disappear from Soviet historiography, and the question of Lenin's theory of revolution to be evaded by Lenin's successors.

Despite his conviction that the Bolshevik seizure of power was not the socialist revolution that Lenin claimed, but merely a 'war communist' one, Bogdanov did not stand aloof from the Soviet regime or go into emigration in the West, as many Russian intellectuals did after 1917. He lent his support to the new regime, applying his organisational theory to the problem of economic planning. Bogdanov never became a political dissident in Soviet Russia, and he never wrote a critique of the increasingly repressive Soviet system. It would probably have served Lenin's purposes better if he had. But in the early 1920s, when opposition movements emerged, all of Bogdanov's existing writings, suffused as they were with the condemnation of authoritarianism, were of themselves subversive. Proletkult, the disparate movement given cogency by Bogdanov's conceptions and by its autonomy, was a challenge to Lenin's centralising government. Since Bogdanov's ideas were incompatible with the Soviet regime and questioned its legitimacy, it was a matter of urgency for Lenin to suppress and discredit Bogdanov as a thinker. To give credit where it is due, Lenin and his successors have been exemplary in the thoroughness with which they erased Bogdanov from the historical record.

What was achieved by this act of intellectual vandalism was that in the absence of Bogdanov's achievement Lenin appeared as the main Russian Marxist thinker of his era. But time has taken its toll. While the Soviet Union existed one would study Lenin's writings because he was the thinker who knew how to bring about a successful socialist revolution. Now one can say that at the cost of millions of lives, Lenin's revolution managed to secure the deferment of a market economy in Russia for a mere seventy years.

It is clear that until at least 1920, Bogdanov was a major figure in Russia's intellectual history, and that many of the generation who made the Russian revolution learned their Marxism and gained their conceptions of socialism from him. His ideas were the inspiration for Soviet economic planning in the 1920s. In later years Bogdanov had an important negative significance, in that Soviet historiography of the Russian revolution was designed to exclude both him and his ideas from the historical record. The interpretation of the revolutionary era in Russia that is centred on Lenin is made possible only by suppressing the evidence that supports views to the contrary. Consequently, restoring Bogdanov to his rightful place in the history of Russia's revolutionary era implies not simply adding a corrective to the existing body of knowledge on the subject, but re-examining the extent to which that body of knowledge has real validity.

Bibliography

Aksel'rod, L. (Ortodoks) 1904, 'Novaia raznovidnost' revizionizma', *Iskra*, 77: 2–4.

Aksel'rod, L. (Ortodoks) 1906, *Filosofskie ocherki. Otvet filosofskim kritikam istoricheskogo materializma*, St Petersburg: Izdanie M.M. Druzhinovoi i A.N. Maksimovoi.

Amiantov, I.N. and Iunitskaia, R.Z. 1962, 'Otchet pervoi partiinoi shkoly v Lonzhiumo', *Istoricheskie zapiski*, 5: 36–56.

Ascher, Abraham 1976, *The Mensheviks in the Russian Revolution*, London: Thames and Hudson.

Ascher, Abraham 1988, *The Revolution of 1905*, 2 vols., Stanford: Stanford University Press.

Avenarius, R. 1868, *Ueber die beiden ersten Phasen des Spinozischen Pantheismus und das Verhältniss der zweiten zur dritten Phase Nebst einem Anhang: Ueber Reihenfolge und Abfassungszeit der älteren Schriften Spinoza's*, Leipzig: E. Avenarius.

Avenarius, R. 1888–90, *Kritik der reinen Erfahrung*, 2 vols., Leipzig: Fues (O.R. Reisland).

Avenarius, R. 1891, *Der menschliche Weltbegriff*, Leipzig: O.R. Reisland.

Avenarius, R. 1905, *Kritika chistogo opyta v populiarnom izlozhenii A. Lunacharskogo*, Moscow: S. Dorovatovskii and A. Charushnikov.

Avenarius, R. 1917 [1876], *Philosophie als Denken der Welt gemäß dem Prinzip des kleinsten Kraftmasses. Prolegomena zu einer Kritik der reinen Erfahrung*, Berlin: J. Guttentag.

Ästhetik und Kommunikation. Beiträge zur politischen Erziehung 1972, Hamburg: Rowohlt Verlag.

Babko, I.V. and Hlavak, T.V. (eds.) 1981, *Ocherki istorii Kievskikh gorodskoi i oblastnoi partiinykh organizatsii*, Kiev: Politizdat Ukrainy.

Bailes, K.E. 1967, 'Lenin and Bogdanov: The End of an Alliance', in *Columbia Essays in International Affairs*, New York & London: Columbia University Press.

Baron, Samuel H. 1953, *Plekhanov: The Father of Russian Marxism*, Stanford: Stanford University Press.

Bazarov, V.A. 1899, *Trud proizvoditel'nyi i trud, obrazuiushchii tsennost'*, St Petersburg: S. Dorovatskii and A. Charushnikov.

Bazarov, V.A. 2004, 'Filosofskie problemy, idei, diskussii, proekty. Iz sokhranivshikhsia arkhivnykh materialov (Predislovie, publikatsiia i primechaniia V.S. Klebanera)', *Voprosy filosofii*, 6: 94–130.

Bellamy, Edward 1888, *Looking Backward 200–1887*, Boston: Ticknor & Co.

Belykh, A.A. 1990, 'A.A. Bogdanov's Theory of Equilibrium and the Economic Discussions of the 1920s', *Soviet Studies*, 42(3), July: 571–82.

Belova, A.A. 1974, *A.A. Bogdanov*, Moscow: "Meditsina".

Berdiaev, N. 1900, 'Friedrich Albert Lange und die kritische Philosophie in ihren Beziehungen zum Sozialismus', *Die neue Zeit*, I 2(32): 132–40, II 2(33): 164–74, III 2(34): 196–207.

Berdiaev, N. 1901, 'Bor'ba za idealizm', *Mir Bozhii*, 10(6): 1–26.

Berdiaev, N. 1902, 'Zametka o knige g. Bogdanova 'Poznanie s istoricheskoi tochki zreniia'', *Voprosy filosofii i psikhologii*, 4: 839–53.

Berdyaev, N. 1950, *Dream and Reality an Essay in Autobiography*, trans. K. Lampert, London: Bles.

Berdiaev, N. 1990 [1947], *Samopoznanie*, Moscow: DEM.

Berdiaev, N. 1999 [1901], *Sub"ektivizm i individualizm v obshchestvennoi filosofii: kriticheskii étiud o N.K. Mikhailovskom*, Moscow: Kanon+.

Berkman, Alexander 1925, *The Bolshevik Myth: Diary 1920–1922*, London: Hutchinson, New York: Boni and Leveright.

Bertalanffy, Ludwig von 1968, *General System Theory. Foundations, Development, Applications*, Harmondsworth: Penguin Books.

Biggart, John 1980, 'Bogdanov and Lunacharskii in Vologda', *Sbornik*, 5: 28–40.

Biggart, John 1981, '"Anti-Leninist Bolshevism": The Forward Group of the RSDRP', *Canadian Slavonic Papers*, 23(2), June: 132–53.

Biggart, John 1989, 'Alexander Bogdanov, Left-Bolshevism and the Proletkult 1904–1932', PhD Diss., University of East Anglia.

Biggart, John 1998, 'The Rehabilitation of Bogdanov', in Biggart, John, Gloveli, G. and Yassour, A. (eds.) 1998.

Biggart, John 1998a, 'Tektology: Editions and Translations', in Biggart, John, Dudley, P. and King, F. (eds.) 1998.

Biggart, John 2001, 'Bogdanov and the Kul'tintern', *Vestnik Mezhdunarodnogo Instituta A. Bogdanova*, 3 (7): 76–87.

Biggart, John 2016, 'Alexander Bogdanov and the short history of the *Kultintern*', https://bogdanovlibrary.files.wordpress.com/2016/08/2016-08-14-biggart-bogdanov-kultintern.pdf

Biggart, John, Dudley, P. and King, F. (eds.) 1998, *Alexander Bogdanov and the Origins of Systems Thinking in Russia*, Aldershot: Ashgate.

Biggart, John, Gloveli, G. and Yassour, A. (eds.) 1998, *Bogdanov and His Work: A guide to the published and unpublished works of Alexander A. Bogdanov (Malinovsky) 1873–1928*, Aldershot: Ashgate.

Bogdanov, A.A. 1897, *Kratkii kurs ekonomicheskoi nauki*, Moscow: Knizhniy sklad A.M. Murinovoi.

Bogdanov, A.A. 1899, *Kratkii kurs ekonomicheskoi nauki*, St Petersburg: S. Dorovatskii and A. Charushnikov.

Bogdanov, A.A. 1899a, *Osnovnye elementy istoricheskogo vzgliada na prirodu*, St Petersburg: Izdatel'.

Bogdanov, A.A. 1901, *Poznanie s istoricheskoi tochki zreniia*, St Petersburg: Tipografiia A. Leiferta.

Bogdanov, A.A. 1902, 'K voprosu o noveishikh filosofskikh techeniiakh (Otvet N. Berdi-aevu)', *Voprosy filosofii i psikhologii*, 11–12: 1049–59.

Bogdanov, A.A. 1902, *Kratkii kurs ekonomicheskoi nauki.*, 3 ed., Moscow: S. Dorovatskii and A. Charushnikov

Bogdanov, A.A. 1903, 'Ideal poznaniia (Empiriokrititsizm i empiriomonizm)', *Voprosy filosofii i psikhologii*, 2(67): 186–233.

Bogdanov, A.A. 1903a, 'Zhizn' i psikhika (Empiriomonizm v uchenii o zhizni)', *Voprosy filosofii i psikhologii*, 4(69): 682–798.

Bogdanov, A.A. 1904, 'Filosofskii koshmar', *Pravda*, 6: 255–9.

Bogdanov, A.A. 1904a, *Iz-za chego voina i chemu ona uchit?*, Geneva: Izdanie Tsent-ral'nogo Komiteta RSDRP.

Bogdanov, A.A. 1904b, *Liberaly i sotsialisty*, Geneva: Izdanie RSDRP.

Bogdanov, A.A. 1904c, *O sotsializme*, Geneva: Izdanie RSDRP.

Bogdanov, A.A. 1904d, 'Sobiranie cheloveka', *Pravda*, 4: 158–75.

Bogdanov, A.A. 1905, *Novyi Mir (Stat'i 1904–1905)*, Moscow: S. Dorovatskii and A. Cha-rushnikov.

Bogdanov, A.A. 1906, *Iz psikhologii obshchestva*, St Petersburg: Delo.

Bogdanov, A.A. 1906a, *Kratkii kurs ekonomicheskoi nauki*, Moscow: S. Dorovatskii and A. Charushnikov.

Bogdanov, A.A. 1908, 'Boikotisty i otzovisty', *Proletarii*, 31 (4 June 1917).

Bogdanov, A.A. 1908a, 'Ernst Mach und die Revolution', *Die neue Zeit* 26(1): 695–700.

Bogdanov, A.A. 1908b, *Prikliucheniia odnoi filosofskoi shkoly*, St Petersburg: Znanie.

Bogdanov, A.A. 1908c, 'Strana idolov i filosofiia marksizma', in *Ocherki po filosofii mark-sizma*, St Petersburg: Bezobrazov.

Bogdanov, A.A. 1909, 'Blagochestivaia redaktsiia', in *Ko vsem tovarishcham!* Paris: Koop-erativnaia tipografiia "Soiuz".

Bogdanov, A.A. 1909a, 'Filosofiia sovremennogo estestvoispytatelia', in *Ocherki filosofii kollektivizma. Sbornik pervyi*, St Petersburg: Znanie.

Bogdanov, A.A. 1909b, 'K istorii partiinoi shkoly', in *Ko vsem tovarishcham!* Paris: Koop-erativnaia tipografiia "Soiuz".

Bogdanov, A.A. 1909c, 'Ne nado zatemniat'', in *Ko vsem tovarishcham!* Paris: Kooperat-ivnaia tipografiia "Soiuz".

Bogdanov, A.A. 1909d, 'Predislovie k russkomy perevodu I–III tomov "Kapitala"', in Marx 1909: III–XII.

Bogdanov, A.A. 1910, *Otchet Pervoi Vysshei Sotsial-demokraticheskoi propagandistsko-agitatorskoi shkoly dlia rabochikh 1910*, Paris.

Bogdanov, A.A. 1910a, *Padenie velikogo fetishizma (sovremennyi krizis ideologii). Vera i nauka (O knige V. Il'ina "Materializm i empiriokrititsizm")*, Moscow: S. Dorovatskii and A. Charushnikov.

Bogdanov, A.A. 1911, *Kul'turnye zadachi nashego vremeni*, Moscow: S. Dorovatskii and A. Charushnikov.

Bogdanov, A.A. 1911a, *Otchet vtoroi vysshei sotsial-demokraticheskoi Propagandistsko-agitarorskoi shkoly dlia rabochikh, 1911*, Paris.

Bogdanov, A.A. 1913, *Mezhdu chelovekom i mashinoiu*, St Petersburg: Priboi.

Bogdanov, A.A. 1914, *Nauka ob obshchestvennom soznanii*, Moscow: Izd. pisatelei.

Bogdanov, A.A. 1916, 'Mirovye krizisy, mirnye i voennye', *Letopis'*, 3: 139–63, 4: 133–53, 5: 113–24, 7: 214–23.

Bogdanov, A.A. 1917 'Chto zhe my svergli?' *Novaia zhizn'*, 25.

Bogdanov, A.A. 1917a, 'O partiinom edinstve', *Novaia zhizn'*, 47.

Bogdanov, A.A. 1917b, *Uroki pervykh shagov revoliutsii*, Moscow: Tipografiia Ia.G. Sazonova.

Bogdanov, A.A. 1917c, *Zadachi rabochikh v revoliutsii*, Moscow: Tipografiia Ia.G. Sazonova.

Bogdanov, A.A. 1918, 'Chto takoe proletarskaia poeziia?' *Proletarskaia Kul'tura*, 1: 12–22.

Bogdanov, A.A. 1918a, 'Metody truda i metody poznaniia', *Proletarskaia Kul'tura*, 4: 3–13.

Bogdanov, A.A. 1918b, 'Nasha kritika. Stat'ia pervaia: O khudozhestvennom nasledstve', *Proletarskaia Kul'tura*, 2: 4–23.

Bogdanov, A.A. 1918c, 'Nasha kritika. Stat'ia vtoraia: Kritika proletarskogo iskusstva', *Proletarskaia Kul'tura*, 3: 12–21.

Bogdanov, A.A. 1918d, 'Proletarskii universitet', *Proletarskaia Kul'tura*, 5: 9–22.

Bogdanov, A.A. 1918e, *Sotsializm nauki. Nauchnye zadachi proletariata*, Moscow: Proletarskaia Kul'tura.

Bogdanov, A.A. 1918f, 'Sud'by rabochei partii v nyneshnei revoliutsii', *Novaia zhizn'*, 19 and 20.

Bogdanov, A.A. 1918g, 'Tovarishchi!', *Proletarskaia Kul'tura* 1: 1.

Bogdanov, A.A. 1920, *Elementy proletarskoi kul'tury v razvitii rabochego klassa*, Moscow: Gosizdat.

Bogdanov, A.A. 1920a, *Filosofiia zhivogo opyta: populiarnye ocherki: materializm, empiriokrititsizm, dialekticheskii materializm, empiriomonizm, nauka budushchego*, Moscow: Gosizdat.

Bogdanov, A.A. 1920b, 'O mezhdunarodnom Proletkul'te', *Proletarskaia Kul'tura*, 15–16: 3–6.

Bogdanov, A.A. 1921, *Ocherki vseobshchei organizatsionnoi nauki*, Samara: Gosizdat.

Bogdanov, A.A. 1922, *Tektologiia: Vseobshchaia organizatsionnaia nauka*, Berlin: Izd-vo Z.I. Grzhebina.

Bogdanov, A.A. 1922a, 'Versal'skoe ustroistvo i Rossiia', *Vestnik Sotsialisticheskoi Akademii*, 1: 106–31; 146–53.

Bogdanov, A.A. 1923, *A Short Course of Economic Science*, London: Communist Party of Great Britain.

Bogdanov, A.A. 1923a, 'Moe prebyvanie v Tule', *Revoliutsionnoe byloe* 2: 16–18.

Bogdanov, A.A. 1923b, 'Pis'mo v redaktsiiu', *Pravda*, 12 January.

Bogdanov, A.A. 1924, 'Ob osnovnom istorizme politicheskoi ekonomii', *Vestnik Kommunisticheskoi Akademii*, 9: 398–400.

Bogdanov, A.A. 1924a, *O proletarskoi kul'ture 1904–1924*, Leningrad and Moscow: "Kniga".

Bogdanov, A.A. 1925, Comment on I.I. Skvortsov-Stepanov's lecture 'Chto takoe politicheskaia ekonomika?' *Vestnik Kommunisticheskoi Akademii*, 11: 301–7.

Bogdanov, A.A. 1925a, 'Uchenie o refleksakh i zagadki pervobytnogo myshleniia', *Vestnik Kommunisticheskoi Akademii*, 10: 87–96.

Bogdanov, A.A. 1926, Commentary on a lecture by P.O. Gorin of 13 November 1925 'Chem zhe byli Sovety Rabochikh Deputatov v 1905 g.?' in Gorin 1926.

Bogdanov, A.A. 1927, 'Predely nauchnosti rassuzhdeniia', *Vestnik Kommunisticheskoi Akademii*, 21: 244–63; 282–90.

Bogdanov, A.A. 1926a, Commentary on a lecture of E.A. Preobrazhenskii: 'Zakon tsennosti v sovetskom khoziaistve', *Vestnik Kommunisticheskoi Akademii*, 15: 210–16.

Bogdanov, A.A. 1929, Reply to the query of the Lenin Institute concerning his exile in Vologda, *Leninskii sbornik*, XI: 333.

Bogdanov, A.A. 1979 [1929], *Krasnaia zvezda: roman-utopiia; Inzhener Menni: Fantasticheskii roman*, Bibliotheca russica, Hamburg: H. Buske.

Bogdanov, A.A. 1984, *Essays in Tektology. The General Science of Organization*, Seaside, California: Intersystems Publications.

Bogdanov, A.A. 1984a, 'Fortunes of the workers' party in the present revolution', *Sbornik* 10.

Bogdanov, A.A. 1984b, *Red Star: The First Bolshevik Utopia*, edited by L.R. Graham, and R. Stites, trans. by C. Rougle, Bloomington: Indiana University Press.

Bogdanov, A.A. 1989, *Tektologiia. Vseobshchaia organizatsionnaia nauka*, 2 vols., Moscow: Ekonomika.

Bogdanov, A.A. 1990, *Voprosy sotsializma: Raboty raznykh let*, Moscow: Izdatel'stvo politicheskoi literatury.

Bogdanov, A.A. 2001, *The Struggle for Viability. Collectivism through Blood Exchange*, translated and edited with commentaries by Douglas W. Huestis, M.D., Philadelphia.: Xlibris Corporation.

Bogdanov, A.A. 2003, *Empiriomonizm: Stat'i po filosofii*, Moscow: Respublika.

Bogdanov, A.A. 2003a, 'K tektologicheskomu preobrazovaniiu nauk', *Voprosy filosofii*, 1: 111–34.

Bogdanov, A.A., Lunacharskii, A.V. and Gorky, M. 1909, 'Pis'mo v redaktsiiu', *Rech'*, December.

Bogdanov, A.A. and Stepanov, I.I. 1910–25, 4 vols., *Kurs politicheskoi ekonomii*, St Petersburg: Znanie.

Bogdanov, A.A., Bogomolov, A.A. 1928, *Na novom pole*, Moscow: Gosudarstvennyi nauchnyi institut perelivaniia krovi.

Bogdanov's Tektology 1996, Book 1, Foreword by Vadim N. Sadovsky and Vladimir V.

Kelle. edited with an introduction by Peter Dudley, Hull: Centre for Systems Studies Press.

Bol'sheviki. Dokumenty po istorii bol'shevizma s 1903 po 1916 god byvshego Okhrannogo Otdeleniia 1990, Moscow: Politizdat.

Bonch-Bruevich, V.D. 1961, *Izbrannye sochineniia*, 3 vols., Moscow: Izdatel'stvo Akademii Nauk SSSR.

Browder, R.P. and A. Kerensky 1961, *The Russian Provisional Government 1917. Documents*, 3 vols., Stanford: Stanford University Press.

Brusnev, M.I. 1923, 'Vozniknovenie pervykh sotsial-demokraticheskikh organizatsii', *Proletarskaia revoliutsiia* 2(14): 17–32.

Brusnev, M.I. 1928, 'Pervye revoliutsionnye shagi L. Krasina' in *Leonid Borisovich Krasin 'Nikitich': gody podpol'ia: sbornik vospominanii, statei i dokumentov*, Moscow: Gosudarstvennoe izdatels'tvo.

Bukharin, N.I. 1915, 'Mirovoe khoziaistvo i imperializm', *Kommunist*, 1: 4–48.

Bukharin, N.I. 1918, Review of Bogdanov's *Voprosy sotsializma* in *Kommunist*.

Bukharin, N.I. 1921, 'K s"ezdu proletkul'ta', *Pravda*, 22 November.

Bukharin, N.I. 1928, 'A.A. Bogdanov', *Pravda*, 8 April, 3.

Bukharin, N.I. 1928a, 'Pamiati A.A. Bogdanova', in *Na novom pole, Trudy gosudarstvennogo nauchnogo instituta perelivaniia krovi im. A.A. Bogdanova*, tom 1, Moscow: Izdanie gosudarstvennogo instituta perelivaniia krovi: IX–XI.

Bukharin, N.I. 1965, *Historical Materialism. A System of Sociology*, New York: Russell and Russell.

Bukharin, N.I. 1972 [1917], *Imperialism and World Economy*, London: The Merlin Press.

Bukharin, N.I. 1990, *Izbrannye proizvedeniia*, Moscow: Ekonomika.

Bukharin, N. and E. Preobrazhensky 1969, *The ABC of Communism*, Harmondsworth: Penguin Books.

Burdzhalov, E.N. 1971, *Vtoraia russkaia revoliutsiia. Moskva. Front. Periferiia.*, Moscow: Nauka.

Bynkina, V.N. 1963, *Iz istorii vozniknoveniia bol'shevistskoi organizatsii Tuly (1894–1904 gg.)*, Tula: Tul'skoe knizhnoe izdatel'stvo.

Byvshii student 1896, 'Besporiadki 1894–95 v moskovskom universitete', *Materialy dlia istorii russkogo sotsial'no-revoliutsionnogo dvizheniia*, 6–7.

Carstanjen, Friedrich 1897, 'Richard Avenarius and his General Theory of Knowledge, Empiriocriticism', *Mind*, 6 (24): 449–475.

Chlebowski, W. and Walewski, W. 1890, *Słownik geograficzny Królestwa Polskiego i innych krajów słowiańskich*, 11, Warsaw: Wladyslaw Walewski.

Chetvertyi (ob"edinitel'nyi) s"ezd RSDRP aprel' (aprel'–mai) 1906 goda. Protokoly 1959, Moscow: Gospolitizdat.

Daniels, Robert V. 1960, *The Conscience of the Revolution. Communist Opposition in Soviet Russia*, Cambridge Mass: Harvard University Press.

Deborin, A. 1927, 'Foreword to the English Translation' of *Materialism and Empirio-Criticism*, London: Martin Lawrence.

Deiateli revoliutsionnogo dvizheniia v Rossii: Sotsial-Demokraty 1880–1904, vol. 5 1931, Moscowi Voocoiuznoe obshchestvo politicheskikh katorzhan i ssyl'no-poselentsev.

Delacroix, Henri 1898, 'Avenarius: Esquisse de l'empiriocriticisme,' *Revue de Métaphysique et de Morale* 6 (1).

Desnitskii, V.A. 1940, *M. Gorkii. Ocherki zhizni i tvorchestva*, Leningrad: "Khudozhestvennaia literatura".

Deutscher, Isaac 1970, *The Prophet Armed: Trotsky 1879–1921*, Oxford: OUP.

Dobrotvorov, N 1923, 'Na zare revoliutsionnogo dvizheniia v Tule', *Revoliutsionnoe byloe* 2: 6–12.

Dodonova, Anna 1967, 'Iz vospominanii o proletkul'te' in *Iz istorii sovetskoi esteticheskoi mysli. Sbornik statei*, Moscow: Iskusstvo.

Donald, Moira 1993, *Marxism and Revolution. Karl Kautsky and the Russian Marxists, 1990–1924*, New Haven: Yale University Press.

Drugov, V.I. (ed.) 1969, *Ocherki istorii Vologodskoi organizatsii KPSS. 1895–1968.*, Vologda: Sev.-Zap. kn. izd.

'Dva pis'ma k N.K. Mikhailovskomu' 1924, *Byloe*, 23: 106–21.

Dvolaitskii, S.M. 1921, 'Nakoplenie kapitala i imperializm', *Krasnaia nov'* 1: 88–100.

Elwood, R.C. 1966, 'Lenin and the Social Democratic Schools for Underground Party Workers, 1909–11', *Political Science Quarterly* 81(3), September: 370–91.

Ermolaev, E.I. 1923, 'Moi vospominaniia', *Sever* 3–4: 1–28.

Fal'kovich, S.M. 1975, *Proletariat Rossii i Pol'shi v sovmestnoi revoliutsionnoi bor'be (1907–1912)*, Moscow: Nauka.

Filosofsko-literaturnoe nasledie G.V. Plekhanova 1973–4, 3 vols., Moscow: "Nauka".

Fitzpatrick, Sheila 1970, *The Commissariat of Enlightenment: Soviet organization of education and the arts under Lunacharsky, October 1917–1921*, Cambridge: Cambridge University Press.

Galerka and Riadovoi [M.S. Ol'minskii and A.A. Bogdanov] 1925, 'Nashi nedorazumeniia', in *Kak rozhdalas' partiia bol'shevikov: Literaturnaia polemika 1903–04 gg. Sbornik*, Leningrad: Priboi.

Genkina, E.B. 1969, *Gosudarstvennaia deiatel'nost' V.I. Lenina 1921–1923*, Moscow: Nauka.

Getzler, Israel 1967, *Martov. A Political Biography of a Russian Social Democrat*, Cambridge: CUP.

Glenny, Michael 1970, 'Leonid Krasin: The Years before 1917. An Outline', *Soviet Studies*, 22(2): 192–122.

Goldman, Emma 1925, *My disillusionment in Russia*, London: Daniel.

Gorelik, George 1983, 'Bogdanov's Tektology: Its Nature, Development and Influence', *Studies in Soviet Thought*, 26 (1): 39–57.

Gorev, B.I. 1924, *Iz partiinogo proshlogo. Vospominaniia 1895–1905*, Leningrad: Gosizdat.

Gorin, P.O. 1926, 'Chem zhe byli Sovety Rabochikh Deputatov v 1905 g.?', *Istorik-marksist*, 1: 201–35.

Gorbunov, V.V. 1974, *V.I. Lenin i Proletkul't*, Moscow: Politizdat.

Gorky, Maxim 1909, 'Razrushenie lichnosti' in *Ocherki filosofii kollektivizma. Sbornik pervyi*, St Petersburg: Znanie.

Gorsen, P. and Knödler-Bunte, E. (eds.) 1974, *Proletkult 1. System einer proletarischen Kultur. Dokumentation*, Stuttgart; Bad Canstatt: Problemata Frommann-Holzboog.

Gorsen, P. and Knödler-Bunte, E. (eds.) 1975, *Proletkult 2. Zur Praxis und Theorie einer proletarischen Kulturrevolution in Sowjetrussland 1917–1925. Dokumentation*, Stuttgart; Bad Canstatt: Problemata Frommann-Holzboog.

Gorzka, G. 1980, *A. Bogdanov und der russische Proletkult: Theorie und Praxis einer sozialistischen Kulturrevolution*, Frankfurt/New York: Campus Verlag.

Grille, Dietrich 1966, *Lenins Rivale: Bogdanov und seine Philosophie*, Cologne: Verlag Wissenschaft und Politik.

Gukovskii, A.I. 1968, 'Kak sozdavalas' "Russkaia istoriia s drevneishikh vremen" M.N. Pokrovskogo', *Voprosy istorii*, 8: 122–32.

Haupt, G. and Scherrer, J. 1978, 'Gor'kij, Bogdanov, Lenin. Neue Quellen zur ideologischen Krise in der bolschewistischen Fraktion (1908–1910)', *Cahiers du Monde russe et soviétique* 19(3): 321–334.

Henning, Hans 1915, *Ernst Mach als Philosoph, Physiker und Psycholog*, Leipzig: Verlag von Johann Ambrosius Barth.

Hilferding, Rudolf 1923 [1910], *Das Finanzkapital: eine Studie über die jüngste Entwicklung des Kapitalismus*, Vienna: Verlag der Wiener Volksbuchhandlung.

Hänggi, Jürg 1984, 'Pod znamenem marksizma', *Studies in Soviet Thought*, 27: 78–279.

Huestis, Douglas 1996, 'The Life and Death of Alexander Bogdanov, physician', *Journal of Medical Biography*, 4(3): 141–7.

Huestis, Douglas 1997, 'The Ironic Death of Dr Bogdanov, Pioneer in Transfusion Medicine', *Transfusion Today*, 31, 31 June: 9–10.

Huestis, Douglas 2001, 'Bogdanov: Poslednii eksperiment', *Vestnik Instituta A Bogdanova*, 3(7): 54–64.

Iakovlev, Ia.A. 1923, Introduction to *Lenin and Plekhanov* 1923.

Iakovlev, Ia.A. 1923b, 'Menshevizm v proletkul'tovskoi odezhde', *Pravda*, 4 January.

Iakhot, Iegoshua 1981, *Podavlenie filosofii v SSSR*, New York: Chalidze Publications.

Iovchuk, M.T., Kurbatova, I. and Chagin, B.A. (eds.) 1973, *Filosofsko-literaturnoe nasledie G.V. Plekhanova*, Vol. 1, Moscow: Nauka.

Istoriia tul'skogo oruzheinogo zavoda, 1712–1972, 1973, Moscow: Mysl'

Ivashko, V.A. and Baskov, P.G. (eds.) 1980, *Ocherki istorii Kharkovskoi oblastnoi partiinoi organizatsii*, Kharkov: "Prapor".

Jensen, K.M. 1978, *Beyond Marx and Mach: Alexander Bogdanov's Philosophy of Living Experience*, Dordrecht: Reidel.

Kak rozhdalas' partiia bol'shevikov. Literaturnaia polemika 1903–04 gg. Sbornik 1925, Leningrad: Priboi.

Kalniņš, Bruno 1972, 'The Social Democratic Movement in Latvia' in *Revolution and Politics in Russia*, edited by A. and J. Rabinowitch, Bloomington: Indiana University Press.

Kapsukas, Vincas 1960–78, *Raštai*, 12 vols., Vilnius: "Vaga".

'K istorii otzovizma' 1924, *Proletarskaia revoliutsiia* 6(29): 193–207.

Kamenev, L.B. 2003, *Mezhdu dvumia revoliutsiiami*, Moscow: Tsentrpoligraf.

Kautsky, Karl 1886, *Karl Marx' ökonomische Lehren*, Stuttgart: Dietz.

Kelly, Eileen M. 1981, 'Empiriocriticism: A Bolshevik philosophy?' *Cahiers du Monde Russe et Soviétique* 21: 89–118.

Kelly, Eileen M. 1990, 'Red Queen or White Knight? The Ambivalences of Bogdanov', *Russian Review* 49(3): 305–15.

Kerzhentsev, V. 1919, 'Mezhdunarodnaia revoliutsiia i proletarskaia kul'tura', *Proletarskaia Kul'tura*, 6: 1–3.

Keynes, Geoffrey 1922, *Blood Transfusion*, London: Hodder and Stoughton.

Keynes, John Maynard 1920, *The Economic Consequences of the Peace*, New York: Harcourt, Brace and Howe.

Khabas 1924, 'Sozdanie bol'shevistskogo tsentra (BKB) i gazety "Vpered"', *Proletarskaia revoliutsiia*, 11: 19–35.

Khait, G.E. 1958, 'V kazanskom kruzhke', *Novyi mir* 4: 189–93.

Khalipov, A.S. 1982, *Bor'ba V.I. Lenina protiv likvidatorstva, 1908–1914*, Minsk: Izd-vo BGU.

Khrustalev-Nosar 1906, 'Istoriia Soveta Rabochikh Deputatov (do 26–Noiabria 1905 g.)' in *Istoriia Soveta Rabochikh Deputatov*, St Petersburg. Tsentral'naia Izvo-Lit M.Ia. Minkova.

Kim, M.P. (ed.) 1972, *Lenin i kul'turnaia revoliutsiia. Khronika sobytii (1917–1923)*, Moscow: "Mysl'".

Kin, D. 1929, 'Vpered', in *Bol'shaia sovetskaia entsiklopediia*, 13, Moscow: Sovetskaia entsiklopediia.

Kindersley, Richard 1962, *The First Russian Revisionists. A Study of "Legal Marxism" in Russia*, Oxford: Clarendon Press.

King, Francis 1994, 'The Political and Economic Thought of Vladimir Aleksandrovich Bazarov (1874–1939)', University of East Anglia.

King, Francis 1996, 'Between Bolshevism and Menshevism: The Social-Democrat Internationalists in the Russian Revolution', *Revolutionary Russia* 9(1), June: 1–18.

Klebaner, V.S. 2000, 'A. Bogdanov i A.A. Malinovskii', in A.A. Malinovskii, *Tektologiia, teoriia sistem, teoreticheskaia biologiia*, Moscow: Editorial URSS.

Klebaner, V.S. 2004, 'V.A. Bazarov–myslitel', uchenyi, grazhdanin', *Problemy prognozirovaniia* 6: 150–6.

Kochański, A. 1971, *Socjaldemokracja Królestwa polskiego i Litwy w latach 1907–1910*, Warsaw: Ksiazka i Wiedza.

Koenker, Diane 1981, *Moscow Workers and the 1917 Revolution*, Princeton: Princeton University Press.

Kokhno, I.P. 1970, 'Vologodskaia ssylka Lunacharskogo', *Literaturnoe nasledstvo*, 82: 603–20.

Kolakowski, Leszek 1972, *Positivist Philosophy. From Hume to the Vienna Circle*, Harmondsworth: Penguin.

Kolakowski, Leszek 1981, *Main Currents of Marxism*, 3 vols., Oxford: OUP.

Kolerov, M.A. 2002, *Sbornik "Problemy idealizma" (1902): istoriia i kontekst*, Moscow: Tri Kvadrata.

Kollontai, Alexandra 1977, *Selected Writings of Alexandra Kollontai*. Translated with an introd. and commentaries by Alix Holt, Westport, Conn.: L. Hill.

Kommunist: Ezhenedel'nyi zhurnal ekonomiki, politiki i obshchestvennosti: organ Moskovskogo Oblastnogo Biuro RKP (bol'shevikov) 1990 [1918], Millwood, N.Y.: Kraus Int. Publ.

Konchalovskii, M.P. 1928, 'Bolezn' i smert' A.A. Bogdanova', in *Na novom pole, Trudy gosudarstvennogo nauchnogo instituta perelivaniia krovi im. A.A. Bogdanova*, tom 1, Moscow: Izdanie gosudarstvennogo instituta perelivaniia krovi: XII–XXVI.

Kosarev, V. 1922, 'Partiinaia shkola na ostrove Kapri', *Sibirskie ogni*, 2: 62–75.

KPSS v rezoliutsiiakh i resheniiakh s"ezdov, konferentsii i plenumov TsK 1953, 2 vols., Moscow: Gospolitizdat.

Krementsov, N. 2011, *A Martian Stranded on Earth. Alexander Bogdanov, Blood Transfusions and Proletarian Science*, Chicago and London: University of Chicago Press.

Krivtsov, S. 1929, 'Ivan Ivanovich Skvortsov-Stepanov', *Vestnik Kommunisticheskoi Akademii*, 30: 7–16.

Krupskaia, N.K. 1989, 'Vospominaniia o Lenine', in *Vospominaniia o Vladimire Il'iche Lenine*, tom 2, Moscow: Partizdat.

Kunavin, V. 1918, 'Pervaia Vserossiiskaia Konferentsiia Proletarskikh Kul'turno-Prosvetitel'nykh Organizatsii', *Proletarskaia Kul'tura*, 5: 26–30.

Lange, F.A. 1877–81, *History of Materialism*, 3 vols., London: Trübner.

Lebedev-Polianskii, P.I. 1918, 'Natsionalizm i sotsializm', *Proletarskaia Kul'tura*, 2: 1–4.

Lebedev-Polianskii, P.I. 1918, 'Tov. N. Lenin', *Proletarskaia Kul'tura*, 4: 1–3.

Lebedev-Polianskii, P.I. 1926, 'Marksistskaia periodicheskaia pechat' 1896–1906 gg.', *Krasnyi arkhiv*, 18.

Lebedev-Polianskii, P.I. and F. Kalinin 1918, 'K sozyvu Vserossiiskoi kul'turno-prosvetitel'noi konferentsii rabochikh organizatsii', *Proletarskaia Kul'tura*, 1: 24–31.

Lenin, V.I. 1929, Comments on N.I. Bukharin's book *Economics of the Transition Period*, *Leninskii sbornik* XI.

Lenin, V.I. 1958–65, *Polnoe sobranie sochinenii*, 5th ed., Moscow: Gospolitizdat.

Lenin, V.I. and Plekhanov, G.V. 1923, *Protiv A. Bogdanova*, Moscow: Krasnaia nov'.

Lesevich, V. 1891, *Chto takoe nauchnaia filosofiia?* St Petersburg: Skorokhodov.

Liadov, M.N. 1956, *Iz zhizni partii v 1903–1907 godakh: vospominaniia*, Moscow: Gospolit-izdat.

Liadov, M.N. 1989–91, 'Iz vospominanii. Moi vstrechi s Leninym', in *Vospominaniia o Vladimire Il'iche Lenine*, tom 3: 117–26.

Listovki Peterburgskikh bol'shevikov, 1902–1920 1939, 3 vols., Moscow: Gospolitizdat.

Listovki Bol'shevistskikh organizatsii v pervoi Russkoi revoliutsii 1905–1907 gg. 1956, 3 vols., Moscow: Gospolitizdat.

Livshits, S.I. 1924, 'Kapriiskaia partiinaia shkola (1909 g.)', *Proletarskaia revoliutsiia*, 6(29): 33–73.

Livshits, S.I. 1926, 'Partiinaia shkola v Bolon'e (1900–1911 gg.)', *Proletarskaia revoliutsiia*, 3: 109–144.

Lorenz, R. (ed.) 1969, *Proletarische Kulturrevolution in Sowjetrussland (1917–1921)*, trans. U. Brügmann, and G. Meyer, Munich: Deutscher Taschenbuch Verlag.

Lowrie, Donald A. 1960, *Rebellious Prophet. A Life of Nikolai Berdyaev*, London: Victor Gollancz Ltd.

Lunacharskaia, I.A. 1979, 'K nauchnoi biografii A.V. Lunacharskogo', *Russkaia literatura*, 4: 110–27.

Lunacharskii, A.V. 1908, 'Ateizm', in *Ocherki po filosofii marksizma*, St Petersburg: Bezobrazov.

Lunacharskii, A.V. 1908–11, *Religiia i sotsializm*, 2 vols., St Petersburg: Shipovnik.

Lunacharskii, A.V. 1909, 'Dvadtsat' tretii sbornik "Znaniia"', in *Literaturnyi raspad. Kriticheskii sbornik. Kniga vtoraia*, St Petersburg: Knigoizdatel'stvo "EOS".

Lunacharskii, A.V. 1909, 'Neskol'ko slov o moem 'bogostroitel'stve'', in *Ko vsem tovarishcham!* Paris: Kooperativnaia tipografiia "Soiuz".

Lunacharskii, A.V. 1928, 'Aleksandr Aleksandrovich Bogdanov', *Pravda*, 10 April.

Lunacharskii, A.V. 1963–67, *Sobranie sochinenii*, 8 vols., Moscow: Khudozhestvennaia literatura.

Lunacharskii, A.V. 1968, *Vospominaniia i vpechatleniia*, Moscow: "Sovetskaia Rossiia".

Lunacharskii, A.V. 1970 [1907], 'Avtobiograficheskaia zametka', *Literaturnoe nasledstvo*, 82: 550–6.

Lutsenko, A.V. 2003, 'Nachalo konflikta mezhdu V.I. Leninym i A.A. Bogdanovym (1907–1909 gg.)', *Voprosy istorii*, 1: 27–47.

Luxemburg, Rosa 1909, 'Revoliutsionnoe pokhmelie', *Proletarii*, 8 (21) April.

Luxemburg, Rosa 1971, *Listy do Leona Jogichesa-Tyszki*, 3 vols., Warsaw: Ksiażka i Wiedza.

Mach, Ernst 1900, *Die Analyse der Empfindungen und das Verhältnis des Physischen zum Psychischen*, Jena: Verlag von Gustav Fischer.

Mach, Ernst 1903, *Die Analyse der Empfindungen und das Verhältnis Des Physischen zum Psychischen*, Jena: Verlag von Gustav Fischer.

Mach, Ernst 1959, *The Analysis of Sensations, and the Relation of the Physical to the Psychical*, New York: Dover Publications.

MacLaine, William 1920, 'Samostoiatel'noe prosveshchenie rabochikh Anglii', *Proletarskaia Kul'tura*, 15–16: 55–7.

Maevskii, Evgenii 1910, 'Obshchaia kartina dvizhenii', in *Obshchestvennoe dvizhenie v Rossii*, Edited by L. Martov, P. Maslov and A. Potresov, tom 2, St Petersburg: "Obshchestvennaia pol'za".

Malinovskii, A.A. 2000, *Tektologiia, teoriia sistem, teoreticheskaia biologiia*, Moscow: Editorial URSS.

Mally, Lynn 1990, *Culture of the future: the Proletkult movement in revolutionary Russia*, Studies on the history of society and culture, Berkeley: University of California Press.

Marksisty 1924, 'Dva Pis'ma k N.K. Mikhailovskomu', *Byloe* 23: 105–26.

Martov, L. 1922, *Zapiski sotsial-demokrata*, Letopis revoliutsii, Berlin: Izd-vo Z.I. Grzhebina.

Marx, Karl 1859, *Zur Kritik der Politischen Oekonomie*, Berlin: Verlag von Franz Duncker.

Marx, Karl 1885, 'Der französische Materialismus des 18 Jahrhunderts', *Die neue Zeit*, 3(9): 385–95.

Marx, Karl 1907–9, *Kapital. Kritika politicheskoi ekonomii*, 3 vols., Kiev and New York: Orenshtein and Maizel.

Marx, Karl 1973, *Grundrisse*, Harmondsworth: Penguin.

Marx Karl 1976, *Capital: a critique of political economy*. Vol. I, translated by Ben Fowkes, Harmondsworth: Penguin Books.

Marx, K. and Engels, F. 1908, *Pis'ma Karla Marksa i Fridrikha Engel'sa k Nikolaiu-onu*, St Petersburg: A. Benke.

Marx, K. and Engels, F. 1969, *Selected Works*, 3 vols, Moscow: Progress Publishers.

Mänicke-Gyöngyösi, K. 1982, *"Proletarische Wissenschaft" und "Sozialistische Menschheitsreligion" als Modelle proletarischer Kultur zur linksbolschewistischen Revolutionstheorie A.A. Bogdanovs und A.V. Lunacarskijs*, Philosophische und soziologische Veröffentlichungen (Osteuropa-Institut an der Freien Universität Berlin), Wiesbaden: In Kommission bei Harrassowitz.

Mehring, F. 1902, *Aus dem literarischen Nachlass von Karl Marx, Friedrich Engels und Ferdinand Lassalle*, Stuttgart: Dietz.

Mikhailov, B.G. 1994, 'Demokraticheskoe dvizhenie v Vologde (XIX v.)', in *Vologda istoriko-kraevedcheskii al'manakh*, Starinnye goroda Vologodskoi oblasti, Vologda: VGPI, izd-vo "Rus".

Mikhailovskii, N.K. 1906, *Sochineniia*, 1, St Petersburg: 'Russkoe bogatstvo'.

Milonov, Iu. 1921, 'Na puti k rabochei entsiklopedii (Vmesto predisloviia)', in Bogdanov 1921: III–XXIV.

Mitelkova, R.S., Kommunisticheskaia partiia Sovetskogo Soiuza. and Vologodskaia oblast (R.S.F.S.R.). 1977, *Marksisty-lenintsy v vologodskoi ssylke (Iz istorii vologod. polit. ssylki 1893–1914 gg.): Sbornik dokumentov i materialov*, Arkhangel'sk: Sev. Zap. kn. izd-vo.

Mitskevich, S.I. 1906, 'Na zare rabochego dvizheniia v Moskve', in *Tekushchii moment*, Moscow.

Mitskevich, S.I. 1937, *Na grani dvukh epokh. Ot narodnichestva k marksizmu: memuarnaia zapis'*, Moscow: Sotsekgiz.

'Nashi tseli', 1912, *Pravda* 1 (22 May).

Najdus, Walentyna 1973, *SDKPiL a SDPRP 1893–1907*, Wrocław: Wydawnictwo Polskiej Akademii Nauk.

Najdus, Walentyna 1980, *SDKPiL a SDPRP 1908–1918*, Wrocław: Wydawnictwo Polskiej Akademii Nauk.

Nechkina, M.V. 1974, *Vasilii Osipovich Kliuchevskii*, Moscow: "Nauka".

Neizvestnyi Bogdanov, 1995, edited by N.S. Antonova and N.V. Drozdova, 3 vols., Moscow: ITs AIRO-XX.

Nevskii, V.I. (ed.) 1924, *Istoriko-revoliutsionnyi sbornik*, 2, Moscow: Gosizdat.

Nevskii, V.I. 1925, *Ocherki po istorii rossiiskoi kommunisticheskoi partii, Vol. 1*, Leningrad.

Nevskii, V.I. 1931 [1920] 'Dialekticheskii materializm i filosofiia mertvoi reaktsii' in V.I. Lenin *Sochineniia*, 13: 317–24.

Nezhdanov, P. 1898, *Nravstvennost'*, Moscow: Tipografiia I.A. Balandina, Volkhonka, D. Mikhalkova.

Nezhdanov, P. (Tscherewanin, A.) 1908, *Das Proletariat und die russische Revolution*, Stuttgart: Dietz Verlag.

Nikolaevskii, B.I. 1995, *Tainye stranitsy istorii*, Moscow: Izdatel'stvo gumanitarnoi literatury.

Noiré, Ludwig 1874, *Die Welt als Entwicklung des Geistes. Baustein zu einer monistischen Weltanschauung*, Leipzig: Veit.

Noiré, Ludwig 1875, *Der monistische Gedanke. Ein Concordance der Philosophie Schopenhauer's, Darwin's, R. Mayer's und L. Geiger's*, Leipzig: Veit.

Noiré, Ludwig 1877, *Der Ursprung der Sprache*, Mainz: Victor von Zabern.

Novoselov, V.I. 1992, 'Novoe o vologodskoi ssylke A.A. Bogdanova', in *Trudy komissii po nauchnomu naslediiu A.A. Bogdanova*, Moscow: Rossiiskaia akademiia nauk institut ekonomiki: 179–86.

Ob agitatsii 1896, Geneva: Izdanie Soiuza Russkikh Sotsialdemokratov.

Obshchestvennoe dvizhenie v Rossii v nachale XX-go veka 1910–14, 4 vols., Edited by L. Martov, P. Maslov and A. Potresov, St Petersburg: Tip. T-va "Obshchestvennaia pol'za".

Ocherki po filosofii marksizma 1908, St Petersburg: Bezobrazov.

Ocherki realisticheskogo mirovozzreniia. Sbornik statei po filosofii, obshchestvennoi nauke i zhizni 1904, St Petersburg: S. Dorovatskii and A. Charushnikov.

'Ogólnopartijna konferencja' 1909, *Czerwony Sztandar* 165 (17 March).

Oreshkin, V.V. 1968, *Voprosy imperializma v rabotakh bol'shevikov-lenintsev dooktiabr'skii period*, Moscow: Nauka.

Ostroukhova, K. 1924, 'Otzovisty i ul'timatisty', *Proletarskaia revoliutsiia*, 6(29): 14–32.

Ostroukhova, K. 1925, 'Gruppa "Vpered" (1909–1917 g.g.)', *Proletarskaia revoliutsiia*, 36: 198–219.

Ostroukhova, K. 1967, 'O rabote v Istparte', *Voprosy istorii KPSS*, 6: 92–101.

Pavlov, A. 1914, 'O nekotorykh chertakh filosofii A. Bogdanova', *Prosveshchenie*, 2: 22–31.

Pavlovskii, O.A. 1980, *Lunacharskii*, Moskva: "Mysl'".

Perepiska V.I. Lenina i redaktsii gazety "Iskra" s sotsial-demokraticheskimi organizatsiiami v Rossii: 1900–1903 gg. Sbornik dokumentov 1969–70, 3 vols., Moscow: "Mysl'".

Perepiska V.I. Lenina i rukovodimykh im uchrezhdenii RSDRP s partiinymi organizatsiiami 1903–1905 gg.: sbornik dokumentov 1969–77, 3 vols., Moscow: "Mysl'".

Peterburgskii komitet RSDRP. Protokoly i materialy zasedanii Iul' 1902–fevral' 1917 1986, Leningrad: Lenizdat.

Petriakov, G.V. 1956, 'Deiatel'nost' V.I. Lenina po rukovodstvu 'Pravdoi' v 1912–1914 godakh', *Voprosy istorii*, 11 (November): 3–16.

Philips Price, M. 1921, *My Reminiscences of the Russian Revolution*, London: Allen and Unwin.

Plekhanov, G.V. 1889, *Novyi zashchitnik samoderzhaviia*, Geneva: Biblioteka Sovremennogo Sotsializma.

Plekhanov, G.V. 1891, 'Zu Hegel's sechzigstem Todestag', *Die neue Zeit*, 1(9): 273–82.

Plekhanov, G.V. 1896, *Beiträge zur Geschichte des Materialismus*, Stuttgart: Dietz.

Plekhanov, G.V. 1923–7, *Sochineniia*, 24 vols., edited by D. Riazanov, Moscow: Gosizdat.

Plekhanov, G.V. 1956–58, *Izbrannye filosofskie proizvedeniia*, 5 vols., Moscow: Gospolitizdat.

Plyutto, P.A. 1992, 'Alexander Bogdanov on the Period of "War Communism"', *Revolutionary Russia*, 5(1): 46–52.

Plyutto, P.A. 1998, 'Bogdanov: A Biographical Chronicle' in Biggart, Gloveli and Yassour 1998: 459–80.

Podliashuk, P. 1973, *Ivan Ivanych*, Moscow: Moskovskii rabochii.

Pokrovskii, M.N. 1905, 'Professional'naia intelligentsiia i sotsial-demokraty: Pis'mo v redaktsiiu', *Proletarii*, 9(22) August.

Pokrovskii, M.N. 1928, 'A.A. Bogdanov (Malinovskii)', *Vestnik Kommunisticheskoi Akademii*, 26 (2): v–x.

Pokrovskii, M.N. 1929, 'Ivan Ivanovich Skvortsov-Stepanov: Skonchalsia 8 oktiabria 1928 g', *Vestnik Kommunisticheskoi Akademii*, 30: 3–6.

Pokrovsky, M.N. 1933, *Brief History of Russia*, 2 vols., London: Martin Lawrence Ltd.

Polosatov, N. 1923, 'Za sem' let', *Revoliutsionnoe byloe*, 2: 25–7.

Preobrazhensky, E. 1965, *The New Economics*, Translated by Brian Pearce, Oxford: Clarendon Press.

Problems of Idealism. Essays in Russian Social Philosophy 2003, translated, edited and introduced by Randall A. Poole, New Haven and London: Yale University Press.

Problemy Idealizmu. Sbornik statei 1902, ed. P.N. Novogrodtsev, Moscow: Izdanie moskovskogo psikhologicheskogo obshchestva.

Prokof'ev, V.A. 1969, *Dubrovinskii*, Moscow: Molodaia gvardiia.

Protokoly pervoi vserossiiskoi konferentsii proletarskikh kul'turno-prosvetitel'nykh organizatsii 15–20 sentiabria 1918 g. 1918, Moscow: Proletarskaia Kul'tura.

Protokoly piatogo s"ezda RSDRP 1935, Moscow: Partizdat.

Protokoly soveshchaniia rasshirennoi redaktsii 'Proletariia'. Iiun' 1909 1934, Moscow: Partizdat.

Prot'ko, T.S. and Gritsanov, A.A. 2009, *Aleksandr Bogdanov*, Minsk: Knizhnyi dom.

Quelch, Tom 1920, 'Angliia kak pole proletarskoi kul'tury', *Proletarskaia Kul'tura*, 15–16: 52–5.

Read, Christopher 1990, *Culture and Power in Revolutionary Russia: the intelligentsia and the transition from tsarism to communism*, Houndmills, Basingstoke, Hampshire: Macmillan.

Read, Christopher 2005, 'Lenin and the 1905 Revolution', in *The Russian Revolution of 1905. Centenary perspectives*, edited by Jonathan D. Smele and Anthony Heywood, London and New York: Routledge.

Remizov, A. 1986, *Iveren zagoguliny moei pamiati*, Modern Russian literature and culture, studies and texts, Berkley, Calif.: Berkley Slavic Specialties.

Rispoli, Giulia 2012, *Dall'Empiriomonismo alla Tectologia. Organizzazione, complessità e approccio sistemico nel pensiero di Aleksandr Bogdanov*, Rome: Aracne.

Rogachevskii, Andrei 1994, 'Social Democratic Party Schools on Capri and in Bologna in the Correspondence between A.A. Bogdanov and A.V. Amfiteatrov', *Slavonic and East European Review*, 72(4), October: 664–79.

Rogachevskii, Andrei 1995, ' "Life Makes No Sense": Aleksandr Bogdanov's Experiences in the First World War', *Proceedings of the Scottish Society for Russian and East European Studies*, Glasgow: 105–16.

Rostunov, I.I. 1976, *Russkii front pervoi mirovoi voiny*, Moscow: Nauka

Rozental', M. and Iudin, P. 1954, *Kratkii filosofskii slovar'*, Moscow, Gospolitizdat.

Rozhkov, N.A. 1903, 'Znachenie i sud'by noveishogo idealizma v Rossii (po povodu knigi "Problemy idealizma")', *Voprosy filosofii i psikhologii*, 11 (67): 314–32.

Rozhkov, N.A. 2010, *Izbrannye trudy*, Moscow: ROSSPEN.

Russell, Bertrand 1903, *The Principles of Mathematics*, Cambridge: CUP.

Russell, Bertrand 1920, *The Practice and Theory of Bolshevism*, London: Allen & Unwin.

Sanburov, V.I. 1978, 'Moskovskii "Rabochii Soiuz" ', *Voprosy istorii*, 5: 95–110.

Saralieva, Z.Kh. 1970, 'Ob izdaniiakh "Kapitala" K. Marksa v Rossii', *Istoriia* SSSR, 5: 114–24.

Schapiro, Leonard 1970, *The Communist Party of the Soviet Union*, London: Methuen.

Scheibert, Peter 1971, 'Lenin, Bogdanov, and the Concept of Proletarian Culture' in *Lenin and Leninism*, edited by Bernard W. Eissenstat, Toronto, London: D.C. Heath and Company: 43–58.

Scherrer, Jutta 1980, 'Un "philosophe-ouvrier" russe: N.E. Vilonov', *Le Mouvement social*, April, 165–87.

Scherrer, Jutta 1988, 'Gor'kij-Bogdanov. Aperçu sur une correspondance non publiée', *Cahiers du Monde russe et soviétique* 29(1): 41–51.

Schwarz, Solomon 1967, *The Russian Revolution of 1905: the Workers' Movement and the Formation of Bolshevism and Menshevism*, Chicago: Chicago University Press.

Semashko, N. 1928, 'Smert' A.A. Bogdanova (Malinovskogo)', *Pravda*, 8 April, 3.

Serge, Victor 1963, *Memoirs of a Revolutionary 1901–1941*, translated by Peter Sedgwick, London and New York: Oxford University Press.

Sharapov, Iu.P. 1997, 'Lenin i Bogdanov: Ot sotrudnichestva k protivostoianiiu', *Otechestvennaia istoriia*, 5: 55–67.

Sharapov, Iu.P. 1998, *Lenin i Bogdanov: Ot sotrudnichestva k protivostoianiiu*, Moscow: RAN, Institut rossiiskoi istorii.

Shkurinov, P.S. 1980, *Pozitivizm v Rossii XIX veka*, Istoriia filosofii., Moskva: Izd-vo Moskovskogo universiteta.

Shuster, U.A. 1976, *Peterburgskie rabochie v 1905–1907 gg.*, Leningrad: Nauka.

Skvortsov-Stepanov, I.I. 1925, 'Chto takoe politicheskaia ekonomiia?', *Vestnik Kommunisticheskoi Akademii*, 11.

Skvortsov-Stepanov, I.I. 1925a, *Ot revoliutsii k revoliutsii. Sbornik statei 1905–1915 gg.* Moscow: Gosizdat.

Skvortsov-Stepanov, I.I. 1928, 'Pamiati A.A. Bogdanova', *Izvestiia*, 8 April.

Skvortsov-Stepanov, I.I. 1930, *Izbrannye proizvedeniia*, Moscow: Gosizdat.

Skvortsov-Stepanov, I.I. 1970, *Izbrannoe*, Moscow: "Izvestiia".

Smirnov, I.S. 1969, 'Leninskaia kontseptsiia kul'turnoi revoliutsii i kritika proletkul'ta', in *Istoricheskaia nauka i nekotorye problemy sovremennosti. Stat'i i obsuzhdeniia*, Moscow: Nauka.

Smirnov, V.I. (ed) 1971, *Ocherki istorii Kalininskoi organizatsii* KPSS, Moskva: Moskovskii rabochii.

Smith, Norman 1906, 'Avenarius' Philosophy of Pure Experience I', *Mind*, 15(57): 13–31; 15(58): 149–60.

Sobolev, I.I. 1992, 'Tovarishch', in *Trudy komissii po nauchnomu naslediiu A.A. Bogdanova*, edited by N.K. Figurovskaia, Moscow: Rossiiskaia Akademiia Nauk Institut Ekonomiki.

Soboleva, Maja 2007, *Aleksandr Bogdanov und der philosophische Diskurs in Russland zu Beginn des 20 Jahrhunderts. Zur Geschichte des russischen Positivismus*, Hildesheim: G. Olms.

Sochor, Zenovia 1988, *Revolution and Culture: The Bogdanov-Lenin Controversy*, Ithaca, New York: Cornell University Press

Sokolov, S.A. 1923, 'Moia vstrecha s Bogdanovym', *Revoliutsionnoe byloe* 2: 18–19.

Solov'ev, A.A. 1983, *S"ezdy i konferentsii KPSS. Spravochnik*, Moscow: Politizdat.

Sol'tsnev, E. and Karev, V. 1930, 'Bogdanov, A'. *Bol'shaia Sovetskaia Entsiklopediia*, 6: Sovetskaia entsiklopediia: 574–82.

Stalin, I.V. 1948–53, *Sochineniia*, 13 vols., Moscow: Gospolitizdat.

Staryi student 1895, 'Peterburgskie studencheskie zemliachestva vo vtoroi polovine 80-kh godov i ikh znachenie', *Materialy dlia istorii russkogo sotsial'no-revoliutsionnogo dvizheniia*, August.

Steila, Daniela 1996, *Scienza e rivoluzione. La recezione dell'empiriocriticismo nella cultura russa (1877–1910)*, Firenze: Casa Editrice Le Lettere.

Steila, Daniela 2009, 'From Experience to Organisation: Bogdanov's Unpublished Letters to Bazarov', in *Aleksandr Bogdanov Revisited*, edited by Vesa Oittinen, Helsinki: Aleksanteri Series.

Steila, Daniela 2013, *Nauka i revoliutsiia. Retseptsiia empiriokrititsizma v russkoi kul'ture (1877–1910 gg.)*, Moscow: Akademicheskii Proekt.

Strumilin, S.G. 1957, *Iz perezhitogo 1897–1917 gg.*, Moscow: Gos. izd-vo polit. lit-ry.

Struve, P.B. 1894, *Kriticheskie zametki ob ekonomicheskom razvitii Rossii*, St Petersburg: Tipografiia I.N. Skorokhodova.

Susiluoto, Ilmari 1982, *The Origins and Development of Systems Thinking in the Soviet Union*, Helsinki: Suomalainen Tiedeakatemia.

Swain, Geoffrey 1983, *Russian Social Democracy and the Legal Labour Movement, 1906–14*, London and Basingstoke: Macmillan.

Tait, A. 1984, *Lunacharsky: Poet of the Revolution (1875–1907)*, Birmingham Slavonic monographs, no. 15., Birmingham: Dept. of Russian Language & Literature University of Birmingham.

Takhtadzhan, A.L. 1998, *Principia tektologica. Printsipy organizatsii i transformatsii slozhnykh sistem: evoliutsionnyi podkhod*, St Petersburg: Izd-vo SPKhFA.

Takhtarev, K.M. [Peterburzhets] 1902, *Ocherk peterburgskogo rabochego dvizheniia 90-kh godov: po lichnym vospominaniiam*, London: Izdanie sotsialdemokraticheskoi organizatsii 'Zhizni'.

Thatcher, Ian D. 2003, *Trotsky*, London and New York: Routledge.

Thatcher, Ian D. 2005, 'Leon Trotsky and 1905', in *The Russian Revolution of 1905. Centenary perspectives*, edited by Jonathan D. Smele and Anthony Heywood, London and New York: Routledge.

Tikhomirov, B.N. 1930, 'Ivan Ivanovich Skvortsov-Stepanov Biograficheskii ocherk', in *I.I. Skvortsov-Stepanov Izbrannye proizvedeniia 1*, Moscow: Gosizdat.

Tretii s"ezd RSDRP *aprel'–mai 1905 goda. Protokoly* 1959, Moscow: Gospolitizdat.

Trifonova, N.A. and Shostak, I.F. 1970, 'A.V. Lunacharskii i "Moskovskoe delo" 1899 goda', *Literaturnoe nasledstvo* 82: 587–602.

Trotsky, Leon 1925, *Sochineniia*, Vol. 2, part 1, Moscow: Gosizdat.

Trotsky, Leon 1930, *Moia zhizn'. Opyt avtobiografii*, 2 vols., Berlin: "Granit".

Trotsky, Leon 1971 [1922] *1905*, New York: Vintage.

Trudy pervoi Vsesoiuznoi konferentsii agrarnikov-marksistov 1930, Moscow: Izd-vo Kommunisticheskoi akademii.

Ul'ianova, A.I. 1989, 'K istorii poiavleniia na svet knigi V.I. Lenina "Materializm i empiriokrititsizm"', in *Vospominaniia o Vladimire Il'iche Lenine*, tom 1, Moscow: Partizdat.

Usyskin, G.S. 1988, 'V.I. Lenin na tret'ei konferentsii RSDRP', *Voprosy istorii*, 4: 13–22.

Utechin, S.V. 1962, 'Philosophy and Society: Alexander Bogdanov', in *Revisionism. Essays on the History of Marxist Ideas*, edited by Leopold Labedz, London: George Allen and Unwin Ltd.

Valentinov, Nikolay 1968, *Encounters with Lenin*, Oxford: Oxford University Press.

Vasin, L.L. 2015, '"Tsennost'" versus "stoimost'"', *Al'ternativy*, 2(87): 122–54.

Viktorov, D. 1905, 'Kritika chistogo opyta', *Voprosy filosofii i psikhologii*, 2: 128–62.

Vladimir Il'ich Lenin, biograficheskaia khronika 1970, 12 vols., Moscow: Politizdat.

Vol'skii, S. 1911, 'O proletarskoi kul'ture', *Vpered*, 2: 71–82.

Vospominaniia o Vladimire Il'iche Lenine 1989–91, 10 vols, Moscow: Politizdat.

Vucinich, Alexander 1976, *Social Thought in Tsarist Russia: The Quest for a General Science of Society, 1861–1917*, Chicago: University of Chicago Press.

Vvedenskii, A.I. 1898, 'Sud'by filosofii v Rossii', *Voprosy filosofii i psikhologii* 2(42): 314–54.

Walicki, A.S. 1990, 'Alexander Bogdanov and the Problem of the Socialist Intelligentsia', *Russian Review* 49(3): 293–304.

White, James D. 1974, 'The First Pravda and the Russian Marxist Tradition', *Soviet Studies* 26(2): 181–204.

White, James D. 1979, 'The Sormovo-Nikolaev *Zemlyachestvo* in the February Revolution', *Soviet Studies*, 31(4): 475–504.

White, James D. 1981, 'Bogdanov in Tula', *Studies in Soviet Thought*, 22 (June): 33–58.

White, James D. 1985, 'Early Soviet Historical Interpretations of the Russian Revolution', *Soviet Studies*, 37 (3): 330–52.

White, James D. 1993, 'Trotsky's *History of the Russian Revolution*', *Journal of Trotsky Studies*, 1, 1: 1–18.

White, James D. 1996, *Karl Marx and the intellectual origins of dialectical materialism*, Basingstoke: Macmillan.

White, James D. 1998, '"No, we won't go that way; that is not the way to take": The Place of Aleksandr Ul'ianov in the Development of Social-Democracy in Russia', *Revolutionary Russia*, 11(2): 82–110.

White, James D. 1998a, 'Sources and precursors of Bogdanov's Tektology', in Biggart, Dudley and King (eds.) 1998.

White, James D. 2001, 'Nikolai Sieber and Karl Marx', *Research in Political Economy* 19: 3–14 In *Marx's Capital and capitalism; Markets in a socialist alternative*, edited by P. Zarembka, vol. 19, Oxford: Elsevier Science.

White, James D. 2011, 'Chugurin's Life before the October Revolution', *Revolutionary Russia*, 24(1), June: 13–21.

White, James D. 2013, 'Alexander Bogdanov's Conception of Proletarian Culture', *Revolutionary Russia*, 26, 1: 52–70.

White, James D. 2015, 'Lenin and Philosophy: The Historical Context', *Europe-Asia Studies*. 67(1): 123–42.

Wildman, A.K. 1967, *The making of a workers' revolution: Russian Social Democracy, 1891–1903*, The history of Menshevism, New York London: University of Chicago Press.

Williams, R.C. 1980, 'Collective Immortality: The Syndicalist Origins of Proletarian Culture, 1905–1910', *Slavic Review* 39(3), September: 389–402.

Williams, R.C. 1986, *The Other Bolsheviks: Lenin and his Critics 1904–1914*, Indiana: Indiana University Press.

Yassour, A. 1968, 'Leçons de 1905: Parti ou Soviet?' *Le Mouvement social*, January, 3–26.

Yassour, A. 1981, 'Lenin and Bogdanov: Protagonists in the "Bolshevik Center"', *Studies in Soviet Thought*, 22.

Yassour, A. 1990, 'Letter on the Bogdanov Issue', *Russian Review* 49(4), October: 467–8.

Zaionchkovskii, A.M. 2002, *Pervaia mirovaia voina*, St Petersburg: Poligon.

Ziber, N.I. 1871, *Teoriia tsennosti i kapitala D. Rikardo v sviazi s pozdneishimi dopolneniiami i raz"iasneniiami. Opyt kritiko-ekonomicheskogo issledovaniia*, Kiev.

Ziber, N.I. 1874, 'Ekonomicheskaia teoriia Marksa', *Znanie*, 1: 43–90.

Ziber, N.I. 1883, *Ocherki pervobytnoi ekonomicheskoi kul'tury*, Moscow: Izd. K.T. Soldatenkova.

Ziber, N.I. 1885, *David Rikardo i Karl Marks v ikh obshchestvenno-ekonomicheskikh issledovaniiakh: opyt kritiko-ekonomicheskogo issledovaniia*, St. Petersburg: Stasiulevich.

Ziber, N.I. 1959, *Izbrannye ekonomicheskie proizvedeniia*, 2 vols., Moscow: Izd-vo sotsial'no-ekonomicheskoi literatury.

Index

CPSIA information can be obtained
at www.ICGtesting.com
Printed in the USA
LVHW030011301019
635746LV00002B/2/P